WHISTLEBLOWING

Law and Practice

WHISTLEBLOWING

Law and Practice

JOHN BOWERS QC
MARTIN FODDER
JEREMY LEWIS
JACK MITCHELL

OXFORD

UNIVERSITY PRESS

OXFORD

UNIVERSITY PRESS

Great Clarendon Street, Oxford ox2 6DP

Oxford University Press is a department of the Univeristy of Oxford.
It furthers the University's objective of excellence in research, scholarship,
and education by publishing worldwide in

Oxford New York

Auckland Cape Town Dar es Salaam Hong Kong Karachi
Kuala Lumpur Madrid Melbourne Mexico City Nairobi
New Delhi Shanghai Taipei Toronto

With offices in

Argentina Austria Brazil Chile Czech Republic France Greece
Guatemala Hungary Italy Japan Poland Portugal Singapore
South Korea Switzerland Thailand Turkey Ukraine Vietnam

Oxford is a registered trade mark of Oxford Unviersity Press
in the UK and in certain other countries

Published in the United States
by Oxford University Press Inc., New York

British Library Cataloguing in Publication Data

Data available

Library of Congress Cataloging in Publication Data

Data available

Typeset by Cepha Imaging Private Ltd, Bangalore, India
Printed in Great Britain
on acid-free paper by
Biddles Ltd, King's Lynn

ISBN 978–0–19–929958–4

1 3 5 7 9 10 8 6 4 2

PREFACE

I believe that the willingness of one health care professional to take responsibility for raising concerns about the conduct, performance or health of another could make a greater contribution to patient safety than any other single factor.

Dame Janet Smith in her introduction to the Shipman Inquiry report

The eight years since the passing of the Public Interest Disclosure Act (PIDA) has seen a major shift of public perception towards the whistleblower. He or she is less likely to be considered to be the 'sneak' who has broken ranks and should be shunned by fellow workers. It is now more likely that he or she will rightly be recognized to be performing an important public service. *Time Magazine* featured whistleblowers on its first front cover in 2003 and dubbed 2003 the 'year of the whistleblower'. As a result of the stimulus given by PIDA for organizations to introduce their own whistleblowing procedures there is also less chance of a worker being left not knowing to whom concerns can be reported.

The consensus which led to the introduction of PIDA has also itself given rise to other developments, with whistleblowing codes being developed in particular areas (for example the Financial Services Authority, NHS, Civil Service), and being extended (to police forces and elsewhere). The Civil Service Code issued in 2006 makes express reference to PIDA for the first time. Consistently with these developments, it has been emphasized[1] that PIDA is not merely to be seen as employment legislation. As the Committee on Standards in Public Life (10th Report, January 2005) has commented: 'effective whistleblowing is a key component in any strategy to challenge inappropriate behaviour at all levels of an organisation. It is both an instrument in support of good governance and a manifestation of a more open organisational culture.'

However the change in perception brought about by PIDA should not be exaggerated. In her 5th report in relation to the Shipman Inquiry, Dame Janet Smith identified a number of natural barriers which might still deter a potential whistleblower from raising concerns. These include the fear of being seen as a troublemaker or maverick, the fear of recriminations and a belief that nothing will be done or that a report will be seen as an attack on an individual or body. As we discuss in Chapter 1, there are continuing frustrations that attitudes are not changing

---

[1]   Ross Cranston, *Hansard*, HC, 5 April 2005, cols 430–431.

quickly enough. Referring specifically to the healthcare sector, Dame Janet Smith referred to the pace of change as 'discouraging' and noted that the evidence which she had heard indicated that reporting concerns about bad behaviour, incompetence or poor performance is still not widely done.[2]

This in turn has focused attention on the detailed terms of PIDA. Several areas of interpretation of the legislation have proved controversial. Foremost amongst these have been the test of reasonable belief for the purposes of a qualifying disclosure, and the requirement of good faith which applies to most categories of protected disclosure.

The second edition of this book provides us with an opportunity to comment on the significant issues which have developed in relation to the meaning of the legislation. We have included consideration of the important case law which has reviewed the complex definitions of the Act, and have completely restructured the chapters on the substance of the Act. We have also extended the scope of the work to include separate chapters on private information and public interest disclosures, remedies, tribunal procedure, the obligation to blow the whistle, alternative dispute resolution and whistleblowing procedures.

We are very grateful to Maurice Kay LJ for his Foreword.

We have many other people to thank for their contribution to the book: in particular Guy Dehn of Public Concern at Work for his general support, Philip Bartle QC for his comments on ADR, Antony Korn for assistance on compensation, J Sturzaker of Russell Jones & Walker for his help on the worked example and Gavin Mansfield of Littleton Chambers on procedural issues.

The law is as stated on 1 November 2006.

J Bowers QC
J Lewis
M Fodder
J Mitchell

---

[2] Lecture given by Dame Janet Smith on 13 October 2005 at Public Concern at Work.

FOREWORD

Recent history contains many examples of industrial, commercial and professional wrongdoing or neglect which has caused devastating injury or loss to innocent people in circumstances where it could have been avoided if some insider had spoken up or, having spoken up, had been taken seriously. However, the workplace is a complex phenomenon, with negative characteristics as well as positive ones. Loyalty is generally a virtue but it can also engender a culture in which serious wrongdoing is covered up, not least because potential whistleblowers fear the consequences of breaking rank. When they have the courage to do so, they may be victimized. All these tensions are well known.

The Public Interest Disclosure Act 1998 was an innovative piece of legislation which provided protection for whistleblowers by incorporating important amendments into the Employment Rights Act 1996. It was described by Lord Borne QC during the passage of the Bill through the House of Lords as 'the most far-reaching piece of whistleblowing legislation in the world'. In common with much modern legislation, it is technical and complex. It may not always have the effect that was intended. In this new book the authors—all practising barristers with great expertise and experience in employment law—have provided an excellent analysis and critique of the law. It is not simply another arid legal textbook which slavishly annotates an Act of Parliament. It combines legal exposition with critical acumen, setting the law in its social context. In so doing, it will, I believe, be of great assistance to all those involved with modern employment law and will take its place as an important addition to the literature.

The Rt Hon Lord Justice Maurice Kay

CONTENTS—SUMMARY

Table of Cases	xxiii
Table of Legislation	xxxvii
1. Introduction	1

I PROTECTING WHISTLEBLOWERS— THE PUBLIC INTEREST DISCLOSURE ACT 1998

2. Structure of the Public Interest Disclosure Act 1998	19
3. Protectable Information	27
4. Good Faith	61
5. The Three Tiers of Protection	81
6. Who is Protected under PIDA?	125
7. The Right not to Suffer Detriment	141
8. Dismissal for Making a Protected Disclosure	189
9. Remedies in Dismissal and Detriment Claims	205
10. Employment Tribunals Procedure and Alternative Dispute Resolution	227

II PROTECTING WHISTLEBLOWERS—OUTSIDE PIDA

11. Private Information and Public Interest Disclosure	255
12. Protection of the Identity of Informants	317
13. Whistleblowing and Copyright (contributed by Richard Price OBE, QC)	329
14. Defamation (contributed by Cameron Doley, Solicitor-Advocate, Managing Partner, Carter-Ruck)	343

III THE OBLIGATION TO BLOW THE WHISTLE

15. Obligations to Blow the Whistle   353

IV RULES, POLICIES, PROCEDURES AND PROBLEMS

16. Whistleblowing Procedures in the Public and Private Sectors:
     Why they are needed and what they should contain   385

Appendices   409

Index   625

CONTENTS

Table of Cases   xxiii
Table of Legislation   xxxvii

1. Introduction   1

  A. Turning a blind eye   2
    (1) The *Piper Alpha* disaster   2
    (2) The Clapham rail disaster   3
    (3) BCCI   3
    (4) Barings Bank   4

  B. Turning a deaf ear   4
    (1) Zeebrugge ferry disaster   4
    (2) Child abuse   4
    (3) Lyme Bay canoe disaster   5
    (4) 1993—Cancer misdiagnosed   5

  C. Blaming the messenger   5
    (1) *R v Ponting* [1985] Crim LR 318   6
    (2) Dr Stephen Bolsin—Bristol Royal Infirmary   6
    (3) Andrew Millar—British Biotech   6
    (4) 1992—Patient abuse   7
    (5) Fraud in the European Commission   8

  D. Triumph of the whistleblower   8
    (1) Scott Report   9
    (2) Abbey National   10

  E. The need for change   10

  F. Momentum for reform   11

  G. The Public Interest Disclosure Act 1998   12

  H. Moving forward the consensus   13

  I. Public awareness   13

  J. The Shipman Inquiry report   14

  K. Beyond PIDA   15

I PROTECTING WHISTLEBLOWERS—
THE PUBLIC INTEREST DISCLOSURE ACT 1998

2. Structure of the Public Interest Disclosure Act 1998   19

  A. Introduction   19

  B. The scheme of the legislation   20

  C. Some initial observations   22

  D. Commencement   23

3. Protectable information   27

  A. Overview of s43B Employment Rights Act 1996   27

  B. Reasonable belief   28

    (1) The *Darnton* guidance   28
    (2) Basis for the information disclosed   31
    (3) Reasonable suspicion or concern   34
    (4) All circumstances relevant to reasonable belief   35

  C. 'Tends to show'   36

    (1) No need to establish truth of the allegation   36
    (2) Extent to which the disclosure must spell out the relevant failure
       and why it is shown   38
    (3) The disclosure must contain 'information'   41
    (4) Information disclosed need not be unknown to the recipient   42
    (5) Disclosures in relation to likely future failures   43

  D. The six categories   47

    (1) Criminal offence   48
    (2) Legal obligation   48
    (3) Miscarriage of justice   53
    (4) Health and safety risks   54
    (5) Damage to the environment   55
    (6) Cover-ups   55

  E. Criminal disclosures   55

    (1) Exclusions for disclosures that are criminal offences   55
    (2) Consequential procedural issues   58
    (3) Standard of proof   59

  F. Legal professional privilege   59

  G. Geographical scope   60

4. Good Faith   61

   A. Overview   61

   B. The meaning of good faith   62
      (1) Good faith is not synonymous with honesty   62
      (2) Ulterior motive must be the predominant or dominant motive
         to negative good faith   63
      (3) Legitimate and illegitimate purposes   64
      (4) Does a predominant non-public interest motive necessarily
         negative good faith?   66

   C. Burden of proof   73

   D. Concerns about the decision in *Street v Derbyshire Unemployed
      Workers' Centre*   74

   E. Counter-arguments in support of the decision in *Street v Derbyshire
      Unemployed Workers' Centre*   77

   F. Reform?   79

5. The Three Tiers of Protection   81

   A. The three tiers   82

   B. First tier disclosures: Section 43C   83
      (1) Overview   83
      (2) Section 43C(1)(a): Disclosure to the employer   84
      (3) Section 43C(1)(b)   85
      Centrality of promoting accountability   85
      Section 43C(1)(b)(i)   86
      Other responsible persons: s43C(1)(b)(ii)   87
      Reasonable belief   90
      (4) Disclosures to employer and disclosure under s43C(1)(b) compared   90
      (5) Section 43C(2): whistleblowing and other authorized procedures   90

   C. First tier disclosures: Section 43D   92
      (1) Overview   92
      (2) From whom can the legal advice be sought?   92
      (3) Capacity in which the legal advice is sought   96

   D. First tier disclosures: Section 43E: Ministers of the Crown
      and government-appointed bodies   97

   E. Regulatory disclosures: Section 43F   98
      (1) Overview   98
      (2) Prescribed persons   99
      (3) Reasonable belief that relevant failure falls within
         a relevant description   100
      (4) Time at which the recipient must be prescribed   101

(5) Reasonable belief that the information disclosed and
any allegation contained in it are substantially true   102
(6) Evidential issues   105

F. Wider disclosures under section 43G   106
(1) Overview   106
(2) 'Personal gain'   107
(3) The s43G(2) preconditions   109
Precondition 1: reasonable belief in victimization; subs (2)(a)   109
Precondition 2: reasonable belief in a cover-up; subs (2)(b)   110
Precondition 3: previous internal disclosure; subs (2)(c)   110
(4) Reasonableness: subs (3)   111
Identity of the person to whom the disclosure is made: subs (3)(a)   112
The seriousness of the failure: subs (3)(b)   114
Whether the relevant failure continues: subs (3)(c)   114
Duty of confidentiality owed to a third party: subs (3)(d)   115
Previous disclosures: subs (3)(e)   116
Whistleblowing procedures: subs (3)(f)   117
Assessment of all the circumstances   117
(5) Disclosure to a trade union   119

G. Wider disclosures of exceptionally serious matters: Section 43H   119

6. Who is Protected under PIDA?   125

A. Employees   125
The identity of 'the employer': special cases   126

B. Workers   127
(1) The ordinary s230(3) definition   127
(2) Extended definition in s43K   129
Agency workers   130
The NHS   131
Trainees   131
Police officers   132
Crown employees   132
(3) Limits of the definition of 'worker'   133
Volunteers   133
Non-executives   136
Members of the armed forces and those involved in national security   136
Parliamentary staff   137
(4) Possibility of more than one employer   137
(5) Workers—summary   137

C. Territorial jurisdiction   137

7. **The Right not to Suffer Detriment**   141

    A. Section 47B ERA: Overview   141

    B. Deployment of the pre-existing models of protection   143

    C. Meaning of 'detriment'   144
        (1) The *Khan* and *Shamoon* guidance   144
        (2) The threat of a detriment   150
        (3) Post-termination detriment   151
        The decision in *Woodward v Abbey National plc*   151
        Outstanding issues as to the scope for post-termination detriment claims 153
        (4) Limitation of detriment claims to the employment field
            during employment   154

    D. 'Act or deliberate failure to act'   155

    E. Subjection by the employer   157
        (1) *London Borough of Harrow v Knight*   157
        (2) Vicarious liability   158
        (3) Action by third parties   160

    F. 'On the ground that'   161
        (1) Guidance in *Nagarajan* and *Khan* on the 'reason why' question   161
        (2) Distinction between the disclosure and the acts connected with
            or manner of the disclosure   165
        Conduct associated with the disclosure   166
        Breach of confidentiality   171
        Distinction between the disclosure and the manner of the disclosure   172
        (3) Failure in the investigation of the subject matter of the disclosure 176
        Detriment   176
        Act or deliberate failure to act by the employer   176
        On the ground that   177
        (4) The burden of proof in relation to the 'reason why' question   177
        (5) Drawing inferences   179

    G. Complaints to an Employment Tribunal in claims
       of victimization   182
        (1) Statutory grievance procedures and whistleblowing claims   182
        (2) Time limits in victimization cases   185
        An act extending over a period   186
        A series of similar acts or failures   187

8. **Dismissal for making a Protected Disclosure**   189

    A. Comparison with the pre-PIDA position   189

    B. The relationship between a protected disclosure dismissal
       and an 'ordinary' unfair dismissal   190

C. Identifying the principal reason in dismissal cases 193

D. Constructive dismissal 194

E. Selection for redundancy 196

F. Unofficial industrial action 196

G. The burden of proof 196

   (1) Ordinary unfair dismissal 196

   (2) Is a burden also on the employer to show the reason was
   not a protected disclosure? 197

H. Unfair dismissal protection for non-protected disclosures 199

I. Extension of time 203

9. Remedies in Dismissal and Detriment Claims 205

A. Unfair dismissal remedies 205

   (1) Overview of remedies 205

   (2) Reinstatement and re-engagement 206

   Practicability of compliance 206

   Contributory fault 207

   Other factors 207

   Permanent replacements 208

   Reasons 208

   Terms of re-engagement 208

   Compensation and back pay in re-employment cases 208

   (3) Compensatory award 209

   (4) Unfair dismissals and contributory fault 211

   (5) Interim relief 213

B. Detriment claims 215

   (1) Overview 215

   (2) Injury to feelings 216

   When can injury to feelings be claimed? 216

   The boundary between detriment and dismissal 216

   Injury to feelings—the appropriate amount 218

   Causation 220

   Knowledge 220

   (3) Personal injury—psychiatric damage 221

   (4) Aggravated damages 222

   (5) Exemplary damages 224

   (6) Victimization by dismissal of a worker who is not an employee 224

   (7) Adjustment of awards for non-compliance with statutory
   disciplinary procedures 225

10. Employment Tribunals Procedure and Alternative Dispute Resolution   227

A. Claim forms   228

B. Responses   229

C. Case management   230
    (1) Case management discussions (CMD)   231
    (2) How to apply for an order   232

D. Additional information: general   233

E. Disclosure   235
    (1) Applicable principles   235
    (2) Disclosure by non-parties   237
    (3) Form of application   237
    (4) Restrictions on disclosure   237
    Confidentiality   237
    Self-incrimination   238

F. Procedure at the hearing   238
    (1) The power to sit in private   238
    (2) Submissions at the close of the claimant's case that there is no case to answer   239

G. Costs   241
    (1) Vexatious   243
    (2) Misconceived   243
    (3) Amount   244
    (4) Wasted costs   245
    (5) When can wasted costs orders be made?   246
    (6) Amount of wasted costs   246

H. Alternative dispute resolution   247
    (1) Introduction   247
    (2) The ADR options   247
    Conciliation   247
    Arbitration   248
    Mediation   248
    The settlement agreement   250
    (3) Issues specific to whistleblowing   250

II PROTECTING WHISTLEBLOWERS—OUTSIDE PIDA

11. Private Information and Public Interest Disclosure   255

A. Introduction   256

B. Identifying obligations of confidentiality/privacy   257

(1) Duties in respect of private information 257
Contractual duties 257
Duties outside contract 260
Sources of obligations to maintain confidentiality 261
Privacy and Article 8 of the European Convention on Human Rights 261

C. The public interest defence of 'just cause and excuse' as a defence
to actions for breach of duty in respect of private information 264
(1) Overview 264
(2) Development of the public interest defence 264
The old 'iniquity' principle 264
From iniquity to public interest 265
(3) What types of information can form the basis of a public
interest defence? 267
The categories corresponding to those covered by the protected
disclosure provisions of ERA 267
Categories of information not covered by the protected disclosure
provisions of ERA where the courts have held that there is
a public interest in disclosure 269
(4) The balancing of interests in domestic law today 274
(5) The context in which the balancing act is carried out 277
Interim relief prohibiting disclosure 277
Cases involving threatened publication 278

D. Protected disclosure provisions as a 'template'? 278
(1) The approach in *Banerjee* 278
(2) PIDA considerations as indicators in the balancing of interests 281
First tier disclosures 281
Second tier/regulatory disclosures 282
Third tier/wider disclosures 288
(3) Proportionality 295
(4) Conclusions in relation to the application of PIDA provisions
as a template 297

E. Agreements rendered void 298

F. European Court of Human Rights decisions 300
(1) Prescribed by law 301
(2) Legitimate aim 301
(3) Necessary in a democratic society and the margin of appreciation 302
(4) Does the whistleblower raise matters of public concern? 303
(5) Duties and responsibilities 305
(6) Manner of the expression 306
(7) Whether the accusations are supported by evidence 308
(8) The recipient of the information 308
(9) Nature of the employing organization 309

(10) Is the sanction imposed by the state?—the scope of the positive
obligation to protect the whistleblower   310
(11) Conclusion on the ECHR authorities   311

G. Criminal law   312

12. **Protection of the Identity of Informants**   317

A. Victimization   317

B. Anonymity of informants and the fairness of disciplinary
and dismissal procedures   318

C. Forcing disclosure of the identity of informants   321
(1) Protection for informants through s10 of the Contempt
of Court Act   323
(2) The public interest defence to a *Norwich Pharmacal* application   326

13. **Whistleblowing and Copyright** (contributed by Richard
Price OBE, QC)   329

A. Infringement   330

B. Defence of fair dealing   330
(1) 'Purpose'   331
(2) Criticism or review of that or another work   331
(3) 'Reporting current events'   333
(4) Sufficient acknowledgment—'identifying the author'   335
(5) 'Fair'   335

C. Public interest defence   337
The effect of the passing of the Human Rights Act 1998   339

D. Interrelation of copyright protection and PIDA   342

14. **Defamation** (contributed by Cameron Doley, Solicitor-Advocate,
Managing Partner, Carter-Ruck)   343

A. The prima facie case   343

B. Justification   344

C. Qualified privilege   345
(1) The 'duty and interest' test   345
(2) The Public Interest Disclosure Act 1998   347
(3) Malice   348
(4) Third tier/wider disclosures   349

III THE OBLIGATION TO BLOW THE WHISTLE

15. Obligations to blow the Whistle   353

   A. *Bell v Lever Brothers*   354

   B. Implied reporting obligations under the contract of employment   356
     (1) Reporting wrongdoing of others   356
     Blowing the whistle on subordinates   356
     Blowing the whistle on superiors   358
     Blowing the whistle on employees of similar seniority   360
     Express terms of the contract   361
     Seriousness of the wrongdoing   361
     Continuing wrongdoing   362
     Deliberate concealment   363
     Has there been a specific request?   364
     Is there someone with whom to raise concerns?   365
     (2) Implied contractual reporting obligations other than misdeeds   365
     (3) Do employees have implied contractual obligations to
        disclose their own wrongdoing?   366
     (4) Conclusion as to the scope of the contractual duty of disclosure   372

   C. Directors and employees who owe fiduciary obligations   373

   D. Duty to investigate   377

   E. Interface with PIDA   377

   F. Statutory and regulatory obligations to disclose information   378

   G. Clarification by a whistleblowing policy   380

IV RULES, POLICIES, PROCEDURES AND PROBLEMS

**16. Whistleblowing Procedures in the Public and Private Sectors:
Why they are needed and what they should contain**   385

   A. Why?   385

   B. How?   392
     (1) Why should concerns be raised?   393
     (2) Who should raise concerns?   393
     (3) How should a report be made?   394
     (4) When should the concern be raised?   394
     (5) Confidentiality or anonymity?   395
     (6) Protection   396
     (7) To whom should reports be made?   397
     (8) Process   398
     (9) Detriments, reprisals, victimization and dismissal   400

(10) Advice or assistance   400
(11) Monitoring   401
(12) Review   401
(13) Advertising   401
(14) Training   402

C. Public sector   402

D. Regulators   403

E. Examples   404

F. Only employees?   405

G. Data Protection   405

H. Future?   407

Appendix 1: Relevant extracts from the Employment Rights Act 1996   411

Appendix 2: Relevant Statutory Instruments   427

Appendix 3: Relevant *Hansard* Extracts   435

Appendix 4: Extracts from Nolan Committee on Standards in Public Life   447

Appendix 5: Extracts from the Shipman Report   459

Appendix 6: Sample Whistleblowing Policies   465

Appendix 7: Case Study   489

Appendix 8: Appellate Whistleblowing Cases   497

Appendix 9: Employment Tribunal Whistleblowing Cases   539

Appendix 10: Precedents   599

Appendix 11: Introduction to Public Concern at Work Guide to PIDA   613

Appendix 12: Useful Addresses   621

Index   625

TABLE OF CASES

A Company, Re [1989] 1 Ch 477 . . . . . 3.88, 5.17, 11.27, 11.36, 11.89, 11.102, 11.119, 16.47
A v B (1907) SC 1154 . . . . 14.11, App 9
A v Company B Limited [1997] IRLR 405 . . . . 12.13
A v X Case No. 2101023/00, 9 March 2001 (Liverpool) . . . . App 9
A-G v Guardian Newspapers Ltd (No. 2) [1990] 1 AC 109 (HL) 5.30, 11.12, 11.17,
11.25, 11.78, 13.24
Abernethy v Mott, Hay and Anderson [1974] IRLR 213 . . . . 8.11
Abrams v United States (1919) 250 US 616 . . . . 11.50
Acikalin v Phones 4 U Ltd, ET, Case No. 3302501/04 . . . . 9.22
Adam v Ward [1917] AC 309 . . . . 14.05
Adlam v Salisbury & Wells Theological College [1985] ICR 786 . . . . 7.102
Alexander v Gloucestershire Partnership Mental Health Trust, ET,
    Case No.1400470/03 . . . . App 9
Alexander v Home Office [1988] ICR 685 . . . . 9.52, 9.62
Alexander v Romania at Heart Trading Co Limited, Brighton ET,
    Case No. 310206/97 . . . . 6.26
Alfred Compton Amusement Machines v Customs & Excise Commissioners
    (No. 2) [1972] 2 QB 102 (CA) 5.14, 10.38
Allison v Sefton M.B. Council (2001) . . . . App 9
ALM v Bladon [2002] EWCA Civ 1085, [2002] IRLR 807, [2002]
    ICR 1444 . . . . 7.63, 10.10, App 8
Almond v Alphabet Children's Services (2001) . . . . App 9
American Cyanamid Co v Ethicon Ltd [1975] AC 396 . . . . 11.59, 11.60
Anya v University of Oxford [2001] EWCA Civ 405, [2001] 847 ICR 7.84
Aoot Kalmneft v Denton Wilde Sapte [2002] 1 Lloyds Rep 417 . . . . 12.11
Armitage, Marsden and HM Prison Service v Johnson [1997] ICR 275 . . . . 9.47, 9.61
Armitage v Relate, Middlesborough ET, Case No. 43238/94 . . . . 6.26
Arrows, Re [1995] 2 AC 75 (HL) 15.72
Artisan Press Ltd v Strawley and Parker [1986] IRLR 126 . . . . 9.18
Asda Stores Limited v Thompson [2002] IRLR 245 . . . . 12.07
Ashdown v Telegraph Group [2002] Ch 149 . . . . 13.30, 13.34, 13.35
Ashworth Hospital Authority v MGN Ltd [2002] 1 WLR 2033 . . . . 12.11, 12.22, 12.24
Asila Elshami v Welfare Community Projects and Leema,
    London North IT, Case No. 6001977/1998 . . . . 6.25, 6.26, 6.31
ASLEF v Brady, EAT/0057/06 and EAT/0130/06, 31 March 2006 . . . . 8.11
Aspinall v MSI Mech Forge Limited, EAT/891/01,
    25 July 2002 . . . . 3.40, 7.45, 7.66, 7.67, App 8
Associated Newspapers Group plc v News Group Newspapers
    Limited [1986] RPC 515 . . . . 13.12, 13.16, 13.17
Associated Newspapers Limited v Wilson; Associated British
    Ports v Palmer [1995] ICR 406 HL 7.08
Attorney General v Guardian Newspapers Ltd [1988] 3 WLR 776 . . . . 11.84, 11.94
Attorney-General v Parry and MGN Limited [2004] EMLR 223 . . . . 11.109
Australian Broadcasting Corporation v Lenah Game Meats Pty Ltd [2001]
    HCA 63 . . . . 11.09

Axa Equity & Law Life Assurance Society plv v National Westminster
  Bank (CA) [1998] CLC 1177 .... 12.11
Aziz v (1) Muskett (2) Tottenham Legal Advice Centre, ET, Case No. 2200560/01,
  3 April 2002 .... App 9
Aziz v Trinity Street Taxis Ltd [1988] IRLR 204 .... 7.60
Azmi v Orbis Charitable Trust (2000) .... App 9
Azzaoui v Apcoa Parking UK Limited, ET, Case No. 2302156/01,
  30 April 2002 .... 5.07, App 9

B v United Kingdom (1985) 45 D&R 41 .... 11.125
Babula v Waltham Forest College, EAT/0635/05, 17 May 2006 ...... 3.56, 3.65, 3.70, App 8
Bachnak v Emerging Markets Partnership (Europe) Limited,
  EAT/0288/05, 27 January 2006 .... 4.15, 4.26, 4.34, App 8
Bahl v The Law Society [2004] EWCA Civ 1070, [2003] IRLR 640,
  [2004] IRLR 799 (CA) 7.89
Bailey v Arrow Consultants Ltd, ET, Case No. 5000328/00,10 October 2000 .... App 9
Bailey v Rolls Royce (1971) Limited [1984] ICR 688 (CA) 3.46
Ballantine (George & Sons) v F.E.R Dixon [1974] 2 All ER 503 .... 10.30
Balmer v Church View Ltd, ET, Case No. 2502583 Newcastle upon Tyne .... App 9
Balston Limited v Headline Filters Limited [1990] FSR 385 .... 15.63, 15.64
Barclays Bank plc v Eustice [1995] 1 WLR 1238 (CA) 11.106
Barclays Bank plc v Kapur (No. 2) [1995] IRLR 87 .... 7.11, 7.12
Barkness and Johnston v Booker Tate Limited, ET, Case No. 2500437;
  2500438/02, 6 January 2004 .... App 9
Barthold v Germany (1985) 7 EHRR 383 .... 11.129, 11.134, 11.150
Bass Taverns Limited v Burgess [1995] IRLR 596 (CA) 7.69
Bastick v James Lane (Turf Accountants) Limited [1979] ICR 778 .... 3.89
BBC v BSB Limited [1992] Ch 141 .... 13.16, 13.17
BCCI v Ali (No. 1) [1999] IRLR 226 .... 15.35, 15.49
BCCI v Ali (No. 3) [1999] IRLR 528 .... 3.46
Beckham v Gibson, 23 April 2005, unreported 11.44
Beggars Banquet Records Ltd v Carlton Television (1993) EMLR 349 .... 13.27
Bekhaled v Pizza Express (Restaurants) Limited Case No. 2204249/2000,
  25 January 2001 .... App 9
Bell v Lever Brothers Limited [1932] AC 161 (HL) 15.02, 15.03, 15.06, 15.07, 15.08,
                                  15.09, 15.10, 15.24, 15.25, 15.27, 15.29, 15.32,
                                  15.34, 15.37, 15.44, 15.46, 15.47, 15.48, 15.55, 15.59
Beloff v Pressdram Limited [1973] 1 All ER 241 .... 11.25, 13.18, 13.23
Belt v Lawes (1882) 51 LJQB 359 .... 14.04
Bennet v Newsquest Media (Southern) plc, ET, Case No.1600464/03 .... App 9
Berriman v Delabole Slate Limited [1985] ICR 546 (CA) 8.14
Beynon v Scadden [1999] IRLR 700 .... 10.56
Bhadresa v SRA (British Transport Police) (2002) .... App 9
Bham v CFM Group Limited, EAT 1254/95, 3 June 1997 .... 4.49
Bhatia v Sterlite Industries (India) Limited, ET, Case No. 2204571/00,
  2 May 2001 .... 3.58, 9.21, App 9
Bill v D. Morgan plc, ET, Case No. 21012981/00, on 2 May 2001 .... App 9
Birds Eye Walls Ltd v Harrison [1985] IRLR 47 .... 10.32
Birmingham District Council v Beyer [1977] 1 IRLR 211 .... 15.38
Blackshaw v Lord [1984] QB 1 .... 14.19
Bladon v AL Medical Services Limited, EAT/709/00 and EAT/967/00,
  19 January 2001, [2002] ICR 1444 .... 5.28
Blaikie v Trustees of Merton Hard of Hearing Resource Centre, ET,
  Case No. 305174/00, 13 February 2001 .... App 9

Boardman v Phipps [1967] 2 AC 46 . . . . 15.58
Bolkavac v DynCorp Aerospace Operations (UK) Ltd, ET,
    Case No. 3102729/01 . . . . App 9
Bolton School v Evans [2006] IRLR 500 (EAT); [2006] EWCA Civ 1653 (CA) 3.27, 3.34,
    3.59, 3.65, 3.66, 3.67, 7.16, 7.45, 7.57, 7.62, 7.65, 7.66, 7.68, 13.42, 15.67, App 8
Bonnard v Perryman [1891] 2 Ch 269 . . . . 11.08
Boots Company Ltd v Lees-Collier [1986] ICR 728 . . . . 9.09
Borah v Stonehill Park Auctions Ltd, ET, Case No. 2202060/02 . . . . App 9
Borley v Suffolk CC (2002) . . . . App 9
Bosman [1995] ECR I-4921 . . . . 11.55
Boughton v National Tyres & Autocentre Ltd (2000) . . . . 16.22, 16.29, App 9
Boulding v Land Securities Trillium (Media Services) Limited, EAT/0023/06,
    3 May 2006 . . . . 3.38, 3.50, 9.27, 10.43, 10.45, 10.46
Bowman v Fels (2005) 1 WLR 3083 . . . . 10.90
Branson v Bower [2001] EWCA Civ 791, [2001] EMLR 809 . . . . 14.14
Bright v Harrow and Hillingdon NHS Trust, ET, Case No. 2201389/00,
    29 November 2000 . . . . App 9
Bristol and West Building Society v Mothew [1998] 1 Ch 1 . . . . 15.58
British Steel Corporation v Granada Television Limited [1981] AC 1096 (HL) 11.45, 11.90
Brooks v Maharajah & Khan trading as Bridges Homes, ET,
    Case No. 3203857/03, 29 June 2004 . . . . App 9
Brooks v Olyslager (UK) Limited [1998] IRLR 590 (CA) 11.05
Brothers of Charity Services Merseyside v Eleady-Cole, EAT/0661/00,
    24 January 2002 . . . . 5.12, 7.87, 7.88, App 8
Bruce v Leeds CAB, EAT/1355/01 . . . . 6.30
Bryanston Finance v de Vries [1975] QB 703 (CA) 14.09
Bryant v Housing Corporation [1999] ICR 123 (CA) 8.08
Bucknor v MAR Contract Cleaning and Support Services Limited, ET,
    Case No. 1101644/02 31 July 2003 . . . . App 9
Bunce v Postworth Limited t/a Skyblue [2005] EWCA Civ 490, [2005]
    IRLR 557 (CA) 6.04
Bunn v BBC [1999] FSR 70 . . . . 11.99
Burton and Rhule v de Vere Hotels Limited [1996] IRLR 596 . . . . 7.35, 7.42
Butcher v Salvage Association, EAT/988/01, 21 January 2002 . . . . 3.63, 8.04, App 9
Butlers v British Railways Board, EAT/510/89 . . . . 9.15
Byford v Film Finances Limited, EAT/804/86 . . . . 8.32, 11.91
Byrne Brothers (Formwork) Limited v Baird [2002] ICR 667 . . . . 6.08
Byrne v Financial Times [1991] IRLR 417 . . . . 10.22

Cable & Wireless plc v Muscat [2006] EWCA Civ 220, [2006]
    IRLR 354 (CA) 6.04, 6.08, 6.11
Callanan v Surrey AHA, COIT/994/36, 5 February 1980 . . . . 9.08
Camelot v Centaur Communications Limited [1998] IRLR 80 . . . . 12.17, 12.20, 12.21, 12.27,
    13.19, 15.31
Campbell v Frisbee [2002] EWHC 328, [2002] EMLR 31 . . . . 11.06, 11.07, 11.45,
    11.108, 11.109
Campbell v MGN [2002] EWCA Civ 1373 (CA) 11.13
Campbell v MGN [2004] UKHL 22, [2004] 2 AC 457 (HL) 11.12, 11.16, 11.17,
    11.43, 11.51, 11.52, 11.53
Cantor Fitzgerald International v Tradition (UK) Limited, 12 June 1998 . . . . 15.23
Carlton Film Distributors Ltd v VCI plc [2003] EWHC 616, [2003] FSR 47 . . . . 12.11
Carmichael v National Power plc [1999] ICR 1226 (HL) 6.08, 6.25
Carroll v Greater Manchester Fire Service, ET, Case No. 2407819/00 . . . . 9.50, App 9
Carter v Credit Change Limited [1979] IRLR 361 (CA) 3.89

Cartiers Superfoods Ltd v Laws [1978] IRLR 315 .... 10.56
Cassell & Co Ltd v Broome [1972] 1 All ER 801 .... 9.67
Cast v Croydon College [1998] IRLR 318 .... 7.101
Cattrall v Plymouth TUC Unemployed Workers Centre, ET, Case No. 1700158/03 ..... App 9
Chantrey Martin v Martin [1953] 2 QB 286 (CA) 5.14
Chard v Glendorgal Health Club, ET, Case No. 1702071/03 .... App 9
Charles v Gillian Radcliffe & Co [2003] EWHC (CH), 5 November 2003 .... 10.65
Chattenton v City of Sunderland City Council, Case No. 6402938/99,
    18 July 2000 .... 7.12, App 9
CHC Software Care v Hopkins and Wood [1993] FSR 241 .... 12.11
Chief Constable of West Yorkshire Police v Khan [2001] UKHL 48, [2001]
    ICR 1065 .... 7.11, 7.12, 7.45, 7.46, 7.48, 7.52, 7.53, 8.13
Chubb v Care First Partnership Limited, ET, Case No. 1101438/99,
    13 June 2001 .... 5.12, 10.35, App 9
Church of Scientology of California v Kaufman [1973] RPC 635 .... 11.33, 11.40
Church of Scientology v Miller, The Times, 23 October 1987 .... 13.27
City & Hackney Health Authority v Crisp [1990] IRLR 47 .... 9.16
Clancy v Cannock Chase Technical College [2001] IRLR 331 .... 9.12
Clark v Oxfordshire Health Authority [1998] IRLR 125 (CA) 6.04, 6.25
Clarke v Watford Borough Council, EAT/4399/0405, 4 May 2000 .... 10.44
Coco v A N Clark (Engineers) Ltd [1969] RPC 41 .... 11.11, 11.17
Coke v Moss Side & Hulme Community Development Trust, ET,
    Case No. 2302271/01, 26 September 2001 .... App 9
Coleman and Stephenson v Magnet Joinery Ltd [1974] IRLR 343 .... 9.07, 9.10
Collins v National Trust, ET, Case No. 2507255/05, 17 January 2006 .... 5.38, App 9
Compagnie Financière v Peruvian Guano Co (1882) 11 QBD 55 .... 10.30
Connolly v Commission (Staff Regulations) [2001] ECJ C-274/99,
    6 March 2001 .... 11.151
Copson v Eversure Accessories Ltd [1974] ICR 636 .... 10.31
Cork v McVicar [1985] The Times, 31 October 1985 .... 5.30
Cornelius v Hackney LBC, EAT/1061/94 .... 8.30
Cotswold Developments Construction Limited v Williams
    [2006] IRLR 181 .... 6.04, 6.08, 6.12
Couper v Lord Balfour of Burleigh (1913) SC 492 .... 14.11
Cream Holdings Limited v Banerjee [2004] UKHL 44, [2005] 1 AC 253 .... 3.45, 11.02,
                11.09, 11.63, 11.64–71, 11.95, 11.96, 11.100, 11.103, 11.114
Credit Suisse First Boston (Europe) Limited v Padiachy [1998] IRLR 504 .... 11.120
Croft v Veta Ltd [2006] UKHL 3 .... 6.39
Crossly v Faithful & Gould Holdings Limited [2004] ICR 1615 .... 15.50
Cruickshank v London Borough of Richmond, EAT/483/97 .... 9.08

Dacas v Brook Street Bureau [2004] IRLR 358 (CA) 6.11
Dalton v Burton's Gold Medal Biscuits Limited [1974] IRLR 45 .... 15.80
Daniel v Toolmex Polmach (2002) .... App 9
Darnton v University of Surrey [2003] ICR 615 .... 3.05, 3.10, 3.12, 3.14, 3.17, 3.21,
                3.23, 5.10, 5.22, 7.65, 10.09, 10.40, 10.46, 11.114, App 8
Davies v Snead (1870) LR 5 QB 608 .... 14.07
Davis v Atkins [1977] ICR 662 .... 8.11
De Freitas v Ministry of Agriculture [1999] 1 AC 69 (PC) 11.55
De Haney v Brent Mind and Lang, EAT/0054/03, 19 March 2004 .... 3.24, App 8
De Jong v The Netherlands, 10280/83 .... 11.142, 11.143, 11.151
De Souza v Automobile Association [1986] ICR 514 .... 7.11, 7.12
Dempsey v Johnstone [2003] EWCA Civ 1134 .... 10.65
Derby & Co Limited v Weldon (No. 7) [1990] 1 WLR 1156 .... 11.94, 11.106

Derby Specialist Fabrication Ltd v Burton [2001] IRLR 69 . . . . 7.100
Devine v Designer Flowers Wholesale Florist Sundries Ltd [1993] IRLR 517 . . . . 9.40
Devis & Sons Limited v Atkins [1977] AC 931 (HL) 9.28
Diocese of Southwark v Coker [1998] ICR 140 . . . . 6.31
Distillers Co (Biochemicals) Limited v Times Newspapers Limited
   [1975] 1 QB 613 . . . . 11.33
Distillers Company (Bottling Services) Limited v Gardner [1982] IRLR 48 . . . . . . 15.78, 15.82
D'Offay v Initial Security Limited, ET, Case No. 1402289/03 . . . . App 9
Dolling Baker v Merett [1990] 1 WLR 1205 . . . . 10.30
Donovan v St Johns Ambulance (2001) . . . . App 9
Douglas v Birmingham City Council, EAT/018/02, 17 March 2003 . . . . 3.32, 5.03,
                                                              5.07, 6.06, App 8
Douglas v Hello! Ltd [2003] 3 All ER 182 . . . . 11.17
Dring v GMB (2002) . . . . App 9
Dubai Aluminium Co Ltd v Salaam [2002] UKHL 48, [2003] 2 AC 366 . . . . 7.38
Dubai Aluminium Co v Al Alawi [1999] 1 All ER 703, [1999] 1 Lloyds Rep 478 . . . . 11.106
Dudin v Salisbury District Council, ET, Case No. 3102263/03,
   20 February 2004 . . . . 5.19, App 9
Dunnachie v Kingston Upon Hull City Council [2004] UKHL 36,
   [2004] IRLR 727 (HL) 9.40, 9.69
Durrant v Norfolk Sheet Lead Limited, ET, Case No. 1500257/01, 30 April 2002 . . . . . . App 9

Eardley and Waldron v Lifeline Care Ltd, ET, Case No. 3300707/03;3300708/03 . . . . . . App 9
Eastelow v Taylor (2001) . . . . App 9
Eastwood v Magnox Electric plc [2004] UKHL 35, [2004] ICR 1064 . . . . 9.44
Edmondson v Birch [1907] 1 KB 371 . . . . 14.08
E.K v Turkey, Case No. 28496/95, 7 February 2002 . . . . 11.123
Electronic Data Processing Ltd v Wright, EAT/292/83 . . . . 9.08
Enessy CO Sa t/a the Tulcan Estate v Minoprio [1978] IRLR 489 . . . . 9.08
England v Baldwin Ltd (in administrative receivership), ET, Case No. 6001820/01 . . . . . . App 9
Essa v Laing Limited [2004] EWCA Civ 2, [2004] IRLR 313 . . . . 9.55
Everett Financial Management Limited v Murrell, EAT/552, 553/02 and
   EAT/952/02, 24 February 2003 . . . . 3.37, 3.40, 7.83, App 8
Everett v Miyano Care Services Ltd, ET, Case No. 3101180/00, 6 April 2000 . . . . App 9
Express Newspapers plc v News (UK) Limited [1990] FSR 359 . . . . 13.15

Faccenda Chicken Ltd v Fowler [1987] Ch 117 . . . . 11.04, 11.07
Fadipe v Reed Nursing Personnel [2001] EWCA Civ 1885, [2005] ICR 1760 . . . . 7.18
Fairhall v Safeway Stores plc, Case No. 2104468/2001, 12 June 2002 . . . . 7.26, App 9
Fairmile Kindergarten v MacDonald, EAT/0069/05 . . . . 12.07
Felter v Cliveden Petroleum Company, EAT/0533/05, 9 March 2006 . . . . 3.61, 3.69,
                                                           7.45, 7.85, 8.12, App 8
Fernandes v Netcom Consultants UK Ltd, ET, Case No. 22000060/00,
   24 January 2000 . . . . 9.21, App 9
Fielden v Total Fitness UK Limited, ET, Case No. 2104937/03 . . . . App 9
Fincham v HM Prison Service, EAT/0925/01 and EAT/0091/01,
   19 December 2002 . . . . 3.30, 3.31, App 8
Flintshire County Council v Sutton, EAT/1082/02, 1 July 2003 . . . . 3.31, 7.03,
                                                              7.29, 8.15, App 8
Francome v Mirror Group Newspapers Ltd [1984] 1 WLR 892 . . . . 5.30, 11.25,
                                                             11.37, 11.77, 11.90
Fraser-Woodward Ltd v (1) British Broadcasting Corporation
   (2) Brighter Pictures Ltd (2005) FSR 36 . . . . 13.05
Freemans plc v Flynn [1984] IRLR 486 . . . . 9.08

Fressoz and Roire v France [2001] 31 EHRR 2 . . . . 11.130, 11.135
Friend v CAA, Unreported, cited in [1998] IRLR 253 . . . . 9.24, 9.25, 14.10
Frost v Boyes & Co (2000) . . . . App 9
Fulham Football Club (1987) Limited v Tigana [2004] EWHC 2585 . . . . 15.51

Gaddafi v Telegraph Group [2000] EMLR 431 . . . . 14.21
Gamlen Chemical Co (UK) v Rochem (No. 2) (1980) 124 SJ 276 (CA) 11.106
Gammon v Stoke Mandeville Hospital NHS Trust, ET, Case No. 2700909/02 . . . . App 9
Garry v Ealing LBC [2001] EWCA Civ 1282, [2001] IRLR 681 . . . . 7.12
Gartside v Outram (1857) 26 Ch 113 . . . . 11.21, 11.25, 11.27, 11.30
GKR Karate (UK) Ltd v Yorkshire Post Newspapers Ltd [2000] 2 All ER 931 . . . . 14.20
Glyn v Weston Feature Film Co [1916] 1 Ch 261 . . . . 11.46
GMB Union v Fenton, EAT/0798/02 and EAT/0046/03, 7 October 2003 . . . . 4.49
Goldman Sachs Services Ltd v Montali [2002] ICR 1251 . . . . 10.18
Goldman v Thomas Cook Retail Ltd, ET, Case No. 3201925/02 . . . . App 9
Goodwin v Cabletel UK Limited [1997] IRLR 665 . . . . 4.50, 7.69, 13.42
Goodwin v United Kingdom [1996] 22 EHRR 123 . . . . 11.123, 11.131, 11.145, 12.17
Gradwell v Council for Voluntary Service, Blackpool, Wyre & Fylde,
    Manchester ET, Case No. 2404313/97 . . . . 6.26
Great Atlantic Insurance v Home Insurance [1981] 1 WLR 529 (CA) 5.14
Green v First Response Training and Development Limited, ET,
    Case No. 250542/03, 13 April 2002 . . . . 4.30, App 9
Green v Warren Grieg & Partners . . . . 10.46, App 9
Greene v Associated Newspapers Ltd [2004] EWCA Civ 1462, [2005] QB 972 . . . . 11.08
Grigoriades v Greece (1998) 4 BHRC 43 . . . . 11.146, 11.151
Group 4 Night Speed Limited v Gilbert [1997] IRLR 398 . . . . 7.102
Guinness Mahon & Co Limited v Kensington & Chelsea LBC [1999] QB 215 . . . . 11.120
Gulwell v Consignia plc, ET, Case No. 1602588/00, 11 June 2002 . . . . 4.46, App 9

H and others, Re [1996] AC 563 . . . . 3.45
Hall v Lorimer [1992] ICR 739, [1994] ICR 218 (CA) 6.04
Halpin v Oxford Brookes University, 30 November 1995 . . . . 14.10
Hamblet v Same, (Ramsey v Walkers Snack Foods Limited) [2004] IRLR 754 . . . . . . 12.05, 12.08
Hands v Simpson Fawcett and Co Limited (1928) 44 TLR 295 . . . . 15.30
Handyside v United Kingdom [1976] 1 EHRR 737 . . . . 11.131, 11.157
Harrow LBC v Knight [2003] IRLR 140 . . . . 3.59, 7.03, 7.29, 7.34, 7.45, 7.53,
                                                                    7.54, 7.77, 7.80, 7.82, App 8
Hassan v YAFA (2001) . . . . App 9
Havers v OCS Cleaning South Ltd, ET, Case No. 3100829/00, 3 October 2000. . . . . App 9
Hayden v Dorchester Trinity Club Ltd, ET, Case No. 3102769/01,
    17 January 2003 . . . . App 9
Hayes v Reed Social Care & Bradford MDC, ET, Case No.1805531/00 . . . . 6.37, App 9
Health Development Agency v Parish [2004] IRLR 550 . . . . 10.54, 10.70
Hebditch v MacIlwaine [1894] 2 QB 54 (CA) 14.08
Hendricks v Metropolitan Police Commissioner [2003] IRLR 96 . . . . 7.100, 7.101, 7.102
Herron v Wintercomfort for the Homeless, ET, Case No.1502519/03,
    11 August 2004 . . . . 5.38, 9.65, App 9
Hinton v University of East London [2005] EWCA Civ 532, [2005] IRLR 552 . . . . App 8
Hittinger v St Mary's NHS Trust & Imperial College (2001) . . . . App 9
HM Prison Service v Salmon [2001] IRLR 425 . . . . 9.53, 9.57, 9.60
Holden v Connex South Eastern Limited, ET, Case No. 2301550/00,
    15 April 2003 . . . . 5.21, 7.103, App 9
Holmes v Grimsby College . . . . 16.49, App 9
Honeyrose Products Ltd v Joslin [1981] IRLR 80 . . . . 10.24

Horcal Limited v Gatland [1983] IRLR 459, [1984] IRLR 288 (CA) 15.59, 15.64
Horrocks v Lowe [1975] AC 135 (HL) 4.07, 4.52, 14.15
Hossack v Kettering BC, EAT/1113/01, 29 November 2002 . . . . 7.73, 13.42, App 8
Hough v Virtual Presence (2001) . . . . App 9
HRH Prince of Wales v Associated Newspapers Limited [2006]
    EWHC 522 (Ch) 11.19, 13.38
Hubbard v Vosper [1972] 2 QB 84 . . . . 11.33, 13.05, 13.16, 13.17, 13.20
Hunt v G.N.Ry [1891] QB 189 . . . . 14.09
Hutcheson v The Key Group (KGI) South, ET, Case No. 3100213/03 . . . . App 9
Hyde Park Residence v Yelland (1999) EMLR 654 . . . . 13.11, 13.16, 13.22, 13.27, 13.33
Hydra plc v Anastasi [2005] EWHC 1559, 20 July 2005 . . . . 15.08

IBM UK Limited v Prime Data [1994] 1 WLR 719 . . . . 10.39
ICTS (UK) Ltd v Tchoula [2000] ICR 1191 . . . . 9.53, 9.63, 9.64
IDC v Cooley [1972] 1 WLR 443 . . . . 15.58
Igen Ltd v Wong [2005] EWCA Civ 142, [2005] IRLR 258 (CA) 7.84
Imutran Ltd v (1) Uncaged Campaigns Ltd (2) Daniel Louis Lyons
    [2001] 2 All ER 385 . . . . 11.61, 11.110, 13.38
Initial Services v Putterill [1968] 1 QB 396 . . . . 5.30, 5.32, 11.02, 11.22, 11.27, 11.31,
                                                        11.40, 11.77, 11.90, 11.100, 11.110
Intelsec Systems Limited v Grech-Cini [2000] 1 WLR 1190 . . . . 11.04
Intercity East Coast Ltd v McGregor, EAT/473/96 . . . . 9.10
International Computers Ltd v Whitley [1978] IRLR 318 . . . . 10.23
Investigating Directorate v Hyundai Motor Distributors (2000) 10 BCLR 1079,
    (Constitutional Court of South Africa) 11.14
Iron and Steel Trades Confederation v ASW Limited [2004] IRLR 926 . . . . 10.60
Island Export Finance v Umunna [1986] BCLC 460 . . . . 15.58
Istil Group Inc v Zahoor [2003] EWHC 165 (Ch), [2003] 2 All ER 252 . . . . 11.106
Item Software (UK) Limited v Fassihi [2004] EWCA Civ 1244, [2004]
    IRLR 928 (CA) 15.02, 15.05, 15.08, 15.34, 15.43, 15.44, 15.55, 15.62, 15.65

Jackson v ICS Group Limited, EAT/499/97, 22 January 1998 . . . . 8.19
Jameel v Wall Street Journal Europe [2006] UKHL 44, [2005]
    4 All ER 356 . . . . 14.18, 14.19
Jeffrey v London Borough of Merton, ET, Case No. 2304242/02 . . . . 16.50, App 9
Jersild v Denmark [1994] 19 EHRR 1 . . . . 11.131
Jiad v Byford [2003] EWCA Civ 135 . . . . 7.12
John Reid Enterprises Limited v Pell [1999] EMLR 675 . . . . 12.20
Johnson v Powerworld Limited, ET, Case No. 2502218/02 . . . . App 9
Johnson v Unisys Limited [2001] UKHL 13, [2001] IRLR 279 . . . . 9.40, 9.44, 9.64
Jones v F Srl & Son (Furnishers) Ltd [1997] IRLR 493 . . . . 8.15
Jones v Gordon (1877) 2 App Cas 616 . . . . 4.39
Jones v Tower Boot Co Limited [1997] IRLR 168 . . . . 7.36

Kajenki v Torrington Homes, ET, Case No. 3302912/01,
    30 September 2002 . . . . 5.24, App 9
Kay v Northumbria Healthcare NHS Trust, ET, Case No. 6405617/00,
    29 November 2001 . . . . 5.36, App 9
Keech v Sandford [1726] Sel Cas 1 King 61 . . . . 15.58
Khashoggi v Smith (1980) 124 SJ 149 (CA) 11.42
King v G.B-China Centre [1992] ICR 516 (CA) 7.84, 7.85, 7.86
Kopel v Safeway Stores [2003] IRLR 753 . . . . 10.58, 10.59
Kraus v Penna [2004] IRLR 260 . . . . 3.07, 3.43, 3.44, 3.46, 3.48, 3.49, 3.51,
                                          3.64, 3.65, 3.66, 3.68, 3.69, 3.73, 5.27, 10.50, App 8

Kuddus v Chief Constable of Leicester Constabulary [2001] UKHL 29 . . . . 9.57

Kuwait Airways Corporation v Iraqi Airways Corporation [2005] EWCA Civ 286 . . . . . 11.106

Ladbroke Racing Limited v King, Daily Telegraph, 21 April 1989 . . . . 15.22, 15.79

Lansing Linde v Kerr [1991] 1 WLR 251 (CA) 11.04, 11.60

Lawrence David v Ashton [1989] ICR 123 . . . . 11.08

Leonard v Serviceteam Limited, ET, Case No. 2306083/01, 30 April 2002 . . . . App 9

Lewer v Railtrack plc, ET, Case No. 2302352/00, 7 December 2000 . . . . App 9

Lewis v Motorworld Garages Ltd [1985] IRLR 465 . . . . 8.15

Lillie and Reed v Newcastle City Council [2002] EWHC 1600 . . . . 14.17

Linfood Cash and Carry Limited v Thomson [1989] IRLR 235 . . . . 12.04, 12.06, 12.07, 12.08

Lingard v HM Prison Service, ET, Case No.1802862/04,

    16 December 2004 . . . . 7.75, 9.21, 16.02, App 9

Lingens v Austria [1986] 1 EHRR 407 . . . . 11.131, 11.145

Lion Laboratories Ltd v Evans [1985] 1 QB 526 (CA) 3.72, 5.30, 11.23, 11.24,

                              11.25, 11.32, 11.94, 13.07, 13.25, 13.27, 13.28

Lister v Hesley Hall [2001] AC 215 (HL) 7.37, 7.38, 15.27, 15.42, 15.52, 15.54, 15.55

Llewelyn v Carmarthenshire NHS Trust (2002) . . . . App 9

Logan v Commissioners of Customs & Excise [2004] IRLR 63 (CA) 10.44

London Regional Transport v The Mayor of London [2001] EWCA Civ 1491,

    [2003] EMLR 88 . . . . 11.20, 11.39, 11.54, 11.61, 11.109

Lord Chancellor v Coker [2001] EWCA Civ 1756, [2001] ICR 507 . . . . 7.11, 7.12

Loveless v Earl [1999] EMLR 530 (CA) 14.05, 14.16

Lucas v Chichester Diocesan Housing Association Limited, EAT/0713/04,

    7 February 2005 . . . . 4.24, 4.34, 4.35, 4.36, 7.63, 8.21, 10.09, 10.44, App 8

Lyon v St James Press Ltd [1976] IRLR 215 . . . . 7.70

Mabrizi v National Hospital for Nervous Diseases [1990] ICR 281 . . . . 9.73

Maini v Department for Work and Pensions, ET, Case Nos: 2202378/01;

    2203653/01 and 2203978/01, 15 October 2002 . . . . App 9

Marchant v The Holiday Place (2000) . . . . App 9

McConnell v Police Authority for Northern Ireland [1997] IRLR 625 . . . . 9.63, 9.64, 9.65

McCormack v Learning and Skills Council, ET, Case No. 3104148/01,

    5 December 2002 . . . . 3.38, 10.46, App 9

MacDonald v Advocate General for Scotland [2003] UKHL 34, [2004] 1 All ER 339 . . . . . 7.42

McGreal v Kingsleigh Holdings Ltd, ET, Case No. 2400030/03, 29 January 2004 . . . . App 9

McKennitt v Ash [2006] EMLR 10 . . . . 11.13, 11.17, 11.20,

                                   11.24, 11.45

McMeechan v Secretary of State for Employment [1997] IRLR 353 (CA) 6.25

McPherson v BNP Paribas [2004] IRLR 558 . . . . 10.54

Maini v Department for Work and Pensions, ET, Case No. 2203978/01,

    15 October 2002 . . . . 3.37, 3.38

Majrowski v Guys & St Thomas NHS Trust [2006] UKHL 234 . . . . 7.37

Malik v BCCI SA [1998] AC 20 (HL) 11.91

Malone v MPC [1979] Ch 344 . . . . 11.27

Marler (E.T.) Ltd v Robertson [1974] ICR 72 . . . . 10.55

Masiak v City Restaurants (UK) Limited [1999] IRLR 780 . . . . 3.75

Maund v Penwith District Council [1984] IRLR 24 (CA) 8.20, 8.23, 8.27

Meek v City of Brimingham City Council [1987] IRLR 250 . . . . 7.84

Mehdaoua v Demipower, ET, Case No. 2201602/04, 11 January 2005 . . . . 4.37, App 9

Melia v Magna Kansei [2005] ICR 874 . . . . 9.28, 9.42, 9.46, App 8

Melluish (Inspector of Taxes) v BMI (No. 3) Limited [1996] 1 AC 454 . . . . 5.14

Mennell v Newell & Wright (Transport Contractors) Ltd [1997] IRLR 519 . . . . 7.15

Meridian Ltd v Gomersall [1977] IRLR 425 . . . . 9.07
Mersey Care NHS Trust v Ackroyd [2006] EWHC 107 . . . . 12.22, 12.24, 12.27
Meteorological Office v Edgar [2002] ICR 149 . . . . 5.20, App 8
Midland Tool Limited v Midland International Tooling Limited [2003]
    2 BCLC 523 . . . . 15.64
Migrant Advisory Services v Chaudri, EAT/11400/97 . . . . 6.26
Miklaszewicz v Stolt Offshore Ltd [2002] IRLR 344 . . . . 2.12, 5.20, App 8
Miles v Gilbank [2006] EWCA Civ 543, [2006] IRLR 538 . . . . 9.48
Miller v 5m (UK) Ltd (EAT/0359/05, 5 September 2005 . . . . App 9
Mingeley v Pennock [2004] EWCA Civ 328, [2004] IRLR 373 (CA) 6.08
Ministry of Defence v Cannock [1994] ICR 918 . . . . 9.21, 9.50, 9.51, 9.53
Ministry of Defence v Jeremiah [1980] ICR 13 . . . . 7.11, 7.12
Mitsui & Co Ltd v Nexen Petroleum UK Ltd [2005] EWHC 625 (Ch),
    29 April 2005 . . . . 12.11
Monaghan v Close Thornton Solicitors, EAT/3/01, 20 February 2002 . . . . 10.58
Montgomery v Universal Services Handling Ltd, ET,
    Case No. 2701150/03 . . . . 9.21, 16.52, App 9
Morissens v Belgium (1988) 56 D&R 127 . . . . 11.126, 11.137, 11.138,
                                                                            11.144, 11.145, 11.151
Morrison v Hesley Lifecare Services Limited, EAT/0262/03 and EAT/0534/03,
    19 March 2004 . . . . 4.13, App 8
Morrow v Safeway Stores plc [2002] IRLR 9 . . . . 15.51
Mounsey v Bradford NHS Trust (2002) . . . . App 9
Moyhing v Barts and London NHS Trust, EAT/0085/06, 9 June 2006 . . . . 7.11, 7.12
Murray v Newham CAB [2001] ICR 708 . . . . 6.30
Murray v Powertech (Scotland) Ltd [1992] IRLR 257 . . . . 9.51
Mustapha v ProTX Ltd, ET, Case No. 2303086/99, 12 February 2001 . . . . App 9
Mutch v Robertson (1981) SLT 217 . . . . 14.08

Nagarajan v London Regional Transport [1999] ICR 877 (HL) 7.45, 7.46, 7.48, 7.49,
                                                                7.51, 7.52, 7.53, 7.65, 8.12, 8.13
Nairne v Highlands and Islands Fire Brigade [1989] IRLR 366 . . . . 9.09
Nationwide Building Society v Various Solicitors [1999] PNLR 52 . . . . 11.106
Neckles v London United Busways Limited, EAT/1339/99, 10 February 2000 . . . . 7.85
New Victoria Hospital v Ryan [1993] ICR 201 . . . . 5.14
Nicholson v Long Products, EAT/0166/02, 19 November 2003 . . . . 7.86
NLA v Marks & Spencers plc [1999] EMLR 369 . . . . 13.10
Noah v Shuba [1991] FSR 14 . . . . 13.02
Norton Tool Co Ltd v Tewson [1972] IRLR 86 . . . . 9.40
Norwich Pharmacal Co v Commissioners of Customs and Excise
    [1974] AC 133 . . . . 12.10, 12.11, 12.13, 12.15, 12.24
Nothman v London Borough of Barnet (No. 2) [1980] IRLR 65 . . . . 9.08
Nottingham University v Fishel (2001) RPC 367 . . . . 13.02, 15.57
Nottinghamshire County Council v Meikle [2004] EWCA Civ 859,
    [2004] IRLR 703 CA 8.15
NWL Ltd v Woods [1979] 1 WLR 1294 . . . . 11.60

O'Connor v MIND Halton (2001) . . . . App 9
Odong v Chubb Security Personnel, EAT/0819/02, 13 May 2003 . . . . 3.33, 3.35,
                                                                                    3.59, App 8
Olesinski v Tameside MBC, ET, Case No. 2400410/04 . . . . 7.57
Olesinski v Tameside MBC, ET, Case No. 2400410/10, 23 February 2005 . . . . App 9
O'Mara Books Limited v Express Newspapers plc [1999] FSR 49 . . . . 12.20, 12.21, 12.27

Omilaju v Waltham Forest London Borough Council [2005]
    EWCA Civ 1493, [2005] ICR 481 . . . . 8.15
Orlando v Didcot Power Stations, Sports and Social Club [1996] IRLR 262 . . . . 9.53
Owalo v Galliford Try Partnership Limited, Case No. 3203344/03, 2
    April 2004 . . . . 3.47, App 9
Owens v Mitsui Babcock Energy Limited, EAT/0732/03, 12 March 2004 . . . . App 8
Owusu v London Fire & Civil Defence Authority [1995] IRLR 574 . . . . 7.100
Oyston v Blaker [1996] 2 All ER 106 (CA) 5.14

P v P (Ancillary Relief: Proceeds of Crime) [2004] Fam 1 . . . . 10.89
P v T Limited [1997] 1 WLR 1309 . . . . 12.11, 12.13, 12.14, 12.21
(1) Painter (2) Collins v Southampton Motor Auction Millbank Ltd, ET,
    Case No. 3103894/03; 3103901/03 . . . . App 9
Parkins v Sodexho [2002] IRLR 109 . . . . 3.61, App 8
Parmiter v Coupland (1840) 6 M&W 105 . . . . 14.02
P. C. v CCC Limited, ET, Case No. 2304244/01, 26 April 2002 . . . . App 9
PCR Limited v Dow Jones Telerate Limited [1998] FSR 170 . . . . 13.12, 13.16, 13.27, 13.28
Peake v Automotive Products Limited [1977] ICR 968 . . . . 7.12
Pearce v Governing Body of Mayfield Secondary School [2001]
    EWCA Civ 1347, [2003] IRLR 512 . . . . 7.42
Pepper v Hart [1993] AC 593 . . . . 5.14
Perera v Civil Service Commission [1980] ICR 699 . . . . 10.34
Perkin v St George's Healthcare NHS Trust, ET, Case No. 2306256/02 . . . . App 9
Persaud (Luke) v Persaud (Mohan) [2003] EWCA Civ 394 . . . . 10.65
Phipps v Bradford Hospitals NHS Trust, EAT/531/02, 30 April 2003 . . . . 8.20, App 8
Pimlott v Meregrove Limited, ET, Case No. 1500625/01, 29 April 2002 . . . . App 9
Pinnington v The City and County of Swansea [2004] EWCA Civ 1180,
    [2005] ICR 685 (CA) . . . . 2.13, 7.02, 7.03, 7.12, 7.30, App 8
Pipes v Bridgeford Lodge (2002) . . . . App 9
Pirelli General Cable Works Ltd v Murray [1979] IRLR 190 . . . . 9.01, 9.13
Polkey v A E Dayton Services [1987] IRLR 503 . . . . 9.08
Porcelli v Strathclyde Council [1986] ICR 564 . . . . 7.12
Port of London Authority v Payne [1994] IRLR 9 . . . . 9.06, 9.12
Power v Hampshire County Council and The Governing Body of Hayling School,
    ET, Case No. 3101406/03 . . . . App 9
Power v Panasonic, EAT/439/04, 9 March 2005 . . . . 10.59
Price Waterhouse v BCCI Holdings (Luxembourg) SA [1992] BCLC 583 . . . . 11.38
Pro Sieben Media AG v Carlton UK Television Limited [1999] 1 WLR 605 . . . . 13.04,
                                 13.05, 13.06, 13.10, 13.12, 13.16, 13.17
Property Guards Ltd v Taylor and Kershaw [1982] IRLR 175 . . . . 9.26
Pullman v Hill [1891] 1 QB 524 . . . . 14.08
Purcell v Sowler [1891] 1 QB 474 . . . . 14.11

Qualcast (Wolverhampton) Ltd v Ross [1979] IRLR 98 . . . . 9.07
Quinn's Supermarket v A-G [1972] IR 1 . . . . 11.55

R (Daly) v Secretary of State for the Home Department [2001] 2 AC 532 . . . . 11.160
R v Broadcasting Standards Commission, ex p BBC [2001] QB 855 . . . . 11.14
R v CAC, ex p BBC [2003] EWHC 1375, [2003] ICR 1542 . . . . 6.08
R v Home Secretary, ex p Simms [2000] 2 AC 11 . . . . 11.50
R v Lancs CC Police Authority, ex p Hook [1980] QB 603 . . . . 14.08
R v Lord Chancellor's Department, ex p Nangle [1991] IRLR 343 (DC) 6.31
R v Loveridge [2001] EWCA Crim 973, [2001] 2 Cr App R 591 . . . . 11.14

R v Ponting [1985] Crim LR 318 . . . . 1.14
R v Secretary of State for the Environment, Transport and the Regions,
        ex p Spath Holme [2001] 2 AC 349 . . . . 5.14
R v Shayler [2002] UKHL 11, [2003] 1 AC 247 . . . . 11.157
Raja v Hoogstraten [2005] EWHC 2890 . . . . 3.91
Ramsey v Walkers Snack Foods Limited [2004] IRLR 754 . . . . 12.05, 12.08
Rank Xerox (UK) Ltd v Stryczek [1995] IRLR 568 . . . . 9.13
Reddington v Straker and Sons Limited [1994] ICR 172 . . . . 10.17
Redrow Homes (Yorkshire) Limited v Wright [2004] EWCA Civ 469,
        [2004] IRLR 720 (CA) 6.08
Reynolds v Times Newspapers Ltd [1999] 3 WLR 1010 . . . . 14.11, 14.18, 14.19
RGB Resources plc (in liduidation) v Rastogi [2002]
        EWHC 2782 . . . . 15.19, 15.25, 15.40, 15.66
Rhys-Harper v Relaxion Group plc [2003] UKHL 33,
        [2003] ICR 867 . . . . 7.18, 7.19, 7.22, 7.23, 7.24, 7.26
Richards v The Trustees of the Oxfordshire Advocacy Development, ET,
        Case No. 2700261/00 . . . . App 9
Riddick v Thames Board Mills [1977] QB 893 (CA) 14.02
Rivaud v Exeter City AFC Ltd, ET, Case No. 1701536/03 . . . . App 9
Robinson v Hartland Forest Golf Club (2001) . . . . App 9
Rodney Harrambeen Organisation Limited, Birmingham ET,
        Case No. 36684/86 . . . . 6.26
Roger Bullivant v Ellis [1987] ICR 464 . . . . 11.04
Rogers v Booth [1937] 2 All ER 751 . . . . 6.31
Rommelfanger v Federal Republic of Germany (1989)
        62 D&R 151 . . . . 11.148, 11.149, 11.151
Rookes v Barnard [1964] AC 1129 HL 9.61, 9.66, 9.67

S (A Child) (Identification: Restrictions on Publication), Re [2004]
        UKHL 47, [2005] 1 AC 593 . . . . 11.53
Sainsburys Supermarkets Limited v Hitt [2002] EWCA Civ 1588,
        [2003] IRLR 23 . . . . 12.04
Salinas v Bear Stearns Holdings Inc [2005] ICR 1117 . . . . 10.54, 10.68
Saltman Engineering Co Ltd v Campbell Engineering Co Ltd (1948)
        65 RPC 203 . . . . 11.11
Saunders v Westminster Dredging Co Ltd, ET, Case No. 1500083/00 . . . . App 9
Schering Chemicals Limited v Falkman Limited [1982] QB 1 (CA) 5.32, 11.89,
        11.93, 11.101
Science Research Council v Nassé [1979] IRLR 465 . . . . 10.38
Scott v Building Management Services (2002) . . . . App 9
Scott v Commissioners of Inland Revenue [2004] EWCA Civ 400,
        [2004] IRLR 713 . . . . 9.50, 10.68
Seager v Copydex Limited [1967] 1 WLR 923 (CA) 11.11
Selkent Bus Co Ltd v Moore [1996] ICR 836 . . . . 8.08, 8.09
Serco Limited v Lawson [2006] UKHL 3, [2006] IRLR 289 . . . . 6.39, 7.65
Service Corporation International plc v Channel Four Television
        Corporation [1999] EMLR 83 . . . . 13.02, 13.26, 13.27
Shamoon v Chief Constable of Royal Ulster Constabulary [2003]
        UKHL 11, [2003] ICR 337 . . . . 7.11, 7.12
Sharma v London Borough of Ealing, EAT/0399/05 . . . . 10.68
Sheffield CAB v Grayson [2004] IRLR 353 . . . . 6.28
Shepherds Investments Ltd v Walters [2006] EWHC 836 (Ch),
        12 April 2006 . . . . 15.57, 15.65

Sheriff v Klyne (Lowestoft) Ltd [1999] IRLR 481 . . . . 9.54
Shillito v van Leer (UK) Limited [1997] IRLR 495 . . . . 4.50, 7.71, 13.42
Sim v Manchester Action on Street Health, EAT/10085/01,
    6 December 2001 . . . . 3.62, App 8
Sim v Stretch [1936] 2 All ER 1237 . . . . 14.02
Sims v MASH (2000) . . . . App 9
Sir Robert McAlpine Limited v Telford, EAT/0018/03, 13 May 2003 . . . . 3.10
SK & F v Department of Community Services [1990] FSR 617 . . . . 11.68
Skyrail Oceanic v Coleman [1981] ICR 864 . . . . 9.52
Smith v Age Concern (Manchester), ET, Case No. 2407595/00, 11 July 2001 . . . . App 9
Smith v Hayle Town Council [1978] ICR 996 . . . . 8.19, 8.22
Smith v Lehman Bros, EAT/0486/05, 13 October 2005 . . . . 8.08
Smith v Ministry of Defence, ET, Case No. 1401537/04,
    26 April 2005 . . . . 4.32, 4.37, 5.03, App 9
SmithKline Beecham Plc v Generics (UK) Ltd BASF [2003]
    EWCA Civ 1109, [2003] 4 All ER 1302 . . . . 11.17
Solicitor, Re A [1992] 2 All ER 335 . . . . 3.91
Speyer v Thorn Security Group Limited, ET, Case No. 2302898/03,
    20 August 2004 . . . . 4.29, 5.12, App 9
Staples v Royal Sun Alliance, ET, 2001 . . . . 5.36, App 9
Steel and Morris v UK, (Application No. 68416/01), [2004] 39 EHRR SE6 . . . . 11.133
Stephens v Avery [1988] 1 Ch 449 . . . . 11.46
Stephenson Jordan & Harrison Limited v MacDonald [1952] RPC 10 . . . . 13.02
Stone v Charrington & Co Ltd [1977] ICR 248 . . . . 10.20
Street v Derbyshire Unemployed Workers' Centre [2004] EWCA Civ 964;
    [2005] ICR 97 (CA) 3.87, 4.07, 4.08, 4.16, 4.17, 4.18, 4.19, 4.27,
                                  4.29, 4.31, 4.33, 4.38, 4.42, 4.45, 4.47, 4.48, 4.49, 5.01,
                                5.14, 5.29, 7.63, 7.67, 8.07, 10.08, 10.09, 10.48, 11.71,
                                                11.86, 16.15, App 8
Stuart v Bell [1891] 2 QB 341 . . . . 14.06
Sugar v Associated Newspapers Ltd, unreported, 6 February 2001 . . . . 14.14, 14.17
Sunday Times v The United Kingdom [1979] 2 EHRR 245 . . . . 11.157
Surrey County Council v Henderson, EAT/0326/05, 23 November 2005 . . . . 12.08
Sutherland v Network Appliance Ltd [2001] IRLR 12 . . . . 11.120
Sutherland v Stopes [1925] AC 47 . . . . 14.04
Swain v West (Butchers) Ltd [1936] 3 All ER 261 . . . . 15.14, 15.17, 15.25,
                                           15.26, 15.28, 15.35, 15.37, 15.39,
                                                     15.42, 15.68
Sybron Corporation v Rochem Limited [1984] 1 Ch 112 . . . . 15.06, 15.07, 15.10,
                                 15.16, 15.17, 15.20, 15.23, 15.24, 15.25, 15.26,
                               15.29, 15.33, 15.34, 15.35, 15.39, 15.46, 15.48,
                                                  15.51, 15.56

Taplin v C Shippam Limited [1978] IRLR 450 . . . . 3.46, 9.33
Tedeschi v Hosiden Besson Ltd, EAT/959/95 . . . . 8.19
Tench v G.W.Ry (1873) 33 UP Can QB 8 . . . . 14.08
Tesco Stores Limited v Pook [2003] EWHC 823,
    [2004] IRLR 618 . . . . 15.02, 15.08, 15.57, 15.61
Thorgeirson v Iceland [1992] 14 EHRR 843 . . . . 11.123, 11.133, 11.140, 11.141,
                                               11.144, 11.145, 11.150, 11.151
Thornley v ARA Ltd, EAT/669/76 . . . . 8.35
Tillery Valley Foods v Channel Four Television [2004] EWHC 1075,
    11 May 2004 . . . . 11.08, 11.14

Tillmanns Butcheries Pty Ltd v Australasian Meat Industry Employees
Union (1979) 42 FLR 331 . . . . 5.21
Time Warner v Channel Four [1994] EMLR 1 . . . . 13.05, 13.19
Timex Corporation Ltd v Thomson [1981] IRLR 522 . . . . 9.08
Todd v British Midland Airways Ltd [1978] ICR 959 . . . . 6.39
Tournier v National Provincial and Union Bank of England [1924]
1 KB 461 (CA) 11.19
Tran v Greenwich Vietnam Community Project [2002] EWCA Civ 553,
[2002] ICR 1101 . . . . 7.84
Trotman v North Yorkshire County Council [1999] IRLR 98 . . . . 15.52
Trustees of Mama East African Women's Group v Dobson, EAT/0219/05
and EAT/0220/05, 23 June 2005 . . . . 7.43, 7.62, 7.65,
7.66, 7.69, App 8
Tse Wai Chun Paul v Cheng, (Court of Final Appeal, Hong Kong), [2001]
EMLR 777 . . . . 14.14, 14.15
Tucht v FRG, 9336/81, unreported 11.141, 11.143, 11.151

Ultraframe (UK) Ltd v Fielding [2005] EWHC 1638 . . . . 15.58
United States ex rel. Copeland v Lucas Western Inc, September 1993 . . . . 16.14
United States ex rel. Merena v SmithKline Beecham Corp, 8 April 1998 . . . . 16.13
University of Nottingham v Eyett [1999] IRLR 87 . . . . 15.50, 15.51

Van Der Heijden v The Netherlands (1985) D & R 42 . . . . 11.147
Van Gestel v Cann, 31 July 1987 . . . . 15.61
Vaseghi v Brunel University, EAT/0757/04 and EAT/0222/05,
3 November 2005 . . . . 7.73
Vaux & McAuley v Bickerton (2002) . . . . App 9
Vento v Chief Constable of West Yorkshire Police (No. 2) [2002]
EWCA Civ 1871; [2003] IRLR 102 . . . . 9.48
Virgo Fidelis Senior School v Boyle [2004] IRLR 268 . . . . 7.85, 9.41, 9.45, 9.49,
9.54, 9.61, 9.62, 9.65, 9.66, 9.67,
16.15, App 8
Vogt v Germany [1996] 21 EHRR 205 . . . . 11.127, 11.131, 11.149, 11.151

W v Edgell [1990] 1 Ch 359 (CA) 5.30, 5.33, 11.87
Wainwright v Home Office [2003] UKHL 53, [2004] 2 AC 406 . . . . 11.14
Watt v Longsdon [1930] 1 KB 130 . . . . 14.08
Weatherby v International Horse Agency & Exchange Limited [1910] 2 Ch 297 . . . . 13.17
Weld-Blundell v Stephens [1919] 1 KB 520 . . . . 5.32, 11.22
Welsh Refugee Council v Brown, EAT/0032/02, 22 March 2002 . . . . 3.18, App 8
West Midlands Passenger Transport Executive v Jaquant Singh [1988] ICR 614 . . . . 7.49
White v University of Manchester [1976] ICR 419 . . . . 10.21
Whiting Designs Limited v Lamb [1978] ICR 89 . . . . 9.27
Wilcox v HGS [1975] ICR 306 . . . . 10.34
Wilgar v Ali t/a Wardour House, ET, Case No. 1700692/04 . . . . App 9
Williams v North Tyneside Council, EAT/0415/05/CK, 31 January 2006 . . . . App 8
Williamson v Karl Suss (GB) Ltd, ET, Case No. 2702198/00, 2 March 2001 . . . . App 9
Wilson v Maynard Shipbuilding Consultants AB [1978] ICR 376 . . . . 6.39
Wood Group Heavy Industrial Turbines Ltd v Crossan [1998] IRLR 680 . . . . 9.08
Woodward v Abbey National plc [2006] EWCA Civ 822 . . . . 7.05, 7.12, 7.18,
7.22, 7.23, 9.38, 9.56, 10.61, App 8
Woodward v Hutchins [1977] 1 WLR 760 (CA) 11.41, 11.45, 11.92
Woolgar v Chief Constable of the Sussex Police [1999] 3 All ER 604 . . . . 11.87

X Ltd v Morgan Grampian (Publishers) Ltd [1991] 1 AC 1 (HL) 12.17
X v UK (1979) 16 D & R 101   . . . . 11.125, 11.147

Yewdall v Secretary of State for Work and Pensions, EAT/0071/05, 19 July 2005   . . . . 7.102
Youssoupoff v MGM Pictures Ltd (1934) 50 TLR 581   . . . . 14.02

Zinnia [1984] Lloyds Rep 211   . . . . 15.27, 15.54
ZYX Music GmbH v King (1995) EMLR 281   . . . . 13.27

TABLE OF LEGISLATION

United Kingdom	xxxvii
Australia	xliii
United States	xliii
European Legislation	xliii

UNITED KINGDOM

Primary legislation

Banking Act 1987 . . . . 15.72
  s 41 . . . . 15.72
Bills of Exchange Act 1882 . . . . 4.39
Building Society 1986 . . . . 15.72
  s 55(3) 15.72
Civil Evidence Act 1968 . . . . 10.39
  s 14 . . . . 10.39
Companies Act 1985 . . . . 15.72
  s 434 . . . . 15.72
Contempt of Court
    Act 1981 . . . . 12.15, 14.21
  s 10 . . . . 12.15, 12.16, 12.17,
                12.20, 12.22, 14.21
Copyright Designs and
    Patents Act 1988 . . . . 13.02, 13.27,
                13.32, 13.35
  s 1 . . . . 13.02
  s 4 . . . . 13.02
  s 10(1) 13.34
  s 10(2) 13.34
  s 11 . . . . 13.02
  s 11(2) 13.02
  s 30 . . . . 13.03, 13.05, 13.14, 13.16
  s 30(1) 13.03, 13.05, 13.06,
           13.08, 13.16, 13.20, 13.41
  s 30(1A) 13.03,
                13.08,13.20
  s 30(1A)(a) 13.03
  s 30(1)(a) 13.03
  s 30(1A)(b) 13.03
  s 30(1A)(c) 13.03
  s 30(1A)(d) 13.03
  s 30(1A)(e) 13.03
  s 30(2) 13.03, 13.09, 13.11, 13.41

  s 30(3) 13.03, 13.14
  s 163 . . . . 13.02
  s 171(3) 13.21, 13.27, 13.33,
           13.36, 13.39, 13.41
  s 178 . . . . 13.14
Criminal Appeals Act 1968 . . . . 3.72
  s 2 . . . . 3.72
Data Protection Act 1998 . . . . 3.27, 3.83,
        4.13, 7.57, 11.13, 13.01
  s 1(1) 3.84
  s 2 . . . . 3.84
  s 55 . . . . 3.83, 3.84, 3.88, 13.01
  s 55(1) 3.83, 3.84, 3.85, 3.86
  s 55(1)(a) 3.83
  s 55(1)(b) 3.83
  s 55(2) 3.85, 3.88
  s 55(2)(a) 3.85
  s 55(2)(a)(i) 3.85
  s 55(2)(a)(ii) 3.85
  s 55(2)(b) 3.85
  s 55(2)(c) 3.85
  s 55(2)(d) 3.85
  Sch 1
    Pt 2
      para 9 . . . . 3.27
Disability Discrimination
    Act 1995 . . . . 4.49, 6.27, 7.19
  s 4 . . . . 7.40
  s 4(2) 7.19
  s 7 . . . . 6.28
  s 17A(1C) 7.84
  s 17A(4) 9.41
  s 55(4) 4.49
  s 68 . . . . 6.28, 6.30
  s 68(1) 6.27
  Sch 3 . . . . 7.102
    para 3(3) 7.102

Drug Trafficking Act 1994 . . . . 15.73
  s 52(1) 15.73
Employment Act 2002 . . . . 5.35, 7.90
  s 31 . . . . 9.72
  s 32 . . . . 7.90
  Sch 2 . . . . 7.90, 7.92
    para 6 . . . . 7.90
    para 9 . . . . 7.90
    para 15 . . . . 7.93, 7.95
    para 15(2) 7.96
    Pt 2 . . . . 7.91, 7.93
  Sch 3 . . . . 7.90
    para 15 . . . . 5.35
  Sch 4 . . . . 7.90
Employment Protection Act 1975 . . . . . 10.74
Employment Relations
    Act 1999 . . . . 6.39, 7.04
  s 32(3) 6.39
  Sch 2 . . . . 7.08
Employment Rights Act 1996 . . . . 1.04,
    1.24, 2.04, 3.01, 6.15, 7.36, 7.63,
    7.91, 7.92, 10.87, 11.02, 11.34,
    11.49, 11.67, 11.86, 12.21, App 1
  Pt 4A 7.93
  Pt IVA 6.09, 6.20, 6.36
  Pt V 2.09, 7.01, 7.07, 7.08, 7.09
    7.14, 7.78, 7.80
  Pt X 6.20, 6.36, 7.01, 9.44
    Chap II 9.68
  s 31(4) 9.72
  s 43(1)(b) 3.33
  s 43(1)(c) 6.18
  s 43(2) 2.13, 11.96
  s 43(2)(aa) 6.14
  s 43(3) 4.45
  s 43A 3.64, 8.05
  ss 43A–43L 11.69
  s 43B 2.05, 2.06, 3.01, 3.13, 3.14,
    3.22, 3.25, 3.37, 3.46, 3.61,
    3.64, 3.66, 3.73, 4.19, 4.22,
    5.21, 5.38, 7.16, 7.60, 8.35,
    10.45, 11.29, 11.35, 11.49, 13.42
  s 43B(1) 3.02, 3.07, 3.09, 3.52, 3.64
  s 43B(1)(a) 3.02, 3.52, 3.87
  s 43B(1)(a)–(f) 3.03
  s 43B(1)(b) 3.02, 3.52, 5.27
  s 43B(1)(c) 3.02
  s 43B(1)(d) 3.02
  s 43B(1)(e) 3.02, 3.52
  s 43B(1)(f) 3.02
  s 43B(2) 3.56, 3.94
  s 43B(3) 3.82, 3.87, 3.88, 3.89, 11.13
  s 43B(4) 3.92, 3.93, 5.13, 5.14
  s 43C 2.13, 3.13, 3.26, 4.05, 4.36,
    5.01, 5.02, 5.04, 5.11, 5.17,
    5.37, 7.65, 11.73, 11.74

ss 43C–43E 2.07
ss 43C–43G 3.13
ss 43C–43H 2.05, 10.03
s 43C(1) 5.02
s 43C(1)(a) 2.07, 4.29, 5.02, 5.03
s 43C(1)(b) 2.07, 5.02, 5.04, 5.05,
    5.07, 5.08, 5.09, 5.10, 5.11,
    5.16, 11.74
s 43C(1)(b)(i) 5.02, 5.05, 5.06,
    5.07, 5.08, 5.09
s 43C(1)(b)(ii) 5.02, 5.06, 5.07,
    5.08, 5.09
s 43C(2) 2.07, 4.29, 5.02, 5.11,
    5.12, 5.37
s 43D 2.07, 2.08, 2.13, 3.67, 4.01,
    5.01, 5.13, 5.14, 5.15, 5.37, 7.65
s 43E 2.07, 5.01, 5.16, 11.119
s 43E(i) 5.16
s 43E(ii) 5.16
s 43F 2.07, 2.08, 2.13, 3.13, 3.14,
    3.25, 3.88, 5.01, 5.07, 5.17, 5.19,
    5.20, 5.21, 5.23, 5.24, 5.34,
    11.75, 11.79, 11.87, 11.119, 16.47
s 43F(1) 5.17
s 43F(1)(a) 5.17, 5.19
s 43F(1)(b) 5.17
s 43F(1)(b)(i) 5.17
s 43F(1)(b)(ii) 5.17, 5.21
s 43G 2.07, 2.08, 2.10, 2.13, 3.13,
    3.14, 3.25, 4.05, 4.19, 4.31, 4.40,
    4.48, 5.01, 5.11, 5.16, 5.21, 5.23,
    5.24, 5.25, 5.26, 5.28, 5.29, 5.36,
    5.37, 5.38, 8.31, 8.34, 8.35, 8.37,
    11.88, 11.94, 11.96, 11.97,
    11.99, 11.104, 11.105
s 43G(1) 5.23
s 43G(1)(a) 5.23
s 43G(1)(b) 4.40, 5.23
s 43G(1)(c) 4.19, 5.23, 5.24
s 43G(1)(d) 2.08, 5.23
s 43G(1)(e) 4.19, 5.23, 5.29, 5.36
s 43G(2) 2.08, 5.21, 5.23, 5.25,
    5.37, 5.38, 8.37
s 43G(2)(a) 2.08, 5.23, 5.25, 5.26, 5.27
s 43G(2)(b) 2.08, 5.23, 5.25, 5.27
s 43G(2)(c) 2.08, 5.23, 5.25, 5.28
s 43G(2)(c)(i) 5.23
s 43G(2)(c)(ii) 5.23
s 43G(3) 5.23, 5.29, 5.30, 5.36, 5.38
s 43G(3)(a) 5.23, 5.30
s 43G(3)(b) 5.23, 5.31
s 43G(3)(c) 5.23, 5.32
s 43G(3)(d) 2.10, 5.23, 5.33
s 43G(3)(e) 5.23, 5.34
s 43G(3)(f) 5.12, 5.23, 5.35, 5.36
s 43G(3)(g) 16.05

Employment Rights Act 1996 (*cont.*)
s 43G(4) 5.23, 5.28
s 43H 2.07, 2.08, 3.13, 3.14, 3.25,
4.48, 5.01, 5.21, 5.23, 5.24, 5.27,
5.29, 5.37, 5.38, 11.88, 11.94,
11.99, 11.105
s 43H(1) 5.38
s 43H(1)(a) 5.38
s 43H(1)(b) 5.38
s 43H(1)(c) 5.24, 5.38
s 43H(1)(d) 5.38
s 43H(1)(e) 5.38
s 43H(2) 5.38
s 43J 2.09, 2.10, 10.88, 11.02,
11.116, 11.118, 11.119, 11.120
s 43K 2.09, 6.09, 6.24, 7.01
s 43K(1) 6.06, 6.14
s 43K(1)(a) 6.10, 6.11
s 43K(1)(a)(i) 6.10
s 43K(1)(a)(ii) 6.10
s 43K(1)(b) 6.12
s 43K(1)(ba) 6.14
s 43K(1)(bb) 6.14
s 43K(1)(c)(ca) 6.14
s 43K(1)(d) 6.16
s 43K(2) 6.09, 7.40
s 43K(2)(a) 6.11
s 43K(2)(ab) 6.14
s 43K(2)(b) 6.14
s 43K(2)(b)(ba) 6.14
s 43K(2)(c) 6.17
s 43KA 2.10, 6.20
s 43KA(2) 6.21
s 43L 5.24, 8.05, 16.16
s 43L(2) 5.24
s 43L(3) 3.03, 3.39, 3.41
s 43M 7.07
s 44 . . . . 1.04, 3.73, 7.07, 7.18
s 44(1)(c) 3.73
s 45 . . . . 7.07
s 45A 7.07
s 46 . . . . 7.07
s 47 . . . . 7.07
s 47A 7.07
s 47B 6.20, 6.36, 7.01, 7.02, 7.04,
7.05, 7.06, 7.09, 7.10, 7.12, 7.17,
7.18, 7.19, 7.39, 7.53, 7.58, 7.65,
7.75, 7.80, 7.81, 7.85, 8.12, 8.13,
9.30, 9.42, 9.44, 9.49, 9.54,
11.03, 12.02, 14.12
s 47B(1) 7.01, 7.02
s 47B(2) 7.01, 7.04,
7.05, 9.43
s 47B(2)(a) 7.01
s 47B(2)(b) 7.01
s 47B(3) 7.01
s 47C 7.07
s 47D 7.07
s 47E 7.07
s 48 . . . . 2.09, 6.20, 7.01, 7.07, 7.18,
7.90, 7.97, 9.36
s 48(1A) 9.68
s 48(2) 7.76, 7.77, 7.79, 7.80, 7.81,
7.82, 7.86
s 48(3) 7.97
s 48(4) 7.28, 7.83, 7.98
s 48(4)(b) 7.28
s 49 . . . . 2.09, 6.20, 7.01, 7.07,
9.36, 9.44
s 49(5) 9.27
s 49(6) 9.39, 9.68
s 94 . . . . 8.03
s 94(1) 6.39, 8.05
s 95(1)(c) 8.14
s 98 . . . . 2.10, 7.80, 7.81, 7.88, 8.02,
8.05, 8.21, 8.36
s 98(1) 7.78, 7.80, 8.03, 8.11,
8.14, 8.19, 8.22, 8.26
s 98(2) 8.03, 8.06, 8.26
s 98(4) 8.01, 8.03, 8.22, 10.44
s 98(6) 8.03, 8.06
ss 99–103 . . . . 8.03
s 100 . . . . 1.04, 3.73
s 100(1)(c) 3.73
s 100(1)(c)(i) 3.73
s 100(1)(c)(ii) 3.73
s 100(1)(e) 3.75
s 103A 2.09, 6.20, 6.36, 7.05,
7.07, 7.58, 7.64, 7.65, 7.75,
7.85, 7.87, 7.88, 8.03, 8.04,
8.05, 8.06, 8.07, 8.10, 8.13,
8.15, 8.20, 8.21, 8.22, 8.28,
9.25, 9.43, 9.68, 12.02
s 105 . . . . 2.09
s 105(1) 8.17
s 105(6) 7.05
s 108(3) 8.19
s 108(3)(ff) 2.09
s 109(2)(ff) 2.09
s 111(2)(a) 10.02
s 111(2)(b) 8.39
s 112 . . . . 9.01
s 112(4) 9.02
s 113 . . . . 9.01
s 114 . . . . 9.03
s 114(4) 9.15
s 115 . . . . 9.03
s 116(1)(a) 9.04
s 116(2) 9.05
s 116(3) 9.05
s 116(4) 9.13
s 116(5) 9.11

Employment Rights Act 1996 (*cont.*)
s 116(6) 9.11
s 117(1) 9.17
s 117(2) 9.17
s 117(3) 9.18
s 118 . . . . 9.02, 9.69
ss 118–126 . . . . 9.01
ss 118–127 . . . . 9.18
ss 119–122 . . . . 9.02
s 123 . . . . 9.02
s 123(6) 9.09, 9.25
s 124 . . . . 9.02
s 124(1) 8.01
s 124(1A) 2.09
s 124(3) 9.14
s 124A 9.72
s 126 . . . . 9.02
s 127 . . . . 9.02
s 128 . . . . 11.02
ss 128–132 . . . . 2.09
s 128(1)(b) 9.31
s 128(2) 9.32
s 128(4) 9.32
s 128(5) 9.32
s 129(1) 9.33
s 129(2) 9.34
s 129(3) 9.34
s 129(3)(b) 9.34
s 129(4)–(6) 9.34
s 129(8) 9.34
s 129(9) 9.35
s 130 . . . . 9.35
s 137(1) 9.20
s 191 . . . . 6.33
s 191(1) 6.22
s 191(2)(aa) 6.22
s 191(3) 6.22
s 192 . . . . 6.33
s 193 . . . . 6.34
s 194 . . . . 6.36
s 195 . . . . 6.36
s 196 . . . . 6.39
s 196(3) 6.39
s 197 . . . . 7.04
s 199(7) 6.39
s 199(8) 6.39
s 200 . . . . 6.18
s 203 . . . . 11.120
s 230 . . . . 7.20
s 230(1) 6.02
s 230(3) 6.07, 6.08, 6.09,
                                                         6.12, 7.20
s 230(3)(b) 6.12
Employment Rights (Dispute
    Resolution) Act 1998 . . . . 10.76
Financial Services Act 1986 . . . . . 5.17, 11.79

Financial Services and Markets
    Act 2000 . . . . 15.72
s 177 . . . . 15.72
s 284 . . . . 15.72
Freedom of Information
    Act 2000 . . . . 11.19, 13.01
Human Rights Act 1998 . . . . 3.45, 8.19,
            11.01, 11.14, 11.15, 11.20, 11.50,
            11.51, 11.111, 11.121, 11.157,
            13.27, 13.28, 13.29, 13.33, 13.36
s 2 . . . . 11.121
s 6 . . . . 11.15
s 12 . . . . 11.62
s 12(3) 3.45, 11.09, 11.62
s 12(4) 3.45, 11.62
Insolvency Act 1986 . . . . 15.72
s 218 . . . . 15.72
s 219 . . . . 15.72
s 235 . . . . 15.72
Local Government Act 2000 . . . . 15.74
National Health Service (Scotland)
    Act 1978 . . . . 6.14
s 17J 6.14
Official Secrets Act 1911 . . . . 11.152
Official Secrets Act 1989 . . . . 1.14, 3.82,
                        11.19, 11.152, 11.157
s 1(1) 11.152, 11.161
s 1(3) 11.153, 11.154
s 1(5) 11.154
s 4 . . . . 11.155
s 4(1) 11.161
s 4(3) 11.161
s 9(1) 11.161
Pensions Act 1995 . . . . 15.71
s 48 . . . . 15.71
Pensions Act 2004 . . . . 15.71
s 70 . . . . 15.71
Pensions Schemes Act 1993 . . . . 15.71
s 33A 15.71
Police Reform Act 2002 . . . . 6.20
s 37 . . . . 6.20
Prevention of Terrorism (Temporary
    Provisions) Act 1989 . . . . 15.73
s 18A(1) 15.73
Proceeds of Crime
    Act 2002 . . . . 10.88, 10.92, 15.73
ss 327–329 . . . . 10.89, 10.91
s 328 . . . . 10.88, 10.90,
                                                         10.91, 10.93
s 328(1) 10.88
s 330 . . . . 15.73
s 331 . . . . 15.73
s 332 . . . . 15.73
Protection from Harassment
    Act 1997 . . . . 7.37

Public Interest Disclosure
    Act 1998 . . . . 1.01, 1.02, 1.22,
        1.23, 1.24, 1.25, 1.26, 1.27, 1.29,
        1.31, 2.04, 2.09, 2.10, 2.11, 2.12,
        3.01, 3.87, 4.41, 4.42, 4.44, 4.51,
        5.20, 6.05, 6.09, 6.14, 6.15, 6.20,
        6.22, 6.23, 7.01, 7.07, 7.12, 7.19,
        7.29, 7.30, 7.32, 7.37, 7.57, 7.59,
        7.61, 7.73, 7.91, 8.01, 8.05, 8.08,
        8.30, 8.32, 8.34, 8.36, 9.24, 9.73,
        10.05, 10.07, 10.09, 10.13, 10.28,
        10.35, 10.37, 10.47, 10.63, 11.64,
        11.67, 11.68, 11.69, 11.70, 11.72,
        11.114, 11.116, 11.147, 11.151,
        12.21, 13.01, 13.42, 14.08, 14.12,
        14.13, 15.01, 15.68, 15.70, 15.82,
        15.83, 16.01, 16.08, 16.09, 16.11,
        16.25, 16.28, 16.32, 16.33, 16.35,
        16.44, 16.49
    s 1 . . . . 11.69
    s 5 . . . . 7.05
    s 6 . . . . 7.05
    s 8 . . . . 2.10
    s 9 . . . . 9.31
    s 12 . . . . 2.10
    s 13. . . . . 2.10, 3.71, 6.18
    s 17 . . . . 1.24
Public Order Act 1986 . . . . 3.70
    s 18 . . . . 3.70
Race Relations Act 1976 . . . . 4.49, 7.10,
        7.17, 7.45, 7.60, 7.65, 8.12
    s 1(1)(a) 7.46, 7.48, 7.49, 7.52
    s 2 . . . . 7.46, 7.52, 7.77
    s 2(1) 7.52
    s 2(2) 4.49
    s 4 . . . . 7.40
    s 4(2) 7.10, 7.12, 7.19
    s 32 . . . . 7.36
    s 54A 7.84
    s 57(4) 9.41
    s 68(7) 7.100
Rehabilitation of Offenders
    Act 1974. 9.26
    s 4(3)(b) 9.26
Restrictive Trade Practices
    Act 1956 . . . . 11.22, 11.31
Sex Discrimination
    Act 1975 . . . . 4.49, 7.10, 7.17
    s 4 . . . . 7.77
    s 4(2) 4.49
    s 6 . . . . 7.40
    s 6(2) 7.10, 7.12, 7.19
    s 41 . . . . 7.36, 7.39
    s 41(3) 7.36
    s 63A 7.84

s 66(4) 9.41
s 76(6) 7.102
Social Security Contributions (Transfer
    of Functions) Act 1999 . . . . 15.71
    Sch 1
        para 44 . . . . 15.71
Terrorism Act 2000 . . . . 15.73
    s 19 . . . . 15.73
    s 20 . . . . 15.73
Trade Union and Labour Relations
    Act 1974 . . . . 8.19
    Sch 1 . . . . 8.19
Trade Union and Labour Relations
    (Consolidation) Act 1992 . . . . 2.09
    s 137 . . . . 7.85
    s 146 . . . . 7.08, 7.09, 7.77, 7.102
    s 147(1) 7.102
    s 152 . . . . 9.27
    s 155 . . . . 9.27
    s 178(2) 10.41
    s 237(1) 8.18
    s 237(1A) 2.09, 8.18
    s 238(2A) 2.09

Secondary legislation

Accountants (Banking Act 1987)
    Regulations 1994,
    (SI 1994/524) 15.72
Auditors (Financial Services Act)
    1986 Rules 1994,
    (SI 1994/526) 15.72
Auditors (Insurance Companies
    Act 1982) Regulations 1994,
    (SI 1994/449) 15.72
Building Societies (Auditors) Order
    1994, (SI 1994/525) 15.72
Civil Procedure Rules,
    (SI 1998/3132) 10.13,
        10.29, 10.62
    Pt 36 . . . . 10.58
    r 1.1–1.3 . . . . 10.13
    r 29PD
        para 6.4 . . . . 10.18
    r 31 . . . . 10.29
    r 31PD.5 . . . . 10.29
Copyright and Related Rights
    Regulations 2003,
    (SI 2003/2498) 13.03,
        13.08, 13.20
Education (Modification of
    Enactments Relating to
    Employment) Order 1999,
    (SI 1999/2256) 6.06
    Art 3(1) 6.06

Employment Act 2002 (Dispute
   Resolution) Regulations 2004,
   (SI 2004/752) 7.91, 8.39,
                            9.32, 9.72
  Reg 2 . . . . 7.94
  Reg 2(1) 7.91
  Reg 5(1) 9.32
  Reg 15 . . . . 7.95, 7.99
Employment Equality (Religion or
   Belief) Regulations 2003,
   (SI 2003/1660) 9.41
  Reg 31(3) 9.41
Employment Equality (Sexual
   Orientation) Regulations 2003,
   (SI 2003/1661) 9.41
  Reg 31(3) 9.41
Employment Protection (Recoupment
   of Jobseekers Allowance and
   Income Support) Regulations
   1996, (SI 1996/2349) 9.16
Employment Rights (Increase of
   Limits) Order 2005,
   (SI 2005/3352) 9.20
Employment Tribunals (Constitution
   and Rules of Procedure)
   Regulations 2004,
   (SI 2004/1861) 5.22,
                         10.10, 10.41
  r 4(4) 10.14
  r 10 . . . . 10.70
  r 10(1) 10.10
  r 10(2) 10.14
  r 10(2)(b) 10.10
  r 10(2)(d) 10.29
  r 10(5) 10.35
  r 11 . . . . 10.36
  r 11(2) 10.14
  r 12(2)(b) 10.17
  r 12(3) 10.17
  r 16(1) 10.41
  r 17(1) 10.14
  r 19 . . . . 10.14
  r 22(8) 10.14
  r 25(5) 10.14
  r 30(5) 10.14
  r 33(1) 10.14
  r 34(1) 10.17
  r 35(1) 10.14
  r 38 . . . . 10.58
  r 38(7) 10.14
  r 38(9) 10.53
  r 39(1) 10.52
  r 40(3) 10.52
  r 40(4) 10.52
  r 41(1)(a) 10.62

r 41(1)(b) 10.62
r 41(1)(c) 10.62
r 42(5) 10.14
r 48(2) 10.63
r 48(4) 10.67
Reg 2 . . . . 10.56
Reg 3(2) 10.13
Reg 3(3) 10.13
Reg 3(4) 10.13
Reg 10(3) 10.13
Sch 1 . . . . 10.41
  para 10(2)(d) 5.22
Sch 2 . . . . 10.14
  r 3(4) 10.14
Financial Investment Management
   Rules 11.36, 11.79, 11.80,
                11.81, 11.82, 11.84, 11.85
Friendly Societies (Auditors) Order
   1994, (SI 1994/132) 15.72
Health and Safety (Enforcing
   Authority) Regulations 1998,
   (SI 1998/494) 5.19
  Reg 4 . . . . 5.19
Management of Health and Safety
   at Work Regulations 1992,
   (SI 1992/2051) 15.73
  Reg 12 . . . . 15.73
Police (Conduct) Regulations 1999,
   (SI 1999/730) 6.19
Police Reform Act 2002
   (Commencement No. 8)
   Order 2004 . . . . 6.20
Public Interest Disclosure Act 1998
   (Commencement) Order 1999
   (SI 1999/1547) . . . . App 2
Public Interest Disclosure
   (Compensation) Regulations
   1999 (SI 1999/1548) . . . . App 2
Public Interest Disclosure (Northern
   Ireland) Order 1998,
   (SI 1998/1763) 1.24, 2.11
Public Interest Disclosure
   (Prescribed Persons)
   (Amendment) Order
   2003, (SI 2003/1993) 5.18
Public Interest Disclosure (Prescribed
   Persons) (Amendment)
   Order 2004, (SI 2004/3265) 5.18
Public Interest Disclosure (Prescribed
   Persons) (Amendment) Order
   2005, (SI 2005/2464) 5.18
Public Interest Disclosure
   (Prescribed Persons) Order,
   (SI 1999/1549) 5.18, 5.19

Response (Employment Tribunal)
    Rules 2004. . . . . 10.02
    r 1 . . . . 10.02
    r 1(3) 10.02
    r 4 . . . . 10.02
    r 10(2)(b). 10.07
Working Time Regulations 1998,
    (SI 1998/1833) 6.08, 6.11

AUSTRALIA

Australian Capital Territory Public
    Interest Disclosure Act 1994. . . . . . . 7.41
Whistleblowers Protection
    Act 1993 . . . . 7.41
Whistleblowers Protection
    Act 1994 . . . . 7.41

UNITED STATES

False Claims Act 1863 . . . . 16.16
Whistleblower Protection
    Act 1989 . . . . 3.54, 8.13

EUROPEAN LEGISLATION

Directives

Directive 76/207, EC Equal
    Treatment Directive 7.84
    Art 2 . . . . 7.84
    Art 7 . . . . 7.84
Directive 89/391, Introduction of
    Measures to Encourage
    Improvements in the Safety
    and Health of Workers at
    Work 15.73
    Art 13 . . . . 15.73

Directive 97/80, EC Burden
    of Proof Directive. 7.84
    Art 1 . . . . 7.84
    Art 2(1) 7.84
    Art 4(1) 7.84
    Art 4(2) 7.84
Directive 2000/43, EC Race
    Discrimination Directive 7.84
    Art 8(1) 7.84
    Art 8(2) 7.84
Directive 2000/78, EC Framework
    Employment Directive. 7.84
    Art 10(1) 7.84
    Art 10(2) 7.84

Treaties and Conventions

European Convention on Human
    Rights. 8.19, 11.01, 11.14
    Art 6 . . . . 10.14
    Art 8. . . . . 11.14, 11.15, 11.16, 11.17,
                 11.51, 11.53, 11.55
    Arts 8–11 . . . . 11.55
    Art 8(1) 11.14
    Art 8(2) 11.14
    Art 10 . . . . 11.14, 11.15, 11.16, 11.20,
                 11.51, 11.53, 11.55, 11.57,
        11.111, 11.133, 11.135, 11.146,
        11.149, 11.150, 11.151, 12.16,
           12.22, 12.27, 13.30, 13.31,
               13.35, 13.40, 14.11
    Art 10(1) 8.19, 11.14, 11.125,
                    11.148, 11.157
    Art 10(2) 11.14, 11.55, 11.122,
                11.129, 11.131, 11.157
Treaty on European Union 11.55
    Art 3b 11.55

1

INTRODUCTION

A.	**Turning a blind eye**	1.03	(4) 1992—Patient abuse	1.17
	(1) The *Piper Alpha* disaster	1.04	(5) Fraud in the European Commission	1.18
	(2) The Clapham rail disaster	1.05	D. **Triumph of the whistleblower**	1.19
	(3) BCCI	1.06	(1) Scott Report	1.20
	(4) Barings Bank	1.07	(2) Abbey National	1.21
B.	**Turning a deaf ear**	1.08	E. **The need for change**	1.22
	(1) Zeebrugge ferry disaster	1.09	F. **Momentum for reform**	1.23
	(2) Child abuse	1.10	G. **The Public Interest Disclosure**	
	(3) Lyme Bay canoe disaster	1.11	**Act 1998**	1.24
	(4) 1993—Cancer misdiagnosed	1.12	H. **Moving forward the consensus**	1.25
C.	**Blaming the messenger**	1.13	I. **Public awareness**	1.26
	(1) *R v Ponting* [1985] Crim LR 318	1.14	J. **The Shipman Inquiry report**	1.28
	(2) Dr Stephen Bolsin—Bristol Royal		K. **Beyond PIDA**	1.32
	Infirmary	1.15		
	(3) Andrew Millar—British Biotech	1.16		

I hope that the Bill will signal a shift in culture so that it is safe and accepted for employees . . . to sound the alarm when they come across malpractice that threatens the safety of the public, the health of a patient, public funds or the savings of investors. I hope that it will mean that good and decent people in business and public bodies throughout the country can more easily ensure that where malpractice is reported in an organisation the response deals with the message not the messenger.

(Standing Committee, Richard Shepherd MP, 11 March 1998, p 4).

1.01 This aspiration was expressed by Mr Richard Shepherd MP, who introduced the Private Member's Bill which led to the enactment of the Public Interest Disclosure Act 1998 (PIDA). It encapsulated the pressing need for a radical change in organizational culture insofar as it affects the whistleblower. We use the term 'whistleblowing' in this book to denote the act of an individual worker or a group of workers raising a concern so as to prevent malpractice or dangers to the public. We refer to the person raising the concern as a 'whistleblower'. These matters raised by the whistleblower typically involve a risk to health and safety, fraud, criminal activity, environmental dangers or miscarriages of justice.

In an organization (whether public or private) the people who are 'on the ground' may be the first to spot trouble or potential trouble, whether threats to health and safety or financial corruption. In the whistleblower, companies and public bodies alike possess a valuable resource to discover or uncover risk. However all too often the culture at work causes staff, through fear of victimization or dismissal, to react by doing and saying nothing. Further, in cases where an employee has spoken up, the reaction is often to regard the employee as a troublemaker, to be at best ignored and ostracized, 'sent to Coventry' and sometimes disciplined or dismissed for speaking up. The IRLB report *Whistleblowers at Work* (Bulletin 563 in February 1997) summarized this ethos as 'the "old" culture of fear, inertia and secrecy' in a situation where such legal protection as existed was, outside the area of health and safety, 'piecemeal and in many respects ineffective'.

1.02   The need to engender a change in the pervasive culture, and to strengthen the pro-tection available to the whistleblower, has been illustrated and acknowledged in the reports upon many tragedies and scandals which could have been prevented, or the impact reduced, had people spoken out or had the warnings of those who did speak out been heeded. These cases also demonstrated the pressing need for a change in the workplace culture relating to whistleblowers and the need to bolster the legal protection afforded to them. At the risk of over-generalization, we categorize events before PIDA came into force under the rubrics 'turning a blind eye', 'turning a deaf ear', 'blaming the messenger' and 'the triumph of the whistleblower'.

A. Turning a blind eye

1.03   In a number of cases, workers were afraid to speak up and this has had the most serious consequences.

(1) *The* Piper Alpha *disaster*

1.04   The Cullen Inquiry[1] was set up following the *Piper Alpha* disaster in 1988, in which 167 people died on a North Sea oil rig some 110 miles off the Scottish coast. The Inquiry uncovered a culture in which staff felt unable to raise health and safety concerns with management. The staff were placed on short-term contracts. This fac-tor, together with the lack of other employment in the region, created job insecurity that manifested itself in the reluctance of staff to raise concerns over safety. The Cullen Report found that when staff were faced with clear health and safety dangers:

> workers did not want to put their continued employment in jeopardy through raising a safety issue which might embarrass management.

---

[1] *Public Inquiry into the Piper Alpha disaster*, Cm. 1310 (1990).

Even though *Piper Alpha* employees had wanted to raise concerns over the health and safety dangers, the endemic culture was enough to prevent staff from doing so. It is doubtful that any of the staff envisaged the disastrous effects of their silence. Nevertheless, such a disaster highlights that, especially where workers are concerned about their job security, staff can be placed in a position where a culture leads them to turn a blind eye to danger, even where the danger is to themselves or their colleagues.

The Cullen Inquiry led directly to legislation specifically designed to protect against victimization of employees carrying out health and safety functions or raising grievances in relation to health and safety. This is now contained in ss 44 and 100 of the Employment Rights Act (ERA) 1996.

(2) The Clapham rail disaster

The Hidden Inquiry into the Clapham rail[2] crash, in which 35 people died and some 500 were injured, heard from one employee who revealed that whilst carrying out an inspection of the rail tracks and the wiring he came across some faulty loose wiring. At 8.10 a.m. on 12 December 1988 a signalling failure resulted in a crowded commuter train running head-on into a stationary train near Clapham Junction. Whilst the signal failure was not necessarily caused solely by the loose wiring, this was a contributory factor. When asked why the employee had not raised his concerns as to the loose wiring, he frankly replied that he did not want to *'rock the boat'*. This response reflected poorly not only on the individual employee whose responsibility was to check the wiring, but also on the organizational culture that contributed to a reluctance to report concerns even where to do so fell squarely within the employee's duties. **1.05**

(3) BCCI

The Bank of Credit and Commerce International SA was compulsorily wound up in 1991 following frauds estimated to run to £2 billion. The Bingham Inquiry[3] investigated BCCI's collapse. It identified an *'autocratic environment'*, where nobody dared to speak up, as a *decisive* factor in the failure to bring an end to the fraud in time to prevent BCCI's collapse. When, in 1990, one brave internal auditor did speak up about fraud he was dismissed purportedly on grounds of redundancy. Such a reaction fuelled fear which was present in the organization. **1.06**

The Bingham Inquiry led to a raft of new regulations imposing specific duties of disclosure on auditors in the banking, building society, insurance, and financial services sector (see Chapter 15).

---

² *Investigation into the Clapham Junction railway accident,* Cm. 820 (1989).
³ *Inquiry into the supervision of the Bank of Credit and Commerce International,* Cm. 198c (1992).

(4) Barings Bank

1.07   In relation to the collapse of Barings Bank the regulator found that a senior manager had failed to blow the whistle loudly or clearly.

B.   Turning a deaf ear

1.08   Even where a worker has, courageously, been willing to come forward with concerns, in all too many cases these have simply been either ignored or not brought to the attention of the relevant decision makers in the employing organization.

(1) Zeebrugge ferry disaster

1.09   The *Herald of Free Enterprise* ferry sunk at Zeebrugge in 1987 because the ferry bow doors were left open at the port resulting in the death of 193 people. The Sheen inquiry[4] found that on five separate occasions staff had raised concerns that the ferries were sailing with the bow doors open. The employees' concerns either were ignored or were not passed on by middle management. The inquiry went to great lengths to examine the many variables that occurred in conjunction to cause the ferry to sink. Nevertheless the failure of the organization to investigate or have proper regard to the concerns raised by staff was a serious and fundamental error. One member of staff had even put forward a constructive suggestion highlighting the possibility that a light in the bridge could alert a captain if the bow doors were still open. The Sheen Inquiry noted that if this sensible suggestion had received the serious consideration it deserved the disaster might well have been prevented.

(2) Child abuse

1.10   Between 1973 and 1986 countless children in care were assaulted and sexually abused in Leicestershire County Council's children's homes. Three men were convicted of assault in 1991, including Frank Beck, director of the homes involved. Mr Beck received five life sentences for crimes of rape and buggery. The Official Inquiry, chaired by Andrew Kirkwood QC, revealed that over the 13-year period there had been no less than 30 occasions on which concerns had been raised about Beck and his colleagues by children, staff and others. However no effective action was taken. The Inquiry noted that:

> the pressures on middle and junior care staff not to be seen to 'rock the boat' with adverse consequences for themselves made it all the more important to take very seriously (their) concern or complaints.

---

[4] Court inquiry, Department of Transport, Ct no. 8074, 1987, HMSO.

As a result of the Kirkwood Inquiry, steps have been taken by Leicestershire County Council to ensure that staff concerns about serious malpractice are properly considered.

(3) Lyme Bay canoe disaster

1.11 The Lyme Bay canoe tragedy is an example of a whistleblower being unable to prevent the tragedy from occurring but enabling action to be taken against the person who was accountable for the tragedy.

Joy Cawthorne worked in an activity centre at Lyme Bay. Her responsibilities included teaching children how to canoe. She became concerned that there were insufficient safety precautions for canoeing. She raised these concerns with the managing director responsible for running the centre but he refused to acquire the necessary equipment. Mrs Cawthorne felt she was unable to continue working and she resigned. However she wrote a letter to the managing director setting out clearly her concerns over the safety standards. In March 1993 four schoolchildren were killed during a canoeing expedition at Lyme Bay. The managing director of the centre was jailed and became the first person in the United Kingdom to be jailed for 'corporate manslaughter'. The prosecution relied heavily on the fact that despite the clear and graphic warning he had been given by Mrs Cawthorne about the grave risk to life if safety standards were not improved, the required improvements were not made and he could not give a good reason for ignoring the warning.

(4) 1993—Cancer misdiagnosed

1.12 Two thousand bone tumour cases had to be re-examined after an inquiry discovered that a senior pathologist at Birmingham's Royal Orthopaedic Hospital had misdiagnosed 42 cancer cases. While some patients unnecessarily underwent treatment, others who had needed attention were given the all clear. The inquiry, headed by Dr Archbald Malcolm, discovered that two consultants had expressed doubts about the diagnoses over several years, and criticized them for failing to speak up through official channels.

C. Blaming the messenger

1.13 In a number of high profile cases, rather than follow up the concerns raised by the worker, the employer instead victimized the worker. The inadequacy of protection for the whistleblower was therefore highlighted.

(1) R v Ponting [1985] Crim LR 318

1.14 A Minister of the Crown provided evidence to a House of Commons Select Committee on Foreign Affairs with regard to the Falklands Conflict and the sinking of the *Belgrano* ship. Subsequently Clive Ponting, a senior Foreign Office civil servant, revealed to Tam Dalyell MP information he had received as a civil servant, which indicated that the then Minister had been less than ' fulsome with the truth' when providing evidence to the Select Committee. Clive Ponting was arrested over this disclosure and charged with a breach of the Official Secrets Act.

On 28 January 1985, the case was heard at the Central Criminal Court. The jury were in effect presented with a defence case that required them to consider whether or not it was Ponting's moral duty to communicate the information to Dalyell. The jury acquitted him and the case resulted in a new Official Secrets Act.

(2) Dr Stephen Bolsin—Bristol Royal Infirmary

1.15 Dr Stephen Bolsin was an anaesthetist who questioned operating techniques at Bristol Royal Infirmary. These techniques were alleged to have been instrumental in the high death rates of infants during heart surgery. Over a period of five years Dr Bolsin sought to raise his concerns through the proper channels. Although he was vindicated by the General Medical Council, he was shunned by the medical profession and was forced to relocate. He now works in Australia.[5] The whole issue became the subject of a public inquiry under the chairmanship of Professor Ian Kennedy.

(3) Andrew Millar—British Biotech

1.16 British Biotech, an Oxford-based company established in 1986 with 10 scientists and shares trading at 40 pence, was applauded as one of the success stories of the 1990s. In 1996 it had the prospect of joining the FTSE 100 with shares valued at 350p, providing it with a market value of approximately £1.6 billion. Although it employed more than 450 people, in the previous 11 years the company had, surprisingly, failed to bring one product to the market. Despite other parties pushing for the company to expand, in 1996 the company faced losses in the region of £30 million against a turnover of less than £10 million.

Dr Andrew Millar joined British Biotech in 1992 as the Director of Clinical Research. His concerns appear to have arisen on 12 May 1997 when British Biotech issued two press releases announcing the result of trials, together with a request for authorization to the European drug safety agency—EMEA. At the same time

---

[5] *The Guardian*, 11 February and 29 June 1999.

many high-level appointments were made to the commercial team which gave the appearance that there was to be a launch of a drug in Europe. However by virtue of his position with the company Dr Millar was aware of disappointing results on drug trials both in Europe and in America. Ironically at the very same time as these press releases were made Dr Millar was in America providing a deposition to the Securities and Exchange Commission with regard to alleged misleading company press releases in America.

In February 1998 EMEA reported that the results of the American trial of the drugs had resulted in no marketing authorization being granted for the drugs. This came as a great shock to the shareholders. An analyst with Goldman Sachs contacted Dr Millar with regard to his not attending some company presentations. Apparently he proffered an explanation that he had problems with the company's business plan. The analyst was concerned and contacted two fund managers who represented one of British Biotech's largest shareholders. Dr Millar spoke candidly to the fund managers. The pattern was easy to establish. Press releases promising new drugs were released followed by further impartial tests failing to support the claims of the earlier press release. Perpetual approached Mercury Asset Management, the biggest shareholder of British Biotech. Dr Millar attended a meeting suggested by Mercury Asset Management with Kleinwort Benson, Biotech's bankers.

Dr Millar was suspended and then summarily dismissed. In a circular to share-holders British Biotech accused Dr Millar of acting 'improperly and unprofessionally'. Biotech then sued Dr Millar for breach of his contractual duty of confidence. In this case, however, the apparent attempt to blacken the name of the whistleblower ultimately failed. In June 1999 Biotech issued a statement exonerating Dr Millar and agreed to pay him substantial compensation (reported to be in the region of £250,000 plus costs).[6] As a result of Dr Millar's disclosures Biotech was censured by the Stock Exchange for making misleading statements about the prospects of one of its drugs.[7]

(4) 1992—Patient abuse

In July 1992, the report of a Committee of Inquiry revealed that patients at **1.17** Ashworth Special Hospital, Merseyside, had been subjected to a brutalizing regime of physical and mental abuse by members of hospital staff for more than three years. The Inquiry, chaired by Sir Louis Blom-Cooper QC, uncovered a 'developed pattern of intimidatory behaviour against staff and professionals who were brave enough to speak out', including death threats, vandalism and physical assault. The Report concluded that the culture at Ashworth had allowed the abuse to

---

6 *The Guardian*, 9 June 1999.
7 *The Guardian*, 25 June 1999.

continue unexposed. It recognized that the problem of non-reporting would be 'endemic' wherever such a culture persists. The Committee recommended that the hospital management make provision for nurses and staff to speak out about malpractice and 'blow the whistle' on abuse.

(5) *Fraud in the European Commission*

1.18 Paul van Buitenen, a Dutch assistant auditor in the European Commission's audit unit, compiled a dossier detailing widescale corruption, fraud and cronyism within the European Commission. It appears that Mr van Buitenen had first raised the matter internally and was threatened with disciplinary action if he passed the matter to the European Parliament.[8] Despite this Mr van Buitenen passed the dossier to the Green Party in the European Parliament. As a result in early December 1998 he was suspended on half pay whilst dismissal proceedings were considered. He was accused of 'imparting information to unauthorised and non-competent persons', notwithstanding that the European Parliament is responsible for assessing whether EU money has been properly spent. He also claims that his family has suffered death threats and that there has been a campaign to blacken his name such as by insinuating that he was politically motivated.

Following receipt of Mr van Buitenen's dossier, on 14 January 1999 the European Parliament resolved that a committee of indendependent experts should be formed to investigate the way in which the Commission detects and deals with fraud, mis-management and nepotism. The Committee delivered its first report on 15 March 1999. The report was so damning that all 20 commissioners felt compelled to resign *en masse* and Mr van Buitenen was able to claim that he had been vindicated by the report. Indeed the Committee's second report (10 September 1999, para 7.6.9) noted 'the value of officials whose conscience persuades them of the need to expose wrongdoings encountered during the course of their duties'. Notwithstanding this, Mr van Buitenen's suspension on half pay was only lifted when the maximum four-month disciplinary period expired. He was reassigned to a department audit-ing the furniture in the Commission's office.[9] He was also issued with a formal reprimand for breach of confidence.[10]

D. Triumph of the whistleblower

1.19 Notwithstanding the litany of cases in which the potential whistleblower has declined to come forward, or in which the whistleblower has been either ignored

---

[8] *The Guardian*, 5 January 1999.
[9] *The Guardian*, 24 July 1999.
[10] Public Concern at Work website <http://www.pcaw.co.uk>.

or victimized, there are other cases in which whistleblowing has prompted a positive response.

(1) Scott Report

Sir Richard Scott V-C's *Report of the Inquiry into the Export of Defence Equipment*   **1.20**
and Dual-Use goods to Iraq and Related Prosecutions, relating to the Arms to Iraq
affair resulted in large part from the actions of a whistleblower. A Matrix Churchill
employee warned the Foreign Office that the company was supplying munitions-
making equipment to Iraq. This letter, which Scott described as 'highly significant',
was kept a secret from ministers for over three years. However the letter played a crucial part in the Rt. Hon. Michael Heseltine's decision not to sign a public interest
immunity (PII) certificate for the purposes of the *Matrix Churchill* trial—which
led to the trial being aborted. With the existence of this letter it was clear to the
officials advising Mr Heseltine that there was a 'whistleblower' who might well go to
the press alleging a cover up. A Department of Trade and Industry official, recognizing the significance of the letter, wrote in a minute that:

> the difficulty of course is not simply that the letter exists but that the writer of the let-
> ter no doubt exists and even if he has not so far been involved in the proceedings by
> either the prosecution or the defense he may well make the existence of his letter pub-
> lic. The chances of his doing so will no doubt be all the greater if he is the one of those
> who is already made redundant or will be made redundant next month. It is tempting
> to suggest that we might claim PII for [the] letter, but I fear that doing so in the face of
> the possibility that the informant in it may well appear across the front of the tabloid
> press during the course of court proceedings, makes me diffident about suggesting it.[11]

The position taken by Mr Heseltine, as demonstrated by his own markings on the
memo and by his evidence to the Inquiry, was that the letter showed that 'everyone
knew'[12] the contract was for military equipment. This became the catalyst to his
refusal to sign the PII certificates and, accordingly, the withdrawal of the charges
taken out against the directors of Matrix Churchill for supplying arms to Iraq.

Whilst the opinion of the DTI official suggested that the whistleblower was still
regarded as a troublemaker, there is also some evidence that others within government
acknowledged, or wished to be seen to acknowledge, the value of the whistleblower.
PII was successfully claimed by the then Foreign Office Minister, Tristan Garel Jones,
to keep the identity of the whistleblower secret. This was because:

> it is undoubtedly in the public interest that the identity of a person carrying out
> his duty to inform the authorities of suspected wrong doing and thereby jeopardise
> himself and his livelihood should as far as possible be kept confidential.

---

[11] At p 1271, para G10.29.
[12] pp 1344–5.

(2) *Abbey National*

1.21   Gary Brown, a manager with Abbey National, received £25,000 from his employers as a reward for blowing the whistle on a superior who he believed was involved in corrupt dealings. Mr Brown was a sales promotion manager in 1993 when his suspicions were aroused over malpractice. He left Abbey National in 1994 but continued to assist the investigators. He appeared in the Old Bailey as a witness in the case against his superior. The superior, who once had been considered a possible chief executive, received an eight-year prison sentence for his malpractice. Shortly after the sentence Mr Brown received a letter from the chairman of Abbey National stating that he had appreciated Mr Brown's behaviour. To express his gratitude in an explicit manner a cheque for £25,000 was sent the following week.

Whilst Mr Brown never embarked upon the whistleblowing for any pecuniary reason, the chairman's gesture demonstrated to staff that Abbey National supported those who came forward to report serious wrongdoing.

E. The need for change

1.22   As the above cases illustrate, there are many people who could have averted a safety or financial disaster had they been encouraged or enabled to speak out. There are a brave few who have managed to succeed in raising their concerns despite facing cultural prejudice and practical barriers in doing so. It may be that there are many more cases in which whistleblowers have been effective in allowing matters to be addressed internally and as such the matter has not needed to come to public knowledge. Nevertheless the above cases illustrate that, prior to the PIDA, there was an urgent need for legislative action. In many cases employees witness serious malpractice but are reluctant to report this for fear of blighting their career by appearing difficult or disloyal. As illustrated by the above cases of 'blaming the messenger', there have been good grounds for fears of physical violence, intimidation or dismissal after blowing the whistle. Indeed a survey of more than 230 whistleblowers in the United Kingdom and the USA. (cited in *The Independent* for 28 January 1999) found that 84 per cent lost their jobs after informing their employer of fraud, even though they were not party to the fraud but were merely reporting the fact that it was going on.

The reluctance of potential whistleblowers to come forward, however, has not been attributable only to justified fears of reprisals. As illustrated by the cases of workers turning a blind eye, an additional factor has often been the prevailing 'culture' within many organizations where the whistleblower is contemptuously regarded as a 'grass' or a 'sneak' to be shunned and avoided. This culture has sometimes been supported (notably in the NHS) by the use of gagging clauses to restrain employees from voicing their concerns. Indeed the Nolan Committee, in its first report on Standards in Public Life,[13] (from which we include extracts in Appendix 4) noted that:

> there is a public concern about 'gagging clauses' in public employees' contracts of employment, which prevent them speaking out to raise concerns about standards of public propriety.

Even in the absence of an express gagging clause, the culture of secrecy might be enhanced by the employee's knowledge that the duty of confidence was owed to the employer and by the example sometimes set by the employing organization in failing to respond to concerns when raised. This culture was further sustained by deficiencies within the law which ensured that staff became trapped in an environment breeding inaction and apathy within the workplace despite the presence of dangers and malpractice.

> it is striking that in the few cases where things have gone badly wrong in local public spending bodies it has frequently been the tip-off to the press or the local Member of Parliament—sometimes anonymous, sometimes not—which has prompted the regulators into action. Placing staff in a position where they feel driven to approach the media to ventilate concerns is unsatisfactory both for the staff member and the organisation.[14]

Nevertheless there will no doubt still be occasions in which the employee justifiably fears that internal disclosure would merely result in reprisals against him or her. In other cases, as illustrated by the examples of 'turning a deaf ear', inadequate notice is taken when the matter is raised internally. One challenge for those legislating to protect the whistleblower was, therefore, to encourage disclosure within the employing organization, whilst providing adequate protection where wide disclosure is appropriate.

F. Momentum for reform

A sea change in the cultural perception of the value of whistleblowers was **1.23** prompted by the Nolan Report and by the observations of a number of public inquiries such as those relating to the Clapham rail crash, the *Piper Alpha* disaster and the collapse of BCCI.

The very term 'whistleblowing' subtly changed in its usage from a generally pejorative label denoting a stance against the establishment, to a word synonymous with openness and informed decision making. This itself reflects changing public

---

13 Cm. 2850–1(1995).
14 Committee on Standards in Public Life, Second Report, Cm. 3270-1 (1996) p 21.

attitudes to someone who is prepared to breach confidence to bring matters to a wider public attention. It may also say something more generally about the perceived need to bring matters to public attention because of a lesser confidence in the integrity of both public and private administration.

By the time the Public Interest Disclosure Bill was introduced to Parliament a wide consensus had developed as to the need for such legislation. There had been previous attempts to legislate for public interest whistleblowing. Dr Tony Wright MP introduced a Ten Minute Rule bill in 1995 for which there was not enough parliamentary time available and this was followed in the next parliamentary session by a Bill introduced by Don Touhig MP. However the Bill which became the 1998 Act was able to sail through Parliament due to an unusual case of cross-party co-operation on a matter impinging on employment law. It also had support from both sides of industry.

The Act is largely a product of the tireless work of Public Concern at Work (PCaW), an independent consultancy and legal advice centre launched in 1993, which has campaigned for many years for such legislation. It was introduced as a Private Member's Bill into the House of Commons by the Conservative MP Richard Shepherd and taken into the Lords by the Labour peer Lord Borrie QC. It received strong support from the Labour Government in its first year in office, especially the Minister of State at the Department of Trade and Industry, Ian McCartney MP. There was, unusually, no debate at the Second Reading in the House of Commons or at the Third Reading in the House of Lords because of the consensus that had developed in support of the measure.

G. The Public Interest Disclosure Act 1998

1.24 The PCaW Consultation Paper, issued before the Public Interest Disclosure Bill was enacted, defined the aim of changing the law as being:

> to make it more likely that where there is malpractice which threatens the public interest, a worker will—rather than turn a blind eye—raise the concern and do so in a responsible way.

The Act offers protection to the whistleblower, in broad terms, provided that the disclosure is proportionate and in relation to one of the specified subjects of public concern. It seeks to do so whilst not giving protection to those making wild allegations or simply 'gold digging'. The difficulty faced by the framers of the legislation in seeking to confine protection to appropriate cases of proportionate disclosure may explain the complex structure of the Act.

Indeed Lord Borrie QC stated in the House Lords debates that 'this is the most far reaching piece of whistleblowing legislation in the world'.

The Act operates by incorporating sections into the Employment Rights Act 1996, and throughout the book we refer to the section as thus incorporated rather than the section of PIDA itself. By section 17, the Act applies only to England, Scotland and Wales. This section enables its provisions to be extended to Northern Ireland by Order in Council, subject to the negative resolution procedure, and this has been the effect of the Public Interest Disclosure (Northern Ireland) Order 1998 (SI 1998 No. 1763 (NI 17)).

H. Moving forward the consensus

The important and hard-won consensus which led to the introduction of PIDA **1.25** has led on to other developments, with whistleblowing codes being developed in particular areas (eg FSA, NHS, Civil Service) and being extended (eg to police), which are covered in our appendices. The Civil Service Code issued in 2006 includes express reference to PIDA for the first time. The role of the whistleblower which was in times past a lonely one (and the whistleblower was often shunned and avoided) has become much more favourably viewed. An example of this was that *Time Magazine* featured whistleblowers on its first front cover in 2003 and dubbed 2003 the 'year of the whistleblower'. Those shown included the woman who blew the whistle which led to the Enron scandal being exposed.

I. Public awareness

One (but only one) barometer of public awareness is the level of claims to employ- **1.26** ment tribunals under PIDA. The number of claims has risen each year. In the first full year of the Act, 2000/2001, there were 416 applications rising to 528, 661, 756 and 869 for 2004/5, the last year for which statistics are available. About two-thirds have settled. The Act has acted as a catalyst for a whole range of developments in both the public and private sectors. PCaW found in 2003 that people are twice as likely to blow the whistle on workplace wrongdoing today as they were five years ago. The top two issues on which callers to the PCaW helpline raised concerns were safety risks and financial misconduct—each making up 30 per cent of calls. The major change over the past decade has been a threefold increase in concern about unfair trading and double standards and a similar increase in calls from the care sector. While consider- ing statistics it is interesting to note that of those who contacted PCaW in 2004/5 (see Biennial Review) 79 per cent had raised their concerns openly, 20 per cent had done so confidentially and only 1 per cent had made an anonymous report.

On the other hand, there is a real question how far consciousness of whistleblowing **1.27** has reached people 'on the ground'. A survey in May 2004 by UNISON (with the involvement of PCaW) showed that 50 per cent of UNISON members did not know whether their hospital or NHS Trust had a whistleblowing policy and 30 per cent said that it would not want to be told if there was a major problem (para 11.62). This lack of knowledge has fuelled increased Government interest in the provision of whistleblowing policies (considered in detail in chapter 16), so that the White Paper on Standards in Public Life issued in December 2005 stated that 'the Government agrees on the importance of ensuring that staff are aware of and trust the whistleblowing process and the need for the boards of public bodies to demonstrate leadership on this issue. It also agrees on the need for regular communication to staff about the avenues open to them to raise issues of concern.'

J. The Shipman Inquiry report

1.28 The next stage in the development of thinking about public interest concerns may come from the long-awaited Government response to Dame Janet Smith's Shipman Inquiry report. It is interesting to note that she states that the term whistleblower has acquired a specific connotation—so that she preferred to avoid that term (para 11.9). She did however call for greater public awareness of its role and more widespread availability of advice to those raising public interest concerns to be provided by PCaW if they were willing to do so or otherwise by a specialist body to be established.

Although not its primary focus the Report had much to say about whistleblowing because there were people who were in a position to disclose material about Dr Shipman from an early stage who were discouraged from doing so by reason of the law as it stood at the time. Had they come forward this might have saved lives. The Report notes that 'the message that emerges from media reports of whistleblowing cases is in essence a negative one; namely that those who put their heads above the parapet and dare to speak out are liable to be penalised in some way' (para 11.7). There were some natural barriers to the raising of concerns by those who had concerns about Shipman, such as being seen as a troublemaker or maverick, fear of recriminations and 'a feeling of impotence grounded in the belief that even if the report is made nothing will be done about it' (para 11.10). This was in addition to the possibility of a claim for defamation. Further 'there is a tendency for attention to be focused on the messenger rather than on the message' (para 11.12). Reading the report causes a feeling that not enough has changed in the underlying ethos of organizations not withstanding several years of PIDA being in force.

1.29 The Report was also concerned that junior doctors are unwilling to raise concerns about a consultant because of the fear that consultants might block their career progression (para 11.79).

Dame Janet made these proposals which at the time of writing await response **1.30** from the Government:

a. the change of language in the Act from disclosure to report since disclosure conveyed the 'presumption that the disclosed facts are true' (para 11.92);

b. disclosure to the General Medical Council or Healthcare Commission should attract second tier protection (para 11.93) ;

c. 'if employers are able to explore and impugn the motives of the messenger when trying to justify having action taken against him/her many messages will not come to light because organizations like PCaW will have to advise those who come to them for advice that their motives can be impugned and they may not be protected by PIDA' (para 11.106). There should thus be a 'public discussion of whether the words in good faith ought to appear in PIDA' (para l 1.108);

d. 'the onus should not be on an individual to establish reasonable belief in the case of internal disclosures and disclosures to external regulators'; rather the public interest would be best served by substituting suspicion for belief (para 11.111); and

e. 'the continued application as a threshold of "reasonable belief in the substantial truth" will result in the regulators remaining unaware of cases of which they should be aware' (para 11.112).

We consider these in more detail in the relevant chapters and in some cases offer our own views.

As to the future the key targets adopted by PCaW include: **1.31**

a. ensuring that business implements whistleblowing as part of risk management; and

b. lobbying policy makers to use whistleblowing as the best way to clarify lines of accountability across public service.

K. Beyond PIDA

In addition to offering our analysis of PIDA and how it has been interpreted by **1.32** tribunals and appellate bodies, this book also considers the common law. In many respects the statute builds on experience gained in common law cases and adopts some concepts derived from the common law. The question of a public interest defence affects actions for breach of confidence, defamation and breach of copyright.[15] Indeed the Act goes along with other developments in the common law, such as

---

[15] For a detailed exposition of the various guises in which a public interest may arise see Cripps, *The Legal Implications of Disclosure in the Public Interest* (2nd ed., London: Sweet and Maxwell, 1994).

the development of public interest defence to claims of breach of confidence, which have facilitated a more sympathetic approach to those acting in the public interest. It is also necessary to take into account the provisions of the European Convention on Human Rights. We discuss the way in which whistleblowing has been and is likely to be treated by the European Court of Human Rights.

One general theme running throughout PIDA, and the thinking of those who have promoted it, is the need to provide support and protection for whistleblowers in order to encourage them to come forward. However since disclosure by a whistleblower might prevent a disaster or perpetuation of fraud, the question arises as to whether there should also be a *duty* to blow the whistle. This has been reflected over the last decade in a number of statutory provisions imposing specific duties of disclosure, such as duties upon an auditor. We therefore consider the development of the common law and statutory duties of disclosure and the inter-relation of these obligations with the new provisions of the Act. Since the Act seeks to foster a new workplace culture which leaves behind the petty schoolyard perception of the whistleblower as a 'sneak', it might be suggested that there should be a fresh emphasis on the responsibilities of workers and therefore on the obligation, rather than merely the right, to disclose matters of genuine concern.

PART I

PROTECTING WHISTLEBLOWERS—
THE PUBLIC INTEREST DISCLOSURE
ACT 1998

2

STRUCTURE OF THE PUBLIC INTEREST DISCLOSURE ACT 1998

A. Introduction   2.01
B. The scheme of the legislation   2.04
C. Some initial observations   2.10
D. Commencement   2.11

A. Introduction

During the passage of the Public Interest Disclosure Bill in the House of Lords, **2.01** Lord Nolan stated that his Committee on Standards in Public Life had been persuaded of the urgent need for protection for public interest whistleblowers. He commended those behind the Bill:

> for so skilfully achieving the essential but delicate balance in this measure between the public interest and the interests of employers.[1]

At the heart of the Act, therefore, was the aim of identifying which sorts of disclo- **2.02** sure required protection, and in which circumstances it would be in the public interest that those making such disclosures be given protection. Those promoting the Bill emphasized that it was not merely an employee rights bill, but a public interest measure. As Lord Borrie explained (introducing the Bill in the Lords for its second reading on 11 May 1998):

> . . . this measure will encourage people to recognise and identify with the wider public interest and not just their own private position. It will reassure them that if they act reasonably to protect the legitimate interests of others who are being threatened or abused, the law will not stand idly by should they be vilified or victimised.

---

[1] *Hansard* HL, 5 June 1998, col. 614.

2.03　In this chapter we outline the scheme adopted to achieve this ambitious aim. The measures are then analysed in more detail in the following chapters of this book.

B. The scheme of the legislation

2.04　At the heart of the legislation were the new concepts of 'qualifying disclosure' and 'protected disclosure'. These brought together a number of different criteria by which to identify whether protection was merited. Only a 'qualifying disclosure' is a candidate to be a 'protected disclosure', and only a 'protected disclosure' attracts the special protection of the measures introduced by PIDA, principally through amendment to the Employment Rights Act 1996 (ERA).

2.05　There is a 'protected disclosure' if:

(a) the disclosure is a 'qualifying disclosure' as defined in s43B ERA; and
(b) there is compliance with one of sections 43C to 43H ERA—which set out different requirements depending on to whom the disclosure is made, becoming more demanding as the recipient of the disclosure becomes more remote from the employer or with a less obvious legitimate interest in receiving the information.

The flow chart at the end of this chapter outlines this process.

2.06　A 'qualifying disclosure' (as defined in s43B ERA) means 'disclosure of information' which, in the *reasonable belief* of the worker making the disclosure, tends to show one or more of six categories of 'relevant failures'. The first five categories of failure concern a past, ongoing, or likely future (a) criminal offence, (b) breach of a legal obligation, (c) miscarriage of justice, (d) danger to health or safety or (e) damage to the environment. The last category relates to cover-ups—that information tending to show that matters falling in one of the previous categories has been or is likely to be deliberately concealed. This initial hurdle of establishing a 'qualifying disclosure' therefore focuses on two elements: the nature of the information being disclosed, and the threshold requirements as to the 'reasonable belief' of the worker making the disclosure. The level of that threshold is a key regulator of the level of protection offered by the legislation. We consider this in more detail in Chapter 3.

2.07　The legislation provides various levels of protection for which different hurdles must be passed. In outline these relate to disclosure:

(a) to the employer (s43C(1)(a), (2) ERA);
(b) to anyone other than the employer legally responsible for the situation in respect of which the disclosure is made or to whose conduct the disclosure relates (s43C(1)(b) ERA);

(c) in the course of obtaining legal advice (s43D ERA);

(d) to a Minister if the individual is appointed under any enactment by the Minister (s43E ERA);

(e) to a regulator as prescribed in Regulations (s43F ERA);

(f) to any other person when it is reasonable to do so according to set criteria (s43G ERA); and

(g) where the disclosure is of exceptionally serious matters (s43H ERA).

Broadly, these levels of protection can be separated into three tiers.　**2.08**

(a) The first tier consists of ss43C–43E. The lowest threshold relates to disclosures in the course of obtaining legal advice (s43D), where there are no requirements above those for a qualifying disclosure. But for the other disclosures in this category the threshold is also low. The only requirement additional to that for a qualifying disclosure is that the disclosure must be made in good faith. This was at the heart of the legislation in encouraging disclosures to the employer, or otherwise to someone accountable for the relevant failure.

(b) The second tier consists of regulatory disclosures under s43F ERA. Here the threshold is set a little higher than first tier disclosures. It is specifically required that the worker must reasonably believe that the information disclosed and any allegation contained in it are substantially true. But the threshold is still deliberately lower than for wider disclosures, in recognition that a disclosure to a prescribed regulator is more likely to be in the public interest.

(c) The third tier comprises wider disclosures under ss43G or 43H ERA. Here the threshold for protection is at its highest, although the threshold is lower for s43H (exceptionally serious failures) than for s43G (other wider disclosures). For both s43G and s43H one of the requirements is satisfying a general test of whether, in all the circumstances, it was reasonable to make the disclosure. The worker opting to make a third tier disclosure therefore has a significantly greater degree of uncertainty as to whether the disclosure will be protected, and is encouraged first to make a first or second tier disclosure. In addition, under s43G, the worker must comply with one of subparagraphs (2)(a), (b) or (c)—which essentially deal with whether it is reasonable for the worker to believe that s/he will be victimized if the disclosure is made to the employer or that evidence will be concealed (where there is no prescribed person under s43F) or where the disclosure has previously been made to the employer or under s43F to a prescribed regulator (s43G(1)(d), (2) ERA).

Whilst the concept of a protected disclosure was a new one which PIDA intro　**2.09** duced, the mechanisms for protection are based principally upon structures that were already in place. Essentially there are three types of protection provided:

(a) Protection from being subjected to a detriment on the ground of having made a protected disclosure. This may include a detriment sustained during or after employment but in the case of employees does not include dismissal (where the remedy is unfair dismissal). This is one of a number of rights not to suffer detriment contained in Part V ERA, with common enforcement mechanisms and provisions for remedy in ss48 and 49 ERA. Protection is available to an extended category of 'workers' (s43K ERA).

(b) In the case of employees, protection by virtue of dismissal being automatically unfair where the reason or principal reason for dismissal was a protected disclosure (s103A ERA), including where the reason or principal reason for selection for dismissal on grounds of redundancy was the making of a protected disclosure (s105 ERA). Various limitations on the right to claim unfair dismissal are also disapplied—the minimum qualifying employment (s108(3)(ff) ERA), the upper age limit (s109(2)(ff) ERA) and the exclusion for taking part in industrial action (ss237(1A) and 238(2A) Trade Union and Labour Relations (Consolidation) Act 1992 (TULRCA)). There are also differences in the remedies available; the limit on the compensatory award is disapplied (s124(1A) ERA) and the provisions for claiming interim relief in ss 128–132 ERA are applied to protected disclosure dismissal cases.

(c) Agreements not to make protected disclosures are rendered void (s43J ERA). Workers therefore have protection against allegations of having acted in breach of contract by having made protected disclosures.

C. Some initial observations

2.10 The following features of the legislation are noteworthy at the outset:

(a) The legislation does not amend the common law, save to the extent that s43J ERA renders void a provision in an agreement prohibiting a worker from making a protected disclosure. Instead, as noted above, the legislation draws upon the existing statutory framework for unfair dismissal and protection against detriment.

(b) The legislation specifically refers to confidentiality only in relation to determining whether a third tier disclosure under s43G is protected. In determining whether it is reasonable for the worker to make such a disclosure, one of the relevant criteria is 'whether the disclosure is made in breach of a duty of confidentiality owed by the *employer* to any other person' (s43G(3)(d)). The issue of confidentiality between *employer* and *employee*, which is the subject matter of most common law claims (and is covered in Paragraphs 7.62–64 and Chapter 11 of this book), is not specifically referred to as something that must be taken into account.

(c) There is no residual class of protection in addition to the six specific defined categories of 'relevant failure'. It is therefore not open to the courts to determine on a case-by-case basis that there are other disclosures which should be protected under the legislation in the public interest. In this the legislation differs from some other jurisdictions which have legislated to protect whistleblowers.

(d) It does not follow that a whistleblower who falls outside the ambit of the Act will have no protection. The worker might still be able to rely upon the general unfair dismissal protection under s98 ERA and may have a contractual claim for wrongful dismissal.

(e) Where a disclosure does not qualify for protection, this may be something which tribunals can be expected to take into account in determining whether dismissal by reason of the disclosure is fair. The legislation is a code that provides guidance as to where protection is appropriate and that workers can be expected to follow, especially if the employer has a properly publicized whistleblowing policy.

(f) PIDA generally operates by amendment of other legislation, primarily the ERA. Its provisions are more easily followed by a review of the legislation which has been amended, rather than PIDA itself.

(g) Some of the provisions of PIDA as originally enacted have been repealed or amended. Section 8 set out provisions for compensation for unfair dismissal, but was repealed without ever coming into force and instead it was provided that there is no limit on the compensatory award. Section 12, which related to work outside the United Kingdom, has been repealed. Section 13, which excluded police officers, has been repealed and replaced with a new s43KA introduced into the ERA which extends the application of the protected disclosure provisions to police officers.

D. Commencement

The substantive provisions of PIDA came into force on 2 July 1999, a year after it **2.11** received Royal Assent. The Act applies only to England, Scotland and Wales. It was extended to Northern Ireland by SI 1998 No.1763 (NI. 17), which was brought into force on 31st October 1999 by SRNI 1999 No. 400.

An employment tribunal may consider a complaint based on a detriment or **2.12** dismissal after PIDA came into force, even though it relates to a protected disclosure made prior to 2 July 1999. In *Miklaszewicz v Stolt Offshore Ltd* [2002] IRLR 344 the EAT held that the employment tribunal had jurisdiction to consider the claimant's complaint that he had been unfairly dismissed by reason of making a 'protected disclosure', even though the disclosure in issue took place six years prior to the PIDA provisions coming into force. It was the dismissal which triggered the entitlement to invoke the statutory remedies.

However, as confirmed by the Court of Appeal in *Pinnington v The City and* **2.13** *County of Swansea and another* [2005] EWCA ICR 685, the detriment and the deliberate failure to act which inflicted the detriment suffered by the employee, must have occurred *after* the Act came into effect.

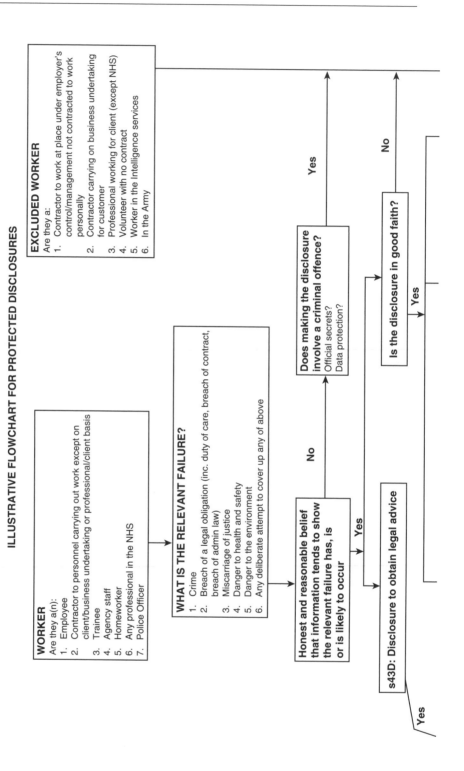

ILLUSTRATIVE FLOWCHART FOR PROTECTED DISCLOSURES

WORKER

Are they a(n):

1. Employee
2. Contractor to personnel carrying out work except on client/business undertaking or professional/client basis
3. Trainee
4. Agency staff
5. Homeworker
6. Any professional in the NHS
7. Police Officer

EXCLUDED WORKER

Are they a:

1. Contractor to work at place under employer's control/management not contracted to work personally
2. Contractor carrying on business undertaking for customer
3. Professional working for client (except NHS)
4. Volunteer with no contract
5. Worker in the Intelligence services
6. In the Army

WHAT IS THE RELEVANT FAILURE?

1. Crime
2. Breach of a legal obligation (inc. duty of care, breach of contract, breach of admin law)
3. Miscarriage of justice
4. Danger to health and safety
5. Danger to the environment
6. Any deliberate attempt to cover up any of above

Honest and reasonable belief that information tends to show the relevant failure has, is or is likely to occur

Does making the disclosure involve a criminal offence?

Official secrets?
Data protection?

Is the disclosure in good faith?

s43D: Disclosure to obtain legal advice

Yes

No

Yes

No

Yes

Yes

No

Yes

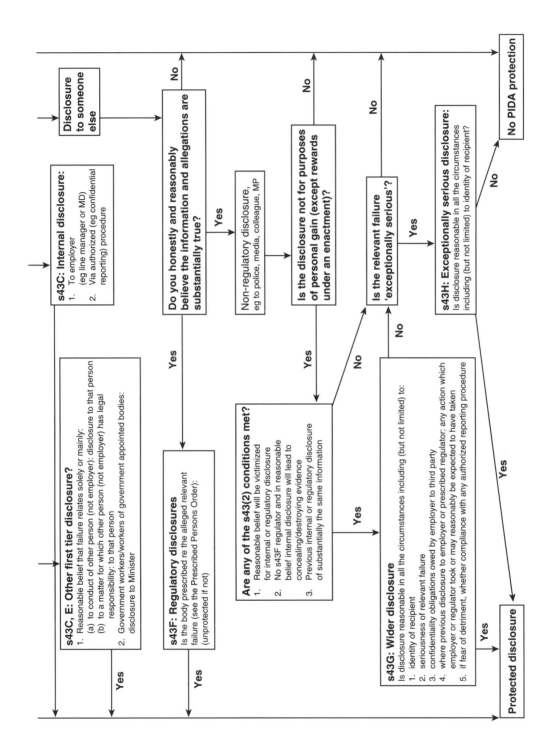

Disclosure to someone else

s43C: Internal disclosure:
1. To employer
   (eg line manager or MD)
2. Via authorized (eg confidential reporting) procedure

s43C, E: Other first tier disclosure?
1. Reasonable belief that failure relates solely or mainly:
   (a) to conduct of other person (not employer): disclosure to that person
   (b) to a matter for which other person (not employer) has legal responsibility: to that person
2. Government workers/workers of government appointed bodies: disclosure to Minister

Do you honestly and reasonably believe the information and allegations are substantially true?

No → **No PIDA protection**

Yes ↓

s43F: Regulatory disclosures
Is the body prescribed re the alleged relevant failure (see the Prescribed Persons Order): (unprotected if not)

Non-regulatory disclosure, eg to police, media, colleague, MP

Are any of the s43(2) conditions met?
1. Reasonable belief will be victimized for internal or regulatory disclosure
2. No s43F regulator and in reasonable belief internal disclosure will lead to concealing/destroying evidence
3. Previous internal or regulatory disclosure of substantially the same information

Is the disclosure not for purposes of personal gain (except rewards under an enactment)?

No → **No PIDA protection**

Yes ↓

Is the relevant failure 'exceptionally serious'?

No

Yes ↓

s43H: Exceptionally serious disclosure:
Is disclosure reasonable in all the circumstances including (but not limited) to identity of recipient?

No → **No PIDA protection**

s43G: Wider disclosure
Is disclosure reasonable in all the circumstances including (but not limited) to:
1. identity of recipient
2. seriousness of relevant failure
3. confidentiality obligations owed by employer to third party
4. where previous disclosure to employer or prescribed regulator: any action which employer or regulator took or may reasonably be expected to have taken
5. if fear of detriment, whether compliance with any authorized reporting procedure

Yes → **Protected disclosure**

Protected disclosure

3

PROTECTABLE INFORMATION

A. Overview of section 43B Employment
   Rights Act 1996   3.01
B. Reasonable belief   3.04
   (1) The *Darnton* guidance   3.04
   (2) Basis for the information disclosed   3.11
   (3) Reasonable suspicion or concern   3.21
   (4) All circumstances relevant to
       reasonable belief   3.24
C. 'Tends to show'   3.25
   (1) No need to establish truth
       of the allegation   3.25
   (2) Extent to which the disclosure must
       spell out the relevant failure and why
       it is shown   3.30
   (3) The disclosure must contain
       'information'   3.37
   (4) Information disclosed need not be
       unknown to the recipient   3.39

   (5) Disclosures in relation to likely
       future failures   3.42
D. The six categories   3.52
   (1) Criminal offence   3.56
   (2) Legal obligation   3.57
   (3) Miscarriage of justice   3.71
   (4) Health and safety risks   3.73
   (5) Damage to the environment   3.79
   (6) Cover-ups   3.80
E. Criminal disclosures   3.82
   (1) Exclusion for disclosures that
       are criminal offences   3.82
   (2) Consequential procedural
       issues   3.89
   (3) Standard of proof   3.90
F. Legal professional privilege   3.92
G. Geographical scope   3.94

A. Overview of section 43B Employment Rights Act 1996

3.01 The starting point in establishing protection for a disclosure is based on the concept of a 'qualifying disclosure'. This focuses on the nature of the information which may attract protection if other conditions set out in The Employment Rights Act (ERA) as modified by PIDA are satisfied in the particular case. But it has also been interpreted as involving threshold requirements in relation to the basis for belief in the information disclosed.

3.02 Section 43B(1) ERA provides that:

> In this Part a 'qualifying disclosure' means any disclosure of information which, in the reasonable belief of the worker making the disclosure, tends to show one or more of the following—
> (a) that a criminal offence has been committed, is being committed or is likely to be committed,

    (b) that a person has failed, is failing or is likely to fail to comply with any legal
obligation to which he is subject,

    (c) that a miscarriage of justice has occurred, is occurring or is likely to occur,

    (d) that the health or safety of any individual has been, is being or is likely to be
endangered,

    (e) that the environment has been, is being or is likely to be damaged, or

    (f) that information tending to show any matter falling within any one of the
preceding paragraphs has been, or is likely to be deliberately concealed.

3.03 Each of the categories of information in subparagraphs (a) to (f) is referred to
as a 'relevant failure'.[1] Together the 'relevant failures' extend to a wide range of
information. Protection is not tied to whether the information is confidential
or to whether a common law defence to breach of confidence can be established.
Indeed only in very exceptional circumstances would a disclosure within the
employing organization constitute a breach of the duty of confidentiality at all,
whether express or implied in the contract of employment. Equally there is no
requirement that the person to whom the disclosure is made is not already aware
of the information from other sources: s43L(3). The whistleblower need not be
telling him something which he did not already know.

B. Reasonable belief

(1) The Darnton guidance

3.04 For there to be a qualifying disclosure, there must be a 'disclosure of information
which, in the reasonable belief of the worker making the disclosure, tends to show
one or more' of the relevant failures. This involves both a subjective test of the
worker's belief, and an objective assessment of whether that belief could reasonably
have been held.

3.05 Guidance as to the appropriate approach for assessing reasonable belief was laid
down by the EAT in *Darnton v University of Surrey* [2003] ICR 615. Mr Darnton
was a senior lecturer at Surrey University's European Management School.
During his short employment with the University he clashed on a number of occasions with the head of the School, Professor Gamble. In June 1999, two months
after the start of his employment, he sent a memorandum to Professor Gamble stating that he felt threatened and harassed and was seeking professional advice.
Following further clashes, it was agreed between Mr Darnton and Professor
Gamble that Mr Darnton's full-time employment would end on 8 September 1999.
A compromise agreement was entered into after Mr Darnton had taken legal advice.

---

[1] s43B(5) ERA.

Pursuant to the agreement, Mr Darnton was to continue working for the School on the basis of a 12-month associate lectureship for which he was to be provided with £20,000 worth of work. Having found another permanent job, Mr Darnton resigned from the teaching part of his lectureship. The University then regarded the obligation to provide £20,000-worth of work as at an end. Mr Darnton disagreed. Mr Darnton wrote a letter to the Vice-Chancellor of the University, and copied it to the Chancellor. It was this letter which was relied upon as containing protected disclosures. The EAT described it as being 'full of intemperate language and complaints about Professor Gamble'. It included allegations of harassment and intimidation and a claim that he had been coerced into signing a compromise agreement. The Management School then wrote to Mr Darnton saying that his services were no longer required. Mr Darnton contended that this amounted to automatically unfair dismissal by reason of having made protected disclosures.

The employment tribunal held that there was no qualifying disclosure and also **3.06** that the disclosures were not made in good faith. In relation to whether there was a qualifying disclosure, the EAT held that the employment tribunal had erred in law by considering whether the allegations were in fact true and then considering in the light of this whether there was a reasonable belief in them. Instead whether there was a reasonable belief must be assessed on the basis of the facts as understood by the worker (or as the worker ought reasonably to have understood them).

The EAT (at para 31) also endorsed the commentary in the previous edition of this **3.07** book as follows:

> We have derived considerable assistance from *Whistleblowing: the new law* by John Bowers QC, Jeremy Lewis and Jack Mitchell. The learned authors write, at p.19, under the heading 'Reasonable belief in truth':
>
> > 'To achieve protection under any of the several parts of the Act, the worker must have a "reasonable belief" in the truth of the information as tending to show one or more of the six matters listed which he has disclosed, although that belief need not be correct (s43B(1)). This had led some to criticise the statute as giving too much licence to employees to cause trouble, since it pays no regard to issues of confidentiality in this respect. Nor need the employee actually prove, even on the balance of probabilities, the truth of what he is disclosing. This is probably inevitable, because the whistleblower may have a good "hunch" that something is wrong without having the means to prove it beyond doubt or even on the balance of probabilities ...[2] The notion behind the legislation is that the employee should be encouraged to make known to a suitable person the basis of that hunch so that those with the ability and resources to investigate it can do so.

---

[2] A sentence was omitted from the passage quoted by the EAT.

The control on abuse is that it must have been reasonable for the worker to believe that the information disclosed was true. This means, we think, that the following principles would apply under the Act:

> (a) It would be a qualifying disclosure if the worker reasonably but mistakenly believed that a specified malpractice is or was occurring or may occur.
> (b) Equally if some malpractice was occurring which did not fall within one of the listed categories, the disclosure would still qualify if the worker reasonably believed that it did amount to malpractice falling within one of those categories.[3]
> (c) There must be more than unsubstantiated rumours in order for there to be a qualifying disclosure. The whistleblower must exercise some judgment on his own part consistent with the evidence and the resources available to him. There must additionally be a reasonable belief and therefore some information which tends to show that the specified malpractice occurred . . .
> (d) The reasonableness of the belief will depend in each case on the volume and quality of information available to the worker at the time the decision to disclose is made. Employment tribunals will have to guard against use of hindsight to assess the reasonableness of the belief in this respect in the same way as they are bound, in considering liability in unfair dismissal cases, to consider only what was known to the employer at the time of dismissal or appeal . . .'

3.08 Summarizing this commentary, the EAT observed (at para 32) that:

> we agree with the authors that, for there to be a qualifying disclosure, it must have been reasonable for the worker to believe that the factual basis of what was disclosed was true and that it tends to show a relevant failure, even if the worker was wrong, but reasonably mistaken.

3.09 The EAT noted that although the issue of whether the information was disclosed was true might not be determinative of whether there was a reasonable belief, it will often be evidentially relevant. It explained (at para 29) that:

> in our opinion, the determination of the factual accuracy of the disclosure by the tribunal will, in many cases, be an important tool in determining whether the worker held the reasonable belief that the disclosure tended to show a relevant failure. Thus if an employment tribunal finds that an employee's factual allegation of something he claims to have seen himself is false, that will be highly relevant to the question of the worker's reasonable belief. It is extremely difficult to see how a worker can reasonably believe that an allegation tends to show that there has been a relevant failure if he knew or believed that the factual basis was false, unless there may somehow have been an honest mistake on his part. The relevance and extent of the employment tribunal's enquiry into the factual accuracy of the disclosure will, therefore, necessarily depend on the circumstances of each case. In many cases, it will be an important tool to decide whether the worker held the reasonable belief that is required by s43B(1).

---

[3] But see the comments in *Kraus v Penna* [2004] IRLR 260 (EAT) considered at 3.43 below, emphasizing that 'likely' means 'probable' or 'more probable than not'.

We cannot accept Mr Kallipetis's submission that reasonable belief applies only to the question of whether the alleged facts tend to disclose a relevant failure. We consider that as a matter of both law and common sense all circumstances must be considered together in determining whether the worker holds the reasonable belief. The circumstances will include his belief in the factual basis of the information disclosed as well as what those facts tend to show. The more the worker claims to have direct knowledge of the matters which are the subject of the disclosure, the more relevant will be his belief in the truth of what he says in determining whether he holds that reasonable belief.

In *Sir Robert McAlpine Limited v Telford* (EATS/0018/03, 13 May 2003) the EAT **3.10** went a step further and suggested that the truth of the information disclosed will always be material. The issue arose in the context of an interim appeal against the refusal of a tribunal to bar the claimant from making allegations of fraud in his oral evidence. Following *Darnton,* the EAT noted that circumstances which related to the claimant's belief at the time when he made the disclosures, and in particular whether there were reasonable grounds for the belief, were relevant even if it turned out that the allegations of fraud were unfounded. The EAT explained (at para 9(iv)), in its summary of the legal principles, that:

> always of assistance in order to decide the question of reasonable belief, would be included the question as to whether, in fact, it was happening; because, if it was happening, then that would assist the Tribunal in deciding that his belief that it was happening was a reasonable one, although it would not of itself be determinative of that aspect, one way or the other.

(2) Basis for the information disclosed

The EAT in *Darnton* therefore rejected a submission that it was sufficient for the **3.11** worker to have a reasonable belief that what s/he is saying on its face (ie if true) tends to show a relevant failure. The point may be illustrated by the following scenario:

> An employee (Ms X) develops concerns that another employee (Ms Y) has been making fraudulent expenses claims. If true this would be a criminal offence and a breach or likely breach of Ms Y's contractual duties to the employer. Ms X's suspicions are based on her analysis of Ms Y's expenses claims and receipts. Ms X reports her concerns and the basis for them to a senior manager (Ms Z). However her allegations were based on a careless and incorrect, albeit honest, analysis of the expenses claims.

Viewed at face value the information (that an analysis of expenses and receipts **3.12** indicated false expenses claims) would indeed tend to show a relevant failure. It would also be reasonable for Ms X to believe that the disclosure would tend to convey to the recipient of the report (Ms Z) that there had been a relevant failure. It would not be necessary to consider further whether the investigation was careless. However if, as the decision in *Darnton* indicates, a tribunal may have regard not only to what was set out in the disclosure, but also the basis for that information, the tribunal would need to consider whether Ms X lacked the requisite reasonable belief in the light of her carelessness in analysing the receipts and expenses.

3.13   How may this be reconciled with the differing tests in ss43C ERA (internal disclosures) and 43F, 43G and 43H (disclosures to a prescribed body or wider disclosures)? In relation to ss43F, 43G and 43H, the worker must reasonably believe that the information disclosed, and any allegation contained in it, are substantially true. There is no equivalent requirement for s43C disclosures, where the only requirement is good faith, and it cannot therefore have been the legislative intention that such a requirement is imposed under s43B ERA. This difficulty would not arise if reasonable belief was to be assessed on the basis of what the information on its face tends to show. This would enable a clear distinction to be drawn between a qualifying disclosure as being concerned with identification of the subject matter capable of being protected, and the further requirements set out in ss43C–43G. It would also be consistent with the policy of encouraging workers to make known their concerns internally so that they can be properly investigated by those best able to do so.

3.14   The EAT in *Darnton* acknowledged (at para 30) that s43B must not be construed in such a way as to import an obligation akin to the requirement in ss43F, 43G and 43H for a reasonable belief that the information disclosed, and any allegation contained in it, are substantially true. It grappled with this, in part, by stressing the lower standard to be applied in order to satisfy the s43B reasonable belief test. It emphasized (at para 30) that the required standard of belief in the truth of what has been disclosed cannot be such as to require the employee in all cases to believe that both the factual basis for the belief and what it tends to show are substantially true.

3.15   The EAT also expressly held (at para 28) that it was unable to accept the University's submission '. . . that the worker must believe in the accuracy of the factual basis of the disclosure on reasonable grounds'. This at first seems difficult to reconcile with the EAT's view that 'it must have been reasonable for the worker to believe that the factual basis of what was disclosed was true . . .' (para 32). In context, the EAT was rejecting the need for 'reasonable grounds' in the sense of a require-ment to have evidence demonstrating that the information was probably true. The EAT's essential point was that the standard of what is reasonable must depend on all the circumstances.[4] Thus (at para 28) the EAT noted that:

> circumstances that give rise to a worker reporting a protected disclosure will vary enormously from case to case. The circumstances will range from cases in which a worker reports matters which he claims are within his own knowledge, or have been seen or heard by him. At the other extreme will be cases where the worker passes on what has been reported to him, or what has been observed by others.

---

[4] Endorsing a passage in the first edition of this book.

In each case there must be some grounds for believing that information disclosed **3.16** is true. But the standard required will depend on the circumstances. As the EAT emphasized, the worker must exercise judgement consistent with the evidence and resources available. This approach affords tribunals the flexibility to distinguish circumstances where the employer will be best able to investigate from, at the other extreme, allegations that the worker ought to have realized were untrue or where the employer has provided an adequate explanation which is unreasonably rejected by the worker.

But if tribunals apply too stringent a test of reasonable belief, there is a risk that **3.17** this will encourage workers either not to make the disclosure or to delay making disclosures which are best investigated by the employer whilst they seek to firm up their suspicions. As noted above, the EAT in *Darnton* (at para 31)[5] endorsed the view that where the whistle blower has a good 'hunch' that something is wrong without the means to prove it, he/ she should be encouraged to make known to a suitable person the basis of that hunch so that those with the ability and resources to investigate can do so.

Some support for this is to be derived from the decision of the EAT in *Welsh* **3.18** *Refugee Council v Brown* (EAT/0032/02, 22 March 2002). Referring to the test for reasonable belief, the EAT (at para 9) commented that:

> . . . a finding that Mrs Brown had a reasonable belief for these purposes necessarily connotes two component matters; thus it necessarily connotes that she *did* in point of fact believe what she was saying, that is, it necessarily connotes a subjective finding to that extent. Second and further, it connotes a finding that that belief was reasonable, that is, it was a tenable belief neither eccentric nor fanciful, it is a belief that withstands objective assessment.

The belief must therefore be 'tenable', and the degree of scrutiny involved will **3.19** necessarily be dependent on the circumstances. Those circumstances are likely to include the basis or source of the information and whether the person making the disclosure is in a position where he or she ought to investigate further, or could reasonably leave it to the recipient of the disclosure to investigate further. In this case Mrs Brown was employed as the regional coordinator of a project run by the respondent, which was an organization set up to assist refugees. The respondent's finance officer raised with Mrs Brown concerns that a director of the respondent had been submitting expenses claims and then also reclaiming the expenses from the City Council, and had also been submitting false expenses claims. Mrs Brown reported the concerns to the respondent's management committee. She claimed that this was a protected disclosure and that she was subjected to detriments,

---

[5] Citing the first edition of this book.

culminating in her dismissal, as a result of her disclosures. She succeeded before the employment tribunal, and its decision was upheld on appeal. The EAT dealt with the question of whether Mrs Brown's belief was reasonable by a series of rhetorical questions as follows (at para 13):

> How could the grounds be other than reasonable as a basis for further disclosure, given the source of the information? What else should Mrs Brown as regional coordinator have done, other than pass the material forward? Should she have kept silent pending her own investigation before passing the matter forward?

3.20 The EAT therefore placed emphasis on the fact that the information came from an apparently credible source and that the standard of reasonable belief was properly to be viewed in the context of the fact that it would not have been appropriate to do other than to make the information available to the employer.

(3) Reasonable suspicion or concern

3.21 Although in *Darnton* reference was made to the need for a reasonable belief in the factual basis of what was disclosed and that this tends to show a relevant failure, there is a danger in applying the test without reference to the statutory language and without regard to the importance, emphasized in *Darnton*, of taking into account the particular circumstances. It might well be that the worker does not and cannot know, or have any belief, as to whether the information is true or reliable. The worker might still have a concern that investigation is needed to identify whether or not the information is true. The policy of the legislation is for the concerns to be reported internally, without risk of reprisal, so that they can be investigated.

3.22 The danger of requiring a belief in the truth of the information and that it tends to show a relevant failure was borne out by the findings in the Shipman Inquiry. In her 5th report,[6] Dame Janet Smith concluded, in relation to the reasonable belief test in s43B, that:

> it seems to me that this requirement . . . may operate against the public interest, especially in cases where the worker has access to incomplete or secondhand information. I am concerned that, in order to make a disclosure even to his/her employer, a worker has to be in the position where s/he could say, for example, 'I believe that this disclosure tends to show that a crime has been committed and my belief is reasonable.' . . . if this threshold were applied to workers having the state of mind of [various people who could have raised early concerns about Shipman], I doubt that they would confidently have been able to cross that threshold. Moreover, I do not think that anyone answering a call on the PCaW [7] helpline could confidently have assured any of those

---

[6] 5th Shipman Inquiry report, 9 December 2004, Cm 6394, 11.110. and 111.
[7] Referring to Public Concern at Work—the whistleblowing charity.

persons (had they been '**workers**') that their state of mind was such that they were guaranteed protection.

The onus should not, in my view, be on an individual to establish '**reasonable belief**' in the case of internal disclosures and disclosures to external regulators. The public interest would, in my view, be best served by substituting 'suspicion' for 'belief'.

The response proposed by Dame Janet Smith was that it should be sufficient to show a 'reasonable suspicion', rather than requiring a 'reasonable belief' that the disclosure tends to show a relevant failure. However, a worker might be sceptical of the information received, yet sufficiently concerned to believe that the matter needs to be properly investigated. It may therefore be more appropriate to refer to a 'reasonable suspicion or concern' that the disclosure tends to show a relevant failure. Whilst this formulation may be clearer, it is suggested that the legislation as currently framed is capable of being construed consistently with this. Once it is accepted, as emphasized in *Darnton*, that the standard of belief will vary according to the circumstances, the legislation is capable of being purposively construed so that the reasonable belief requirement is satisfied where an employee, though sceptical of information, reasonably believes that it has sufficient credence to warrant further investigation, and that this information if true would tend to indicate a breach of an obligation (albeit there may be other factors or explanations that ultimately show this not to be the case). We consider this further below in relation to the meaning of the phrase 'tends to show'. **3.23**

(4) All circumstances relevant to reasonable belief

The EAT in *Darnton* emphasized the need to have regard to all the circumstances in assessing whether the requisite reasonable belief was held. This applies not only to assessing whether there were reasonable grounds for the belief, but also to considering what the worker subjectively believed. As indicated by the EAT in *de Haney v Brent Mind and Lang* (EAT/0054/03, 19 March 2004), this may extend to the circumstances in which the allegation is raised before the employment tribunal. Mrs de Haney alleged that in a meeting with her line manager she had complained about the appointment of a colleague which she claimed was in breach of her employer's equal opportunity policy. The claimant had raised a concern about the appointment in writing prior to her dismissal, but the allegation that her concerns in relation to this amounted to a protected disclosure was not contained in the originating application or the claimant's further particulars of her claim, but was first made in her witness statement. In those circumstances the EAT held that the tribunal had been entitled to find that the allegation was put in as a 'makeweight' and as such was not a qualifying disclosure (in that she did not hold the requisite reasonable belief). **3.24**

C. 'Tends to show'

(1) No need to establish truth of the allegation

3.25   There is no need to have a reasonable belief that the information disclosed actually establishes a relevant failure. It is sufficient if it 'tends to show' a relevant failure. This is an important qualification. It lies at the heart of the distinction drawn between the reasonable belief requirement in s43B and the requirement under ss43F, 43G and 43H that the worker must have a reasonable belief that the allegations are substantially true. Especially in relation to internal disclosures, the legislation recognizes that the worker may only have access to part of the evidential picture. The information available to the worker might indeed tend to show a relevant failure, in the sense of being one piece of evidence which merits a concern being raised. It might however not be reasonable to hold the belief that the allegation is substantially true prior to an investigation of the matter by the employer.

3.26   There may be a variety of reasons for the worker only having part of the picture. It might be that this arises because the information is only received secondhand. Thus, for example, if a worker hears from a colleague that another colleague has been stealing from the company, that might well be sufficient to found a reasonable belief that this was information that tended to show a colleague had been stealing. But it might be premature to hold a belief that the allegation is substantially true without investigation as to the reliability of the source, or further details of the circumstances of the alleged thefts or the explanation provided by the person alleged to have been stealing. The employer might be best placed to investigate those matters. As such it is appropriate that the further requirement of a substantial belief in the truth is not applied to an internal disclosure (ie within the employing organization or otherwise within s43C ERA), but is required only for an external disclosure.

3.27   This was reflected in the reasoning of the EAT in *Bolton School v Evans* [2006] IRLR 500. Mr Evans disclosed that he was going to break into the school's computer system in order to demonstrate that the system was insecure and would too readily lead to unauthorized disclosures. The employment tribunal found that Mr Evans had a reasonable belief that his employer was likely to breach the seventh Data Protection principle. This principle requires that appropriate technical and organizational measures be taken against unauthorized or unlawful processing of personal data and against accidental loss or destruction of, or damage to, personal data. The Data Protection Act (para 9 of pt 2 of Sch 1) contains principles of interpretation relating to this, providing that having regard to the state of technological development and the cost of implementing any measures, the measures to be taken must ensure a level of security which is appropriate to the harm that might result and the nature of the data to be protected. On behalf of the respondent school, it was argued that Mr Evans could not have held a reasonable belief that the seventh Data Protection principle would be infringed without appreciating what that principle obliged the employer to do, and that this required him to weigh up the considerations set out in the principles of interpretation in order to determine whether or not the information tended to show a likely breach. In rejecting this argument the EAT held (in paras 51 and 52) that:

> we do not think that the protection is lost merely because the employer may be able to show that, for reasons not immediately apparent to the employee, the duty will not apply or that he has some defence to it. The information will still, it seems to us, tend to show the likelihood of breach. It is potentially powerful and material evidence pointing in that direction even although there may be other factors which ultimately would demonstrate that no breach is likely to occur.
>
> There may indeed be cases where a relatively detailed appreciation of the relevant legal obligation is required before an employee can establish that he reasonably believed that the information tended to show that a breach of a legal obligation was likely. But it would undermine the protection of this valuable legislation if employees were expected to anticipate and evaluate all potential defences, whether within the scope of their own knowledge or not, when deciding whether or not to make that disclosure.

3.28 The EAT recognized therefore that the legislation is constructed to cater for the fact that the employee may only be aware of part of the evidential picture. What matters is that the employee reasonably believes that the disclosure points in the direction of a breach being likely to occur, even though there might ultimately be other considerations which are raised which indicate that this is not the case.

3.29 This is an essential aspect of the legislation, since it avoids pushing workers into extreme positions in order to attract the protection of the legislation. It is easy to envisage that the worker might be reticent about making allegations, yet believe that the information is indicative of a relevant failure and therefore needs to be investigated. Thus, for example, if an internal accountant discovers various irregularities which are reasonably believed to be indicators of fraud, there is no additional requirement for him to believe that once the matter has been fully investigated it will be found that there has in fact been a fraud. The irregularities may be potentially powerful and material evidence tending to show a fraud even though ultimately there will be sufficient countervailing evidence to demonstrate that there has been no fraud. This may also be seen as an application of the principles set out in *Darnton* that all the relevant circumstances must be taken into account in determining whether there is the requisite reasonable belief. One important circumstance may be that the worker only has part of the evidential picture and it is reasonable in the circumstances not to require further investigation. Plainly, however, this can only apply where the worker only has part of the evidential picture and the evidence available or which ought to be ascertained could reasonably be regarded as indicating a relevant failure. If in the above example the internal accountant discovered the various irregularities, but also knew that there was an innocent explanation, there could be no question of the requisite reasonable belief existing even though taken in isolation the irregularities could be regarded as an indicator of potential fraud.

(2) *Extent to which the disclosure must spell out the relevant failure and why it is shown*

3.30 The legislation does not specify the extent to which the disclosure must spell out which relevant failure the information disclosed tends to show. This issue was addressed by the EAT in *Fincham v HM Prison Service* (EAT/0925/01 and EAT/0991/01, 19 December 2002). Ms Fincham made various complaints about the conduct of other members of staff (who were not her managers) which she alleged amounted to harassment. She contended that these tended to show a breach of the implied trust and confidence term in their contracts of employement. The tribunal decided that it was not permissible to look at the various disclosures collectively to determine whether taken together they tended to show a breach of a legal obligation. It further decided that none of the disclosures individually tended to show such a breach, on the basis that an employer cannot be taken to have acted in breach of contract every time one employee behaves badly to another. The decision and reasoning on this issue was upheld by the EAT. It emphasized (at para 33) that, whilst there could be a series of acts that collectively gave rise to a breach of the trust and confidence term:

> . . . there must in our view be some disclosure which actually identifies, albeit not in strict legal language, the breach of legal obligation on which the employers are relying.

3.31 This might be read as indicating that there has to be a reference to the particular legal obligation which the employee has in mind, albeit precise legal language need not be used. However it is doubtful whether the EAT intended to set out any such general rule. First, the difficulty in *Fincham* was not a failure to identify the relevant legal obligation, but a failure to set out in one disclosure the facts which collectively might have indicated a breach of that legal obligation. Identifying the legal obligation in the letter, without referring to the earlier series of complaints which the tribunal considered needed to be taken together to show a breach of a legal obligation, would not have been sufficient.[8] Second, the legislation does not provide, as it could easily have done, that the particular relevant failure must be identified. In some cases, identifying the relevant failure may be important in

---

[8] But compare *Flintshire v Sutton* (EAT/1082/02, 1 July 2003) where the EAT held that there was no need to distinguish between four memoranda to members of a Council raising concerns, where the memoranda made up a series.

order to explain the significance attached to the other information disclosed so that it does tend to show a relevant failure. In other cases, it will be apparent that the information disclosed tends to show a relevant failure without having to spell this out. Indeed in *Fincham* the EAT accepted that there was a qualifying disclosure as a result of Ms Fincham having complained that she was under pressure and under stress. Contrary to the decision of the employment tribunal, the EAT considered that this could not be anything other than a statement that her health and safety was being or at least was likely to be endangered. The EAT therefore accepted that (subject to the reasonable belief test) it was sufficient that the relevant failure was identifiable from the information disclosed notwithstanding that the particular failure (in this case health and safety being endangered) was not mentioned in terms.

A more relaxed approach to what is required to identify the relevant failure **3.32** was adopted in *Douglas v Birmingham City Council and others* (EAT/018/02, 17 March 2003). The claimant, Mrs Douglas, was a staff governor of a local education authority school. She initially raised concerns in confidence with a fellow governor (C) about her perception of a lack of equal opportunities at the school. C however reported the discussion to the head teacher. Mrs Douglas then wrote to the Chair of Governors complaining about C and the attitude of the head teacher. She complained that in the head teacher's eyes speaking up about equality was worse than discrimination and that staff were expected to ignore discrimination. The EAT construed the disclosure as a complaint that the head teacher was not carrying out policies relating to equal opportunities and equal rights. Mrs Douglas did not identify a specific policy but the EAT noted that realistically there must have been a policy to carry out equal opportunities policies. The EAT held that an allegation that the head teacher was acting contrary to equal opportunities policies tended to show a breach of contract insofar as the policies were apt for incorporation in contracts of employment, as well as a breach of the anti-discrimination legislation. It was not a bar to this conclusion that Mrs Douglas had not in terms alleged a breach of contract.

Similarly in *Odong v Chubb Security Personnel* (EAT/0819/02, 13 May 2003) the **3.33** EAT did not require that a specific legal obligation be identified. Mr Odong was employed as a security officer by Chubb at an American Express site. The tribunal found that he was removed from the site because he failed to obey a reasonable instruction to conduct temperature checks. The tribunal rejected his case that his removal was due to a protected disclosure in relation to health and safety. It decided that his refusal to enter the room to carry out the checks was not due to health and safety concerns, nor was that the reason for removal. Allowing the appeal, the EAT accepted that on the ET's own findings of fact there was capable of being in the alternative a protected disclosure under s43(1)(b) of failing or being likely to fail to comply with a legal obligation. Mr Odong had stated that he was not prepared to enter the room to carry out the checks because the room was marked 'no entry' and he did not accept that the person instructing him to do so had authority to give that instruction. Mr Odong did not further identify any legal obligation as being in play. However the EAT accepted that his disclosure raised issues in relation to a breach of his own contract if he entered the room without proper authority or if he was given an unauthorized instruction and a breach of obligations owed to American Express who had designated the room as 'no entry'.

3.34 Again in *Bolton School v Evans*[9] the EAT was willing to find that there had been a qualifying disclosure notwithstanding that the disclosure itself did not identify the particular relevant failure. Mr Evans disclosed that he was going to break into the school's computer system in order to demonstrate that the system was insecure and would too readily lead to unauthorized disclosures. He also told the headmaster, after the event, what he had done. The EAT accepted that this amounted to a qualifying disclosure in relation to a breach or likely breach of a legal obligation. It was noted that Mr Evans did not in terms identify any specific legal obligation. However the EAT considered that this did not matter as it would have been obvious to all that the concern was that private and sensitive information about pupils could get into the wrong hands and it was appreciated that this could give rise to a potential liability. This was sufficiently shown by the information disclosed without the need to specify any particular legal obligation.

3.35 As the decision in *Odong* illustrates, concerns as to wrongdoing may be raised in a range of contexts within the workplace, and it may be unrealistic to expect specific legal obligations to be identified. Where the relevant failure is a breach or likely breach of a legal obligation or commission of a criminal offence, the underlying purposes of the legislation might be undermined by a requirement to specify the particular legal obligation or offence. The need to refer to a specific legal obligation or offence might discourage workers from raising concerns. For example a worker might identify financial irregularities and recognize them as indicators of fraud, but also be reluctant to allege in terms that the information tended to indicate a fraud. Instead the worker might prefer simply to draw the information to the employer's attention so that it could be properly investigated. It would not be consistent with the purpose of the legislation if the worker could be victimized for so doing.

3.36 Further, in some cases whilst it may be apparent that the information disclosed is likely to breach some legal obligation or amount to a criminal offence, the worker might not have knowledge of the specific obligations. In such circumstances it would be surprising if the employee was unprotected in bringing the information

---

[9] See above, para 3.27.

to the employer's attention, or was required to delay in doing so, due to the need first to obtain legal advice as to the specific legal obligation engaged.

(3) *The disclosure must contain 'information'*

In order for there to be a qualifying disclosure, there must be a 'disclosure of **3.37** information'. In some cases this has led to issues as to whether a bare allegation or expression of concern as to a relevant failure involves any disclosure of information.

In *Everett Financial Management Limited v Murrell* (EAT/552,553/02 and EAT/952/02, 24 February 2003) the claimant was one of nineteen dealers who signed a petition seeking a written assurance from the directors that they were not engaged in any unlawful activity. The employment tribunal concluded by a majority that this constituted a protected disclosure, but the EAT disagreed. It concluded that merely expressing a concern and seeking reassurance that there was no breach of a legal obligation did not involve any disclosure of information within s43B.

In *Maini v Department for Work and Pensions* (ET, Case No. 2203978/01, 15 October 2002) the claimant was employed by the DWP. His role involved visiting those claiming benefits to discuss their individual cases with them. He made allegations of corruption to the Chief Executive Officer of the Benefit Agency and to the National Audit Office. Although he alleged that there was 'a huge amount of corruption', and urged the need to investigate the Benefit Agency in London, he failed to provide any further details. The ET held that these were not qualifying disclosures as they merely made allegations rather than containing any information tending to show one or more relevant failures.

By contrast in *McCormack v Learning and Skills Council* (ET, Case No. 3104148/01, **3.38** 5 December 2002) an employment tribunal rejected a submission that a bare allegation of 'financial irregularities' would not have disclosed information. The ET commented that it could not see how a person could disclose their belief without thereby disclosing information. Thus the bare allegation of corruption in the *Maini* case at least involved the disclosure that the claimant believed that there was indeed corruption. The real issue, it is suggested, is not whether there was information disclosed, but whether it was reasonable for a worker to believe that it tended to show a relevant failure. Having regard to the purposes of the legislation, there may be circumstances where a bare allegation tends to show a relevant failure. Where a worker initially raises a concern it may be that a bare allegation of the relevant failure is made in the expectation that there will then be an opportunity given to discuss and expand on the concerns with a view to them being investigated by the recipient of the disclosure. It would sit uneasily with the purposes of the legislation if in those circumstances the employer, rather than investigating the allegation or seeking further details, could subject the worker to a detriment. In that context, and applying the approach that 'there is a certain generosity in the construction of the statute and in the treatment of the facts',[10] the bare allegation or concern as to the relevant failure might be said to be information tending to show a relevant failure. By contrast that would no longer be the case if, when details of the basis of the belief are sought, the worker declines to provide these.

(4) Information disclosed need not be unknown to the recipient

3.39   However the information disclosed need not be previously unknown to the recipient of the information. Section 43L(3) ERA provides expressly that in a case where the person receiving the information is already aware of it, the references to disclosure of information must be treated as references to bringing the information to that person's attention. Without this provision workers could be discouraged from making public interest disclosures because, not knowing what information the employer already had, they could not be confident of being protected.

3.40   In *Everett Financial Management* the EAT recorded that it was common ground between (leading) counsel in that case that there could be no disclosure of information if the provider of the information was aware that the recipient already knew of the information. A similar view was expressed in *Aspinall v MSI Mech Forge Limited* (EAT/891/01, 25 July 2002). Mr Aspinall arranged for a colleague to make a video of how certain factory equipment worked as evidence in support of the claimant's personal injury claim. Although the video could be said to convey information tending to show that health and safety was or was likely to be endangered, the EAT said it was unconvinced that the making of the video by a fellow worker to whom nothing new was disclosed could amount to a protected disclosure.

3.41   However s43L(3) does not draw a distinction between cases where the worker did or did not know that the employer was already aware of the information. Such a distinction could readily have been drawn if that was the legislative intention. Nor is such a limitation consistent with the policy of the legislation. For example a worker might disclose the same information to the employer on a second occasion because of a concern that the matter is not being adequately investigated. Because of those concerns the second disclosure might be put in more strident language, but it would not be consistent with the aims of the legislation if an employer who took exception to the second disclosure and subjected the worker to a detriment as a result, could say that it was not protected because the same information had

---

[10] *Boulding v Land Securities Trillium (Media Services) Limited* (EAT/0023/06, 3 May 2006)—discussed at paragraph 3.50 below.

previously been disclosed. There may be cases where the fact that it is known that the recipient of the information is already aware of the information is material to the assessment of whether the disclosure is made in good faith. But in the light of s43L(3) it is not a basis for saying there was no disclosure of information at all.

(5) Disclosures in relation to likely future failures

Several of the categories of relevant failure relate to concerns in relation to the **3.42** future. There may be a disclosure about a criminal offence which is 'likely to be committed', or a likely failure to comply with a legal obligation or that a miscarriage of justice is likely to occur, or that health and safety or the environment is likely to be endangered or damaged respectively. In each case this raises issues as to the degree of likelihood that is required. In evaluating whether it was reasonable to believe that the relevant failure was likely, a tribunal might not be able simply to assume that an existing state of affairs will continue. There might be a need to consider whether the circumstances giving rise to the concerns are likely to be rectified before there is a relevant failure. For example, if there is a disclosure by an in-house accountant as to inadequacy in accounting records kept by the company, a tribunal will need to consider not only whether the information *tends to show* that the records did not satisfy statutory requirements, but also whether there is evidence tending to show that this *would be likely to be the case* by the time at which the records must be compliant.

This issue arose in *Kraus v Penna plc* [2004] IRLR 260 (EAT). Mr Kraus' services **3.43** were provided to Syltone by Penna plc for human resources advice in relation to Syltone's proposed reorganization and redundancy programme. Kraus alleged that he had been told that a representative of Syltone had made it clear that he intended to reduce the workforce significantly beyond the number identified as being redundancies likely to result from the reorganization, and then to recruit back at a later date. He asserted that he had warned Syltone that it 'could breach employment legislation and would be vulnerable to claims for unfair dismissal in pursuing this course of action'. Shortly afterwards Syltone dispensed with Kraus' services. He alleged that this was in response to his disclosures warning of possible breaches of employment legislation. The employment tribunal struck out the claim on the basis that it had no reasonable prospect of success. The EAT upheld this decision. It emphasized that the word 'likely' means 'probable' or 'more probable than not'. Thus, in relation to a future breach of a legal obligation: 'The information disclosed should, in the reasonable belief of the worker at the time it is disclosed, tend to show that it is probable or more probable than not that the employer will fail to comply with the relevant legal obligation.' Since, on Kraus' own case, he had only warned that Syltone 'could' breach employment legislation and be vulnerable to unfair dismissal claims, the EAT concluded that 'Mr Kraus's belief was limited, at this early stage, to the possibility or the risk of a breach of employment legislation, depending on what eventually took place.'

3.44 There are some difficulties with this analysis. First, the decision was made at a pre-hearing review without hearing any evidence. It does not necessarily follow that because the disclosure is couched in cautious terms (such as referring only to a possibility of a breach) the worker could not have subjectively believed that there was a likely failure to comply. A worker may well be concerned to couch the disclosure in moderate terms, perhaps for fear of the reaction of management if more serious allegations are made. In each case there must therefore be consideration of the substance of the information disclosed, and of the worker's own case as to his or her state of belief and of the circumstances in which that stated belief is asserted. The decision in *Kraus* might be supportable on the basis that not only was the disclosure couched in terms of possibility rather than probability of breach, but that it was, as the EAT noted, merely a proposed course of conduct, in its preliminary stages, on which Mr Kraus had been engaged specifically to advise. As such the tribunal could have concluded that even if Mr Kraus did believe that Syltone would have failed to comply, there was no reasonable basis for the belief at the time of the disclosure. However, rather than adopting this approach, the EAT (at para 21) founded its decision on the conclusion that, based on the terms of the disclosure, Mr Kraus did not himself believe the information tended to show a likely breach, so that the issue of reasonableness of the belief did not arise.

3.45 Second, a line of high authority supporting the proposition that 'likely' does not necessarily mean 'more probable than not' was not cited to the EAT. This line of authorities was considered by the House of Lords in *In re H and others* [1996] AC 563. It was noted that 'likely' in ordinary language may mean probable or might include what might well happen. The meaning therefore has to be considered in the light of the particular context. The case concerned care and supervision orders where a child was 'likely to suffer significant harm'. In that context 'likely' meant 'a real possibility, a possibility that cannot sensibly be ignored'. Similarly in *Cream Holdings Limited v Banerjee* [2005] 1 AC 253 the various possible shades of meaning of the word 'likely' were considered in the context of the test for granting interim relief in freedom of expression cases. Section 12(4) of the Human Rights Act 1998 provides that relief should not be granted to restrain publication before trial unless the court is 'likely' to be satisfied that the applicant is likely to establish that publication should be allowed. In context the House of Lords concluded that 'likely' did not mean that it was necessary to establish in every case that success at trial was more likely than not. Further Lord Nicholls, who gave the only substantive speech, noted (at para 12) that:

> as with most ordinary English words 'likely' has several different shades of meaning. Its meaning depends upon the context in which it is being used. Even when read in context its meaning is not always precise. It is capable of encompassing different

degrees of likelihood, varying from 'more likely than not' to 'may well'. In ordinary usage its meaning is often sought to be clarified by the addition of qualifying epithets as in phrases such as 'very likely' or 'quite likely'. In section 12(3) the context is that of a statutory threshold for the grant of interim relief by a court.

However the decision in *Kraus* contains no acknowledgment that the term 'likely' **3.46** may have more than one ordinary meaning. Nor does it set out any explanation as to why the context indicates that the meaning 'more probable than not' should be applied. Instead reliance was placed on cases in other contexts where 'likely' has been interpreted as more probable than not.[11] However given the high judicial recognition that 'likely' can have more than one meaning, this reveals nothing as to why the context requires the more limiting option to be applied in the context of s43B.

The context may indeed be said to support the construction of 'likely' as meaning **3.47** only a real possibility that cannot be ignored. This would sit well with the aim of the legislation in encouraging workers to come forward, and thereby provide an early warning of a relevant failure. Conversely the implication of *Kraus* is that, if a worker discloses information in order to prevent wrongdoing, the disclosure will be unprotected. Indeed this was the conclusion of an employment tribunal in *Owalo v Galliford Try Partnership Limited* (Case No. 3203344/03, 2 April 2004). Mr Owalo was a design and build contractor employed by a construction company. Acting in good faith, he disclosed that the design for a proposed building would be in breach of building regulations. The ET held that there was no qualifying disclosure precisely because on his own evidence he made the disclosure 'in order to rectify a problem before it arose'—although on the facts the dismissal was found not to be by reason of the disclosures.

As this illustrates, the logic of the reasoning in *Kraus* is that if a worker identifies a **3.48** real risk of serious wrongdoing, but is not confident that the information discovered renders it more likely than not that the wrongdoing will take place, the worker will act at his own peril in bringing this to the attention of the employer to be investigated. It would be strange if a worker who has the courage to come forward and report concerns should be unprotected because s/he believes that if s/he had not come forward someone else would probably, though not certainly, have done so, and thereby prevented the future wrongdoing. It would be all the more strange, if the worker believes that the result of reporting concerns to the employer is likely to be that the employer will prevent the future wrongdoing, that as a result the worker

---

[11] *Bailey v Rolls Royce (1971) Limited* [1984] ICR 688 (CA) relating to legislation setting out restrictions on lifting, carrying or moving a heavy load 'likely to cause injury'; *Taplin v C Shippam Limited* [1978] IRLR 450 (EAT) concerning the power of a tribunal to grant interim relief continuing a contract, and *dicta* of Lightman J in *BCCI v Ali (No.3)* [1999] IRLR 528 as to the meaning of 'likely' to destroy or seriously damage trust and confidence.

cannot be said to have the requisite belief in a likely failure to comply with a legal obligation and be protected.

3.49 There is also a particular difficulty in factoring in the employer's likely response to the disclosure. The EAT in *Kraus* placed some emphasis (at para 20) on the fact that Mr Kraus had been engaged specifically to advise on the proposed course of conduct. The implication is that because he was to advise on the proposals, and there was nothing at that early stage to indicate that his advice would not be followed, it could not be said that there was a likely failure to comply with a legal obligation. However there is a risk of absurd results if it is necessary to take account of the employer's likely reaction to the disclosure in order to ascertain whether a future relevant failure is likely. Take the example of an employee who has reasonable grounds to believe that a colleague, who is working out notice, is likely to copy unlawfully and take away the employer's confidential database unless prevented from doing so. If the employee simply says nothing the database is likely to be stolen. However if she makes a report to the employer, there will not be a likely breach because the colleague will immediately be placed on garden leave and will not have the opportunity to remove the database. It would be anomalous, and wholly contrary to the underlying policy of the legislation, if the employer could contend that there was no qualifying disclosure because, by reason of making the disclosure, the worker could not reasonably have believed that there was a likely relevant failure. Indeed this would suggest that a worker who has no faith in his or her employer's ability or willingness to prevent a relevant failure may make a qualifying disclosure, but a worker who does have faith in the employer's willingness and ability to act appropriately may not. This is hardly conducive to the aim of encouraging internal disclosures to the employer.

3.50 The danger of reaching a conclusion contrary to the policy of the legislation was recognized by the EAT in *Boulding v Land Securities Trillium (Media Services) Limited*.[12] Mr Boulding was a senior engineer who was responsible for monitoring compliance with regulations for safety of equipment. He raised concerns that certain certificates, known as 'CE markings', which indicated safety compliance, were missing from some of the equipment. This did not indicate a present breach of regulations, but there would be a breach if the equipment was supplied to a customer without the CE markings. At first instance the tribunal dismissed the claim at the completion of the claimant's evidence, and before hearing the respondent's evidence. It held that although Mr Boulding had made the disclosure to his employer in good faith it was clear on his own evidence that he did not have a reasonable belief in a likely failure to comply with a legal obligation. The tribunal relied in part on a finding that the equipment would not be supplied unless

---

[12] See n 10 above.

Mr Boulding agreed that compliance was complete, and also that on the evidence the employer's response to the concerns raised by Mr Boulding indicated that it intended to obtain the documentation.

The EAT allowed the appeal on the basis that the claimant should have been **3.51** allowed to test the respondent's evidence. It emphasized that once a subjective belief in the likely failure is established, an objective standard is then to be applied to the finding of fact as to what was believed. This required consideration of the employer's evidence bearing on what was likely to happen, rather than just looking at the evidence of the employee. However, the EAT appears to have been willing to contemplate that there could be a likely failure to comply with the obligation to supply the equipment with CE markings even though Mr Boulding's own evidence was that he was confident that documentation would be obtained. Whilst the *ratio* of the decision may be limited to the conclusion that the case should not have been stopped without hearing full evidence, this does not sit easily with the emphasis in *Kraus* that a 'likely' failure is one that is probable or more probable than not. The approach taken by the EAT reflected an expressly purposive approach to the legislation and the facts. The EAT emphasized (at para 24) that in whistleblowing cases 'there is a certain generosity in the construction of the statute and the treatment of the facts. Whistle-blowing is a form of discrimination claim.' In assessing whether the disclosure could be protected, the EAT noted (at para 31) that, given that Mr Boulding had acted in good faith in raising appropriate compliance issues, and had done so after obtaining appropriate advice, it would be 'out of step with the regime of protection for an employee in such a situation not to have the statutory protection, as he saw it, although steps were being taken to provide documentation'.

D. The six categories

There are six defined categories of protectable disclosure which are described by **3.52** the Act in s43B(1) as 'qualifying disclosures'. There is scope for considerable overlap between the six categories in particular cases. Damage to the environment may for example fall within subsections (a), (b) and (e) of s43B(1) ERA.

It is also noteworthy that there is no necessity for a link between the matters **3.53** disclosed and the actual employment of the worker. The discloser might simply be acting as a concerned employed citizen, although gratuitous interference in a matter of no concern to the employee might reflect on the good faith requirement, which we consider in Chapter 4.

These six categories constitute a complete statutory regime. There is no concluding **3.54** catch-all provision to give flexibility to the concept of protected disclosure. Tribunals therefore have no licence to go outside the parameters of these six protected areas. There is also no specific reference to financial irregularities, although these will usually fall within the rubric of criminal offences of one sort or another, such as fraud, theft or false accounting. In the USA, by contrast, the Whistleblower Protection Act 1989 covers disclosures of 'gross mismanagement', 'gross waste of funds' and 'abuse of authority'. These are more elastic concepts in the hands of the courts.

3.55 We now consider in turn the scope of the categories of information referred to in the statute:

(1) Criminal offence

3.56 The first of the relevant failures is that 'a *criminal offence* has been committed, is being committed or is likely to be committed'. This involves a criminal offence of whatever degree of seriousness, and may include breach of a minor regulation. There is no specific geographical scope placed on where the crime may be committed or whether it is a crime under the law of the United Kingdom or any other country or territory (s43B(2)). There must however be an actual criminal offence; it is not sufficient that the employee believes reasonably that there is such a criminal offence if the employee's belief is incorrect: see *Babula v Waltham Forest College* (EAT/0635/05, 17 May 2006) which is considered at paragraph 3.70 below.[13]

(2) Legal obligation

3.57 Failure to comply with a *legal obligation* includes a breach of any statutory requirement, contractual obligation, common law obligation (eg negligence, nuisance, defamation) or an administrative law requirement.

3.58 Again, this might include a legal obligation imposed by a different jurisdiction. This was the case in *Bhatia v Sterlite Industries (India) Limited and another* (ET, Case No. 2204571/00, 2 May 2001). Mr Bhatia was employed in London by a company listed on the National Stock Exchange of India which also had operations in Australia and, through a subsidiary company, in the United States. His role involved responsibility for documentation in relation to mergers and acquisitions. It was decided that the respondent's optical fibre cable division should be listed on the New York Stock Exchange via an Initial Public Offering (IPO). While preparing for a presentation in relation to this, the claimant was told by the respondent's chairman to include reference to a particular product as an existing business line. But the claimant knew that this was untrue. He told the chairman that if the IPO documentation included the product as being an existing business line this would be illegal under American legislation. The claimant later also had occasion to inform

---

[13] Permission to appeal was granted by the Court of Appeal on 21 July 2006 ([2006] EWCA Civ 1154). This was on the basis that there was a real prospect of success in establishing that it is sufficient to have a reasonable belief as to the existence of a legal obligation even if there was in fact no such obligation or it was not yet in force.

the chairman that proposals in relation to conversion of preference shares in the Australian subsidiary into ordinary shares would be in breach of Australian law. The tribunal concluded that the claimant had a reasonable belief that the disclosures tended to show likely criminal offences and likely breaches of legal obligations under American and Australian law.

There is no requirement that the disclosure must relate to breach of a legal obligation **3.59** by another person. It may relate to disclosure by a worker of his own breach of an obligation: see *Odong v Chubb Security Personnel* [14] and *Bolton School v Evans*.[15] However where the disclosure relates to a worker's own wrongdoing, the employer may well be able to show that detriment was not on grounds of the disclosure, but due to the breach of the obligation. It would not be sufficient for the worker to show that the wrongdoing would not have been discovered but for the protected disclosure: see *Harrow LBC v Knight* [2003] IRLR 140 (EAT) and Chapter 7.

There is no requirement that the obligation must reach a minimum level of **3.60** seriousness. It may be however that if the concerns are trivial this will be material in assessing whether the concerns were raised in good faith. The triviality of the concerns may be indicative that they are raised for an ulterior motive, rather than being raised in the public interest (see also the discussion below in relation to health and safety).

The issue as to the scope of what may constitute a 'legal obligation' was considered **3.61** in *Parkins v Sodexho* [2002] IRLR 109. The EAT (Altman J) held that the term 'legal obligation' was wide enough to cover obligations under the claimant's contract of employment.[16] It held (paras 15 and 16) that:

> it is obviously not sufficient under Section 43B that there should simply be a breach of contract but what has to be shown is first a breach of the employment contract as being a breach of a legal obligation under that contract. Secondly, there must be a reasonable belief that this has, is, or is likely to happen on the part of the worker. Thirdly, there must be a disclosure of that which is alleged to be the reason for dismissal. In other words, where it is a breach of the contract of employment, the worker is bound to make his case on the basis that the reason for dismissal is that he has complained that his employer has broken the contract of employment.

> Subject to that as being the necessary basis for the whole complaint, under the protection from protected disclosures, we can see no real basis for excluding a legal obligation which arises from a contract of employment from any other form of legal obligation. It seems to us that it falls within the terms of the Act. It is a very broadly drawn provision.

---

[14] See above para 3.33.

[15] See above para 3.27.

[16] But in *Felter v Cliveden Petroleum Company* (EAT/0533/05, 9 March 2006) the EAT noted (at para 12) that counsel had reserved the right to argue on appeal that *Parkins v Sodexho* was wrongly decided and that 'legal obligations' refers only to statutory, not common law obligations. There is no proper basis for implying any such limitation.

3.62   The Act does not, however, cover a failure to fulfil what might be considered to be
a moral (but not legal) obligation of the employer. Nor does it cover a generalized
allegation such as a statement, without more, that the employee is 'concerned
with financial probity': *Sim v Manchester Action on Street Health* (EAT 10085/01,
6 December 2001) at para 4). Further, whether disclosure of a breach of a self-
regulatory code qualifies for protection will turn upon whether there is a legal
obligation to comply with the rule. In some cases this might give rise to difficult
issues of construction. Whilst a breach of a Code of Conduct might enable the
self-regulatory organization to take disciplinary action it may in some contexts be
difficult to identify a *legal* obligation which has been flouted.

3.63   Similarly a 'professional obligation' will not suffice unless it amounts to a legal
obligation. This was one of the bases for rejecting a protected disclosure dismissal
claim in *Butcher v Salvage Association* (EAT/988/01, 21 January 2002). The claimant,
Mr Butcher, was employed by the respondent as Chief Financial Officer. The Chief
Executive disagreed with the way Butcher presented financial reports to the respondent's Governing Committee. The choice of styles was presented to the committee,
and it preferred the Chief Executive's position. Butcher raised a concern internally
that in being asked to adopt the approach of the Chief Executive to the financial
reporting he was being asked to change figures and monthly management reports
to the Board in a way which he believed would be misleading. He addressed the
Governing Committee about his complaints, but they were rejected. The employment
tribunal, which heard expert evidence on the point, concluded that Mr Butcher's
concerns were about acting professionally and that it was 'contrived to seek to promote an issue as to professional ethics into a legal obligation'. It also rejected the
contention that requirements of professional ethics were incorporated into his contract since the accounts were only internal (so there was no question of misleading
a third party or the Board—who were aware of the issues), and in preparing the
accounts in the way required he was acting on the instructions of the Board and
the Governing Committee. The appeal on this issue was dismissed by the EAT at
a preliminary hearing, and permission to appeal was refused by the Court of
Appeal ([2002] EWCA Civ 867).

3.64   Further there must be an actual legal obligation. In *Kraus*[17] the EAT rejected a
submission that it would be sufficient if the worker had a reasonable, albeit
incorrect, belief that the obligation existed. The EAT explained that:

> . . . the worker's reasonable belief in s43B(1) relates to the information which he is
> disclosing and not to the existence of a legal obligation which does not actually exist.
> In other words if the employers are under no legal obligation, as a matter of law, a
> worker cannot claim the protection of this legislation by claiming that he reasonably
> believed that they were. His belief and the reasonableness of it in our view relates to
> the factual information in his possession, namely what he perceives to be the facts

---

[17] See above, para 3.43.

and the basis on which he considers it reasonable to rely upon them. This can only properly be tested against the background of the legal obligation, 'to which [the employer or other person] is subject'. If there is no obligation to which they actually are subject the worker's suggestion that he reasonably believed they were cannot render the disclosure a protected one within ss43A and B.

This decision was qualified to some extent in *Bolton School v Evans*. The EAT held that **3.65** there may be a qualifying disclosure even though for some reason not immediately apparent to the employee the duty alleged to have been breached does not apply or there is some defence to it. However in *Babula v Waltham Forest College*,[18] the EAT held that, as qualified in *Bolton School v Evans*, the decision in *Kraus* remained good law.[19]

This construction in *Kraus* is difficult to support. It introduces an unwarranted **3.66** gloss on the language of s43B. There need be no insuperable difficulty in testing whether the information tends to show a breach of a legal obligation which is reasonably, but incorrectly, believed to exist. This would involve ascertaining what legal obligation was believed to exist, whether it was reasonable to believe this and whether the information disclosed tended to show a breach (or likely breach). Further the reasoning in *Kraus*, referring to the difficulties in testing reasonable belief if the obligation did not exist, is undermined by the decision in *Bolton School v Evans*. The difficulty of testing whether there is a reasonable belief may be no greater in a case where the legal obligation is reasonably but incorrectly believed to exist (eg because not yet in force) than in a case where (as contemplated in *Bolton School v Evans*) although it exists, it does not apply or there is a defence.

The EAT recognised in *Bolton School v Evans* that the aims of the legislation would **3.67** be undermined by requiring employees to anticipate and evaluate all defences in order to establish a qualifying disclosure. This concern applies equally to the decision in *Kraus*. This is apparent when the subsequent provisions of the scheme for protection are considered. Section 43D ERA relates to a disclosure made in the course of obtaining legal advice. Thus if an employer intercepted a communication from an employee seeking advice in relation to legal obligations, and disciplined the employee, it would be open for the employer to argue that there was *in fact* no legal obligation. Even though the employee had acted wholly reasonably, and was properly seeking legal advice as to the legal obligations in play, the disclosure would then be unprotected.

---

[18] See above, para 3.56.

[19] The issue is however due to be considered by the Court of Appeal in *Babula v Waltham Forest College*. Permission to appeal was granted by the Court of Appeal on 21 July 2006 ([2006] EWCA Civ 1154). The Court accepted that there was a real prospect of success in the contention that it is sufficient to have a reasonable belief as to the existence of a legal obligation even if there was in fact no such obligation. Whilst not pre-judging the merits of this issue, Lord Justice Maurice Kay commented that 'It may be that applying a purposive construction, a broader approach would be justifiable.' Lord Justice Buxton agreed and said that 'the jurisprudence of *Kraus v Penna* clearly merits further consideration by' the Court of Appeal.

3.68 Similarly, the approach in *Kraus* would enable the employer to penalize an employer who genuinely raises concerns internally with the employer in relation to legal obligations which the employee reasonably, but incorrectly, believes to exist. Thus, for example, this would apply if an employee disclosed information showing that another manager had discriminated against employees on grounds of age prior to October 2006 in circumstances that would become unlawful once age discrimination legislation had come into force. There might have been good reason for the employee to believe that the legislation was already in force. For example the employee might have received literature which was misleading as to when the legislation came into force. Yet the disclosure would be unprotected even if made reasonably and in the public interest, except possibly if the employee could rely on an estoppel if the misleading communication to the effect that the legislation was in force came from the employer. Similarly there might be genuine difficulty in establishing whether there is a legal obligation, such as where the issue is as to whether rules or practices give rise to an implied contractual obligation which has been breached. In such circumstances the margin for error permitted by a test of reasonable belief in the legal obligation would be valuable.

3.69 These difficulties are illustrated by the decision in *Felter v Cliveden Petroleum Company*.[20] Dr Felter was appointed as director and Executive Chairman of an oil company, Cliveden SA. Cliveden owned eight geological basins, known as the 'Chad Convention', that were to be explored for oil. 50 percent of Cliveden's interest in the Chad Convention was sold to a Canadian corporation, Encana. The deal was negotiated by Dr Felter. An agreement was entered into between Encana and Cliveden. It was common ground between the parties, and recorded by the EAT (at para 25), that the agreement was 'impenetrable'. Subsequently 50 percent of Cliveden's shares were sold to two Chinese companies. It was alleged by Dr Felter that he had made a protected disclosure by advising Cliveden (the respondent) that it was obliged to tell Encana of the share sale before it took place or immediately afterwards. This turned on whether there was either an express or implied obligation under the agreement with Encanca to do so. The tribunal held that there was no such obligation and this conclusion was upheld by the EAT. Following *Kraus*, the EAT held that this finding that there was no such legal obligation was decisive of the issue. Notwithstanding the impenetrable nature of the agreements, and the difficult legal issues which arose as to what obligations should be implied under the agreement, there was no issue as to whether it was reasonable for Dr Felter to believe that there was a legal obligation. As the decision illustrates, even if a disclosure is only to be made internally to the employer or even to a legal adviser for the purposes of obtaining legal advice, some complex legal issues might have to be addressed with certainty before a worker could be confident that a disclosure would be protected. This sits uneasily with the aims of the legislation in deliberately setting a low threshold for

---

[20] See n 16 above.

achieving protection for internal disclosures with a view to encouraging workers to raise their concerns internally.

Further, given that the legal obligation must be established, rather than being a **3.70** matter of reasonable belief, it is particularly important that the appropriate legal obligations are identified within the tribunal proceedings. The dangers of failing to do so are indicated by the decision in *Babula v Waltham Forest College*.[21] Mr Babula was employed as a lecturer. He passed on information that a previous lecturer (Mr Jalil) had divided students into an Islamic group and non-Islamic groups and had told the Islamic group that he wished a September 11-type incident would occur in London. Babula's case was that he reasonably believed that the disclosures tended to show a criminal offence of incitement to racial hatred contrary to s18 of the Public Order Act 1986. However the EAT concluded that the disclosures tended to show conduct directed against a group based on religion rather than race. In the EAT's view, therefore, the claimant could not reasonably have believed that the disclosures tended to show a breach of legislation relating to racial, rather than religious, hatred. It would appear that the facts disclosed by Babula tended to show at least a breach by Jalil of his contract with the respondent college. However this does not appear to have been argued. Equally, the disclosures appear to have shown a breach of the Employment Equality (Religion or Belief) Regs 2003 insofar as they related to events after this came into force on 2 December 2003. However, this was not pursued, having not been raised at first instance. The EAT emphasized that the case could only be decided on the claim as formulated by the claimant.

(3) Miscarriage of justice

The third heading of relevant failure is 'that a miscarriage of justice has occurred, **3.71** is occurring or is likely to occur'. This would include all interference with the proper judicial process, such as perjury or failure to disclose evidence.

'Miscarriage of justice' is not a widely used term of art, although it is mentioned **3.72** in s2 of the Criminal Appeals Act 1968. As such there is little case law to guide tribunals and they can be expected to adopt a common sense broad brush approach to this term. An instructive case in this context, which shows the potential ambit of the term, is *Lion Laboratories v Evans* [1985] 1 QB 526 (CA). Two employees of Lion Laboratories disclosed to the press information casting doubt on the reliability of breathalyser equipment produced by the employer company. These machines were used by the police to measure levels of intoxication in drink-driving cases. The Court of Appeal decided that because of the public interest in the matter wide disclosure was justified since it related to potential miscarriages of justice. An injunction was therefore refused.

---

[21] See above, para 3.56. Permission to appeal was granted on 21 July 2006 ([2006] EWCA Civ 1154).

(4) Health and safety risks

3.73 The ERA 1996 (in ss. 44 and 100) already provides some protection on victimization for health and safety matters, being protection against detriment and dismissal if the employee is (in summary) disadvantaged or dismissed for carrying out health and safety activities or because he is a member of a works safety committee or refuses to work in circumstances of danger which the employee 'reasonably believed to be serious and imminent and which he could not reasonably have been expected to avert'. This test is naturally a difficult one to satisfy. However it also includes disclosures as to future health and safety risks to the employer which is in some respects more widely drawn than s43B, as interpreted in *Kraus*. Employees are protected from detriments other than dismissal (by s44(1)(c) ERA) and are to be regarded as automatically unfairly dismissed (pursuant to s100(1)(c) ERA) if:

> (c) being an employee at a place where—
>> (i) there was no such representative or safety committee, or
>> (ii) there was such a representative or safety committee but it was not reasonably practicable for the employee to raise the matter by those means,
>
> he brought to his employer's attention, by reasonable means, circumstances connected with his work which he reasonably believed were harmful or *potentially harmful* to health or safety [emphasis added].

3.74 In this context, therefore, the bar is set at a lower level than 'likelihood' of danger to health and safety. Potential harm is sufficient.

3.75 The protection relating to disclosure of health and safety risks applies whether the risk threatens a worker or any individual. As such, this could apply to employees, visitors to public places, or customers in a restaurant or the general public. In *Masiak v City Restaurants (UK) Limited* [1999] IRLR 780 (EAT) it was held that s100(1)(e) ERA is not confined to concerns as to the health and safety of other employees but covers concerns as to the health and safety of the general public. It may also relate to the claimant's own health and safety, as in *Fincham*.[22] As noted above (see paragraph 3.31), the EAT considered that the claimant's complaint that she was under pressure and under stress could not be anything other than a statement that her health and safety was being or was at least likely to be endangered.

3.76 Again, there is no provision excluding trivial concerns. This issue was raised in the Parliamentary debates in Standing Committee. Ian McCartney, the Minister of State, Department of Trade and Industry, commented[23] that:

> we would not want the full protection of the law to apply to, for example, a worker who discloses that his boss smokes, drives a car, or quite legitimately manufactures hazardous chemicals. If, however, his boss smokes in a munitions factory, that might

---

[22] See above, para 3.30.
[23] Standing Committee D: Wednesday 11 March 1998.

be a different matter, as might the fact that the firm pollutes a river by discharging poisonous waste into it, or that the manufacturing process cuts corners on safety, or that the disposal of dangerous chemical by-products is unregulated. Disclosures about such matters will be covered by the Bill.

3.77 However Mr McCartney explained that the Government was not in favour of the proposed amendment as:

> . . . it could have deterred people from raising issues of proper concern and led to legalism and complex case law.

> The Government are satisfied that the Bill contains sufficient safeguards to ensure that workers will not be encouraged to disclose trivial matters or concerns. Individuals must act in good faith if they are to attract protection. External disclosures are protected only if a worker acts reasonably.

3.78 As this indicates, whilst trivial concerns are not in terms excluded, it may be that if the concerns are trivial it will raise questions as to whether it was genuinely believed that there was a danger to health and safety and whether that belief was reasonable.

(5) Damage to the environment

3.79 The fifth category is 'that the environment has been, is being or is likely to be damaged'. This would cover potential oil spills, toxic waste emissions, and threats to the rain forest.

(6) Cover-ups

3.80 The final category of relevant failure is 'that information tending to show any matter falling within any of the preceding paragraphs has been, or is likely to be deliberately concealed'.

3.81 It is one of the first reactions (and perhaps a natural reaction) in those about whom the whistle is blown to seek to restrict information about the malpractice. If that is done deliberately, disclosures about the cover-up are as well protected as would be the original information about the malpractice itself. This would not, however, cover accidental or unintended concealment.

E. Criminal disclosures

(1) Exclusion for disclosures that are criminal offences

3.82 There is special provision (s43B(3)) that where the disclosure of the information is itself a crime (eg it breaches the Official Secrets Act 1989) it does not qualify as being a 'qualifying disclosure' under the Act. This is especially controversial since it might be said that one area where the whistle might most usefully be blown in the public interest is in the civil service or the security services where to do so would often amount to a breach of the Official Secrets Act, and therefore be a crime.

3.83 Of more general application, particular difficulties may arise in relation to offences under the Data Protection Act 1998 (DPA). In particular, s55 of the DPA provides for an offence in the following terms:

> (1) A person must not knowingly or recklessly, without the consent of the data controller—
>   (a) obtain or disclose personal data or the information contained in personal data, or
>   (b) procure the disclosure to another person of the information contained in personal data.

3.84 On its face this is potentially of wide application. The word 'data' is widely defined. It includes any information which 'is being processed by means of equipment operating automatically in response to instructions given for that purpose' or which is 'recorded with the intention that it should be processed by means of such equipment' (DPA s1(1)). It also includes non-automated records where these are part of a 'relevant filing system' as defined in s1(1) of the DPA. 'Personal data' is widely defined as data which relates to living individuals who can be identified from the data. There are also certain categories of data identified in s2 DPA, which constitute 'sensitive personal data'. These include matters such as the racial or ethnic origin of the data subject (ie the person who is the subject of the personal data) or his 'physical or mental health or condition'. However, the offence under s55 is not restricted to this narrower category, but includes personal data generally. Subject to the defences which are set out in s55 DPA, where a person obtains information relating to one or more identifiable individuals from the employer's electronic records and knowingly discloses that information without the permission of the employer (as the data controller), s55(1) DPA would apply. Since the disclosure would involve the commission of a criminal offence, it could not be a qualifying disclosure.

3.85 Section 55(2) DPA sets out circumstances where disclosing the personal data is not a defence. It provides:

> (2) Subsection (1) does not apply to a person who shows—
>   (a) that the obtaining, disclosing or procuring—
>   (i) was necessary for the purpose of preventing or detecting crime, or
>   (ii) was required or authorised by or under any enactment, by any rule of law or by the order of a court,
>   (b) that he acted in the reasonable belief that he had in law the right to obtain or disclose the data or information or, as the case may be, to procure the disclosure of the information to the other person,

(c) that he acted in the reasonable belief that he would have had the consent of the data controller if the data controller had known of the obtaining, disclosing or procuring and the circumstances of it, or

(d) that in the particular circumstances the obtaining, disclosing or procuring was justified as being in the public interest.

The issues raised by s55(2) DPA will be in play in most cases where there would **3.86** be a qualifying disclosure but for s43B(3) ERA. In many cases section 55(2)(b) DPA will apply, since the scheme of PIDA is to encourage disclosure to an appropriate person, and having regard to the further tests for protection where there is a wider disclosure. Nevertheless, the test of a reasonable belief in the right to obtain or disclose the data or information is conceptually different from the test of a reasonable belief in information tending to show a relevant failure. An employee who does not believe he or she has any right to disclose information consisting of personal data, may opt to make the disclosure in spite of this because of a belief that it tends to show a relevant failure.

In those circumstances the employee may still be able to fall back on the exceptions **3.87** in s55(2)(a) and (d) DPA. In neither case is reasonable belief part of the test. It may be argued, therefore, that this connotes that a court must make an objective assessment of whether the disclosure is in fact in the public interest or necessary to prevent crime. We suggest, however, that a court would be entitled to have regard to a protected disclosure legislative scheme as providing an indication of whether the disclosure is justified in the public interest. Thus, if an employee makes a disclosure which (apart from s43B(3)) would be a qualifying disclosure and would be protected, this of itself will often be a compelling basis for determining that the disclosure is justified in the public interest.[24]

By way of an illustration of the difficulties which might arise, suppose an employee **3.88** believes his employer has been defrauding the Revenue by under-declaring amounts paid by way of salary to employees. The employee provides information which is the basis for the concerns to the Inland Revenue (being the relevant prescribed body under s43F ERA), but the information supplied is from the employer's tax records relating to its employees. Authorization from the employer to make the disclosures is neither provided nor sought. If the employee had a reasonable belief that the information disclosed tended to show a criminal offence, and acted in good faith and with a reasonable belief that the information disclosed and any allegations contained in it were substantially true, then subject to s43B(3) ERA, the disclosure

---

[24] But see the discussion in chapter 4 of *Street v Derbyshire Unemployed Workers' Centre* [2005] ICR 97 (CA) at para 4.41 where the Court of Appeal regarded the opening words of PIDA as requiring the worker to act in the public interest rather than denoting that disclosures made in accordance with the PIDA requirements were thereby to be regarded as having been made in the public interest.

would be protected under s43F. We suggest that this should also be a sufficient basis to demonstrate that the disclosure was justified in the public interest under s55(2)(d) DPA, even if on investigation the concerns proved not to be correct.[25] Similarly it would be likely that the employee could show a reasonable belief in the right to disclose the information to the appropriate authorities.

(2) Consequential procedural issues

3.89 Because of s43B(3) ERA there may be an overlap of jurisdictions dealing with a particular disclosure. Where the disclosure is alleged to constitute a criminal offence and proceedings are in progress or anticipated, the employment tribunal might be willing, upon application by either party, to postpone the tribunal proceedings. In relation to whether to grant a postponement the tribunal has a broad discretion taking into account what the interests of justice require: *Carter v Credit Change Limited* [1979] IRLR 361 (CA). In considering whether to allow an adjournment the tribunal will ordinarily consider the degree of similarity between the issues before the tribunal, the extent of the delay likely to be caused, how late the application is made and the reasons for the delay in making an application for an adjournment. However the arguments in favour of a postponement are likely to be more powerful where, as in the case of s43B(3) the tribunal has directly to consider whether the disclosure constituted an offence, than when the issue of criminal conduct arises in ordinary unfair dismissal proceedings. This is illustrated by the leading case of *Bastick v James Lane (Turf Accountants) Limited* [1979] ICR 778 (EAT). Mr Bastick was dismissed from his employment in a betting office for dishonestly paying out on losing bets. There were also criminal charges of theft arising out of the same activities. It was argued that if the tribunal proceedings took place first, Mr Bastick would be prejudiced either because he might lead evidence in the employment tribunal proceedings which would prejudice him in the criminal trial, or by being inhibited in advancing evidence in the tribunal proceedings. Despite this, his application for a postponement of the employment tribunal proceedings was refused and the decision was upheld by the EAT as a legitimate exercise of discretion. In refusing the postponement the ET placed emphasis on the unacceptable delay that would result from postponement, since the issues before the criminal court and the tribunal were different. The issue in the criminal court would focus on whether Mr Bastick had acted dishonestly, whereas the focus in the tribunal proceedings was on what the employer knew and on the reasonableness of the decision to dismiss. That consideration would not however apply where the issue of criminality was directly raised, as where s43B(3) is in issue.

---

[25] See by analogy *In re a Company* [1989] 1 Ch 477, discussed in Chapter 11.

(3) Standard of proof

During the Parliamentary debates on the Public Interest Disclosure Bill 1998, at   **3.90**
the House of Lords Committee stage on 5 June 1998 an unsuccessful attempt was
made to introduce an amendment limiting the exclusion in s43B(3) to where the
worker acted knowingly or recklessly in some way. It was argued that the exclusion
could otherwise work unfairly especially as it could apply to strict liability
offences. In rejecting this argument, Lord Borrie QC emphasized that protection
is intended to apply to disclosures in the public interest and that 'it is very difficult
to say that the commission of a criminal offence by a discloser can nonetheless be
in the public interest'.[26]

Lord Nolan[27] and Lord Borrie QC,[28] speaking on the Bill in the House of Lords,   **3.91**
opined that where no such proceedings were in prospect but the employer alleges
that the disclosure constituted a crime, the standard of proof which the tribunal
should apply should be effectively a criminal one. Both based their comments
on the decision in *In Re A Solicitor* [1992] 2 All ER 335. The Government
spokesman, Lord Haskell,[29] while pointing out that the effects of such a finding
would not be the same as in a criminal court, stated that a 'high standard of proof'
would be required. This is consistent with the ordinary approach where matters
which would constitute a criminal offence are raised in civil proceedings.
Ordinarily the civil standard of proof on the balance of probabilities will continue to
apply but the evidence required to satisfy this standard will be at the high end of the
scale because the court will take into account the improbability of guilt as part of the
range of circumstances to be weighed in determining the balance of probability.[30]

F. Legal professional privilege

Section 43B(4) ERA makes special provision to prevent a legal advisor claiming   **3.92**
protection under the Act if he discloses information which was supplied by a
worker, if the worker could have claimed legal professional privilege in relation
to such information. The legal advisor will not be able to assert that he has made
a qualifying disclosure if he discloses the information without authority from the
worker client.

On a literal reading of s43B(4), it might be argued that if the lawyer then discloses   **3.93**
the privileged information to the employer on the client's instructions to do so,

---

[26] *Hansard* HL, 5 June 1998, col. 616.
[27] *Hansard* HL, 5 June 1998, col. 614.
[28] ibid, cols. 616/7.
[29] ibid, col. 616.
[30] *In re H and others*, para 3.45 above; *Raja v Hoogstraten and others* [2005] EWHC 2890.

this is not a qualifying disclosure. Section 43B(4) states in terms that disclosure of the privileged information by a person to whom it was given in the course of obtaining legal advice is not a qualifying disclosure. There is no express mention of an exception if the disclosure was authorized by the client. However it would be wholly inconsistent with the approach of the legislation to deny a worker protection for a disclosure made in good faith to his employer which otherwise satisfies the requirements of a qualifying disclosure, merely because the disclosure is made through the solicitor. The better view therefore is that s43B(4) does not affect the lawyer's ability to make disclosures to others on the express instructions of a worker who is his client, in which case there would be a disclosure as agent for the worker client and that would be judged in the normal way. This can be reconciled with the wording of s43B(4) on the basis that once the client has given authority to the lawyer to disclose the information, and that information is duly disclosed, there could no longer be a claim to legal privilege in relation to that information.

G. Geographical scope

3.94 To fall within the Act, the relevant failure or malpractice may occur or be anticipated to occur either inside or outside the United Kingdom (s43B(2) ERA). Thus, an employee in the UK might raise concerns about the felling of rainforests in South America, or human rights violations in East Timor (provided that this amounted to a crime or other breach of a legal obligation): see para 3.58 above. Nor does it matter what law applies to the disclosure as a matter of private international law (s43B(2) ERA).

4

GOOD FAITH

A. **Overview**	4.02	C. **Burden of proof**	4.34
B. **The meaning of good faith**	4.04	D. **Concerns about the decision in**	
(1) Good faith is not synonymous		*Street v Derbyshire Unemployed*	
with honesty	4.04	*Workers' Centre*	4.38
(2) Ulterior motive must be the		E. **Counter-arguments in support**	
predominant or dominant motive		**of the decision in** *Street v*	
to negative good faith	4.07	*Derbyshire Unemployed*	
(3) Legitimate and illegitimate purposes	4.08	*Workers' Centre*	4.45
(4) Does a predominant non-public		F. **Reform?**	4.51
interest motive necessarily negative			
good faith?	4.16		

The concept of 'good faith' lies at the heart of the protected disclosure legislation. **4.01** It is a requirement which applies in every case except where the disclosure is made in the course of obtaining legal advice (under s43D). The concept has attracted some controversy in the light of the way in which it has been interpreted by the courts. Indeed this led to a call, in the Report of the Shipman Inquiry by Dame Janet Smith,[1] for the requirement to be removed altogether.

A. Overview

In summary, these propositions have been established in relation to the meaning **4.02** and effect of the good faith requirement:

(a) Good faith is not simply to be equated with honesty. It requires consideration of the motive of the person making the disclosure. A disclosure might therefore be in bad faith, by reason of an 'ulterior motive', even though a worker

---

[1] 5th Report, 9 December 2004, Cm 6394, paras 11.6 and 11.10.

reasonably believes that the information disclosed and the allegations contained in it are true and that it tends to show a relevant failure.

(b) Good faith may only be negatived if the ulterior motive is the dominant or predominant one.

(c) An ulterior motive is a motive for the disclosure that is other than the public interest.

(d) Examples of ulterior motives which have been held to negative good faith are personal antagonism, pursuing a personal campaign and seeking to obtain a personal employment advantage.

(e) Ultimately the question of whether a disclosure was or was not made in good faith is one of fact. The test is not whether there were mixed motives or a predominant ulterior motive, but whether the disclosure was made in good faith.

(f) The burden of proving bad faith is on the respondent employer and must be specifically alleged.

4.03 We consider each of these propositions in more detail below.

B. The meaning of good faith

(1) Good faith is not synonymous with honesty

4.04 The leading case on the meaning of 'good faith' in the context of protected disclosures is *Street v Derbyshire Unemployed Workers' Centre* [2005] ICR 97 (CA). The Court of Appeal rejected a submission that good faith merely connoted that the disclosure was made 'honestly' or with 'honest intention'. Instead, in context, good faith focuses on the motive of the person making the disclosure, so that it is open to a tribunal to find that a disclosure was not made in good faith if it was made for some ulterior purpose, being a purpose other than acting in the public interest. Second, however, the Court of Appeal accepted that, in a case of mixed motives, protection is not to be denied merely because there was some ulterior motivation unless that was the dominant or predominant purpose of the disclosure.

4.05 Mrs Street worked as an administrator for the Derbyshire Unemployed Workers' Centre. She was dismissed after making a series of allegations against the manager, which she claimed were made under s43G ERA (being made to the treasurer of one of the borough councils that funded the Centre) and under s43C ERA (being made to a councillor who sat on the Centre's management committee, and therefore being a disclosure to her employer). Her disclosures included that the manager had committed fraud in setting up a secret account so as to conceal the true level of the Centre's assets for the purposes of obtaining funding which was means-tested. She also alleged that the manager had made trips abroad for the benefit of other organizations during his working time, that he had frequently instructed the claimant to work for other organizations in her working time for the Centre and that he had shown double standards in the implementation of the Centre's equal opportunities policy. At the instigation of the Centre's management committee, an investigation was carried out into each of the allegations other than the allegations of fraud (which were believed to be for another body—the local TUC—to look into). Mrs Street refused to cooperate with the investigation by being interviewed because, she said, she did not regard the investigation as truly independent. The internal investigation found the allegations to be unfounded. Following a disciplinary interview, she was dismissed on the grounds that she had made unfounded and libellous allegations and had then refused to cooperate with the investigation. The employment tribunal found that Mrs Street satisfied all the requirements of ss43C and 43G except good faith. The tribunal therefore found that she had reasonably believed that the information disclosed and the allegations contained in it were substantially true, that she had reasonably believed that she would be subjected to a detriment if she made the disclosure to her employer and that she had not made the disclosure for the purposes of personal gain. It also found that in all the circumstances it was reasonable for her to make the disclosures. However the tribunal found that the disclosures had not been made in good faith because Mrs Street had been motivated by personal antagonism to the manager against whom she made the allegations. This decision was upheld by the Court of Appeal.

4.06 In the Court of Appeal Auld LJ (giving the leading judgment) questioned the validity of the finding that the disclosure was reasonable in all the circumstances. He noted that this sat uneasily with the finding that it was not made in good faith, and there were indications that the tribunal had focused on the identity of the recipients of the disclosure rather than considering all the circumstances. Notwithstanding this, the findings raised in stark terms the meaning of good faith. The Court of Appeal upheld the finding that, even though Mrs Street disclosed what she honestly and reasonably believed constituted serious wrongdoing (in this case including fraud), and was subjected to detrimental treatment as a result, the protection of the protected disclosure provisions was lost by the disclosure having been made for an ulterior motive (personal antagonism) and therefore not in good faith.

(2) Ulterior motive must be the predominant or dominant motive to negative good faith

4.07 The Court of Appeal in *Street* acknowledged one potential difficulty in relation to the negativing of good faith on the basis that the worker was actuated by personal antagonism. It was noted that the very fact of the belief that someone has been guilty of a relevant failure, or dissatisfaction with the way a disclosure is handled, may itself lead to hostility or antagonism in the worker. As Lord Diplock put it in *Horrocks v Lowe* [1975] AC 135 at 150 (a defamation case),[2] it is 'difficult to hate the sin but love the sinner'. In the light of this, the test of dominant or predominant purpose was adopted. If the dominant or predominant purpose of the disclosure was in the public interest then personal antagonism or hostility would not be a basis for removing protection.

(3) Legitimate and illegitimate purposes

4.08 The Court of Appeal in *Street* referred to the 'public interest purpose' of the protected disclosure legislation[3] and that protection is for those making the disclosure 'in the public interest'.[4] This did not mean that there must be some wider public significance of the disclosure, such as to exclude for example disclosures by workers as to a breach of their own contracts of employment. That would be to give 'good faith' a meaning which it could not reasonably bear. Instead, it connoted that the motive must be consistent with the aims of the legislation, being principally to remedy, prevent or facilitate investigation in relation to a relevant failure.

4.09 To this end, Wall LJ commented (at para 71, p 117) that:

> ... the primary purpose for the disclosure of such information by an employee must, I think, be to remedy the wrong which is occurring or has occurred; or, at the very least, to bring the s43B information to the attention of a third party in an attempt to ensure that steps are taken to remedy the wrong. The employee making the disclosure for this purpose needs to be protected against being victimised for doing so; and that is the protection the statute provides.

4.10 Similarly Auld LJ (at para 55, p 114) noted that resentment against the person who was the subject of the disclosure should not necessarily negative good faith 'if, when making the disclosure, the worker is still driven by his original concern to right or prevent a wrong'.

4.11 The Court of Appeal however did not purport to set out a comprehensive list of what could be a legitimate or proper purpose. It left scope for there to be argument (on the facts of a particular case) not only as to what constitutes the dominant purpose, but as to what constitutes a legitimate purpose. Wall LJ emphasized

---

[2] But as discussed below, as construed in *Street*, the test is more difficult to satisfy in relation to protected disclosures than in defamation, which is a point on which the Shipman report commented adversely.

[3] *Per* Auld LJ at para 56 p 114.

[4] *Per* Auld LJ at para 47 p 112.

(at para 74, p 118) that it would 'be folly to attempt to list what could constitute ulterior motivation or bad faith'.

In many cases it may be apparent that particular purposes are not legitimate. **4.12** There might be various reasons for this such as the pursuance of a grudge, retaliation against a colleague who has in some way harmed the person making the disclosure, general resentment against the employer's policy, a desire for publicity or deployment of the disclosure as a tactic to obtain some personal advantage.

In *Morrison v Hesley Lifecare Services Limited* (EAT/0262/03 and EAT/0534/03, **4.13** 19 March 2004), Mr Morrison resigned from his position as a special support assistant in a school for children exhibiting challenging behaviour. He claimed he had been constructively dismissed for a reason connected with protected disclosures. Prior to the alleged protected disclosures he had been disciplined for using inappropriate language to colleagues. He had received a further verbal warning in respect of his language and had received a written warning after his line manager had complained of harassment. Mr Morrison in turn made threats through his solicitors against the respondent alleging serious violations of his rights under the Data Protection Act, libel and slander. The tribunal concluded that Mr Morrison had not acted in good faith, but had instead sought to deploy the protected disclosure legislation as part of a campaign he had waged against the respondent. The finding was upheld by the EAT which commented (at para 32) that:

> we bear in mind that this legislation is designed to protect people who no doubt would be regarded as officious, at best and bloody minded at worst. It is in the public interest that people be protected if they make disclosures meeting the specific conditions, and do so in good faith reasonably believing the material before them. It is not Parliament's intention to protect those who simply wage a campaign against their employer.

In context it was not the mere fact of a campaign which drove the tribunal to its **4.14** conclusion of bad faith, but the nature of the campaign and the way the legislation was being deployed. Thus mere persistence in pursuing an allegation, or waging a campaign out of a determination to have the employer investigate or remedy a relevant failure would not negative good faith. However here the disclosures were not being made for their own end but as a tactical ploy. Essentially the protection provided by the legislation was being abused.

There might be particular suspicion as to the claimant's motives for making a **4.15** disclosure where the claimant has some other claim or dispute with the employer. The disclosure might then be seen or portrayed as seeking to procure a personal employment advantage rather than being made in the public interest. In *Bachnak v Emerging Markets Partnership (Europe) Limited* (EAT/0288/05, 27 January 2006) the claimant was employed by an infrastructure investment adviser. He made disclosures which included allegations that investors had been misled. Some of the disclosures were made after Mr Bachnak had been given notice of termination of his employment and whilst he was serving out his notice. Another was made after he had been summoned to a meeting for copying documents without permission and yet another after his suspension but before his dismissal. The EAT upheld the tribunal's findings that the disclosures had primarily been made by Bachnak to strengthen his hand in negotiations for a new contract with the respondent or to put pressure on the respondent not to dismiss him. The EAT held that the tribunal had therefore been entitled to find that he had not acted in good faith because he had acted in his personal interest rather than in the public interest.

(4) Does a predominant non-public interest motive necessarily negative good faith?

4.16   The decision in *Street* makes clear that once it is established that a worker's predominant motive for making a disclosure was something other than the public interest, it is at least open to a tribunal to consider whether the disclosure was made other than in good faith. But is such a finding determinative of the good faith issue, or must the tribunal still stand back and consider whether, taking into account the findings as to motive, the disclosure was not in good faith? Put another way, having found that the predominant motive was not the protection of the public interest, can a tribunal still find that the motive was not sufficiently illegitimate as to render the disclosure made other than in good faith?

4.17   Suppose, for example, an employee (X) provides information about suspected wrongdoing by his line manager (Y) because the employer has threatened X that unless he provides full information relating to the allegations he will be disciplined. X then provides the information primarily because he is concerned that it is in his own personal interest to do so. The decision in *Street* makes clear that, at minimum, it is open to a tribunal to consider whether this renders the disclosure made other than in good faith. But is it open to the tribunal to conclude that although X's primary motivation was his own personal interest, this was not sufficient in the circumstances to negative good faith? X might have been genuinely cooperating with the investigation. There might be good reasons why X did not come forward earlier, such as fear of victimization by Y. In such circumstances it may be thought a strange use of the term for the worker to be depicted as having acted in 'bad faith'. Suppose, alternatively, that X came forward and disclosed wrongdoing, not under threat of disciplinary action but principally due to a concern that if the disclosure was not made the worker himself would be blamed for not doing so should the failure come to light (rather than principally due to concern to remedy the wrongdoing). Again, it would be strange to taint this as a disclosure made in bad faith and it may be regarded as entirely contrary to the policy of the legislation in encouraging workers to raise concerns internally, if the worker was consequently denied protection against victimization for having raised the concerns with his employer.

We suggest that the decision in *Street* does not compel a tribunal to find, if an **4.18** employee primarily acts in his own personal interest, that this necessarily negatives good faith. Indeed, that issue did not arise in *Street*. It was only necessary to determine whether a tribunal had been entitled to find that Mrs Street had not acted in good faith due to having acted out of personal antagonism, not to determine that it was bound to find this. *Street* was not a case in which the court was faced with a tribunal having found that an employee had acted in good faith despite primarily acting in her own personal interest.

Dame Janet Smith, in her analysis of the decision in *Street* contained in the **4.19** Shipman report,[5] suggested a distinction between the judgments of Auld LJ (with whom Jacob LJ agreed) and the concurring judgment of Wall LJ. In her view, Auld LJ concluded that good faith would be absent if the predominant purpose of the worker was other than the public interest, whereas Wall LJ considered that a tribunal was not bound to do so. However whilst Auld LJ concluded that an ulterior motive would have to be a predominant motive in order to negative good faith, he did not directly address the question as to whether it would necessarily lead to that conclusion. Further, there are indications in his judgment that even where the primary motive is not one of acting in the public interest, good faith might not be negatived. Thus, in comparing the good faith test with other requirements in s43G—that the disclosure must (a) not be made for personal gain and (b) be reasonable in all the circumstances—Auld LJ commented (at para 50) that:

> . . . there is clearly scope for motivation of personal gain to negative good faith. But it *may be a sufficiently justified motivation to pass the good faith requirement* but not that of the absence of motivation of personal gain. So, depending on the outcome, it may be academic where personal gain is the, or the main, motivation for disclosure, whether it also serves to negative good faith—the disclosure loses its protection anyway. And here the specific requirement of the absence of a motivation of personal gain in s43G(1)(c) may not be otiose any more than that of reasonableness in s43G(1)(e), depending on the circumstances, for example, where the ulterior motive is not for personal gain and might be considered reasonable, but is not made for any of the purposes for which s43B provides protection. (Our emphasis)

Auld LJ therefore contemplated that whilst good faith might be negatived even **4.20** though the motive could be considered reasonable, nevertheless a motivation of personal gain might be 'sufficiently justified' so as not to negative good faith. It may be that Auld LJ had in mind that the motive might be 'sufficiently justified'

---

5 5th Report of the Shipman Inquiry by Dame Janet Smith (9 December 2004, Cm 6394) at paras 11.103 and 11.104.

because it was mixed up with some other predominant interest which was in the public interest. There are however other indications which suggest that Auld LJ contemplated that, even where a predominant interest was a personal interest (rather than a public interest motive), a tribunal should still assess whether it was such as to negative good faith. Thus (at para 53, p 113) he said that:

> . . . in considering good faith as distinct from reasonable belief in the truth of the disclosure, it is clearly open to an employment tribunal, where satisfied as to the latter, to consider nevertheless whether the disclosure was not made in good faith because of some ulterior motive, which may or may not have involved a motivation of personal gain, and/or which, in all the circumstances of the case, may or may not have made the disclosure unreasonable. Whether the *nature or degree of any ulterior motive* found amounts to bad faith . . . is a matter for its assessment on a broad basis. (Our emphasis)

4.21 As this emphasizes, ultimately the tribunal must apply the statutory test of whether the disclosure was made in good faith. Whilst, having regard to the underlying purposes of the legislation, motive is relevant to good faith, the tribunal must still consider not only the degree of any ulterior motive (including whether it is the predominant motive), but also the nature of the ulterior motive, and whether this is such that, in all the circumstances, good faith is negatived. Auld LJ (at para 54, p 113) rejected as 'too prescriptive' the suggestion by Public Concern at Work that 'an ulterior motive should only negative good faith when it is so wicked and/or malicious as to be or approach dishonesty and is the predominant motive'. But this did not exclude a tribunal from taking into account the nature of the disclosure, and considerations of the extent to which it undermines or conflicts with the purposes of the legislation, in making an overall factual assessment of whether it negatives good faith.

4.22 The concurring judgment of Wall LJ might be relied upon as stronger support for a proposition that a predominant motive other than the public interest necessarily negatives good faith. As noted above, Wall LJ observed (at para 71, p 117) that the primary purpose of the disclosure 'must . . . be to remedy the wrong which is occurring or has occurred; or at the very least, to bring the s43B information to the attention of a third party in an attempt to ensure that steps are taken to remedy the wrong'. However he also stressed the need ultimately to apply the statutory language, noting (at para 72, p 117) that:

> it will, of course, be for the tribunal to identify those different motives, and nothing in this judgment should derogate from the proposition that the question for the tribunal at the end of the day as to whether a person was acting in good faith will not be: did the applicant have mixed motives? It will always be: was the complainant acting in good faith?

4.23 Wall LJ added that he was persuaded that it 'should be *open* to tribunals' (emphasis added) to conclude that a claimant was not acting in good faith if the predominant motivation was other than to achieve the objectives of remedying the wrong or at least bring it to the attention of a third party for it to be addressed. As noted by Dame Janet Smith in the Shipman Report,[6] this appears to contemplate that while a tribunal would be able to find bad faith, it is not bound to do so.

Two subsequent EAT decisions contain *dicta* which might be taken as indicating **4.24** that if the dominant or predominant motive for a disclosure is not the public interest, this necessarily negatives good faith. In *Lucas v Chichester Diocesan Housing Association Limited* (EAT/0713/04, 7 February 2005) at para 39 the EAT commented that:

> . . . an Employment Tribunal must consider all the evidence and decide for itself whether the dominant or predominant motive is an ulterior one in which case it will not attract the protection.

In context, however, we suggest that this was not indicating that good faith must **4.25** necessarily be negatived where the predominant motive for the disclosure was a personal rather than public interest.

(a) Again the issue did not directly arise on the facts. The tribunal made a finding of bad faith, and the EAT found it had not been entitled to do so.

(b) The EAT emphasized the cogent evidence required to establish bad faith because, the EAT said, 'bad faith is a surprising and unusual feature of working relationships' (para 39). This indicated the continuing need to apply the statutory test of good faith, which is not necessarily simply to be equated with acting in the public interest. It might be that the EAT intended that the designation of the motive as 'ulterior' itself indicated a judgement that the nature of the motive is sufficiently illegitimate or inconsistent with the legislation as to negative good faith. But it is unlikely that the EAT considered that a finding that the employee was acting in his personal interest necessarily negatived good faith. It is very doubtful if it could be said to be a surprising and unusual feature of a working relationship for an employee to act primarily in his own personal interest rather than in the public interest. A tribunal must still consider whether by virtue of an employee acting in his personal interest he is to be regarded as having acted in bad faith.

(c) The EAT also commented (at paragraph 33) that 'it is *open* to a tribunal to consider whether disclosure was not made in good faith if an ulterior motive exists which is the dominant or predominant purpose for making the disclosure'. This appears to indicate an acceptance that the tribunal was not bound to make such a finding.

---

[6] 5th Report of the Shipman Inquiry by Dame Janet Smith (9 December 2004, Cm 6394) at paras 11.95 and 11.104.

4.26 In *Bachnak v Emerging Markets Partnership (Europe) Limited* (EAT/0288/05, 27 January 2006) (at para 24), however, the EAT commented that:

> . . . the statutory protection is afforded to those who make disclosures in the public interest; thus where the predominant purpose is the employee's personal interest, or in the case of *Street*, personal antagonism against a manager, the disclosure will not be made in good faith.

4.27 The EAT therefore expressed themselves in more unequivocal terms. However, we suggest for the reasons set out above, that this goes further than *ratio* of the decision in *Street*. It risks substituting a different test in place of the statutory language, rather than, having identified the predominant motives, standing back and considering whether in all the circumstances this establishes that good faith has been negatived. Again, however, on the facts the issue did not arise as to whether a personal interest necessarily negatives good faith. It was sufficient that, on the facts, the tribunal had been entitled (rather than bound) to find that good faith was negatived by virtue of disclosures having been deployed for an ulterior purpose of strengthening the claimant's hand in negotiations or putting pressure on the employer not to dismiss him.

4.28 Several employment tribunal decisions illustrate the proposition that a disclosure might be made in good faith even though there is no predominant motive of furthering the public interest, and the need to stand back and consider directly the statutory test of 'good faith' rather than focusing only on the question of whether there is a predominant ulterior motive.

4.29 *Speyer v Thorn Security Group Limited and others* (ET, Case No. 2302898/03, 20 August 2004) concerned disclosures made by the claimant in the course of an investigation by the Manhattan District Attorney into potential fraud and financial irregularity by the parent company of the claimant's employer. Mr Speyer was asked by his employer to assist it in cooperating with the investigation. A meeting was held with the District Attorney, which his employers attended, when information relied on as being protected disclosures was provided by Speyer. The disclosures were treated as made under s43C(1)(a) as the employers were represented at the meeting with the District Attorney, and under s43C(2) as they were made in accordance with a procedure authorized by the employer, albeit on an ad hoc basis. The tribunal found that the disclosures were made in good faith notwithstanding that Speyer had emphasized that he was only acting on instructions in making the disclosures. Although (since the decision preceded the Court of Appeal's decision in *Street*) the tribunal equated good faith with honest intention, it was apparent from the tribunal's findings that this did not affect the decision. In particular, although the tribunal found that Speyer had used the opportunity to seek to establish his own innocence of any illegality, the tribunal regarded this as incidental only. However even if the predominant purpose had been to establish Speyer's own innocence, or if his predominant purpose had been to act in accordance with instructions to cooperate, it may be questioned why that should necessitate a finding of bad faith, especially when set against the tribunal's finding that he disclosed all that he knew that might be of interest to the enquiry.

Similarly *Green v First Response Training and Development Limited* (ET, Case No. **4.30** 250542/03, 13 April 2002) illustrates that the line between workers acting in their own personal interest and acting in the public interest may not be easy to draw, and that in some cases a focus on this question may unnecessarily complicate the issue of whether the worker was acting in good faith. Mr Green was employed by a company which provided training and education services, and which was partly funded by the local council. He became concerned that the employer was invoicing for more hours of training than were being provided to the students. He raised concerns with the employer, in the form of the sole director and shareholder (E), but there was a failure to provide him with documentary evidence to allay his concerns. Subsequently Mr Green's employment was terminated, but he was allowed to continue working whilst he sought alternative employment. Whilst still working for the respondent he raised further concerns. These included concerns raised with the relevant examination body about E's conduct of examinations and, having looked at the employer's paperwork and records, concerns raised with the principal of the funding college that E had submitted exaggerated and fraudulent claims for funding.

The tribunal was satisfied that Mr Green had been dismissed for making a **4.31** protected disclosure under s43G. It rejected the employer's contention that the disclosures had not been made in good faith. However, in the context of considering motive in the light of the EAT's decision in *Street*, the tribunal noted that Green had been 'rightly concerned about the impact upon his own reputation and that of his colleagues, had the wrongdoing come to light in other circumstances'. The tribunal plainly regarded this as a legitimate motive for the disclosure. Although he was also concerned about his colleagues' reputations, it is most unlikely that the tribunal would have come to a different conclusion if he had been concerned only as to the damage to his own reputation should the wrongdoing he believed had occurred have been discovered other than by Green reporting it. If the issue is considered in terms of whether there was an ulterior motive it might be argued that in those circumstances Green would have been acting in his own personal interest rather than in the public interest. But if the question is cast in terms of whether he was acting other than in good faith, in acting out of concern as to his own reputation had wrongdoing not been disclosed, the answer is much easier. It would be wholly inconsistent with the aims of the legislation if a worker was held not to have acted in good faith in such circumstances in revealing wrongdoing which he genuinely and reasonably believed was occurring.

The decision of the employment tribunal in *Smith v Ministry of Defence* (ET, Case **4.32** No. 1401537/04 and others, 26 April 2005) also illustrates the difficulties which may arise in applying a test of predominant motive, rather than considering whether there is bad faith. The claimants were part of the Ministry of Defence Guard Force (known as MGS) stationed at a base in Bristol. Their concerns arose because a colleague (T) was permitted to return to work after a period of suspension and investigation following his conviction for indecent assault on an 8-year-old girl. Outside the base, about 50 metres from one of the guard points, there was a nursery used by children of the staff engaged at the base. The team initially raised internally their objections to T being permitted to return to work. They were told that the decision was final and that disciplinary action would follow if they did not abide by this and work alongside T. The claimants then raised their concerns both with the local MP and with the press. There were further steps that could have been taken to pursue the matter internally with higher levels of management or through the whistleblowing procedure but this was not done. The claimants were dismissed for gross misconduct following the press reports. It was argued that they had made protected disclosures to the press consisting of information tending to show that the health and safety of the children in the nursery had been, was being or was likely to be endangered. The tribunal held that there was no qualifying disclosure as the requisite reasonable belief was lacking. It also held that the disclosure was not made in good faith. The proximity of the nursery was part of the claimants' concerns but, in the tribunal's view, their principal motivation was their 'strongly held revulsion' at having to work with T due to the crime for which he had been convicted. The concerns expressed in relation to the nursery, though genuine, were (the tribunal held) the vehicle through which the claimants sought to justify their instinctive feelings of revulsion towards T and their objections to working with him.

4.33 The ET therefore drew a distinction between the concern as to health and safety at the nursery (which it regarded as a genuine but subsidiary and unreasonable concern) and the revulsion towards T due to his crime and the consequent objection to working with him (which it considered to be an ulterior motive). But it is notable that the ET directed itself, purporting to follow *Street*, that 'the disclosure will not be made in good faith if an ulterior motive was the dominant or predominant purpose of making it'. It therefore did not go on expressly to consider whether, on the basis that it had identified an ulterior motive, this meant that the disclosure was made in bad faith having regard to both the nature of the identified ulterior motive, and the fact that the concerns in relation to health and safety were genuine. Applying the test of whether there was a predominant ulterior motive may not necessarily have led to the same conclusion as might have been reached if the tribunal had then asked whether the fact that the primary motivation was revulsion at T's crime meant that the (genuine) concerns had not been raised in good faith.

C. Burden of proof

The burden of proving that a disclosure was not made in good faith is on the **4.34** employer: *Bachnak* at para 25; *Lucas*.[7]

As noted above (para 4.25) in *Lucas* the EAT emphasized that the evidence as a **4.35** whole must be cogent in order to establish absence of good faith. This was because absence of good faith is an unusual feature in an employment relationship. However this might not always be the case. If the disclosure is in the context of a strained relationship or where a worker has some other apparent grounds for dissatisfaction, such as where the worker has been passed over for a promotion or a pay rise, it may be less surprising that there is an ulterior motive. Further, whistleblowers are often regarded as 'troublemakers' by employers and as such there may be a natural inclination in many cases to challenge the good faith of the whistleblower.

The EAT in *Lucas* also emphasized that if an allegation of improper motivation **4.36** is to be made this should be made explicit in advance and put squarely to the claimant in cross-examination. Ms. Lucas raised concerns about financial irregularities. The tribunal decided that the disclosures were made out of spite because her hours had been reduced. However this was not an allegation that had been trailed in the Notice of Appearance. Nor was it put to her in cross-examination in relation to a crucial meeting when disclosures had been made. Further, disclosures as to financial irregularities had been made before there had been any basis for inferring that Lucas had been acting out of spite. In those circumstances the EAT reversed the finding of the ET and held that protected disclosures had been made under s43C ERA.[8]

A wide range of factors may be relied on in the circumstances of a particular case **4.37** to demonstrate that a disclosure was not made in good faith. Relevant considerations are likely to include:

• the potential ulterior motives arising out of the personal circumstances of the employee. Thus, if the employee has reason to be resentful of the employer, or has an opportunity to gain an employment advantage, an employer may seek to identify this as the predominant motivation for the disclosure.
• the means by which the disclosure is made—which may be regarded as telling in relation to the true motivation. Thus in the case of *Smith v Ministry of Defence* (see para 4.32 above), the fact that disclosure was made to the press was influential in the tribunal's decision. The ET's view was that if the safety of the

---

[7] See above, para 4.15 and 4.24.
[8] *Lucas* was followed by the EAT in *Doherty v British Midland Airways Ltd* (2006) IRLR 90 (at para 39). The EAT emphasized the need clearly to put allegations of malice by the claimant in the context of a claim of constructive dismissal on the ground of trade union activities.

children in the nursery had been the claimants' primary concern, they would not have broadcast this to the public at large, but would have used the respondent's whistleblowing procedure or approached the nursery or the relevant regulator (Ofsted) or the appropriate Minister.

• the timing of the disclosure. Thus if the disclosure is made long after the employee became aware of the alleged relevant failures despite opportunities to raise the matter earlier this may, if unexplained, be regarded as material. This was regarded by the tribunal as significant in *Mehdaoua v Demipower* (ET, Case No. 2201602/04, 11 January 2005) where an allegation of fraud was made by the claimant's manager. The unexplained delay between the alleged wrongdoing and the disclosure, taken together with the fact the disclosure was made when a colleague had been or was about to be dismissed, was treated by the tribunal as indicating an absence of good faith and that the disclosure had in fact been made in support of the colleague.

• the employee's conduct after making the disclosure. An ulterior motive might (as in *Street*) be indicated by a refusal to cooperate with the investigation and to provide further details without good reason, thereby undermining the policy of enabling the matter to be investigated.

D. Concerns about the decision in *Street v Derbyshire Unemployed Workers' Centre*

4.38 Because of the scope which it affords to focus on the messenger rather than the message, the Court of Appeal's decision in *Street* has attracted some controversy.[9] The breadth of matters which might be relied upon as constituting an ulterior motive means that this will be an issue in many protected disclosure cases. It will often be possible to point to some employment advantage which an employee may hope to attain or some reason for dissatisfaction, and to contend that this is the primary motivation. This has prompted concerns that the impact of the decision in *Street* will cause uncertainty as to whether protection is likely to be conferred and accordingly make those able to bring to light important relevant failures reticent about doing so. This is contrary to the intention of the legislation.

4.39 There is scope for criticism both as to the reasoning which led to the decision in *Street* and as to the policy implications. As to the reasoning, Auld LJ began his analysis by acknowledging that 'shorn of context, the words "in good faith" have a core meaning of honesty'. The Court of Appeal reasoned, however, that the statutory context

---

[9] For example, criticism by Public Concern at Work in their comment on *Street* on the PCaW website, and recommendations for reform in the Shipman report.

demonstrated that good faith required a focus on the motive for the disclosure rather than merely on whether it was made honestly. The court emphasized that it was necessary to have regard to the specific context and as such it was not helpful to have regard to other contexts, where good faith has been equated with honesty.[10]

A central element in the Court of Appeal's reasoning was that the term good faith **4.40** in s43G would be otiose if it merely connoted a requirement of honesty. The court considered that this would add nothing to the requirement in s43G(1)(b) that the worker 'reasonably believes that the information disclosed, and any allegation contained in it, are substantially true'. But this is unconvincing. Suppose a worker collects together evidence of fraud by a colleague, but in the course of his investigation also discovers some evidence which might indicate the contrary. If the worker only discloses the damning evidence, and conceals all contrary evidence, it might legitimately be said that the worker does not act in good faith—in the core sense of not acting honestly—even though he reasonably believes that the information disclosed and the allegation contained in it are substantially true.

The other principal plank of the Court of Appeal's reasoning was that the heading **4.41** of the Public Interest Disclosure Act 1998 (PIDA) provides that it is: '*An Act to protect individuals who make certain disclosures of information in the public interest . . .*'. This was taken to indicate that the protection was intended to apply to those who are motivated by the public interest. It might be countered that where the disclosure satisfied the requirements of the legislation it is then to be regarded as being in the public interest that the disclosure is made. In the 5th report of the Shipman Inquiry, Dame Janet Smith suggested (at para 11.102) that Mrs Street might have been on stronger ground if the introductory words had provided that PIDA was an Act 'to protect individuals who disclose information, the disclosure of which is in the public interest'. Yet the introductory words would seem easily capable of this construction. A disclosure may be 'in the public interest' even if not made with the motive of promoting the public interest. The scheme of the legislation, it might be argued, is to identify what sorts of disclosure are in the public interest—rather than for this to be an additional requirement. That was brought into sharp focus by the Shipman case, which concerned the investigation into the circumstances surrounding his murder of a large number of his patients. If an employee had given early warning of Shipman's actions, this would plainly have been in the public interest even if done out of personal antagonism towards him. As this illustrates, the public policy in encouraging the disclosure of concerns may be no less compelling merely because there are ulterior motives. Wrongdoing may

---

[10] For example, the term 'good faith' in the Bills of Exchange Act 1882 has been interpreted to mean that a person who was 'honestly blundering and careless' was acting in good faith: *Jones v Gordon* (1877) 2 App Cas 616.

be brought to light by someone motivated by personal antagonism as well as by public-spirited individuals.

4.42 Further, it might be argued that the approach in *Street* will encourage employers to 'shoot the messenger'—in the sense of challenging his/her motives—rather than listen to the message conveyed. The employer is encouraged to search for ulterior reasons for the blowing of the whistle and it might seek to do so even in the case of an internal disclosure. This undermines the good corporate governance aims underlying PIDA. These concerns were voiced by Dame Janet Smith in her report in the Shipman Inquiry,[11] where she commented that:

> if employers are able to explore and impugn the motives of the 'messenger', when trying to justify having taken action against him/her, many 'messages' will not come to light because organisations like PCaW will have to advise those who come to them for advice that, if their motives can be impugned, they may not be protected by the PIDA.

4.43 Nor would it be an answer that in Shipman's case the very gravity of the disclosure would make a tribunal unlikely to find that a disclosure was not made in good faith. That is to view the matter with the benefit of hindsight having regard to the fact that the disclosures would have been well-founded. However a person considering making a disclosure might well have no means of knowing with certainty that the investigation would demonstrate that the concerns were correct. If the allegations turned out to be incorrect, the very gravity of the disclosures might be relied upon to portray the worker as prone to wild and libellous allegations, and so to question the motivation behind the disclosure.

4.44 The Court of Appeal reasoned that even if PIDA did not apply, this did not prevent employees bringing an ordinary unfair dismissal claim. But this may not apply either if the worker is not an employee, or lacks sufficient qualifying service, or the detriment does not take the form of dismissal. Ordinary unfair dismissal may also be of little comfort if an employee is to face character assassination for bringing a claim. Automatic unfairness is required precisely because of the need to encourage whistleblowers to step forward, not least as an early warning system for revealing concerns. Lifting of the cap on compensation is also important due to the difficulties that workers sometimes experience in finding alternative work once they are branded as whistleblowers. One of the key reasons why whistleblowers have historically been reluctant to disclose concerns is the worry that they will be seen as troublemakers, disloyal or as attacking the employer.[12] The decision in *Street* may be seen as offering unwarranted encouragement for employers to take that course.

---

[11] Fifth Report of the Shipman Inquiry by Dame Janet Smith (9 December 2004, Cm 6394) at para 11.106.
[12] ibid, para 11.10.

E. Counter-arguments in support of the decision in
Street v Derbyshire Unemployed Workers' Centre

The arguments against the decision in *Street* tend to focus on adverse public policy **4.45** consequences in terms of the 'chilling effect' deterring workers from coming forward if their motives will be questioned, and on the public interest in serious disclosures being made irrespective of the motivation. Clearly this was the context of the recommendations in the Shipman report. The circumstances in Shipman illustrate that it may be in the public interest to make a disclosure irrespective of motive, notably because of the particular seriousness of the relevant failure. Conversely there are circumstances where it would be strange if motivation could not be taken into account. It is a feature of the protected disclosure legislation that it covers a wide range of circumstances. The matters which may be said to constitute relevant failures range from the most serious, to the much less significant or more limited. Further, in an extreme case it is conceivable that a disclosure might be made for purposes approaching blackmail (although if the disclosure did amount to a criminal offence it would be unprotected pursuant to s43(3) ERA). A worker might raise an allegation to pressurize the employer into a pay rise or better severance terms.

The decision of the ET in *Gulwell v Consignia plc* (ET, Case No. 1602588/00, **4.46** 11 June 2002) provides an illustration of the importance of being able to refer to motive. Mr Gulwell made allegations of fraud and malpractice within his department. The tribunal found that he lacked the requisite reasonable belief for a qualifying disclosure, but it also made findings as to lack of good faith which would have applied even if he did have a reasonable belief. It found that the disclosures were made 'in order to achieve his own ends to be appointed as sales adviser and were being used as a crude form of bullying tactics . . .'. His conduct included keeping a diary on the activities of colleagues. Further, some of his allegations were made in vague terms and the tribunal found there was force in the submission that he should have provided the detail to his employers long before the tribunal hearing so as to enable them to investigate whether the allegations were made in good faith. It would be strange if a worker in such circumstances could benefit from automatic unfair dismissal and no cap on compensation, and be better placed than more meritorious claimants who are limited to ordinary unfair dismissal claims.

In circumstances such as these, there is force in the observations of the Court of **4.47** Appeal in *Street* that, whilst ordinary unfair dismissal protection may be available, the worker should not have the special protection offered by legislation relating to disclosures in the public interest. If the worker was to be protected irrespective of a malign motive, provided only that the allegation was made honestly and with the requisite reasonable belief for a qualifying disclosure, this could lead to protection being afforded in circumstances which would undermine the wide-ranging support which the legislation has attracted.

4.48 Further, whilst it may be in the public interest that disclosures are made so as to prevent or enable detection of relevant failures, the legislation does contemplate that this is not necessarily a sufficient basis to attract protection even though such a disclosure be made on reasonable grounds. This is indicated by the requirement in relation to ss43G and 43H that the disclosure must not be made for the purposes of personal gain. It was argued in *Street* that the express reference to motive in the context of personal gain would have been rendered otiose if good faith was concerned with motive. This was rejected by the Court of Appeal on the basis that the legislation includes overlapping requirements and that motivation of personal gain might be sufficiently justified in particular circumstances that good faith would not be negatived.[13] However the requirement does show that even though a disclosure is in the public interest it might be unprotected. Section 43H makes specific provision for disclosures which *are* (not merely reasonably believed to be) 'of an exceptionally serious nature'. In such cases, if the requirement of a reasonable belief that the information disclosed is substantially true is satisfied, it would almost inevitably be in the public interest that the disclosure is made even though made for an illegitimate purpose. Yet, even aside from the good faith requirement, by virtue of the prohibition of a personal gain motivation, the disclosure might be unprotected.

4.49 In *Street* the Court of Appeal noted that it may not be helpful to refer even to closely related legislation, such as the sex,[14] race[15] and disability discrimination[16] legislation, for guidance as to the meaning of good faith (*per* Auld LJ at para 41). In that legislation the notion of good faith is deployed in relation to victimization claims, in that it is not unlawful to treat a person less favourably for making an allegation (eg of race discrimination) if the allegation is 'false and not made in good faith'. The Court of Appeal rejected an argument that reference could be made to that legislation as indicating that good faith should be equated with honesty because unlike the protected disclosure legislation, in the victimization provisions good faith is the only vehicle for considering the honesty with which the allegation was advanced. However, far from supporting an argument that good faith is to be equated only with honesty, the good faith requirement has also been interpreted in the context of the discrimination legislation as encompassing the possibility of a finding of bad faith where there is an ulterior motive. In *Bham v CFM Group Limited* (EAT 1254/95, 3 June 1997) the EAT upheld a finding that a complaint of race discrimination had been made in bad faith in circumstances

---

[13] *Per* Auld LJ in *Street* at para 50.
[14] s4(2) Sex Discrimination Act 1975.
[15] s2(2) Race Relations Act 1976.
[16] s55(4) Disability Discrimination Act 1995.

where Mr Bham complained that his dismissal constituted victimization for having made a discrimination complaint. The employment tribunal found that Bham had deliberately declined to raise any complaint of discrimination as part of a grievance which he had brought but had indicated to an employee of the respondent that he would do so if the grievance hearing did not appear to be going well. Bham subsequently wrote to local authority councillors indicating a concern that he was the victim of race discrimination. He was later dismissed after he failed to attend a meeting to investigate his absences from work on the grounds of ill health. The tribunal found that Bham was unfairly dismissed but that there was no discrimination on grounds of race and no victimization. It also held that the complaint of victimization had not been made in good faith because it had been raised as a 'tactical tool' in the hope of extending Bham's employment by any means at his disposal. The tribunal appear to have concluded that if there had been a genuine belief in the complaint it would have been raised earlier rather than being held back for tactical purposes. Further the EAT upheld the decision of the tribunal to take account of the finding that the complaint had been made in bad faith in reducing compensation for unfair dismissal.[17]

Similarly in the context of victimization on health and safety grounds, in *Shillito* **4.50**
v van Leer (UK) Limited [1997] IRLR 495, the EAT held that a health and safety representative might be said to have acted in bad faith since he had been pursuing a personal agenda of embarrassing the company, but that there was no requirement that he generally behave reasonably.[18]

F. Reform?

Proposals for reform have been highlighted in the Report of the Shipman Inquiry **4.51**
by Dame Janet Smith DBE.[19] The Report recommends that the good faith requirement should be removed altogether, commenting that:

> . . .if disclosure is in the public interest, it should not matter whether the person making the disclosure has mixed (or, possibly, even malicious) motives.

> . . .I think that there should be public discussion about whether the words 'in good faith' ought to appear in the PIDA. In my view, they could properly be omitted. The three tiered regime of the PIDA, with its incrementally exacting requirements, should afford sufficient discouragement to those minded maliciously to raise baseless concerns.

---

[17] See to similar effect *GMB Union v Fenton* (EAT/0798/02 and EAT/0046/03, 7 October 2003), where in the context of a victimization claim against a union under the SDA, the claim was remitted to consider whether good faith was negatived by the claim having been pursued for a collateral purpose of bringing pressure on the union to settle the claimant's pension claims.

[18] See also *Goodwin v Cabletel UK Limited* [1997] IRLR 665 (EAT).

[19] 5th Report, 9 December 2004, Cm 6394, paras 11.105 and 11.108.

I think that it would be appropriate also if the preamble to the PIDA made it plain that the purpose of the PIDA is to protect persons disclosing information, the disclosure of which is in the public interest. That would serve to focus attention on the message rather than the messenger. The public interest would be served, even in cases where the motives of the messenger might not have been entirely altruistic.

4.52   The removal of the good faith requirement altogether may go too far for the reasons addressed in section E above. However Dame Janet Smith further explained that her proposal was intended to make the test in relation to protected disclosure more closely aligned to the test which applies in the context of defamation where qualified privilege may be negatived by malice.[20] In that context it has been emphasized that courts should be very slow to draw an inference that a defendant was actuated by improper motives amounting to malice, unless satisfied that (s)he did not believe that what was said or written was true or was indifferent to its truth or falsity: *Horrocks v Lowe*.[21] As such, if removal of the good faith test altogether is regarded as unpalatable, an appropriate alternative might be to replace it with a test of malice so as to make clear that the quality or nature of the ulterior motive must be sufficiently bad as to disbar the defendant from protection.

---

[20] ibid, para 11.124.
[21] At 150: see above, para 4.07.

5

THE THREE TIERS OF PROTECTION

A. **The three tiers**   5.01

B. **First tier disclosures: (1) Section 43C**   5.02
   (1) Overview   5.02
   (2) Section 43C(1)(a): Disclosure
       to the employer   5.03
   (3) Section 43C(1)(b)   5.04
   Centrality of promoting
       accountability   5.04
   Section 43C(1)(b)(i)   5.05
   Other responsible persons:
       s43C(1)(b)(ii)   5.07
   Reasonable belief   5.10
   (4) Disclosures to employer and
       disclosure under s43C(1)(b)
       compared   5.11
   (5) Section 43C(2): Whistleblowing
       and other authorized procedures   5.12

C. **First tier disclosures: Section 43D**   5.13
   (1) Overview   5.13
   (2) From whom can the legal advice
       be sought?   5.14
   (3) Capacity in which the legal advice
       is sought   5.15

D. **First tier disclosures: Section 43E:
   Ministers of the Crown and
   government-appointed bodies**   5.16

E. **Regulatory disclosures:
   Section 43F**   5.17
   (1) Overview   5.17
   (2) Prescribed persons   5.18
   (3) Reasonable belief that relevant
       failure falls within a relevant
       description   5.19

   (4) Time at which the recipient must
       be prescribed   5.20
   (5) Reasonable belief that the
       information disclosed and any
       allegation contained in it are
       substantially true   5.21
   (6) Evidential issues   5.22

F. **Wider disclosures under section 43G**   5.23
   (1) Overview   5.23
   (2) 'Personal gain'   5.24
   (3) The s43G(2) preconditions   5.25
   Precondition 1: reasonable belief in
       victimization; subs (2)(a)   5.26
   Precondition 2: reasonable belief in a
       cover-up; subs (2)(b)   5.27
   Precondition 3: previous internal
       disclosure; subs (2)(c)   5.28
   (4) Reasonableness: subs (3)   5.29
   Identity of the person to whom the
       disclosure is made: subs (3)(a)   5.30
   The seriousness of the failure:
       subs (3)(b)   5.31
   Whether the relevant failure
       continues: subs (3)(c)   5.32
   Duty of confidentiality owed to a
       third party: subs (3)(d)   5.33
   Previous disclosures: subs (3)(e)   5.34
   Whistleblowing procedures:
       subs (3)(f)   5.35
   Assessment of all the circumstances   5.36
   (5) Disclosure to a trade union   5.37

G. **Wider disclosures of exceptionally
   serious matters: Section 43H**   5.38

A. The three tiers

5.01 At the heart of the scheme of the protected disclosure legislation are the differing thresholds for protection dependent on to whom the disclosure is made. The scheme was described in *Street v Derbyshire Unemployed Workers' Centre* [2005] ICR 97 as setting out a 'three tiered disclosure regime':

1. The first tier was said to include disclosures under ss43C (employer or other responsible person) and 43E (Minister of the Crown). These, together with s43D (disclosures in the course of legal advice), set the lowest threshold for protection. They are sometimes referred to by way of shorthand as 'internal disclosures'. This reflects the fact that the most significant category of disclosures within this group are disclosures to the employer. However it also encompasses other disclosures which may be outside the employing organization, including disclosures to those whose conduct is in question or who have legal responsibility for the relevant failure. We therefore prefer to refer to disclosures within this category (ss43C, 43D and 43E) as *'first tier disclosures'*. In each case the legislation acknowledges that the recipient of the disclosure is likely to be an appropriate choice for raising concerns in the first instance, and a low threshold is therefore set for protection. In each case (other than s43D where there are no additional requirements), the only requirement over and above that to establish a qualifying disclosure is that the disclosure must be made in good faith.

2. The second tier is disclosures to a prescribed body under s43F ERA. We refer to these as *'regulatory disclosures'*. The threshold for protection is set higher than for first tier disclosures, but still at a level which reflects the fact that the recipient is likely to be an appropriate person to whom to make the disclosure.

3. The third tier comprises wider disclosures under ss43G or 43H ERA. For these disclosures the thresholds for protection are set at their highest. For ease of reference we refer to these as *'third tier disclosures'*.

Broadly, therefore, the stringency of the requirements in each tier of disclosure relates to whether the recipient of the disclosure has a direct interest in receiving the information, or is readily identifiable as a party well placed to investigate or address the relevant failure. In this chapter we consider in turn each of the heads of protection within each of the three tiers.

B. First tier disclosures: Section 43C

(1) Overview

Section 43C ERA provides: **5.02**

Disclosure to employer or other responsible person

(1) A qualifying disclosure is made in accordance with this section if the worker makes the disclosure in good faith—
  (a) to his employer, or
  (b) where the worker reasonably believes that the relevant failure relates solely or mainly to—
    (i) the conduct of a person other than his employer, or
    (ii) any other matter for which a person other than his employer has legal responsibility,
    to that other person.
(2) A worker who, in accordance with a procedure whose use by him is authorised by his employer, makes a qualifying disclosure to a person other than his employer, is to be treated for the purposes of this Part as making the qualifying disclosure to his employer.

This was described by Lord Borrie QC (one of the promoters of the Public Interest Disclosure Bill) as being 'absolutely at the heart' of the Act.[1] Similarly Lord Haskell, speaking for the Government at the Lords Committee Stage said:[2]

> When my noble friend Lord Borrie spoke to the first amendment, he reminded us that we want to encourage the use of proper internal procedures. That is why the purpose of Section 43C in Clause 1 of the Bill is to encourage workers to raise their concerns with the employer first, whether directly or through proper internal company procedures. They need only act in good faith in doing so, which is deliberately not an onerous condition.

> The Bill is therefore very much in line with the Government's partnership approach, which seeks to encourage greater co-operation between employers and workers and trade unions.

No additional evidential test applies in this section beyond the requirement to act in good faith and, by virtue of the need to establish a qualifying disclosure, that the worker 'reasonably believes the information tends to show' the malpractice or misconduct.

---

[1] *Hansard* HL, 19 June 1998 cols. 1801–2, during the Lords Report Stage.
[2] *Hansard* HL, 5 June 1998, col 621.

(2) Section 43C(1)(a): Disclosure to the employer

5.03 Where a disclosure is made internally within the employer's organization an issue may arise as to whether this constitutes disclosure to the employer. Some guidance can be drawn from the decision of the EAT in *Douglas v Birmingham City Council and others* (EAT/018/02, 17 March 2003). As summarized in Chapter 3 (para 3.32), the claimant, Mrs Douglas, was a staff governor of a local education authority school. She raised concerns in relation to a perceived lack of equal opportunities at the school. Her concerns were initially raised in confidence with a fellow governor (C). The EAT held that this did not fall within s43C(1)(a) ERA because the disclosure was made to C 'in a confidential manner and not to her *qua* employer'.

The test of whether the disclosure is made *qua* employer provides a helpful yardstick. It indicates that the concept would ordinarily include a disclosure to any person senior to the worker, who has been expressly or implicitly authorized by the employer as having management responsibility over the worker. But it also indicates that there might be circumstances where even a disclosure to someone more senior in the hierarchy will not be a disclosure to that person *qua* employer. Thus if the disclosure is made to a more senior colleague but on the basis of confiding confidentially in a friend, it may be that the disclosure was not made to the colleague *qua* employer.

Equally s43C(1)(a) does not cover a disclosure to a more junior colleague unless that person has a particular role in receiving complaints whether pursuant to a special whistleblowing policy or just the normal chain of command. It would ordinarily not cover disclosure to a colleague on the same level. There might however be exceptions at the most senior levels of a company. Thus where one director makes a disclosure to a co-director this may be regarded as a disclosure to that director *qua* employer.

The scope of the persons to whom the disclosure can be made might be covered expressly in a whistleblowing procedure, and it is best practice for the employer to do this, although there is no such statutory requirement. If there is a whistleblowing procedure covering these matters, this might influence the determination by the tribunal whether the employee is acting in good faith. An employee who wholly fails to abide by the terms and conditions of that policy may be more likely to be held not to be acting in good faith (see eg *Smith v Ministry of Defence* (ET, Case No. 1401537/04 and others, 26 April 2005), which is discussed in Chapter 4 at paragraph 4.32).

(3) Section 43C(1)(b)

Centrality of promoting accountability

Section 43C(1)(b) ERA provides that, if the worker reasonably believes that the **5.04** relevant failure relates solely or mainly to the conduct of a person other than the employer or to matters for which that other person has legal responsibility, there is a protected disclosure if the disclosure is made to that person in good faith. At the Lords Report stage of the Public Interest Disclosure Bill, Lord Borrie (a promoter of the Bill) emphasized that s43C(1)(b) was central to the scheme of the legislation in that it encourages disclosure to those accountable for relevant failures, and encourages accountability within employing organizations. He explained[3] that:

> Subsection (b) demonstrates that the 'other responsible person' refers to the person responsible for the malpractice because it is his misconduct which is in issue or because he has a legal responsibility for the malpractice.

> This clause is absolutely at the heart of the Bill because this is the provision which will assert and help to ensure that those who are responsible for the concern or malpractice—be it crime, other kinds of illegality, danger to health or safety—are made aware of the concern and can investigate it.

> The effect is that if the concern proves well-founded and there is concern on behalf of the public interest, the employer will, in law, be accountable for the response. Your Lordships will all recall the tragic loss of life in connection with the Zeebrugge ferry. Even though the official inquiry found that on five occasions staff had voiced concerns that the ferries were sailing with their bow doors open, the company was not liable in criminal law, as the board—known in law as the controlling heart and mind of the organisation—had not been informed on those concerns and was unaware of the resultant risk.

> By contrast, when four schoolchildren were killed during a canoeing expedition at Lyme Bay, the managing director of the Outward Bound centre was gaoled for two years because a member of staff had written to him with a clear and graphic warning about the grave risk to life if safety standards were not dramatically and considerably improved. Unable to give good reason as to why he had ignored that warning, the managing director was the very first person in the United Kingdom to be gaoled for what is called corporate manslaughter. Therefore, what will be Section 43C of the 1996 Act signals that concerns should be raised with those who, in law, are responsible for the matter—normally the employer. However, where someone else is legally responsible, then it will be that person.

> In practical terms the clause as it stands, unamended, is right to emphasise the vital role of those who are in law accountable for the conduct or practice in question. . . .

The provision is central to the aims of the legislation in encouraging disclosure to those who are best able to investigate concerns or are responsible for addressing them.

---

[3] *Hansard* HL, 19 June 1998 at cols. 1801–1802.

It highlights accountability in two senses. First, it places an onus on those who are in law accountable to take appropriate action in relation to disclosures as to relevant failures. Second, it promotes and fosters accountability, by helping to ensure that those who have a legal responsibility for relevant failures are properly held accountable, and do not escape appropriate censure for failing to take action on the basis of professed ignorance as to the relevant failures. The provision is therefore an important part of the scheme for encouraging good corporate governance.

Section 43C(1)(b)(i)

Conduct of a person other than his employer

5.05 Section 43C(1)(b) has two limbs which are alternatives. The first limb is where the worker reasonably believes that the relevant failure relates solely or mainly to the conduct of someone other than the employer and the disclosure is made to that person. There is a very substantial overlap with the second limb of s43C(1)(b) ERA. In many, perhaps most, cases, if there is a relevant failure which relates solely or mainly to the conduct of a particular person, that person will have a legal responsibility in relation to the matter.

A potential complication arises where the conduct is of an employee or director of the employer. Can it be said that this person's conduct is properly attributable to the employer and therefore that it does not relate wholly or mainly to a person *other than the employer*? We suggest not. It would be inappropriate to construe the legislation narrowly so as to restrict the ability of an employee to take up concerns in good faith with the individual whose conduct is at the heart of the relevant failure.

Solely or mainly conduct of the other person

5.06 Where more than one person is involved in the relevant conduct, s43C(1)(b)(i) ERA involves a comparison of the degree of involvement of that person in the relevant failure with that of the employer or others. The issues which may arise can be illustrated by the following example. Suppose an employee (A) suspects that his employer has been conspiring to distort market prices and that a third party (T) has also been involved in this. It may be that the employee could not make a disclosure under s43C(1)(b)(i) to T. Although the disclosure relates to the conduct of T it might not relate 'solely or mainly' to T's conduct. On the contrary it might relate at least equally to the conduct of the employer. The appropriate and safer course would be to make the disclosure to the employer.

This indicates a potential difficulty where there are several people other than the employer involved in the relevant failure. It may be difficult to say that the relevant failure relates wholly or mainly to the conduct of any one person. But if T also has a legal responsibility for causing the market distortion, a disclosure could be made to T under s43C(1)(b)(ii) ERA.

Other responsible persons: s43C(1)(b)(ii)

Legal responsibility

The second limb of s43C(1)(b) contemplates disclosure to someone with 'legal **5.07** responsibility' for the relevant failure. The phrase 'legal responsibility' needs to be construed in context. We suggest it encompasses someone who may be responsible, in the sense of being held responsible or being accountable, for the wrongdoing. This is consistent with the aims of the provision in promoting accountability. It does not, we suggest, extend to disclosure to any person who has a legal responsibility for investigating another person's wrongdoing. Otherwise the distinction with s43F ERA would collapse. It would be difficult to conceive of a case where a disclosure to a prescribed body would not be to a person legally responsible for the relevant failure. Equally it would mean that any disclosure to the police would fall within s43C(1)(b) if there was a qualifying disclosure relating to a criminal offence. This would be inconsistent with the scheme of the legislation in encouraging the investigation of matters internally.

Consistently with the emphasis on accountability, Public Concern at Work (PCaW) has suggested on its website[4] (and we agree) that s43C(1)(b) would entail protection in the following circumstances:

(a) A nurse employed by an agency who, in the care home where she works (ie is placed by the agency), raises a concern about malpractice in that home. The care home might have vicarious liability for the malpractice and therefore this might be regarded as conduct of the care home or a matter for which it has legal responsibility.

(b) A worker in an auditing firm who raises a concern with the client (in relation to a matter for which the client would be legally responsible, such as a potential liability for inadequate accounts).

(c) Someone who works for a local authority highway contractor who raises a concern with the local authority that the performance of the contract exposes the authority to negligence claims from injured pedestrians.

Difficulties may arise however in distinguishing between whether there is legal responsibility in the sense of accountability for a relevant failure, or simply a responsibility to investigate or address another's failure without being accountable for that failure. The distinction may be illustrated by reference to the employment tribunal's decision in *Azzaoui v Apcoa Parking UK Limited* (ET, Case No. 2302156/01, 30 April 2002). A parking attendant disclosed that undue pressure was being placed on parking attendants to meet production targets, thereby forcing them into the position of issuing false parking contravention notices (PCNs) and making

---

4 <http://www.pcaw.co.uk>.

inaccurate reports which were used as evidence against motorists in appeals. The disclosure was made both to the claimant's employer and to the local council, which was the employer's client and on behalf of whom parking fines were levied. The tribunal concluded that the disclosure to the council fell within s43C(1)(b)(ii). This finding was not further explained. It is understandable that the tribunal concluded that the council was legally responsible, given that the alleged wrongdoing involved the council (albeit unwittingly) in the wrongdoing by relying on inaccurate reports as evidence against motorists in appeals. Indeed on this basis it would have been open to the tribunal to find that the disclosure fell within s43C(1)(b)(i) as it related to the conduct of the council. The tribunal did not however rely on this provision. We suggest that in order to rely on s43C(1)(b)(ii) it was necessary for the tribunal to address further the issue of whether the council could be held responsible for the failures of employees of its clients. This issue was not directly addressed.

Indeed in cases where reliance had been placed on s43C(1)(b), there has generally been no analysis of what is meant by legal responsibility. The issue arose at an appellate level in *Douglas v Birmingham City Council and others*.[5] Following the initial confidential disclosure, Mrs Douglas made a further disclosure to the Chair of the governing body in relation to failure to carry out the policies relating to equal opportunities. The EAT concluded that this constituted a disclosure to the employer, but accepted that if this was not correct, it fell within s43C(1)(b)(ii) as disclosure to 'another responsible person'. The reasoning in support of this conclusion was not set out, though it can be explained on the basis that the governors were responsible for ensuring the proper implementation of the equal opportunities policy, and they were accountable for a failure to do so.

Solely or mainly to conduct of another person

5.08 Although the phrase 'solely or mainly' applies to both limbs of s43C(1)(b) ERA there may be an important difference in how it applies to the two limbs. In relation to the second limb of s43C(1)(b), in contrast, the phrase 'solely or mainly' is not applied to the degree of responsibility for the matter to which the relevant failure relates. The issue is instead whether the relevant failure relates solely or mainly to a particular matter, rather than whether the recipient of the disclosure has sole or main responsibility for that matter. It is possible that the relevant failure might be solely or mainly about something for which a number of people, including the recipient of the disclosure, have legal responsibility. Thus in the market distortion example (para 5.06 above), there might be a number of people and entities involved with various degrees of culpability but all with some legal responsibility. If the disclosure relates solely or mainly to the market distortion, the disclosure

---

[5] See above, para 5.03.

could be made to each person with legal responsibility without need for further consideration of who has greatest legal responsibility provided the disclosure was made in good faith.

Conversely if the disclosure related only in small part to something for which the recipient of the disclosure had a legal responsibility, the disclosure could not be made under s43C(1)(b)(ii). Thus suppose that a worker makes a disclosure that the employer has been damaging the environment by dumping excessive pollution into a local river and that some of the pollutant material has been leaking from pipes en route to the river. The construction company which built the pipes might have a legal responsibility for flaws in the construction giving rise to the leaks, but the disclosure would not be solely or mainly about a matter for which the construction company had legal responsibility. It would not be a disclosure solely or mainly about defective pipes, but about the employer's conduct in causing the pollution.

A person other than his employer

The phrase 'other than his employer' may be thought to contain an ambiguity. **5.09** Does it mean simply that the recipient of the disclosure is not the employer, or does it connote that the employer does not have a legal responsibility for the matter? It might be argued that the policy of the legislation indicates that it only applies where the employer has no legal responsibility, so that where the employer does have legal responsibility the employee is encouraged to raise the matter internally with the employer. We suggest however that the better view is that the phrase 'other than his employer' simply means that the recipient of the disclosure is not the employer—and does not preclude the employer also having a legal responsibility for the matter. As to this:

(a) the phrase 'other than his employer' appears in both limbs of s43C(1)(b). In the first limb, s43C(1)(b)(i), it plainly does not connote that the employer has no involvement in the relevant failure. The employer may have some involvement provided the failure does not relate mainly to the employer's conduct rather than that of the person to whom the disclosure is made. The same phrase in s43C(1)(b)(ii) does not, we suggest, have a wholly different connotation as requiring that the employer have no legal responsibility.

(b) if the intention was that the disclosure could only be made to a third party where the employer did not have a legal responsibility, clear language could have been used to indicate this. It could readily have been stipulated as a requirement that the employer have no legal responsibility for the relevant failure.

(c) those with a legal responsibility for a relevant failure have a proper and compelling interest in receiving a disclosure in relation to it, and this is recognized in the scheme of the legislation.

Reasonable belief

5.10   In relation to both limbs of s43C(1)(b), the requirements that the failure relate
solely or mainly to the conduct of another person, or another matter for which
another person has legal responsibility, are qualified by the 'reasonable belief' test.
The guidance in *Darnton v University of Surrey* [2003] IRLR 133 as to the meaning
of 'reasonable belief' in relation to a qualifying disclosure (discussed in Chapter 3),
is likely also to be material here. The worker must not only have a genuine belief but
also, objectively, there must be some reasonable basis for holding that belief.
However, as emphasized in *Darnton*, the standard of reasonableness will depend very
much on the circumstances, such as whether the worker reports matters which he
claims are within his own knowledge, or have been seen or heard by him, or merely
raises matters which have been reported to him by others (*Darnton* at para 28).

(4) Disclosures to employer and disclosure under s43C(1)(b) compared

5.11   Whilst s43C ERA encompasses disclosures to someone other than the employer,
this does not have all the same consequences as a disclosure to the employer. The
following special aspects about disclosure under s43C(1)(b) should be noted:

(a) Subject to s43C(2) (see below) this does not amount to raising the matter
with the employer for the purposes of a subsequent wider disclosure (under
s43G), when it is in some cases possible to build on the failure to act on one
disclosure to make another.

(b) The Act does not place any obligation on the person responsible to respond
to the concern or to investigate it in any way.

(c) If the worker is victimized for making a disclosure under this subsection, any
claim which he may have is only to be made against his employer, and not
against the person to whom he made this disclosure.

(5) Section 43C(2): Whistleblowing and other authorized procedures

5.12   Section 43C(2) ERA expressly provides that where the organization has a whistleblowing procedure which involves raising the concern with someone other than
the employer, a disclosure to that person will be treated as if it were a disclosure to
the employer. Typically this would apply to a procedure authorizing a disclosure
to a health and safety representative, a union official, its parent company, a retired
non-executive director, its lawyers or external auditors, or to a commercial reporting
hotline.

However s43C(2) is not limited to a procedure which is specifically designated as
a whistleblowing procedure. It applies wherever the employer has authorized

a procedure for raising matters other than with the employer and the disclosure is made in accordance with that procedure. In *The Brothers of Charity Services Merseyside v Eleady-Cole* (EAT/0661/00, 24 January 2002), the claimant was employed by a charity in a hostel run by his employer. The respondent employer engaged another company (PPC) to run a confidential telephone report service by which employees could raise and discuss concerns. PPC would then report on concerns to the employer where the circumstances so required. The claimant reported his concerns to this telephone service, and the EAT held that this fell within s43C(2). The EAT specifically rejected a submission that s43C(2) applied only to a situation where an employer set up a specific procedure for employees to make qualifying disclosures, or where the employer sets up another person or body with some authority to take specific action in consequence of whatever a worker discloses to him or it. The EAT declined to provide an exhaustive definition of the kind of procedures to which s43C(2) would apply. However it emphasized that in the reporting procedure in that case, all employees had access to the service and that in the event of a disclosure of criminal activities within the employers' homes or organization, a disclosure of that fact would in turn be made by PPC to the employer, albeit preserving the anonymity and confidentiality of the informant.[6]

It is not however a prerequisite of s43C(2) for the procedure to provide for the report ultimately to be passed on to the employer. It might also apply for example where, under a procedure authorized by the employer, a complaint is made about the employer to a third party with a view to that party investigating the employer. Thus in *Chubb and others v Care First Partnership Limited* (ET, Case No. 1101438/99, 13 June 2001) it was conceded that s43C(2) applied to a complaint made to a local authority about alleged mistreatment of residents at the respondent care home. The disclosures were made in accordance with the employer's complaints procedure.

Further there is no requirement for a standing procedure, or one of general application, for reporting concerns. It is sufficient if there is an ad hoc procedure which may be set out for a particular occasion or disclosure. This was the case in *Speyer v Thorn Security Group Limited and others* (ET, Case No. 2302898/03, 20 August 2004).[7] Here an employee was specifically requested to assist in an investigation by the Manhattan District Attorney. As such disclosures made in a specific meeting with the District Attorney fell within s43C(2).

The Act does not require employers to set up whistleblowing procedures. However, a worker who makes a wide, public disclosure is more likely to be

---

[6] EAT decision paras 19–21.
[7] See Chapter 4 at 4.06.

protected if there was no such procedure or it was not reasonable to expect him to use it (s43G(3)(f)).

C. First tier disclosures: Section 43D

(1) Overview

5.13 Section 43D ERA as inserted by PIDA is a short section which covers a disclosure made in the course of seeking legal advice about a concern. It provides that:

> a qualifying disclosure is made in accordance with this section if it is made in the course of obtaining legal advice.

This is the only sort of disclosure within the Act which does not have to be made in good faith in order to be protected. The legal advisers, in turn, cannot of their own volition make a protected disclosure of the information if it would be covered by legal professional privilege (s43B(4)). They can make only such disclosure as the client instructs them to make on the client's behalf. If the legal advisers disclose the privileged information without authority, they will be unable to assert that they made a qualifying disclosure. If the disclosure is authorized by the client, this will be judged as having been a disclosure made by the client, and it will only be protected if it is made in accordance with the other provisions of the Act.

(2) From whom can the legal advice be sought?

5.14 Section 43D is headed 'disclosure to legal adviser'. However the section itself does not refer to a 'legal adviser'. It merely requires that the disclosure is made in the course of obtaining 'legal advice'. As such there is no express limit on the categories of people from whom that advice might be sought. Thus on its face it would apply to obtaining legal advice not only from a lawyer, but also a union representative, the CAB or a lay adviser. It would also apply if advice is obtained from PCaW. Further, it would apply where legal advice is being obtained from other professionals who are not lawyers, such as if an accountant advises on tax law or an auditor advises in relation to whether accounts are compliant with company law obligations.

The issue therefore arises as to whether this apparently wide scope of s43D is, as a matter of construction, properly to be cut down by virtue of either to the reference to 'legal adviser' in the heading, or to the context or purpose of the legislation or by reference to *Hansard*. In principle, the heading of s43D is properly to be taken into account in construing the section. The applicable principle is summarized in Bennion, *Statutory Interpretation* (4th ed, London: Butterworths, 2002) at p 635 as follows:

> A heading within an Act, whether contained in the body of the Act or a Schedule, is part of the Act. It may be considered in construing any provision of the Act, provided

due account is taken of the fact that its function is merely to serve as a brief, and therefore necessarily inaccurate, guide to the material to which it is attached.[8]

The heading can therefore be taken into account as an indication that s43D cannot have such a wide scope as to encompass, for example, obtaining legal advice from an accountant. However, especially as the heading is a 'necessarily inaccurate' guide to the meaning, we suggest that this is an insufficient basis to override the plain wording of s43D. As a short and inaccurate guide to the content of s43D, the heading is capable of being reconciled with the wording of the section on the basis that someone who provides advice, irrespective of whether they are a lawyer, is in that specific respect regarded as a 'legal adviser'.

An argument might be constructed to cut down the scope of s43D by reference to the purpose of the legislation. If the scope of s43D was too wide, it might undermine the structure of encouraging internal disclosures. Further, the fact that a disclosure may be made under s43D without any need to comply with the good faith requirement is strongly indicative that the section is intended to be of limited ambit. This is particularly so in the light of the emphasis in *Street*[9] on the central role of the good faith requirement in limiting protection to disclosures made in the public interest. As against this, however, irrespective of who is a legal adviser, the scope of s43D is limited by the fact that it only applies to a disclosure in the course of obtaining legal advice.

A further argument for limiting the scope of s43D to legal advice from a lawyer may be founded on the inter-relation with s43B(4), which makes specific provision for the situation where there is a disclosure in breach of legal professional privilege of information obtained in the course of legal advice. This was emphasized during the progress of the Public Interest Disclosure Bill through Parliament. The issue arose in the context of proposed amendments, at the Lords Committee stage (on 5 June 1998) and again at the Lords Report stage (on 19 June 1998), to provide for disclosures to trade union officials. In opposing the proposed amendments both Lord Haskell (for the Government) and Lord Borrie (a proposer of the Bill) emphasized the distinction between lawyers and union officials in relation to legal professional privilege and, specifically, the obligation under s43B(4) restricting unauthorized disclosure by the lawyer. It was canvassed that one possibility would be to make similar provision in relation to disclosures to union officials, but it was noted that this was problematic because the information might be required for the officials' collective role. Thus Lord Borrie commented:[10]

> Where a member makes a disclosure to his union in the course of obtaining legal advice—and here, if you like, I am talking about the union solicitor—then, irrespective

---

[8] This passage was applied by Henry LJ in *Oyston v Blaker* [1996] 2 All ER 106 (CA) at 104.

[9] See above, para 5.01.

[10] *Hansard* HL, 5 June 1998, cols. 624–626.

of whether the union is recognised at the workplace, if there is such a disclosure and a seeking of legal advice on how to raise the matter, that disclosure to the union solicitor will be protected under Section 43D.

. . .

Where a person is approached for confidential legal advice, protection under Section 43D will apply. As with all disclosures for legal advice, Section 43B(4) ensures that the lawyer cannot do as he pleases with the information. That is a most important point. As it stands, the amendment would not impose on advice agencies and unions the linked obligation under Section 43B(4). Unless the advice agency or union accepts that the information is subject to clear obligations of confidence, it will be free to do as it pleases with the information.

It is possible that certain advice agencies—or, indeed, unions—will accept as a matter of practice strict obligations of confidence. However, the amendment does not deal with that aspect of the matter. . . . One solution would be to say that the disclosures to unions under the provision should be subject to obligations of confidence. Therefore, that would make it the same as disclosures to lawyers. But to do so would have a significant effect on the role of unions in labour relations. It would mean that the information could be used for no other purpose than the one to which the client had agreed. It could not be used in the course of general negotiations with the employer. More significantly, if the information related to some safety risk, but the whistle blower decided that he did not want to raise it or pursue it, it would not be open to the union to take up the matter itself even though the well-being of some of its members might well be affected.

Without such an obligation of confidence as a *quid pro quo* to trade union officials being equated with lawyers, one possible effect of the amendment would be to give irresponsible whistle blowers a potential passport to media and more public disclosures if they were to find an individual union member or officer who would brief the media. The publication would be effected by that person on his own behalf. The employer would have no recourse against the employee whose disclosure would be protected.

The scope of s43D was therefore expressly linked to that of s43B(4) ERA. But s43B(4) relates specifically to restriction of information which could be subject to a claim of legal professional privilege. This would include only a subset of the communications which, as indicated above, might be covered by the phrase 'made in the course of obtaining legal advice'. It covers members of the legal profession when exercising professional skill as a lawyer in a relationship of lawyer and client, including foreign lawyers,[11] and in-house lawyers.[12] But privilege does not apply where someone who does not have formal legal professional qualifications performs the functions of a legal adviser, such as a personnel consultant in an industrial dispute.[13] Nor does it apply where legal advice is given by other non-lawyer professionals such as accountants.[14]

---

[11] *Great Atlantic Insurance v Home Insurance* [1981] 1 WLR 529 (CA) at 536A.
[12] *Alfred Compton Amusement Machines v Customs & Excise Commissioners (No.2)* [1972] 2 QB 102 (CA) at 129.
[13] *New Victoria Hospital v Ryan* [1993] ICR 201 (EAT).
[14] *Chantrey Martin v Martin* [1953] 2 QB 286 (CA) at 293–294.

Whilst s43B(4) ERA provides a further indication that s43D is more limited in scope than its literal wording suggests, it can be said that there is no necessity for s43B(4) and s43D to be similar in scope. If s43D was not limited in scope to legal professional advisers, it would still have been appropriate to provide that a disclosure in breach of legal privilege information would not be a qualifying disclosure. Further, if s43D was intended to apply only in circumstances giving rise to legal professional privilege, this could readily have been stated in the section. It would not only serve to exclude other professionals (eg accountants) from giving legal advice but also others such as a personal consultant who performs the function of a legal adviser. This would therefore go further even than is suggested by reference to the heading to s43D.

An attempt might also be made to rely directly on the comments made during the passage of the Bill through Parliament, and specifically the above comments by Lord Borrie, as showing that s43D has a more limited ambit and applies only in circumstances giving rise to legal professional privilege. However there are significant obstacles to reliance on *Hansard* for this purpose. Reference may only be made to *Hansard* as an aid to construction in rare cases[15] and if three conditions are satisfied. These are '(a) legislation is ambiguous, obscure or leads to an absurdity; (b) the material relied upon consists of one or more statements by a minister or other promoter of the Bill together if necessary with such other Parliamentary material as is necessary to understand such statements and their effect; (c) the statements relied upon are clear.': *Pepper v Hart* [1993] AC 593 *per* Lord Browne-Wilkinson at 640B–C; *R v Secretary of State for the Environment, Transport and the Regions, ex p Spath Holme* [2001] 2 AC 349 at 391E, 392D–E. Further, the statement must be directed to the very issue which is in question in the litigation: *Pepper v Hart per* Lord Bridge at 617A–B; *Melluish (Inspector of Taxes) v BMI (No.3) Limited* [1996] 1 AC 454 *per* Lord Browne-Wilkinson at 481F–482A.

Whilst the above statement by Lord Borrie was by a promoter of the Bill, we suggest that the other conditions for reliance on the statement are not satisfied. Even if it could be said, despite the apparently plain wording of s43D, that it was ambiguous (by reference to the considerations outlined above), Lord Borrie was not directly addressing the issue as to the breadth of s43D and in what circumstances legal advice would be covered. Instead he was opposing an amendment directed at providing specific reference to unions.

Taking the above arguments together there is a possibility that the courts will determine that s43D is to be construed as containing an implicit limit as to the categories of persons from whom legal advice must be sought, and that it applies only to a legal adviser in circumstances where the advice would give rise to legal professional privilege. Certainly the safer course is to seek legal advice from a lawyer.

---

15 *Pepper v Hart* [1993] AC 593 *per* Lord Bridge at 617A–B.

However we suggest that the better view of the construction of s43D is that it is not appropriate to cut down the plain meaning of the words 'made in the course of obtaining legal advice'. Where the disclosure is to someone who does not ordinarily provide legal advice, there will be a question of fact in each case for a tribunal where the issue is raised as to whether the advice being obtained is legal advice. Thus if a worker approaches a trade union official who is not legally qualified and seeks guidance as to what to do in relation to concerns as to a relevant failure, the natural interpretation might be that the worker is not specifically obtaining legal advice but guidance generally as to what to do in relation to the concerns. However the worker may have asked the official for advice as to his/her legal rights or obligations in the event that she makes a wider disclosure. The union official might then be expected to make appropriate enquiries within the union organization so as to be able to provide appropriate legal advice. We suggest that s43D is of ample scope to cover such a disclosure, and it is not appropriate to construe the section purposively so as to deny protection under it to a worker in such circumstances. The position might be otherwise if the worker makes a request for legal advice from someone who cannot reasonably be expected to provide, and does not provide, any legal advice. In such a situation we suggest that it could not be said that this was in the course of obtaining (rather than merely requesting) legal advice.

(3) Capacity in which the legal advice is sought

5.15 Further, s43D does not expressly state in what capacity the advice must be sought. It is therefore not (at least expressly) limited to the situation where a worker seeks advice on his own behalf from his own lawyer. It would on its face cover a situation where a worker seeks advice, at the employer's expense, on behalf of the employing company from the employer's lawyers. It may however be doubted whether the provision would be construed in this way. The underlying rationale of s43D, and for not having threshold requirements over and above those for establishing a qualifying disclosure, might be seen to be undermined if it extended to obtaining legal advice from the employer's lawyers. Where workers seek legal advice from their own lawyer it would plainly be an unacceptable infringement of client–lawyer confidentiality for such communications to be subjected to scrutiny to identify whether they are made in good faith. It may also be seen as appropriate that if an employee does have in mind to make a disclosure for ulterior motives, (s)he should be able to obtain advice as to this, and to ascertain that it would not be covered, without losing protection. But these considerations do not necessarily apply with the same force where the worker seeks legal advice from the employer's lawyers rather than taking his own advice. It may be questioned why there should be a lower threshold for protection in such circumstances than for a disclosure to the employer—where there would be a requirement of good faith.

We suggest, however, that the better view is that s43D may still apply notwithstanding that the disclosure is to the employer's rather than the employee's own, legal adviser. There may be circumstances where, notwithstanding the absence of a good faith requirement, the presence of an ulterior motive might indicate that the disclosure to the employer's lawyers was not in fact in the course of obtaining legal advice. But there will also be circumstances where the worker turns to the employer's lawyers as the most immediate, and in some cases appropriate, source of advice in relation to concerns encountered in the course of employment. If a disclosure with a view to obtaining advice in such circumstances was to be excluded from the ambit of s43D, much clearer words of exclusion would be required.

D. First tier disclosures: Section 43E: Ministers of the Crown and government-appointed bodies

Section 43E ERA provides that workers are protected if, in good faith, they disclose **5.16** their concerns to a Minister of the Crown provided that their employer is:

(i) an individual appointed under any enactment by a Minister of the Crown, or
(ii) a body any of whose members are so appointed.

This therefore applies to government employees. It would also apply to, amongst others, employees of utility regulators such as OFWAT, OFTEL and OFGAS and to NHS Trusts, tribunals and all kinds of non-departmental public bodies whose members are appointed by a Minister of the Crown. The section refers to disclosure to a Minister as, legally, this is taken to be the effect of a disclosure to a Department.

This provision is based on the recommendations that the Committee on Standards in Public Life made in its First[16] and Second Reports.[17] We include relevant extracts in Appendix 4. An employee may be more comfortable making the disclosure to the Department since it is at one remove from the work relationship, and thus disclosure may not be seen so directly as diminishing trust and confidence in the relationship with the employer. The Department may also have far greater ability to put matters right in response to the concerns expressed.

The following matters should be noted about this subsection:

(a) As under s43C(1)(b), a disclosure under this section is not treated as one to the employer for the purposes of any subsequent, wider disclosure (s43G).

---

[16] May 1995, Cm 2850–I pp 60 and 91–92.
[17] May 1996, Cm 3270–1 p 22.

(b) If the worker is victimized for making a disclosure under this subsection, any claim he may have is made against his employer and not against the Minister to whom he made this disclosure.

(c) Subs 1(b) requires the worker to act in 'good faith'.

E. Regulatory disclosures: Section 43F

(1) Overview

5.17 The second tier of disclosure identified by Auld LJ in *Street* was disclosure to a prescribed person under s43F. Section 43F(1) ERA provides:

> (1) A qualifying disclosure is made in accordance with this section if the worker—
>> (a) makes the disclosure in good faith to a person prescribed by an order made by the Secretary of State for the purposes of this section, and
>> (b) reasonably believes—
>>> (i) that the relevant failure falls within any description of matters in respect of which that person is so prescribed, and
>>> (ii) that the information disclosed, and any allegation contained in it, are substantially true.

In addition to the good faith requirement, therefore, the worker must reasonably believe that the malpractice falls within the matters prescribed for that regulator and reasonably believe 'that the information disclosed, and any allegation in it, are substantially true' (s43F(1)(b)). Thus, although the worker must meet a higher evidential burden than in s43C relating to first tier whistleblowing, where a regulator has been prescribed, there is no requirement:

(a) that the particular disclosure was reasonable (although it must be made in good faith);

(b) that the malpractice was serious; nor

(c) that the worker should have first raised the matter internally.

The favoured position of the whistleblower who makes disclosure to a regulator is explicable on the basis that:

(a) the regulators will have a statutory duty to investigate such matters and they can only perform their role if members of the public are prepared to come to them with information. Employees will only do so if there is no danger of retaliation in the workplace for disloyalty;

(b) the regulator can usually be relied upon to maintain confidentiality of the material once it is in his domain, whether the allegation is right or wrong;

(c) the motivation of anyone revealing material to a regulator is likely to be one of concerned public interest because the regulator will not pay money for the material (although someone who makes such a disclosure may qualify for a Community Action Trust award).

These considerations have also been persuasive in forging a preferential position under the common law of confidence for disclosures made to prescribed regulators over other external disclosures. In *In re A Company* [1989] 1 Ch 477, where an employee reported an internal matter to FIMBRA which was then the relevant regulator under the Financial Services Act 1986 (and whose functions are now performed by the Financial Services Authority), Scott J said:

> it may be the case that the information proposed to be given, the allegations to be made by the defendant to FIMBRA and for that matter by the defendant to the Inland Revenue, are allegations made out of malice and based upon fiction or invention. But if that is so, then I ask myself what harm will be done. FIMBRA may decide that the allegations are not worth investigating. In that case no harm will have been done. Or FIMBRA may decide that an investigation is necessary. In that case, if the allegations turn out to be baseless, nothing will follow from the investigation. And if harm is caused by the investigation itself, it is harm implicit in the regulatory role of FIMBRA.

Notwithstanding these considerations, even where the disclosure is made to a prescribed regulator it may be important to consider whether it can also be characterized as a first tier disclosure. Where there is a prescribed regulator, it is often the case that the employing organization will provide, whether in a whistleblowing policy or otherwise, that disclosure to the prescribed regulator is permitted. The effect is that where the disclosure is made in accordance with a procedure deployed by the prescribed regulator, it can be said that s43C(2) applies, which entails a lower threshold for protection than under s43F.

(2) Prescribed persons

5.18 The Public Interest Disclosure (Prescribed Persons) Order (SI 1999 No. 1549)[18] sets out a list of the persons who are prescribed for the purposes of this section (see Appendix 2). In each case there is a corresponding description of the matters in respect of which the person is prescribed. In addition to listing over 50 prescribed bodies, there is also a general provision so as to encompass successor bodies of any of the specifically prescribed bodies.

An amendment was made to the Bill in Committee[19] for the purposes of enabling classes of person to be prescribed so as to ensure that health and safety representatives

---

[18] As amended, principally by the Public Interest Disclosure (Prescribed Persons) (Amendment) Orders 2003 (SI 2003/1993), 2004 (SI 2004/3265) and 2005 (SI 2005/2464).

[19] Parliamentary Debates HC, Standing Committee D, 11 March 1998.

might be prescribed, should it transpire that employers were not including them within internal reporting procedures. In the event, however, health and safety representatives were not included in the list of prescribed persons.

(3) Reasonable belief that relevant failure falls within a relevant description

5.19 The worker must make the disclosure in good faith to a prescribed person and reasonably believe that the relevant failure falls within any description of matters in respect of which that person is prescribed. It is to be noted that the reasonable belief test does not apply to whether a person or body is prescribed. If, for example, a disclosure is made to the police, not being a prescribed body, there is no scope to argue that there was a reasonable but mistaken belief that the police were prescribed.

Nor does the reasonable belief test apply to what matters are prescribed in relation to a particular body or person. Thus suppose a worker has a reasonable and genuine but mistaken belief that the relevant failure amounts to fraud by a company. If the worker made a disclosure to the Secretary of State for Trade and Industry he could then be said to hold a reasonable belief that the relevant failure falls within the description of 'Fraud, and other misconduct, in relation to companies . . . ' which applies to that prescribed person. However if the worker was mistaken as to the description of matters for which the Secretary of State for Trade and Industry was prescribed, and made a disclosure in relation to a matter for which the Secretary of State was not prescribed, that would not fall within s43F. As such, it would be good practice, if there is any uncertainty as to whether the matter is appropriately raised with a prescribed person, for the worker or his adviser first to contact the particular regulator informally to discuss the nature of the concern in order to establish whether it is within the regulator's remit and to explore what action the regulator considers appropriate.

This may be particularly important in cases where more than one body is identified in the Public Interest Disclosure (Prescribed Persons) Order as being responsible for the same matter. This arose in *Dudin v Salisbury District Council* (ET, Case No. 3102263/03, 20 February 2004). Mrs Dudin was employed as a Tenant Participation Officer by a district council. She became convinced that bullying was endemic in the council. She raised concerns and allegations about this with the council's Scrutiny Committee, which was a committee charged with reviewing and scrutinizing decisions made and actions taken in connection with discharge of council functions. She argued that this was a disclosure within s43F ERA. The Health and Safety Executive, and also local authorities with responsibility for enforcement of health and safety legislation, are both prescribed in the Public

Interest Disclosure (Prescribed Persons) Order in relation to matters which may affect the health or safety of any individual at work and matters which may affect the health and safety of any member of the public, arising out of or in connection with the activities of persons at work. On its face, therefore, the disclosure to the council fell within the description of prescribed matters in the Order. However, although not specified in the Public Interest Disclosure (Prescribed Persons) Order, the relevant enforcing authority for employees of the local authority was the HSE rather than the local authority.[20] On this basis the tribunal held that s43F did not apply. The decision may be doubted on the basis that it added a gloss to s43F(1)(a). On the face of that provision it should have sufficed to have a reasonable belief that the concerns related to health and safety at work, and so fell within the description of matters in respect of which the council was prescribed. As against this, the decision may be explained as being consistent with the underlying rationale that s43F is concerned with disclosure to an appropriate body.

(4) Time at which the recipient must be prescribed

In *Miklaszewicz v Stolt Offshore Limited* [2002] IRLR 344 (Court of Session) the **5.20** issue arose as to whether, for the purposes of s43F, it was necessary that the recipient of the disclosure had to be prescribed at the time of the disclosure or at the time of the detriment. In 1993, six years before the Public Interest Disclosure Act came into force, Mr Miklaszewicz reported to the Inland Revenue that his employer had engaged in unlawful tax evasion in changing his employment status to self-employed when that was a false description of his status. As a result he was dismissed later that year. However he continued to work in the same industry and, by virtue of transfers of undertakings, in December 1999 he came to be employed again by the same employer. He was dismissed purportedly on grounds of redundancy but claimed that the real reason was his disclosures in 1993. The employment tribunal decided that it did not have jurisdiction because the protected disclosures were made before PIDA came into force, but the EAT and Scottish Court of Session disagreed. As the EAT had decided in *Meteorological Office v Edgar* [2002] ICR 149, the court held that there could be a claim if the detriment or dismissal was after PIDA came into force. However the more difficult issue related to s43F. It was argued that its plain wording made clear that there could not have been a protected disclosure under s43F in 1993 since the Inland Revenue was not at that stage a prescribed body, there being no prescription order until 1993. The Court of Session held that since the claim under the legislation is triggered by the dismissal (or other detriment), 'the making of the disclosure requires

---

[20] Pursuant to reg 4 of the Health and Safety (Enforcing Authority) Regulations 1998 SI 1998/494.

to be considered at the point in time; and it is then that the criteria for treating it as a protected disclosure are applicable, on a proper construction of the relevant statutory provisions.' On that basis, since by the time of dismissal the Inland Revenue was a prescribed person, and the disclosure was in relation to matters for which it was prescribed, that was sufficient.

In adopting this approach, the Court of Session followed a purposive construction of the legislation. At the heart of s43F is the principle that a lower threshold for protection should apply where there is a disclosure to an appropriate prescribed body, as identified in the relevant Order. On the facts in *Miklaszewicz* the result was consistent with this in that the Inland Revenue was plainly the appropriate body with which to raise concerns about tax evasion. The emphasis on assessing whether there is a protected disclosure by reference to the position at the date of dismissal might however be regarded as problematic. It is not generally the case that the criteria for a protected disclosure are assessed at the time of the detriment. Thus in relation to whether there is the requisite reasonable belief for the purposes of a qualifying disclosure, the position must be assessed on the basis of the circumstances of the worker, and what he knew, at the time of making the disclosure, rather than the worker's knowledge by the time of being subjected to a detriment.[21] The decision in *Miklaszewicz* might be reconciled with this on the basis that the worker must still have had a reasonable belief, at the time of making the disclosure that it involved a relevant failure within the description of matters which were subsequently prescribed for the Inland Revenue. Thus it was sufficient that, at the time of the disclosure, he had a reasonable belief that the disclosure related to a relevant failure in relation to National Insurance and income tax, being matters in relation to which the Inland Revenue was subsequently prescribed. The decision did not necessitate assessing what he reasonably believed at the time of dismissal. It is not to be regarded as supporting any wider principle that a worker's state of mind or belief is to be assessed at a time subsequent to the making of the protected disclosure.

(5) Reasonable belief that the information disclosed and any allegation contained in it are substantially true

5.21   In each of ss43F, 43G and 43H ERA, the worker must reasonably believe that (a) the information disclosed and (b) any allegation contained in it, are substantially true. In Chapter 3 we discuss how the reasonable belief test for a qualifying disclosure has been construed against the context that it must differ from the reasonable belief test in s43F(1)(b)(ii). Equally the comparison with the reasonable

---

[21] *Darnton,* above para 5.10.

belief test for a qualifying disclosure casts light on the construction of the test in s43F. We suggest that the following considerations are relevant.

(a) As in the case of the reasonable belief test for a qualifying disclosure, the worker's belief must be tested by reference to the circumstances as they were understood, or ought to have been understood, by the worker, rather than simply by the facts as ultimately found to have existed by the tribunal.

(b) The worker will not lose protection if his belief was mistaken, provided it was reasonable for him to hold it. But as with the test for reasonable belief in s43B, whether the allegation was in fact true is likely to be relevant in ascertaining the reasonableness of the belief.

(c) Again, as in the reasonable belief test for a qualifying disclosure, all the circumstances must be considered in order to ascertain whether the belief was reasonable. However the standard to be applied in relation to whether it was reasonable to hold the belief is likely to be higher than that for a qualifying disclosure. In particular the worker may be required to have done more to look into the matter, or have had it looked into at the first tier of disclosure. Thus in relation to a disclosure to the employer (or other first tier disclosure) there may be a reasonable belief even though the worker has done little to investigate the matter, because the policy of the legislation is to encourage workers to raise their concerns with the employer who may be best placed to investigate. Under section s43F, there is no obligation first to raise the matter with the employer. However, if it was raised with the employer it will be relevant to take into account any response by the employer, or any failure to respond or inadequacies in the response, in relation to how this affects the reasonableness of the belief.

The decision of the employment tribunal in *Holden v Connex South Eastern Limited* (ET, Case No. 2301550/00, 15 April 2002), illustrates the potential inter-relation between internal disclosures and regulatory disclosures when it comes to assessment of the worker's reasonable belief. Mr Holden was a train driver employed by Connex and was appointed as a health and safety representative. He had a track record of raising a number of genuine and legitimate concerns. Mr Holden became concerned about measures to be introduced by his employers which he believed would be in breach of regulations prohibiting train operators from undertaking safety-critical work for such long hours as to cause them fatigue. By a code of practice his employers were required to carry out suitable and sufficient assessment before introducing the changes. Mr Holden raised his concerns with the Managing Director of Connex as to a breach of the regulations and requested a copy of the risk assessment. He was refused a copy and, after the restructure was implemented, his concerns were reinforced when he received a number of complaints from other drivers who felt increasingly tired. He carried out his own investigations which led him to believe that many of the incidences where a signal had been passed at danger could be attributed to tiredness or fatigue. He then reported his finding to HM Railway Inspectorate. He later also sent a second report to the Inspectorate and provided copies to his members. The tribunal decided that the two reports constituted protected disclosures under s43F. It concluded that even if it had not been established that all the allegations made were true, he held a reasonable belief that they were true. In so concluding the tribunal emphasized that it was the employers who held all the detailed information, and it was as a result of their failure to provide Mr Holden with the necessary health and safety information which he sought that he had needed to investigate the matter himself. Thus the fact that he had raised concerns with his employer (albeit not the specific findings which he then reported to the Inspectorate in his first report), and had requested and been denied information and documentation which the employer possessed, and by reference to which the concerns could have been verified, played an important part in demonstrating that his belief was reasonably held.

(d) The differing considerations which are likely to apply to a disclosure under s43F are indicated by the fact that the phrase 'tends to show', which appears in s43B, does not appear in ss43F (or 43G or 43H ERA). As discussed in Chapter 3, the phrase is important in the context of s43B. It accommodates the possibility that the worker may only have access to part of the evidential picture. As such it might be premature to require, prior to making a disclosure to the employer (or other first tier disclosure), that the worker hold a reasonable belief that the allegation is substantially true. It might be sufficient that the worker has come across information which tends to show a relevant failure, even though it is possible that on further investigation the full evidential picture may show this not to be the case. By contrast, for the purposes of ss43F (and 43G and 43H), the worker cannot merely say that the information disclosed tends to point in the direction of a relevant failure, and needs further investigation. The worker must reasonably believe that the allegations are substantially true.

(e) The worker making the disclosure has a degree of leeway because the requirement to believe in the truth of the allegations is qualified on the basis that it is sufficient to have a reasonable belief that the information and allegations are 'substantially' true. There is an ambiguity in this phrase:
   (i) used in a quantitative sense, it might mean a belief that most of the information or the allegations are true,[22] but
   (ii) used in a qualitative sense, it refers to a belief that the substance, in the sense of the gist, of what is disclosed is true.

---

[22] In the Australian authority, *Tillmanns Butcheries Pty Ltd v Australasian Meat Industry Employees Union* (1979) 42 FLR 331 at 348, the court declared that when used in a quantitative sense it does not necessarily mean 'most' but may mean only 'much' or 'some'. But in the context of ss43F, 43G and 43H it plainly means more than merely some of the information/allegations.

We suggest that a tribunal is likely to have regard to both the quantitative and qualitative sense, in order to form an overall view as to whether there was the requisite reasonable belief. There must be a reasonable belief that the gist or core of what has been disclosed is true. Further, if there is a core truth in the allegations but they are embroidered with a series of false and wild allegations which the worker could not reasonably believe to be true, a tribunal might conclude that there was not the requisite reasonable belief in substantial truth. It might therefore be important that the worker does not exaggerate the allegations. We suggest however that tribunals need to exercise care not to overlook the degree of leeway afforded by the term 'substantially'. There is a public interest in concerns as to relevant failures being raised with the appropriate prescribed body. It would be unfortunate if those with the courage to come forward and raise such concerns were to lose protection because of a degree of lack of circumspection in the terms in which the concerns are raised.

(6) Evidential issues

Where the disclosure is made to a prescribed body, it will be important to give **5.22** careful consideration to the evidence which may be relevant arising from this, including identifying issues in relation to disclosure of documents. There might be an issue as to whether the employer was aware of the disclosure to the prescribed body prior to the alleged detriment or dismissal. The approach taken by the prescribed body might also be material to the issue of whether the worker had the requisite reasonable belief that the information and the allegations were substantially true. Just as the truth of the allegations was recognized in *Darnton* as being a material consideration, so if the prescribed body has treated the allegations as raising sufficient concerns to merit serious investigation, a tribunal may regard this as persuasive on the issue of the reasonableness of the belief. If the prescribed body has not pursued the concerns, or has rejected them, the respondent employer may seek to place reliance on this in challenging the reasonableness of the belief. Thus if the employer has had no or minimal contact from the prescribed body, the employer might point to this as indicating a lack of substance in the allegations made. Conversely it may be important for the worker to ascertain in such circumstances why an investigation has not been progressed. In some cases it may be, for example, that the prescribed body is awaiting the outcome of the employment tribunal proceedings.

It will therefore be important to consider not only any disclosure from the employer in relation to its dealings with the prescribed body, but also what evidence might be gathered from the prescribed body itself. This may include consideration of whether relevant documentation or information in relation to communications with the employer can be obtained from the prescribed body. The employment tribunal has power to order the provision of information and documentation from a third party: see Employment Tribunals (Constitution and Rules of Procedure) Regulations 2004 Sch 1 para 10(2)(d).

F. Wider disclosures under section 43G

(1) Overview

5.23 Sections 43G and 43H set out the circumstances in which other disclosures, including those to the media, may be protected. These provisions give the tribunal much more scope for determining the reasonableness of aspects of the employee's behaviour than the earlier provisions. Section 43G provides:

Disclosure in other cases

(1) A qualifying disclosure is made in accordance with this section if—
  (a) the worker makes the disclosure in good faith,
  (b) he reasonably believes that the information disclosed, and any allegation contained in it, are substantially true,
  (c) he does not make the disclosure for purposes of personal gain,
  (d) any of the conditions in subsection (2) is met, and
  (e) in all the circumstances of the case, it is reasonable for him to make the disclosure.

(2) The conditions referred to in subsection (1)(d) are—
  (a) that, at the time he makes the disclosure, the worker reasonably believes that he will be subjected to a detriment by his employer if he makes a disclosure to his employer or in accordance with section 43F,
  (b) that, in a case where no person is prescribed for the purposes of section 43F in relation to the relevant failure, the worker reasonably believes that it is likely that evidence relating to the relevant failure will be concealed or destroyed if he makes a disclosure to his employer, or
  (c) that the worker has previously made a disclosure of substantially the same information—
    (i) to his employer, or
    (ii) in accordance with section 43F.

(3) In determining for the purposes of subsection (1)(e) whether it is reasonable for the worker to make the disclosure, regard shall be had, in particular, to—
  (a) the identity of the person to whom the disclosure is made,
  (b) the seriousness of the relevant failure,
  (c) whether the relevant failure is continuing or is likely to occur in the future,
  (d) whether the disclosure is made in breach of a duty of confidentiality owed by the employer to any other person,
  (e) in a case falling within subsection (2)(c)(i) or (ii), any action which the employer or the person to whom the previous disclosure in accordance with section 43F was made has taken or might reasonably be expected to have taken as a result of the previous disclosure, and

(f) in a case falling within subsection (2)(c)(i), whether in making the disclosure to the employer the worker complied with any procedure whose use by him was authorised by the employer.

(4) For the purposes of this section a subsequent disclosure may be regarded as a disclosure of substantially the same information as that disclosed by a previous disclosure as mentioned in subsection (2)(c) even though the subsequent disclosure extends to information about action taken or not taken by any person as a result of the previous disclosure.

The approach of the legislation is therefore to build additional requirements upon those which apply for regulatory disclosures. In addition to the requirements of good faith and reasonable belief in the substantial truth of the information and allegations, there are three further requirements. The first additional requirement relates to motive; the disclosure must not be for purposes of personal gain. The second (s43G(2)) sets out three preconditions, one of which must be met if the disclosure is to be capable of protection. Finally, to be protected the disclosure must be reasonable in all the circumstances (s43G(1)(e) and (3)). If the concern has been raised internally beforehand or with a prescribed regulator, the reasonableness of the worker's belief in the substantial truth of the information disclosed will be assessed having regard to what happened in a first tier disclosure and any response which he may have received from management or the prescribed regulator to the original complaint. Thus, if the response was a stony silence or an ineffectual remedy, the employee may be justified in continuing with his campaign and taking the matter further to a wider audience.

(2) 'Personal gain'

A disclosure under s43G or s43H does not qualify for protection unless the **5.24** disclosure is not made for purposes of personal gain.[23] As to this:

(a) Although the provision is primarily aimed at the grosser excesses of 'cheque book journalism', it is not expressly limited to *financial gain*. It is capable of encompassing other forms of personal advantage. This was the view of the employment tribunal in *Kajencki v Torrington Homes* (ET, Case No. 3302912/01, 30 September 2002). Mrs Kajencki worked as manager of a residential care home. She raised concerns with the Council's Joint Inspection Unit about standards of food hygiene and staff training. The tribunal decided that the disclosure was made for the purposes of personal gain in that Mrs Kajencki had made the disclosures in order to secure effective control over running the home from her employer.

---

[23] s4G(1)(c); s43H(1)(c).

(b) We suggest that, consistently with the rationale of the exception for personal gain, the provision would also catch a situation where the benefit did not go directly to the worker but to a member of his family, provided that its purpose was personal gain. The position would, we suggest, be otherwise if the payment was to be made to charity, and as such could not be regarded as direct or indirect personal gain for the worker making the disclosure.

(c) The concept of personal gain does not, however, catch any reward payable by or under any enactment (s43L(2)), such as a payment made by Customs and Excise for information received.[24] The exception does not cover private rewards of any sort such as an award by the Community Action Trust. The effect of s43L is that where a reward is made by a regulator who is not prescribed under s43F, it is not a bar to protection. Such rewards are occasionally made by statutory agencies in return for information supplied. Banks also often provide rewards for such information.

(d) Protection is not lost merely because the worker receives a payment or otherwise benefits from the disclosure. The focus is on the *purposes* for which the disclosure was made.

(e) Section 43G(1)(c) does not specify how it applies in a case of mixed motives. As discussed in Chapter 4, it has been held that an ulterior motive may only negative good faith if it is a predominant motive. It might be argued that the same should apply in relation to personal gain, as it would be unfortunate if a worker who satisfies the other requirements of s43G, including acting reasonably, and who acts primarily in the public interest (eg to prevent a relevant failure), could be subjected to a detriment for so doing. There are also *dicta* in *Street* which support this view. Thus Auld LJ noted that 'whether the motive of personal gain was of such a nature or strength as to "make the disclosure for the purposes of personal gain"' is for the tribunal to assess.[25] As against this, the legislation does not expressly distinguish between a principal or subsidiary purpose in this context. If it was intended that protection is lost only where the predominant purpose of the loan was personal gain, this could have been readily provided for. Further the personal gain provision is plainly intended to be an additional important restriction. However it would in practice add little to the good faith requirement if it only applied, as in the good faith requirement, in the case of a predominant purpose of personal gain. We suggest therefore that there is not an exception in the case of mixed motives. There may be cases where any motivation of personal gain is *de minimis* so that it cannot be said that this was a purpose of the disclosure. But we suggest that if one of the purposes which materially influences the making of the disclosure was personal gain, protection under ss43G and 43H does not apply.

---

[24] Standing Committee D, *Hansard*, 11 March 1998.
[25] At para 53; see above, para 5.01.

(3) The s43G(2) preconditions

Even where an allegation is made in good faith, not for personal gain, and it is rea-   **5.25**
sonably believed to be substantially true, a third tier disclosure will still only qualify for protection under s43G if one or more of the three further preconditions
(sometimes referred to as gateways to protection) are met. These conditions are
that the worker reasonably believes that he *will be victimized* by the employer if he
makes the disclosure (s43G(2)(a)); that he reasonably believes that there is likely
to be a cover-up such that 'evidence relating to the relevant failure will be
concealed or destroyed if he makes a disclosure to his employer' (s43G(2)(b)); or
that the matter or substantially the same matter had previously been raised internally or with a prescribed regulator (s43G(2)(c)). It is only necessary to meet one
of these three preconditions. Albeit not raised as a specific condition, there is
clearly underlying these preconditions the presumption that, before any wider
disclosure is protected, there should ordinarily be a first tier or regulatory disclosure and that only if this has not addressed the problem should the matter be taken
outside the organization. Even if the precondition is met the tribunal must
still consider whether the worker acted *reasonably in all the circumstances of the
particular case*.

Precondition 1: reasonable belief in victimization; subs (2)(a)

The first of the alternative preconditions which may be met is that the worker rea-   **5.26**
sonably believes that he will (not may) be subjected to a detriment by his employer
were he to raise the matter internally or with a prescribed regulator. The relevant
belief must exist at the time when he makes the external disclosure and must be
objectively reasonable. As such, if the worker does not address his mind to the
question of whether to make a disclosure to the employer, neither of the first two
preconditions in s43G can be satisfied.

Relevant considerations may include:

(a) the nature of the relevant failure. Thus if disclosure involves an allegation of a
breach of a legal obligation or a criminal offence by the employer it is likely to
be easier to establish the requisite reasonable belief than if the concern is about
a risk to health and safety which the employer could remedy.
(b) the identity of the person alleged to have been responsible for the relevant
failure. Thus if there is an allegation of wrongdoing made against the most
senior levels of the employing organization, the reasonable belief might be
more readily established than if it relates to a more junior employee or relates
to an allegation against someone other than the employer.
(c) whether there is an effective whistleblowing policy which makes clear to
whom the concern should be addressed, and that workers will not be subjected to detrimental treatment for raising concerns in good faith.

(d) the employer's culture, internal policies, and track record in relation to the raising of concerns.

(e) in relation to regulatory disclosures, whether it would be necessary for the employer to be informed of the identity of the employee making the disclosure, and whether this would be apparent in any event to the employer.

In order to reduce the risk of wider disclosures, it is therefore important that there be an effective whistleblowing policy, that staff are made sufficiently aware of it, that victimization of those raising concerns in good faith is regarded as unacceptable within the employing organization and that a disclosure in good faith to a prescribed regulator is a permissible option.

Precondition 2: reasonable belief in a cover-up; subs (2)(b)

5.27   The second precondition deals with circumstances where the worker reasonably believes a cover-up of the malpractice is likely to occur if he makes the disclosure at the first tier. It can only be satisfied where there is no regulator prescribed under s43F to whom the reporting of that malpractice should be made. Accordingly where there is a prescribed regulator, the Act states that a concern about a cover-up should be raised with that regulator before any wider disclosure might be capable of protection unless the matter is exceptionally serious (s43H). However in contrast to s43G(2)(a), which requires a belief that the worker 'will' be subjected to a detriment, s43G(2)(b) requires only that concealment is likely. This therefore connotes a lesser degree of certainty. However if construed in the same way as s43B(1)(b) ERA, this would still require a belief that the concealment or destruction of evidence is more likely than not to occur: see *Kraus v Penna* [2004] IRLR 260 (EAT) (considered in Chapter 3).

Precondition 3: previous internal disclosure; subs (2)(c)

5.28   The third approach is that the wider disclosure may be protected where the matter has previously been raised internally or with a prescribed regulator. It should be noted that the disclosure at this third tier does not have to be of *exactly* the same information as was disclosed at the first, provided it is *substantially* the same. Typically the employee will build into the third tier disclosure additional information identified since the disclosure to the employer, and also specifically cover the failure of the employer to respond to the initial concerns. Indeed the brush-off or contemptuous response to the first disclosure will often light the touch-paper for more explosive and wider disclosure. Section 43G(4) specifically deems a disclosure to be 'substantially the same' where the subsequent disclosure 'extends to information about action taken or not taken by any person as a result of a previous disclosure'.

The EAT decision in *Bladon v ALM Medical Services Limited* (EAT/709/00, EAT/967/00, 19 January 2001)[26] supports a particularly broad approach to the meaning of 'substantially the same'. The decision needs to be treated with a degree of caution as it was a preliminary hearing attended only by the appellants, although the EAT did say (at para 21) that its comments might give assistance to tribunals. In relation to the phrase 'substantially the same', the EAT explained (at para 31) that:

> it would, in our judgment, be wholly inappropriate for tribunals to embark upon an exercise of nice and detailed analysis of the disclosure to the employer, compared with the disclosure to the outside body, for the purpose of deciding whether the test in section 43G(2)(c) has been made out. The correct approach, in our judgment, is for tribunals to adopt a commonsense broad approach when deciding whether or not the disclosure is 'substantially the same'.

Mr Bladon was employed in a nursing home. He raised concerns about patient welfare and care with his employer and then also with the Nursing Home Inspectorate within the local authority. Because both the concerns raised internally and with the Inspectorate related to concerns about patients being put at risk by failures of care, the EAT held that the disclosures satisfied the requirement under s43G of being 'substantially the same'. This was so irrespective of whether the examples given by Mr Bladon of lack of care were similar or the same in both cases or if additional examples were given in the disclosure to the employer or to the Inspectorate.

Where this precondition applies, it is specifically provided that, in assessing whether it was reasonable to make the disclosure, the tribunal must have particular regard to whether the worker, in raising the matter with the employer, had complied with the terms of any authorized procedure for raising such concerns. This need not be an expressly agreed procedure since the statute refers to 'any procedure whose use by [the worker] was authorized by the employer'. Thus, for example, if the whistleblowing procedure provides a right to appeal against the conclusions reached in response to the concerns, but the employee makes a third tier disclosure before exhausting the internal appeal process, this might be a factor pointing against it being reasonable to make the third tier disclosure.

(4) Reasonableness: subs (3)

5.29 The final requirement under s43G ERA is that it must be reasonable in all the circumstances of the case for the worker to have made the disclosure. Subsection (3) expounds some of the factors in determining reasonableness. The tribunal is obliged to take into account each of these factors: the identity of the recipient, the seriousness of the relevant failure and whether the relevant failure is continuing or

---

[26] The decision was overturned on appeal to the Court of Appeal ([2002] ICR 1444) but this issue as to the meaning of 'substantially the same' was not addressed.

is likely to occur in the future, any duty of confidentiality to a third party and the nature of previous disclosure(s). However s43G(3) ERA does not purport to set out a comprehensive list of all the relevant considerations. Whilst a tribunal must take into account the factors identified in s43G(3), as emphasized by Auld LJ in *Street*,[27] in accordance with s43G(1)(e) ERA the tribunal is required to take into account 'all the circumstances of the case'.

The particular considerations identified can be seen as drawing on factors that have been recognized as important in the context of the common law of confidentiality and in particular whether confidentiality has been overridden in the public interest. During the passage of the Public Interest Disclosure Bill, Richard Shepherd MP (a promoter of the Bill), referring to the relationship with the common law of confidentiality, commented[28] that:

> in consultations, the Minister and I agreed that any cross-reference to the law of confidence in the Bill was inappropriate for a number of reasons. First, we were keen to make the public interest in all disclosure of wrong-doing the pre-eminent factor. Secondly, we feared that it would not be sufficiently clear to employers and employees how this area of case law might apply if there were some umbilical link. Thirdly, we recognised that workers who reported a serious wrong-doing should not forfeit protection because it later transpired that that information was [not][29] in law confidential. When the courts have granted or refused an injunction to stop the disclosure of that same confidential information, the view of the Minister, with which I acquiesced, was that those decisions should be relevant, but not binding on the tribunal. As such, no reference was made to the law of confidence in the Bill.

The common law of confidence, and whether confidentiality has been overridden in favour of disclosure in the public interest, is therefore not determinative of how the issues arising under ss43G and 43H, and in particular the issue of reasonableness, would be resolved.[30] In some instances, however, it helps illustrate the considerations which might arise, and we make some reference below to cases drawn from the common law of confidence for that purpose. We discuss this in more detail in Chapter 11.

Identity of the person to whom the disclosure is made: subs (3)(a)

5.30 The tribunal must have regard to 'the identity of the person to whom the disclosure is made'. There is no limit on the range of people to whom such a disclosure might be made. It could include the police, a professional body, a non-prescribed regulator, a union official, an MP, the relatives of a patient at risk, a contracting party whose rights were being flouted, colleagues who cannot be regarded as the

---

[27] At 105 (para 28); see above para 5.01.

[28] *Hansard*, Standing Committee D, 11 March 1998.

[29] The word 'not' appears to have been a typographical error or to have been mis-spoken.

[30] See also *Street*, above para 5.01, where the Court of Appeal held that cases drawn from the common law of confidence were not material to the proper construction of the 'good faith' requirement in the context of protected disclosures.

employer (such as if more junior colleagues are informed of concerns so that they can assist in investigating the concerns), shareholders (who have a role as stakeholders in the business), friends and neighbours, members of voluntary groups or the media. Whilst the list of potential recipients is vast, however, in each case it will be important to show why this was an appropriate person to whom to make the disclosure and it will be relevant whether there was a more appropriate recipient of the disclosure.

In any given case it may be possible to identify a hierarchy in terms of the most appropriate recipients of a disclosure. This might for example be as follows: internal within the organization; to a regulator with power to redress the concern; to a trade union; to the responsible Minister; to a Secretary of State-appointed body; to an MP; to shareholders; to interested third parties eg to a concerned citizens group; to the local or trade media; to the national media. In each case however this will turn on all the circumstances including the other express factors identified in s43G(3) ERA.

An illustration of some of the considerations that may be material in relation to the identity of the recipient is provided by decisions in relation to the public interest defence in respect of duties of confidentiality (see Chapter 11 below). Disclosures of confidential information to the media were held to be justified in *Initial Services v Putterill* [1968] 1 QB 396, where a disclosure to the *Daily Mail* about price-fixing was held to be lawful by the Court of Appeal because the public were being misled. Lord Denning MR (at 405G to 406B) observed that ordinarily any disclosure should be to a person with a 'proper interest to receive the information' but that there might be cases 'where the misdeed is of such a character that the public interest may demand, or at least excuse, publication on a broader field, even to the press'. Similarly in *Lion Laboratories v Evans* [1985] 1 QB 526 the Court of Appeal held the press was an appropriate recipient of the information in relation to suspect roadside breathalysers as it was important that people had the information needed to challenge criminal charges and it seemed that the Home Office—which had approved the breathalyser—was an interested party. In *Cork v McVicar* [1985] The Times, 31 October 1985 the High Court allowed the *Daily Express* to publish allegations of corruption in the Metropolitan Police.

However the Court of Appeal in *Francome v Daily Mirror* [1984] 1 WLR 892, held that the *Daily Mirror* could not publish confidential information which suggested that a jockey had been engaged in misconduct as the public interest would be just as well served by a disclosure to the police or the Jockey Club. This position was explained in *A-G v Guardian Newspapers Ltd (No 2)* [1990] 1 AC 109 (HL) (*per* Lord Griffiths at p 268):

> In certain circumstances the public interest may be better served by a limited form of publication perhaps to the police or some other authority who can follow up a suspicion that wrongdoing may lurk beneath the cloak of confidence. Those authorities will be under a duty not to abuse the confidential information and to use it only for the purpose of their inquiry.

W v Edgell [1990] 1 Ch 359 (CA) provides a further illustration of a disclosure being regarded as legitimate due to the identity of the recipient, where a wider disclosure would not have been. The claimant suffered from paranoid schizophrenia and was detained in a secure hospital after killing five people. He applied to a mental health review tribunal and, to support his application, sought a report from the defendant who was an independent consultant psychiatrist. The defendant's report revealed that the claimant had a continuing interest in home-made bombs and expressed the opinion that the claimant was a continuing danger to the public. The claimant then withdrew his application and refused to consent to the defendant disclosing the report. However the defendant disclosed the report to the medical officer at the secure hospital and a copy was sent to the relevant Secretary of State. Whilst there would have been an obvious breach of confidence if the medical report had been disclosed to the public, the Court of Appeal held that there was no such breach where the report was made available to the authority concerned with deciding whether the claimant should be released from a secure hospital.

The seriousness of the failure: subs (3)(b)

5.31 A further consideration in assessing reasonableness is 'the seriousness of the relevant failure'. Thus if the matter is very serious, that may justify a wider disclosure than would otherwise be the case. A lower level of seriousness would for example be expected where a third tier disclosure of confidential information is made to the police or a non-prescribed regulator, than if the same information was disclosed to the media.

Whether the relevant failure continues: subs (3)(c)

5.32 The third matter which must be weighed in the balance of reasonableness is 'whether the relevant failure is continuing or is likely to occur in the future'. This is closely connected with the question of the seriousness of the concern. The sense of this provision is that it will be reasonable if the disclosure is about a continuing or future threat as opposed to something which has blown over, in the sense that it has already happened and it is not considered likely that it will happen again.

Conversely disclosure to the media is likely to be more difficult to justify where the concern has already been satisfactorily addressed, whether within the employment organization or otherwise, or where the person making the disclosure does so for the purposes of personal gain rather than to right a wrong. This picks up on a theme in the jurisprudence on the law of confidence (see Chapter 11). This has been touched on in, for example, *Weld-Blundell v Stephens* [1919] 1 KB 520; *Initial Services v Putterill* [1968] 1 QB 396 at 405; *Schering Chemicals v Falkman* [1982] QB 1 at 27. Where the threat has passed, there must be a particularly clear public interest in any confidential information being disclosed.

Duty of confidentiality owed to a third party: subs (3)(d)

This provision was inserted in the House of Commons at Committee stage in   **5.33**
order to ensure that tribunals took account of the interests of a third party to
whom a duty to maintain confidentiality of information was owed. In introducing the amendment the sponsoring Minister, Ian McCartney, commented that it
was necessary in order to deal with information which was subject to particular
confidence, such as arising out of a banker–client or doctor–patient relationship.
He explained[31] that:

> . . . the amendment would ensure that tribunals take into account the damage that
> may occur to a third person by disclosure. The tribunal may already take that into
> account, but it is not obliged to do so. One example might be that of a doctor's recep-
> tionist who disclosed medical records in good faith and in accordance with informa-
> tion available to her. But she could be wrong and the patient might have suffered an
> irreversible invasion of privacy.
>
> Another example might arise out of a business relationship. A bank employee might
> disclose that one of the bank's clients appeared to be insolvent. That could be very
> damaging to the client, who trusted the bank's duty of confidentiality to protect him.
> It would certainly damage his relationship with the bank and there might be damage
> to the bank's wider reputation and future business. Any potential damage might be
> justified by the circumstances, but the amendment has neither the intention nor the
> effect of suggesting that a duty of confidence to a third party will override all other
> factors. It would merely ensure that the tribunal will take that and any damage
> caused into account.

The effect of the reference to the duty of confidentiality to third parties is therefore
not to set an absolute bar to protection where such confidentiality is infringed.
Rather it is one matter which is expressly declared to be material in determining the
reasonableness of the particular disclosure. This was also stressed by Richard
Shepherd MP, one of the promoters of the Bill, who commented[32] that:

> . . . during consultation, the point was made that there are some particularly impor-
> tant obligations of confidence for example, those owed by a doctor to his patient or
> a bank to its customer. A fear was expressed that the Bill as drafted might unwittingly
> permit or encourage a secretary in a doctor's surgery or a clerk in a bank to disclose
> a concern about malpractice or misconduct without regard to the fact that that
> information was subject to an important obligation of confidence owed by the
> employer to a third party. The amendment has been tabled simply to allay those
> fears. Its purpose is not to thwart protection simply because the information was
> subject to a routine claim of confidentiality. It covers those exceptional cases in which
> there is a particularly important duty of confidence, as between doctors and patients,
> when a worker's disclosure breaches that duty and harms the third party. In such
> cases, it is right that the tribunal should consider the breach and the degree of any
> harm that it causes in deciding whether the disclosure was reasonable.

---

31 *Hansard,* Standing Committee D, 11 March 1998.
32 *Hansard,* Standing Committee D, 11 March 1998.

Again therefore, it was emphasized that not all obligations of confidentiality would have the same weight, but rather that tribunals were expected to be able, when assessing reasonableness, to recognize certain obligations of confidentiality as being of particular importance. Further, this subparagraph does not refer to confidentiality as between *employer and employee*—though there is scope to take account of this in considering all the circumstances of the case.

An example of circumstances of disclosure of information despite confidentiality obligations owed to a third party is provided by the decision in *W v Egdell* [1990] 1 Ch 359 (CA), summarized at paragraph 5.30 above. A further example would be the position of a doctor who carries out a blood test on an individual and becomes aware that he is HIV-positive. The doctor might find it difficult to argue that it is in the public interest to inform the public about this through the media. In the event that the patient had a partner, the disclosure might be reasonable.

Previous disclosures: subs (3)(e)

5.34 In a case where the worker has previously made a disclosure of substantially the same information to his employer or to a prescribed person under s43F, the tribunal must also take into account action which the employer or prescribed person took or might reasonably be expected to have taken. This may be a factor either pointing in favour of or against the disclosure being reasonable. Thus if the employer has investigated the concern and taken all reasonable action in respect of it, the further disclosure is unlikely to be reasonable unless, perhaps, the whistleblower does not know the action has been taken and could reasonably believe that it had not been taken. It is likely to be a strong factor against the disclosure being reasonable if the employer was in the process of taking appropriate action, or if the worker jumped the gun and made a wider disclosure before awaiting a response from the employer and when the employer might reasonably be expected to have taken appropriate action if afforded sufficient time to act. Conversely, if the action taken was inadequate and fell short of the action which the employer or prescribed person could reasonably be expected to have taken, or indicated that the concerns were not being treated seriously, this might point strongly in favour of a wider disclosure being reasonable.

The provision therefore makes clear that it is important that the worker who made the disclosure is kept informed as to the outcome of any investigation which has taken place into the concern he has expressed and what action has been taken if the allegation is found to be substantiated. If the employer investigates and does not report back any outcome or reasons for the outcome to the worker, it might be reasonable for the worker to take the matter further, perhaps to the media. Conversely, should the employer openly investigate and report back to the worker, with a thorough explanation as to why the allegation is not substantiated, it might be unreasonable for the worker to proceed further down the line of disclosure. It might also make sense for employers to press the regulators to report back as promptly and fully as possible so as to avoid such further disclosure being held to be reasonable.

Whistleblowing procedures: subs (3)(f)

Where a third tier disclosure is to be made on the basis that the worker has previously made a disclosure of substantially the same information to the employer, in determining reasonableness the tribunal must consider whether the worker complied with any whistleblowing procedure authorized by the employer. However it is suggested it will not be enough simply to introduce such a procedure in a workplace. Reasonable steps should also be taken to promote the whistleblowing procedure amongst the workforce. Ideally once such a procedure is introduced, its use should be monitored and its role should be explained to the workforce, for example, (depending on the size of the organization), through team briefings, newsletters or posters. We discuss in Chapter 16 what would be appropriate to put in these procedures, and set out a number of sample procedures at Appendix 5. **5.35**

It should be noted that a grievance procedure is different from a whistleblowing procedure—a point made by Lord Borrie[33]—in that under a grievance procedure it is for the worker to prove his case, whereas under a whistleblowing procedure he raises the matter so that it may be investigated. This may be significant in relation to the extent of any evidence which the worker must adduce. This is also reflected in the specific distinction drawn between whistleblowing procedures and grievance procedures in para 15 of Sch 3 to the Employment Act 2002 relating to the scope of statutory grievance procedures. This provides that the standard grievance procedures are only applicable to a protected disclosure if the information disclosed relates to a matter which could have been raised as a grievance with the employer and it was the intention of the worker that the disclosure should constitute the raising of a grievance.

Assessment of all the circumstances

Provided that the tribunal does take into account each of the factors in s43G(1)(e), and properly directs itself as to the need to take into account all relevant circumstances, its judgment as to whether it was reasonable to make the disclosure is likely to be difficult to disturb on appeal. It will be for the tribunal to determine which circumstances in addition to the specific factors in s43G(3) are relevant, and what weight to give to each of the factors taken into account, including the factors in s43G(3) ERA. Whilst, as indicated above, consideration of how the public interest defence has been applied in the context of confidentiality may provide an illustration of some of the relevant considerations, decisions in that different **5.36**

---

[33] *Hansard* HL, 5 June 1998, col. 627.

statutory context are in no way binding and each case must be considered on its own facts by the tribunal against the touchstone of reasonableness.

The following two cases are examples of how the tribunals have taken account of the competing considerations in first instance decisions which have considered questions of reasonableness specifically in the context of s43G ERA.

In *Staples v Royal Sun Alliance* (ET, 2001), the claimant was a part-time negotiator in the respondent's estate agency division. Concerns were raised internally by the claimant about health and safety of customers and the way financial services were being sold. But the claimant also subsequently mentioned one concern to a customer. The tribunal held that the raising of the concern with the customer fell within s43G as (a) it concerned a breach of consumer law, (b) the claimant had already raised it internally and (c) it was reasonable to tell the customer as the tribunal noted that it could understand why the claimant felt obliged to inform potential customers so they would not be deceived.[34] The nature of the concern, together with the fact that the disclosure was made to those with a proper interest in receiving the information, was therefore determinative.

In *Kay v Northumbria Healthcare NHS Trust* (ET, Case No. 6405617/00, 29 November 2001) the ET found that a disclosure fell within s43G even though made to the press, having regard in particular to the response when the issues were raised internally, and the issues of serious public concern which were raised. Mr Kay was a ward manager employed by an NHS Trust. He managed a ward for the elderly. He raised internally concerns he had as to bed shortages, but it was made clear to him that there were no resources available to address this. The situation deteriorated and some elderly patients were moved to a gynaecological ward. As a means of highlighting his concerns, he then wrote a satirical letter, framed as an open letter to the Prime Minister, which was published in his local paper. As a result he was disciplined for unprofessional conduct. The ET found that there was a protected disclosure. Kay had a reasonable belief that the disclosure tended to show a danger to health and safety in that elderly patients were being directed from a ward dedicated to their needs to one not so dedicated, and he was entitled to take the view that this would compromise their health care. In concluding that it was reasonable to make the disclosure to the press, the tribunal took into account (a) the previous internal disclosure, (b) the fact that it had been made clear that no action would be taken due to lack of resources, (c) that Kay was not aware of any authorized procedure for raising concerns within the meaning of s43G(3)(f) ERA, (d) that it was a matter of serious public concern that elderly patients should be moved around in the way described and (e) that it was in the public interest that the information and concerns be raised.

---

[34] This summary is drawn from summaries of cases published by PCaW. Ultimately the claim failed on the basis that the protected disclosure was not the reason for dismissal.

(5) Disclosure to a trade union

There is no express provision relating to disclosure to a trade union. However an **5.37** attempt was made during the passage of the Protected Information Disclosure Bill to make specific reference to disclosure to a union. In favour of the amendment it was argued that officials (who will often not be employed by the same company as the whistleblower) were in reality in a similar position to legal representatives, and would often be the first port of call especially in a health and safety issue. In rejecting a proposed amendment to refer to unions in s43C, it was said that this would not be consistent with the scheme of the legislation in encouraging concerns to be raised first internally with the employer or the person legally responsible for the failure.[35] It was also noted that disclosure to a trade union solicitor would be covered under s43D, and that it can be expected that where there is a whistleblowing procedure it will provide for disclosures to trade union officials so that there would be protection under s43C(2) ERA.

There remains an issue however as to the adequacy of coverage in relation to union officials. If an employee approaches a union official (other than a union lawyer) for initial guidance as to how to address concerns this will not fall within s43C unless such a disclosure is authorized under the employer's procedures. But nor will there be protection under s43G unless the employee could satisfy one of the preconditions in s43G(2) or the guidance can be regarded as obtaining legal advice and s43D is to be construed as applying to non-lawyers (see para 5.14 above). If the union official is the first port of call for initial guidance, it will not be possible to show that substantially the same information has been disclosed to the employer. If the gateway requirements of s43G(2) are not satisfied, and it is not an exceptionally serious failure falling within s43H, the employee will not have protection for making a protected disclosure.

G. Wider disclosures of exceptionally serious matters: Section 43H

Section 43H provides an alternative basis for protecting disclosures relating to **5.38** matters of an exceptionally serious nature. It provides:

Disclosure of exceptionally serious failure

(1) A qualifying disclosure is made in accordance with this section if—
   (a) the worker makes the disclosure in good faith,
   (b) he reasonably believes that the information disclosed, and any allegation contained in it, are substantially true,

---

[35] *Hansard*, 19 June 1998, Lords Report Stage *per* Lord Haskell (at cols. 1800–1801), *per* Lord Borrie (at cols. 1801–1802).

   (c) he does not make the disclosure for purposes of personal gain,

   (d) the relevant failure is of an exceptionally serious nature, and

   (e) in all the circumstances of the case, it is reasonable for him to make the disclosure.

(2) In determining for the purposes of subsection (1)(e) whether it is reasonable for the worker to make the disclosure, regard shall be had, in particular, to the identity of the person to whom the disclosure is made.

The essential difference between s43H ERA and s43G, therefore, is that in place of the three alternative preconditions in s43G(2), under s43H it is sufficient to establish that the relevant failure is exceptionally serious in nature. As in s43G, there is still a requirement that the worker must act in good faith, must possess a reasonable belief that the information disclosed is substantially true, must not be acting for personal gain and it must be reasonable for him in all the circumstances to make that disclosure. Even where the relevant failure is 'exceptionally serious', therefore, the disclosure is not protected unless it was reasonable in all the circumstances for the worker to make it. However in relation to reasonableness the only factor which *must* be taken into consideration is the identity of the person to whom the disclosure is made. The other factors listed in s43G(3) in relation to reasonableness *may* still be taken into account but there is no express statutory requirement to do so.

The requirements as to the identity of the recipient of the disclosure and the requirement for reasonableness in all the circumstances (s43H(1)(e), (2)) were inserted by a Government amendment in Committee in the Commons.[36] The Minister said:

> The Government firmly believe that where exceptionally serious matters are at stake, workers should not be deterred from raising them. It is important that they should do so, and that they should not be put off by concerns that a tribunal might hold that they should have delayed their disclosure or made it in some other way. That does not mean that people should be protected when they act wholly unreasonably: for example, by going straight to the press when there could clearly have been some other less damaging way to resolve matters.

> The amendment will encourage people to act reasonably even in serious matters, but it should not make them afraid that they will lose protection when they do so. It restores the balance between the need to make a disclosure and the need to do so in an effective and reasonable manner. Such disclosures should not be made in an offhand, rushed way to the press, as if that were the first or only way to raise the complaint or allegation. The amendment re-tilts the balance to an even keel by recognising employers' needs as well as the dangers of discouraging urgent and serious disclosures.[37]

During the passage of the Public Interest Disclosure Bill through the House of Lords, an attempt was made to amend clause 43H so as to replace the 'exceptionally serious'

---

[36] Parliamentary Debates HC, Standing Committee D, 11 March 1998.
[37] ibid, col. 10.

requirement, with the words 'very serious'. In support of the amendment it was argued that the exceptionally serious test set the threshold too high, and might lead tribunals down a cul-de-sac in considering whether a small enough percentage of failures was of a particular type.[38] In rejecting the proposed amendment it was emphasized that the 'exceptionally serious' test deliberately set a very high threshold with the intention that it would apply only in rare circumstances. Lord Haskell (for the Government) explained[39] that:

> . . . the new section is meant to apply only in very rare cases. The purpose of inserting 'exceptional' is to indicate that the case is indeed a rare case. Nobody wants individuals disclosing confidential information to other bodies unless the circumstances are exceptional.
>
> However, we all recognise that there will be concerns that are rare, but so grave that they need to be disclosed and dealt with as soon as possible. We believe that the current wording conveys that very clearly.
>
> . . .
>
> We believe that the best way to convey the order of seriousness under new Section 43H is by referring to failures that are objectively judged to be exceptionally serious. There may be disclosures which are very serious, but hardly exceptional, and such disclosures would be protected under other provisions in the Bill.

It was intended therefore, that the term 'exceptionally serious' would connote a very high standard, meaning something more than 'very serious'. The scope of what is 'exceptionally serious' is a matter of fact and degree for the tribunal. It is a matter on which there may be legitimate room for disagreement, and not much room for appeal to the Employment Appeal Tribunal since this is pre-eminently a matter of appreciation by the tribunal hearing all the evidence.

In some cases it will be apparent from the nature of the failure itself that it is exceptionally serious. Thus in *Herron v Wintercomfort for the Homeless* (ET, Case No. 1502519/03, 11 August 2004), s43H was found to apply where the relevant failure was that there had been a murder. The claimant met with a client (B) who displayed signs of bruising and said that her partner had threatened to set fire to her. B was then admitted to hospital with serious burns and later died from her injuries before she was able to give any information to the police. The claimant was contacted by the police and told them about her meeting with B. She was pressed by the police to hand over the file. She initially resisted because she wanted to contact her superior first. After she had been unable to contact her superior she handed the file over. Her employer regarded her disclosures as a breach of confidentiality. She was already serving out her notice at the time of the events, but she

---

[38] Lords Committee Stage, 5 June 1998, *per* Lord McCarthy at col. 629.
[39] Lords Committee Stage, 5 June 1998, at cols. 629–630.

was subjected to detriments including being required to attend a disciplinary hearing and then being told that she was no longer trusted to work at the same office and would be relocated. This was found to be a detriment on the grounds of protected disclosures under s43H ERA. Since the relevant failure related to a murder it was indeed exceptionally serious in nature. Further the disclosure was regarded as reasonable even if made in breach of an obligation of confidentiality in the light of the fact that it was made to the police and in response to approaches by them. The serious nature of the relevant failure, and the fact that it was made to an appropriate body (the police) was also regarded as material in relation to whether there was a qualifying disclosure. The file handed over contained much material which did not amount (if taken separately) to a disclosure within s43B, but a more broad-brush approach was regarded as appropriate given that the police required to see the whole file in relation to a murder investigation and would not have allowed her to select individual parts of the file to hand over.

In other cases, there might be a combination of factors which, taken together, lead a tribunal to conclude that the failure is exceptionally serious. This was the case in *Collins v National Trust* (ET, Case No. 2507255/05, 17 January 2006), which concerned and the disclosure to the press of a draft report relating to contamination on land owned and managed by Mr Collins' employer, The National Trust. Mr Collins genuinely and reasonably believed that the draft report showed (a) the environment was likely to be damaged and (b) health and safety was likely to be endangered as the contamination had potential to cause damage to workers and public, including children. Further he reasonably believed that information about this was being concealed, in that the report was not disclosed by the local council to the National Trust for over a year and was to be kept confidential pending further investigation. Mr Collins was dismissed purportedly on the grounds that he had disclosed the report to the press in breach of a lawful instruction that queries about the report should be referred either to his employer's press officer, or its property manager. The tribunal however held that the real reason for dismissal was the disclosure of the content of the report to the press.

In relation to the requirement that the disclosure be of an 'exceptionally serious nature', the tribunal accepted that to gain protection the relevant failure must be 'very serious indeed'. In concluding that this test was satisfied it took into account in particular that:

1. there were three relevant failures: damage to the environment, endangerment of health and safety to the public and concealment of information;
2. the public were invited onto the land for recreational purposes; children played there and were identified in the report as especially at risk; and
3. the respondent (The National Trust) was a well-known and well-respected conservation charity in which the public places special trust and confidence, and the disclosure related to land which the Trust owned and managed.

The tribunal accepted that the respondent may have acted reasonably in adopting a strategy of further consultation before disclosing the report. However the tribunal stressed that the fact that the respondent may have been acting reasonably did not necessarily imply that Mr Collins had been acting unreasonably. In this case the tribunal concluded that he had been acting reasonably in the light of his genuine and reasonable concerns about public safety, that there was reason to believe that disclosure of the report would be delayed and that the public should be able to obtain their own advice on the risks indicated in the report. Accordingly Mr Collins' claim succeeded.

Whilst ultimately the tribunal will be required to make a broad-brush assessment in all the circumstances, we suggest that the following considerations are likely to be significant in the assessment of whether something is 'exceptionally serious'.

(a) By their nature, and by virtue of the fact that the good faith requirement has been construed as connoting that a disclosure is made in the public interest, most disclosures falling within s43B will be of quite serious matters. Section 43H connotes something of a different order, which can properly be regarded as exceptional.

(b) Taking a purposive approach, in assessing whether the failure is exceptionally serious in nature, it may be helpful to consider whether the seriousness justifies making a wider disclosure without satisfying any of the gateways to protection in s43G(2) ERA.

(c) The seriousness of the harm caused is fundamental. A danger to public safety, as in *Collins* may be more likely to qualify than financial concerns.

(d) Whether it is an ongoing or imminent failure is important—although *Herron* illustrates that if the matter is serious (in that case murder) it may still qualify.

(e) The decision in *Collins* indicates that the number of failures may cumulatively affect whether, taken together, they can each be regarded as exceptionally serious.

(f) The number of potential victims may be important.

(g) The nature of the person responsible for the failure may be relevant, as was the case in *Collins*.

6

WHO IS PROTECTED UNDER PIDA?

A. Employees	6.02	Crown employees	6.22
The identity of 'the employer':		(3) Limits of the definition of 'worker'	6.23
special cases	6.05	Volunteers	6.24
B. Workers	6.07	Non-executives	6.32
(1) The ordinary s230(3) definition	6.07	Members of the armed forces and those	
(2) Extended definition in s43K	6.09	involved in national security	6.33
Agency workers	6.10	Parliamentary staff	6.36
The NHS	6.14	(4) Possibility of more than one employer	6.37
Trainees	6.16	(5) Workers—summary	6.38
Police officers	6.18	C. Territorial jurisdiction	6.39

The protection of individuals from action taken against them by their employer is **6.01** afforded not just to an 'employee' but also (with certain important differences and modifications which are set out below) to the wider class of those who come within the definition of a 'worker.'

A. Employees

An 'employee' is defined by s230 (1) ERA as: **6.02**

> . . . an individual who has entered into or works under (or, where the employment has ceased, worked under) a contract of employment.

A 'contract of employment' is defined as: **6.03**

> . . . a contract of service or apprenticeship, whether express or implied, and (if it is express) whether oral or in writing.

The following principles are applicable in relation to whether there is a contract **6.04** of employment:

(a) The first essential prerequisite for 'employment' is that there must be a contractual relationship, express or implied, between the worker and the employer.

The need to consider whether there is an implied contract is particularly important where there is a 'triangular' relationship, such as where a worker is supplied by an agency to an end-user/client. There are typically written contracts between the end-user and the agency, and the worker and the agency, but there needs to be an assessment of whether there is an implied contract directly between the worker and the end-user. A contract can be implied if it is necessary to give business reality to the relationship and arrangements between the worker and the end-user and to establish the enforceable obligations that one would expect to see between them: *Cable & Wireless plc v Muscat* [2006] IRLR 354 (CA) at para 51.

(b) Second, there must be mutuality of obligation.[1] The obligations must relate to the personal provision of work for remuneration and an obligation to perform it, though the remuneration need not be paid directly by the employer.[2]

(c) There must also be a sufficient degree of control to be consistent with an employment relationship.[3]

(d) In addition it is necessary to identify whether the other provisions of the contract indicate that it is a contract of service.[4] It is necessary to paint a picture from the accumulation of detail: *Hall v Lorimer* [1994] ICR 218 (CA) at 226; [1992] ICR 739 (EAT) at 744–745.[5]

The identity of 'the employer': special cases

6.05 As explained in Chapter 5, the degree to which, and method by which, a worker is protected by PIDA will depend on whether the disclosure in issue is made to that worker's employer or to another person or entity, and if so what the legal status is of that other person or entity *vis-à-vis* the worker. Usually the identity of the employer will be a straightforward question. In some cases it will not be.

6.06 One of the issues in *Douglas v Birmingham City Council* (EAT/0518/02, 17 March 2003) was the identity of the employer of the claimant for the purposes of the whistleblowing legislation. The claimant was a paid classroom assistant. The disclosure in question was made to the chairman of the governors of the

---

[1] See eg *Clark v Oxfordshire Health Authority* [1998] IRLR 125 (CA).

[2] *Cable & Wireless plc v Muscat* [2006] IRLR 354 (CA) at para 35; *Cotswold Developments Construction Limited v Williams* [2006] IRLR 181 (EAT) at para 48, 49.

[3] See eg *Bunce v Postworth Limited t/a Skyblue* [2005] IRLR 557 (CA) where there was insufficient control for there to be an employment relationship between an agency worker and the agency.

[4] *Cable & Wireless plc v Muscat*, above n 2, at paras 31, 32.

[5] There is, of course, a plethora of authority on the distinction between a contract of service and a contract which is not a contract of service. The principles are set out in more detail in *Chitty on Contracts* (29th Ed, London: Sweet & Maxwell, 2004) Vol 2 Chapter 39 paragraphs 39–010 to 39–028 and Bowers, *A Practical Approach to Employment Law* (Oxford: Oxford University Press, 2005) pp 15 to 22.

school where she worked. The claimant's contract of employment was with the local authority. The EAT upheld the ET's ruling that the claimant was not deemed, for the purposes of the whistleblowing legislation, to be an employee of the governors (contrary to the more general position under Art 3(1) of the Education (Modification of Enactments Relating to Employment) Order 1999 SI 1999/2256). However, it concluded that the claimant was a worker within the extended definition given by s43K(1) because she was supplied by a contract of employment, effected by the City Council, to do work for the governing body of the school and the terms on which she was engaged to do that work were in practice determined not by her, but by the governing body or by the council or both. She thus fell within s43K(1) as a 'worker.' She was therefore entitled to bring proceedings against the person who fitted the definition of her 'employer.' A disclosure to the Chair of the governors was a disclosure to the governing body (her employer). The Chair was the appropriate 'natural person' since he led the governing body which was the body which employed the claimant. In those circumstances, the disclosure to the Chair constituted a disclosure to the claimant's employer.

B. Workers

(1) The ordinary s230(3) definition

The ordinary meaning of 'worker' contained in s230(3) ERA is someone who is either an employee or any other: **6.07**

> individual who has entered into or works under (or, where the employment has ceased, worked under)—
>
> . . .
>
> (b) any other contract, whether express or implied and (if it is express) whether oral or in writing, whereby the individual undertakes to do or perform personally any work or services for another party to the contract whose status is not by virtue of the contract that of a client or customer of any profession or business undertaking carried on by the individual.

The definition of worker therefore has the following key elements. **6.08**

(a) There must be an express or implied contract. It has been said on many occasions that there must be 'mutuality of obligations', but in *Cotswold Developments Construction*[6] the EAT held that there is no such requirement in relation to the definition of a worker over and above the mutuality required to establish a contract.

(b) It must be a contract 'whereby the individual undertakes to do or perform personally any work or services for another party to the contract'. There must

---

[6] Above n 2.

be a contractual obligation to do work personally; it does not necessarily follow from the fact that the work is in fact done personally that there was a contractual obligation to do so: *Redrow Homes (Yorkshire) Limited v Wright* [2004] IRLR 720 (CA) at para 21. However unless the parties to the agreement have agreed that a document or series of documents was intended to constitute an exclusive record of their agreement, any question arising as to the nature or terms of the contract is a question of fact to be determined from a consideration of all the evidence, including written documents, oral statements and conduct, including what happened in practice: see *Cable & Wireless v Muscat* at para 33.[7] In the context of the slightly differently worded definition of 'employer' in race discrimination legislation,[8] it has been held that the dominant purpose must be the personal execution of work or labour,[9] but it has subsequently been doubted by the EAT whether this applies to the definition of worker in s230(3): *Cotswolds Developments Construction* at paragraph 50.

(c) The status of the other party (ie the 'employer') must not be that of 'a client or customer of any profession or business undertaking carried on' by the putative worker. The meaning of business undertaking was considered in *Byrne Brothers (Formwork) Limited v Baird* [2002] ICR 667 (EAT) where Mr Recorder Underhill QC provided guidance in relation to this provision:

> (2) '[Carrying on a] business undertaking' is plainly capable of having a very wide meaning. In one sense every 'self-employed' person carries on a business. But the term cannot be intended to have so wide a meaning here, because if it did the exception would wholly swallow up the substantive provision and limb (b) would be no wider than limb (a). The intention behind the regulation is plainly to create an intermediate class of protected worker, who is on the one hand not an employee but on the other hand cannot in some narrower sense be regarded as carrying on a business. . . . It is sometimes said that the effect of the exception is that the 1998 Regulations do not extend to 'the genuinely self-employed'; but that is not a particularly helpful formulation since it is unclear how 'genuine' self-employment is to be defined.
>
> (3) . . . Possibly the term 'customer' gives some slight indication of an arm's-length commercial relationship—see below—but it is not clear whether it was deliberately chosen as a key word in the definition or simply as a neutral term to denote the other party to a contract with a business undertaking.
>
> (4) It seems to us that the best guidance is to be found by considering the policy behind the inclusion of limb (b). That can only have been to extend the benefits of protection to workers who are in the same need of that type of protection as employees *stricto sensu* . . . The reason why employees are thought to need such protection is that they are in a subordinate and dependent position *vis-à-vis* their employers: the purpose of the Regulations is to extend protection

---

[7] Above n 2, summarizing the effect of *Carmichael v National Power plc* [1999] ICR 1226 (HL).
[8] Referring to 'a contract personally to execute any work or labour'.
[9] *Mingeley v Pennock and another* [2004] IRLR 373 (CA).

to workers who are, substantively and economically, in the same position. Thus the essence of the intended distinction must be between, on the one hand, workers whose degree of dependence is essentially the same as that of employees and, on the other, contractors who have a sufficiently arm's-length and independent position to be treated as being able to look after themselves in the relevant respects.

(5) Drawing that distinction in any particular case will involve all or most of the same considerations as arise in drawing the distinction between a contract of service and a contract for services—but with the boundary pushed further in the putative worker's favour. It may, for example, be relevant to assess the degree of control exercised by the putative employer, the exclusivity of the engagement and its typical duration, the method of payment, what equipment the putative worker supplies, the level of risk undertaken, etc. The basic effect of limb (b) is, so to speak, to lower the passmark, so that cases which failed to reach the mark necessary to qualify for protection as employees might nevertheless do so as workers.

This guidance has been followed in several cases.[10] It was supplemented in *Cotswolds Developments Construction* where the EAT said (at para 53):

The distinction is not that between employee and independent contractor. The paradigm case falling within the proviso to 2(b) is that of a person working within one of the established professions: solicitor and client, barrister and client, accountant, architect etc. The paradigm case of a customer and someone working in a business undertaking of his own will perhaps be that of the customer of a shop and the shopowner, or of the customer of a tradesman such as a domestic plumber, cabinet maker or portrait painter who commercially markets services as such. Thus viewed, it seems plain that a focus upon whether the purported worker actively markets his services as an independent person to the world in general (a person who will thus have a client or customer) on the one hand, or whether he is recruited by the principal to work for that principal as an integral part of the principal's operations, will in most cases demonstrate on which side of the line a given person falls.[11]

(2) Extended definition in s43K

Section 43K ERA provides that, for the purposes of Part IVA ERA (ie that Part **6.09** dealing with victimization for whistleblowing), the category of 'worker' is extended in various respects to also include individuals who would not be workers as defined by s230(3) ERA. Accordingly the scope of PIDA protection extends to persons who do not have other rights accorded to 'workers'. As amended by PIDA, ERA expressly protects independent contractors who provide services other than in a professional–client or business–client relationship. It also expressly covers certain

---

[10] See *Cotswolds Developments Construction*, above n2, at paragraph 33, listing the cases that have followed *Byrne Bros v Baird*.

[11] See also *R v CAC ex p BBC* [2003] ICR 1542, where the meaning of 'profession' was considered, and it was held that the existence of a regulatory body may be relevant but is not necessarily determinative.

agency workers, homeworkers, NHS doctors, dentists, ophthalmologists and pharmacists, and trainees on vocational or work experience schemes. Section 43K(2) ERA identifies who constitutes the worker in relation to the various extended categories of worker.

Agency workers

6.10 Section 43K(1)(a) ERA provides that a worker includes a person who:

(a) works or worked for a person in circumstances in which—
(i) he is or was introduced or supplied to do that work by a third person, and
(ii) the terms on which he is or was engaged to do the work are or were in practice substantially determined not by him but by the person for whom he works or worked, by the third person or by both of them.

6.11 Section 43K(1)(a) therefore makes special provision to cover agency workers, where the agency introduces workers or finds them the post and the terms of employment are substantially determined by the agency or the organization where they perform the work. In this case 'the person who substantially determines or determined the terms' of the engagement is deemed to be the employer (see s43K(2)(a) ERA). This will normally be the organization where the person performs the work. This widening of scope represents a somewhat different provision to that introduced (controversially) into the Working Time Regulations 1998 which treats as the employer the body which actually pays the worker. The person or body determining the terms of engagement seems to denote the person or body who or which provides the details of the work to be performed and the level and terms of remuneration. In many cases, however, workers in this category will fall within the narrower category of employee on the basis that it is necessary to category a contract in order to give business reality to the relationship: *Cable & Wireless v Muscat*, following *Dacas v Brook Street Bureau* [2004] IRLR 358 (CA).

6.12 The ordinary definition of a worker under s230(3) ERA covers an independent contractor who *personally* provides services other than in a professional–client or business–client relationship. The definition is a wide and flexible one which includes the self employed.[12] This definition is further extended by s43K(1)(b) ERA to an individual who:

. . . contracts or contracted with a person, for the purposes of that person's business, for the execution of work to be done in a place not under the control or management of that person and would fall within section 230(3)(b) if for 'personally' in that provision there were substituted '(whether personally or otherwise)'.

6.13 Accordingly the requirement of personal service is removed but only if the work is not to be done at a place under the control or management of the employer.

---

[12] For a recent review of the case law see *Cotswold Developments Construction*, above n 2.

This would therefore encompass a homeworker irrespective of whether they engage others to carry out the work.

The NHS

Subsection (1) of s43K (as amended) brings within the category of 'worker' for the **6.14** purposes of PIDA protection a person who:-

(a) 'works or worked as a person performing services under a contract entered into by him with a Primary Care Trust or Local Health Board . . .', and in relation to such a worker the Primary Care Trust or Local Health Board referred to will be 'the employer' (ss43K(1)(ba), 43(2)(aa) ERA);

(b) 'works or worked as a person providing services under a contract entered into by him with a Health Board under section 17J of the National Health Service (Scotland) Act 1978', in relation to whom the Health Board is the employer (ss43K(1)(bb); 43K(2)(ab) ERA); or

(c) 'works or worked as a person providing general . . . dental services, general ophthalmic services or pharmaceutical services in accordance with arrangements made—
    (i) by a Primary Care Trust or Health Authority . . . ., or
    (ii) by a Health Board . . .'
    and the relevant authority or board is the employer (ss43K(1)(c)(ca), 43K(2)(b),(ba) ERA).

Accordingly PIDA protection applies across virtually the whole of the NHS. **6.15** Doctors, dentists, ophthalmologists and pharmacists in the NHS are usually independently contracting professionals and are covered under the Act although they would not necessarily otherwise come under the definition of employee or worker in the ERA.

Trainees

A trainee on work experience or on a vocational scheme receives protection, **6.16** if he/she is a person who is:

> . . . . provided with work experience pursuant to a training course or programme or with training for employment otherwise than (i) under a contract for employment or by an educational establishment on a course run by that establishment (s43K(1)(d) ERA).

For these people the person providing the training is deemed to be the employer **6.17** for the purposes of the Act (see s43K(2)(c). This does not, however, cover trainees or students in education. It would probably cover a student on a sandwich year since the training is not run by the educational establishment. Whilst this is supported by and often set up by, or with the help of, an educational establishment, the year out does not possess the necessary integration with the educational establishment to fall within the relevant words 'run by'.

Police officers

6.18 Until 1 April 2004 s13 of PIDA extended s200 of the ERA to, and thereby excluded, police officers from protection under the PIDA-inserted provisions. This did not affect the rights of civilian staff in the police service to claim protection. The exclusion of police officers from protection was criticized by the Police Complaints Authority, the Association of Chief Police Officers and other consultees, in particular given that miscarriages of justice are one of the specified malpractices expressly covered by the Act (see s43(1)(c)).

6.19 When the proposed public interest disclosure legislation was before Parliament, the Government gave an absolute commitment that police officers, whilst they would be outside the coverage of the Act, would be given equivalent protection by regulation. The Police (Conduct) Regulations were indeed amended to permit the making of an internal grievance complaint where a police officer complains of victimization as a result of a disclosure.

6.20 However subsequently a different and much more effective mechanism was adopted. Section 37 of the Police Reform Act 2002[13] inserted a new s43KA into ERA which provides that for the purposes of the PIDA-inserted provisions,[14] a person who holds, otherwise than under a contract of employment, the office of constable or an appointment as a police cadet shall be treated as an employee employed by the 'relevant' officer under a contract of employment; and any reference to a worker being 'employed' and to his 'employer' shall be construed accordingly.

6.21 By subs(2) of s43KA the 'relevant officer' is defined in relation to members of a police force or special constables as the chief officer of police. In relation to a member of a police force seconded to the Serious Organised Crime Agency to serve as a member of its staff, *that* agency is the relevant officer. In relation to any other person holding the office of constable or an appointment as police cadet, the relevant officer is the person who has the direction and control of the body of constables or cadets in question.

Crown employees

6.22 Except as described below (that is in relation to the armed forces and national security personnel) the PIDA-inserted provisions of ERA apply in relation to Crown employment and persons in Crown employment as they have effect in relation to other employment and other employees or workers (s191(1) and 2(aa) ERA).

---

[13] The Police Reform Act 2002 (Commencement No. 8) Order 2004, 24 March 2004 brought into force s37 on 1 April 2004.

[14] Part IVA and s47B, and ss48 and 49 so far as relating to that section, and s103A and the other provisions of Part X so far as relating to the right not to be unfairly dismissed in a case where the dismissal is unfair by virtue of s103A.

'Crown employment' means 'employment under or for the purposes of a government department or any officer or body exercising on behalf of the Crown functions conferred by a statutory provision' (s191(3) ERA).

(3) Limits of the definition of 'worker'

Whilst the category of 'workers' under the PIDA provisions is a wide one it is not all-embracing. We address below categories of individuals who carry out work but are (or may be) not covered either because they do not fall within the general definition of 'worker' even as extended or who are specifically excluded. **6.23**

Volunteers

Although s43K provides for an extended definition of the term 'worker,' there must still be a contractual relationship. In order for there to be a contractual relationship there must be an agreement supported by consideration, an intention to create legal relations and reasonable certainty of terms. Where a person works as a volunteer it may be that the requirements for consideration and for an intention to create legal relations are not satisfied and the tribunal will have regard to the reality of the situation. **6.24**

As to the requirement of consideration, one common feature of a volunteering relationship is the absence of any obligation to provide the volunteer with work and of any minimum commitment of time from the volunteer. If so there will not be an umbrella or global contract of employment linking each occasion on which the volunteer has worked for the 'employer'.[15] However on the facts it might be that there is an obligation to offer and accept work even if the work is only of a sporadic or casual nature.[16] Even where there is no minimum commitment of time, the volunteer may be a 'worker' as a result of entering into a contractual relationship on the occasions when work has in fact been done by the volunteer.[17] **6.25**

A further common feature of a volunteering relationship is the absence of any payment for the work done except in respect of expenses incurred. Payments made to workers will not constitute consideration if they are genuinely *ex gratia* (although tribunals may be sceptical of this if the payments are made as a matter of course). Nor will payments made genuinely by way of reimbursement of expenses constitute consideration. In these cases, even where there may be a right to terminate the volunteer relationship which is akin to a dismissal, and even though the volunteer **6.26**

---

[15] *Clark v Oxfordshire Health Authority*, above n1.

[16] Though see *Carmichael v National Power plc* [2000] IRLR 43 HL.

[17] *Clark*, above n1; *McMeechan v Secretary of State for Employment* [1997] ILRR 353 (CA); *Asila Elshami v Welfare Community Projects and Leema* (London North IT, Case No. 6001977/1998).

may gain status and skill from acting as a volunteer, the volunteer is unlikely to be a 'worker', at least where there is no mutual time commitment and no other mutual obligations such as an obligation to provide training.[18] However whilst it may be that expenses have merely been estimated in broad-brush terms to save administrative costs, in a series of cases flat-rate payments made to volunteers have been a crucial factor leading to a finding that the volunteer was in employment (either under a contract of services or personally providing work or labour). The fact that the payment is low is irrelevant since the tribunal is not concerned with assessing the value of the consideration.[19] Further, where there is no or no immediate payment, it may be that other mutual obligations are accepted such as an obligation to train, supervise and provide a safe system of work.[20]

6.27 A series of cases against Citizens' Advice Bureaux arising out of claims under the Disability Discrimination Act 1995 have explored the extent and circumstances in which 'volunteers' may be said to be employed. The cases were concerned with the (now repealed) small employer exemption section which excluded claims against employers with less than 15 employees—employees being defined for this purpose by s68(1) of the DDA. Whilst that section provides a particular (and extended) meaning to the word 'employee' the principles emerging from these cases are of some general application.

6.28 In *Sheffield CAB v Grayson* [2004] IRLR 353 Mr Grayson, who was accepted to be an employee of the CAB, claimed discrimination contrary to the DDA. The CAB raised the defence under s7, that there were only eleven paid employees. The issue was whether volunteers at the CAB in question fell within s68, thus raising the headcount above fifteen. They were engaged pursuant to a 'volunteer agreement' which was construed by the ET which also heard oral evidence. The EAT said that the central question for the employment tribunal was whether the CAB's volunteer workers were subject to a contract under which they were obliged to work for the Bureau. Rimer J, giving the judgment of the EAT, said at paragraph 12 that:

> . . . . it would appear to us surprising if the answer to that question were yes, since it is of the essence of volunteer workers that they are ordinarily under no such contract. As volunteers, they provide their services voluntarily, without reward, with the consequence that they are entitled to withhold those services with impunity. However that starting position is not necessarily also the finishing point. In every case, including this one, if a question arises as to the legal relationship between an

---

[18] *Gradwell v Council for Voluntary Service, Blackpool, Wyre & Fylde* (Manchester ET, Case no. 2404313/97); *Alexander v Romania at Heart Trading Co. Limited* (Brighton ET, Case No. 310206/97).

[19] *Migrant Advisory Services v Chaudri* (EAT/ 11400/97); *Asila Elshami*, above n 18); *Rodney Harrambeen Organisation Limited* (Birmingham ET, Case 36684/86).

[20] See *Armitage v Relate* (Middlesborough ET, Case No. 43238/94) where there was a minimum time commitment and a provision for recouping training expenses if obligations were not met.

alleged employer and a so-called voluntary worker, it is always necessary to analyse that relationship to see exactly what it amounts to. But if the proposition is that the volunteer worker is in fact an employee under a contract of service, or under a contract personally to do work, for the purposes of section 68 of the 1995 Act, then in our view it is necessary to be able to identify an arrangement under which, in exchange of valuable consideration, the volunteer is contractually obliged to render services to or else to work personally for the employer.

The EAT noted that the CAB did not require its volunteers to sign the volunteer **6.29** agreement, the stated purpose of which was 'to clarify the reasonable expectation of both the volunteer and the Bureau'. In the EAT's view the agreement was: 'directed at clarifying each side's "reasonable expectations" and this was not the language of contractual obligation. Respective contractual obligations were not usually expressed in terms of "reasonable expectation". They would ordinarily be expressed in terms of unqualified obligation, or at any rate the primary obligations will be so expressed, in particular those relating to the employee's hours of work and his reward for it'. The EAT went on to consider various aspects of the Volunteer Agreement and came to this conclusion at paragraph 18:

> We are prepared to accept that this element of the Agreement, and also the provision in it to the effect that the Bureau will indemnify advisers against negligence claims by disgruntled clients, probably do, or at least may, evidence a binding contractual relationship between the Bureau and the volunteer, namely a unilateral contract in the nature of what is sometimes referred to as an 'if' contract, one which can be expressed as follows: 'if you do any work for the Bureau and incur expenses in doing so, and/suffer a claim from a client you advise, the Bureau will indemnify you against your expenses and any such claim'. But that contract is still not one which imposes on the volunteer any obligation actually to do any work for the Bureau.

They concluded that 'the contract imposed no obligation on the volunteer to do **6.30** anything . . .'. The provision requiring the volunteer to undertake training did not constitute consideration (para 21). The 'crucial question' was not whether any benefits flowed from the Bureau to the volunteer in consideration of any work actually done by the volunteer for the Bureau, but whether the Volunteer Agreement imposed a contractual obligation upon the Bureau to provide work for the volunteer to do and upon the volunteer personally to do for the Bureau any work so provided, being an obligation such that, were the volunteer to give notice immediately terminating his relationship with the Bureau, the latter would have a remedy for breach of contract against him. The Volunteer Agreement imposed no such obligation. It was open to a volunteer at any point, either with or without notice, to withdraw his or her services from the Bureau, in which event the Bureau would have no contractual remedy against him. It followed that the advisers and other volunteers were not employed by the Bureau within the meaning of the definition in s68 ERA.[21]

---

[21] See also *Murray v Newham CAB* [2001] ICR 708 and *Bruce v Leeds CAB* (EAT/1355/01).

6.31 Even where there is an agreement supported by consideration this will not be binding unless there is an intention to create legal relations, rather than an agreement which is 'purely voluntary or is binding in honour only'.[22] The label placed on the agreement by the parties, such as whether the worker is referred to as a 'volunteer' may be relevant but it is not determinative as to whether there was an intention to create legal relations. The tribunal can also have regard to the context in which an agreement was made in order to ascertain whether there was the requisite intention. On this basis, in *Rogers v Booth* [1937] 2 All ER 751 the Court of Appeal held that an officer of the Salvation Army had no contract because the relationship was purely a spiritual one. This was so even though she was paid a maintenance payment. The payment was expressly stated to be purely hardship money since the officer had no other means of earning a living.[23] More recently, however, in *Percy v Church of Scotland Board of National Mission* [2006] 2 AC 28 (HL) it was emphasized that there is no necessary inconsistency between there being a contract and the obligations being exclusively spiritual, and that the issue now needs to be considered in the modern context of statutory protection provided for workers and employees (*per* Lord Nicholls at paras 25, 26). Where the agreement lacks precision and is informal this may be consistent with an absence of intention to create legal relations.[24] The mere fact that there is a recognized practice of using volunteers and an informal relationship may not however be sufficient to persuade a tribunal of an absence of an intention to create contractual relations.[25]

Non-executives

6.32 Non-executive directors who blow the whistle on malpractice are unlikely to be protected. They are self-employed and would not be a person performing work or services even allowing for the extended definition in s43K ERA.

Members of the armed forces and those involved in national security

6.33 There are various exclusions from the scope of protection offered under the Act which broadly mirror those found in other parts of employment legislation. As we have noted the Act applies to people who are employees of, work for, or are in the service of the Crown (s191 ERA). However it is not extended to those in the armed forces (s192 ERA).

---

[22] See Stuart-Smith LJ in *R v Lord Chancellor's Department ex p Nangle* [1991] IRLR 343 (DC) at para 23.

[23] See also *Diocese of Southwark v Coker* [1998] ICR 140 (assistant curate in Church of England not an employee as no contractual intention).

[24] *Chitty on Contracts*, above n 5, p 211 para 2–176.

[25] See eg, *Asila Elshami*, above n 17.

Nor does it extend to those involved in national security (s193 ERA). The general **6.34**
rule in s193 ERA applies, to the effect that a Crown servant is protected under the
Act, unless the worker is the subject of a ministerial certificate that his work
safeguards national security. This is a conclusive answer to a claim and would not
be open to review by the employment tribunal.

A worker in the security service or at GCHQ will therefore not be protected by the **6.35**
Act even where he or she raises a concern only internally. Concern was expressed
in the House of Commons Committee debate as to whether the scope of the
definition of security service was clear enough. A proposed amendment sought
to apply the Act to non-operational employees, for example office cleaners and
messengers who might come across waste or maladministration which did not
impinge on sensitive and secret matters. This proposal was withdrawn.

Parliamentary staff

Sections 194 and 195 apply provisions of ERA to House of Lords and House **6.36**
of Commons staff respectively but do not include an application of Part IVA
or s47B (detriment as the grounds of a protected disclosure). Part X (unfair dismissal)
is applied and s103A is not expressly excluded.

(4) Possibility of more than one employer

The application of the extended definition of worker may result in the worker **6.37**
having more than one employer. This was found to be the case in *Hayes v Reed
Social Care & Bradford MDC* (ET, Case No. 1805531/00), where the claimant
was held to be employed both by the agency who supplied his services and by the
local authority for whom he worked and which substantially determined the
terms of the engagement.

(5) Workers—summary

The broad definition of a 'worker' allows the protection of the Act to extend to a **6.38**
very wide range of circumstances in which a person who would not be an
'employee' might come across malpractice. All of the following circumstances
would be covered:

(a) trainees aware of abuse of public money on government-funded programmes;
(b) employed accountants working in private practice who become aware of
    financial malpractice in a company or charity;
(c) actuaries who blow the whistle on a pension fund fraud; and
(d) an employed book-keeper who becomes aware of a VAT or Revenue fraud.

C. Territorial jurisdiction

6.39 The Employment Rights Act used to contain a provision—s196 (3)—that, under the heading 'Employment outside Great Britain', provided that the right to claim unfair dismissal did not apply 'to any employment where under his contract of employment the employee ordinarily works outside Great Britain'. By s32(3) of the Employment Relations Act 1999 the whole of s196 was repealed and nothing was put in its place (a special provision for mariners was re-enacted in slightly different form as s199(7) and (8)). The courts were left to imply an appropriate limitation to the substantive right. They proceeded to do so, but not in unanimity. In *Serco Limited v Lawson* [2006] IRLR 289 the issue reached the House of Lords. Lord Hoffman gave the only reasoned speech. Detailed analysis of the problem and the conclusion of the House is outside the scope of this book[26] but in summary the House of Lords held that:

(a) it was a mistake to try to formulate an ancillary rule of territorial scope, in the sense of a verbal formula such as s196 used to provide (and as had been formulated by the Court of Appeal in *Serco*), which had then itself to be interpreted and applied.

(b) the question of construction should be decided according to established principles, giving effect to what Parliament may reasonably be supposed to have intended and attributing to Parliament a rational scheme.

(c) the decision as to whether the employment tribunal had jurisdiction was a question of law, although involving judgement in the application of the law to the facts, but was a question of degree on which the decision of the primary fact-finder was entitled to considerable respect.

(d) the standard, normal or paradigm case of the application of s94(1) was the employee who was working in Great Britain: ordinarily the question should simply be whether he is working in Great Britain at the time when he is dismissed. This would be in accordance with the spirit of the Posted Workers Directive, even though that Directive was not applicable to the right not to be unfairly dismissed.

(e) as the facts of *Croft v Veta Ltd*[27] showed, the concept of employment in Great Britain might not be easy to apply to peripatetic employees. The solution adopted under the old 'ordinarily works outside Great Britain' formula (which preceded s196(3)) had been to ask where the employee was based.[28] That was the correct approach following the repeal of s196(3).

---

26 See Linden, T, ILJ Vol 35 No. 2 June 2006, p 186 for an analysis.

27 Which concerned airline pilots working out of London for the Hong Kong airline, Cathay Pacific.

28 *Todd v British Midland Airways Ltd* [1978] ICR 959, Lord Denning MR at p 964 and *Wilson* [1978] ICR 376, Megaw LJ at p 387.

(f) the problem of expatriate employees and the concept of a base, which was useful to locate the workplace of a peripatetic employee, provided no help in the case of an expatriate employee. But only in exceptional cases would the right to bring unfair dismissal proceedings apply to such an employee and it was necessary to try, without drafting a definition, to identify the characteristics which such exceptional cases will ordinarily have. It would be very unlikely that someone working abroad would be within the scope of s94(1) unless he was working for an employer based in Great Britain.

(g) the fact that the employee also happens to be British or even that he was recruited in Britain, so that the relationship was 'rooted and forged' in this country, should not in itself be sufficient to take the case out of the general rule that the place of employment is decisive. Something more is necessary. That 'something more' might be provided by the fact that the employee was posted abroad by a British employer for the purposes of a business carried on in Great Britain as representative of a business conducted at home.

(h) two examples of cases in which s94(1) might apply to an expatriate employee were given: the employee posted abroad to work for a business conducted in Britain and the employee working in a political or social British enclave abroad. It was possible that there were others but Lord Hoffman said that he had not been able to think of any and if there were such employees then they would have to have equally strong connections with Great Britain and British employment law.

The House of Lords therefore has not laid down a 'test', but rather a set of guiding principles, indicating that ordinarily the question of whether the claim is within the territorial scope for protection will be resolved by whether the claimant was working in Great Britain at the time of the dismissal or, in non-dismissal claims, the detriment.

7

THE RIGHT NOT TO SUFFER DETRIMENT

A. **Section 47B ERA: Overview**	7.01	
B. **Deployment of the pre-existing**		
models of protection	7.07	
C. **Meaning of 'detriment'**	7.11	
(1) The *Khan* and *Shamoon* guidance	7.11	
(2) The threat of a detriment	7.13	
(3) Post-termination detriment	7.17	
The decision in *Woodward v Abbey*		
National plc	7.17	
Outstanding issues as to the scope		
for post-termination detriment		
claims	7.22	
(4) Limitation of detriment claims		
to the employment field during		
employment	7.26	
D. **'Act or deliberate failure to act'**	7.27	
E. **Subjection by the employer**	7.34	
(1) *London Borough of Harrow v*		
Knight	7.34	
(2) Vicarious liability	7.36	
(3) Action by third parties	7.40	
F. **'On the ground that'**	7.44	
(1) Guidance in *Nagarajan* and *Khan*		
on the 'reason why' question	7.44	

(2) Distinction between the disclosure		
and the acts connected with or		
manner of the disclosure	7.56	
Conduct associated with the disclosure	7.57	
Breach of confidentiality	7.66	
Distinction between the disclosure and		
the manner of the disclosure	7.68	
(3) Failure in the investigation of the		
subject matter of the disclosure	7.75	
Detriment	7.75	
Act or deliberate failure to act by the		
employer	7.75	
On the ground that	7.75	
(4) The burden of proof in relation		
to the 'reason why' question	7.76	
(5) Drawing inferences	7.82	
G. **Complaints to an employment**		
tribunal in claims of victimization	7.90	
(1) Statutory grievance procedures and		
whistleblowing claims	7.90	
(2) Time limits in victimization cases	7.97	
An act extending over a period	7.100	
A series of similar acts or failures	7.102	

A. Section 47B ERA: Overview

PIDA inserted a new section 47B into Part V of ERA which is now in the following **7.01**
terms:

Protected disclosures
(1) A worker has the right not to be subjected to any detriment by any act, or any
deliberate failure to act, by his employer done on the ground that the worker has
made a protected disclosure.

141

(2) . . . this section does not apply where—
  (a) the worker is an employee, and
  (b) the detriment in question amounts to dismissal (within the meaning of Part X).
(3) For the purposes of this section, and of sections 48 and 49 so far as relating to this section, 'worker,' 'worker's contract,' 'employment' and 'employer' have the extended meaning given by section 43K.

7.02 Section 47B ERA therefore provides that a worker has the right not to be subjected to any detriment as a result of any act, or any deliberate failure to act, by his employer done on the ground that the worker has made a protected disclosure. As explained by Mummery LJ in *Pinnington v Swansea City Council and another* [2005] ICR 685 (CA) at p 691, para 27, once it is established that there were protected disclosures, there are four further elements of the cause of action under section 47B ERA:

> It is a necessary ingredient of her cause of action under section 47B(1), first, that she was subjected to 'detriment,' secondly, she was subjected to detriment 'by any act, or any deliberate failure to act,' and, thirdly, that it was by the employer, and, fourthly, that it was on the ground that 'the worker has made a protected disclosure'.

7.03 We consider each of these steps in more detail below. They are consistent with, but further elucidate, the approach identified as appropriate by the EAT in an earlier case, *London Borough of Harrow v Knight* [2003] IRLR 140. Mr Recorder Underhill QC (at paragraph 5), emphasized that 'it is particularly important in victimization cases, which are still rather unfamiliar and require careful analysis, that a tribunal should, in reaching and explaining its conclusions, set out the elements necessary to establish liability and consider them separately and in turn'. The EAT identified three steps once protected disclosures had been identified, namely that:

1. the worker has suffered an identifiable detriment or detriments;
2. there has been an act or deliberate failure to act by the respondent by which the worker has been subjected to the identified detriment or detriments. This therefore focuses on the link between the detriment and the act or omission; and
3. the act or deliberate failure to act was 'done on the ground that' the worker made the protected disclosure or disclosures. This focuses on the reason for the act or omission.

This was cited with approval in *Flintshire County Council v Sutton* (EAT/1082/02, 1 July 2003) at paragraph 26. The four step approach in *Pinnington* essentially separates out two issues implicit in the second step of the *Harrow v Knight* approach.

7.04 Paragraph 47B(2) was amended by the Employment Relations Act 1999 to reflect the repeal of provisions for contracting out of unfair dismissal protection in relation to fixed-term contracts. As originally enacted subpara (2) made provision that where an employee was on a fixed-term contract of more than a year and had agreed in accordance with the then s197 ERA to waive any claim for unfair dismissal if the contract was not renewed, the employee could bring a claim under s47B that his contract was not renewed because he had made a protected disclosure.

Section 47B ERA protects employees[1] from action other than dismissal and pro-   **7.05**
tects other workers (who cannot be unfairly dismissed—within the meaning of the term as used in ERA) from any form of victimization, including the termination of their contract. By s47B(2) an employee who is dismissed cannot claim under this section but must claim under ss103A and 105(6) of ERA. Claims by an employee in respect of a dismissal are considered below. There is no reason why an employee cannot claim both in respect of victimization before dismissal and in respect of the dismissal itself, and indeed this is often done.

There is no qualifying period for protection under s47B ERA, nor is the right   **7.06**
excluded by any upper age limit.

B. Deployment of the pre-existing models of protection

Prior to PIDA, Part V ERA provided a set of categories in which employees, and   **7.07**
in some cases workers, had a right not to suffer detriment. The addition of protection in relation to protected disclosures has been part of a trend towards substantially expanding the categories in which this protection applies. When the ERA was enacted the protection encompassed employees who had been designated to carry out health and safety duties or were members of health and safety committees (s44), those who declined to work on a Sunday (s45 ERA), trustees of occupational pension schemes (s46 ERA) and employee representatives (s47). In addition to the protected disclosure provisions it has now been expanded to include victimization in relation to jury service (s43M); working time (s45A); employees exercising the right to time off work for study or training (s47A); leave for family and domestic reasons (s47C); tax credits (s47D); and flexible working (s47E). For each of the categories of protection in Part V, s48 ERA sets out common provisions in relation to enforcement and s49 ERA sets out common provisions for remedies, subject to specific provision in relation to compensation in dismissal cases covered by s103A ERA.

---

[1] And ex-employees, together with ex-workers. See paras 7.17 to 7.21 and discussion of the Court of Appeal's decision in *Woodward v Abbey National plc* [2006] IRLR 677.

7.08 The original model for this mechanism was the forerunner of what is now s146 of the Trade Union and Labour Relations (Consolidation) Act 1992 (TULRCA). The formula initially used in that context gave employees the right not to have 'action short of dismissal' taken against them for the purposes of preventing or deterring them from being or seeking to become a member of an independent trade union, or penalizing them for so doing. However in Part V ERA the protection is instead framed as the 'right not to be subjected to any detriment as an individual by any act, or any deliberate failure to act' on specified grounds, including on the ground that the worker has made a protected disclosure. This is also the formula which has since been adopted in s146 TULRCA[2] following the decision in *Associated Newspapers Limited v Wilson; Associated British Ports v Palmer* [1995] ICR 406 HL to the effect that the previous formula did not cover omissions.

7.09 Helpful guidance as to the approach to s47B ERA, and the enforcement and remedy provisions, can therefore be drawn from cases in the other categories of protection in Part V ERA and on s146 TULRCA. This is however subject to the caveat that the phrase 'action short of dismissal', formerly found in the old s146 TULRCA, is an inadequate description of the entitlement under s47B in two important respects. First it does not cover deliberate omissions to act. Second it carries the implication that the focus is only on an event up to but not including dismissal itself. However the s47B entitlement also covers post-termination detriment. We consider further the demarcation between dismissal and detriment cases in Chapter 9 at paragraphs 9.42 to 9.46.

7.10 In addition, guidance as to the meaning of s47B ERA is to be drawn from long-standing anti-discrimination legislation. Both the Sex Discrimination Act 1975 (s6(2)) and the Race Relations Act 1976 (s4(2)), as well as subsequent anti-discrimination legislation, provide that it is unlawful to discriminate, in the manner prohibited by that legislation, by dismissing an employee 'or subjecting him to any other detriment'.

C. Meaning of 'detriment'

(1) The Khan *and* Shamoon *guidance*

7.11 The meaning of 'detriment' has been considered by the House of Lords in two decisions in the contexts of sex and race discrimination or victimization. The principles

---

[2] As amended by Sch 2 of the Employment Relations Act 1999.

to be drawn from those cases were summarized by Elias J in *Moyhing v Barts and London NHS Trust* [2006] IRLR 860 (EAT), in the context of a sex discrimination claim, as follows:

> ... In *Chief Constable of West Yorkshire Police v Khan* [2001] UKHL 48; [2001] ICR 1065, a case of victimisation discrimination, Lord Hoffmann observed (para 53):
>
>> 'Being subject to a detriment ... is an element in the statutory cause of action additional to being treated "less favourably" which forms part of the definition of discrimination. A person may be treated less favourably and yet suffer no detriment. But, bearing in mind that the employment tribunal has jurisdiction to award compenzation for injured feelings, the courts have given the concept of the term "detriment" a wide meaning. In *Ministry of Defence v Jeremiah* [1980] ICR 13, 31 Brightman LJ said that "a detriment exists if a reasonable worker would or might take the view that the [treatment] was in all the circumstances to his detriment". Mr Khan plainly did take that view ... and I do not think that, in his state of knowledge at the time, he can be said to have been unreasonable.'
>
> A similarly broad analysis was adopted in *Shamoon v Chief Constable of Royal Ulster Constabulary* [2003] UKHL 11; [2003] ICR 337. The Northern Ireland Court of Appeal in that case had held, following a decision of the Employment Appeal Tribunal in *Lord Chancellor v Coker* [2001] ICR 507 that in order for there to be a detriment there had to be some physical or economic consequence arising as a result of the discrimination which was material and substantial. The House of Lords rejected that approach. Lord Hope said this (paras 34–35):
>
>> 'The statutory cause of action which the applicant has invoked in this case is discrimination in the field of employment. So the first requirement if the disadvantage is to qualify as a "detriment" within the meaning of article 8(2)(b), is that it has arisen in that field. The various acts and omissions mentioned in article 8(2)(a) are all of that character and so are the words "dismissing her" in section 8(2)(b). The word "detriment" draws this limitation on its broad and ordinary meaning from its context and from the words with which it is associated. *Res noscitur a sociis*. As May LJ put it in *De Souza v Automobile Association* [1986] ICR 514, 522G, the court or Tribunal must find that by reason of the act or acts complained of a reasonable worker would or might take the view that he had thereby been disadvantaged in the circumstances in which he had thereafter to work.
>>
>> But once this requirement is satisfied, the only limitation that can be read into the word is that indicated by Brightman LJ. As he put it in *Ministry of Defence v Jeremiah* [1980] ICR 13, 30, one must take all the circumstances into account. This is a test of materiality. Is the treatment of such a kind that a reasonable worker would or might take the view that in all circumstances it was to his detriment? An unjustified sense of grievance cannot amount to "detriment": *Barclays Bank plc v Kapur (No 2)* [1995] IRLR 87. But contrary to the view that was expressed in *Lord Chancellor v Coker* [2001] ICR 507 on which the Court of Appeal relied, it is not necessary to demonstrate some physical or economic consequence.'
>
> Lord Hutton (para 91) and Lord Scott (paras 103–105) both expressly approved this analysis. Lord Scott said that 'if the victim's opinion that the treatment was to his or her detriment was a reasonable one to hold, that ought ... to suffice'.

7.12 We draw attention to the following points:

(a) We suggest that the meaning to be given to 'detriment' in the context of protected disclosures is at least as wide as that in the context of race and sex discrimination. This is supported by the decision of the Court of Appeal in
Woodward v Abbey National plc.[3] In the context of considering whether s47B
protection covered detriments imposed after the termination of employment,
Ward LJ (with whom Maurice Kay LJ and Wilson LJ agreed), observed that:

> Victimization is established by showing inter alia the discrimination of the employee
> by 'subjecting him to any other detriment'—see s6(2) of the 1975 Act and s4(2) of the
> 1976 and 1995 Acts. Under s47B of the ERA a worker likewise has the right 'not to
> be subjected to any detriment'. Although the language and the framework might be
> slightly different, it seems to me that the four Acts are dealing with the same concept,
> namely, protecting the employee from detriment being done to him in retaliation for
> his or her sex, race, disability or whistle-blowing. This is made explicit by the long title
> to the Public Interest Disclosure Act 1998, which is, as I have already set out:
>
> > 'An Act to protect individuals who make certain disclosures of information in the
> > public interest; to allow such individuals to bring action *in respect of victimisation*.'
> > (Emphasis added)
>
> All four Acts are, therefore, dealing with victimisation in one form or another. If the
> common theme is victimisation, it would be odd indeed if the same sort of act could
> be victimisation for one purpose, but not for the other.

(b) There is some scope for a submission that the term 'detriment' has an even
broader meaning in the context of s47B than in the context of race and sex
discrimination legislation. As noted above (in the comments of Lord Hoffmann
in *Chief Constable of West Yorkshire Police v Khan*), in the area of sex and race
discrimination legislation, the statutory context demands that 'detriment' be
attributed a meaning distinct from 'less favourable treatment.' There is no
equivalent requirement in the context of s47B ERA. This was not in issue in
Woodward itself.

(c) The limitation identified by Lord Hope, that the detriment must arise in the
employment field, does not mean that the detriment must be imposed *during* employment: *Woodward*. Similarly, although Lord Hope in *Shamoon*
made reference to detriment involving the worker being 'disadvantaged in
the circumstances in which he had thereafter to work', this is properly to be
regarded as only one example of a detriment. It also encompasses a detriment
imposed by the employer *after* the employment has terminated, such as in
relation to the provision of a reference. We consider below in more detail the
implications of the decision in *Woodward*, and the scope of the limitation to
detriment in the employment field, both (a) in relation to the post-termination

---

[3] See above n 1.

of employment protection and (b) in relation to detriments covered during the employment relationship.

(d) The term 'detriment' has a wide meaning. It merely means putting at a disadvantage (*Ministry of Defence v Jeremiah* [1980] ICR 13 *per* Brandon LJ at p 26). There is no requirement that there must be some physical or economic consequence for there to be a detriment. Instead there is a test of materiality. As emphasized in the above observations in *Khan* and *Shamoon*, this involves an objective element. The tribunal must consider whether in all the circumstances, including the worker's state of knowledge at the time, a reasonable worker would or might take the view that in all the circumstances the act or deliberate failure to act was to his or her detriment.

(e) In *de Souza v Automobile Association* [1986] ICR 514, the Court of Appeal held (at 524) that there would only be a detriment if both the employee was, and a reasonable employee would be, disadvantaged. The test is an objective one by reference to a reasonable person in the shoes of the particular worker. Thus if a worker is the subject of banter for having made a protected disclosure, notwithstanding that a hypothetical reasonable worker might find the banter offensive, there would not be a detriment if the particular worker was not at all bothered by the banter. The perspective of the particular worker is highly material to whether the act is detrimental or disadvantageous at all. Conversely if the worker is subjected to objectively detrimental treatment, such as being treated with unwarranted suspicion by the employer, this might be a detriment even though the worker is unaware of this treatment. This is apparent from the decision in *Garry v Ealing LBC* [2001] IRLR 681 where the Court of Appeal held, in the context of the Race Relations Act 1976, that a worker had been subjected to a detriment when an investigation into her activities was continued longer than an ordinary investigation would have been. This was held to be a detriment even in relation to the period during which the claimant was unaware that the investigation was going on. As explained by Pill LJ (at para 29):

> the fact that the appellant was unaware at the time of what was going on (if that be the case) does not provide the respondents with a defence if, on analysis, their treatment of her was to her detriment. In the circumstances, it was no less a detriment in that for a time she was unaware of it. The adage relied on by the Employment Appeal Tribunal that 'ignorance is bliss' is in the present circumstances misplaced. The analogy drawn by the Employment Appeal Tribunal with an Inland Revenue investigation is also misplaced. That type of investigation is one confidential to the Revenue and the member of the public concerned. The present investigation was known to officers of the council whose attitude to the appellant and her work was important in the context of her present and future employment with the council.

(f) In *Shamoon*, the House of Lords rejected the requirement that the detriment must be 'substantial.' Notwithstanding this, in *Moyhing*, it was accepted on behalf of the claimant, with apparent approval by the EAT (at paragraph 20) that a *de minimis* difference in treatment could not amount to a relevant detriment. The EAT noted that this exception was recognized in *Jeremiah*, approving on this ground only the earlier decision of the Court of Appeal in *Peake v Automotive Products Limited* [1977] ICR 968.[4] In relation to a s47B claim in *Pinnington v The City and County of Swansea and another* [2004] EWCA Civ 1180, on an application for permission to appeal, a panel of the Court of Appeal (Keane LJ and Neuberger LJ) also contemplated a *de minimis* exception in a post-*Shamoon* case. However the substantive appeal was upheld on other grounds without considering it necessary to determine if there was a detriment ([2005] ICR 685 at paras 46, 47). A *de minimis* exception does not sit easily with the emphasis in *Shamoon*, that once the detriment was established as being in the employment field, the only limitation was one of materiality in the sense explained by Lord Hope (above). Nor, in the light of the objective element in the test for detriment, and the opportunity to reflect lower levels of detriment in the size of any award for injury to feelings, is there any necessity to construe the legislation so as to exclude detriments which might be regarded as trivial or *de minimis*.

(g) Lord Hope stated in *Shamoon* that 'an unjustified sense of grievance will not suffice' as a detriment. This was applied by the employment tribunal in *Pinnington*. The claimant made disclosures including that the school in which she was employed was implementing a policy of non-resuscitation of terminally ill children at the school. An inquiry was ordered by the local council which found no basis for the allegations. The claimant fell ill, but the tribunal held that the claimant had an 'unjustified sense of grievance' and if that caused her ill health it could not amount to a detriment for the purposes of PIDA. The decision was ultimately upheld on other grounds by the Court of Appeal, as we discuss below (paragraph 7.30).

However the guidance that an unjustified sense of grievance is not covered should not be elevated to a principle which obscures the statutory language. It is intended to be an application of the principle that there is no detriment if a reasonable person in the position of the worker would not consider himself to have been disadvantaged: see *Barclays Bank Plc v Kapur (No. 2)* [1995] IRLR 87 (CA) at paras 43–44. It is not intended to connote that detrimental

---

[4] See also *Porcelli v Strathclyde Council* [1986] ICR 564 (Ct of Session), referring (at p 573H) to gender-based unpleasant conduct being sex discrimination unless the harm inflicted was 'a mere scratch'. Also in *Jiad v Byford* [2003] EWCA Civ 135 the Court of Appeal accepted that a trivial disadvantage would not suffice. But this was in the context of following the test in *Lord Chancellor v Coker* in the Court of Appeal [2002] ICR 321—since rejected in *Shamoon*—that the detriment must be substantial and material.

treatment does not constitute a detriment if the worker ought to have appreciated that the treatment was justified. This is confirmed by the guidance provided by the EAT in *Moyhing v Barts and London NHS Trust* [2006] IRLR 860. The claimant was a male student nurse who complained of discrimination in that male nurses had to be chaperoned when carrying out intimate procedures on female patients, whereas the same did not apply where female nurses carried out intimate procedures on male patients. The claimant felt that this stigmatized him as being someone who was likely to attack a female patient, but the ET held that there was no detriment because there was good reason for the chaperoning policy and the claimant's objection to it was unjustified. The EAT however held that there was a detriment, and that the ET's approach effectively introduced a defence of justification to direct discrimination. The objective element in the test of detriment required consideration of whether the claimant could reasonably have perceived the treatment to be detrimental. The reason for the treatment was a relevant circumstance because the perception of a reasonable employee will often be affected by this. But ultimately, however justified the respondent's policy, it was not unreasonable for the claimant to feel demeaned and irritated by it.

This reasoning is potentially of significance in protected disclosure cases. Suppose, modifying the facts in *Pinnington*, a potential protected disclosure is made which raises issues as to an apparent breach of confidentiality. It might be reasonable for the employer to investigate and, further, in order to facilitate the investigation, it might be reasonable for the worker to be suspended on full pay for a short period during the investigation. In considering whether a reasonable worker would regard this as a detriment, one of the relevant circumstances is that a reasonable worker might recognize the need to investigate and therefore not regard the suspension as indicating a lack of trust on the part of the employer. Yet the worker might still reasonably consider that being suspended is detrimental, perhaps on the basis that it might lead to stigma among colleagues. It does not follow from the fact that the suspension might be justified that it cannot amount to subjecting the worker to a detriment.

(h) The EAT decision in *Moyhing* indicates the need, in assessing whether a reasonable worker could consider treatment to be detrimental, to take into account all the circumstances. In addition to what the worker ought to realize as to any justification for treatment, an important factor might be whether the worker is treated any less favourably than others. An example of this is the ET decision in *Chattenton v City of Sunderland City Council* Case No. 6402938/99, 18 July 2000 (Newcastle upon Tyne) (see Appendix 9 case no. 29) where the claimant employee disclosed his concern over the downloading of pornography from the internet onto a shared computer that he used. He went on holiday and when he returned found that his office was locked and he had been moved to an open-plan office. The respondents explained that they had changed working practices to prevent access to the internet and porn sites; the change to open-plan work applied to everyone. The tribunal found that the decision to move the claimant was not a disadvantage as everyone was treated the same.

(2) The threat of a detriment

7.13 The legislation does not expressly cover threats of detrimental treatment. But it is unlikely that there could be a threat of a detriment which does not itself amount to a detriment. That certainly seems to have been the Government's intention. Speaking on behalf of the Government during the Lords Committee stage of the Public Interest Disclosure Bill, Lord Haskell explained that:

> an employee who has made a disclosure to his employer could be threatened with relocation to a remote branch of a company, for instance, where promotion prospects are poorer. That kind of threat is a detriment and even though the worker can be assured that the employer could not lawfully carry out the threat, the fear of the threat may well amount to detrimental action. Any threat which puts a worker at a disadvantage constitutes in itself detrimental action.[5]

7.14 Lord Haskell further explained the Government's reluctance specifically to include reference to threats of detriment. Such a provision would have cast doubt on whether threats were covered in the other cases (contained in Part V ERA) where there is protection against suffering a detriment.

7.15 During the debate[6] Lord Wedderburn had expressed a concern that the then recent decision of the Court of Appeal in *Mennell v Newell & Wright (Transport Contractors) Ltd* [1997] IRLR 519 would lead to a construction of the proposed legislation that would not regard threats of a detriment as detriments. However this case related to a claim of dismissal for asserting a statutory right. In relation to that cause of action, it was held that there could be no claim until the statutory right had been asserted. The closer parallel is therefore with a separate point which was made during the same debate: that threats to prevent disclosures being made would not be covered as there would not be protection until the disclosure was made. In response it was said that whilst what was merely in somebody's head could not be covered, if it was mentioned to someone in the position of employer that a disclosure was going to be made, that would itself constitute a disclosure. It was accepted that, whilst it might be possible to imagine cases not covered, ordinarily a disclosure made to the employer or via internal procedures was likely to get through rather than merely be attempted.[7]

---

[5] Lord Haskell, *Hansard* HL, 5 June 1998, col. 634.
[6] Lord Wedderburn, *Hansard* HL, 5 Jun 1998, col. 631.
[7] Lord Haskell, *Hansard* HL, 5 June 1998, col. 635.

This did not fully meet the concern however. Because of the need to establish the **7.16** requisite reasonable belief for a qualifying disclosure, there might in some cases be a stage where an employee is engaged in conducting his own investigations in relation to a suspected relevant failure. If an employer got wind of this and made threats to discourage the worker from continuing the investigation or making allegations arising from those investigations, this would not be covered if the worker has not yet made a disclosure or does not yet have the requisite reasonable belief for a qualifying disclosure. Consistently with this, in *Bolton School v Evans* [2006] IRLR 500 the EAT commented (at para 68) that:

> putting it simply, it seems to us that the law protects the disclosure of information which the employee reasonably believes tends to demonstrate the kind of wrongdoing, or anticipated wrongdoing, which is covered by section 43B. It does not protect the actions of the employee which are directed to establishing or confirming the reasonableness of that belief. The protection is for the whistleblower who reasonably believes, to put it colloquially if inaccurately, that something is wrong, not the investigator who seeks either to establish that it is wrong or to show that his concerns are reasonable.

(3) Post-termination detriment

The decision in *Woodward v Abbey National plc*

As noted above in the guidance set out in *Shamoon*[8] as to the meaning of detri- **7.17** ment, it was identified that the detriment must be 'in the employment field'. This analysis was based on considerations material to the specific statutory context of the Sex Discrimination Act 1975 and the Race Relations Act 1976. The material provisions are contained in a part of those Acts headed 'Discrimination in the Employment Field,' and the reference to detriment comes at the end of a series of provisions identifying unlawful discriminatory treatment in relation to offering employment and during employment. Notwithstanding this, parallel reasoning can properly be applied to s47B ERA. This provision is contained in a part of the ERA headed 'Protection from Suffering Detriment *in Employment*' (our emphasis). This connotes a similar limitation to detriment in the employment field.

However in *Woodward v Abbey National plc*[9] the Court of Appeal concluded **7.18** (*per* Ward LJ at para 64) that there could be a detriment imposed after the end of the employment contract. The term 'in employment' was properly to be construed as meaning 'in the employment relationship' and that this could survive the termination of the contract itself. The claimant claimed that some years after the termination of her employment, she was caused detriment by her ex-employers,

---

[8] See above, para 7.11.
[9] See above, n 1.

including by their not providing a reference for her due to her having been a whistleblower. She made claims pursuant to s48 (and s47B) of ERA 1996. The Court of Appeal[10] reversed the EAT[11] and its own earlier decision in *Fadipe v Reed Nursing Personnel* [2005] ICR 1760 holding that, although it was not expressly overruled, *Fadipe* could not stand with the decision of the House of Lords in *Rhys-Harper v Relaxion Group plc* [2003] ICR 867. In *Fadipe* s44 ERA, which is in the same terms as s47(B), had been held not to apply where the alleged detriment was inflicted and suffered after the employee had ceased to be employed.

7.19　Ward LJ, giving the only substantive judgment, rejected the primary submission for the employer that *Rhys-Harper* had no application at all to claims under the ERA because different statutes were in play. The context was not different. In the discrimination statutes victimization was established by showing *inter alia* the discrimination of the employee by 'subjecting him to any other detriment'—(s6(2) of the Sex Discrimination Act 1975 and s4(2) of the Race Relations Act 1976 and Disability Discrimination Act 1995). Under s47B of the ERA a worker likewise had the right 'not to be subjected to any detriment'. Although the language and the framework were slightly different, the four Acts were dealing with the same concept, namely, protecting the employee from detriment being done to him in retaliation for his or her sex, race, disability, related protected act or whistleblowing. This is made explicit by the long title to PIDA, which was to allow whistleblowers 'to bring action *in respect of victimisation*'. It would be odd if the same sort of act could be victimization for one purpose but not for the other. Second, as Lord Nicholls had said, no sensible distinction could be drawn between giving a reference the day before employment ends and giving a reference the day after. Further, in *Fadipe* Mummery LJ was clearly confining the 'employment relationship' to the duration of the contract and that could not stand with the wider scope of an employment relationship given to the concept in *Rhys-Harper*.

7.20　This conclusion was supported by the general definition in s230 ERA[12] which covered the whole spectrum of the ERA. Thus 'worker' means not only an individual who currently works under a contract of employment but one who formerly worked under such a contract. Although a provision framed in this way served the purpose of giving a former employee the right to bring his claim under s48 or a claim for unfair dismissal, it did not follow that this is its *only* purpose and if that was the intention one would have expected the point to have been more

---

[10] [2006] EWCA Civ 822.

[11] [2005] ICR 1750.

[12] '(1) In this Act 'employee' means an individual who has entered into or works under (or, where the employment has ceased, worked under) a contract of employment.' And similarly for 'worker' in subsection 3.

clearly made in a provision explaining that a right accruing during the currency of a contract of employment can be enforced by the victim after the contract is at an end. Drafted as it was, it was an omnibus definition of 'employee, worker etc' and it was accordingly more likely that the legislature intended the purpose to be served and the meaning to be ascribed to take colour from the context of the section in which 'worker' appears. Under s47B 'worker,' in its ordinary meaning, was just as naturally to be construed as including a former employee.

The Court of Appeal emphasized that the underlying purpose of s47B would be **7.21** sold short by allowing the former employer to victimize his former employee with impunity and it made no sense at all to protect the current employee but not the former employee. If it was in the public interest to blow the whistle, then the whistleblower should be protected when he becomes victimized for doing so, whenever the retribution is exacted.

Outstanding issues as to the scope for post-termination detriment claims

Whilst establishing the principle that there could be a claim based on detriment **7.22** after the termination of employment, the Court of Appeal left a number of issues unresolved. Indeed it did not even proceed to decide whether the particular allegations and facts of *Woodward's* case would lead to a remedy being afforded to her. The reason for this was, first, that there had been no argument on this point, but second because of the diversity of the ways in which those constituting the majority in the House of Lords in *Rhys-Harper* had described the test. It was not appropriate to resolve this without determination of the facts in the case and without hearing argument on the facts.

The various tests suggested in *Rhys-Harper* in relation to whether relief should be **7.23** afforded after termination of employment were summarized by Ward LJ in *Woodward* (at para 53):

(1) for Lord Nicholls, the employment relationship triggered the employer's obligation not to discriminate in all the incidents of the employment relationship whenever they arise, provided the benefit in question arises between the employer or former employer as such and the employee or former employee as such (44, 45);

(2) for Lord Hope the test was whether there is still a continuation of the employment relationship (114, 115);

(3) for Lord Hobhouse the test was one of proximity: does the conduct complained about have a sufficient connection with the employment (139) or a substantive and proximate connection between the conduct complained of and the employment by the alleged discriminator (140);

(4) for Lord Rodger, one must look for a substantive connection between the discriminatory conduct and the employment relationship, with the former employer discriminating *qua* former employer (205);

(5) for Lord Scott, it depends on whether the relationship between employer and employee brought into existence when the employee entered into the employer's service is still in existence (200) or is still continuing notwithstanding the termination of the employment (204).

In other words Lord Hope and Lord Scott seem to tie the application of the Act to the continuance of the employment relationship whereas the majority look for a connection (variously described) between the former employee as such and the former employer as such.

7.24 Lord Nicholls (at para 45) further expanded in *Rhys-Harper* on his preferred test, explaining that:

to be an 'incident' of the employment relationship for this purpose the benefit in question must arise between employer or former employer as such and employee or former employee as such. A reference is a prime example. Further, save perhaps in exceptional circumstances which it is difficult to envisage, failure to provide a non-contractual benefit will not constitute a 'detriment', or discrimination in an opportunity to receive a 'benefit', within the meaning of the anti-discrimination legislation unless the non-contractual benefit in question is one which normally is provided, or would be provided, to others in comparable circumstances. This is so with regard to current employees. It is equally so with former employees. But I stress this is not to say that an employer's practice regarding current employees is to be treated as equally applicable to former employees. This is emphatically not so. The two situations are not comparable. What is comparable is the way the employer treats the claimant former employee and the normal way he treats or would treat other former employees in similar circumstances.

7.25 As this indicates, it is fairly clear that an employer who victimizes a whistleblower by declining to give an appropriate reference within a short period after the termination of employment would now be vulnerable to a claim. More remote claims will be problematic. Further, the Court of Appeal expressly left over the question as to whether the protected disclosure must precede the termination of employment.

(4) Limitation of detriment claims to the employment field during employment

7.26 The limitation of detriment claims to the employment field may also give rise to some issues pertinent to claims of detriment during the currency of an employment contract. Again, this involves consideration of what is encompassed within the employment field and what degree of connection is required between the disclosure and the employment relationship. Suppose for example that, in response to a worker's protected disclosure, his colleagues and managers continue to deal with him as normal at work but cold-shoulder him socially outside work.[13] Can it be

---

[13] See eg case number 43 in Appendix 9, *Fairhall v Safeway Stores plc* Case No. 2104468/2001, 12 June 2002.

said that this does not qualify as a detriment because it is outside the employment field? In the search for a demarcation between the employment field and the area outside that field, no doubt the courts will build on the various tests suggested in *Rhys-Harper* (see paras 7.23 and 7.24 above) albeit they were framed in relation to whether relief should be afforded after termination of employment.

D. 'Act or deliberate failure to act'

7.27 An employer subjects a worker to a detriment both by *acts* to the worker's detriment and also by *deliberately failing to act* so as to cause detriment. Examples would include refusing promotion, not giving a pay rise, disciplining the worker, singling the worker out for relocation or being denied facilities or training which would otherwise have been made available, provided in each case that the failure was 'deliberate.'

7.28 The requirement that the failure be 'deliberate' connotes that there must be a decision rather than merely an oversight leading to a failure to act. This is further indicated by the statutory context. First, this involves consideration of the reason for the failure to act. Second, s48(4)(b) ERA provides that 'a deliberate failure to act shall be treated as done when it was decided on'. However s48(4) ERA provides that:

> in the absence of evidence establishing the contrary, an employer shall be taken to decide on a failure to act when he does an act inconsistent with doing the failed act or, if he has done no such inconsistent act, when the period expires within which he might reasonably have been expected to do the failed act if it was to be done.

7.29 A prima facie case of a failure to act can therefore be made out in the absence of identifying a specific decision. But this is only 'in the absence of evidence establishing the contrary'. Thus, for example, where information leaks out of an investigation into a disclosure which embarrasses the worker who made the disclosure, prima facie a decision to leak the information is deemed to have been made when the information was leaked. But the employer might be able to show that the leak was due to an oversight or organizational error rather than a decision to disseminate the information. A similar scenario arose in *Harrow LBC v Knight*.[14] A complaint was made that the claimant suffered stress as a result of the way in which his protected disclosures were handled. There was a failure by the employer to keep the matter confidential, resulting in the claimant being cold-shouldered by colleagues. The failure by the employer to counteract the difficulties which this caused the claimant may have commenced prior to PIDA coming into force, but

---

[14] See above, para 7.03.

continued after this. However, the EAT emphasized (at para 12) that there was no finding that the failure to act was '"deliberate", as opposed to merely insensitive or careless'.[15]

7.30 The absence of an act or 'deliberate' failure to act was crucial to the Court of Appeal's reasoning in *Pinnington*.[16] Mrs Pinnington was a nurse at a special needs school. As noted above, from 1997 she made allegations that a policy of non-resuscitation of terminally ill children was being implemented at the school. An inquiry was ordered by the local council which found no basis for the allegations. Mrs Pinnington was away from work on certificated sick leave from 17 September 1997 to 31 March 1998, suffering from stress and anxiety. She returned to work for a short period between 31 March and 29 April 1998 but then went sick again and did not return prior to her dismissal. On 2 July 1998, that is after she had begun the second period away sick, she was suspended by the employer. This was for breach of confidence about records relating to children at the school. There was then a second inquiry. It was carried out by the governors following further complaints of the same kind that the claimant had made before: again it was found that there was no evidence of the policy of non-resuscitation of the kind the claimant alleged. Following a capability hearing (and thereafter an appeal) the claimant was dismissed with effect from 3 July 1999. PIDA only came into effect on the previous day, 2 July 1999.

7.31 The tribunal held that the dismissal of the claimant was fair and that the principal reason for the dismissal of the claimant was incapability due to illness. The reason for her dismissal was *not* (as she alleged) that she had made protected disclosures about the alleged policy of non-resuscitation. The tribunal also held that the employer was entitled to suspend the claimant in July 1998 because of disclosures she had made in breach of confidence. The tribunal identified, as the only relevant period in which detriment *could* have been suffered, the two days, 2 and 3 July 1999. No period earlier than that was relevant, because the protected disclosure provisions did not come into effect until 2 July 1999. Even in that short period the claimant was prevented by ill-health from going to work. It was not simply a question of her having been suspended and that suspension still being in force. She was unable to go to work because of her ill-health.

7.32 For Mrs Pinnington it was argued that there was a 'deliberate failure to act' by the employer after the PIDA provisions came into force on 2 July 1999, the deliberate failure being *not* terminating the suspension, which had been in force

---

[15] See also *Flintshire v Sutton* (EAT/1082/02, 1 July 2003) where a failure to support was due to 'perception of the Applicant as a problem because he had made the relevant protected disclosures' (see Appendix 7).

[16] See above, para 7.02.

since 2 July 1998. This was rejected by the Court of Appeal on the basis that whilst there was a failure to act, in the sense of the failure to terminate the suspension, this was not a *deliberate* failure. There was neither any evidence of a deliberate failure nor any basis upon which one could be inferred. There was no question of needing to make a decision because prior to 2 July 1999 the employers had already decided that they were going to dismiss her on grounds of incapability and it was unrealistic in those circumstances to expect that they should have considered, on 2 July, terminating the suspension.

Mummery LJ did say (at paragraph 45) that: **7.33**

> if she was to remain in employment, then I can see the argument that there might have been, I say no more than that, some duty on the part of the employers to revisit the question of continuing her original suspension in the light of the provisions relating to protected disclosure which had come into force on 2 July 1999. But that is not this case.

In context this was not a suggestion that there could be a deliberate failure to act in the absence of any decision having been made. Rather it was said in the context of considering whether there was any basis for inferring that a decision had been made.

E. Subjection by the employer

(1) London Borough of Harrow v Knight

The cause of action requires that something must be done or omitted to be done **7.34**
which subjects the worker to a detriment. This requirement was considered in *Harrow v Knight*.[17] Mr Knight, a technical officer in its environmental services department, made a report to the council's chief executive and director of finance, Mr Redmond, in accordance with the provisions of the council's whistleblower procedures, raising concerns that his immediate superior might have been complicit in breaches of regulations by a business that was under investigation. It was conceded by Harrow that this was a protected disclosure. Harrow had commenced an investigation into Mr Knight's allegation but this took a long time and whilst it was ongoing Mr Knight wrote several letters complaining of the time that was being taken and contending that he was being victimized because of his disclosure. Harrow did not reply to those letters and Mr Knight said that this had caused him to have a nervous breakdown. The tribunal found that that the exacerbation of Mr Knight's medical condition was 'related to the disclosure'. They accepted that he had suffered over the months, especially when his letters were

---

[17] See above, para 7.03.

ignored both by the chief executive and the investigators. He had suffered a detriment which was 'directly related to the protected disclosure that he has made'. The tribunal concluded that the complaint succeeded. The appeal succeeded in part because the tribunal had not properly applied the test that any detriment be 'on the ground that' the worker had made a protected disclosure. We discuss this further below.[18] But the EAT also commented on the need to consider whether Mr Knight had been 'subjected to' the detriment by the employer.

7.35 The EAT noted that in some cases the doing of the act and the suffering of the detriment are essentially two sides of the same coin. This will be so, for example, where the detriment consists of being subject to disciplinary action by the employer. However this was not so in the present case. The alleged detriment was the claimant's ill health. It was therefore an important part of the analysis to identify the act or deliberate failure to act and on what basis this was said to have subjected the claimant to the detriment. The tribunal had failed to set this out and had instead asked simply whether Mr Knight suffered a detriment 'related to' his having made a protected disclosure; and found that 'the applicant's medical condition [was] related to the disclosure'. The EAT was however satisfied that in two respects—the failure by the chief executive to respond to his letters, and the failure to look after him—the tribunal had properly found that the claimant had been subjected to a detriment.[19]

(2) Vicarious liability

7.36 The victimization provisions of the ERA contain no equivalent of s41 of the Sex Discrimination Act.[20] Section 41(1) provides that anything done by a person in the course of his employment shall be treated for the purposes of that Act as done by the employer as well as him, whether or not it was done with the employer's knowledge or approval but that the employer has a defence if he proves that he has taken such steps as were reasonably practicable to prevent the employee from doing that act (s41(3)). The construction given by the Court of Appeal in *Jones v Tower Boot Co Limited* [1997] IRLR 168 is that the words 'course of employment' should be interpreted in the sense in which they are employed in everyday speech and not restrictively by reference to the principles laid down by case law for establishing an employer's vicarious liability for the torts committed by an employee.

---

[18] At paragraph 7.44ff.

[19] But the EAT followed the test in *Burton and Rhule v de Vere Hotels Limited* [1996] IRLR 596 which has subsequently been disapproved by the House of Lords: see para 7.42 below.

[20] Or the other discrimination statutes, eg s32 of the Race Relations Act 1976.

In PIDA cases it is not appropriate to ask whether the employer has taken such **7.37** steps as were reasonably practicable to prevent the employee from doing the act or acts in question by reason of the absence of those words (which could easily have been adopted) from the relevant provisions. We think it instead likely that the courts will apply the broad vicarious liability test in *Lister v Hesley Hall* [2001] 1 AC 215 (HL); that is whether there is a sufficient connection between the work the person was employed to do and the acts committed of which complaint was made (in that case the sexual abuse of boys by the warden of the boarding house). This principle was applied in the case of a statutory tort in *Majrowski v Guys & St Thomas NHS Trust* [2006] ICR 1199 (a case decided on the Protection from Harassment Act 1997).

Mr Majrowski claimed that his departmental manager, a Mrs Freeman, bullied **7.38** and intimidated him, but he sued their joint employers (not her). The employers said that the legislation did not impose vicarious liability. This argument was rejected. Lord Nicholls explained that although vicarious liability is a 'common law principle of strict no fault liability' (para 7), there is no basis for confining the principle to common law wrongs. The policy reasons underlying the principle were to facilitate compensation since employers were likely to be better placed financially than the wrongdoing employee, to spread the economic burden through insurance and higher prices and 'and importantly, imposing strict liability on employers encourages them to maintain standards of "good practice" by their employees'.[21] The breadth of application of vicarious liability principles was emphasized (*per* Lord Nicholls at para 10):

> With these policy considerations in mind, it is difficult to see a coherent basis for confining the common law principle of vicarious liability to common law wrongs. The rationale underlying the principle holds good for equitable wrongs. The rationale also holds good for a wrong comprising a breach of a statutory duty or prohibition which gives rise to civil liability, provided always the statute does not expressly or impliedly indicate otherwise. A precondition of vicarious liability is that the wrong must be committed by an employee in the course of his employment. A wrong is committed in the course of employment only if the conduct is so closely connected with acts the employee is authorised to do that, for the purposes of the liability of the employer to third parties, the wrongful conduct may fairly and properly be regarded as done by the employee while acting in the course of his employment: see *Lister v Hesley Hall Ltd* [2002] 1 AC 215, 245, para 69, per Lord Millett, and *Dubai Aluminium Co Ltd v Salaam* [2002] UKHL 48, [2003] 2 AC 366, 377, para 23. If this prerequisite is satisfied the policy reasons underlying the common law principle are as much applicable to equitable wrongs and breaches of statutory obligations as they are to common law torts.

Lord Nicholls (at para 16) considered that statutes were presumptively to be con- **7.39** strued as imposing liability on employers *unless* the statutory provision expressly

---

[21] *Per* Lord Nicholls at para 9.

or impliedly excluded such liability. Lady Hale, Lord Carswell and Lord Brown (at para 81) all agreed with this presumption.[22] We suggest therefore that notwithstanding that the ERA contains no equivalent of s41(1) of the Sex Discrimination Act, the general vicarious liability principle applies to the statutory tort created by s47B ERA.

(3) Action by third parties

7.40   The section does not confer a right of action against any third party who victimizes the worker other than the employer (as widely defined by the statute). As such there may not be a claim under the Act against clients of the employer (unless that third party comes within the extended definition of employer in s43K(2)). Nor can a prospective employer be liable for discriminating against a whistleblower by declining to employ him or her on that ground. The Act does not provide protection against a refusal to offer employment. As such a prospective employer who declines to employ a whistleblower by reason of the whistleblowing can do so with impunity. A whistleblower may therefore still run the risk that if he/she speaks out then his/her future job prospects will be damaged. The failure to offer protection against this contingency contrasts with the position under discrimination law in relation to sex, race and disability.[23]

7.41   This may be compared with the position in Australia. Several states provide that reprisals for making a public interest disclosure is a tort or criminal offence or in some cases both, as in Queensland's Whistleblowers Protection Act 1994 and the Australian Capital Territory's Public Interest Disclosure Act 1994.[24]

7.42   In some circumstances it may be possible to attribute liability to the employer for the failure of the employer to protect the worker against such action by others for which he is not liable on ordinary principles of vicarious liability. However the scope for this has been substantially restricted following the disapproval of the decision in *Burton and Rhule v de Vere Hotels* [1996] IRLR 596 (EAT). In that case the EAT expressed the view that an employer subjects an employee to a detriment if it causes or allows the detriment to occur in circumstances where it can control whether it happens or not. *Burton* was subsequently disapproved by the House of

---

[22] At paragraphs 72, 78 and 81.

[23] 'Providing Rights for Whistleblowers: Would an Anti-Discrimination Model be More Effective?' Lewis, ILJ Vol. 34 Number 3 September 2005 p 239 referring to s6 of the Sex Discrimination Act 1975. See also s4 of the Race Relations Act 1976 and s4 of the Disability Discrimination Act 1995.

[24] See further in relation to the approach in Australia, David Lewis, 'Whistleblowing statutes in Australia: is it time for a new agenda?' [2004] Deakin Law Review Vol. 8 no 2 pp 318–334.

Lords in *Macdonald v Advocate General for Scotland* and *Pearce v Governing Body of Mayfield Secondary School* [2003] IRLR 512 and is no longer good law. It would be necessary to establish that there was an act or deliberate failure to act by the employer to prevent the action by the third party or to protect the worker from it, and that this act or deliberate failure to act was on the grounds of the protected disclosure.

However if an employer does fail to take reasonable steps to protect a whistleblow- **7.43** ing employee from consequential adverse action by others, and this exacerbates the consequences of a breach by the employer, the failure to act may lead to the employer being saddled with the consequences of this failure. This is illustrated by *The Trustees of Mama East African Women's Group v Dobson* [25] where the tribunal was concerned with a claim by a whistleblowing teacher. The employer submitted that the compensation should be capped to take account of the fact that there had been a loss of confidence by the students in the claimant and accordingly the claimant could not have carried on teaching anyway. The employment tribunal disagreed. The tribunal's conclusion was that, assuming that the respondent's students were not prepared to be taught by the claimant, then that situation was itself caused by the respondent's mishandling of the inquiry following the claimant's disclosure. That situation was unlikely to have arisen if the respondent had dealt with the matter properly. Even if it had occurred, it would in any event have been for the employer to manage the situation. The employer would have had a duty to protect the claimant from suffering any detriment because a disclosure had been made. The EAT agreed that to allow the employer's submission would be to allow the employer to save itself money on compensation by relying upon its own wrongful acts: that could not be correct.

F. 'On the ground that'

(1) Guidance in Nagarajan and Khan on the 'reason why' question

In order to establish victimization, it must be shown that the detriment was **7.44** inflicted 'on the ground that' the worker made a protected disclosure. The reason is thus crucial and it is also necessary to stress that the reason and causation are to be distinguished, albeit the two concepts are often not differentiated properly.

The phrase 'on the ground that' involves a consideration of the reasons, whether **7.45** conscious or unconscious, for the act or deliberate failure to act by which the worker was subjected to a detriment. This in turn requires consideration of the

---

[25] EAT/0219/05/ & UKEAT/0220/05/TM, 23 June 2005.

mental processes which led to the act or failure to act. The leading guidance was set out by the House of Lords in *Chief Constable of West Yorkshire Police v Khan*[26] and *Nagarajan v London Regional Transport* [1999] ICR 877 (HL), in the context of victimization under the Race Relations Act 1976. This statute contained different language—the requirement that treatment be 'on racial grounds' for the purposes of direct race discrimination, and in relation to victimization that detrimental treatment be 'by reason that' the person victimized had done a protected act. But the guidance in *Khan* and *Nagarajan* has subsequently been followed in several protected disclosure cases.[27]

7.46 In *Khan* Lord Nicholls (at p 1072 at para 29) explained that:

> contrary to views sometimes stated, the third ingredient ('by reason that') does not raise a question of causation as that expression is usually understood. Causation is a slippery word, but normally it is used to describe a legal exercise. From the many events leading up to the crucial happening, the court selects one or more of them which the law regards as causative of the happening. Sometimes the court may look for the 'operative' cause, or the 'effective' cause. Sometimes it may apply a 'but for' approach. For the reasons I sought to explain in *Nagarajan v London Regional Transport* [1999] ICR 877, 884–885, a causation exercise of this type is required either by s1(1)(a) or s2. The phrases 'on racial grounds' and 'by reason that' denote a different exercise: why did the alleged discriminator act as he did? Unlike causation, this is a subjective test. Causation is a legal conclusion. The reason why a person acted as he did is a question of fact.

7.47 Lords Hoffman and Hutton agreed with the speech of Lord Nicholls. Lord Scott also agreed (at p 1083). He also commented (at para 77) that the test was not one of strict causation, and that the words 'by reason that' suggested that 'it is the real reason; the *causa causans*, the motive, for the treatment complained of that must be identified'.

7.48 In his speech in *Khan* Lord Nicholls drew upon and clarified the guidance he gave in *Nagarajan*. Addressing the role of consideration of the mental processes leading to a decision, in *Nagarajan* Lord Nicholls had explained (at 884) that:

> to be within section 1(1)(a) the less favourable treatment must be on racial grounds. Thus, in every case it is necessary to inquire why the complainant received less favourable treatment. This is the crucial question. Was it on grounds of race? Or was it for some other reason, for instance, because the complainant was not so well qualified for the job? Save in obvious cases, answering the crucial question will call for some consideration of the mental processes of the alleged discriminator. Treatment, favourable or unfavourable, is a consequence which follows from a decision. Direct evidence of

---

[26] See above, para 7.11.

[27] *Aspinall v MSI Mech Forge Limited* (EAT/ 891/01, 25 July 2002 (following Lord Scott in *Khan*)), *Harrow v Knight*, above, para 7.03, *Bolton School v Evans* above, para 7.16 and *Felter v Cliveden Petroleum Company* (EAT/0533/05, 9 March 2006).

a decision to discriminate on racial grounds will seldom be forthcoming. Usually the grounds of the decision will have to be deduced, or inferred, from the surrounding circumstances.

The crucial question just mentioned is to be distinguished sharply from a second and different question: if the discriminator treated the complainant less favourably on racial grounds, why did he do so? The latter question is strictly beside the point when deciding whether an act of racial discrimination occurred.

The focus on mental processes does not however exclude consideration of sub-   **7.49** conscious motivation. As Lord Nicholls explained in *Nagarajan* (at 885–886):

> I turn to the question of subconscious motivation. All human beings have precon-ceptions, beliefs, attitudes and prejudices on many subjects. It is part of our make-up. Moreover, we do not always recognise our own prejudices. Many people are unable, or unwilling, to admit even to themselves that actions of theirs may be racially motivated. An employer may genuinely believe that the reason why he rejected an applicant had nothing to do with the applicant's race. After careful and thorough investigation of a claim members of an employment tribunal may decide that the proper inference to be drawn from the evidence is that, whether the employer realised it at the time or not, race was the reason why he acted as he did. It goes without saying that in order to justify such an inference the tribunal must first make findings of primary fact from which the inference may properly be drawn. Conduct of this nature by an employer, when the inference is legitimately drawn, falls squarely within the language of section 1(1)(a). The employer treated the com-plainant less favourably on racial grounds. Such conduct also falls within the purpose of the legislation. Members of racial groups need protection from conduct driven by unrecognised prejudice as much as from conscious and deliberate discrimination. Balcombe LJ adverted to an instance of this in *West Midlands Passenger Transport Executive v Jaquant Singh* [1988] ICR 614, 620C. He said that a high rate of failure to achieve promotion by members of a particular racial group may indicate that 'the real reason for refusal is a conscious or unconscious racial attitude which involves stereotyped assumptions' about members of the group.
>
> . . . Although victimization has a ring of conscious targeting, this is an insufficient basis for excluding cases of unrecognized prejudice . . .

Similarly in a protected disclosure case, it may be important for a tribunal to be   **7.50** alive to the possibility of subconscious as well as conscious motivation. The nature of stereotypical assumptions is of course likely to be different from the context of race discrimination, but may still be present. Thus it may be that the organizational culture is such as to indicate the presence of stereotypical assumptions that those who speak up or reveal wrongdoing are regarded as disloyal or troublemakers.[28]

---

[28] In the ET decision in *Lingard* (Appendix 9, case number 68) the tribunal appears to have concluded that two of the governors of the prison victimized the claimant subconsciously (see paragraphs (e) and (j) of the summary and paragraphs 15.6 and 15.11 of the ET's judgment).

7.51 Lord Nicholls also dealt in *Nagarajan* (at 886) with the appropriate approach where there are mixed reasons for action or a failure to act:

> Decisions are frequently reached for more than one reason. Discrimination may be on racial grounds even though it is not the sole ground for the decision. A variety of phrases, with different shades of meaning, have been used to explain how the legislation applies in such cases: discrimination requires that racial grounds were a cause, the activating cause, a substantial and effective cause, a substantial reason, an important factor. No one phrase is obviously preferable to all others, although in the application of this legislation legalistic phrases, as well as subtle distinctions, are better avoided so far as possible. If racial grounds or protected acts had a significant influence on the outcome, discrimination is made out.

7.52 Both *Nagarajan* and *Khan* were victimization cases where the 'by reason that' test applied, rather than cases of direct race discrimination where the 'on racial grounds' test applied. However in *Nagarajan* Lord Nicholls (at 886) explained that there was no difference between the approach to be taken:

> 'On racial grounds' in section 1(1)(a) and 'by reason that' in section 2(1) are interchangeable expressions in this context. The key question under section 2 is the same as under section 1(1)(a): why did the complainant receive less favourable treatment? The considerations mentioned above regarding direct discrimination under section 1(1)(a) are correspondingly appropriate under section 2. If the answer to this question is that the discriminator treated the person victimised less favourably by reason of his having done one of the acts listed in section 2(1) ('protected acts'), the case falls within the section. It does so, even if the discriminator did not consciously realise that, for example, he was prejudiced because the job applicant had previously brought claims against him under the Act.

7.53 The guidance in *Nagarajan* and *Khan* was applied in the context of s47B ERA, and further explained, in *Harrow v Knight*.[29] The tribunal applied a test of whether the detriment suffered by the claimant (ill-health) was 'related to' the protected disclosures. The EAT held that this betrayed a fatal misdirection since:

(a) Applying *Nagarajan* and *Khan* the tribunal was required to focus on the reason (conscious or unconscious) for the acts or deliberate failures to act of which complaint was made. It was necessary to show that the protected disclosures at least influenced the acts or failures to act by which the claimant was subjected to a detriment. It was not sufficient to show that 'but for' the act or omission the detriment would not have occurred.

(b) The 'related to' test imported an even lower threshold than the 'but for' test. It 'imports a different and much looser test than that required by the statute: it merely connotes some connection (not even necessarily causative) between the act done and the disclosure'.

---

[29] See above, para 7.03.

164

The difference between a 'but for' test of causation, and a focus on the (conscious   **7.54**
or subconscious) reasons for the act or deliberate failure to act, is significant. It presents potentially a substantially more difficult hurdle for the claimant. This was
starkly illustrated on the facts in *London Borough of Harrow v Knight*. Mr Knight
reported allegations that his line manager had condoned breaches of food regulations by a food business in the borough. The report also criticized a Mr Esom, the
chief environmental health officer, to whom his line manager reported. It took
nine months to produce a final report. In the interim Knight wrote to the chief
executive (Mr Redmond) expressing concerns as to the progress of the investigation and alleging victimization as a result of having made the original disclosure.
On the findings of the ET, the case turned on the allegation that Redmond had
failed to respond to letters from the claimant and that there had been a failure to look
after him so as to protect him from (amongst other things) being cold-shouldered
by colleagues including Esom, and that as a result he sustained an illness of a depressive nature. Referring to this, the EAT commented (at para 16) that:

> on any view the failure of Mr Redmond to answer Mr Knight's letters was *related to*
> the protected disclosure: after all, the disclosure was the fundamental subject matter
> of the letters and they would never have been written but for the fact that the disclosure had been made. Likewise any failure on the part of the Council to look after
> Mr Knight *related to* the disclosure: the awkward situation created by the disclosure was
> the very reason why he needed help. But that does not answer the question whether
> that formed part of the motivation (conscious or unconscious) of Mr Redmond or
> Mr Esom. Mr Redmond, for example, might have failed to answer the letters because
> he was annoyed by the original report and regarded whistleblowers as disloyal and a
> nuisance: that would indeed be a deliberate omission 'on the ground that' he had
> made the protected disclosure. But he might in principle equally have failed to do so
> for one of a number of other reasons.

Thus it would not be sufficient to say that but for the disclosures there would not   **7.55**
have been a train of events, including a failure to respond promptly to the claimant's
letters, which led to the claimant becoming unwell. It was necessary to consider
the reason for the failure to respond to his letters.

(2) Distinction between the disclosure and the acts connected with or manner of the disclosure

The need to focus on the reason for the act or deliberate omission alleged to give   **7.56**
rise to the detriment may raise some difficult issues as to whether a distinction can
be drawn between detrimental action 'on the ground' of a protected disclosure,
and on the ground of other things, for example:

(a) steps taken associated with the disclosure, including in the investigation leading to the disclosure;
(b) a breach of confidentiality in making the disclosure; and/or
(c) the manner or form of the disclosure (such as the use of intemperate language).

Conduct associated with the disclosure

7.57   PIDA protects disclosure: it does not protect the employee from the consequences of acts which might be regarded as connected to the disclosure but are not disclosures in themselves. This issue arose in *Bolton School v Evans* [2006] IRLR 500.[30] The claimant, a technology teacher at the respondent school, was concerned that the school's new computer system was insecure, and that information might be obtained by pupils in breach of the Data Protection Act, due to the school having adopted a single network for educational and administrative purposes. In order to test his concerns, and to demonstrate that they were well-founded, he hacked into confidential information on the network from a computer used by pupils in the technology department. He gave prior warning of his intentions to the member of staff designated by the headmaster as the individual to be contacted in relation to any concerns about the system (Mr Edmundson), and also to the Head of Computing. He also told them, and also the Headmaster, after he had hacked into the system. However he was disciplined, the headmaster having reached the decision that the claimant had deliberately hacked into the network. It was accepted that the claimant was acting in good faith and further that the claimant might have been justified in his belief that he was not being properly listened to in relation to his security concerns. A written warning was nevertheless issued. The claimant appealed but the appeal was dismissed. The claimant decided that his position was untenable and he resigned. He felt he had been victimized for highlighting security concerns and he was aggrieved that the school had focused on his conduct rather than tackling what he considered to be the much more important question of why the system had been established in what he perceived to be an insecure way.

7.58   Before the tribunal the claimant argued that the warning (a detriment) had been imposed contrary to s47B because he had made a public interest disclosure. He further contended that the imposition of the warning in those circumstances amounted also to a breach of the duty of trust and confidence and that he had resigned in response to that breach. It followed, he contended, that he had been automatically unfairly dismissed contrary to s103A ERA.

7.59   The employment tribunal did not accept that it was reasonable for the school to take the view that the hacking into the computer was unauthorized, but it did not doubt that the school had genuinely taken that view. The school believed that the claimant had committed an act of misconduct. The tribunal held that there had been a protected disclosure, reasoning that it was wrong to treat the claimant's conduct in hacking into the system as distinct from the disclosure of information itself. The tribunal considered it would emasculate the public policy behind the legislation to accept the school's submission that the claimant was the subject of

---

[30] See above, para 7.16; see also the Court of Appeal decision ([2006] EWHC (Admin) 1653). In the ET case of *Olesinski v Tameside MBC* (ET, Case No. 2400410/04) the ET rejected an argument that the claimant's dismissal was the result of her protected disclosure because this had preoccupied her to the extent that it affected her ability to do her job, leading to her dismissal.

disciplinary action not because he had blown the whistle on a suspected failure to comply with the legal obligation, but rather because he had hacked into the respondent's computer system without authority. It said that to allow an employer to defeat a PIDA case in this way would be to drive a coach and horses through the intention of the legislature that whistleblowers should have employment protection. In order to obtain sufficient evidence to found a reasonable belief, the claimant had to do more than simply express misgivings about what had happened over the summer of 2003. The investigation undertaken by the employee to found his reasonable belief could not be divorced from the disclosure itself. Accordingly the claimant had established that the reason that disciplinary action was taken against him was because he made a protected disclosure.

The EAT disagreed. It concluded that the statute protected disclosures but not **7.60** other conduct by the employee even if that conduct was connected in some way to the disclosures. They contrasted this with the wider scope of the victimization provisions under the Race Relations Act as reflected in the decision in *Aziz v Trinity Street Taxis Ltd* [1988] IRLR 204. The law only protected the claimant if he had reasonable grounds for his belief and it did not allow him to commit what would otherwise be acts of misconduct in the hope that he might be able to establish the justification for his belief to his employer. The law protects the disclosure of information which the employee reasonably believes tends to demonstrate the kind of wrongdoing, or anticipated wrongdoing, which is covered by s43B. It does not protect the actions of the employee which are directed to establishing or confirming the reasonableness of that belief.

Sedley LJ gave permission to appeal to the claimant (See [2006] EWCA Civ 710, **7.61** 9 May 2006). He considered that the employment tribunal's findings were 'cogently reasoned'. He also commented that the appeal arguably raised issues of public importance since:

> there are likely to be few cases where a whistle-blower has not been dismissed for what the employer genuinely believes to be misconduct; so that the purpose and effectiveness of the 1998 Act may themselves be in question.

However the Court of Appeal dismissed the appeal ([2006] All ER (D) 198, 15 November 2006). It held that it was wrong to give a special purposive meaning to the term 'disclosure' so as to encompass Mr Evans' act of hacking into the system. It was not sufficient that the school had found out about the misconduct as a result of the disclosure. Mr Evans was dismissed for his misconduct in hacking into the system, not for making a disclosure that the system was vulnerable.

The decision in *Bolton School v Evans* may be contrasted with the earlier decision **7.62** of the EAT in *The Trustees of Mama East African Women's Group v Dobson*.[31]

---

31 EAT/0219/05 and EAT/0220/05, 23 June 2005.

Mrs Dobson was employed as an English teacher by the respondent, a small charity whose aim is to support Somali women in Sheffield and to provide them with training in English as a second language. She received information from a student that a former student had mistreated children at a crèche which the respondent operated. The former student was the sister of the manager (S) to whom the claimant would normally have first reported the allegation. For this reason Mrs Dobson first reported the matter to another employee or ex-employee of the respondent, but she was advised to report it to S and then did so. S purported to investigate the allegations and found them unfounded. Following a disciplinary hearing Mrs Dobson was then dismissed on three grounds: (1) making a false allegation, (2) not following the procedure thereby damaging the reputation of the respondent and (3) breach of confidentiality (referring to the report to a colleague or former colleague). The tribunal found that Mrs Dobson had a reasonable belief for her report, based on the information she had received, and it amounted to a protected disclosure. The tribunal also found that the reason for dismissal was the protected disclosure. Of the reasons given in the dismissal letter, the fact that the disclosure was false did not prevent it being protected and the other matters were intimately connected with the protected disclosure.

7.63 In the appeal it was argued that the reasons given in the letter were indeed distinct from the disclosure itself. This was rejected by the EAT primarily on the basis that the tribunal had made a finding of fact which was open to it, being that it was the protected disclosure that was the principal reason for dismissal. However the EAT also made clear that fine distinctions between the disclosure and matters associated it with it were unlikely to be successful in the context of the legislation (paras 19 and 25):

> There is a very strong public interest in the vindication of whistle blowers so that their action is protected. This does not mean that all of their claims and allegations have to be supported. They have to be investigated and provided the disclosure meets the terms of the Employment Rights Act 1996, action against them is unlawful. See for the social policy behind the Act and its application in employment cases *ALM v Bladon* [2002] ICR 1444, *Street v Derbyshire* above, our judgement in *Lucas v The Chichester Diocesan Housing Association* EAT/0731/04, and the approach of Dame Janet Smith in the Shipman Enquiry which adopted evidence given to it by Public Concern at Work.
>
> . . .
>
> . . . it cannot be right for an employer to assert a non-tainted reason and yet in the social context of this legislation avoid its connection to the protected activity. The reason or the principal reason the Tribunal found was that the Claimant had raised a disclosure.

7.64 This reasoning had considerable force in relation to the attempt to draw a distinction between the disclosure and its falsity. However it was more problematic in relation to the other two grounds set out in the letter of dismissal. As regards failing to follow the correct procedure, this related to a contention that Mrs Dobson ought to have obtained the assistance of an interpreter to clarify what had been said. The tribunal rejected the need for this. Insofar as an inference was drawn that this was not the real reason, then this was unexceptional. However insofar as it was rejected as the reason because it was associated with the disclosure this was problematic. What mattered was the respondent's reasons for dismissal rather than (in relation to s103A) whether they were reasonable. The obtaining of an interpreter was an aspect of the investigation which preceded the disclosure. Similarly the allegation of breach of confidentiality related to a matter preceding the disclosure consisting of the (unprotected) disclosure to the colleague.

We suggest that in the context of the legislation it is indeed appropriate that tribunals should be wary of too readily drawing a distinction between a disclosure and the way it is made. However, it is apparent from not only the wording of s47B, but also the structure of the legislation, that there is a distinction to be drawn between the steps to investigate concerns as to relevant failures, and the disclosures themselves. The EAT in *Bolton School* were, in our view, right to conclude that the ET adopted an incorrect approach in construing the legislation purposively so as to conclude that 'the investigation undertaken by the employee to found his reasonable belief should not be divorced from the disclosure itself'.[32] Equally in *Trustees of Mama* if the employer's principal reason for dismissal had been a previous breach of confidentiality in what was not a protected disclosure (as opposed to breaching confidentiality by making a protected disclosure) that ought not to have been found to infringe s103A ERA. As to this: **7.65**

(a) The ET's approach in *Bolton School* would potentially produce absurd results. Plainly, for example, where one employee bullies and assaults a colleague in order to obtain information to sustain a protected disclosure, an employer must be free to take disciplinary action for such conduct. It could not be an answer to say that the bullying was part of an investigation for the purposes of making a protected disclosure. A somewhat analogous point was considered in *Serco Ltd v Redfearn* [2006] IRLR 623 (CA), in the context of the Race Relations Act. It was argued by a claimant who had been dismissed due to being a member of the British National Party, which is a 'whites only' organization, that 'racial grounds' encompass grounds that are 'significantly informed by racial considerations or racial attitudes' or 'referable to race'. Just as it is insufficient for protection under PIDA that conduct (eg the worker's previous investigation) is referable to the disclosure, so being referable to race

---

[32] It was argued in *Bolton School v Evans* in the Court of Appeal [2006] EWHC (Admin) 1653 that breaking into the system was itself a disclosure by conduct in so far as it was designed specifically to demonstrate the weakness in security. This was rejected. It is considered further at paragraph 7.68 below.

was identified as being far too wide a test under the RRA. Mummery LJ drew attention to the absurd consequences if this was taken to its logical conclusion, including that an employee could not be disciplined for discriminatory conduct.

(b) As in *Redfearn* there is a policy background. If all investigatory action or other steps associated with but previous to the protected disclosure were deemed to be protected as part of the disclosure this would fatally undermine the structure of the legislation. There is a low threshold for protection for disclosures to an employer precisely because employees are encouraged to raise concerns with an appropriate person who may be better placed to investigate them further. If all investigatory steps by the employee were also protected, however disruptive, a significantly higher threshold would be appropriate in some cases, even in first tier disclosures under s43C.

(c) In relation to s43D disclosures for the purposes of obtaining legal advice, there is not even a requirement to act in good faith. It would be highly surprising if, by a sidewind, employees making such a disclosure also received protection for all investigatory steps, however disruptive or unlawful, subject only to satisfying the reasonable belief requirement for a qualifying disclosure.

(d) The structure of the legislation is premised on there being a reasonable belief for a qualifying disclosure. In many cases the investigatory steps will precede there being such a belief, and be carried out in order to gather the information for such a belief. The logic of the ET's position in *Bolton School v Evans* would be to provide protection to workers where it turns out that there is information to sustain a reasonable belief and where the worker then makes a disclosure, but not for those who satisfy themselves from their investigations that the concern is not well-founded and so do not make the disclosure. Yet there is no strong reason why the two cases, each relating to workers investigating genuine concerns which may merit further investigation by them, should be treated so differently.

(e) There remains a concern that workers might be discouraged from raising concerns if they are advised that there must be a reasonable belief sufficient to satisfy the qualifying disclosure test, yet that investigations to substantiate that belief will not be specially protected. The risk of this is however mitigated in two ways:

(i) The Tribunal can be expected to analyse critically the reasons for the disciplinary action or dismissal and whether to accept an assertion by the employer that the real reason was the conduct preceding or associated with the disclosure rather than the disclosure itself. This is a process which tribunals are accustomed to undertaking in the context of other discrimination cases, where employers will rarely admit to having taken discriminatory action and it is necessary to assess whether the alleged non-discriminatory reason is true or sufficient. Further, as noted above,

Nagarajan provides guidance for tribunals as to how to deal with mixed reasons cases. As such, in a detriment case under s47B, it is sufficient if the disclosure was 'a significant influence on the outcome', even though other aspects of the employee's conduct might also have been a factor. In relation to dismissal, it is sufficient if the disclosure was the principal reason for dismissal even if not the sole reason.

(ii) As discussed in Chapter 3, in *Darnton* the EAT stressed the need to have regard to all the relevant circumstances in deciding whether the requisite belief was held for the purposes of a qualifying disclosure, and in *Bolton School v Evans* it was emphasized that an employee might only have part of the evidential picture. As such, in assessing whether a worker held a reasonable belief that information tends to show a relevant failure, there is scope to take into account potential difficulties in investigating further the basis for a concern, and also to take into account the policy consideration that workers are to be encouraged to make concerns known at an early stage to those best placed to investigate.

Breach of confidentiality

Whilst *Bolton School v Evans* drew a distinction between the disclosure and the **7.66** preceding investigation, it is far more problematic to contend that something about the disclosure itself, such as that it was a breach of confidence, should be a legitimate basis for disciplinary action or dismissal. As noted above, the decision in *Trustees of Mama* indicates that tribunals ought to be wary of such a submission in the context of the protected disclosure legislation. However the EAT's decision in *Aspinall v MSI Mech Forge Limited* (EAT/891/01, 25 July 2002)[33] might be regarded as providing some support for such a submission. Mr Aspinall arranged for a colleague to make a video of how certain factory equipment worked as evidence in support of Aspinall's personal injury claim. He passed this to his solicitor, and this amounted to a protected disclosure in relation to health and safety. When the video came to light he was subjected to disciplinary proceedings and put under pressure to name the person who made the video. He was told that if he named the person he would be given a final written warning and if he did not, there would be further discussion as to action to be taken. He resigned in response. The EAT disposed of the case on the basis that he had not been threatened with dismissal and had instead resigned of his own accord. However it also expressed views on the protected disclosure issues. It expressed reservations as to whether making the video amounted to a protected disclosure—and this was cited in *Bolton School v Evans* as support for the distinction it drew between a protected disclosure and the investigation.

---

[33] See above, n 26.

7.67 The EAT also held that dismissal in any event (ie even if making the video had amounted to a protected disclosure) was not by reason of a protected disclosure, but solely because of the perceived breach of confidentiality of the employer's manufacturing process. The perceived breach of confidentiality appears to have related to the employer's misapprehension that the video might have been made by an outside third party—whereas in fact the claimant had said that it was made by a colleague (EAT decision para 6). As to this:

(a) one difficulty with the brief reasoning in *Aspinall* is that it does not directly address what was alleged to be the breach of confidentiality and whether it was regarded as permissible for the employer to discipline the claimant even if the breach consisted of the making of a protected disclosure.

(b) it would not, we suggest, be acceptable for a tribunal to permit an employer to draw a distinction between the information conveyed in a protected disclosure, and whether the disclosure is in breach of confidence. This would permit a coach and horses to be driven through the legislation. The structure of the legislation carefully identifies the requirements for protection at each stage. That protection would be illusory if an employer could argue that, for example, although all the requirements of s43G are satisfied, the employee could be disciplined for making the disclosure in breach of confidence. This would be particularly unsatisfactory since the legislation deliberately avoids tying protection to the law of confidentiality. Indeed in *Street v Derbyshire Unemployed Workers' Centre* [2005] ICR 97, the Court of Appeal specifically drew attention to the differing tests for protection that apply in relation to the law of confidentiality.

(c) there may be some cases where a breach of confidentiality is relevant. This might be the case, for example, if a protected disclosure is accompanied by a disclosure of other information, which does not amount to a protected disclosure, and which is disclosed in breach of an obligation of confidentiality. But the employer would have to persuade a tribunal that it was this breach of confidentiality, and not the protected disclosure, which was the reason for the disciplinary action.

Distinction between the disclosure and the manner of the disclosure

7.68 A related particular difficulty is that an employer may well contend that the action he took against the employee was not by reason of or on the ground of the disclosure itself but the manner in which the disclosure was made. In some circumstances such a distinction might indeed need to be drawn. This can be illustrated by reference to the situation considered in *Bolton School v Evans*. It was argued in the Court of Appeal that there were two aspects to Mr Evans' decision to hack into the school's computer network. It was in part to test his concerns and as such was part of the investigation in order to establish reasonable belief. But it was also to demonstrate the validity of his concerns as to security weaknesses. In relation to this, the conduct of breaking into the system might be regarded as part and parcel of the disclosures which Mr Evans made. By hacking into the computer system Mr Evans was communicating, and evidencing by his conduct, that the system was inadequate. Further, he did so in the context of having raised these concerns expressly both before and after having hacked into the system. Nothing in the legislation expressly requires that the disclosure has to be by words or in writing. This argument was rejected on the facts in *Bolton School* on the basis that breaking into the computer did not involve communication with anyone. If however a disclosure could be by conduct (which was not the finding in *Bolton School*) it is plain that it must be permissible in some circumstances for an employer to assert that it is disciplining the employee by reason of that conduct rather than for the message which the conduct is intended to convey. Otherwise, to adapt the facts in *Bolton School*, Mr Evans would have been insulated against disciplinary action even if he had caused wholly disproportionate damage to the computer network, and acted precipitately when there was no reason to believe his concerns were not being heeded. But equally where the disclosure is made expressly in writing or verbally, there could be absurd results if it were in no circumstances permissible to distinguish between the disclosure and the manner of the disclosure. To take an extreme example, plainly an employee who enters his manager's office and sprays graffiti on the walls might legitimately be disciplined for so doing even if the graffiti consisted of protected disclosures.

Whilst it must therefore in principle be permissible in some circumstances to **7.69** draw a distinction between the protected disclosure and the manner in which it is made, the approach taken in relation to victimization for carrying out health and safety or trade union duties, and the policy considerations identified in *Trustees of Mama* (para 7.62 above), suggests that in most cases it will be difficult for an employer to draw such a distinction, for example by relying upon the intemperate language used. The dangers of permitting too fine a distinction to be drawn, based on the way in which a protected activity is carried out, was emphasized in *Goodwin v Cabletel UK Limited* [1997] IRLR 665.[34] Mr Goodwin was employed by the respondents as a construction manager and a health and safety representative. He raised concerns about the safety record of one particular firm of subcontractors. He wanted to take a strong line against the firm but his employers favoured a more conciliatory approach. Ultimately, his employer decided that he should be removed from direct dealings with the firm in question and his job was changed to that of assistant construction manager reporting to a manager who was formerly his equal. In the light of the demotion, he resigned and claimed constructive dismissal.

---

[34] The EAT purported to follow the Court of Appeal's decision in *Bass Taverns Limited v Burgess* [1995] IRLR 596 (CA), relating to dismissal for union activities, although the policy considerations were set out less firmly in that case, and it turned largely on a finding as to the scope of union activities in the context.

He claimed he had been dismissed automatically (constructively) unfairly for carrying out or proposing to carry out his health and safety duties. The EAT held that the tribunal had erred in law in dismissing his claim on the basis that it was the way in which he carried out his health and safety activities, rather than the actual doing of them, which led to his dismissal. The EAT commented (at paragraph 40) that:

> the protection afforded to the way in which a designated employee carries out his health and safety activities must not be diluted by too easily finding acts done for that purpose to be a justification for dismissal; on the other hand, not every act, however malicious or irrelevant to the task in hand, must necessarily be treated as a protected act in circumstances where dismissal would be justified on legitimate grounds.

7.70 The EAT (at para 39) cited with approval the judgment of Phillips J in *Lyon v St James Press Ltd* [1976] IRLR 215, where he said (at paragraphs 16 and 20), in relation to the protection for trade union activities, that:

> . . . trade union activities must not be allowed to operate as a cloak or an excuse for conduct which ordinarily would justify dismissal; equally, the right to take part in the affairs of the trade union must not be obstructed by too easily finding acts done for the purpose to be a justification for dismissal. The marks are easy to describe, but the channel between them is difficult to navigate.
>
> . . .
>
> We do not say that every such act is protected. For example, wholly unreasonable, extraneous or malicious acts done in support of trade union activities might be a ground for a dismissal which would not be unfair.

7.71 The tenor of these cases is therefore to recognize the caution required before allowing a tribunal to draw a distinction between the manner in which union or health and safety activities are carried out (and by extension the manner in which a disclosure is made) and the activities themselves, whilst recognizing that this may be permissible in extreme circumstances such as 'wholly unreasonable, extraneous or malicious acts'. *Shillito v van Leer (U.K.) Ltd* [1997] IRLR 495 provides an example of where such a distinction could be drawn. The claimant was a senior shop steward of a recognized union. Following a concern about an odour on a production line, he raised these concerns but did not follow the agreed safety procedures. Instead he went to see the staff member responsible for first aid and insisted, allegedly in a belligerent way, that those concerned should be seen by the company doctor or sent to hospital. He was disciplined for failing to follow agreed procedures and for acting in a way which was not to be expected of a union representative. The EAT reasoned that whether this was permissible turned not on whether he had acted reasonably, but on the reasons for the employer having taken the disciplinary action. Thus (at paragraph 18), the EAT noted that:

> the question for the industrial tribunal was whether the appellant was disciplined (that is, subjected to a detriment) on the ground that he was performing the functions of a safety representative, acknowledged by the employer. If that was the reason for his being disciplined, it is no defence that he intended to embarrass the company in

front of external safety authorities, or that he performed those functions in an unreasonable way, unacceptable to the employer. The complaint is made out.

On the facts of the case, however, the EAT concluded that the tribunal had been **7.72** entitled to find that the claimant's health and safety activities were not the reason for the disciplinary action. The reasons were that (a) he was not the health and safety representative for the line in question; (b) that he was not acknowledged as a safety representative for the purpose of acting outside the agreed procedures and (c) he acted in bad faith in that his purpose was not to pursue a genuine health and safety matter but to pursue a personal agenda to embarrass the company. The decision did not therefore enable the employer merely to draw a distinction between conducting health and safety activities and unreasonable conduct. There was a more limited distinction based on the claimant having acted in an unauthorized way and in bad faith *and in addition*, it had to be shown that this was the reason for the disciplinary action.

The issue was ventilated in a PIDA context in *Hossack v Kettering BC* (EAT/ **7.73** 1113/01, 29 November 2002). It was argued for the employee that once the tribunal had accepted (as it had in that case) that there had been a protected disclosure, it was not open to an employer to discipline or dismiss an employee for the 'manner' in which the disclosure was made because this would undermine the specific provisions set out by Parliament as to how a disclosure must be made in order to gain protection. The EAT agreed that a differentiation between the content of a disclosure and the manner in which it is made, if not carefully analysed, could emasculate the legislation and that any tribunal approaching a protected disclosure would need to be alert to that danger. However the tribunal that had heard Mrs Hossack's complaint had been alert to that danger and its ruling could not be impeached. Ms Hossack was dismissed from her position as Policy Research Officer to the Conservative group on the council after writing a letter to the district auditor with allegations of wrongdoing against officers of the council and Labour councillors. The EAT held that the tribunal had been entitled to find that the reason for her dismissal was not the protected disclosure she made, but her inability to distinguish her role as a Research Officer employed by the council, from a political role as an elected member of the Conservative group, resulting in a loss of confidence in her as an employee. The tribunal had been entitled to find that the disclosures were not the reason for the dismissal and the councillor who dismissed her had no difficulty with the disclosure itself. But the disclosure, and comments within it such as that the Conservative group was her group, evidenced the claimant's inability to understand her advisory role.[35]

---

[35] See also *Vaseghi v Brunel University* (EAT/0757/04 and EAT/0222/05, 3 November 2005) where, in the context of a claim of race and union victimization, the EAT rejected a submission that in principle it was impermissible to draw a distinction between a protected act and the disruptive manner in which it was carried out, and referred to a submission to that effect as one 'that impresses only by its audacity'.

7.74   In the context of a dismissal it is arguable that even if the tribunal concludes that the reason or principal reason for the dismissal was the making of a protected disclosure then the manner in which it was made contributed to the ensuing dismissal. We consider this aspect in Chapter 9.[36]

(3) Failure in the investigation of the subject matter of the disclosure

7.75   In practice, although the 'reason why' question is often the most significant issue once a protected disclosure is established, each of the elements of s47B may require careful consideration. The nature of the analysis which is required may be illustrated by reference to the question of whether failure in the investigation of the subject matter of the disclosures gives rise to a PIDA claim. Whilst it is possible for a failure to investigate to give rise to a claim under s47B (or s103A) there are likely to be a number of significant hurdles to overcome.

Detriment

An employer will be under a duty to investigate disclosures where these amount to grievances and accordingly a failure to investigate a disclosure which also amounted to a grievance is likely to amount to a detriment. It may also be a breach of the term of trust and confidence because it might indicate that the employer condones wrongdoing or the continuance of a hazard. If the employee's disclosure relates to a matter which does not concern the employee's own job then in some cases it may be arguable that a failure to investigate that disclosure would not amount to a detriment. Given the wide meaning of the term 'detriment', however, this may remain problematic. The worker might be caused considerable anxiety by the failure to investigate serious concerns and the implication that the employer is either unwilling to address them or does not treat them seriously.

Act or deliberate failure to act by the employer

Where the objection is to a specific step taken in the investigation, such as failing to respect a request for anonymity, there is no difficulty in establishing an act by the employer. The position is less straightforward where there is a failure to take steps, such as a delay in commencing the investigation. It will be necessary to establish that this is a 'deliberate' failure.

In *Lingard v HM Prison Service*, (ET, Case No. 1802862/04, 16 December 2004)[37] the claimant prison officer complained of a large and wide-ranging number of

---

[36] Paras 9.23 to 9.30.
[37] Case 68 in Appendix 9.

detriments visited upon her on the ground that she had made protected disclosures about practices in the prison where she was working. The detriments included failures in the investigation. The ET concluded that it was a detriment to a whistleblower to fail, deliberately or by maladministration or negligence, to investigate legitimate concerns which directly affected the duties the whistleblower had to carry out and which she was contractually obliged to disclose. However this formula, referring to maladministration or negligence, does not take into account the need for the failure to be deliberate.

On the ground that

In many cases, however, the principal difficulty will be in showing that a failure in the investigation was 'on the ground that' the worker made the protected disclosure, rather than merely that the failure 'relates to' the disclosure and would not have happened 'but for' the disclosure. Clearly failings in the investigation of a protected disclosure will relate to the disclosure and would not have happened but for it. But that is not of itself sufficient. If an employer who receives a disclosure of a relevant failure regards the employee as causing trouble in making the disclosure, and for that reason decides to put off or otherwise avoid dealing with the concerns, and the employee suffers stress due to the failure to deal with the concerns, it can be said that there has been a detriment on the ground of the making of the disclosure. If, on the other hand, the employer does not investigate because of a pre-existing dislike of the employee, or because he simply cannot be bothered to get round to doing so, then the pre-existing dislike of the employee or perhaps just apathy, rather than the protected disclosure, would be the reason for the failure to act. The *detriment* sustained by the worker might still be due to having raised protected disclosures, for example because making the disclosure or the absence of a satisfactory response is highly stressful and upsetting. But the test is not whether the *detriment* is on the grounds of the protected disclosure, but *whether the act or deliberate failure to act* is on those grounds. This focuses on the employer's reasons, rather than on the reason for the employee considering that he is disadvantaged.

(4) *The burden of proof in relation to the 'reason why' question*

In general terms the burden is on the claimant to prove the facts constituting the **7.76** protected disclosure. There are two important exceptions. The first relates to the good faith requirements for protected disclosures and is considered in Chapter 4. The second relates to establishing the grounds for an act or deliberate failure to act. Workers may face particular difficulties in establishing why an employer acted or deliberately failed to act in a manner alleged to have caused detriment. It will be the employer who is best placed to adduce evidence in relation to this and to explain its conduct. In recognition of this, s48(2) ERA provides that 'on [a complaint of victimization to a tribunal by a worker] it is for the employer to show the ground on which any act, or deliberate failure to act, was done'.

7.77 In *Harrow v Knight* (referred to in paragraph 7.34 above) Mr Knight cited s48(2) in defence of the tribunal's approach in his case. The EAT noted that they had not been referred to any authority as to the effect of this subsection and that it did not appear to have any equivalent in the 'victimization' provisions of other statutes (eg s4 of the Sex Discrimination Act 1975, s2 of the Race Relations Act 1976 and s146 of the Trade Union and Labour Relations (Consolidation) Act 1992).

7.78 The EAT considered that the subsection might seem to be intended to have the same effect as s98(1) of the 1996 Act, which, as we note below, requires an employer in a claim of unfair dismissal to prove what the reason for the dismissal was and that it was within one of the categories of admissible reasons: if the employer fails to establish either of those matters the dismissal is generally unfair. But the EAT reasoned that the concept of 'unfair dismissal' did not require the tribunal to be satisfied of anything save that the section had not been complied with and in that sense it had no positive content. By contrast 'victimization' requires the ingredient that the employer had acted on the prohibited ground. The EAT thought that there was no reason in principle why the statute could not have provided that the employer be deemed to have so acted where he did not prove any other reason, but would have expected such a provision to be clearly spelt out. Furthermore if s48(2) were construed as having such a deeming effect, the result would appear to be that an employer who could not prove his 'ground' could be liable to a series of claims under each (and, they might have added, *all*) of the anti-victimization provisions of Part V ERA. That would no doubt be highly unlikely to happen in practice, but even the theoretical possibility cast doubt on the correctness of the approach.

7.79 The employer (Harrow LBC) contended that all that s48(2) ERA did was to make it clear to employers that they have to be prepared to say in the tribunal why they acted in the respect complained of, with the result that if they failed to do so they might find inferences drawn against them (though only if such inferences are justified by the facts as a whole). Whilst stating that it did not need to resolve this issue, the EAT indicated that it found this submission persuasive.

7.80 The EAT's tentatively expressed views on the issue have attracted criticism[38] and, we suggest, they are not correct. Most cases are decided on the basis of positive findings rather than on the burden of proof, but it is open to a tribunal to decide a case on the basis that an employer has not discharged the burden of showing that

---

[38] *Harvey on Industrial Relations and Employment Law*, paragraph DII R[631].

the reason for an act or deliberate failure to act was the making of a protected disclosure. As to this:

(a) it is notable that s48(2) ERA uses the same language as s98(1) ERA: 'it is for the employer to show' the reason for dismissal or the ground on which an act or deliberate failure to act took place. It would be surprising if, within the same statute, these words carried very different meanings.

(b) the risk (raised in *Harrow v Knight*) that an employer who provides no evidence could be found to have acted for all the impermissible reasons in Part V will only apply where the other elements of the cause of action are made out. Thus, in relation to protected disclosures, the tribunal will need to be satisfied that there was a protected disclosure and of each of the other elements of a claim under s47B.

(c) the tentative view expressed in *Harrow v Knight* involves a gloss on the plain words of s48(2) ERA which in unambiguous terms places the burden of proof on the employer. If it was intended only to impose a lesser evidential burden this could readily have been made clear by the draughtsman. Further, there was no more a need for the legislation to point out the consequences of failing to discharge the burden of proof, than for this to be stipulated expressly in relation to s98 ERA.

7.81 It is to be noted that one consequence of s48(2) ERA is that[39] a worker (whatever the length of his or her employment) would appear to be in a more advantageous position as regards the burden of proof than an employee who has not qualified for the right not to be unfairly dismissed under s98 ERA. Such an employee will bear the burden of proving that a protected disclosure was the reason or principal reason for dismissal, and if unable to establish this will not be able to fall back on a claim in respect of the dismissal under s47B. By contrast, under s48(2) ERA the employer will bear the burden of proof in relation to a worker who is not an employee, but whose contract is terminated.

(5) Drawing inferences

7.82 The extent to which tribunals are able to draw inferences as to the real reason for an act or deliberate failure to act is likely to play an important role in many cases, most significantly in relation to the grounds or reason for an act or deliberate failure to act of which complaint is made. Tribunals will need to consider whether to accept the reasons advanced by the employer for the act or deliberate failure to act. Whilst a tribunal may be able to fall back on the failure of an employer to discharge the burden under s48(2), in many cases a tribunal will prefer to make

---

[39] As pointed out by Professor Lewis, ILJ (2002).

positive findings as to the reason or grounds for an act or deliberate failure. Indeed in *Harrow v Knight* the EAT counselled that, whether or not its tentative view as to the effect of s48(2) ERA was correct,

> prudent tribunals in dealing with victimisation claims will no doubt prefer, wherever possible, to make positive findings as to the grounds on which the employer acted rather than to rely on s48(2) until its effect has been authoritatively established.

7.83 Such positive findings will often turn not only on the findings of primary fact, but also on the inferences which can properly be drawn from those findings, such as in relation to the adequacy of the explanation for the employer's acts or deliberate failures to act.[40] The drawing of inferences may also be relevant to other issues, such as whether a failure to act was deliberate, though again there is some statutory assistance in relation to this in the terms of s48(4) as discussed above (para 7.28).

7.84 Before statute intervened[41] tribunals hearing discrimination claims applied the approach stated by Neil LJ in *King v G.B.–China Centre* [1992] ICR 516 (CA) at 529. The outcome of a claim of discrimination would usually depend on what inferences it was proper to draw from the primary facts found. The tribunal would have looked to the employer for an explanation of the conduct complained of and if no satisfactory explanation was put forward for that conduct it would be legitimate for the tribunal to infer that the conduct was on racial grounds. This, as Neil LJ put it, was not a matter of law but 'almost common sense'. It did not help to think in terms of shifting evidential burdens; instead the tribunal would have to make findings as to the primary facts and draw such inferences as they considered proper from those facts. This guidance was built on by Sedley LJ in *Anya v University of Oxford*[42] where he stressed the importance of the tribunal making proper findings of primary fact so as to show their process of reasoning (and setting this out in their reasoning.[43])

---

[40] See eg *Everett Financial Management Ltd v Murrell* (EAT/552/02, 24 February 2003) where in paragraph 23 the EAT referred to the following passage in the Employment Tribunal's decision: 'the Respondent did not in their evidence produce any plausible explanation for their conduct and the majority of the Tribunal thus infers a link between the Applicant's signature of the petition and his later treatment'. The EAT made this reference without criticizing this approach (although the employer's appeal was allowed for other reasons).

[41] Section 63A of the Sex Discrimination Act 1975; s54A of the Race Relations Act 1976; s17A(1C) of the Disability Discrimination Act 1995; Arts 2 and 7 of the EC Equal Treatment Directive 76/207 (as amended); Arts 1, 2(1), 4(1), 4(2) EC Burden of Proof Directive 97/80; Arts 8(1), 8(2) EC Race Discrimination Directive 2000/43; Arts 10(1), 10(2) EC Framework Employment Directive 2000/78; for an analysis see *Igen Ltd v Wong* [2005] IRLR 258 (CA).

[42] [2001] EWCA Civ 405 [2001] 847 ICR.

[43] See more generally on the need to set out reasons, *Meek v City of Birmingham City Council* [1987] IRLR 250 and *Tran v Greenwich Vietnam Community Project* [2002] EWCA Civ 553, [2002] ICR 1101.

Whilst, in relation to other discrimination statutes, the guidance in *King* has been **7.85** displaced by the intervention of statute, it might be argued that the guidance remains of assistance in relation to consideration of the reasons for acts or failures to act alleged to be on grounds of protected disclosures. Claims under ss47B and 103A ERA are a species of discrimination claim: *Virgo Fidelis Senior School v Boyle* [2004] IRLR 268 (EAT) at para 44(b); *Felter v Cliveden Petroleum Company* (EAT/0533/05, 9 March 2006) at para 15. The *King* guidelines have also on occasion been suggested as having wider application. In *Neckles v London United Busways Limited* (EAT/1339/99, 10 February 2000) the EAT at a preliminary hearing held (at para 12) that a tribunal had directed itself correctly in applying the *King* guidelines by analogy in a case of alleged refusal to offer employment on grounds related to union membership contrary to s137 TULRCA.

We suggest however, that the better view is that the process of fact-finding might **7.86** be unduly complicated by referring to the *King* guidelines. First, the guidelines were framed in a context where there was no equivalent of s48(2) ERA. Second, the reasoning of the EAT in *Nicholson & Others v Long Products* (EAT/0166/02, 19 November 2003) is persuasive. The EAT rejected a submission that the approach endorsed in *King* was applicable in the case of a dismissal for trade union reasons. The EAT explained (para 20) that the guidance in *King* had been deemed necessary in the specific context of alleged discrimination which required a tribunal to consider whether there was differential treatment and the adequacy of the explanation for it. This was not to suggest that the drawing of appropriate inferences as secondary findings of fact was not an important part of the fact finding process, but that:

> what a Tribunal is, of course, required to do . . . is to scrutinise the evidence and, so far as is relevant and necessary, to find the primary facts and then to proceed, again insofar as it is necessary to do so to inform the parties as to why they have won or lost, to reach factual conclusions or secondary findings of fact based on the primary findings of fact.

The importance of a tribunal setting out clearly its findings of primary facts, and **7.87** how its secondary findings flow from those primary facts, was emphasized by the EAT in the context of a protected disclosure dismissal claim in *The Brothers of Charity Services Merseyside v Eleady Cole* (EAT/0661/00, 24 January 2002). The tribunal had drawn an inference that the real reason for the dismissal of the claimant was not his poor performance (as the employers contended), but his having made a protected disclosure. The EAT allowed an appeal on the basis that the decision was insufficiently reasoned. It observed (at para 31) that there was force in the submission that:

> . . . under Section 103A where a finding of unfair dismissal in circumstances such as those in this case necessarily involves a finding that the reasons put forward by the employer were not genuine and that evidence given before the Tribunal was untruthful,

it is incumbent on the Tribunal to base its conclusions on clear findings as to the primary facts about which of the persons before it were responsible for what happened, and to explain clearly how those findings lead causally to the conclusion that the protected disclosure had been the true reason for the employee's dismissal.

7.88 The decision in *The Brothers of Charity* also raised an issue as to the extent to which inferences can properly be drawn from the fact of unreasonable conduct. The tribunal had drawn inferences from the fact that it regarded the criticisms of the claimant's performance as trivial and not sufficient to justify terminating the claimant's employment. The EAT regarded this as indicating that the tribunal was focusing on the reasonableness of the decision to dismiss, rather than whether the complaints as to the claimant's performance were in fact the reason for dismissal—whether or not reasonably so. The EAT emphasized that issues as to reasonableness were relevant for ordinary unfair dismissal under s98 ERA, but that under s103A ERA, the focus was on the reason for dismissal.

7.89 The extent to which the unreasonable nature of behaviour might give rise to adverse inferences has been considered further in the context of race and sex discrimination. A tribunal cannot draw an inference of discrimination from the mere fact of unreasonable treatment. However an inference may be drawn where there is no explanation for the unreasonable treatment: *Bahl v The Law Society* [2004] IRLR 799 (CA) at para 101. Further, in considering whether to accept an employer's explanation for an act or deliberate failure to act by which an employee was subjected to a detriment, a tribunal is more likely to regard the explanation with suspicion if the explanation relies on unreasonable conduct: *Bahl v The Law Society* [2003] IRLR 640 EAT at paras 99 to 101.

G. Complaints to an employment tribunal in claims of victimization

(1) Statutory grievance procedures and whistleblowing claims

7.90 Section 32 of the Employment Act 2002 provides that an employee shall not present a complaint to an employment tribunal under a jurisdiction to which the section applies if it concerns a matter in relation to which the requirement in para 6 or 9 of Sch 2 applies, and that requirement has not been complied with. In essence a complaint will be rejected if the employee has not attempted to invoke the statutory grievance procedure.[44] One of the complaints which is listed

---

[44] For a fuller description of the mechanisms by which employees are compelled to comply with statutory grievance procedures see, eg Bowers, *A Practical Appproach to Employment Law* (7th Ed, Oxford: Oxford University Press, 2005) para 4.76ff.

in Schs 3 and 4 of the 2002 Act is a complaint under s48 ERA which is, as we have seen, the section by which claims in respect of victimization for whistleblowing are made.

Standard and modified grievance procedures are provided for in Part 2 of Sch 2 **7.91** of the Employment Act 2002 and duties are imposed on employees and employers to bring and entertain grievances. When the Employment Relations Bill was before Parliament[45] there was discussion as to the interaction between the statutory procedures and the system for making and protecting public interest disclosures. Concerns were expressed that the statutory grievance procedure might undermine or cut across the working of the PIDA-inserted provisions of ERA. It was felt that, rightly or wrongly, employees might feel compelled to use the statutory grievance procedure when they wanted to make a public interest disclosure not relating to their own personal treatment. They might feel constrained from raising their concern in a less formal way with their employer or via dedicated disclosure procedures, they might also feel that they could not make the disclosure to third parties. The purpose of the resulting amendment was to make it clear that employees were free to decide how they wish to pursue a concern which could be treated either as a public interest disclosure or as a grievance.

> If they wish to take up an issue as a grievance, they can do so. If they wish to disclose their concern in other ways consistent with the Public Interest Disclosure Act 1998, then they are free to pursue that course of action either as an alternative to raising the matter as a grievance or, indeed, as an addition to raising it as a grievance.[46]

Lord Borrie agreed that the amendment made it clear that the grievance proce- **7.92** dure did not undermine the legislative framework for whistleblowing in the public interest contained in the protected disclosure provisions of ERA. In a speech which illuminates the nature and purpose of the exception to the general scheme of grievance procures he continued:[47]

> The view of Public Concern at Work is that the key element of a grievance procedure is that its purpose is to remedy or redress some harm or damage suffered by an employee. That differs from whistleblowing, where the purpose is to alert or to put on notice the employer or the relevant authority so that they can assess what action, if any, is needed. As the new statutory dispute regime is concerned only with grievances which may ground a tribunal claim, a definition of grievance that recognises the essential element of remedy for personal harm is appropriate. That is because the pre-eminent reason claims are brought to a tribunal is to seek a personal redress, especially, and usually, compenzation for a detriment or harm the employee believes that he has suffered at the employer's hands.

---

[45] See *Hansard* HL, 11 Jun 2002: col. 186.
[46] Lord McIntosh of Haringey, ibid at col. 187.
[47] *Hansard* HL, 11 Jun 2002: cols. 187–188.

We trust that Her Majesty's Government will confirm that there will now be full and open consultation on what is a grievance before regulations are introduced. We trust too that they will confirm that the key element of a grievance in the new regime will be that the employee is seeking a remedy or redress for harm or detriment.

When the Bill becomes an Act, the new statutory regime will be explained in various ways to employers and employees, who can all usefully be reminded of the nature and value of whistleblowing. If an employee is concerned about wrongdoing in his workplace, be it fraud, public danger, danger to public health or cover up of wrongdoing, he should feel able to raise that matter as a witness and be seen as such by managers and fellow employees rather than as a complainant who may have a personal interest in the outcome.

If, sadly, as we all know happens only too frequently, an employee is victimised as a result of blowing the whistle perfectly legitimately within the public interest disclosure regime and seeks a personal remedy, the grievance procedure set out in Schedule 2 will apply as it does to any other kind of grievance. I warmly welcome the amendment.

7.93　Paragraph 15 of Sch 2 EA 2002 provides that the procedures set out in Part 2 are only applicable to matters raised by an employee with his employer '*as a grievance*' (our emphasis) and that:

> accordingly, those procedures are only applicable to the kind of disclosure dealt with in Part 4A of the Employment Rights Act 1996 (c 18) (protected disclosures of information) if information is disclosed by an employee to his employer in circumstances where—
>
> (a) the information relates to a matter which the employee could raise as a grievance with his employer, and
> (b) it is the intention of the employee that the disclosure should constitute the raising of the matter with his employer as a grievance.

7.94　'Grievance' was given a definition as Lord Borrie had suggested it should be:

> . . . a complaint by an employee about action which his employer has taken or is contemplating taking in relation to him.[48]

7.95　Of course, as Lord Borrie noted in the passage set out above, a disclosure might not 'relate . . . to a matter which the employee could raise as a grievance with his employer': a disclosure might concern a matter which the employee believes constitutes a wrong against other employees or a third party or parties. All that para 15 of Sch 2 does is to allow the employee to sidestep the statutory grievance procedure where his/her disclosure concerns a perceived wrong against the employee which could be raised as a grievance. The employee is not disabled from bringing a tribunal claim because he/she has not followed one of these statutory grievance procedures. But equally it is important to note that the statutory extension in the time limits applicable where a grievance has been submitted within the period

---

[48] Employment Act 2002 (Dispute Resolution) Regulations 2004 (SI 2004/752), Reg 2.

allowed,[49] would not apply if the concerns as to a protected disclosure are not or could not be raised as a grievance.

It is also important to note that, whilst the employee may be able to avoid going **7.96** through the statutory grievance procedure in respect of his/her original disclosure, para 15(2) does not disapply the statutory grievance scheme where the employee is complaining about victimization which *follows* the disclosure.

(2) Time limits in victimization cases

Section 48 (3) provides that a tribunal shall not consider a complaint under s48 **7.97** (that is to say a tribunal will have no jurisdiction to entertain such a complaint) unless it is presented before the end of the period of three months beginning with the date of the act or failure to act to which the complaint relates or, where that act or failure is part of a series of similar acts or failures, the last of them, or within such further period as the tribunal considers reasonable in a case where it is satisfied that it was not reasonably practicable for the complaint to be presented before the end of that period of three months.[50]

Section 48(4) ERA provides that where an act extends over a period, the 'date of **7.98** the act' means the last day of that period, and a deliberate failure to act shall be treated as occurring when it was decided on. In the absence of evidence establishing the contrary, an employer is to be taken to decide on a failure to act when he acts in a way inconsistent with doing the failed act or, if no such inconsistent act has occurred, when the period expires within which he might reasonably have been expected to carry out the failed act if it was to be performed.

Time may also be extended by three months where at the time the normal time **7.99** limit expired it was believed on reasonable grounds that a statutory disciplinary procedure was being followed in respect of the substance of the tribunal complaint, or there is an applicable statutory disciplinary or grievance procedure. This would apply if the detriment consisted of disciplinary action and, for example, an appeal was being pursued in relation to this at the time of the expiry of the normal three-month time limit. Similarly the time limit will be extended by three months if either of the statutory grievance procedures applies and if a step 1 grievance letter was sent within the primary limitation period or the claim was presented within the primary period in circumstances where it was not permissible to do so. This might occur if the worker failed to begin by taking the first step in the standard or

---

[49] Employment Act 2002 (Dispute Resolution) Regulations 2004 (SI 2004/752), Reg 15.
[50] For a more detailed exposition of the law relating to time limits in unfair dismissal and victimization cases see Bowers, Brown, Mansfield (eds), *Blackstone's Employment Practice* 2006 (Oxford: Oxford University Press, 2006) 3.02 pp 28–29.

modified grievance procedure (sending the written statement of the grievance to the employer) and then waiting 28 days before making the application to the tribunal.[51]

An act extending over a period

7.100 When will an act 'extend over a period'? This is essentially an issue of fact and degree but there is an equivalence with the discrimination statutes in the use of the concept of a continuing act. The Race Relations Act s68(7)[52] provides that 'any act extending over a period shall be treated as done at the end of that period'. In *Hendricks v Metropolitan Police Commissioner* [2003] IRLR 96 the Court of Appeal accepted that a female police officer who contended that numerous alleged incidents of sex discrimination over an extended period were linked to one another might be able to demonstrate that those incidents were 'evidence of a continuing discriminatory state of affairs covered by the concept of "an act extending over a period"' (Mummery LJ at paragraph 48). Having referred in paragraph 51 to earlier authorities from *Owusu v London Fire & Civil Defence Authority* [1995] IRLR 574 through to *Derby Specialist Fabrication Ltd v Burton* [2001] IRLR 69, Mummery LJ said this at paragraph 52:

> The concepts of policy, rule, practice, scheme or regime in the authorities were given as examples of when an act extends over a period. They should not be treated as a complete and constricting statement of the indicia of 'an act extending over a period'. I agree with the observation made by Sedley LJ, in his decision on the paper application for permission to appeal, that the Appeal Tribunal allowed itself to be sidetracked by focusing on whether a 'policy' could be discerned. Instead, the focus should be on the substance of the complaints that the Commissioner was responsible for an ongoing situation or a continuing state of affairs in which female ethnic minority officers in the Service were treated less favourably. The question is whether that is 'an act extending over a period' as distinct from a succession of unconnected or isolated specific acts, for which time would begin to run from the date when each specific act was committed.

7.101 Accordingly a continuing act is not merely the maintenance of a rule, practice, scheme or regime but also may consist of the 'act' of being responsible for an ongoing situation in which the less favourable treatment occurs. The 'act' or 'acts' in *Hendricks* were not the alleged individual acts of the officers for whom the Commissioner was responsible but the overarching act of the Commissioner. The starting point is to determine what is the specific act of which complaint is made (see Auld LJ in *Cast v Croydon College* [1998] IRLR 318 at paragraph 24).

---

[51] Employment Act 2002 (Dispute Resolution) Regulations 2004 (SI 2004/752), Reg 15.
[52] Identical provisions to those in the Race Relations Act are contained in the Sex Discrimination Act 76(6) and the Disability Discrimination Act Sch 3 para 3(3).

A series of similar acts or failures

An alternative possibility, which does not feature in the discrimination statutes, **7.102** is that an act or failure to act was 'part of a series of similar acts or failures'. To use the *Hendricks* case as an example, would the alleged individual acts of the officers have been a series of similar acts if there were a similar provision in the Sex Discrimination Act? The similarly worded s147(1) of TULRCA provides the time limit for a complaint under s146 of that Act in relation to victimization for trade union activities. In relation to s147(1), in *Yewdall v Secretary of State For Work & Pensions* (EAT/0071/05, 19 July 2005), Burton P, giving the judgment of the EAT, said this (at paragraph 28):

> [Counsel] has referred us to two authorities on the issue of a series of acts, although he accepts that there is little in the law books on the definition of the word 'series'. The first such authority is *Adlam v Salisbury & Wells Theological College* [1985] ICR 786 and the other is *Group 4 Night Speed Limited v Gilbert* [1997] IRLR 398. Mr Powell has produced extracts from dictionaries. It appears to us that there is not a great deal of help to be gained from dictionaries or from authorities. The words are relatively clear. What is required to be shown is a series of similar acts. Mr Powell made the submission, by reference to *Group 4 Night Speed Limited*, that when one is addressing in similar legislation (in that case under what was then the Wages Act), where there are so many different kinds of unlawful deductions of wages that can be found, the need for the series of deductions to be similar indicates that it is not simply their unlawfulness which is going to create the similarity, and we agree. Thus, acts which are all capable of amounting to breaches of section 146 are not, for that reason or, indeed, for the reason that they cause detriment, similar. They must be, in our judgment, similar by way of nature.

Accordingly the EAT considered that it was not sufficient to establish 'similarity' by **7.103** reference to the underlying reason for the acts or failures. It will be a question of fact as to whether the acts or failures to act are sufficiently alike to be 'similar'.[53]

However a different approach has recently been taken by the Court of Appeal, in **7.104** a PIDA context, in *Arthur v London Eastern Railway Ltd (trading as One Stansted Express)* ([2006] EWCA Civ 1358, 25 October 2006). The ET (which did not hear any evidence) said that for the acts to be 'part of a series' required 'a significant degree of linkage' and rejected the claimant's contention that it was sufficient that there was a common motive for the acts or failures to act. The EAT endorsed this approach but the Court of Appeal remitted the issue for a rehearing including the admission of evidence. Mummery LJ said that the ET erred in law in determining the important time limit point without hearing any evidence or making any

---

[53] See eg *Holden v Connex South Eastern Limited* (ET Case No. 2301550/00, 15 April 2003) (case number 58 in Appendix 9) where the employment tribunal found that the whole of the respondent's conduct could be treated as acts of continuing detrimental treatment forming part of a series of similar acts and failures the last of which was in time.

findings of fact. He emphasized (at paragraph 35) that some evidence was needed to determine what link, if any, there is between the acts within the 3 month period prior to presentation of the claim and the acts outside the three month period. It was necessary to look at all the circumstances surrounding the acts including:

> Were they all committed by fellow employees? If not, what connection, if any, was there between the alleged perpetrators? Were their actions organised or concerted in some way? It would also be relevant to inquire why they did what is alleged.

He also said that, 'depending on the facts', he would not rule out the possibility of a series of apparently disparate acts being shown to be part of a series of similar acts by reason of them all being on the ground of a protected disclosure. Lloyd LJ disagreed on this point on the basis that it would give no meaning to the requirement that the acts or failures to act be 'similar'. However he was in a minority on this issue. Sedley LJ offered the example that there could be a series of acts made up of different acts of harassment, such as putting chewing gum on a chair and salt in tea, where the only link between different acts by different aggressors might be the perpetrators' inferred reasons for their actions.

8

DISMISSAL FOR MAKING A PROTECTED DISCLOSURE

A.	Comparison with the pre-PIDA position	8.01	F. Unofficial industrial action	8.18
			G. The burden of proof	8.19
B.	The relationship between a protected disclosure dismissal and an 'ordinary' unfair dismissal	8.03	(1) Ordinary unfair dismissal	8.19
			(2) Is a burden also on the employer to show the reason was not a protected disclosure?	8.20
C.	Identifying the principal reason in dismissal cases	8.11	H. Unfair dismissal protection for non-protected disclosures	8.28
D.	Constructive dismissal	8.14	I. Extension of time	8.39
E.	Selection for redundancy	8.17		

A. Comparison with the pre-PIDA position

In relation to protection against dismissal, the PIDA provisions improved the **8.01** protection for workers making protected disclosures in the following principal respects:

(a) protection previously applied only to employees under a contract of employment rather than the wider class of worker, including protection against termination of contract for non-employee workers;

(b) there is no equivalent minimum service qualification, in contrast to the one-year service qualification before accruing the right not to be unfairly dismissed;

(c) if the disclosure is protected, compensation is not capped, whereas under s124(1) ERA 1996 compensation for ordinary unfair dismissal is capped at £60,000 (with effect from 1 February 2007);

(d) there is a right to claim interim relief; and

(e) dismissal by reason of the disclosure having been made is automatically unfair, whereas under the general law of unfair dismissal it is not; the ordinary test of reasonableness under s98(4) ERA must be applied.

8.02 In this section we consider first the scope of protection provided against unfair dismissal where protected disclosures were made. We then consider the inter-relation with an 'ordinary' unfair dismissal under s98 ERA, including in relation to disclosures that do not meet the requirements for protection.

B. The relationship between a protected disclosure dismissal and an 'ordinary' unfair dismissal

8.03 The legislation makes dismissal by reason of a protected disclosure, or where this is the principal reason, a prohibited reason for dismissal under ss99 to 103 ERA. In summary the structure of the legislation is as follows.

(a) Section 94 ERA gives an employee the right not to be unfairly dismissed.

(b) Section 98(1) requires an employer facing a claim of unfair dismissal to show the reason or principal reason for the dismissal and that it falls within the potentially fair reasons set out in s98(1) and (2).

(c) If a potentially fair reason is shown, then in an ordinary unfair dismissal case the question of whether the dismissal is fair would depend on the test in s98(4) of whether in the circumstances the employer acted reasonably or unreasonably in treating it as a sufficient reason for dismissing the employee. However s98(6) provides that this is subject to the various provisions for automatic unfairness including s103A ERA. The effect is that a tribunal is not to consider whether or not the employer's actions were reasonable (although reasonableness may conceivably become relevant to the amount of compensation).

(d) Section 103A provides that:

> an employee who is dismissed shall be regarded for the purposes of this Part as unfairly dismissed if the reason (or, if more than one, the principal reason) for the dismissal is that the employee made a protected disclosure.

(e) If there were a number of reasons for the dismissal then the dismissal will be automatically unfair only if the protected disclosure was the principal reason.

8.04 The nature of the relationship between s103A and ordinary unfair dismissal arose as an issue in *Butcher v The Salvage Association* (EAT/988/01, 21 January 2002). The claimant raised various issues in relation to his employer's internal accounts. The tribunal held that the concerns related to professional but not legal obligations, and so there was no protected disclosure. It further held that the principal reason for dismissal was irreconcilable differences with the Chief Executive, who had disagreed with the way that the claimant wanted to present the financial reports. On appeal the claimant sought to argue that the finding on the protected disclosure issue was wrong, but also that it was incumbent upon the Tribunal to reach a separate conclusion in respect of this, which gave him a separate and distinct right of appeal. Both contentions were rejected by the EAT at a preliminary hearing and by Peter Gibson LJ in refusing permission to appeal to the Court of Appeal.[1]

The EAT (at a preliminary hearing) held that there was no separate right given by **8.05** ss43A and 43L to complain of a dismissal for that reason. The right to complain of unfair dismissal was given by s94(1) which simply stated the right of an employee not to be unfairly dismissed by his employer. Although the sections that follow dealt with the way in which a tribunal had to approach the determination of the issues caused by that right, that section did not give a separate and free-standing right in respect of PIDA. A finding in favour of the claimant on a complaint of unfair dismissal, if reached on one basis, gave him no right to complain that it should have been reached on a different basis. This approach was, perhaps, understandable on the facts where the only basis on which it was suggested that a finding under s103A would make a difference was in relation to contributory fault, and that submission was rejected. But the decision cannot be taken as authority to the effect that a claimant who succeeds under s98 but fails under s103A would be unable to appeal where the difference would be significant, such as in relation to the cap on the compensatory award.

In refusing permission to appeal Peter Gibson LJ placed emphasis on the impor- **8.06** tance of establishing the reason for dismissal both in relation to ordinary and automatically unfair dismissal. In this case the tribunal had made a finding of fact that the reason for the dismissal was the irreconcilable differences,[2] rather than the reason advanced by Mr Butcher, and that this amounted to a substantial reason such as potentially to justify dismissal. On this analysis a finding of ordinary unfair dismissal was inconsistent with a finding under s103A where there had been found to be a potentially fair reason within s98(2) ERA. That has force where, as in *Butcher*, the potentially fair reason is within the category of a substantial reason such as to justify dismissal. It is difficult to see how dismissal by reason of a protected disclosure could fall within that category. The position is less clear where the potentially fair reason is conduct. It might be argued that making a protected disclosure can be both a conduct reason and automatically unfair within s103A. The structure of the legislation is that having found that the dismissal amounted to conduct, the tribunal would then have to consider under s98(6) whether s103A applies.

A related point as to the relation between ordinary unfair dismissal and **8.07** s103A arose in the EAT in *Street v Derbyshire Unemployed Workers' Centre* [2004]

---

[1] [2002] EWCA Civ 867, 31 May 2002.
[2] But this may beg the question as to the reason for 'irreconcilable differences'—were they due to a protected disclosure?

ICR 213.[3] There the claim had been (at least primarily) pleaded as one of protected disclosure leading to dismissal. During the hearing the claimant sought to run a claim of 'ordinary' unfair dismissal as well, it having initially been conceded that no claim of ordinary unfair dismissal was pleaded. One of the issues for the EAT was whether the tribunal was correct in declining to entertain the ordinary unfair dismissal claim (it had gone on to dismiss the PIDA-based claim).

8.08 The EAT said that this raised an issue of construction in relation to the originating application, to see whether it contained the basis of a claim so that this could be adduced. This was a technical issue, involving a pure point of law and not the assessment of the reality of the circumstances.[4] *Selkent Bus Co Ltd v Moore* [1996] ICR 836[5] laid down the guidelines upon which a decision about raising a new and additional claim might be made.[6] Amongst the considerations are whether the amendment sought is a substantial alteration pleading a new cause of action. If a new complaint or cause of action was proposed to be added by way of amendment, it was essential for the Tribunal to consider whether that complaint is out of time and, if so, whether the time limit should be extended under the applicable statutory provisions. The EAT then analysed the originating application. In box 1 Mrs Street had described the 'type of complaint' as 'Unfair Dismissal—Right not to be dismissed or victimised following disclosure of wrongdoing by employer under PIDA 1998'. Under the 'details of complaint' she had written:

> I conclude that I have been disciplined and dismissed unfairly, that I was protected under PIDA and the allegations I made were made in good faith at the time and were made to organisations . . . because I feared victimisation and eventual dismissal, which has come to pass.

8.09 The EAT's analysis was that on this wording there was within the originating application the basis of a claim for ordinary unfair dismissal. They went on (in paragraphs 36–39) to say this:

> We accept [the submission on behalf of Mrs Street] that there is what we described as a single channel, that is, one complaint is made under the sole basis which is section 94, a complaint of unfair dismissal. It may take different forms and different facts will be relevant to different specific forms . . . If what was thought to be advanced was a completely new ordinary unfair dismissal claim, *Selkent* would have

---

[3] The decision in the Court of Appeal ([2005] ICR 97) is discussed in detail in Chapter 4.

[4] *Bryant v Housing Corporation* [1999] ICR 123 (CA): see Buxton LJ at p 130.

[5] See now the summary of the applicable principles in *Smith v Lehman Bros* (EAT/0486/05, 13 October 2005), deciding that the balance of hardship and injustice test applies even to new claims brought out of time.

[6] See the principles set out at p 842.

been directly relevant. In *Selkent* it is not decided whether or not such a change constitutes a new cause of action. The principal basis upon which *Selkent* was decided was that new facts, not previously pleaded, would have to be put in evidence and it was unfair to allow that to be done at the stage that had then been reached. . . . we have come to the conclusion that the Employment Tribunal focused incorrectly on section 111 and did not focus upon the other factors in *Selkent* and did not correctly analyse the Originating Application as containing in itself a claim for ordinary unfair dismissal which simply needed particularisation. It will be borne in mind that the onus then would fall on the employer to produce reasons. As it happens, the Respondent did so, for it met a claim of ordinary unfair dismissal by its answer that the dismissal was nothing to do with public interest disclosure, was to do with gross misconduct and was fair; and it demonstrated the procedure adopted.

The EAT's approach is that claims of 'ordinary' unfair dismissal and a dismissal **8.10** contrary to s103A are indeed the same 'cause of action' as each other—the cause of action being unfair dismissal.

C. Identifying the principal reason in dismissal cases

Once a protected disclosure is established, the focus is on the reason for dismissal. **8.11** In an ordinary dismissal context, the test for the reason for dismissal was recently summarized by Elias J in *ASLEF v Brady* (2006) IRLR 576:

51. In *Devis v Atkins* [1977] ICR 662 at 677–678 Viscount Dilhorne addressed the reason for dismissal in the following terms:

'The decision of the Court of Appeal in *Abernethy v Mott, Hay and Anderson* [1974] IRLR 213, was on the 1971 Act. Lord Denning MR said that the reason shown for the dismissal "must be a reason in existence at the time when he is given notice. It must be the principal reason which operated on the employer's mind." He went on to say that it must be made known to the man before he is given notice or told to him at the time. I do not see anything in the Act which makes it a condition of fair dismissal that the man dismissed must know before he is given notice or told at the time that he is given notice the reason for it. I prefer the view of Cairns LJ, who said:

"A reason for the dismissal of an employee is a set of facts known to the employer, or it may be of beliefs held by him, which cause him to dismiss the employee. If at the time of his dismissal the employer gives a reason for it, that is no doubt evidence, at any rate as against him, as to the real reason, but it does not necessarily constitute the real reason. He may knowingly give a reason different from the real reason out of kindness. . ."'

52. So the question is: why did the employers dismiss him? If the principal reason was the act or acts of misconduct, then the requirements of section 98(1) are met. If, on the other hand, there was some other reason, they will not be.

8.12   This indicates that the test of the reason for dismissal therefore involves the same considerations as arise in the 'on the ground that' test in s47B (see Chapter 7). Both focus on the mental processes of the employer. Indeed as noted in Chapter 7, in *Nagarajan*, Lord Nicholls emphasized that the tests of 'on racial grounds' and 'by reason that' in the context of the Race Relations Act 1976 were the same. In the context of protected disclosures, in *Felter v Cliveden Petroleum Company* (EAT/0533/05, 9 March 2006) it was accepted (at paragraph 15) that 'the words "on the ground that" in s47B and "the reason . . . for the dismissal" in s103A require the same approach'.

8.13   There is however a significant distinction between the approaches in s47B and in s103A. Following the *Nagarajan* and *Khan* guidance, it is sufficient for the purposes of s47B that the protected disclosure 'had a significant influence on the outcome' (*per* Lord Nicholls in *Nagarajan*).[7] That does not however suffice in the context of unfair dismissal. In a case where there are mixed reasons, s103A only applies where the protected disclosure was the principal reason. This also contrasts with the United States' Whistleblower Protection Act 1989 which merely requires the employee to demonstrate that the whistleblowing was a contributory factor in the dismissal.

D. Constructive dismissal

8.14   In cases of constructive dismissal, the burden is on the employee first to show that he resigned in response to a repudiatory breach of contract. Having established the dismissal within s95(1)(c) ERA, it remains necessary to identify the reason for dismissal. As explained by Browne-Wilkinson LJ in *Berriman v Delabole Slate Limited* [1985] ICR 546 (CA):

> . . . in our judgment, even in a case of constructive dismissal, [s98(1) of the ERtsA 1996] imposes on the employer the burden of showing the reason for the dismissal, notwithstanding that it was the employee, not the employer, who actually decided to terminate the contract of employment. In our judgment, the only way in which the statutory requirements of the [ERA] can be made to fit a case of constructive dismissal is to read [s98(1)] as requiring the employer to show the reasons for their conduct which entitled the employee to terminate the contract thereby giving rise to a deemed dismissal by the employer.

8.15   The focus is therefore on the reason for the conduct which the employee is able to show amounted to a repudiatory breach of contract. The issues considered in Chapter 7 in relation to the whether an act or deliberate failure to act was

---

[7] *Nagarajan v London Regional Transport* [1999] ICR 877 (HL), at 886.

on the grounds of a protected disclosure are therefore also liable to arise here. However there is the additional potential complication of identifying the principal reason. This may be straightforward enough where there is only one act or omission of the employer which is relied upon by the employee as constituting 'the conduct' amounting to a repudiatory breach or where there has been a practice of detrimental treatment due to protected disclosure.[8] But what if the employee establishes that he or she terminated the contract because of a series of acts and omissions of the employer which cumulatively was such as to lead to a breach of the implied term of trust and confidence in the employer? Do *all* of those acts or omissions have to have been done for the reason or principal reason that the employee made a protected disclosure? The last action of the employer which leads to the employee leaving need not itself be a breach of contract; the question is, does the cumulative series of acts taken together amount to a breach of the implied term. Whilst the final act might not be blameworthy or unreasonable it had to contribute something to the breach even if relatively insignificant.[9] Is it sufficient to ground a case of constructive dismissal contrary to s103A that the last 'relatively insignificant' act by the employer was a response to or by reason of the protected disclosure having been made when the rest of the chain of events upon which the employee relies had nothing to do with it, indeed perhaps preceded it having been made?[10]

Ultimately it will be a matter for the tribunal, as a question of fact, to assess in all the circumstances whether the protected disclosure was the principal reason. We suggest though that in such cases it will assist to take into account three aspects of the matter. First and foremost there will need to be a qualitative assessment of how important the protected disclosure was in the erosion of trust and confidence. But together with this, or as part of it, there may need to be a quantitative assessment of how much of the matter complained about can be identified as by reason of the protected disclosure, and also a temporal assessment, in that those events that come later in the story, especially the last straw, may thereby be regarded as more important. **8.16**

---

[8] See also *Flintshire v Sutton* (EAT/1082/02, 1 July 2003) where there was a continuing failure to provide support to which the claimant was entitled due to a *'perception of the Applicant as a problem because he had made the relevant protected disclosures'* (see Appendix 8).

[9] See Glidewell LJ in *Lewis v Motorworld Garages Ltd* [1985] IRLR 465; *Omilaju v Waltham Forest London Borough Council* [2005] EWCA Civ 1493, [2005] ICR 481, paragraph 20 Dyson LJ.

[10] The question discussed here is of course distinct from the issue as to whether the repudiatory breach (or breaches) by the employer are the cause of the employee leaving on which see *Jones v F Sirl & Son (Furnishers) Ltd* [1997] IRLR 493, (there may be another cause as well) and *Nottinghamshire County Council v Meikle* [2004] EWCA Civ 859, [2004] IRLR 703, CA which appears to set an even lower threshold (the resignation being, *at least in part*, due to the repudiatory breach of the employer).

E. Selection for redundancy

8.17 Specific provision is made in relation to redundancies so as to stop employers using redundancy as a way of ridding themselves of whistleblowing employees. If the reason for the dismissal was a redundancy affecting more than one employee then, by s105(1) ERA, it is unfair to select a particular employee for dismissal for redundancy on the ground that he made a protected disclosure. A dismissal will be unfair if (a) the principal reason for it was redundancy, (b) other employees in a similar position (ie potentially subject to redundancy) were not dismissed 'in the same circumstances' and (c) the reason or principal reason for the selection of the complainant employee was because he had made a protected disclosure.

F. Unofficial industrial action

8.18 Whilst s237(1) Trade Union and Labour Relations (Consolidation) Act 1992 provides that generally an employee who is taking part in unofficial industrial action at the time of his or her dismissal cannot bring a claim for unfair dismissal, this bar will not apply where the employee was dismissed or made redundant because he or she had made a protected disclosure (s237(1A)).

G. The burden of proof

(1) Ordinary unfair dismissal

8.19 It is for the employee to prove that he was dismissed and (except in relation to the issue of good faith) that he/she made a protected disclosure. By contrast, at least in relation to 'ordinary' unfair dismissal, the burden is on the employer to show the reason for dismissal and that it was a potentially fair reason (s98(1) ERA). This is subject to an exception where an employee has not accumulated one year's continuous employment prior to dismissal. In *Smith v Hayle Town Council* [1978] ICR 996, Eveleigh LJ, with whom Sir David Cairns agreed, considered the relevant wording (then contained in Schedule 1 to the Trade Union and Labour Relations Act 1974). Once the employer has established that the employee has not been employed for a sufficient period to claim ordinary unfair dismissal then the burden of proof was upon the employee to show that the reason for the dismissal was the proscribed ground. The majority's decision and reasoning in *Smith* was followed by the Employment Appeal Tribunal in *Tedeschi v Hosiden Besson Ltd* (EAT/959/95). Further, in *Jackson v ICS Group Limited* (EAT/499/97, 22 January 1998), the EAT rejected a claimant employee's argument that the position was altered by changes in the wording of the statute to that now contained in s108(3) of the Employment Rights Act 1996.[11]

(2) Is a burden also on the employer to show the reason was not a protected disclosure?

Does it follow that where an employee has sufficient qualifying service, in a claim **8.20** made by reference to s103A, there remains a burden on the employer to show that the reason or principal reason for dismissal was *not* the fact that the employee had made a protected disclosure? The decision of the Court of Appeal in *Maund v Penwith District Council* [1984] IRLR 24 (CA) may be thought to support this proposition. Indeed it was cited in support of this proposition in the context of s103A ERA in *Phipps v Bradford Hospitals NHS Trust* (EAT/531/02, 30 April 2003), where the EAT commented (at para 4):

> The Applicant having raised an automatically unfair reason for dismissal, that is a **8.21** protected disclosure, the burden of establishing a potentially fair reason for dismissal and thus negativing that impermissible reason, lay on the Respondent.

Thus, in the EAT's view, the onus on the employer included an onus to disprove the automatically unfair reason under s103A. Similarly, in another protected disclosure case, *Lucas v Chichester Diocesan Housing Association Limited* (EAT/0713/04, 7 February 2005), the EAT expressed the view (at paragraph 39) that 'the burden of proof, even in an automatically unfair dismissal, remains on the employer pursuant to section 98'.

In our view, however, this does not correctly reflect the effect of the decision in *Maund*, **8.22** nor is it consistent with the wording of the legislation. As to the terms of the statute:

(a) the opening words of s98(1) ERA provide:

> in determining for the purposes of this Part *whether the dismissal of an employee is fair or unfair*, it is for the employer to show . . . (Our emphasis)

> The onus on the employer is therefore imposed specifically for the purposes of determining if the dismissal is fair or unfair. The logical corollary is that if the burden is not discharged, the dismissal is unfair, but not that it is unfair for any particular reason.

---

[11] For criticism of the effect of these provisions in a whistleblowing context see Lewis, 31 ILJ 79 (2002) who argues that it should be considered whether the Human Rights Act (HRA) and the requirement to give effect to Article 10 (1) of the European Convention on Human Rights enables a different approach to be taken and proposes that tribunals could adopt the position that, irrespective of length of service, where a claimant produces evidence to suggest that the reason for dismissal fell within s103A or s105 (6A) ERA, the HRA requires the employer to show that this was not in fact the reason or principal reason. The author argues that this would put the approach in dismissal cases more in line with that taken by s48(2) ERA in cases of detriment but would also deal with the anomaly that workers who are not employees are more favourably treated in this regard by virtue of the reversal in the burden of proof (see paras 7.76–7.81 above).

(b) the reasoning in *Smith v Hayle Town Council*,[12] in holding that the burden of proof was on the employee to show the reason for dismissal where (s)he lacked the requisite qualifying service, also indicates that the burden would be on the employee to show a reason under s103A. Eveleigh LJ (at p 1002) emphasized that the provision permitting a claim to be brought without the requisite qualifying service where there was an inadmissible reason was 'an exceptions paragraph'. It was therefore for the employee to show that (s)he came within the exception. Equally s103A is in several respects an 'exceptions paragraph'. It is an exception to the application of the fairness test in s98(4) ERA, to the requirement for qualifying service, to the upper age limit and to the limit on the compensatory award. By parity of reasoning with that in *Smith v Hayle Town Council* it is to be expected that it would be for the employee to show that the exception applies.

8.23 We turn therefore to the decision in *Maund*.[13] The employee was dismissed by the council on the grounds of redundancy but claimed that the true reason for his dismissal was not redundancy but the council's dislike of his trade union activities, which would have been an automatically unfair reason. In relation to the onus of proof, Griffiths LJ explained (at 149):

> it is not for the employee to prove the reason for his dismissal, but merely to produce evidence sufficient to raise the issue or, to put it another way, that raises some doubt about the reason for the dismissal. Once this evidential burden is discharged, the onus remains upon the employer to prove the reason for the dismissal.

8.24 To similar effect Purchas LJ commented (at 154–155) that:

> the onus that rests upon the employee is to show that there is an issue which warrants investigation existing, against which an alternative reason, or competing reason, may be established. I emphasise that the onus resting upon the employee is not to prove, on a balance of probabilities, that his contending reason is the principal reason, but he must prove, on the balance of probabilities, that the issue exists. The gravity of the accusations, if any, involved in raising the issue will reflect upon the quality of the evidence necessary to establish the existence of the issue. Once the employee has adduced evidence to establish, on the balance of probabilities, the existence of the issue, the onus of showing which of the two competing reasons, or more if there are more, is the principal reason, remains as it always had been, on the shoulders of the employer.

8.25 Stephenson LJ stated (at 157) that:

> the legal burden is placed by the statute on the employer and it remains there. If the employee raises on the evidence before the industrial tribunal an issue as to another reason being the real one, he has not to go further and prove that other reason to be the real one, even if it is an inadmissible reason and to disguise it would be very wrong

---

[12] See above, para 8.19.
[13] See above, para 8.20.

for any employer and even more serious misconduct on the part of a public authority like the respondent council.

The Court of Appeal therefore held that there was an evidential onus on the **8.26** employee to establish an issue as to another reason for dismissal, but the burden of proof remained on the employer even in a case where the alternative reason contended for by the employer was an automatically unfair reason. The tribunal had erred in transferring to the employee the burden of establishing the alternative reason, rather than merely that there was an issue as to an alternative reason. But the court was concerned with the consequences of the employer failing to establish its asserted reason. If so, the dismissal would be unfair by virtue of (the predecessor of) s98(1) and (2). The court was not concerned with issues in relation to the positive benefit of establishing an automatically unfair reason in order, for example, to remove the ceiling on compensation. The relevance of adducing evidence as to an alternative reason was that it was one way of casting doubt on whether that was the true reason. Indeed, as Purchas LJ noted (p 155) there might be more than one competing reason.

Put at its highest, therefore, *Maund* might be relied on for the proposition that if **8.27** the employer does not discharge the onus of proving its reason for dismissal, and the employee has discharged the evidential burden of establishing an issue as to whether the protected disclosure was a reason for dismissal, then this is sufficient to satisfy the principal reason test under s103A. But the better view, we suggest, is that the consequence of a failure by the employer to establish a reason for dismissal is only that the dismissal is unfair. In order to establish that the dismissal is automatically unfair, and to benefit from the exceptional consequences of this, the employee would have the onus of showing that the principal reason for dismissal was the protected disclosure.

H. Unfair dismissal protection for non-protected disclosures

Notwithstanding a finding that a disclosure did not amount to a protected disclosure **8.28** there might still be an issue as to whether a dismissal by reason of the disclosure was (procedurally or substantively) unfair. This was a point stressed by Auld LJ in *Street*.[14] He commented that:

> it has to be remembered that even if a worker might be deterred from making a relevant disclosure because of concern that his employer might raise against him a suggestion of bad faith in the sense of a mix of motives, including personal antagonism, or fails in his section 103A claim on that account, all is not lost. His automatic protection provided by that section is lost, but he can still maintain an 'ordinary'

---

[14] At 112; see above, para 8.07.

claim for unfair dismissal against his employer in which a mix of motives may not be fatal to his claim.

8.29 Whilst there remains the possibility of an ordinary unfair dismissal claim, the fact that a disclosure does not meet the requirements for a protected disclosure, and the reasons that it fails to do so, are likely to be material to the decision as to whether dismissal was a reasonable sanction.

8.30 Further, even in pre-PIDA cases, the factors which would now be material to whether there was a protected disclosure can be seen at play in the determination of whether a dismissal was fair. In *Cornelius v Hackney LBC* (EAT/1061/94) Mr Cornelius, who was employed by Hackney as an internal auditor, discovered that a stores officer also employed by Hackney had acted illegally and in a manner detrimental to his employer's interests. He reported on these matters to his employers but became concerned about what he perceived to be an unwillingness amongst senior management to deal with corrupt practices. He passed on details of his concerns, and of documentary evidence in support, to his trade union and to the chairman of the Performance Review Sub-Committee. The employment tribunal held that the dismissal was procedurally unfair. However even though Mr Cornelius had genuinely been seeking to address a perceived cover-up of corrupt practices, the tribunal held that he was substantially to blame for his dismissal by reason of having disclosed his concerns to his trade union and to the chairman of the Performance Review Sub-Committee, especially as his report was annotated with unflattering remarks about his colleagues. Compensation was therefore reduced by 50 per cent. On appeal, however, the EAT concluded that the decision to reduce compensation was perverse. As the EAT explained:

> there is a high duty upon local government officers in the Appellant's position to report dishonesty in any form, and to persist if need be in ensuring that it is brought to the attention of those in authority and that appropriate action is taken. . . . It is difficult to see how the Appellant could be criticised for passing the documents in his possession, all of which related to his duty to uncover corruption, to the Chairman of the Committee which was concerned in investigating the matter, and who had expressly requested to see them. Equally we are at a loss to understand why the Appellant should be criticised for sending documents to his Union in order to obtain advice from them, if he was unable to resolve the matter satisfactorily by other means.

8.31 Although the tribunal had proceeded only on the basis of procedural unfairness, the EAT plainly regarded the dismissal as substantively unfair. It is likely that an employee in Mr Cornelius' position would now be able to succeed under ERA. Reliance could now be placed on s43G of the ERA in the light of the fact that the concerns had previously been raised with management. Having done so it was then reasonable to make the wider disclosure in the light of the genuine concern that there was a cover-up, together with the fact that the disclosure was made to those with a genuine and legitimate interest in receiving the information either to provide assistance and advice (in the case of the union) or to investigate the handling of corruption (in the case of the councillor).

In *Byford v Film Finances Limited*[15] there were again echoes of reasoning that **8.32** would be material in a post-PIDA case. Although the claimant had a genuine belief in serious allegations against her employer, other considerations led to a finding that dismissal was fair. Mrs Byford was a long-serving employee who felt that she owed obligations of loyalty not only to the company that employed her, but also to its former chairman who was a minority shareholder in the company and had been ousted from a role in managing the company by the majority shareholders. Out of loyalty to the former chairman, Mrs Byford was persuaded to spy on the activities of the company for the minority shareholders. She discovered what she genuinely believed was evidence of improper and fraudulent conduct by the directors of the employing company (who were associated with the majority shareholders), including conduct constituting a fraud on the minority. She reported her findings to the minority shareholders and, as a result, unfair prejudice proceedings were commenced. Upon discovering Mrs Byford's role, the respondent company dismissed her.

The EAT upheld the employment tribunal's finding that the dismissal was fair. The **8.33** dismissal had been for 'some other substantial reason' in that there was a breakdown in trust in Mrs Byford as a result of her having gone behind the directors' back to report her findings to the minority shareholders. Further, the EAT considered that not only was the decision to dismiss within the range of reasonable responses but there was really no other alternative since Mrs Byford plainly could not be trusted.

Neither the employment tribunal nor the EAT resolved the issue as to whether **8.34** the allegations made by Mrs Byford were true. As such the decision proceeded on the basis that the employer was entitled to demand loyalty irrespective of the truth of the serious allegations. It may be, however, that the decision would have been different if the allegations had not been raised for the ulterior motive of assisting the minority. In a post-PIDA decision this might have led to a conclusion that the disclosure was not made in good faith. Nor had the disclosure been raised with a person responsible for investigating the allegations. Further, although the minority shareholders might be said to have had a legitimate interest in the information as to a fraud on them, the EAT emphasized that if there was to be a disclosure of the concerns it would have been more appropriate to make disclosure to the auditors or if, as Mrs Byford alleged, they could not be trusted, to the Department of Trade and Industry. In the post-PIDA world this

---

[15] EAT/804/86.

would no doubt have been reflected in a finding that the disclosure fell outside s43G ERA.

8.35 The employer's entitlement to expect loyalty was similarly emphasized in *Thornley v ARA Ltd*.[16] Mr Thornley raised concerns about the aircraft design of the Tornado aircraft. He was not satisfied with the response. Ultimately he sent a letter to *The Guardian* and was then dismissed. The EAT was unimpressed with the argument that unless Mr Thornley publicized his concerns, the aircraft would be sold with flaws. It was not for him to denigrate his employer's product. On the facts, the matters Mr Thornley disclosed might have fallen within the health and safety, or, possibly, the relevant failures relating to likely breach of legal obligation now enacted within s43B ERA. But in any event it is most unlikely that disclosure to the press would have fallen within s43G unless it could be shown that there was no more appropriate recipient of the information. Again, the factors which would be likely to take the case outside a protected disclosure, also led to the finding of unfair dismissal.

8.36 The considerations relevant to whether there was protected a disclosure are therefore likely to be of importance where the issue of reasonableness under s98 needs to be addressed. Further, one of the aims of the promoters of PIDA was to encourage a change in culture so that there would be a different and more sympathetic attitude to those who raise concerns in a reasonable way. One corollary of this may be that those who do not meet the requirements of a protected disclosure attract less sympathy. For example one consequence of the protected disclosure legislation has been to encourage much more widespread adoption of whistleblowing procedures. Where there is such a procedure, and despite this a disclosure is made which does not meet the requirements for a protected disclosure, an employer may be on stronger ground in contending that dismissal fell within the range of reasonable responses.

8.37 Despite the above considerations, each case will turn on its facts. It is possible to contemplate circumstances where dismissal may not fall within the range of reasonable responses. For example if a worker reports suspected fraud by a colleague to the police, but fails to report this first to the employer, this would fall outside s43G ERA if it did not meet the gateway requirements in s43G(2). But if the employee held an honest and reasonable belief in the fraud and had merely failed to follow correct procedures internally, an employer would no doubt have difficulty in persuading a tribunal that dismissal fell within the range of reasonable responses. The employer is entitled to expect loyalty from the employee but, to take an extreme, the duty of fidelity could not extend to requiring an employee to conceal fraud.

---

[16] EAT 669/76.

In considering the substantive fairness of the decision to dismiss, we suggest **8.38** therefore that the factors material to whether there was a protected disclosure are likely to be important but not necessarily determinative. The important considerations are likely to include the nature and seriousness of the allegation, whether the person receiving the information had a proper interest in receiving it, whether there are others to whom the information could more appropriately have been communicated, the motive for the disclosure, the extent to which the employer can legitimately regard it as showing disloyalty and the evidential basis for the disclosure.

I. Extension of time

The tribunal can only extend time if: (a) it was not reasonably practicable for the **8.39** employee to claim within the period of three months and then only if the time within which the claim was actually made was a reasonable one (s111(2)(b) ERA) or (b) pursuant to the provisions of the Employment Act 2002 (Dispute Regulations) 2004 SI 2004/752 (see Chapter 7 paragraph 7.97–7.101).[17]

---

[17] For a consideration of the general law on time limits and extension of time limits see Bowers, *A Practical Approach to Employment Law* (7th Ed, Oxford: Oxford University Press, 2005) paras 11.06–11.24.

9

REMEDIES IN DISMISSAL AND DETRIMENT CLAIMS

A. **Unfair Dismissal Remedies** 9.01
  (1) Overview of remedies 9.01
  (2) Reinstatement and
    re-engagement 9.03
  Practicability of compliance 9.06
  Contributory fault 9.09
  Other factors 9.10
  Permanent replacements 9.11
  Reasons 9.12
  Terms of re-engagement 9.13
  Compensation and back pay in
    re-employment cases 9.14
  (3) Compensatory award 9.19
  (4) Unfair dismissals and
    contributory fault 9.23
  (5) Interim relief 9.31
B. **Detriment Claims** 9.36
  (1) Overview 9.36

  (2) Injury to feelings 9.40
  When can injury to feelings be
    claimed? 9.40
  The boundary between detriment
    and dismissal 9.42
  Injury to feelings—the appropriate
    amount 9.47
  Causation 9.51
  Knowledge 9.52
  (3) Personal injury—psychiatric
    damage 9.54
  (4) Aggravated damages 9.61
  (5) Exemplary damages 9.66
  (6) Victimization by dismissal of
    a worker who is not an employee 9.68
  (7) Adjustment of awards for
    non-compliance with statutory
    disciplinary procedures 9.72

A. Unfair Dismissal Remedies

(1) Overview of remedies

The primary remedies for unfair dismissal are provided for in s112 ERA. Where an **9.01** employment tribunal finds that the grounds of complaint are well-founded the tribunal is to explain to the complainant what orders may be made under s113 for reinstatement or re-engagement and in what circumstances they may be made, and ask him whether he wishes the tribunal to make such an order. If the complainant expresses such a wish, the tribunal may make an order under s113. If no order for reinstatement or re-engagement is made under s113 then the tribunal *shall* make an award of compensation for unfair dismissal which is to be calculated in accordance with ss118 to 126.

The requirements of s113 are mandatory and a failure to explain the orders amounts to an error of law (*Pirelli General Cable Works Ltd v Murray* [1979] IRLR 190).

9.02 Section 118 ERA provides that where a tribunal makes an order of compensation for unfair dismissal under s112(4) (ie where no order is made for reinstatement or re-engagement), the award is to consist of:

(a) a basic award (calculated in accordance with ss119–122 and 126), and
(b) a compensatory award (calculated in accordance with ss123, 124, 126 and 127).

(2) Reinstatement and re-engagement

9.03 An order for reinstatement is an order that the employer shall treat the complainant in all respects as if he had not been dismissed (s114 ERA). An order for re-engagement is an order, on such terms as the employment tribunal may decide, that the complainant be engaged by the employer, or by a successor of the employer or by an associated employer, in employment comparable to that from which he was dismissed or other suitable employment (s115).

9.04 In exercising its discretion whether to make a re-employment order, the tribunal must first consider whether to make an order for reinstatement and in so doing the tribunal must take into account (s116(1)(a) ERA):

(a) whether the complainant wishes to be reinstated;
(b) whether it is practicable for the employer to comply with an order for reinstatement; and
(c) where the complainant has caused or contributed to some extent to the dismissal, whether it would be just to order reinstatement.

9.05 If the tribunal decides not to make an order for reinstatement, it must then consider whether to make an order for re-engagement and, if so, on what terms (s116(2) ERA). In so doing the tribunal must take into account:

(a) any wish expressed by the complainant as to the nature of the order to be made;
(b) whether it is practicable for the employer (or a successor or an associated employer) to comply with an order for re-engagement; and
(c) where the complainant caused or contributed to some extent to the dismissal, whether it would be just to order his re-engagement and if so, on what terms (s116(3) ERA).

Practicability of compliance

9.06 The practicability of compliance is generally an important factor in determining whether such an order should be made but has particular resonance in whistleblowing cases. It is also relevant to the issue of enforcement of such an order: a tribunal must consider this factor at both stages and cannot postpone its consideration until the enforcement stage (*Port of London Authority v Payne and Others* [1994] IRLR 9).

In deciding whether a re-employment order is practicable, the tribunal should **9.07** consider whether, having regard to the employment relations realities of the situation, it is capable of being put into effect with success (*per* Stephenson LJ in *Coleman and Stephenson v Magnet Joinery Ltd* [1974] IRLR 343). What is 'practicable' should not be equated with what is 'possible' and in this context, the tribunal may take into account the impact the order has on other staff (*Meridian Ltd v Gomersall and another* [1977] IRLR 425). However mere inexpediency is no bar to re-employment (*Qualcast (Wolverhampton) Ltd v Ross* [1979] IRLR 98).

When initially deciding whether to make a re-employment order, the tribunal is **9.08** only required to 'consider' the issue of practicability. At that stage, the tribunal's assessment on the issue of practicability is provisional. It is not uncommon for tribunals to make an order to test whether or not employer claims of impracticability are justified (*Timex Corporation Ltd v Thomson* [1981] IRLR 522 and *Freemans plc v Flynn* [1984] IRLR 486). A tribunal may therefore make an order where an employer claims that there is no vacancy (*Electronic Data Processing Ltd v Wright* (EAT/292/83)) or where the reason for dismissal was redundancy (*Polkey v A E Dayton Services* [1987] IRLR 503). An order is unlikely where there has been a fundamental loss of trust between the parties (*Nothman v London Borough of Barnet (No 2)* [1980] IRLR 65) particularly where the employer is small and the job involves a close working relationship (*Enessy CO SA t/a the Tulcan Estate v Minoprio* [1978] IRLR 489). It has been suggested that where there has been a breakdown in trust and confidence such a re-employment order will only be made in the rarest cases (*Wood Group Heavy Industrial Turbines Ltd v Crossan* [1998] IRLR 680) but tribunals should not necessarily conclude that re-employment is impracticable because of the claimant's conduct of litigation against the employer (*Cruickshank v London Borough of Richmond* (EAT/483/97)). This argument is often used in resistance to an order for reinstatement or re-engagement in whistle-blowing cases (eg *Callanan v Surrey AHA* (COIT 994/36, 5 February 1980).

Contributory fault

Tribunals are also required to consider whether re-employment is just in the light **9.09** of the employee's contributory conduct. The test to be applied is the same as under s123(6) ERA (*The Boots Company Ltd v Lees-Collier* [1986] ICR 728), ie the conduct involved must be blameworthy. However, a finding of contributory conduct does not rule out the possibility of a re-employment order being made, although such an order is unlikely where the employee is substantially to blame for the dismissal (*Nairne v Highlands and Islands Fire Brigade* [1989] IRLR 366).

Other factors

In addition to these requirements, a tribunal may take into account other factors **9.10** in deciding whether or not to make a re-employment order. For example, tribunals may take into account the impact the order would have on employment relations generally (*Coleman v Magnet Joinery Ltd* [1974] ICR 46) or the personal relationships with other employees (*Intercity East Coast Ltd v McGregor* (EAT/473/96): reinstatement was not practicable because of the acrimonious relationship between employee and supervisor, to which the employee had contributed).

Permanent replacements

9.11 Reinstatement or re-engagement are not necessarily considered impracticable simply because the employer has taken on a permanent replacement. Section 116(5) ERA provides that where an employer has engaged a permanent replacement, this shall not be taken into account in deciding whether or not to make a re-employment order unless 'it was not practicable for [the employer] to arrange for the dismissed employee's work to be done without engaging a permanent replacement' or the employer engaged the replacement 'after the lapse of a reasonable period without having heard from the dismissed employee that he wish to be reinstated or re-engaged', and at the time the replacement was taken on, 'it was not practicable for [the employer] to arrange for the dismissed employee's work to be done without engaging a permanent replacement' (s116(6) ERA).

Reasons

9.12 The tribunal must give its reasons for making or refusing such an order and in particular the reasons why it considers the order to be practicable or otherwise (*Port of London Authority v Payne and ors* [1992] IRLR 447 and *Clancy v Cannock Chase Technical College* [2001] IRLR 331).

Terms of re-engagement

9.13 Other than in cases where the claimant is found to have contributed to the dismissal, the tribunal is required to order re-engagement on such terms which are, so far as is reasonably practicable, as favourable as reinstatement (s116(4) ERA) but the tribunal cannot order re-engagement on terms that are *more* favourable than if the employee had been reinstated (*Rank Xerox (UK) Ltd v Stryczek* [1995] IRLR 568). The order should specify the place of employment and the nature of employment (*Stryczek*, ibid) and the date by which the order should be complied with (*Pirelli General Cable Works Ltd v Murray* [1979] IRLR 190).

Compensation and back pay in re-employment cases

9.14 The tribunal is entitled to award the full amount of back pay which has accrued between dismissal and the date when the order will take effect and the claimant may also recover compensation for any improvements in such terms and conditions between the date of dismissal and the date on which the order takes effect. Even in an ordinary unfair dismissal claim there is no statutory limit on the amount the tribunal can award in this regard (s124(3) ERA).

However, in calculating the amount payable by the employer, tribunals must **9.15** deduct the payments set out in s114(4) ERA namely:

(a) wages in lieu of notice or any *ex gratia* payment received by the employee from the employer in respect of the period between the date of termination and the date of reinstatement (see *Butlers v British Railways Board* (EAT/510/89));

(b) any payments received by the employee in respect of employment with another employer in the same period; and

(c) such other benefits as the tribunal thinks fit in the circumstances.

No deduction should be made for contributory fault or a failure to mitigate **9.16** (*City & Hackney Health Authority v Crisp* [1990] IRLR 47). The Employment Protection (Recoupment of Jobseekers Allowance and Income Support) Regulations 1996 (SI 1996/2349) apply to the award.

The statutory provisions distinguish between partial compliance with the tribunal's **9.17** order and non-compliance. s117(1) ERA provides that if an order for reinstatement or re-engagement is made and the complainant is reinstated or re-engaged but the terms of the order are not complied with, then the tribunal 'shall make an award of compensation'. In such circumstances, the amount of the award 'shall be such as the tribunal thinks fit having regard to the loss sustained by the complainant in consequence of the failure to comply fully with the terms of the order' (s117(2) ERA). There is no power to make an additional award in these circumstances.

Section 117(3) ERA provides that if the claimant is not reinstated or re-engaged, the **9.18** tribunal is required, subject to the defence of impracticability, to make an additional award of between 26 and 52 weeks' pay as well as a standard award of compensation for unfair dismissal calculated in accordance with ss118-127. Note: reinstatement on different terms from those ordered by the tribunal amounts to non-compliance (*Artisan Press Ltd v Strawley and Parker* [1986] IRLR 126).

(3) Compensatory award

Section 123 ERA directs that the amount of the compensatory award shall be such **9.19** as the tribunal considers just and equitable in all the circumstances having regard to the loss sustained by the complainant in consequence of the dismissal insofar as that loss is attributable to action taken by the employer. There are specific provisions as to expenses and losses of benefits consequential upon dismissal similar to those in relation to victimization.

9.20 The compensatory award for ordinary unfair dismissal claims is subject to a ceiling which is index linked and currently stands at £60,000.[1] However there is no ceiling on compensation for a dismissal where the reason or principal reason was that the employee made a protected disclosure (s137(1) ERA). This provision was introduced at the Report Stage of the Bill on 30 March 1999. When introducing the amendment the then Secretary of State for Trade and Industry, Stephen Byers, explained that 'we must send out a clear message underlining how seriously we regard this issue.' He also stated in responding to criticism that the absence of a ceiling on compensation would be difficult for small firms:

> Any tribunal can take into account the size of an organisation or company in deciding whether an approach has been fair and reasonable in particular circumstances .... If a small business does not have the amount of back-up that is available to a larger company, the tribunal can take that factor into account in deciding the appropriate level of compensation to apply.[2]

9.21 The principles as to recovery of financial loss may be found in *Blackstone's Employment Law Practice 2006* (Oxford: Oxford University Press, 2006) chaps 24–26. Very large awards are often made for pecuniary loss because employees may be able to convince the tribunal that because they have blown the whistle they will find it very difficult to work in the particular industry in which they operate. In *Fernandes v Netcom Consultants UK Ltd* (ET, Case No. 22000060/00, 24 January 2000) Mr Fernandes was awarded £293,441 on the basis that the 58-year-old chief financial officer would not secure similar work in the future. Again in *Montgomery v Universal Services Handling Ltd* (ET, Case No. 2701150/03) the employee successfully showed that the reason he could not gain security clearance to work in the security industry as he wished was because of his dismissal and his subsequent period of employment.[3] The tribunal will consider the percentage likelihood chances of gaining another job at a specific time and at a specific rate (eg *MOD v Cannock* [1994] ICR 918, *Lingard v HM Prison Service* (ET, Case No. 1802862/04, 16 December 2004).

9.22 It is often appropriate, in assessing what income the employee would have earned if he had not blown the whistle, for the claimant to focus on another employee who has not blown the whistle and to consider what has happened to his or her career path by way of comparison with the claimant (eg *Acikalin v Phones 4 U Ltd* (ET, Case No. 3302501/04). This may be particularly important in predicting what bonus the employee would have received if he had not blown the whistle.

---

[1] Employment Rights (Increase of Limits) Order 2006 SI 2006/3045.
[2] *Hansard*, 30 March 1999, Col. 877.
[3] See also *Bhatia v Sterlite Industries (India) Ltd* (ET, Case No. 2204571/00, 2 May 2001) where there was an award of £805,384.

(4) Unfair dismissals and contributory fault

As noted in Chapter 7 there has been some judicial recognition that the legitimate **9.23** protection against victimization could be undermined by too readily allowing employers to draw a distinction between the protected activity or disclosure and the manner in which it was carried out or made. These considerations are also apposite in relation to the extent to which awards may be subject to deductions for contributory fault due to, for example, the intemperate way in which a disclosure was made.

In the pre-PIDA case of *Friend v CAA*[4] an employment tribunal held that a **9.24** whistleblower had contributed 100 per cent to his dismissal. Captain Friend was employed by the CAA as a flight operations inspector. As a result of expressing strong views as to safety matters, he enjoyed a poor relationship with some of his colleagues. Ultimately, following allegations made by some of his colleagues, he was dismissed. The employment tribunal held that the dismissal was procedurally unfair but that his compensation should be reduced by 100 per cent due to his contributory fault. In upholding this decision the Court of Appeal explained that there was no need for the tribunal to have investigated whether Captain Friend's safety concerns were well-founded since in relation to compensation:

> the question for the industrial tribunal . . . was not whether he was right or wrong, reasonable or unreasonable, in the views he expressed; but whether his way of expressing them, and the steps he took, or omitted to take, as a means of emphasising them, amounted to action which caused or contributed to his dismissal . . . [F]or the purpose of answering that question it was unnecessary to enlarge the ambit of an already long hearing by going into the rights and wrongs of the controversy engendered by the helicopter safety issue.

The issue arises as to whether the approach in the *Friend* case could be applied **9.25** in the case of someone automatically dismissed under s103A ERA. Could it be argued that the manner of disclosure in a particular case contributed to the employee's dismissal and accordingly that compensation ought to be reduced under s123(6) ERA on the ground that the dismissal was to an extent 'caused or contributed to by [an] action of the complainant'?

On one level it is difficult to see how contributory fault has any part to play in **9.26** assessment of compensation where the tribunal has concluded that the dismissal was automatically unfair because the reason or principal reason for the dismissal was the making of a protected disclosure. How can the employee ever be said to have contributed to a dismissal which is for that reason save in the sense that he or she made the disclosure? Further, the protected conduct cannot be the ground of a reduction for contributory fault. This was established in *Property Guards Ltd v Taylor and Kershaw* [1982] IRLR 175. The employee security guards were dismissed

---

4 Unreported, cited in [1998] IRLR 253.

because they had failed to disclose 'spent' convictions. This was argued to constitute contributory action. But by S4(3)(b) of the Rehabilitation of Offenders Act it was provided that 'a conviction which has become spent or any circumstances ancillary thereto, or any failure to disclose a spent conviction or any such circumstances, shall not be a proper ground for dismissing or excluding a person from any office, profession, occupation or employment'. Accordingly the dismissals were effectively automatically unfair. The EAT said, at paragraph 13, that no question of contribution could arise, because there was no obligation to disclose and there was no question of any fault by the claimants or either of them, which could form the subject matter of a claim that there was contribution to their dismissal.

9.27 However it is clear that contributory fault *can* be found in a case of automatic unfair dismissal. This is shown by terms of other provisions for automatic unfair dismissal. Section 152 of TULRCA makes dismissal of an employee on grounds related to union membership or activities automatically unfair. Section 155 TULRCA specifies certain matters which are to be disregarded in assessing contributory fault. It therefore follows that conduct other than those specified matters may lead the tribunal to conclude that the dismissal was caused or contributed to by the action of the complainant. This is also consistent with the express provision for contributory fault to be taken into account in detriment claims (s49(5) ERA). There is no inconsistency with the finding that the principal reason for dismissal was a protected disclosure, because it is sufficient if contributory conduct played a material part in the dismissal albeit it was not the principal reason: see *Robert Whiting Designs Limited v Lamb* [1978] ICR 89 (EAT). Notwithstanding this, whilst in principle the way in which a worker behaves when making a protected disclosure might properly be blameworthy conduct justifying a reduction in compensation, such as due to being unnecessarily abusive, a good deal of leeway is to be permitted. This is consistent with the policy, as noted in *Boulding v Land Securities Trillium (Media Services) Limited* (EAT/0023/06, 3 May 2006 at paragraph 24) that having regard to the public interest in the legislation, 'there is a certain generosity in the construction of the statute and in the treatment of the facts'.

9.28 A related issue was highlighted by the decision of the EAT in *Melia v Magna Kansei* [2005] ICR 874.[5] In addition to the deductions that can be made on the grounds of contributory fault, the tribunal may reduce compensation on the basis of the likelihood that a fair dismissal would have occurred in any event or that it is just and equitable to do so.[6] One potential difficulty arising from this is if it

---

[5] This decision (at Court of Appeal level) is considered further below in relation to the scope of injury to feelings awards.

[6] *Devis & Sons Limited v Atkins* [1977] AC 931 (HL). Deductions can also be made for failing to follow an applicable statutory disciplinary or grievance procedure (see paras 9.72 and 9.73 below).

encourages a search for evidence to hold against the person who has blown the whistle. This was found to have occurred in *Melia*. The claimant complained that, having made a disclosure in May 2001 in respect of alleged bullying by a manager, he was subjected to various detriments by his employer over the succeeding months and up to November 2001. He was then suspended pending an investigation of an allegation of gross misconduct. He said that this confirmed to him that his employer was not capable of, nor willing to perform his contract of employment, nor its legal duties under various statutory instruments including the Health and Safety at Work Act. He purported to accept the repudiatory breaches and terminated the contract with immediate effect. As Chadwick LJ put it in the Court of Appeal,[7] 'In short, he alleged that he was forced to resign because he was a "whistleblower"'.

The tribunal upheld Mr Melia's complaints of victimization and that the principal **9.29** reason for his constructive dismissal was that he had made a protected disclosure. However they also ruled that prior to and unconnected with his dismissal, Mr Melia had seriously misused the respondent's computer system for which he might, but not necessarily would, have been fairly dismissed in any event. An award of £6,000 was made for detriment and the respondent had to pay a compensatory award of £11,601.87. There was a reduction of 50 per cent in both the basic and compensatory award on the grounds that it was just and equitable to do so in the light of Mr Melia's misconduct prior to dismissal. This reduction was made notwithstanding the tribunal's finding that the evidence of wrongdoing was:

> discovered after a concerted effort to find material which—as a result of the protected disclosure—could be used to ensure the termination of the claimant's employment, if possible without the need for any form of negotiated settlement.

The EAT (at para 55) note the force of the submission that the employers should **9.30** not be permitted 'to scrabble around after a protected disclosure to try to find some misconduct which it could then use as a justification or excuse for dismissal, or at any rate by way of self-defence to claim against it . . .' Indeed this in itself would appear to have been an unlawful detriment under s47B ERA. Notwithstanding this, the EAT considered that there was no basis to interfere with the tribunal's decision on this issue.

(5) Interim relief

Pursuant to s128(1)(b) ERA (as amended by s9 PIDA) employees (but not other **9.31** workers) who are dismissed because they have made a protected disclosure are able to seek interim relief. This emphasizes the importance of public interest disclosure cases and puts them on a par with dismissals for trade union activities. If a tribunal

---

[7] [2006] IRLR 117 (CA).

finds that the employee is likely to win at the full hearing it will order that the employee is re-employed or, if the employer is not willing to accept this, make an order for the continuation of the employment contract so that the claimant will receive his pay and normal benefits. If after the full hearing the tribunal finds for the employee, such an interim order is likely to increase the chances that the tribunal finds that it is practicable for the employer to comply with any re-employment order made at the full hearing.[8]

9.32 For interim relief to be available the claim for it must be made within seven days of the dismissal (s128(2) ERA)—that is to say that the normal 3-month time limit is abrogated. The tribunal must determine the application as soon as possible thereafter (s128(4) and cannot postpone the hearing of the application unless there are exceptional circumstances (s128(5) ERA). This also has ramifications for the operation of statutory disciplinary or dismissal procedures. The parties are treated as having complied with the appeal stage of the standard or modified disciplinary or dismissal procedures, provided that there has been compliance with the previous stages by the time the application for interim relief is presented.[9]

9.33 If at the interim relief hearing the tribunal considers it likely that, at a full hearing, it will find that the reason or principal reason for the dismissal was on the ground of whistleblowing, then a series of provisions apply (s129(1) ERA). In the parallel provisions in respect of interim hearings in trade union activities cases 'likely' has been interpreted as meaning a 'pretty good chance of succeeding', which equated to better than 'more likely than not'.[10]

9.34 The procedure in PIDA cases is the same as that for other applications for interim relief. The tribunal first explains its powers to the parties (s129(2) ERA) and asks the employer if it will re-employ the employee pending the full hearing (s129(3) ERA). If the employer is willing to do so then an order is made to that effect: s129(4)–(6) ERA. If the employee does not accept re-engagement (that is a different post though on terms no less favourable: s129(3)(b) ERA) the tribunal decides whether that refusal is reasonable. If it is reasonable the employee's contract is deemed to continue until the full hearing. If the refusal is not reasonable no order is made pending full hearing: s129(8) ERA.

9.35 If the employer fails to attend the hearing or says that he is unwilling to re- employ the employee (s129(9)) the tribunal makes an order, under s130 ERA, that the employee's contract is deemed to continue until the full hearing. Even if the employee does not actually return to work, such an order will strengthen the employee's bargaining position in negotiations and may have some influence

---

[8] An order for interim relief was made in *Fernandes*, above para 9.21.

[9] The Employment Act 2002 (Dispute Resolution) Regulations 2004 (SI 2004/752), reg 5(1).

[10] *Taplin v C Shippam Limited* [1978] IRLR 450 (EAT).

on the tribunal's decision whether to grant a re-employment order at the full hearing and on whether it was practicable for the employer to comply with it. As far as we are aware interim relief has only been awarded in three cases but seeking interim relief will frequently cause the tribunal to put the case down for an earlier hearing than it would otherwise achieve.

B. Detriment Claims

(1) Overview

So far as detriment complaints are concerned s49 ERA provides that, where an **9.36** employment tribunal finds a complaint under s48 well-founded, the tribunal *shall* make a declaration to that effect, and *may* make an award of compensation to be paid by the employer to the complainant in respect of the act or failure to act to which the complaint relates. The amount of the compensation awarded shall be such as the tribunal considers just and equitable in all the circumstances having regard to:

(a) the infringement to which the complaint relates, and
(b) any loss which is attributable to the act, or failure to act, which infringed the complainant's right.

The section specifically provides that the loss shall be taken to include: **9.37**

(a) any expenses reasonably incurred by the complainant in consequence of the act, or failure to act, to which the complaint relates, and
(b) loss of any benefit which he might reasonably be expected to have had but for that act or failure to act.

Substantial pecuniary losses in detriment cases which do not also include claims **9.38** of dismissal are less common than in unfair dismissal claims for the straight-forward reason that the employee usually remains employed (though as discussed in Chapter 7, the detriment might also be inflicted after the employment has ended).[11] There might still be substantial financial loss, such as where the detriment consists of the impact on discretionary bonus payments, or where it has resulted in being passed over for a promotion or where a detrimental reference results in loss of other employment.

In contrast with unfair dismissal claims, compensation for detriment claims **9.39** can, and invariably does, include non-pecuniary losses. This is however subject to s49(6) ERA where the detriment consists of termination of a contract which is not

---

[11] *Woodward v Abbey National plc* [2006] IRLR 677 (CA).

a contract of employment. In such a case compensation is limited to that which would be available in an unfair dismissal claim. We consider this further below.[12]

(2) Injury to feelings

When can injury to feelings be claimed?

9.40 Since *Norton Tool Co Ltd v Tewson* [1972] IRLR 86 it had been almost universally accepted that unfair dismissal compensation could not include compensation for injury to feelings[13] occasioned by the dismissal. But following Lord Hoffman's remarks in *Johnson v Unisys Limited* [2001] IRLR 279, to the effect that they had the power to do so, various employment tribunals began to make awards for injury to feelings in unfair dismissal cases. The issue reached the House of Lords in *Dunnachie v Kingston Upon Hull City Council* [2004] IRLR 727, and it was held that tribunals could not do this.[14]

9.41 Injury to feelings may be taken into account in respect of detriments but not dismissal. It is determined on a basis similar to that used in discrimination cases (ie Sex Discrimination Act 1975, s66(4), Race Relations Act 1976, s57(4), Disability Discrimination Act 1995, s17A(4), Employment Equality (Sexual Orientation) Regulations 2003, reg 31(3) and Employment Equality (Religion or Belief) Regulations 2003, reg 31(3)) as the EAT put beyond doubt in *Virgo Fidelis Senior School v Boyle* [2004] IRLR 268.

The boundary between detriment and dismissal

9.42 It is quite common for dismissed employees (or workers) to allege (successfully) that prior to their dismissal on the ground of their having made a protected disclosure they were subjected to victimization on that ground which caused a detriment. The dismissal may of course take the form of straightforward dismissal or a constructive dismissal. Because there can only be an injury to feelings award for detriment claims, it becomes important to identify what is regarded as part of the dismissal claim, and what constitutes detriment. Thus, if a disciplinary hearing is conducted in a vindictive manner, compensation for this could only be claimed if the case could be brought under s47B ERA, rather than regarding the disciplinary proceedings as part of the dismissal. Similarly, in a constructive dismissal case, the issue arises as to whether the repudiatory conduct can lead to a s47B detriment

---

[12] At paragraphs 9.68–9.71.

[13] Or for personal injury.

[14] But financial losses flowing from damage to health are recoverable in an unfair dismissal claim: see eg *Devine v Designer Flowers Wholesale Florist Sundries Ltd* [1993] IRLR 517 (EAT).

claim or whether it is part of the dismissal. This issue was addressed in *Melia*,[15] making it clear that in both of these instances, the claim could proceed as a detriment claim, alongside a claim of unfair dismissal for losses arising out of the dismissal itself.

As noted above,[16] Mr Melia succeeded in claims that he had been subjected to   **9.43** a detriment by reason of protected disclosures, and also that he had been constructively unfairly dismissed under s103A in that he resigned in response to being victimized for having made protected disclosures. In reaching its conclusion as to the appropriate compensation for being subjected to detriment, the tribunal only compensated for the detriment up until June 2001, rather than for the whole period to his resignation in November 2001, taking the view that s47B (2) meant that it had to separate from that and effectively discount such of the treatment (and thus its consequences) as effectively amounted to the unfair dismissal. This was because it could not award within compensation for unfair dismissal a sum of money to reflect the injury to feelings caused by the manner, still less the fact, of that dismissal. Accordingly the tribunal would only compensate for detriment up to the point at which the treatment of Melia became so serious that it amounted to a fundamental breach of contract. That point was not the date by which Melia decided that his employment had to end but the date, which they decided was late June 2001, by which the conduct moved from being a detriment to being a matter of dismissal.

The EAT supported this approach but the Court of Appeal allowed Melia's   **9.44** appeal. The proper meaning to be given to the phrase 'the detriment in question amounts to dismissal' is that it excluded detriment which could be compensated under the unfair dismissal provisions. If the detriment could not be compensated under the unfair dismissal provisions because it was not a loss sustained *in consequence of the dismissal* then there was nothing to take it out of s47(B); and the provisions in s49, which require compensation for that detriment, should apply. An employee who was dismissed whether expressly or constructively, was entitled to recover in respect of detriment right up to the point of dismissal. 'Dismissal' in s47B should be construed to have the same meaning as the meaning given to it in Part X of the ERA—which was the point in time when the employment was terminated. Chadwick LJ said:

> When the two sections are read together, the proper meaning to be given to the phrase 'the detriment in question amounts to dismissal' is that it excludes detriment which can be compensated under the unfair dismissal provisions. If the detriment cannot be compensated under the unfair dismissal provisions—for the reason that it is not a loss sustained in consequence of the dismissal—then there is nothing to take it out

---

[15] [2006] IRLR 117 (CA).
[16] At paragraphs 9.28 to 9.30.

of section 47(B); and the provisions in section 49, which require compensation for that detriment, should apply.[17]

9.45 In a constructive dismissal case, it is not the repudiatory breach that constitutes the dismissal, but the acceptance of that repudiatory breach by the employee, thereby terminating the contract. Melia was therefore entitled to compensation for injury to feelings right up to 9 November 2001. Equally in a case of dismissal by the employer it would be open for the employee to assert that the manner in which disciplinary proceedings were conducted amounted to a detriment for which there could be an injury to feelings award, notwithstanding that the proceedings culminated in dismissal. Thus in *Virgo Fidelis* an injury to feelings award was made arising in part from deficiencies in the disciplinary steps leading up to dismissal for whistleblowing. It is only injury to feelings consequential on the dismissal itself which is excluded.

9.46 This approach considerably simplifies the issue as to where a detriment amounts to dismissal thereby excluding an injury to feelings claim. One residual issue however relates to appeals against dismissal. Clearly a detriment in relation to the conduct of an appeal can be taken into account in calculating injury to feelings. What of the decision to uphold the dismissal itself? Strictly the dismissal might already have taken effect by that time and so the decision on appeal may be said not to amount to dismissal. However it would be bizarre if injury to feelings were unavailable for a detriment consisting of the fact of the dismissal but were available for a detriment consisting of the fact of the dismissal being upheld. Nor would this be consistent with the reasoning in *Melia*, which emphasizes that the scheme of the legislation is to draw a distinction between detriments which can be compensated by an unfair dismissal claim (albeit restricted to financial losses) and those which cannot. We think the better view, therefore, is that there cannot be an award of injury to feelings in respect of a detriment consisting of the upholding of an appeal on the grounds of a protected disclosure, but we recognize that there is no direct authority on the point.[18]

Injury to feelings—the appropriate amount

9.47 Translating hurt feelings, such as upset, anxiety, frustration and humiliation, into an award is inevitably a somewhat artificial exercise but employment tribunals

---

[17] This closely paralleled the approach taken in *Eastwood v Magnox Electric plc* [2004] ICR 1064 (HL) to the scope of what is excluded by the decision in *Johnson v Unisys Limited* [2001] ICR 480 (HL), that damages are not recoverable at common law for the manner of dismissal. In that context also, the '*Johnson* exclusion area' has been drawn by distinguishing between breaches of contract prior to dismissal and the termination of the contract itself.

[18] See further Bowers and Lewis 'Non-economic Damage in Unfair Dismissal cases: What's Left After *Dunnachie*?' (2005) 34 ILJ 83.

have to do the best they can on the evidence before them. The general considerations (some based on public policy) which tribunals should take into account in applying the law were summarized by Smith J in *Armitage, Marsden and HM Prison Service v Johnson* [1997] ICR 275:

> Awards for compensation for injury to feelings are compensatory. They should be just to both parties. They should compensate fully without punishing the tortfeasor. Feelings of indignation should not be allowed to inflate the award. Awards should not be too low as that would diminish respect for the policy of the legislation. On the other hand, awards should be restrained as excessive awards may be seen as the way to untaxed riches. Awards should bear some broad general similarity to the range of awards in personal injury cases. In exercising their discretion, tribunals should remind themselves of the value in everyday life of the sum they have in mind. This can be done by reference to purchasing power or by reference to earnings. Tribunals should have regard to the need to retain public respect for the level of awards made.

In *Vento v Chief Constable of West Yorkshire Police (No 2)* [2003] IRLR 102, the   **9.48** Court of Appeal (Mummery LJ) gave guidance with regard to the level of awards for injury to feelings in discrimination cases.[19] At paras 65 to 68 Mummery LJ said this:

> Employment tribunals and those who practise in them might find it helpful if this court were to identify three broad bands of compensation for injury to feelings, as distinct from compensation for psychiatric or similar personal injury.
>
> (i) The top band should normally be between £15,000 and £25,000. Sums in this range should be awarded in the most serious cases, such as where there has been a lengthy campaign of discriminatory harassment on the ground of sex or race. This case falls within that band. Only in the most exceptional case should an award of compensation for injury to feelings exceed £25,000.
>
> (ii) The middle band of between £5,000 and £15,000 should be used for serious cases, which do not merit an award in the highest band.
>
> (iii) Awards of between £500 and £5,000 are appropriate for less serious cases, such as where the act of discrimination is an isolated or one-off occurrence. In general, awards of less than £500 are to be avoided altogether, as they risk being regarded as so low as not to be a proper recognition of injury to feelings.

Mummery LJ added that there was within each band 'considerable flexibility,   **9.49** allowing tribunals to fix what is considered to be fair, reasonable and just compensation in the particular circumstances of the case'. This guidance was followed in the context of a s47B protected disclosure detriment claim in *Virgo Fidelis Senior School v Boyle* [2004] IRLR 268. The EAT reduced the award made by the tribunal for injury to feelings from £42,500 to £25,000. The EAT did however draw attention to the fact that under the *Vento* guidelines the seriousness of the offence

---

[19] In *Miles v Gilbank* [2006] IRLR 538, however, the Court of Appeal reminded litigants that *Vento* provided guidance and is not a rule of law.

is an important factor in assessing the impact in terms of injury to feelings and the level of award. In relation to this, the EAT commented (at para 45) that:

> ... detriment suffered by 'whistleblowers' should normally be regarded by tribunals as a very serious breach of discrimination legislation.

9.50   An award for injury to feelings includes compensation for loss of congenial employment (*Ministry of Defence v Cannock* [1994] ICR 918) but, in England and Wales, such an award does not include aggravated damages (*Scott v Commissioners of Inland Revenue* [2004] IRLR 713). The injury to feelings may sometimes arise from the conduct of co-workers as well as directly by the employer (eg *Carroll v Greater Manchester Fire Service* (ET, Case No. 2407819/00)).

Causation

9.51   Such an award for injury to feelings will not be made automatically: it is for the claimant to show that such injury has been suffered as a result of the unlawful act (*Cannock*, para 9.50 above). It is then for the tribunal to consider the extent of the injury (*Murray v Powertech (Scotland) Ltd* [1992] IRLR 257).

Knowledge

9.52   It has been suggested in *Skyrail Oceanic v Coleman* [1981] ICR 864 and *Alexander v Home Office* [1988] ICR 685 that such an award can only be made where the claimant knows the act which led to the injury to be discriminatory, although there is nothing in the statutory provisions to support such a requirement, but knowledge may be an aggravating factor.

9.53   These principles apply:

(a)   Where there is more than one act of detriment, a tribunal may use a global approach in assessing injury to feelings rather than making a separate award for each complaint as it may be unrealistic to make a separate award for each act of discrimination particularly where the acts form a pattern of conduct (*ICTS (UK) Ltd v Tchoula* [2000] ICR 1191).

(b)   In some cases, it may be relevant to take into account the nature of the employment, ie whether the employment was full-time or part-time. In *Orlando v Didcot Power Stations Sports and Social Club* [1996] IRLR 262 the EAT observed that a 'person who unlawfully loses an evening job may be expected to be less hurt and humiliated ... than a person who loses their entire professional career'.

(c)   In principle, it is open to a tribunal to make an award for both injury to feelings and injury to health provided compensation is not awarded twice for the same loss (*HM Prison Service v Salmon* [2001] IRLR 425).

(d)   A tribunal should ignore the fact that the claimant will receive interest on the award (*Cannock*, para 9.50 above).

(3) Personal injury—psychiatric damage

Compensation can be awarded in respect of personal injury resulting from **9.54** discrimination under the race, sex and disability statutes: see *Sheriff v Klyne (Lowestoft) Ltd* [1999] IRLR 481 where the Court of Appeal ruled that the tribunal (or the county court) can award compensation by way of damages for physical or psychiatric injury consequent upon or caused by the statutory tort of discrimination since the claimant is entitled to be compensated for the loss and damage actually sustained as a result of the statutory tort. It is clear from the decision in *Virgo Fidelis* that such a claim could also be made arising out of a s47B protected disclosure detriment claim. Stuart Smith LJ in *Sheriff* said that care needed to be taken in any complaint to an employment tribunal under this head where the claim includes, or might include, injury to health as well as injury to feelings. Obtaining a medical report would be well advised especially since the time within which to make a complaint was limited and an adjudication might follow quite shortly.

An issue which might need to be addressed is whether the psychiatric damage was **9.55** foreseeable. This was the subject of the Court of Appeal's decision (by a majority) in *Essa v Laing Limited* [2004] IRLR 313, a case of direct racial discrimination by use of racist words. There the Employment Tribunal's conclusion that the claimant was not entitled to compensation for psychiatric loss suffered in that case because it was not reasonably foreseeable was overturned. A victim of direct discrimination— at least in the form of racial abuse— is entitled to be compensated for the loss which arises naturally and directly from the wrong. Pill LJ said (at para 39) that it is possible that different considerations will apply where the discrimination takes other forms than that in *Essa's* case.

We have seen how the appellate courts have tended to assimilate the principles **9.56** from sex, race and disability discrimination law into the protections afforded to whistleblowers, most notably in *Woodward v Abbey National plc*.[20] It is difficult to find a rational distinction between a victim in the position of Mr Essa and a whistleblower who can show a direct (but not reasonably foreseeable) link between the treatment meted out to him or her and ensuing psychiatric illness.

It is for the claimant to prove injury to health as a result of a discriminatory act. **9.57** Where there is no specific medical evidence to support such a claim the award for injury to feelings should reflect general stress and emotional upset suffered by the claimant (*HM Prison Service v Salmon*, para 9.53 above) and tribunals might refuse to award additional compensation for injury to health in such circumstances.

---

[20] See paras 7.17–7.21 above.

9.58 The most common form of personal injury claim in discrimination cases involves psychiatric injury. Awards are often made with reference to the *Judicial Studies Board Guidelines* (8th ed, 2006, Oxford: Oxford University Press) by which relevant factors to be taken into account in valuing such damage include the injured person's ability to cope with life and work, the effect on the injured person's relationships, the extent of treatment and future vulnerability, prognosis, whether medical help is being sought, the nature of the abuse, and its duration.

9.59 There are within these Guidelines four categories of award for psychiatric injury:

severe (£32,000–£67,200) where the claimant has serious problems and the prognosis is poor;

moderately severe (£11,200–£32,000) where there are significant problems in relation to the above factors but where the prognosis is more optimistic;

moderate (£4,825–£13,500) where there has been a significant improvement and the prognosis is good; and

minor (£2,300–£4,825) where the illness is of limited duration, such as temporary anxiety.

9.60 However a discount should be made where the illness is not solely attributable to the discriminatory conduct, for example, where there is some previous medical history or there are other contributory factors. In *HM Prison Service v Salmon* [2001] IRLR 425 compensation for psychiatric injury was reduced by 25 per cent on the basis that the depressive illness contracted by the claimant was not entirely caused by the unlawful discrimination suffered.

(4) Aggravated damages

9.61 Aggravated damages were another issue on the appeal in *Virgo Fidelis* where the tribunal had decided that they did not have the power to make a separate award for aggravated damages. The EAT disagreed and made an award of £10,000 in this respect. In *Armitage, Marsden and HM Prison Service v Johnson* [1997] IRLR 162, the EAT had held (after citing *Rookes v Barnard*[21]) that, as a matter of principle, aggravated damages ought to be available to claimants for the statutory torts of sex and race discrimination: the commission of the torts might be sufficiently intentional as to enable the claimant to rely upon malice or the defendant's manner of committing the tort or other conduct as aggravating the injury to feelings.

---

[21] [1964] AC 1129 HL and in particular p 1221, Lord Devlin).

Subsequently[22] the Court of Appeal appeared to have assumed that aggravated **9.62** damages were available in discrimination cases. In *Virgo Fidelis* the EAT said this:

> The decision whether or not to award aggravated damages and, if so, in what amount must depend on the particular circumstances of the discrimination and on the way in which the complaint of discrimination has been handled. Common sense requires that regard should also be had to the overall magnitude of the sum total of the awards of compensation for non-pecuniary loss made under the various headings of injury to feelings, psychiatric damage and aggravated damage. In particular, double recovery should be avoided by taking appropriate account of the overlap between the individual heads of damage.

The EAT considered that the extent of overlap would depend on the facts of **9.63** each particular case, referring to what Carswell LCJ said in *McConnell v Police Authority for Northern Ireland* [1997] IRLR 625, at paragraph 19, that an award of aggravated damages should not be an extra sum over and above the sum which the tribunal of fact considers appropriate compensation for the injury to the claimant's feelings. Any element of aggravation ought to be taken into account in reckoning the extent of the injury to his feelings, for it is part of the cause of that injury. It should certainly not be treated as an extra award which reflects a degree of punishment of the respondent for his behaviour. This approach had been followed in *ICTS (UK) Ltd v Tchoula* [2000] IRLR 643. His Honour Judge Peter Clark had remarked that tribunals sometimes include an element of aggravated damages in their award for injury to feelings and sometimes the awards were expressed separately. However that was a matter of form rather than substance. The first question must always be, 'do the facts disclose the essential requirements for an award of aggravated damages'?

Finally, in *Vento*, where the decisions in *Johnson* and *Tchoula* appeared to have **9.64** been cited with approval, (although *McConnell* was not referred to in the judgment) the Court of Appeal had stated at para 67 that the decision whether or not to award aggravated damages depended on the particular circumstances of the discrimination and the way in which the complaint of discrimination had been handled. An award was made of £5,000 for aggravated damages.

In *Virgo Fidelis* the EAT rejected the argument that the element of aggravation can **9.65** be included in the compensation for injury to feelings as was the *McConnell* approach. The tribunal were in error in coming to the conclusion that they did not have the authority to make an award of aggravated damages, and the EAT decided that a figure of £10,000 should be awarded by way of aggravated damages.[23]

---

[22] *Alexander v Home Office* [1998] IRLR 190, CA and *Noone v North West Thames Regional Health Authority* [1988] IRLR 195 CA.

[23] For a case in which the employment tribunal found that the employer behaved in a misguided way but not one deserving of aggravated damages see *Herron v Wintercomfort for the Homeless* (ET, Case No. 1502519/03).

(5) Exemplary damages

9.66 The EAT also considered the question of exemplary damages in *Virgo Fidelis* though these were not granted in that particular case. The EAT started their discussion with *Rookes v Barnard* (para 9.61 above) where the House of Lords identified the two circumstances in which exemplary damages might be available, namely:

(1) oppressive arbitrary or unconstitutional action by the servants of the government and

(2) where the defendant's conduct had been calculated by him to make a profit for himself.

9.67 The object of an award of such damages was to punish or deter. Lord Devlin said[24] that the fact that the injury to a claimant had been aggravated by the malice or by the doing of the injury would not normally be justification for an award of exemplary damages; aggravated damages would be sufficient in that type of case. In *Cassell & Co Ltd v Broome* [1972] 1 All ER 801, the class of 'servants of government' was extended to 'those who by common law or statute are exercising functions of a governmental character'.[25] Finally the decision in *Kuddus v Chief Constable of Leicester Constabulary* [2002] 2 AC 122 clarified that the availability of exemplary damages was not confined to cases where the tort in question existed prior to 1964 and that 'once the cause of action test no longer exists and the *Rookes v Barnard* test becomes fact-sensitive rather than cause-of-action-sensitive' the EAT could 'see no reason why in principle exemplary damages could not be awarded, provided that the other conditions are made out'. However 'in the majority of cases aggravated damages would be sufficient to mark the employer's conduct'. The decision in *Kuddus* was applied to a protected disclosure claim in *Virgo Fidelis*, where it was decided that the tests for making such an award were not satisfied.

(6) Victimization by dismissal of a worker who is not an employee

9.68 By s49(6) ERA it is provided that where a complaint is made under s48(1A), and the detriment to which the worker is subjected is the termination of his worker's contract, and that contract is not a contract of employment, any compensation must not exceed the compensation that would be payable under Chapter II of Part X if the worker had been an employee and had been dismissed for the reason specified in s103A (ie on the ground that he made a protected disclosure). However since there is in fact no limit on the compensation that is payable to such an employee this subsection bites only in one important respect. It operates to limit any sums

---

[24] At p 412D–I.
[25] Lord Reid at 838C.

that can be recovered for non-pecuniary damage since these could not be recovered in an unfair dismissal claim.

It does not follow that no sums can be recovered for injury to feelings in a termination of contract case. But any such award would be limited to sums which an employee could receive as 'compensation' in the unfair dismissal claim. It is relatively clear that the basic award should be taken into account as part of the 'compensation' that would be received for unfair dismissal. Although it does not consist of compensation for financial loss, the introductory words of s118 ERA make clear that it is part of the award of compensation for unfair dismissal. It is also notable that in the Court of Appeal in *Dunnachie*,[26] Sedley LJ expressed the view (at paragraph 48) that: **9.69**

> for the ordinary case of unfair dismissal, assuming that there is no reinstatement or re-engagement, it is the basic award which is there to compensate for the unfairness.

It might be argued that compensation in an unfair dismissal case could also include the sum of between 26 to 52 weeks' pay by way of an additional award for failing to comply with a re-employment order. However it is most unlikely that this could be taken into account. There would be no way of assessing in the case of a non-employee whether, if he had been an employee, the employer would fail to comply with such an order, and such a claim flows from the refusal to comply with the order, rather than otherwise being payable by reason of the unfair dismissal.   **9.70**

In substance, therefore, in the case of a non-employee dismissal, the non-pecuniary damage award has a ceiling equivalent to the basic award that would have been payable to an employee in the position of the claimant since the financial loss would also be recoverable by an employee through the compensatory award.   **9.71**

(7) Adjustment of awards for non-compliance with statutory disciplinary procedures

Section 31 of the Employment Act 2002 provides for an uplift or reduction in award in cases of non-completion of statutory disciplinary or grievance procedures. This applies both to unfair dismissal (where the adjustment is made only to the compensatory award[27]) and detriment claims. Where the non-completion of the statutory procedure is 'wholly or mainly attributable to failure by the employer to comply with a requirement of the procedure', the tribunal must (other than in exceptional circumstances[28]) increase the award to the employee by 10 per cent and may, if it considers it just and equitable, increase the award by a further amount up to a total increase of 50 per cent. Conversely, if the non-completion of   **9.72**

---

[26] *Dunnachie v Kingston upon Hull City Council* [2004] ICR 481 (CA).
[27] Section 124A ERA.
[28] Section 31(4) ERA.

the applicable statutory procedure was wholly or mainly attributable to the employee's failure to comply with a requirement of the procedure or to exercise a right of appeal under it, there must be a reduction in the award of at least 10 per cent (again save for exceptional circumstances) and up to 50 per cent. In relation to unfair dismissal claims, the adjustment is made before the compensatory award is reduced for contributory fault or on account of a payment of an enhanced redundancy payment (s124A ERA). The Employment Act 2002 (Dispute Resolution) Regulations 2004 (SI 2004/752) makes detailed provision as to where the statutory procedures apply and where the parties are treated as having complied with procedures.

9.73   There is no statutory guidance as to the amount by which the award should be increased above the 10 per cent minimum as this is left to the discretion of the tribunal. Some assistance may be derived by analogy with the approach to the uplift of 26 to 52 weeks by way of an additional award for non-compliance with a re-employment order. In *Mabrizi v National Hospital for Nervous Diseases* [1990] ICR 281 the EAT emphasized the width of the discretion afforded to tribunals in determining what factors ought properly to be taken into account. The EAT observed that the award is intended to be a *solatium* rather than a precisely calculated substitute for financial loss, although it would be permissible to take into account the extent to which the imposition of the statutory cap resulted in loss not being fully compensated by the compensatory award. The EAT also noted that the degree of fault on the part of the employer is likely to be an important factor. These considerations are likely also to be applicable to the uplift for non-compliance with the statutory disciplinary/dismissal and grievance procedures. It is likely that any increase (or reduction) will reflect a number of factors including the seriousness of the procedural default, the degree of culpability on the part of the employer (or employee), and the size and resources of the employer.[29] This may be important in PIDA cases where the awards tend to be large in any event and could lead to a big increase, or decrease, in a large award.

---

[29] See by analogy the broad discretion tribunals have in relation to the uplift for failure to comply with a re-employment order.

10

EMPLOYMENT TRIBUNALS PROCEDURE AND ALTERNATIVE DISPUTE RESOLUTION

A. Claim forms	10.02	G. Costs		10.47
B. Responses	10.07	(1) Vexatious		10.55
C. Case management	10.10	(2) Misconceived		10.56
(1) Case management		(3) Amount		10.62
discussions (CMD)	10.13	(4) Wasted Costs		10.63
(2) How to apply for an order	10.15	(5) When can wasted costs orders		
D. Additional information: general	10.19	be made?		10.69
E. Disclosure	10.28	(6) Amount of wasted costs		10.70
(1) Applicable principles	10.28	H. Alternative dispute resolution		10.71
(2) Disclosure by non-parties	10.35	(1) Introduction		10.71
(3) Form of application	10.36	(2) The ADR options		10.74
(4) Restrictions on disclosure	10.37	Conciliation		10.74
Confidentiality	10.38	Arbitration		10.76
Self-incrimination	10.39	Mediation		10.79
F. Procedure at the hearing	10.41	The settlement agreement		10.87
(1) The power to sit in private	10.41	(3) Issues specific to whistleblowing		10.88
(2) Submissions at the close of the				
claimant's case that there is no				
case to answer	10.43			

General questions of procedure are dealt with in other texts to which the reader is **10.01** referred.[1] We deal here with points which are or may be peculiarly apposite to whistleblowing cases and begin with tactical considerations as to what should go into claim forms and responses, then move to points about the hearing and conclude with alternative dispute resolution.

---

[1] *Blackstone's Employment Practice 2006* (Oxford: Oxford University Press, 2006), at pp 1–224.

A. Claim forms

10.02 A claim must be made by an employee to an employment tribunal within three months of the effective date of the dismissal (s111(2)(a) ERA) or detrimental act or deliberate failure to act (or last in a series of such acts or failures) complained of, save when time is extended (see para 8.39). It is now mandatory under the Response (Employment Tribunal) Rules 2004 Rule 1 (3) to use the claim form as set out in the ET Rules. Rules 1 and 4 require the claimant to set out the details of a claim and the respondent to state the grounds for resisting a claim.

10.03 It is important that claimants state in their application precisely what disclosures are relied on, to whom they were made (especially whether internally or externally and which of ss43C to 43H are said to apply) and why they fall within the six statutory categories of relevant failure. The making of each disclosure should be linked to the precise detriment (or dismissal) said to have been the result of each disclosure. Each cause of action should thus be stated as precisely as possible. Although many employment tribunals will give some leeway for employees to refine their cases some will not, with potentially calamitous results for claimants. It is not worth the employee running that risk and seeking leave to amend at a later stage.

10.04 In practice however the employee may not know with certainty precisely which disclosure was the reason for the detriment and will be relying on inference. It may therefore be necessary instead to put the case in relation to which of the disclosures was the reason for the detriment. The employee has to prove that he made disclosures and thus should know precisely what is relied on. The employee also has to prove that the disclosures were protected, other than the element of good faith where the employer has the burden of proof.[2]

10.05 Setting out each cause of action will render it easier to decide what evidence must be led at the hearing and to found any application for disclosure, which might often be very important in PIDA cases. It is also useful at this early stage to sketch out the extent of any injury to feelings alleged.

10.06 Whilst taking care to address the various elements of the cause of action, however, it is important that the essential 'story' is not lost. The claim form and response form will probably be the first documents that an employment tribunal read when dealing with an interim application or the main hearing. It is not the role of the pleadings to set out the detailed evidence, but it is to the claimant's advantage if the initial claim conveys in a logical and persuasive way the claimant's essential cases. In some cases, such as where the contentions as to the existence of protected

---

[2] See Chapter 4, paras 4.34–4.37.

disclosures are complicated or cover a protracted period, it may help for there to be a summary section at the outset identifying the causes of action and the essential nature of the claim.

B. Responses

Frequently employers find applications in PIDA cases unclear, and seek further information or written answers about what is alleged (Rule 10(2)(b)). It is important (especially in the employers' interest) that cases do not reach the employment tribunal hearing without the issues being properly specified. **10.07**

We suggest that these factors are borne in mind by employers' representatives in making their responses: **10.08**

(a) if it is contended that no disclosure was in fact made that should be stated in clear terms;

(b) if it is contended that any disclosure was not made in good faith this should be spelt out and the basis for the contention given. Clearly representatives should only plead this if they have good grounds for doing so. Indeed pleading this without good grounds may result in discipline by professional bodies and/or an order for costs in serious cases—although it might be argued that this is less likely having regard to the meaning attributed to good faith in *Street v Derbyshire Unemployed Workers' Centre* [2005] ICR 97 (CA) (see Chapter 4); and

(c) in many PIDA cases, the parties are seeking to gain the 'moral high ground' before the tribunal whatever may be the legal niceties of the respective positions. As with the claim form, this may involve painting the general picture at an early stage. The response can thus be used to tell the story from the employer's point of view and to rebut the atmosphere which the employee is seeking to cultivate.

There are real tactical issues surrounding what matters the employer wishes to put in issue in a PIDA case. In particular: **10.09**

(a) if reasonable belief is put in issue (eg in relation to a qualifying disclosure) the impact may be that the tribunal will need to hear evidence about the underlying allegation—which the employer may wish to avoid in a public forum (especially given what is said in *Darnton v University of Surrey* [2003] ICR 615, discussed in Chapter 3, about it being relevant whether the allegations are true). There may be a number of reasons why the employer might seek not to fight on that ground. One might be an issue as to costs and proportionality, as an issue as to 'reasonable belief' for the purposes of a qualifying disclosure might substantially widen the hearing and it might be held unreasonable to have put it in issue. The strength of other parts of the case, such as the 'reason why' question (see Chapter 7), might affect the assessment. Another might be that the employer wants to avoid going into all the details of the allegations (and in a serious case the tribunal might refer matters to appropriate authorities for investigation such as HM Revenue & Customs). On the other hand if other elements of the protected disclosures are in issue, this still might not be effective in wholly excluding consideration of the issue since truth of the allegation might be argued to be relevant to good faith—though *Street v Derbyshire Unemployed Workers Centre* [2004] IRLR 687 (discussed in Chapter 4) shows this is not necessarily determinative.

(b) whether good faith should be challenged. Ordinarily bad faith is not to be asserted without cogent evidence and *Lucas v Chichester Diocesan Housing Association Limited* (EAT/0713/04, 7 February 2005) indicates that applies here. As noted above, set against this is the argument that *Street* gives good faith a wider meaning and so might lessen the risk in challenging good faith.

C. Case management

10.10 In *ALM Services Limited v Bladon*[3] the Court of Appeal said that there should be directions hearings in protected disclosure cases in order to identify the issues and ascertain what evidence the parties intend to call on those issues. Rule 10(1) of the 2004 Rules of Procedure[4] provides the Tribunal with various powers to manage tribunal cases: these powers may be exercised in or out of a case management discussion, which is often held by telephone. In particular Rule 10(2)(b) provides a power to order a party to provide 'additional information'.

10.11 The Tribunal (and the respondent) will be concerned to elicit from the claimant (if these details are not already pleaded) for example:

(a) when and to whom the disclosure was made;
(b) precisely which act or acts are alleged to constitute the disclosure of information which is or are relied upon;
(c) what act or omission or apprehended act or omission and which of the relevant failures subsections 43B(1)(a)–(f) is relied upon;
(d) where the claim is one of victimization, what acts or omissions of the employer are relied upon as constituting a detriment; and
(e) what facts and matters are relied upon by the claimant in support of the allegation that he or she was subjected to a detriment and/or (as the case may be) dismissed on the ground of or by reason that he or she had made a protected disclosure.

---

[3] [2002] EWCA Civ 1085; [2002] IRLR 807.
[4] The Employment Tribunals (Constitution and Rules of Procedure) Regulations 2004 (SI 2004/1861).

Likewise the Tribunal (and the claimant) will wish to elicit from the respondent **10.12**

(a) whether it is accepted that a qualifying disclosure was made as alleged by the claimant, and
(b) whether it is accepted that the qualifying disclosure is a protected disclosure and if not why not and, in particular, whether, and if so in reliance on what facts and matters, the respondent intends to contend that the disclosure was not made in good faith.

(1) Case management discussions (CMD)

The 2004 Employment Tribunal Rules formalize provision for these interim **10.13** hearings, at which hopefully the issues are defined (a particularly important matter for PIDA cases) and any outstanding matters can be dealt with before the main hearing. It is the overriding objective of the Employment Tribunal rules to deal with cases justly (reg 10(3)). Dealing with a case justly includes, so far as is practicable: (a) ensuring that the parties are on an equal footing; (b) dealing with cases in ways which are proportionate to the complexity of the issues; (c) ensuring that cases are dealt with expeditiously and fairly; and (d) saving expense (reg 3(2)). This is largely a replication of the overriding objective in the Civil Procedure Rules (rr1.1–1.3) and a tribunal or chairman must seek to give effect to the overriding objective either when exercising any power given to it or him by the regulations or the rules in the schedules, or when interpreting any of the Employment Tribunal rules (reg 3(3)). There is also an obligation on the parties to assist the tribunal to further the overriding objective which ought not to be overlooked (reg 3(4)).

A CMD is held by a Chairman alone and may be held in private (r17(1)) but may **10.14** not, however, determine a person's 'civil rights or obligations'. This language is borrowed from Article 6 of the European Convention on Human Rights and the aim is to ensure that Article 6 does not apply to the conduct of the CMD (which would include a requirement that it be heard in public). As a consequence matters such as striking out a claim or part of it may not be determined at a CMD. Rule 10(2) sets out a list of examples of orders that may be dealt with at a CMD but this is not exhaustive. They include:

(a) the manner in which the proceedings are to be conducted, including any time limit to be observed—this will include a time estimate and possibly the timetabling of witnesses;
(b) that a party provide additional information—for example because the claim or response is not clear or that a schedule of loss should be provided—this may be particularly important in such hearings;
(c) requiring the attendance of any person in Great Britain either to give evidence or to produce documents or information;

(d) requiring any person in Great Britain to disclose documents or information to a party to allow a party to inspect such material as might be ordered by a County Court (or in Scotland, by a sheriff);

(e) extending any time limit, whether or not expired (subject to rr 4(4) extension of time limit for response, 11(2) application for an order to be not less than ten days before the date of the hearing, 25(5) time limit for withdrawal of proceedings, 30(5) time limit for requesting written reasons, 33(1) time limit for a review of default judgment, 35(1) time limit for a review, 38(7) time limit for costs application and 42(5) time limit for preparation time order, and to r 3(4) of Sch 2 time limit in national security cases);

(f) requiring the provision of written answers to questions put by the tribunal or chairman;

(g) that, subject to r 22(8), a short conciliation period be extended into a standard conciliation period;

(h) staying (in Scotland, sisting) the whole or part of any proceedings;

(i) that part of the proceedings be dealt with separately—this may cover a split liability and remedy hearing;

(j) that different claims be considered together;

(k) that any person who the chairman or tribunal considers might be liable for the remedy claimed should be made a respondent in the proceedings;

(l) dismissing the claim against a respondent who is no longer directly interested in the claim;

(m) postponing or adjourning any hearing;

(n) varying or revoking other orders;

(o) giving notice to the parties of a pre-hearing review or the hearing;

(p) giving notice under r 19;

(q) giving leave to amend a claim or response;

(r) that any person who the chairman or tribunal considers has an interest in the outcome of the proceedings may be joined as a party to the proceedings;

(s) that a witness statement be prepared or exchanged; or

(t) as to the use of experts or interpreters in the proceedings.

(2) How to apply for an order

10.15 A party may apply for an order to be issued, varied or revoked at any stage in the proceedings. An application for an order must be made not less than ten days before the hearing at which it is to be considered unless it is not reasonably practicable to do so or the chairman or tribunal considers it in the interests of justice that shorter notice should be allowed.

10.16 The application must be made in writing to the Employment Tribunal, unless otherwise directed, and include the case number and the reasons for the request.

If the application is for a CMD to be held it should identify the precise orders sought there. It should also set out a brief explanation as to why the orders are sought and how the order will assist the Chairman in dealing with the proceedings efficiently and fairly. There is a right to make an objection to the order sought within seven days and this must be communicated to all other parties by the legal representative or (if a party is not legally represented) by the secretary to the tribunal.

An order made at a CMD is an interim order and cannot therefore be reviewed **10.17** (see r34(1)). Where an order has been made by a Chairman of his own initiative and the parties have not been given an opportunity to make representations, or only one party has had the opportunity to do so, the matter may be reconsidered by the Tribunal upon application by the absent party (see *Reddington v Straker and Sons Limited* [1994] ICR 172). An application to vary or revoke such an order must be made before the time for complying with the order has expired and must include the reasons for the application (r12(2)(b) and (3)).

An order made or refused by one Chairman cannot simply be revisited. If there **10.18** is a subsequent application, tribunals should ordinarily follow the same principles applicable under the CPR and only set aside or vary such an order where there has been a change in the circumstances since it was made (see CPR, 29PD, para 6.4). In *Goldman Sachs Services Ltd v Montali* [2002] ICR 1251 a tribunal reversed an interim order (made by a different tribunal) providing for a limitation issue to be heard at a directions hearing, and instead ordered it to be dealt with at the substantive hearing. It was held on appeal that, in the absence of any change of circumstances, this was both 'a wrong exercise of discretion and wrong in principle'. In *Onwuka v Spherion Technology UK Limited* [2005] ICR 576 (EAT), Rimer J expressed the 'provisional view' that tribunals had jurisdiction to hear renewed interim applications (in that case for amendment). However he commented that in the absence of any material change in circumstances he would not ordinarily expect a chairman to exercise that jurisdiction.

D. Additional information: general

Requests for further information or for written answers may be particularly **10.19** important in protected disclosure cases—where claims are frequently poorly drafted yet there are a number of stages through which the claim must pass to succeed. The general principles are:

(a) a tribunal may order a party to provide further details of the allegations in a claim or response;

(b) the tribunal can so order at the request of a party or at the tribunal's own motion either before or at a hearing;

(c) parties should try to avoid long and complicated requests, and the earlier requests are made the more likely they are to be granted;

(d) the purpose of a request for further information is to inform the other side of the case that they have to meet, to prevent parties from being taken by surprise by enabling them to prepare rebutting evidence and to define the issues in dispute; and

(e) a party who fails to comply with an order to provide further information may find his claim or response, or relevant parts, dismissed or struck out.

10.20 Tribunals are, in general, anxious that cases do not become a complex battle of pleadings reminiscent of some cases in the High Court. In *Stone v Charrington & Co. Ltd* [1977] ICR 248 the EAT stated that:

> industrial tribunals were set up with the purpose of operating cheaply, quickly and informally and as far as possible therefore it is desirable that the formalities of the regular courts should be avoided. To introduce a formal system of discovery and inspection, interlocutories and so forth might in the abstract produce more perfect justice but it would be at such great cost in time, money and manpower that the whole machine would grind to a halt.

10.21 Important guidance on the proper scope of orders for further information under the old Rules (but still relevant to the new) was given in *White v University of Manchester* [1976] ICR 419 at 423 by Phillips J, who said:

> it is a matter of straightforward sense. In one way or another the parties need to know the sort of thing which is going to be the subject of the hearing. Industrial tribunals know this very well and, for the most part, seek to ensure that it comes about. Of course, in the end, if there is surprise they will ordinarily grant an adjournment to enable it to be dealt with, but by and large it is much better if matters of this kind can be dealt with in advance so as to prevent adjournment taking place . . .

10.22 The EAT thus required particulars of the generalized allegation made by the employers that the employee, a typist, was 'unable to cope with her job duties'. This guidance was echoed by Wood J in *Byrne v Financial Times* [1991] IRLR 417.

10.23 An employer was also held to be entitled to particulars of an allegation that the employers condoned fraudulent claims for expenses so that they should know precisely the case which was going to be put against them, and to enable them to prepare their evidence (*International Computers Ltd v Whitley* [1978] IRLR 318).

10.24 In *Honeyrose Products Ltd v Joslin* [1981] IRLR 80 Waterhouse J pointed out the essential principles. Claims should be sufficiently simple to enable the (employers) to identify with reasonable clarity the case that they have to meet and the range of argument that is likely to occur before the tribunal. On the other hand, it would be 'most unfortunate if it became the general practice for employers to make requests when the nature of the case is stated with reasonable clarity'.

10.25 An order for further information will however be refused where it is unnecessary or overly burdensome or oppressive. Part of the overriding objective relates to proportionality in any event. Thus a request for details of incidents that occurred many years ago might be refused as both unnecessary and burdensome since the witnesses are unlikely to recall the matters. Requests that are very detailed and relate to statistical or other matters might also fail on the grounds that they are too burdensome.

A request for particulars of evidence, as opposed to particulars of facts, may be ordered **10.26** since the request is not limited to the pleadings but might encompass any issue in the case. The old distinction which was drawn between a request for information and for evidence was always a difficult one and turned on the facts being the material parts of the story and the evidence being the means of showing that the story is true.

Well-targeted requests for further information are likely to be of particular impor- **10.27** tance in relation to those parts of the other side's case where only the other party has full access to the information. From the employer's perspective, in considering the approach to take in the litigation on issues such as whether the claimant had the requisite reasonable belief for a qualifying disclosure, it may be particularly important to hone in on the information and evidence which was available to the worker at the time of making the disclosure. For the employee, it will be important to consider what information might be available to test the employer's contentions as to the reasons for alleged detrimental action. In some cases, for example, it may be appropriate to seek information as to how comparators were treated in a comparable situation in order to support an inference that the difference in treatment was due to a protected disclosure. Similar considerations are also applicable when identifying documents which may need to be sought.

E. Disclosure

(1) Applicable principles

Each party might need documents in the possession of the other to prove its case. **10.28** In PIDA cases, it is necessary to consider carefully what categories of documentation are likely to exist which may be relevant, in particular so as to obtain evidence in relation to those parts of the case which are not within a party's own knowledge. In relation to the reason for treatment, for example, it will be important to identify who might have been party to or consulted about the decision and to ensure there is disclosure of internal e-mails bearing on the reaction to the disclosure(s) made.

On the application of a party or of its own motion, a tribunal may order a party to **10.29** grant disclosure or inspection of a document to another party. Such orders are not limited to documents, and photographs and video evidence may also be obtained. In contrast with the position under CPR 31, there is no general duty on the parties to give disclosure in tribunal proceedings. Tribunals are nevertheless directed by r 10(2)(d) to adopt the same principles as the county court. The principles of standard disclosure under the CPR require a party to disclose those documents on which he relies, any documents which support or adversely affect his or another party's case, and any other documents which a party is required to disclose pursuant to a relevant practice direction. CPR 31PD.5 states that in deciding whether to make an order for specific disclosure the court will take into account all the circumstances of the case and, in particular, the overriding objective (to deal with cases justly and in a cost effective manner).

10.30 The general rule is that a document is relevant 'which it is reasonable to suppose contains information which may, not which must, either directly enable the party either to advance his own case or to damage the case of his adversary (including) a document which may fairly lead him to a train of inquiry which may have either of these two consequences' (*Compagnie Financière v Peruvian Guano Co.* (1882) 11 QBD 55; see also *Ballantine (George & Sons) v F.E.R. Dixon* [1974] 2 All ER 503). The documents sought must be relevant and necessary for the fair disposal of the proceedings (*Dolling Baker v Merrett* [1990] 1 WLR 1205) and the fact that they are available and would be disclosed normally is not the correct approach.

10.31 In *Copson v Eversure Accessories Ltd* [1974] ICR 636, Sir John Donaldson said:

cases are intended to be heard with all the cards facing upwards on the table. The tribunal's power of ordering further and better particulars, discovery or issuing witness orders will be of little value in the pursuit of justice if the parties do not know they exist. Tribunals should therefore be vigilant to ensure that their existence is known in appropriate cases.

10.32 In *Birds Eye Walls Ltd v Harrison* [1985] IRLR 47 Waite J stated the important general principle that:

no party is under any obligation, in the absence of an order upon the Industrial Tribunal, to give discovery in the Tribunal proceedings. That is subject, however to the important qualification that any party who chooses to make voluntary discovery of any documents in his possession or power must not be unfairly selective in his disclosure. Once, that is to say, a party has disclosed certain documents (whether they appear to him to support his case or for any other reason) it becomes his duty not to withhold from discovery any further documents in his possession or power (regardless of whether they support his case or not) if there is any risk that the effect of withholding them might be to convey to his opponent or to the tribunal a false or misleading impression as to the true nature, purport or effect of any disclosed document.

10.33 There are two principles to be borne in mind so that no party should suffer injustice. The first is that the duty of every party not to withhold from disclosure any document whose suppression would render the disclosed document misleading is a high duty which the tribunals should interpret broadly and enforce strictly. The second is that the tribunal should use its wide and flexible powers as master of its own procedure to ensure that if any party can be shown at any stage of the proceedings to have been at risk of having his claim or defence unfairly restricted by the denial of an opportunity to become aware of a document in the possession or power of the other side material to the just prosecution of his case, he does not suffer any avoidable disadvantage as a result.

The tribunal will take into account considerations of proportionality and in **10.34** certain circumstances an application for an order for disclosure will be refused if to grant it might lead to such significant expenditure of time and cost to the respondent as to be oppressive (see *Wilcox v HGS* [1975] ICR 306 and *Perera v Civil Service Commission* [1980] ICR 699).

(2) Disclosure by non-parties

It may be important in PIDA cases to gain documents from non-parties, for **10.35** example statutory regulators. A tribunal may make an order, either on application or of its own motion, requiring a person who is not a party to attend and to produce any document relating to the matter to be determined. Rule 10(5) states that such an order may be made only when the disclosure sought is necessary in order to dispose fairly of the claim or to save expense. In the case of *Chubb and ors v Care First Partnership Ltd.*[5] (ET, Case No. 1101438/99B) Mrs Chubb and the other claimants were care assistants who made an external disclosure of abuse at a care home where they worked. The Tribunal encouraged third party disclosure from the local authority of their notes of the initial disclosure and copies of reports made following investigations into the allegations.

(3) Form of application

The party requiring the information should initially approach the other side by **10.36** letter with a copy to the tribunal. If the other side refuses a reasonable request an order for disclosure should be sought from the tribunal (in accordance with r 11). The letter should set out the documents sought and the request may be facilitated by a schedule or draft order identifying the documents sought so that the chairman considering the application can tick off the documents to be disclosed.

(4) Restrictions on disclosure

The following restrictions on disclosure may be particularly relevant in PIDA cases. **10.37**

Confidentiality

In *Science Research Council v Nassé* [1979] IRLR 465, it was held that where a **10.38** party claims that it is not appropriate to disclose a document, the tribunal may

---

5   See Appendix 9, case 30 for a summary of this decision.

inspect the document and decide whether the claim is valid. Confidentiality is a consideration, not a determinative factor and the test is whether discovery would fairly dispose of the proceedings. There is however no rule whereby confidential documents are excluded from discovery merely because they are confidential. This was emphasized in *Alfred Compton Amusement Machines Ltd v Customs and Excise Commissioners (No. 2)* [1974] AC 405, where it was stated that, in the absence of some additional factor, such as the fact that the claimant is exercising a statutory function which would be impeded by disclosure, confidentiality would not justify the non-disclosure of a document.

Self-incrimination

10.39 Section 14 of the Civil Evidence Act 1968 provides that a party does not have to give disclosure if it would tend to incriminate him or his spouse or expose them to proceedings which might lead to a penalty.[6] Mere assertion of the privilege will not necessarily be accepted. The tribunal must decide from the circumstances of the case and the nature of the evidence whether there are grounds to invoke the privilege. The privilege must be claimed before the evidence is supplied or it will be too late.[7]

10.40 Where does this Act leave a respondent who has evidence that they have committed a criminal act and a claim in regard to a disclosure of that act? First, if the respondent has to rely upon asserting the privilege against self-incrimination then that does not bode well for the defence of the claim and the view the tribunal is likely to form of them. Second, consideration will need to be given as to whether (a) it is possible and (b) it is tactically advantageous to dispute that there is a qualifying disclosure having regard to the fact that whether the allegation is true may be a relevant consideration in assessing reasonable belief (*Darnton*). In theory it might be possible to assert that the claimant had no reasonable belief at the time. But in practice this is unlikely to carry any force in a case where it is necessary to plead the privilege against self-incrimination.

F. Procedure at the hearing

(1) The power to sit in private

10.41 Where the subject matter of the disclosure which is in issue consists of information that is still sensitive, as it often will be, the respondent employer may wish to consider applying for an order that the hearing or part of it be conducted in private.

---

[6] See Hollander, *Documentary Evidence*, 9th ed (London: Sweet & Maxwell, 2006) chapter 9.
[7] *IBM UK Limited v Prime Data* [1994] 1 WLR 719.

The general principle is that hearings of claims are held in public. Rule 16(1) of the 2004 Rules of Procedure[8] however provides that a hearing or part of one may be conducted in private for the purpose of hearing from any person evidence or representations which in the opinion of the tribunal or chairman is likely to consist of information:

(a) which he could not disclose without contravening a prohibition imposed by or by virtue of any enactment;

(b) which has been communicated to him in confidence, or which he has otherwise obtained in consequence of the confidence placed in him by another person; or

(c) the disclosure of which would, for reasons other than its effect on negotiations with respect to any of the matters mentioned in s178(2) of TULRCA,[9] cause substantial injury to any undertaking of his or any undertaking in which he works.

Rule 16(2) provides that where there is a decision to hold a hearing or part of one **10.42** in private, then reasons for doing so shall be given.

(2) Submissions at the close of the claimant's case that there is no case to answer

In *Boulding v Land Securities Trillium (Media Services) Ltd* (EAT/0023/06, **10.43** 3 May 2006) the EAT held that the employment tribunal had erred in acceding to a half-time submission of 'no case to answer' made in a whistle-blowing claim. The claimant alleged that he had been unfairly dismissed for having blown the whistle on what he said was the respondent's wrongdoing. Having less than one year's continuous employment, the burden was on the employee to show that the reason or principal reason for dismissal was a protected disclosure. For this reason the claimant's case was heard first. As discussed in Chapter 3 (paras 3.50 to 3.51), the claimant raised concerns to his employer that equipment lacked certain markings. This would have led to a breach of the employer's obligations had the equipment been supplied to a customer without this being rectified. However the tribunal decided that, although the claimant had made a disclosure to his employer in good faith, it was clear on his own evidence that he did not have a reasonable belief that his employer was likely to fail to comply with a legal obligation, and that there was therefore no qualifying disclosure.

---

[8] Schedule 1 to the Employment Tribunals (Constitution and Rules of Procedure) Regulations 2004, SI 2004/1861.

[9] Terms and conditions of employment, or the physical conditions in which any workers are required to work.

10.44   The EAT reasoned (following *Lucas v Chichester*[10]) that a whistleblowing claim is
in the nature of a claim of discrimination and it should normally be heard in full.
In *Logan v The Commissioners of Customs & Excise* [2004] IRLR 63 (CA) the Court
of Appeal approved the statement of principles by Judge Clarke in *Clarke v
Watford Borough Council* (4 May 2000):

> (1) There is no inflexible rule of law and practice that a tribunal must always hear
> both sides, although that should normally be done:
> (2) The power to stop a case at 'half-time' must be exercised with caution:
>> (a) it may be a complete waste of time to call upon the other party to give
>> evidence in a hopeless case:
>> (b) even where the onus of proof lies on the applicant, as in discrimination
>> cases, it will only be in exceptional or frivolous cases that it would be right to
>> take such a course:
>> (c) where there is no burden of proof, as under s98(4) of the Employment Rights
>> Act 1996, it will be difficult to envisage arguable cases where it is appropriate
>> to terminate the proceedings at the end of the first party's case . . .

10.45   The EAT said that the question under s43B ERA of the likelihood of the employer
not responding to the claimant's allegation of wrongdoing, and stopping uncerti-
fied electrical equipment being used, did not depend solely on the claimant's
appreciation. The employment tribunal should have considered, by examining
evidence from the respondent, what its response was likely to be. At first blush this
might seem a contrived conclusion. The fact that the statutory protection to
whistleblowers is akin to a discrimination statute is of relevance where the issue is
why the respondent acted in the way it did. In such cases it is usually unwise to
stop a case before the respondent's evidence on that issue has been heard. However
the issue which the EAT focused on in *Boulding* was the reasonableness of the
claimant's belief that wrongdoing would be likely to occur. That might be thought
to depend on the claimant's appreciation of what he knew (or thought) at the
time. Unless his own evidence as to what he thought and believed and why he did
so persuaded the tribunal that there was a triable issue in that regard then it might
be thought that he was not going to win the case.

10.46   However in *Darnton v University of Surrey* [2003] IRLR 133 the EAT emphasized
that in assessing the reasonableness of a worker's belief, the fact of whether the
allegations are true or not may be highly material. Applying this principle, the
approach in *Boulding* has more force. As the EAT decision in *Boulding* makes
clear, if the worker does not have a subjective (or genuine) belief in the allegations,
then nothing in the employer's evidence can rescue the situation. However once
the requisite subjective belief is made out, the tribunal is concerned with whether

---

[10]   See above, para 10.09.

there was a sufficient objective basis for the belief. The sufficiency of the grounds for the belief *may* look quite different when viewed with the perspective of the evidence that the concerns were in fact well-founded. Thus if evidence was secured from the employers in cross-examination that they were in fact unlikely to respond to the claimant's concerns about the markings, that might affect the way in which the tribunal viewed the quality of the evidence upon which the claimant in fact relied for his belief. Put another way, it would sit uneasily with the public policy of the legislation if the worker had some grounds to believe that there was wrongdoing, and the concerns in fact proved well-founded, yet the worker who raised the concerns was still deprived of protection on the basis that the grounds relied upon were regarded as insufficient to establish a reasonable belief. For further cases on a qualifying disclosure not being a protected disclosure on the ground that the claimant did not possess a reasonable belief see the cases of *Green v Warren Grieg & Partners* and *McCormack v Learning & Skills Council* in Appendix 9 (cases 50 and 72).

G. Costs

An important distinction between proceedings in the courts and those in the **10.47** tribunal is that the tribunal's power to award costs to a successful party are very limited. Given the passions aroused, and often the very great effort that goes into preparing a PIDA case, and (as we discuss below) due to the ingredients in the cause of action, costs may be more likely to be awarded than in some other areas. In other words it might be said that when a PIDA claim or response falls flat it really falls flat, and it is easier to establish that the losing party has behaved in a misconceived or unreasonable manner.

For many disclosures the structure of the legislation effectively presses the employer **10.48** into challenging good faith as the only way of taking issue with whether there was a protected disclosure. If successful that might lead on to a costs application. As noted above, set against this, in view of the wider meaning on one view of *Street*,[11] there might be more scope in this context to resist a costs order where there was a finding that a disclosure was not in good faith in the sense of being a disclosure in personal interest rather than public interest—and the grounds for costs might be considered in that light.

Similarly, in order to show that there was no protected disclosure, an employer **10.49** might press hard the argument that the worker lacked the requisite reasonable

---

[11] See above, para 10.09(a).

belief for a protected disclosure. Again, although the questions are not precisely the same, a tribunal that is persuaded that a worker has made the disclosure without any reasonable belief, especially if a third tier disclosure was made, might be open to arguments the worker acted unreasonably in so doing.

10.50 Further, in the light of the decision in *Kraus v Penna plc* [2004] IRLR 260 (EAT), there may be some pressure on workers to overstate their case. As noted in Chapter 3, the EAT held that in relation to future breaches it must be shown that in the reasonable belief of the worker the information disclosed tends to show that the relevant failure is more likely than not to occur. Again there is the risk of costs applications being made against workers who are tempted into overstating their case.

10.51 Furthermore, in the hope of achieving a settlement, sometimes the respondent will fight all points until a time close to trial and then make late admissions so as to avoid going into the protected disclosures in a public forum. This might be visited in costs in a serious case.

10.52 Costs orders can be made in the following circumstances:

(a) an adjournment occasioned by a failure to adduce evidence to deal with a request for reinstatement or re-engagement (r39(1));

(b) vexatious, abusive, disruptive or otherwise unreasonable conduct (r40(3)); and

(c) failing to comply with an order or practice direction (r40(4)).

10.53 An order can be made at any stage in the proceedings. An application which is made at the end of a hearing can either be oral or in writing. In each case it must be made within 28 days of an oral judgment or the date on which any reserved judgment was sent to the parties (r38(9)). The Secretary to the Tribunal must send notice to the party against whom an order is sought allowing them the opportunity to give reasons as to why the order should not be made. There is no requirement to send a notice where the party has had the opportunity to respond orally.

10.54 There is also the discretion to order costs against a party who, in bringing the proceedings, has acted vexatiously, abusively or disruptively or otherwise unreasonably. Costs might also be ordered against the paying party where the bringing or conducting of the proceedings has been misconceived. In *Health Development Agency v Parish* [2004] IRLR 550 the EAT held that the conduct of a party prior to proceedings, or unrelated to proceedings, cannot form the basis of an order for costs. However in *McPherson v BNP Paribas* [2004] IRLR 558 the Court of Appeal held that there is no requirement for a causal link between the party's unreasonable behaviour and the costs incurred by the receiving party. The tribunal should have regard to the nature, gravity and effect of the unreasonable conduct as factors relevant to the exercise of its discretion, but there is no need to link the conduct to any specific loss (this was subsequently followed in *Salinas v Bear Stearns Holdings Inc and another* [2005] ICR 1117).

(1) Vexatious

In the rules before 1993 the formulation used to describe conduct attracting an award of costs was 'frivolous and vexatious' and the classic description of this was given by Sir Hugh Griffiths in *Marler (E. T.) Ltd v Robertson* [1974] ICR 72 at 76D: **10.55**

> If the employee knows that there is no substance in his claim and that it is bound to fail, or if the claim is on the face of it so manifestly misconceived that it can have no prospect of success, it may be deemed frivolous and an abuse of the procedure of the tribunal to pursue it. If an employee brings a hopeless claim not with any expectation of recovering compensation but out of spite to harass his employers or for some other improper motive or acts vexatiously and likewise abuses the procedure [his action is vexatious].

(2) Misconceived

Misconceived 'includes having no reasonable prospect of success' (reg 2). The definition is not exhaustive and clearly leaves the tribunal with a wide discretion. The categorization extends not only to a party who knows that there is no merit in the case but also to one who ought to have known that the case had no merit. In *Cartiers Superfoods Ltd v Laws* [1978] IRLR 315 the EAT held that a tribunal should enquire as to what a party knew or ought to have known had he gone about the matters sensibly. The question of whether a party knew or ought to have known that a claim was without merit should be considered throughout the hearing and not just at the beginning. So, while it might be reasonable to commence proceedings, it may later become clear that they are misconceived. In *Beynon v Scadden* [1999] IRLR 700 the EAT suggested that it may be unreasonable conduct to fail to seek further and better particulars, written answers or disclosure in order to assess the merits of a case (para 28). **10.56**

The fact that a party has sought legal advice is a relevant factor but not determinative of itself. The tribunal ought, however, to be wary of the dangers of hindsight. The fact that a party loses before the tribunal does not mean that the case was misconceived or vexatious. What becomes clear to the parties, for example after cross-examination, at the end of the proceedings may not have been clear at the start. **10.57**

In proceedings in the civil courts a winning party who fails to do better than an offer made to him by the losing party will usually expect to pay the losing party's costs from the date of the offer (see generally CPR Part 36). The use of '*Calderbank* letters' is common—an offer to settle without prejudice, save as to costs. The letter is not revealed to the court until the end of the trial. Initially the **10.58** practice of *Calderbank* letters was not looked upon favourably in tribunals (see Lindsay J in *Monaghan v Close Thornton Solicitors* (EAT/3/01, 20 February 2002). In *Kopel v Safeway Stores* [2003] IRLR 753, it was held that a failure by a party to beat a *Calderbank* offer will not, by itself, result in an award of costs against him. What must be shown is 'that the conduct of an appellant in rejecting the offer was unreasonable before the rejection becomes a relevant factor in the exercise of its discretion under [r 38]' (para 18). On the facts of that case, the EAT upheld a tribunal's award of £5,000 costs against the claimant where she had failed in her unfair dismissal and sex discrimination claims, and had not only turned down a 'generous' offer to settle the case but had persisted in alleging breaches of the provisions of the European Convention on Human Rights prohibiting torture and slavery, which the tribunal categorized as 'frankly ludicrous' and 'seriously misconceived'. In the circumstances, the EAT held that the tribunal was entitled to find that the rejection of the offer was unreasonable conduct of the proceedings justifying the award of costs that was made.

10.59   In *Power v Panasonic* (EAT 439/04, 9 March 2005) the EAT again stressed that the rule in *Calderbank* has no place in the Employment Tribunal jurisdiction and cited *Kopel* with approval. However where a party has obstinately pressed for some unreasonably high award despite its excess being pointed out and despite a warning that costs might be asked for against that party if it were persisted in, the tribunal could in appropriate circumstances take the view that the party had conducted the proceedings unreasonably.

10.60   However, it is worth considering *Iron and Steel Trades Confederation v ASW Limited* [2004] IRLR 926 where Burton P said (at para 11):

> We do not encourage, indeed we would not welcome, a situation in which threats of costs are fired across the bows as a matter of course between the parties. There are many cases in which this will be seen almost to amount to emotional or financial blackmail, and certainly in any sort of race or sex discrimination cases it could be said, and has been I think in some cases said, that a threat of costs could amount to victimisation.

10.61   Further in this regard, the case of *Woodward v Abbey National plc* [2006] EWCA Civ 822 (CA) dealing with post-dismissal detriments should be borne in mind, since it indicates that it is not a bar to a claim that the detriment post-dates the termination of employment.

(3) Amount

10.62   Where it has been decided to make a costs order against a party, a tribunal or chairman may make one of the following orders (see r 41(1)):

(a) an order for a specified sum not exceeding £10,000;
(b) an order for a specified sum agreed by the parties; or

(c) an order that the whole or a specified part of the costs be determined by way of a detailed assessment in a county court in accordance with the CPR or, in Scotland, as taxed according to such part of the table of fees prescribed for proceedings in the sheriff court as shall be directed by the order.

(4) Wasted Costs

10.63 Tribunals can make a wasted costs order against a party's representative but only where an application was presented after 1 October 2004. Representatives include legal or other representatives (r48(2)). Wasted costs means any costs incurred by a party as a result of any improper, unreasonable or negligent act or omission or any costs incurred by such conduct which the Tribunal considers it unreasonable for a party to pay. This is especially important in PIDA cases because allegations of serious wrongdoing might well be made and representatives may need to be satisfied that there are proper bases to make such allegations.

10.64 The Tribunal must ask itself three questions:

(1) Has the legal representative acted improperly, unreasonably or negligently?
(2) Did such conduct cause the party to incur unnecessary costs?
(3) If so, is it unreasonable that the other party should pay those costs?

10.65 Improper conduct includes that which is very serious under the representative's professional code of conduct (*Medcalf v Weatherill and another* [2003 1 AC 120]). Negligent is to be used in the normal sense of failing to act with reasonable competence but also something akin to abuse of process (see *Persaud (Luke) v Persaud (Mohan)* [2003] EWCA Civ 394 and *Charles v Gillian Radford & Co* [2003] EWHC (CH) 5 November 2003). Problems of privilege have arisen, for example, where a hopeless case has been pursued. A representative against whom the application is made cannot waive privilege on advice given unless the client permits this. The Court of Appeal has held that it cannot be inferred from those circumstances that the representatives have advised the course of action taken. The task for the Court is to ask whether or not a reasonably competent legal adviser would have evaluated the chances of success such as to continue with it, but the judge may only come to a conclusion adverse to the party's advisers if he has seen their advice (*Dempsey v Johnstone* [2003] EWCA Civ 1134).

10.66 The order may be one, or a combination, of the following:

(a) that the representative pays costs to another party;
(b) that the representative pays costs to his own client; and/or
(c) that the representative pays any witness allowances of any person who has attended the Tribunal by reason of the representative's conduct of the proceedings.

10.67 Representatives means a party's legal or other representatives and any employee of such representatives (r48(4)). Excluded from wasted costs orders are representatives who do not act in pursuit of profit—principally law centres and Citizens' Advice Bureaux representatives—although those acting under conditional fee arrangements are deemed to be acting in pursuit of profit. Wasted costs orders may not be made against representatives who are the employees of a party. Wasted costs orders can be made in favour of a party regardless of whether they are legally represented.

10.68 If the claimant knows that the allegations they are making are 'false or alternatively, without merit, costs should follow as the claims were misconceived'.[12] In *Salinas v Bear Stearns* (EAT/0596/04, 21 October 2004) a cost order of £120,000 was upheld by Burton P where the claimant was found to have altered documents using typing correction fluid and was found to be dishonest and unreasonable in calling witnesses whose evidence was irrelevant. Against this it must be remembered that the power to award costs is a disciplinary power not a compensatory one[13] and relates to a two-stage process, namely a finding of such conduct as to entitle costs to be awarded and the exercise of discretion in making an order for costs.

(5) When can wasted costs orders be made?

10.69 An order does not have to be made at the end of the case but the party's representative should be given the notice in writing of the wasted costs proceedings and any order sought. The representative should be given a reasonable opportunity to make oral or written representations as to why the order should not be made. The Tribunal may have regard to the representative's ability to pay when considering whether to make an order or the amount.

(6) Amount of wasted costs

10.70 There is no limit to the amount of a wasted costs order and the order should specify the amount to be paid or disallowed. The Tribunal should give written reasons for any order provided a request for such reasons has been made within 14 days of the date of the order. It is expressly provided that no extension may be made to this time limit under r10. There must however be a causal connection between the conduct of the party and the amount of costs ordered.[14]

---

[12] *Sharma v London Borough of Ealing* UKEAT/0399/05/DM.
[13] *Scott v Commissioners of Inland Revenue* [2004] IRLR 713.
[14] *Health Development Agency v Parish* [2004] IRLR 550.

H. Alternative dispute resolution

(1) Introduction

Dissatisfaction with the legal process in employment tribunals and courts, in terms **10.71** of the remedies offered there and its cost in financial and human terms, has meant that alternative forms of dispute resolution—known collectively as ADR—are finding an increasing role because of the different processes and different outcomes that they offer.

The ADR options for employment and workplace cases are essentially concilia- **10.72** tion, arbitration and mediation. Central features of these processes are that they are voluntary, (hopefully) speedy, informal, private and independent of employment tribunals and use the services of a neutral third party. Proving facts, presenting evidence and making legal arguments are largely absent from most types of ADR and the focus shifts instead to exploring the issues and negotiating a settlement. The solutions available through ADR are not necessarily limited to the legal remedies.

They may be of particular relevance in whistleblowing cases because of the desire **10.73** of the employer to keep embarrassing matters away from the public realm of the tribunal. Further the employee may have a wish not to be seen as a whistle-blower—which may have the effect of limiting his job opportunities.

(2) The ADR options

Conciliation

The Advisory, Conciliation and Arbitration Service (ACAS) provides an inde- **10.74** pendent and impartial service to resolve statutory employment disputes. ACAS was established as an independent industrial relations organization in 1974 and became a statutory body under the terms of the Employment Protection Act 1975. Once a claim has been made to an employment tribunal the conciliation officer will make contact with the parties or their representatives. The role of the conciliation officer is to inform parties of their legal rights, examine the strengths and weaknesses of their case and explore the options open to them. The conciliation officer may encourage some bargaining to take place and if settlement is reached it is the parties and not the conciliation officer who determine the settlement.

The process normally does not involve any face-to-face meetings between the parties. **10.75** Rather, conciliation officers relay the perspectives of one party to the other. Officers will not reveal information that one party wishes to keep from the other and information given to a conciliation officer in connection with conciliation is not admissible in evidence before a tribunal without the consent of the person who gave it.

Arbitration

10.76 ACAS has responsibility for an arbitration scheme under the Employment Rights (Dispute Resolution) Act 1998 as a means to resolve claims of unfair dismissal. The arbitrator hears from both sides and then makes a binding decision. The decision is therefore the arbitrator's and the parties lose their power over the settlement. The arbitrator's award is final and the case cannot then proceed to a tribunal. Parties therefore make a choice between arbitration and going to court.

10.77 Hearings are private and confidential, and inquisitorial rather than adversarial. No cross-examination is permitted and clarification or questioning is conducted only through the arbitrator and with the arbitrator's permission. The parties are given the opportunity to state their own cases and comment on the case of the other side. The arbitrator rules on procedural and evidential matters rather than directly on points of law. The arbitrator can only make awards of compensation, reinstatement and re-engagement, so the settlements reached are limited to those provided by law.

10.78 There is no appeal in respect of the arbitrator's award, except on grounds of serious irregularities. The scheme is voluntary so both parties will have to opt for it.

Mediation

10.79 In a mediation the mediator, an independent neutral third party, assists disputing parties to reach a settlement. The mediator is not a judge or arbitrator of the dispute before him and will not seek to impose a solution. He is a facilitator. Like all ADR processes, mediation is voluntary, private and informal. The process usually involves bringing the parties together for at least one face-to-face meeting but the degree to which parties continue to meet in joint session will vary depending on the practice of the mediator and the willingness of the parties to have joint meetings. In addition to the joint session, the mediator will speak to the parties privately and in confidence so that he can reveal to party B what took place at a private meeting with party A only if he has A's consent. Mediators may give an opinion on the merits of the dispute or make suggestions for settlement.

10.80 Mediation is flexible in terms of both process and outcomes and may be ideally suited for problems concerned with relationships or behaviour, where the employee remains in employment, as will often be the case with whistleblowers. Mediated agreements can include protocols about future behaviour such as how complaints are to be aired in the future, a written apology, an explanation of what took place and decisions about what might happen in the future. None of these are within the direct power of an employment tribunal or the court.

A mediation can be set up at short notice. The majority of mediations last no more than one day (8 hours). Mediation may be particularly beneficial where the employee is still with the employer and all parties want to continue the relationship. **10.81**

Nothing said during mediation can be used against a party at a later time; the entire process is strictly 'without prejudice' to legal rights. If a satisfactory outcome is not reached through mediation, parties can still pursue a grievance or bring a claim to an employment tribunal (subject to time limits). **10.82**

The general principle for the time to mediate is 'the earlier the better', not least in order that the issue does not become more bitter as time goes on, but also because the cost and time savings are the greatest. However, it may be inappropriate to hold a mediation if further documents or information have to be provided by one party to enable the other party fully to understand the first party's allegations. Also, part of mediation's flexibility is that it can be used at any stage in a dispute and can run in parallel to a formal grievance or tribunal process and should not be used as an excuse to hold up an existing timetable. Sometimes, conversely, time is a healer and the best time to mediate will be some time after a claim has been lodged. Therefore, the right time to mediate in each case will depend on a variety of factors. **10.83**

The terms on which the mediation is to take place are outlined in a short document ('the mediation agreement') that must be agreed by the parties and the mediator. The mediation agreement sets out the practical details of the mediation such as the paying parties, date, time, venue, selected mediator etc. In mediated employment disputes in which the employee cannot afford to pay the mediator's costs, the employer frequently agrees to pay all the costs of the mediation. The agreement also establishes the legal features of the mediation such as 'without prejudice', confidentiality, mediator immunity and authority to settle. The document should be simple and straightforward so that all parties will be willing to sign it. The mediation should be attended by those parties with first-hand knowledge of the issues and full authority to settle the dispute. If lawyers or other representatives do attend the mediation with their clients, it is important that they understand that their role is not to represent their client in the traditional sense, but rather to support them in seeking a solution going forward. Court-room behaviour is wholly inappropriate in a mediation and achieves nothing. Unrepresented parties should consider bringing a 'friend' to the mediation, that is someone who can play a supportive and largely observational role. Union representatives might also have such a role. **10.84**

It is common for parties to submit to the mediator a brief written summary of the dispute highlighting the key issues from each of their perspectives. This can help parties **10.85** to focus on the real issues in dispute that they wish to address. In many disputes there will also be some relevant documentation which it is appropriate for the mediator to see in advance. The case summaries and relevant documents are then exchanged between the parties and copied to the mediator, at an agreed date before the mediation. Parties may bring additional documents to the mediation for only the mediator to see or send such documents to the mediator before the mediation.

10.86 Most mediations (not including the pre-mediation meetings) take no longer than one day, (ie about 8 hours) but, occasionally, mediations can last two or three days for particularly complex cases. The parties will decide in advance how long they want the mediation to last. Even if the mediation is agreed at 8 hours, parties are usually keen for it to continue on the same day if there has been no settlement at the end of the 8 hours and one is in sight. If so, the mediation will continue by consent either until the dispute is resolved or it is agreed that there will be no resolution. Occasionally, mediations are adjourned after they have started if, during the course of the mediation, it is agreed that the parties require further information and that the mediation cannot be resolved without that information.

The settlement agreement

10.87 At the conclusion of the mediation, the mediator may assist the parties to prepare a list of the points they have agreed upon although it is the parties' responsibility to draw up such agreement. Once the agreement has been written, it must be signed. It can be formally typed up later. No agreement will be legally binding until it is written down and signed by the parties or their authorized representatives in the form of a compromise agreement or ACAS COT3 form. It is important to ensure that the settlement which comes out of an employment mediation meets the criteria of compromise agreements within the Employment Rights Act 1996 including a statement that the employee has been independently advised by a relevant advisor.

(3) Issues specific to whistleblowing

10.88 These specific issues may be relevant to ADR and whistleblowing:

(a) the terms of s43J ERA which render void any provision which purports to preclude the worker from making a protected disclosure (see further paras 11.116ff);

(b) the fact that employers may frequently welcome ADR since it avoids embarrassing disclosures having the full glare of publicity;

(c) the terms of the Proceeds of Crime Act 2002 (POCA) may be relevant— Section 328 provides that:

(1) A person commits an offence if he enters into or becomes concerned in an arrangement which he knows or suspects facilitates (by whatever means) the acquisition, retention, use or control of criminal property by or on behalf of another person.

There was concern that obligations to report would cause difficulties in media- **10.89**
tions because parties to the mediation would feel restrained in what they could
say. This was heightened by the decision in *PvP (Ancillary Relief: Proceeds of
Crime)* [2004] Fam 1, although it was argued on behalf of mediators that, even if
lawyers were caught by ss 327-329, mediators were not caught because they were
not concerned in an arrangement.

The central issue in *Bowman v Fels* (2005) 1 WLR 3083 was whether s328 applied **10.90**
to the ordinary conduct of legal proceedings or any aspect of such conduct—
including, in particular, any step taken to pursue proceedings and the obtaining
of a judgment. The court also considered whether s328 POCA applies to any con-
sensual steps taken or settlement reached during legal proceedings and the extent
to which POCA overrode legal professional privilege.

The court concluded that: **10.91**

(a) section 328 was 'not intended to cover or affect the ordinary conduct of
    litigation by legal professionals. That includes any step taken by them in
    litigation from the issue of proceedings and the securing of injunctive relief or
    a freezing order up to its final disposal by judgment. We do not consider that
    either the European or the United Kingdom legislator can have envisaged that
    any of these ordinary activities could fall within the concept of "becoming
    concerned in an arrangement which . . . . facilitates the acquisition, retention,
    use or control of criminal property"' (para 83).

(b) proceedings or steps taken by lawyers in order to determine or secure legal
    rights and remedies for their clients would not involve them in 'becoming
    concerned in an arrangement which . . . facilitates the acquisition, retention,
    use or control of criminal property'; even if they suspected that the outcome
    of such proceedings might have such an effect (para 84). Therefore, the issue
    or pursuit of ordinary legal proceedings with a view to obtaining the court's
    adjudication upon the parties' rights and duties is not to be regarded as an
    arrangement or a prohibited act within ss 327–329 POCA. The policy reasons
    which persuaded the Court of Appeal to exclude settlements of existing or
    contemplated litigation from POCA apply equally to mediations. Section
    328 does not override legal professional privilege (paras 85–87 and 90).

(c) That privilege could only be overridden by express words or by necessary impli-
    cation. There was nothing in the language of s328 to suggest that Parliament
    expressly intended to override legal professional privilege and much stronger
    language would have been required if s328 could be interpreted as bearing a
    necessary implication that legal professional privilege was to be overridden.

Part II

PROTECTING WHISTLEBLOWERS—
OUTSIDE PIDA

11

PRIVATE INFORMATION AND PUBLIC INTEREST DISCLOSURE

A.	Introduction	11.01
B.	Identifying obligations of confidentiality/privacy	11.04
	(1) Duties in respect of private information	11.04
	Contractual duties	11.04
	Duties outside contract	11.11
	Sources of obligations to maintain confidentiality	11.13
	Privacy and Article 8 of the European Convention on Human Rights	11.14
C.	The public interest defence of 'just cause and excuse' as a defence to actions for breach of duty in respect of private information	11.19
	(1) Overview	11.19
	(2) Development of the public interest defence	11.21
	The old 'iniquity' principle	11.21
	From iniquity to public interest	11.23
	(3) What types of information can form the basis of a public interest defence?	11.29
	The categories corresponding to those covered by the protected disclosure provisions of ERA	11.29

	Categories of information not covered by the protected disclosure provisions of ERA where the courts have held that there is a public interest in disclosure	11.35
	(4) The balancing of interests in domestic law today	11.50
	(5) The context in which the balancing act is carried out	11.58
	Interim relief prohibiting disclosure	11.59
	Cases involving threatened publication	11.62
D.	Protected disclosure provisions as a 'template'?	11.64
	(1) The approach in *Banerjee*	11.64
	(2) PIDA considerations as indicators in the balancing of interests	11.72
	First tier disclosures	11.73
	Second tier/regulatory disclosures	11.75
	Third tier/wider disclosures	11.88
	(3) Proportionality	11.110
	(4) Conclusions in relation to the application of PIDA provisions as a template	11.114
E.	Agreements rendered void	11.116

F. **European Court of Human Rights decisions** 11.121
  (1) Prescribed by law 11.123
  (2) Legitimate aim 11.124
  (3) Necessary in a democratic society and the margin of appreciation 11.128
  (4) Does the whistleblower raise matters of public concern? 11.133
  (5) Duties and responsibilities 11.137
  (6) Manner of the expression 11.139
  (7) Whether the accusations are supported by evidence 11.144

  (8) The recipient of the information 11.145
  (9) Nature of the employing organization 11.147
  (10) Is the sanction imposed by the state?—the scope of the positive obligation to protect the whistleblower 11.148
  (11) Conclusion on the ECHR authorities 11.150
G. **Criminal law** 11.152

A. Introduction

11.01 This chapter describes in broad terms the sources and nature of common law, and equity-based and statutory protections in respect of private information including the overlay of the rights to privacy contained in the European Convention on Human Rights as applied by the Human Rights Act 1998 (HRA). It then considers the nature, extent and application of the public interest defence to those protections including the effect of the right to free expression contained in Article 10 of the Convention.[1]

11.02 The main thrust of the protected disclosure provisions in the ERA, including the powers it contains for interim relief in s128, is to protect a worker from the consequence of losing employment or suffering some other form of lesser detriment by reason or on the grounds that the worker has made[2] a protected disclosure. Those provisions impact upon the subject matter of this chapter in three ways:

(a) By s43J of the ERA, under the heading 'Contractual duties of confidentiality', it is provided that any provision in an agreement between a worker and his employer (whether a worker's contract or not), including an agreement to refrain from instituting or continuing any proceedings under the ERA or any proceedings for breach of contract, is void insofar as it purports to preclude the worker from making a protected disclosure.[3]

---

[1] For an exhaustive, though now slightly dated, treatment of this subject see Cripps, *The Legal Implications of Disclosure in the Public Interest*, 2nd Edn 1994.

[2] Or in the case of interim relief is likely to have made it.

[3] The section reflects the approach of, eg, Salmon LJ and Winn LJ in *Initial Services v Putterill* [1968] 1 QB 396 at 409–410 and 410–411: a contract which obliges an employee to keep secret a

(b) It has been suggested that the template established by the protected disclosure provisions is now of considerable relevance to the approach of the courts as to whether an injunction should be granted to restrain disclosure of information by a worker or former worker.[4]

(c) In addition the making of a claim for an injunction or damages by an employer **11.03** against an employee might constitute a 'detriment' under s47B ERA. This would depend on satisfying the tests for protection against detriment which are considered in detail in Chapter 7.

B. Identifying obligations of confidentiality/privacy

(1) Duties in respect of private information[5]

Contractual duties

A duty of confidentiality may arise as a matter of contract, in which case the **11.04** contract may impose duties, not only during the period of the active relationship between the parties, but also afterwards. During the employment an implied term protects as confidential a very wide range of information. The information does not have to be in the nature of a trade secret, but comprises all information of the employer not in the public domain which might be of advantage to a trade rival (see *Faccenda Chicken Ltd v Fowler* [1987] Ch 117; *Roger Bullivant v Ellis* [1987] ICR 464 at 473–475; *Lansing Linde v Kerr* [1991] 1 WLR 251 (CA)). The confidential information protected after employment by the implied terms of the contract is more limited. It covers trade secrets in the nature of secret formulae and highly confidential information of a non-technical nature which if disclosed to a competitor would cause real or significant harm: see *Lansing Linde v Kerr per* Staughton LJ at 259–260 and *Intelsec Systems Limited v Grech-Cini* [2000] 1 WLR 1190 at 1205–1206.

This distinction was applied against the employer when the Court of Appeal held **11.05** that there had been no breach of confidence by a former managing director in *Brooks v Olyslager OMS (U.K.) Limited* [1998] IRLR 590 (CA). After entering into a compromise agreement terminating his employment, the managing director

---

wrong that ought to be disclosed would be illegal on the ground that it was clearly contrary to the public interest. Other examples are cited by Toulson and Phipps in *Confidentiality* (London: Sweet & Maxwell, 1996) at pages 75–78.

⁴ See the discussion of *Cream Holdings v Banerjee* [2005] 1 AC 253 below.

⁵ The following is only a brief outline of the law in relation to the circumstances giving rise to obligations of confidentiality.

disclosed to an investment banker, who was interested in the company as a professional adviser and option holder, that the company was insolvent and that its budgets were considered too optimistic by its holding company. The claimant argued that the defendant was thereby in breach of the terms of the compromise agreement. The Court of Appeal upheld the trial judge who had ruled that the disclosures were not a breach of any implied term of the agreement. Since the employment had ended there was no implied duty to keep secret information that was merely confidential and no information akin to a trade secret had been disclosed by the defendant.

11.06 Although there is little direct analysis of the point in the case law, it would seem logical that similar principles as those applying to parties to employment contracts will apply to those where the relationship is that of employer and independent contractor. See eg *Campbell v Frisbee* where the contract was said to be one for services rather than of service.

11.07 In *Faccenda Chicken* the Court of Appeal said that where the parties are, or have been, linked by a contract of employment, the obligations of the employee are to be determined by the contract between him and his employer.[6] This approach has its attractions: its principal difficulty is that if the employer is held to have repudiated the contract then all obligations of confidentiality under that contract will presumably come to an end. This issue was considered in *Campbell v Frisbee* which we consider below (at paragraph 11.108ff).

11.08 In order to grant relief, courts have required obligations of confidentiality, especially if relied upon to impose obligations beyond implied obligations of confidentiality, to be identified with particularity.[7] *Tillery Valley Foods v Channel Four Television & anor* [2004] EWHC 1075 (Ch) (11 May 2004) (Mann J) provides an illustration. Tillery produced chilled and frozen meals for NHS hospitals. A journalist obtained employment at Tillery's factory and filmed whilst employed there. Channel Four intended to broadcast some of his film and stated that it showed alleged practices including employees routinely sneezing and coughing over food, employees eating on the production line and improper re-heating procedures. Tillery sought an injunction to prevent the broadcasting of parts of a television programme in relation to its operation, at least until it could view and respond to what was contained in the programme. Clearly, as the judge remarked, these

---

6 At [1987] Ch 135.

7 In many cases this is also tied to the 'cardinal rule that any injunction must be capable of being framed with sufficient precision so as to enable a person injuncted to know what it is he is to be prevented from doing': *Lawrence David v Ashton* [1989] ICR 123 *per* Balcombe LJ at 132.

allegations were serious for Tillery and might have had a serious effect on its business. Tillery did not accept the truth of any of the allegations but the defendants said they intended to justify all the allegations and, because of the principle in *Bonnard v Perryman* [1891] 2 Ch 269,[8] Tillery could not obtain an interim injunction restraining the broadcast. Instead the company sought to base the claim in the law of confidentiality arguing that the activities of the journalist amounted to a breach of his duties of trust and confidence as an employee and that the film that he took amounted to confidential information. The company contended that Channel 4 received and held the information in the form of the film knowing that it was confidential and so could be restrained from using it.

Mann J said that he was 'nowhere near satisfied' that the test under s12(3) of the **11.09** Human Rights Act 1998 was met.[9] Tillery had not shown that it was likely that Channel Four had come into possession of information that was confidential. Mann J dismissed Tillery's argument that it was self-evident that where an employee filmed his workplace, working activities and workmates, it was inevitably going to have the quality of confidential information. There would have to be something more to produce that effect.[10] The terms of the employee/journalist's contract with Tillery did not assist Tillery either. Clause 15 of that contract read:

> Confidentiality
>
> You may not disclose figures or other information about the company's or client's business to anyone outside the company which may injure or cause loss to the company or customer. In the event of a request for information from the press or for information likely to be of interest to the press, the request must be referred to your managing director.
>
> Any information regarding any supplier's business must also be treated confidentially.

Mann J rejected the contention that this term created confidentiality if it would **11.10** otherwise not exist. It was a contractual bar on disclosure applying to all information and did not depend on the information in issue being confidential. Nor did it vest

---

[8] See also *Greene v Associated Newspapers Ltd* [2004] EWCA Civ 1462 [2005] QB 972 (5 November 2004). Where a defendant to a defamation action intends to plead justification it will only be in exceptional cases that an interim injunction will be granted to restrain publication. A claimant would not be able to obtain an interim injunction unless it were plain that the plea of justification was bound to fail.

[9] Mann J applied the Court of Appeal's ruling in *Cream v Banerjee* as to the proper construction of the subsection. The House of Lords subsequently arrived at a different conclusion: see paras 11.64ff below, although this would not have affected the decision that Mann J reached in *Tillery*.

[10] Mann J referred to the Australian authority of *Australian Broadcasting Corporation v Lenah Game Meats Pty Ltd* [2001] HCA 63 where the High Court of Australia held that the activities of a company which processed possum meat for export were not such as to attract the quality of being confidential for the purpose of the law protecting confidentiality.

all information with the character of confidentiality it would not otherwise have had, either expressly or implicitly.

Duties outside contract

11.11 It has been pointed out that the underlying conceptual basis of the action for breach of confidence is not easy to identify.[11] Property, contract, bailment, trust, fiduciary relationship, good faith, unjust enrichment, have all been claimed as the basis of judicial intervention and these concepts have been intermingled between themselves as well. However by 1969 the law had become fairly clear: aside from cases where the parties were bound by contract, the gist of the cause of action of breach of confidence was that private information had been disclosed by one person to another in circumstances importing an obligation of confidence even though no contract of non-disclosure existed: Megarry J in *Coco v A N Clark (Engineers) Ltd* [1969] RPC 41, 47–48. A party who received information in confidence was subject to an obligation in equity not to take unfair advantage of it: *Seager v Copydex Limited* [1967] 1 WLR 923 (CA) at 931B–F. In *Coco* Megarry J put it this way at p 47:

> In my judgment, three elements are normally required if, apart from contract, a case of breach of confidence is to succeed. First, the information itself, in the words of Lord Greene MR in *Saltman Engineering Co Ltd v Campbell Engineering Co Ltd* (1948) 65 RPC 203, 215, must have the necessary quality of confidence about it. Secondly, that information must have been imparted in circumstances importing an obligation of confidence. Thirdly, there must be an unauthorized use of that information to the detriment of the party communicating it.

11.12 Now, as Lord Nicholls put it in *Campbell v MGN* [2004] 2 AC 457 (at para 14), the cause of action has shaken off the limiting constraint of the need for an initial confidential relationship. In *A-G v Guardian Newspapers Ltd (No 2)* [1990] 1 AC 109, the *Spycatcher* case, Lord Goff stated the broad principles as follows:

> . . . a duty of confidence arises when confidential information comes to the knowledge of a person (the confidant) in circumstances where he has notice, or is held to have agreed, that the information is confidential, with the effect that it would be just in all the circumstances that he should be precluded from disclosing the information to others. I have used the word 'notice' advisedly, in order to avoid the (here unnecessary) question of the extent to which actual knowledge is necessary, though I of course understand knowledge to include circumstances where the confidant has deliberately closed his eyes to the obvious. The existence of this broad general principle reflects the fact that there is such a public interest in the maintenance of confidences, that the law will provide remedies for their protection.

---

[11] Cripps, p 17 citing Jones, 'Restitution of Benefits obtained in breach of another's confidence', (1970) 86 LQR 463.

. . . in the vast majority of cases, in particular those concerned with trade secrets, the duty of confidence will arise from a transaction or relationship between the parties, often a contract, in which event the duty may arise by reason of either an express or an implied term of that contract. It is in such cases as these that the expressions 'confider' and 'confidant' are perhaps most aptly employed. But it is well-settled that a duty of confidence may arise in equity independently of such cases.

Sources of obligations to maintain confidentiality

It follows from these principles that the relationships and situations which will engender a duty to respect private information are many and various. Professionals owe duties of confidence. Friends or former friends may be held to owe them.[12] In addition to common law obligations, there are also statutory obligations which restrict the use or disclosure of information, including intellectual property rights and obligations as to processing of data pursuant to the Data Protection Act 1998.[13] We consider in Chapter 3 the specific relevance this potentially has in relation to s43B(3) ERA which provides that a disclosure is not a qualifying disclosure if the making of it is a criminal offence.

11.13

Privacy and Article 8 of the European Convention on Human Rights

The common law has not developed an overall remedy for the invasion of privacy and the courts will not invent a new cause of action to cover types of activity which were not previously covered: *Wainwright v Home Office* [2004] 2 AC 406. But the courts do protect the privacy of the individual and, indeed arguably, that of corporations.[14] This is a rapidly developing area of law, driven in large measure by the effect given to the European Convention on Human Rights through the Human Rights Act 1998. Article 8 of the Convention provides:

11.14

Right to respect for private and family life

1. Everyone has the right to respect for his private and family life, his home and his correspondence.

---

[12] See for example *McKennitt v Ash* [2006] EMLR 10.

[13] The detailed provisions of the Data Protection Act are beyond the scope of this book. In *Campbell v MGN* [2002] EWHC QB 499 Morland J (at para 17) associated himself with the remark by counsel that the DPA was a 'thicket'. In the Court of Appeal in that case ([2002] EWCA Civ 1373 at paragraph 75) Lord Phillips MR described the Act as 'a cumbersome and inelegant piece of legislation'.

[14] Clayton and Tomlinson, *Law of Human Rights*, (Oxford: Oxford University Press, 2000) 22.22 p 1486 citing *R v Broadcasting Standards Commission ex p BBC* [2001] QB 855 and *Investigating Directorate v Hyundai Motor Distributors* (2000) 10 BCLR 1079 (Constitutional Court of South Africa) where the court took the view that a company could have privacy rights. Clayton and Tomlinson also cite *R v Loveridge* [2001] 2 Cr App R 591 where *ex p BBC* was applied. We are not aware of a case where Article 8 has been prayed in aid by a company in a whistleblowing context. In the *Tillery* case referred to above the claimant expressly declined to argue any right of action based upon privacy.

2. There shall be no interference by a public authority with the exercise of this right except such as is in accordance with the law and is necessary in a democratic society in the interests of national security, public safety or the economic well-being of the country, for the prevention of disorder or crime, for the protection of health or morals, or for the protection of the rights and freedoms of others.

The right in Article 8 (1) is qualified by 8 (2) and is to be balanced against the right contained in Article 10:

Article 10

Freedom of expression

1. Everyone has the right to freedom of expression. This right shall include freedom to hold opinions and to receive and impart information and ideas without interference by public authority and regardless of frontiers. This article shall not prevent States from requiring the licensing of broadcasting, television or cinema enterprises.
2. The exercise of these freedoms, since it carries with it duties and responsibilities, may be subject to such formalities, conditions, restrictions or penalties as are prescribed by law and are necessary in a democratic society, in the interests of national security, territorial integrity or public safety, for the prevention of disorder or crime, for the protection of health or morals, for the protection of the reputation or rights of others, for preventing the disclosure of information received in confidence, or for maintaining the authority and impartiality of the judiciary.

11.15 Whilst the Human Rights Act does not create any new cause of action between private persons, if there is a relevant cause of action applicable, the court as a public authority must act compatibly with both parties' Convention rights. The relevant vehicle will usually be the action for breach of confidence. Lord Woolf CJ said in *A v B plc*:[15]

> [Articles 8 and 10] have provided new parameters within which the court will decide, in an action for breach of confidence, whether a person is entitled to have his privacy protected by the court or whether the restriction of freedom of expression which such protection involves cannot be justified. The court's approach to the issues which the applications raise has been modified because, under section 6 of the 1998 Act, the court, as a public authority, is required not to 'act in a way which is incompatible with a Convention right'. The court is able to achieve this by absorbing the rights which articles 8 and 10 protect into the long-established action for breach of confidence. This involves giving a new strength and breadth to the action so that it accommodates the requirements of these articles.

11.16 Accordingly Article 8 operates as a protective mechanism for private information. The touchstone of private life is whether in respect of the disclosed acts the person in question had 'a reasonable expectation of privacy'.[16] If the interest in privacy is

---

[15] [2003] QB 195, 202, para 4.
[16] Lord Nicholls in *Campbell* [2004] 2 AC 457 at paragraph 21.

engaged, the focus then shifts to the balance between Article 8 and Article 10. We consider below how that balance is applied.

The modern approach to identifying confidentiality/privacy was considered **11.17** by Eady J in *McKennitt v Ash* [2006] EMLR 10 in the context of an application to restrain publication of a book containing revelations about the private life of Ms McKennitt. Summarizing the position, Eady J said (paras 60, 61 and 63):

> . . . Lord Hope observed in *Campbell v MGN Ltd* at [85], that '. . . a duty of confidence will arise whenever the party subject to the duty is in a situation where he knows or ought to know that the other person can reasonably expect his privacy to be protected. The difficulty will be as to the relevant facts, bearing in mind that, if there is an intrusion in a situation where a person can reasonably expect his privacy to be respected, that intrusion will be capable of giving rise to liability unless the intrusion can be justified'.

> Reference was made to the 'three limiting principles' identified by Lord Goff in *Attorney General v Guardian Newspapers Ltd (No.2)* [1990] 1 AC 109 at 282:

> 'The first limiting principle . . . is that the principle of confidentiality only applies to information to the extent that it is confidential. In particular, once it has entered what is usually called the public domain (which means no more than that the information in question is so generally accessible that, in all the circumstances, it cannot be regarded as confidential) then, as a general rule, the principle of confidentiality can have no application to it. . . .

> The second limiting principle is that the duty of confidence applies neither to useless information, nor to trivia. . . .

> The third limiting principle is of far greater importance. It is that, although the basis of the law's protection of confidence is that there is a public interest that confidences should be preserved and protected by the law, nevertheless that public interest may be outweighed by some other countervailing public interest which favours disclosure. This limitation may apply, . . . to all types of confidential information. It is this limiting principle which may require a court to carry out a balancing operation, weighing the public interest in maintaining confidence against a countervailing public interest favouring disclosure'.

> . . .

How to decide whether Article 8 is engaged

It thus becomes clear that, with respect to any given piece of information, the first task confronting a court is to identify whether there would be a reasonable expectation of privacy such as to engage Art 8 at all. If not, the balancing exercise becomes unnecessary and any claim based solely upon breach of confidence and/or privacy would fail. Another way of putting it, in the conventional language of claims for breach of confidence, would be to say that the relevant information does not have about it the necessary 'quality of confidence': see, eg *Coco v AN Clark (Engineers) Ltd* [1969] RPC 41; *Douglas v Hello! Ltd* [2003] 3 All ER 182 [sic]; *SmithKline Beecham plc v Generics (UK) Ltd BASF* [2003] EWCA Civ 1109; [2003] 4 All ER 1302 at [31].

As noted by Eady J, Lord Goff identified three limiting principles. The third limit- **11.18** ing principle was that the public interest in confidentiality may be outweighed by a countervailing public interest. We now turn to the scope of this principle.

C. The public interest defence of 'just cause and excuse' as a defence to actions for breach of duty in respect of private information

(1) Overview

11.19   A defence of 'just cause or excuse' may be founded on the basis that the disclosure was under compulsion of law, that there was express or implied consent of the person to whom the duty is owed to make disclosure or that the disclosure was in the public interest.[17] It is the last of these defences which is the subject of this section. As we shall see it applies to someone who is bound by statutory obligations of 'confidentiality' to the Crown contained in the Official Secrets Act 1989 as well as to common law obligations of confidentiality.

11.20   The public interest principle is invoked in a variety of situations which do not easily fit into notions of what constitutes 'whistleblowing'. Mr Livingstone's disclosure of elements of Deloitte's report, the subject matter of *London Regional Transport v The Mayor of London*, and Ms Ash's disclosure through publication of a book on aspects of the life and activities of Ms McKennitt which was in issue in *McKennitt v Ash* [2006] EMLR 10, would not on first impression appear to belong in a survey of whistleblowing where the emphasis is on disclosures by employees of relevant failures. However it is appropriate and necessary to have regard to those cases. It is becoming clear that the essential balancing function for the courts to carry out in situations such as those in the *London Regional Transport* and *McKennitt* cases on the one hand, and 'ordinary' whistleblowing cases on the other, has a single source: the European Convention as applied by the Human Rights Act 1998 and, in particular, Articles 8 and 10 of the Convention, with the principle of proportionality read into them.

(2) Development of the public interest defence

The old 'iniquity' principle

11.21   The defence of disclosure in the public interest has developed from a principle which initially required 'iniquity'. The starting point is *Gartside v Outram*[18] in which Wood V-C stated the general principle thus:[19]

---

[17] *Tournier v National Provincial and Union Bank of England* [1924] 1 KB 461 (CA) *per* Bankes LJ at 473. The Freedom of Information Act 2000 (FOIA) may conceivably provide an additional defence in relation to information within its scope (see eg *HRH the Prince of Wales v Associated Newspapers Limited* [2006] EWHC 522 (Ch), where in Prince Charles' action to prevent the further publication of his private diaries, the newspaper appears to have argued that the Prince had or might have filed with a public authority records of the tours to which the eight journals relate or, possibly, a copy of the eight journals. On the facts however Blackburne J noted this was '. . . speculation without the least evidential foundation'.
[18] (1857) 26 Ch 113.
[19] At 114.

there is no confidence as to the disclosure of iniquity. You cannot make me the confidant of a crime or a fraud, and be entitled to close up my lips upon any secret which you have the audacity to disclose to me relating to any fraudulent intention on your part: such a confidence cannot exist.

In *Initial Services Limited v Putterill*[20] Lord Denning MR increased the reach of the principle saying[21] that: **11.22**

Counsel suggested that this exception was confined to a case where the master has been 'guilty of a crime or fraud'; but I do not think that it is so limited. It extends to any misconduct of such a nature that it ought in the public interest to be disclosed to others . . . . . . In *Weld-Blundell v Stephens* ([1919] 1 KB 520 at p 527) Bankes LJ rather suggested that the exception was limited to the proposed or contemplated commission of a crime or a civil wrong; but I should have thought that that was too limited. The exception should extend to crimes, frauds and misdeeds, both those actually committed as well as those in contemplation, provided always—and this is essential—that the disclosure is justified in the public interest . . . The disclosure must, I should think, be to one who has a proper interest to receive the information. Thus it would be proper to disclose a crime to the police; or a breach of the Restrictive Trade Practices Act, 1956, to the registrar. There may be cases where the misdeed is of such a character that the public interest may demand, or at least excuse, publication on a broader field, even to the press.

From iniquity to public interest

In the *Lion Laboratories*[22] case the principle developed from the notion of the need to demonstrate 'iniquity' or something like it to the wider, though rather less precise, concept of 'public interest'. Griffiths LJ said this: **11.23**

I am quite satisfied that the defence of public interest is now well established in actions for breach of confidence and, although there is less authority on the point, that it also extends to breach of copyright . . . I can see no sensible reason why this defence should be limited to cases in which there has been wrongdoing on the part of the plaintiffs. I believe that the so-called iniquity rule evolved because in most cases where the facts justified a publication in breach of confidence, it was because the plaintiff had behaved so disgracefully or criminally that it was judged in the public interest that his behaviour should be exposed. No doubt it is in such circumstances that the defence will usually arise, but it is not difficult to think of instances where, although there has been no wrongdoing on the part of the plaintiff, it may be vital in the public interest to publish a part of his confidential information . . . . [it] is not an essential ingredient of this defence that the plaintiffs should have been guilty of iniquitous conduct.

---

[20] [1968] 1 QB 396 (CA).
[21] At 405G–406B.
[22] *Lion Laboratories Ltd v Evans* [1985] QB 526.

11.24   As Eady J explained in *McKennitt* (at para 95):

> Nowadays the principle is not regarded as confined to unlawful activity, or even 'iniquity', and it is customary to address the question in terms of a broader 'public interest'. On the other hand, as Mr Browne has fairly pointed out, it is necessary to confine the concept of 'public interest', especially in this context, in a fairly disciplined way. . . . The *Lion Laboratories* case represented something of a departure, in the sense that the emphasis shifted away from the old 'iniquity rule' and on to the somewhat wider, albeit less precise, concept of 'public interest'.

11.25   This development was reflected in Lord Goff's third limiting principle in the *Spycatcher* case, *A-G v Guardian Newspapers (No 2)*.[23] Referring to this principle, Lord Goff said:

> Embraced within this limiting principle is, of course, the so called defence of iniquity. In origin, this principle was narrowly stated, on the basis that a man cannot be made 'the confidant of a crime or a fraud': see *Gartside v Outram* (1857) 26 LJCh 113, 114, *per* Sir William Page Wood V-C. But it is now clear that the principle extends to matters of which disclosure is required in the public interest: see *Beloff v Pressdram Ltd* [1973] 1 All ER 241, 260, *per* Ungoed-Thomas J, and *Lion Laboratories Ltd v Evans* [1985] QB 526, 550, *per* Griffiths LJ. It does not however follow that the public interest will in such cases require disclosure to the media, or to the public by the media. There are cases in which a more limited disclosure is all that is required: see *Francome v Mirror Group Newspapers Ltd* [1984] 1 WLR 892. A classic example of a case where limited disclosure is required is a case of alleged iniquity in the Security Service.

11.26   It has been pointed out that the language used by their Lordships was imperative in tone: Lord Goff saying that the disclosure had to be required in the public interest. From this it is suggested that:

> . . . the true principle is not . . . that the court will permit a breach of confidence whenever it considers that disclosure would serve the public interest more than non-disclosure, but rather that no obligation of confidence exists in contract or in equity, in so far as the subject matter concerns a serious risk of public harm . . . and the alleged obligation would prevent disclosure appropriate to prevent such harm.[24]

11.27   Viewed in this way the principle does not amount to a defence to a claim of breach of confidence but instead has the effect that there is no confidentiality to be breached in the first place. The phraseology used in *Gartside* and by Denning MR in *Initial Services* and, for example, Scott J in *In Re A Company* discussed below, supports this contention. If, on the other hand, the principle is a defence, then the obligation presumably lies on the defendant to establish the public interest

---

[23] See above, para 11.12.
[24] Toulson and Phipps, above n 3, page 80.

in question. Cripps[25] suggests that the increasing popularity of the second or 'defence' basis for the principle may be attributable to judicial recognition of the desirability of allowing confidential material to be disclosed or intercepted on the basis of a reasonable belief that the course of action is in the public interest even if that belief subsequently turns out to be unfounded: in such a case it cannot be said that an obligation of confidence never arose in the first place.

So far as the burden of proof is concerned, the factual basis for establishing that **11.28** otherwise confidential information lacks the quality of confidentiality due to iniquity, must itself be raised at any interim application and proved at trial (and cannot merely be the subject of an assertion). The practical difference between the approaches may therefore be more apparent than real. In any event, as we shall see, the most recent cases do not approach the matter as one depending on the burden of proof but as a balancing act in which an assessment is made as to whether the interests of confidentiality/privacy trump the interest in disclosure/publication or vice versa.

(3) What types of information can form the basis of a public interest defence?

The categories corresponding to those covered by the protected disclosure provisions of ERA

As described in Chapter 3, s43B ERA sets out the categories of information, 'relevant **11.29** failures' in the terminology used by the Act, the disclosure of which can attract the protections of the protected disclosure provisions of ERA (see para 3.02 above). In this section we consider the extent to which the public interest defence mirrors those categories, although it is clear that the public interest defence is of wider scope than the 'relevant failures' which can form the subject matter of qualifying disclosures under ERA. The identification of a type of information which potentially provides a defence to a breach of confidentiality is not the end of the matter. Considerations of proportionality and the balancing of the interest in disclosure against any interest in privacy/confidentiality still require consideration.

Crime

Information that a criminal offence has been, is being or is likely to be committed **11.30** is a legitimate subject of disclosure: see *Gartside v Outram*. That case concerned disclosure by an ex-employee of accounting and business information which it was alleged showed that the employer had been carrying on business in a fraudulent manner. Wood V-C held that this would be a good defence if the factual basis for it was made out at trial.

---

25 At page 25 referring to Megarry V-C in *Malone v MPC* [1979] Ch 344 at 377.

Failure to comply with a legal obligation

11.31   The decision in *Initial Services*[26] provides an example falling within the category of information that a person has failed, is failing or is likely to fail to comply with any legal obligation to which he is subject. On resigning as sales manager of the claimant launderers, Mr Putterill removed documents belonging to the claimant which he passed to *Daily Mail* reporters. Relying upon these documents, the newspaper alleged that there was an unlawful price-fixing agreement and that the laundries had misled the public in claiming to have increased their prices to offset tax when in reality they then were increasing their profits. Breach of the Restrictive Trade Practices Act 1956 was not a criminal offence and it was argued that the disclosure could only be justified in cases of information relating to crime and fraud. The Court of Appeal rejected this submission and refused to strike out the defence that the disclosures were made in the public interest.

Miscarriage of justice

11.32   The decision of the Court of Appeal in *Lion Laboratories*[27] provides an example of information that a miscarriage of justice has occurred, is occurring or is likely to occur. Unless there was full disclosure of the information in issue, there might have been unsafe convictions for drink driving. The claimants manufactured breathalyser equipment. The defendants had been employed by the claimants as technicians. When their employment ended they removed documents which cast doubt on the reliability of the equipment. These documents were passed on to the press. It was admitted that the documents were confidential but an interlocutory injunction was overturned because of the public interest in the public being informed that the equipment might not be reliable.

Health and safety concerns

11.33   As to information that the health or safety of any individual has been, is being or is likely to be endangered, see *Hubbard v Vosper* [1972] 2 QB 84. Lord Denning MR (at 96A–B) considered that, in relation to material on Scientology which had been published in breach of confidence, a public interest defence might be established at trial on the basis that it was dangerous material including 'medical quackeries of a sort which might be dangerous if practised behind closed doors'. Similarly in *Church of Scientology of California v Kaufman* [1973] RPC 635 Goff J held that disclosure by a former student of Scientology was justified on the basis

---

[26] See above n 3.
[27] See above n 22.

of possible danger to the public in the light of evidence that Scientology had caused some followers to be become ill.[28]

Damage to the environment/concealment of information

Equally the public interest principle would plainly be wide enough to cover **11.34** disclosures of information that the environment has been, is being or is likely to be damaged, or, specifically information tending to show that one of the other relevant failures has been, or is likely to be deliberately concealed.

Categories of information not covered by the protected disclosure provisions of ERA where the courts have held that there is a public interest in disclosure

The scope for a public interest defence however extends beyond the categories of **11.35** 'relevant failures' provided for by s43B.

Breaches of rules of self-regulatory schemes

Disclosure of a breach of the rules of a self-regulatory scheme, particularly in the **11.36** financial services sector, is capable of being justified at least where the disclosure is to the relevant regulatory body. In *In re A Company's Application* [1989] 1 Ch 477, which is considered in more detail below,[29] the claimant company provided financial advice and management. It was alleged that the defendant, a former employee, had threatened that if he was not paid £10,000 as compensation for his having been dismissed he would report breaches of the Financial Investment Management Rules to the Financial Investment and Brokers' Regulatory Authority (FIMBRA) and would also report allegations of tax improprieties to the Inland Revenue. The defendant sought an injunction to prevent any disclosures using their confidential information. Scott J refused to grant an interlocutory injunction to this effect: the duty of confidentiality did not extend to a duty not to make disclosure to the appropriate regulatory body of a possible breach of that body's regulatory rules.

Similarly in *Francome v Mirror Group Newspapers Limited* [1984] 1 WLR 892 **11.37** secret tapes were made of telephone conversations involving John Francome, a well-known jockey. The tapes were then sold to the press. An attempt was made to justify the apparent breach of Mr Francome's confidence on the basis that the tapes revealed breaches of the rules of racing. The Court of Appeal restrained publication until trial but held that there was a triable issue as to whether the publication could be justified.

---

[28] The decision of Talbot J in *Distillers Co (Biochemicals) Limited v Times Newspapers Limited* [1975] 1 QB 613 at 622 that negligence, even if it could be proved, could not be within the same class as crime, fraud or misdeed so as to constitute an exception to the need to protect confidentiality, is out of line with other authority. See Cripps, above n 1, p 102.

[29] In paras 11.79ff.

Damage to financial interests of investors/the public

11.38 Damage to the financial interests of the public which might not involve breaches of a legal obligation, may also be justified. In *Price Waterhouse v BCCI Holdings (Luxembourg) SA* [1992] BCLC 583 the Court of Appeal expressly recognized that the public interest in effective supervision of banking institutions could justify overriding a duty of confidence. Price Waterhouse had acted as auditors to the BCCI Group. After the collapse of the Group the Bank of England and the Treasury set up a non-statutory enquiry into the supervision of BCCI. The Bank of England and the Serious Fraud Office served notices on Price Waterhouse to disclose various confidential documents and Price Waterhouse sought a declaration that it was entitled to disclose the documents. Millet J considered that in this case the public interest in preserving the confidentiality of the documents relating to Price Waterhouse's client—BCCI—was outweighed by the public interest in the effective supervision of authorized banking institutions, having regard to the need to protect depositors, and the public interest in ensuring that the inquiry into the adequacy of such supervision should have access to all relevant material.

11.39 In *London Regional Transport v Mayor of London* [2001] EWCA Civ 1491; [2003] EMLR 88, London Regional Transport sought to prevent publication by the Mayor of London, Ken Livingstone, of a report prepared by a firm of accountants, Deloitte's, concerning the London Underground. The report went into the supposed flaws in the methods used to assess the efficacy of the public–private partnership that was proposed for the Underground. London Regional Transport argued that, because of written confidentiality agreements which bound the Mayor and which applied to his receipt of the Deloitte's report, the court had no option but to prevent disclosure. At first instance Sullivan J held that it was genuinely in the public interest for a redacted version of the Deloitte's report to be published. He reached that conclusion having balanced 'the desirability in the public interest of upholding confidentiality agreements and the public interest in freedom of access to information'. The Court of Appeal held that the judge was correct to have conducted such a balancing exercise and agreed with his conclusion. We consider their approach to the balancing exercise in more detail below.

Where the public has been/will be misled

11.40 A series of cases suggest that disclosure could be justified in order to prevent the public being misled. In *Initial Services* it was alleged that the public had been misled into believing that laundry prices had been increased due to tax when in fact there was substantial additional profit being made. This was held to be a further arguable ground justifying disclosure of otherwise confidential material. Similarly in *Scientology v Kaufman* (at 654) one ground for resisting an injunction was that otherwise the public might be deceived into paying for 'nonsensical mumbo-jumbo' (being the judge's description of the teachings of the Church of Scientology). It was therefore in the public interest that there should be disclosure of the type of thing for which payment was being requested.

The theoretical possible breadth of this ground was illustrated by the controversial decision in *Woodward v Hutchins* [1977] 1 WLR 760 (CA). A former public relations officer and press agent wrote a series of articles about the activities of pop stars by whom he had been employed (via a management company). An interim injunction was refused. Although the injunction sought was too wide in any event since it covered information in the public domain, Lord Denning MR and Bridge LJ both emphasized that since the pop stars had invited publicity they could not complain if the truth was then told. The information in issue in *Woodward* tended to show that the image that the pop group had fostered was not a true image and it was in the public interest that it be corrected. Of course in no sense did the alleged hypocrisy represent any form of danger to the public. It may be however that the decision turned not so much upon whether there was a defence to breach of confidence as a matter of law but on whether the discretion of the court should be exercised in favour of granting the claimant an injunction. Bridge LJ left open the possibility that if the defendants could show that the information was true there would only be nominal damages for breach of confidence. Further Lawton LJ explained the decision on the basis that the breach of confidence was interwoven with the allegations of libel and that the ordinary principle in the case of libel was to allow publication where justification was alleged. **11.41**

The decision in *Woodward* was followed in *Khashoggi v Smith* (1980) 124 SJ 149 (CA) where the claimant sought unsuccessfully to restrain her former housekeeper from disclosing information about her private affairs including allegations of criminal conduct. Roskill LJ accepted that the allegations about the claimant's private life could not be disentangled from the allegations of offences and that disclosure was therefore justified since there could not be any confidence where the information was to be exploited (by the press) for investigation into the alleged offences. However he also held that the claimant had allowed herself into the public eye to such an extent that she 'ran the risk of the whole story being made public', in the sense of giving a full account of matters where only a partial or misleading account had previously been given. **11.42**

In *Campbell v MGN* [2004] 2 AC 457 it was conceded that the *Daily Mirror* was entitled to publish the fact of Naomi Campbell's drug dependency and the fact that she was seeking treatment because she had specifically given publicity to the very question of whether she took drugs and had falsely said that she did not. This created a sufficient public interest in the correction of the impression she had previously given. Lord Nicholls observed at 467D, albeit the point was not in issue in *Campbell*, that: **11.43**

> . . . where a public figure chooses to present a false image and make untrue pronouncements about his or her life, the press will normally be entitled to put the record straight.

11.44   Langley J ruled to a similar effect when David and Victoria Beckham sought an interim injunction against their former nanny, Abbie Gibson,[30] who had signed a confidentiality agreement. On behalf of Ms Gibson (and the *News of the World*) it was argued that because the Beckhams used their marriage as a marketing tool, the public was entitled to know what Ms Gibson and the newspaper contended was the reality of that marriage. Langley J appears to have accepted this argument.

11.45   However the decision in *Woodward* may be seen as failing adequately to observe the distinction between what is interesting to the public and what is in the public interest to be made known.[31] In *Campbell v Frisbee* [2002] EMLR 31 it was argued before Lightman J that the disclosures were legitimate because they corrected a false impression that Ms Campbell had placed before the public and reliance was placed on *Woodward*. Lightman J said that he did not see how it was seriously maintainable that the public had any interest in the content of the disclosures (most particularly that the claimant was cheating on her partner) or any need to know, or that the defendant had any such reason or justification for making her disclosures, and there was no real prospect of the court holding at the trial that the disclosure by the defendant could possibly be justified. In the Court of Appeal [2003] ICR 141 Lord Phillips MR said that Lightman J 'might well have been right to suggest that *Woodward* should no longer be applied'. Further, in *McKennitt v Ash*, Eady J noted the range of criticism of *Woodward* and expressed the view that for personal misbehaviour which was not unlawful to justify disclosure, 'a very high degree of misbehaviour must be demonstrated'.

Alleged immorality

11.46   In *Stephens v Avery*[32] *The Mail on Sunday* published an article containing details of a lesbian affair on the basis of information passed on by a third party in whom the claimant had confided. The claimant brought a claim for breach of confidence. The defendants applied to have the action struck out as disclosing no reasonable cause of action, or as being scandalous, frivolous or vexatious on the basis that there could be no confidence in respect of information concerning grossly immoral conduct. The Master refused to strike out the proceedings and Sir Nicholas Browne-Wilkinson V-C upheld this decision. The defendants relied on the 1915 decision of Younger J in *Glyn v Weston Feature Film Co.* [1916] 1 Ch 261 where the claimant alleged that an episode in her novel had been pirated in breach

---

[30] *Beckham v Gibson*, 23 April 2005, unreported.

[31] *Per* Lord Wilberforce in *British Steel Corporation v Granada Television Limited* [1981] AC 1096 (HL) at 1168G. In the same case Viscount Dilhorne at 1176C was of the view that disclosure would not have been justified in order to establish that it was not true that there had been no government intervention in the steel strike.

[32] [1988] 1 Ch 449.

of copyright. Younger J refused to grant relief on various grounds including that the episode in question was:

> grossly immoral in its essence, in its treatment, and in its tendency. Stripped of its trappings, which are mere accident, it is nothing more nor less than a sensual adulterous intrigue. And it is not as if the plaintiff in her treatment of it were content to excuse or palliate the conduct described. She is not even satisfied with justifying that conduct. She has stooped to glorify the liaison in its inception, its progress, and its results; and she has not hesitated to garnish it with meretricious incident at every turn. Now it is clear law that copyright cannot exist in a work of a tendency so grossly immoral as this, a work which, apart from its other objectionable features, advocates free love and justifies adultery where the marriage tie has become merely irksome.

Browne Wilkinson V-C did not suggest that *Glyn* was incorrect as a matter of law: **11.47** that which was grossly immoral might not attract the law's protection.

> But at the present day the difficulty is to identify what sexual conduct is to be treated as grossly immoral. In 1915 there was a code of sexual morals accepted by the overwhelming majority of society. A judge could therefore stigmatize certain sexual conduct as offending that moral code. But at the present day no such general code exists. There is no common view that sexual conduct of any kind between consenting adults is grossly immoral. I suspect the works of Elinor Glyn if published today would be widely regarded as, at the highest, very soft pornography.
>
> The sexual conduct of the plaintiff was not so morally shocking in this case as to prevent the third defendant, a major national Sunday newspaper, from spreading the story all over its front and inside pages. The submission on behalf of these defendants that the actions of the plaintiff in this case are so grossly immoral as to produce a tendency towards immoral conduct and thereby to be without the law lies ill in their mouths, since they have themselves spread the news of such conduct nationwide for their own personal profit.
>
> If it is right that there is now no generally accepted code of sexual morality applying to this case, it would be quite wrong in my judgment for any judge to apply his own personal moral views, however strongly held, in deciding the legal rights of the parties. The court's function is to apply the law, not personal prejudice. Only in a case where there is still a generally accepted moral code can the court refuse to enforce rights in such a way as to offend that generally accepted code.

The practical problem is therefore likely to be how to satisfy the Court that there **11.48** is in the 21st century a 'generally accepted moral code' with regard to the subject matter of the information in question, whatever it may be.

Conclusions as to the nature of the information that can form the basis of a public interest defence

The protected disclosure provisions of ERA set out a finite list of the categories of **11.49** information which can form the subject of qualifying disclosures. The principle of public interest disclosure which we are considering in this chapter is more flexible and matters not listed in s43B might attract its application. There is no reason whatsoever to suppose that the categories are closed or even that the courts will proceed on the basis that they should find a precedent in a previous case involving information of an analogous nature to that under consideration. That is not to say that the nature, importance and seriousness of the 'harm' in issue is not relevant: it most certainly is, and the distinction between what is of interest to the public and what is of public interest to be made known remains important.

(4) The balancing of interests in domestic law today

11.50 It is now arguably the case that there is an overarching right to freedom of expression, the curtailment of which is to be balanced against the competing right of the claimant to the continued confidentiality of his or her information. We consider how the overall balancing test is developing along these lines below and how the courts are in the process of formulating, or rather adopting from European models, 'rules' to guide the process of carrying out that balance. The balancing of interests has now to be applied in the context of the incorporation of the Convention rights into domestic law through the medium of the Human Rights Act. The most recent cases emphasize the importance of freedom of expression: see for example Lord Steyn in *R v Home Secretary ex p Simms* [2000] 2 AC 11:

> The starting point is the right of freedom of expression. In a democracy it is the primary right: without it an effective rule of law is not possible. Nevertheless, freedom of expression is not an absolute right. Sometimes it must yield to other cogent social interests. . . .
>
> Freedom of expression is, of course, intrinsically important: it is valued for its own sake. But it is well recognized that it is also instrumentally important. It serves a number of broad objectives. First, it promotes the self-fulfilment of individuals in society. Secondly, in the famous words of Holmes J (echoing John Stuart Mill), 'the best test of truth is the power of the thought to get itself accepted in the competition of the market': *Abrams v United States* (1919) 250 U.S. 616, 630, *per* Holmes J (dissenting). Thirdly, freedom of speech is the lifeblood of democracy. The free flow of information and ideas informs political debate. It is a safety valve: people are more ready to accept decisions that go against them if they can in principle seek to influence them. It acts as a brake on the abuse of power by public officials. It facilitates the exposure of errors in the governance and administration of justice of the country: see Stone, Seidman, Sunstein and Tushnet, *Constitutional Law,* 3rd ed. (1996), pp 1078–1086. (pp 125–6)

11.51 However in *Campbell v MGN* Lord Hope concluded (at paragraphs 85–86) that although some of the language has changed (notably focusing on the concept of proportionality), the process remains substantially the same:

> The third limiting principle is particularly relevant in this case. This is the principle which may require a court to carry out a balancing operation, weighing the public interest in maintaining confidence against a countervailing public interest favouring disclosure.
>
> The language has changed following the coming into operation of the Human Rights Act 1998 and the incorporation into domestic law of article 8 and article 10

of the Convention. We now talk about the right to respect for private life and the countervailing right to freedom of expression. The jurisprudence of the European Court offers important guidance as to how these competing rights ought to be approached and analysed. I doubt whether the result is that the centre of gravity, as my noble and learned friend, Lord Hoffmann, says, has shifted. It seems to me that the balancing exercise to which that guidance is directed is essentially the same exercise, although it is plainly now more carefully focused and more penetrating. As Lord Woolf CJ said in *A v B plc* [2003] QB 195, 202, para 4, new breadth and strength is given to the action for breach of confidence by these articles.

This applied even though *Campbell* was not a 'whistleblowing' case in any usually **11.52** accepted sense: there were major differences between it and the *Spycatcher* case in which Lord Goff gave the exposition to which Lord Hope was referring. Peter Wright was 'whistleblowing' in respect of irregularities he alleged had occurred in the security services. The information he was disclosing was nothing like the information about Naomi Campbell's treatment for drug addiction, the disclosure of which was the subject matter of her claim against the *Daily Mirror.*

In *Re S (A Child) (Identification: Restrictions on Publication)* [2005] 1 AC 593 at **11.53** paragraph 17 Lord Steyn referred to the opinions in the House of Lords in *Campbell* as having illuminated the interplay between articles 8 and 10 and continued (at paragraph 17):

> for present purposes the decision of the House on the facts of *Campbell* and the differences between the majority and the minority are not material. What does, however, emerge clearly from the opinions are four propositions. First, neither article has *as such* precedence over the other. Secondly, where the values under the two articles are in conflict, an intense focus on the comparative importance of the specific rights being claimed in the individual case is necessary. Thirdly, the justifications for interfering with or restricting each right must be taken into account. Finally, the proportionality test must be applied to each. For convenience I will call this the ultimate balancing test.

Further guidance as to the approach required by the concept of proportionality is **11.54** provided by the decision in *London Regional Transport v Mayor of London* [2003] EMLR 88. London Regional Transport sought to prevent publication by the Mayor of London of a report commissioned by accountants concerning the London Underground. Sullivan J held that it was genuinely in the public interest for a redacted version of the report to be published. He arrived at that conclusion having balanced 'the desirability in the public interest of upholding confidentiality agreements and the public interest in freedom of access to information': see para 42 of the Court of Appeal judgment. Walker LJ (para 50) clearly thought that the information in question raised very serious issues:

> The guiding principle is to preserve legitimate commercial confidentiality while enabling the general public (and especially the long-suffering travelling public of London) to be informed of serious criticism, from a responsible source, of the value for money evaluation which is a crucial part of the PPP for the London Underground.

That is a very important public interest which goes far beyond the transitional purposes of the 1999 Act, and it is the interest which must go into the scales on proportionality.

11.55 Sedley LJ's judgment expressed full agreement with that of Robert Walker LJ. In his view the discharge of the injunction by Sullivan J was justified on the straightforward ground that there was nothing of genuine commercial sensitivity in the redacted version of the Deloitte's report and nothing therefore to justify the stifling of public information and debate by the enforcement of a bare contractual obligation of silence. However addressing the issue as to how the balance was to be struck between the interest in confidentiality and the article 10 interest in disclosure he said:

> Article 10 of the European Convention on Human Rights is not just about freedom of expression. It is also about the right to receive and impart information . . . . Whether or not undertakings of confidentiality had been signed, both domestic law and Art. 10(2) would recognise the propriety of suppressing wanton or self-interested disclosure of confidential information; but both correspondingly recognise the legitimacy of disclosure, undertakings notwithstanding, if the public interest in the free flow of information and ideas will be served by it.

> The difficulty in the latter case, as Miss Appleby's argument has understandably stressed, is to know by what instrument this balance is to be struck . . . .

> It lies in the methodical concept of proportionality. Proportionality is not a word found in the text of the Convention: it is the tool—the *metwand*—which the Court has adopted (from 19th-century German jurisprudence) for deciding a variety of Convention issues including, for the purposes of the qualifications to Arts. 8 to 11, what is and is not necessary in a democratic society. It replaces an elastic concept with which political scientists are more at home than lawyers with a structured inquiry: does the measure meet a recognized and pressing social need? Does it negate the primary right or restrict it more than is necessary? Are the reasons given for it logical? These tests of what is acceptable by way of restriction of basic rights in a democratic society reappear, with variations of phrasing and emphasis, in the jurisprudence of (among others) the Privy Council, the Constitutional Court of South Africa, the Supreme Court of Zimbabwe and the Supreme Court of Canada in its Charter jurisdiction (see *de Freitas v Ministry of Agriculture* [1999] 1 AC 69, 80, PC), the courts of the Republic of Ireland (see *Quinn's Supermarket v A-G* [1972] IR 1) and the Court of Justice of the European Communities (see Art. 3b, Treaty on European Union; *Bosman* [1995] ECR I–4921, §110).

11.56 Central importance was therefore attached to the principle of proportionality. The claimants in *London Regional Transport* were a public authority, but Sedley LJ noted that, whilst it did not necessarily follow from the court's own status as a public authority that all its judgments had without more ado to be Convention-compliant, it did follow that where it is deciding whether or not to grant an injunction its judgment had to respect both the relevant Convention rights and their qualifications. Sedley LJ however concluded by saying:

> In the present case, as one would hope in most cases, the human rights highway leads to exactly the same outcome as the older road of equity and common law. But it may

be that it is in some respects better signposted, and it is therefore helpful that it has played a central role in the argument.

However as noted above, prior to the need to apply Article 10 of the Convention, **11.57** in a case between private litigants the burden of proof appears to have been on the defendant to show that disclosure is justified, whereas the government had the burden of establishing a public interest in establishing confidentiality.[33] This must now be read subject to the need to apply proportionality to both the interests in confidentiality and in free expression with no presumption in favour of either interest.

(5) *The context in which the balancing act is carried out*

It is important to bear in mind, when considering the way the courts balance the **11.58** competing public interests of confidentiality on the one hand, and exposure of 'relevant failures' on the other, the context in which the decisions have been made. There are relatively few cases of a public interest defence being tested at a full trial and in practical terms the interim hearing will very often resolve the matter. The strength of the defence is tested at an interim hearing with limited evidence and limited time to consider it. Most of the cases discussed in this chapter arose out of applications for interim injunctions.

Interim relief prohibiting disclosure

The basic test for the consideration of whether interim relief should be granted is **11.59** that set out by Lord Diplock in *American Cyanamid Co v Ethicon Ltd*:[34] the court must be satisfied 'that there is a serious question to be tried'. It is no part of the court's function at this stage of litigation to try to resolve conflicts of evidence on affidavit or in witness statements nor to decide difficult questions of law calling for detailed argument and mature consideration. Unless the applicant fails to show he has 'any real prospect of succeeding in his claim for a permanent injunction at the trial', the court should proceed to consider where the balance of convenience lies. As to that, where other factors appear to be evenly balanced 'it is a counsel of prudence' for the court to take 'such measures as are calculated to preserve the status quo'.

However the *American Cyanamid* approach is not of universal application. The **11.60** law recognizes that there is a category of case in which a more stringent threshold than serious arguable case is required. In *NWL Ltd v Woods*[35] Lord Diplock said this:

> Where . . . the grant or refusal of the interlocutory injunction will have the practical effect of putting an end to the action because the harm that will have been already

---

[33] See the *Spycatcher* case *per* Lord Griffiths (at 328), *per* Lord Keith (at 256), *per* Lord Griffiths (at 270) and *per* Lord Goff (at 283).
[34] [1975] AC 396.
[35] [1979] 1 WLR 1294, 1307.

caused to the losing party by its grant or its refusal is complete and of a kind for which money cannot constitute any worthwhile recompense, the degree of likelihood that the plaintiff would have succeeded in establishing his right to an injunction if the action had gone to trial, is a factor to be brought into the balance by the judge in weighing the risks that injustice may result from his deciding the application one way rather than the other.[36]

11.61 This is apposite in the context of the balance to be struck at an interim stage between disclosure and non-disclosure[37] because a disclosure once made cannot be unmade. But in a case where publication is involved (ie wider disclosure discussed below) different principles apply in any event, to which we now turn.

Cases involving threatened publication

11.62 Section 12 of the Human Rights Act 1998 makes special provision regarding the right to freedom of expression. When considering whether to grant relief which, if granted, might affect the exercise of the Convention right to freedom of expression, s12(4) provides that the court must have particular regard to the importance of this right. Section 12(3) imposes a threshold test which has to be satisfied before a court may grant interlocutory injunctive relief:

> No such relief [which might affect the exercise of the Convention right to freedom of expression] is to be granted so as to restrain publication before trial unless the court is satisfied that the applicant is likely to establish that publication should not be allowed.

11.63 This provision was the subject of the House of Lords' decision in *Cream Holdings Ltd and others v Banerjee and another*[38] where it was concluded that it did not necessarily require that the applicant must establish that he is more likely than not to succeed at trial. Whilst likelihood of success is an essential element to be considered, the degree of likelihood will depend on all the circumstances.

D. Protected disclosure provisions as a 'template'?

(1) The approach in Banerjee

11.64 Whilst the decision in *Banerjee* is therefore to be seen in the context that it concerned an application for interim relief, it raised an issue as to the interface between the public interest defence, and the structure for protection introduced

---

[36] See also *Lansing Linde Limited v Kerr* (para 11.04 above) at 258A–C.
[37] See Morritt V-C in *Imutran* (see para 11.110 below) para 15 and Sullivan J in *London Regional Transport* para 55 at first instance together with the Court of Appeal's judgment in the latter case at para 44.
[38] 2004 UKHL 44; [2005] 1 AC 253.

by PIDA. The Cream group of companies ran businesses including nightclubs, dance festivals and the franchising of their brand name and logo and merchandising clothes and other items. Lord Nicholls described them as 'an important business in Liverpool featuring both on general news pages and financial pages of newspapers'. Ms Banerjee was a chartered accountant and worked as the financial controller of one of the companies in the Cream group for three years from February 1998 to January 2001. Prior to that she worked for a firm of accountants and was responsible for dealing with the Cream group's financial affairs between 1996 and 1998. The second defendant, was the publisher of Liverpool's *Daily Post* and the *Liverpool Echo*. In January 2001 Cream dismissed Ms Banerjee. When she left she took with her copies of documents she subsequently claimed showed illegal and improper activity by the Cream group which she passed to the *Echo* with additional information. She received no payment for this. In June 2002 the *Echo* published articles about alleged corruption involving one director of the Cream group and a local council official. The Cream group sought injunctive relief to restrain publication by the newspaper of any further confidential information given to it by Ms Banerjee. The defendants admitted the information was confidential but contended that disclosure was in the public interest.

At first instance, Lloyd J granted interim injunctive relief, restraining disclosure of **11.65** confidential information except to criminal or regulatory authorities. He considered that, given the undoubted obligation of confidentiality inherent in Ms Banerjee's employment contract, the disputes of fact on some matters, and the possibility that Ms Banerjee's complaints of defaults by the Cream group might be met adequately by disclosure to certain regulatory authorities as distinct from publication at large by the press, the right course was to maintain the status quo and direct a speedy trial if desired.

The majority in the Court of Appeal, Simon Brown and Arden LJJ, dismissed the **11.66** appeal, and Sedley LJ dissented. However this was reversed by the House of Lords who concluded that the prospects of establishing at trial the interest in confidentiality were insufficient to justify maintaining the injunction.

The precise way in which the conclusion was reached on the balancing exercise **11.67** must be a matter of inference because the detail was set out in closed judgments. However Sedley LJ placed PIDA at the centre of his reasoning. He identified that there was a public interest in disclosure of the information. He also noted that there may be an interest in maintaining confidentiality given that the information was disclosed by a former employee, albeit he also referred to the principle that no confidence attaches to confidentiality. As to these competing considerations he said (at paras 90–91):

> How are these two principles to be reconciled? It is said by the claimants that to let the second trump the first is to give carte blanche to any employee to go straight to

the press with damaging disclosures about his or her employers; and if employees, why not independent professional advisers? The answer lies in the concept of graduated responses for which the Employment Rights Act 1996 as amended by the Public Interest Disclosure Act 1998 now provides a template. Lloyd J derived assistance from it. But what it seems to me he failed to recognise was that the first defendant had exhausted these responses. The detail, regrettably, has to be relegated to my closed judgment.

In these circumstances I see no real possibility of the claimants' succeeding at trial. They could do so only on the footing that the duty of confidentiality was inviolable, and in law it is well established that it is not. The argument from consequences has to be taken seriously, but there are several answers to it. So far as concerns employees, there is now a statutory framework which the employee will step outside at his or her peril; but this the first defendant did not do. So far as concerns auditors, lawyers and others, there is a strong code of professional standards the breach of which may result in the loss of their livelihoods; but it is not suggested that the first defendant faces any such charge. The essential story is in my view one which, whatever its source, no court could properly suppress.

11.68 Sedley LJ therefore considered that the PIDA provisions provided a 'template' to balance the competing principles in relation to confidentiality and the public interest and that employees would step outside that protection at their peril. This approach has obvious attractions. It would provide a set of clear principles which will squarely meet the criticism by Gummow J (in *SK & F v Department of Community Services* [1990] FSR 617, 663) of the case law as it stood at the time. He made this remark:

> . . . an examination of the recent English decisions shows that the so-called 'public interest' defence is not so much a rule of law as an invitation to judicial idiosyncrasy by deciding each case on an ad hoc basis as to whether, on the facts overall, it is better to respect or to override the obligation of confidence.

11.69 However, although Lord Nicholls (who gave the only speech in the House of Lords) agreed with the conclusion reached by Sedley LJ, he did not endorse the observations as to the use of PIDA as a template. He explained (at paragraph 24) that:

> . . . I am satisfied that in one particular respect the judge fell into error in any event. The error was identified by Sedley LJ and sufficiently explained by him at para 88[39] of his judgment [2003] Ch 650, 677, and para 1 of his 'private' judgment. I agree with him that the principal happenings the *Echo* wishes to publish are clearly matters of serious public interest. The graduated protection afforded to 'whistleblowers' by sections 43A to 43L of the Employment Rights Act 1996, inserted by the Public Interest Disclosure Act 1998, section 1, does not militate against this appraisal. Authorities such as the Inland Revenue owe duties of confidentiality regarding the affairs of those with whom they are dealing. The 'whistleblower' provisions were intended

---

[39] In paragraph 88 Sedley LJ noted that the disclosure was essentially true (otherwise there would have been a defamation claim) and that there was a serious public interest in disclosure.

to give additional protection to employees, not to cut down the circumstances where the public interest may justify private information being published at large.

11.70 Lord Nicholls therefore emphasized the differing considerations that may arise in relation to whether the public interest might justify private information being published and whether to grant protection under PIDA. It was relevant to draw this distinction because the defendant had raised potential defences under the protected disclosure provisions as a reason to refuse relief. At first instance Lloyd J had identified the question arising in the case as being:

> whether Cream is likely to be able to succeed at trial despite the defendants' defences based on the public interest and the Public Interest Disclosure Act.[40]

11.71 Whilst Sedley LJ referred to a worker stepping outside the protected disclosure provisions at his peril, Lord Nicholls' approach identified that a defence under the protected disclosure provisions would not necessarily resolve the balance of where the public interest lies. This mirrored the approach of Auld LJ in *Street v Derbyshire Unemployed Workers' Centre* [2005] ICR 97 (CA) who rejected a submission that the tests applied in relation to publishing confidential information were of relevance in relation to the meaning of good faith in the protected disclosure provisions.

(2) PIDA considerations as indicators in the balancing of interests

11.72 We consider in this section the extent to which, notwithstanding Lord Nicholls' caution that protected disclosure defences do not necessarily negate an interest in disclosure, factors material to a protected disclosure are material when assessing the balance of public interest in relation to confidentiality. Whilst not necessarily determinative, the factors taken into account in relation to protected disclosures are likely to be material considerations in relation to whether a public interest defence to confidentiality is made out. Indeed this is unsurprising given that, without tying protection to common law confidentiality obligations, the legislation drew upon principles established in the body of case law principally in the context of confidentiality. We consider below how factors central to the PIDA legislation also play an important role in relation to confidentiality obligations.

First tier disclosures

11.73 First tier disclosure is disclosure either to the employer or to a person other than the employer in respect of a relevant failure for which a person other than the employer has legal responsibility. No issue as to breach of confidentiality would arise upon disclosure to the employer in cases where the duty of confidentiality is owed to the employer. But issues might arise where the duty is owed to a third

---

[40] See paragraph 24 of the judgment of Simon Brown LJ in the Court of Appeal ([2003] Ch 650 at 662).

party. One instance would be where an employee discloses information about a previous employer to the new employer. Ordinarily these issues arise in the context of disclosing valuable business information to a competitor, rather than disclosing issues of public concern. However it might engage protected disclosure issues. The position can be illustrated by the example of an employee who provides the new employer with sensitive salary information belonging to the old employer, which he believes shows that the old employer has been defrauding the Revenue. In terms of protected disclosure provisions, the key issues under s43C ERA would be whether the disclosure was made in good faith and whether there was a reasonable belief that the information tends to show a relevant failure. There might be an absence of good faith due to a grudge against the old employer or because the employee's motivation was to assist the new employer unfairly in competing with the old employer by providing information which could be used to poach its staff. However if the good faith requirement, and reasonable belief in the relevant failure requirements were satisfied there would be a protected disclosure. By contrast the balancing of public interests permits a more flexible approach. A court would be expected to take into account that there are far more appropriate recipients of the information, such as the Revenue, than a trade rival.

11.74   As against this, in many cases the considerations relevant to protected disclosures and the balance of public interest will be similar. In relation to s43C(1)(b) ERA, where the disclosure is to the person with legal responsibility or the person whose conduct is primarily involved, there may well be a breach of confidence owed to the employer in making the disclosure. However it is inherent within these categories, as it ordinarily is with the employer despite the example considered above, that the disclosure is to someone with a proper interest in receiving the information. As identified by Lord Denning in *Initial Services*, that is an important consideration in favour of disclosure. Again, however, it cannot be assumed that the approach to protected disclosures will necessary be identical to the public interest balance. If there is an absence of good faith this will be determinative against protected disclosure under s43C ERA. That might not however be the case in relation to the public interest balance, as other factors such as the nature and importance of the information will also be relevant. We consider further the role of motive in the context of second tier/regulatory disclosures.

Second tier/regulatory disclosures

11.75   As we have noted in Chapter 5 a second tier disclosure to the appropriate prescribed person under s43F will be made if:

(a) the worker makes the disclosure in good faith, and
(b) he or she reasonably believes that:
    1. the relevant failure falls within any description of matters in respect of which the person to whom the disclosure is made is the prescribed person, and

2. the information disclosed, and any allegation contained in it, are substantially true.

Rationale for protection

The favoured position of the whistleblower who makes disclosure to a regulator **11.76** (as opposed to a wider class of recipient) is explicable on the basis that:

(a) The regulators will have a statutory duty to investigate such matters and they can only perform their role if members of the public are prepared to come to them with information, free from the threat of retaliation. Further, the regulator is likely to have the expertise to investigate the allegations and to identify those matters that are of legitimate concern.

(b) The regulator can usually be relied upon to maintain confidentiality of the material once it is in his own domain, whether the allegation is right or wrong.

(c) The motivation of anyone revealing material to a regulator is likely to be one of concerned public interest because the regulator will not pay money for the material (although someone who makes a such a disclosure might qualify for a Community Action Trust award).

Importance of recipient of disclosure

The courts have always regarded the identity of the intended recipient as being **11.77** important to the question of whether disclosure should be permitted. As noted above, this was emphasized by Lord Denning MR in *Initial Services*.[41] In *Francome v Mirror Group Newspapers Limited*, referred to at paragraph 11.37 above, the Court of Appeal was sceptical as to whether disclosure to the press was justified but was more sympathetic to the claim that publication might be justified if it was made to the police or to the Jockey Club (which had supervisory powers in relation to racing), *per* Sir John Donaldson MR at 899A–C, and *per* Stephen Brown LJ at 902B.

In *A-G v Guardian Newspapers (No. 2)*[42] Lord Griffiths[43] similarly emphasized the **11.78** importance of the recipient of the information, stating that even if the balance comes down in favour of publication, it did not follow that publication should be to the world through the media and, in certain circumstances, the public interest may be better served by a limited form of publication via authorities who would be under a duty not to abuse the confidential information and to use it only for

---

[41] [1968] 1 QB 396 at 405G–406B.
[42] See above, para 11.12.
[43] ibid, (at 268A–C).

the purpose of their inquiry. Similarly Lord Goff (at 282H–283B) emphasized that more limited disclosure might sometimes be required and, in the Court of Appeal (at 176F–G), Lord Donaldson MR explained this on the basis that the nature and degree of communication must be proportionate to the cause of or excuse for the disclosure. On this basis both Lord Goff and Lord Griffiths in *A-G v Guardian (No. 2)* emphasized that, since in that case there were a number of avenues of proper complaint, it was difficult to envisage a case in which it would be in the public interest for allegations of iniquity to be published in the media (although no issue arose as to what steps could be taken if other avenues of complaint failed to advance the matter).

Approach to good faith and substantial belief in truth in relation to regulatory disclosures

11.79 However whilst the identity of the recipient is important, it does not necessarily follow that the issues are precisely the same as in relation to a protected disclosure under s43F ERA. One area of potential difference relates to the good faith requirement and the degree of supporting evidence required. This is illustrated by *In re A Company*.[44] The claimant carried on business in the supply of financial advice and financial management of clients' investment portfolios and was subject to the regulatory scheme imposed by the Financial Investment Management and Brokers' Regulatory Authority (FIMBRA), pursuant to the provisions of the Financial Services Act 1986. The defendant had been an employee of the claimant in a fairly senior position. His duties had included those of being the claimant's compliance officer. FIMBRA was entitled at its discretion from time to time to make spot checks on companies subject to its regulatory umbrella for the purpose of ensuring compliance with its regulations. Scott J said that it would be expected that any details which came to the attention of FIMBRA in the discharge of its regulatory role would be kept confidential by FIMBRA

11.80 Following the termination of his employment (but while a form of self-employed consultancy continued) a telephone conversation took place between the defendant and a senior executive, the content of which was in dispute in the proceedings. The claimant said that the defendant sought to extract £10,000 under threat of reporting the claimant to FIMBRA for breaches of the FIMBRA regulations and to the Inland Revenue for tax irregularities. The defendant denied any such blackmail saying that he had indicated that he intended to seek compensation for unfair dismissal and that £10,000 was the right amount for him to receive. He had then gone on to raise with the senior executive various misfeasances which represented, in his view, breaches of the FIMBRA regulations and tax improprieties.

---

[44] [1989] 1 Ch 477.

The claimant obtained injunctions to restrain any disclosure to the authorities based upon the confidential information or confidential documents and for a search order to locate and remove all the claimant's documents from the defendant's home. The question for Scott J was whether the injunction against disclosure should be continued given the defendant's expressed intention to communicate information to FIMBRA and to the Inland Revenue. The claimant argued that the full injunction ought to be continued to trial subject only to an undertaking by the claimant itself to place before FIMBRA and the Inland Revenue respectively such documents as it might have relating to the specific matters identified by the defendant as being matters which he thought merited investigation. **11.81**

Scott J did not think this was the right approach. It was 'easy to agree' that details about the claimant's clients' personal affairs should be regarded as confidential information and should be so treated by all the claimant's employees and if there were any question or threat of general disclosure by the defendant of confidential information concerning the way in which the claimant carried on its business or concerning any details of the affairs of any of its clients, there could be no answer to the claim for an injunction. However intended disclosure was limited to FIMBRA, the regulatory authority, and, in relation to a particular case, to the Inland Revenue. Scott J continued: **11.82**

> I ask myself whether an employee of a company carrying on the business of giving financial advice and of financial management to members of the public under the regulatory umbrella provided by FIMBRA owes a duty of confidentiality that extends to barring disclosure of information to FIMBRA. It is part of the plaintiff's case, although not essential to its confidential information cause of action, that the defendant in communicating with FIMBRA will be motivated by malice. The defendant's professed intention is, in the plaintiff's view, associated with the blackmail attempt made by the defendant. At the present stage, and until cross-examination, I must accept that that may be true. It is not necessarily true. The defendant's explanation may be a genuine one. But the plaintiff's case may be true. It may be the case that the information proposed to be given, the allegations proposed to be made by the defendant to FIMBRA, and for that matter by the defendant to the Inland Revenue, are allegations made out of malice and based upon fiction or invention.
>
> But if that is so, then I ask myself what harm will be done. FIMBRA may decide that the allegations are not worth investigating. In that case, no harm will have been done. Or FIMBRA may decide that an investigation is necessary. In that case, if the allegations turn out to be baseless, nothing will follow the investigation. And if harm is caused by the investigation itself, it is harm which is implicit in the regulatory role of FIMBRA. It may be that what is put before FIMBRA includes some confidential information. But that information would, as it seems to me, be information which FIMBRA could at any time obtain by the spot checks that it is entitled to carry out. I doubt whether an employee of a financial services company such as the plaintiff owes a duty of confidence which extends to an obligation not to disclose information to the regulatory authority FIMBRA.

11.83 Scott J considered that, so far as the Inland Revenue was concerned, the point was a narrower one as that authority was not concerned in any general way with the business of a financial services company but tax. If confidential details which did not relate to fiscal matters were disclosed to the Inland Revenue, that would be as much a breach of the duty of confidentiality as the disclosure of that information to any other third party. On the other hand it would be difficult to accept that disclosure would be a breach of such a duty if what was disclosed to the Inland Revenue related to fiscal matters which were the concern of the Inland Revenue.

11.84 Scott J then rejected a submission on behalf of the claimant that he could and should conduct some sort of preliminary investigation into the substance of the allegations proposed to be made by the defendants to FIMBRA and to the Inland Revenue respectively, for the purpose of deciding whether there was any case warranting investigation either by FIMBRA or by the Inland Revenue. The submission was based on what Lord Keith of Kinkel said in the *Spycatcher* case:[45]

> as to just cause or excuse it is not sufficient to set up the defence merely to show that allegations of wrongdoing have been made. There must be at least a prima facie case that the allegations have substance.

11.85 Scott J said that Lord Keith's remark was in the context of a disclosure threatened to be made to the world at large, a disclosure which would have taken place in the national press. Where the disclosure which is threatened was no more than a disclosure to a recipient which had a duty to investigate matters within its remit, it was not for the court to investigate the substance of the proposed disclosure unless there was ground for supposing that the disclosure goes outside the remit of the intended recipient of the information. He continued:

> . . . it is for FIMBRA on receiving whatever information the defendant puts before it, to decide whether there is a matter for investigation. If there is not then I cannot see that any harm has been done to the plaintiff. If there is, then it is right for FIMBRA rather than the court to investigate. Similarly, it is not for the court but for the Inland Revenue, if information is placed before them by the defendant, to decide whether there is material that warrants investigation or explanation. . . .

> . . . I think it would be contrary to the public interest for employees of financial services companies who thought that they ought to place before FIMBRA information of possible breaches of the regulatory system, or information about possible fiscal irregularities before the Inland Revenue, to be inhibited from so doing by the consequence that they might become involved in legal proceedings in which the court would conduct an investigation with them as defendants into the substance of the information they were minded to communicate.

> If it turns out that the defendant's allegations are groundless and that he is motivated by malice then, as it seems to me, he will be at serious risk of being found liable in damages for defamation or malicious falsehood. But that is for the future.

---

45 [1988] 3 WLR 776. Lord Keith of Kinkel, at p 787.

In the context of the application for prior restraint of disclosure to the prescribed **11.86** person which was sought by the company against the defendant, there were therefore both parallels and differences with the approach of the protected disclosure provisions of ERA. The similarity lay in the fact that Scott J clearly thought it was essential that the intended disclosure was to the correct regulator and that the intended disclosure to that regulator was limited to the information which was relevant to the failure which was or would be the concern of that particular regulator. As against this:

(a) Scott J was not prepared to investigate the issue of whether the defendant was acting in good faith (or whether the threatened disclosure was blackmail); this was irrelevant to the question of prior restraint and would be relevant only if the allegations turned out to be 'groundless' in which case the sanction would be that the defendant might be liable in damages for defamation or malicious falsehood.

In *Street* this was distinguished by Auld LJ specifically on the basis that different considerations apply in relation to confidentiality. He emphasized (para 46) that the 'issue of motive arose not, as in Mrs Street's case, out of any conditional obligation imposed by law to make such disclosure in good faith, but out of an assertion inessential to the company's cause of action, based on confidentiality of the information, that the former employee was motivated by malice'. He therefore distinguished between a protected disclosure claim— where good faith was an essential ingredient—and the claim in confidentiality where good faith was not an ingredient. On that basis the particular comments as to malice could be dismissed as 'more of a practical observation on the facts of the case than a proposition of law'.

(b) Whilst the court would have entered into a factual enquiry as to whether the intended disclosure was to the appropriate regulator, Scott J was not prepared to enter upon such an enquiry with regard to whether there was a prima facie case of a relevant failure that should be disclosed to the appropriate regulator. There was no threshold of reasonable belief that the information disclosed and any allegation contained it in be substantially true.

Seriousness of wrongdoing

Scott J did not expressly address the seriousness of the alleged irregularities as a **11.87** factor to be brought into account as to whether disclosure to the regulator ought to be restrained. As we shall see the seriousness of the failure or the harm involved will be an important factor in the assessment of whether disclosure to the wider public and the media should be permitted. But it has also been regarded as a factor in cases of disclosure to persons in the position of a 'regulator'. In *W v Edgell*[46] the

---

[46] [1990] 1 Ch 359 (CA).

claimant suffered from paranoid schizophrenia and was detained in a secure hospital after killing five people. He applied to the mental health review tribunal and, to support his application, sought a report from the defendant who was an independent consultant psychiatrist. The defendant's report revealed that the claimant had a continuing interest in home-made bombs and expressed the opinion that the claimant was a continuing danger to the public. The claimant then withdrew his application and refused to consent to the defendant disclosing the report. Notwithstanding this, the defendant disclosed the report to the medical officer at the secure hospital and a copy was sent to the relevant Secretary of State. When the claimant's case was subsequently referred to a mental health review tribunal it became apparent that the report had been disclosed and the claimant applied for an injunction to restrain the defendant from communicating the contents of the report and requiring all copies to be delivered up. In refusing the injunction the Court of Appeal held that the public interest in confidentiality was outweighed by the public interest in protecting others against possible violence. The Court of Appeal emphasized the degree of danger to the public, as demonstrated by the nature of the crimes which the claimant had previously committed, and the fact that the disclosure had been made to the appropriate regulatory bodies who should have all relevant information in relation to the claimant before considering his release from hospital.[47] Again, however, this involved taking into account a consideration, namely the seriousness of the wrongdoing, which is not part of the test for protection under s43F ERA.

Third tier/wider disclosures

11.88 In relation to third tier/wider disclosures, s43G ERA in particular, and to a lesser extent s43H ERA, set out detailed criteria to be taken into account for there to be a protected disclosure. It is therefore in relation to disclosures within these categories that protected disclosure legislation provides the most significant assistance by way of a checklist of appropriate considerations to take into account.

Good faith and personal gain

11.89 Whilst good faith was not treated as significant in *In re A Company* in relation to a second tier/regulatory disclosure, it tends to be of greater importance in relation to third tier disclosures. In *Schering Chemical Limited v Falkman Limited* [1982] QB 1 (CA) it was alleged that confidential information had been used to make a film

---

[47] See also *Woolgar v Chief Constable of the Sussex Police* [1999] 3 All ER 604 where an application to restrain disclosure by the police to the United Kingdom Central Council for Nursing, Midwifery and Health Visiting (the UKCC) of information given under caution failed and the court considered the police were best placed to decide if the information should be disclosed, but should first give notice to the person whose confidentiality was breached so this could be challenged if appropriate.

relating to the drug Primodos. The claimant company had withdrawn Primodos from the market after suspicions had arisen that it had caused abnormalities in new-born children. The Court of Appeal refused to grant an injunction restraining the broadcast of the film. Shaw and Templeman LJJ appeared to consider it relevant that the motive of the discloser was financial, albeit there were other powerful reasons for granting the injunction quite apart from the motive of the discloser.

In *British Steel Corporation v Granada Television Ltd*[49] Lord Fraser referred to   **11.90**
weighing up the public interest for and against publication, and went on (at 1202) to say that the informer's motives were in his opinion irrelevant. However in *Francome v Mirror Group*[50] Lord Donaldson MR noted that it is almost unheard-of for compliance with the moral imperative to make disclosure to be in the financial interests of the person making the disclosure. Again in *Initial Services* Lord Denning MR (at 406G) suggested that differing considerations might apply depending on the motive for the disclosure. He commented that:

> I say nothing as to what the position would be if he disclosed it out of malice or spite or sold it to a newspaper for money or for reward. That indeed would be a different matter. It is a great evil when people purvey scandalous information for reward.

Even if there is a public interest defence in relation to confidentiality, if the disclo-   **11.91**
sure is in bad faith the employee is likely to be in breach of the duty of fidelity and of the duty not without reasonable and proper cause to conduct himself in a manner calculated or likely to destroy or seriously damage the relationship of confidence and trust between the employee and employer.[51] Additionally, an employee who owes fiduciary duties would in general be required to account for secret profits made from his employment through acting other than bona fide in the best interests of the employer.

Similarly there may be an obligation upon an employee to make restitution of   **11.92**
any profits resulting from the disclosure if it is something which the employee had specifically contracted not to do. In *Woodward v Hutchins*, for example, although the Court of Appeal considered that publication by the press of material 'putting the record straight' as to the private lives of various pop stars, the conduct of the employee who leaked the story for reward was clearly regarded with distaste. As Lawton LJ put it (at 75SF), 'persons like the first defendant cannot expect much in the way of admiration when they sell their employers' secrets for money'.

---

[49] See above n 31.
[50] See above, para 11.37.
[51] *Malik v BCCI SA* [1998] AC 20 (HL); *Byford v Film Finances Limited* (EAT/804/86).

11.93 In any event if the allegation proves to be false, the employee motivated by malice may also be liable in damages for defamation or malicious falsehood. The motive of the person responsible for the disclosure may also be taken into account when the court exercises its discretion as to costs.[52]

Evidential basis

11.94 In the *Spycatcher* case[53] Lord Keith referred to the need for there to be 'at least a prima facie case that the allegations have substance'. This might be regarded as a broad equivalent to the statutory test in ss43G and 43H that there must be a reasonable belief that the information disclosed and any allegation contained in it are substantially true, except that in contrast to the protected disclosure position, the test of substantiality is not expressly tied to the belief of the person making the disclosure. In *Lion Laboratories*[54] Griffiths LJ emphasized that it was necessary at least that a fair reading of the documents disclosed to the press should cast doubt on the accuracy of the breathalyser equipment. Further it was said to be necessary to evaluate the strength of the defence at the interlocutory stage since otherwise the defence of public interest could be a 'mole's charter'.[55] The strength of the evidence required might also vary according to the importance of the public interest in preserving confidentiality in the particular case. In the context of the burden of proof required to remove the cloak of privilege on grounds of iniquity, for example, the balance of authority is that at least prima facie evidence that the allegation of fraud is well founded will be required before privilege is lifted. The evidential burden will however vary according to the particular circumstances—including the public interest in confidentiality, the recipient of the disclosure and the matters being disclosed. As Vinelott J explained in *Derby & Co. Limited v Weldon (No.7)* [1990] 1 WLR 1156 at 1173E—F:

> There is a continuous spectrum and it is impossible to, as it were, calibrate or express in any simple formula the strength of the case that the plaintiff must show in each of these categories. An order to disclose documents for which legal professional privilege is claimed lies at the extreme end of the spectrum.

11.95 The evidential burden was not a point expressly addressed in *Cream v Banerjee* save that Sedley LJ said that the proposed disclosure in that case was 'essentially true; otherwise the action would be in defamation'. In a case where the facts were disputed the court would presumably enter into *some* evaluation of the substantiality of the allegations and the wider the disclosure and the greater the degree of confidentiality in issue, the higher the burden on the defendant to substantiate the allegations.

---

[52] See *Schering Chemicals Limited v Falkman Limited* (above para 11.89).
[53] Above, 45. Lord Keith of Kinkel, at p 787.
[54] See above, para 11.23.
[55] At 550G–551A,G.

Other responses inapplicable or exhausted

For the purposes of s43G ERA one of the three gateway requirements in s43(2) **11.96**
must be satisfied. One of these is that the worker has previously made a disclosure
of substantially the same information to the employer or a prescribed person. The
decision in *Cream v Banerjee* indicates that similar considerations might also arise
in relation to confidentiality. Sedley LJ placed particular emphasis on the finding
that Ms Banerjee had exhausted responses short of going to the press (albeit the
detail had to be relegated to his closed judgment).

Reasonableness of disclosure

Over and above these matters, s43G ERA contains a general reasonableness test **11.97**
subject to the requirement to take into account specific considerations. The factors which must be taken into account are also liable to be material in relation to
a defence to confidentiality.

The identity of the recipient to whom the disclosure is made   As noted above **11.98**
in the context of regulatory disclosures, the identity of the recipient is an important consideration in the context of obligations of confidentiality.

The seriousness of the relevant failure   The seriousness of the relevant failure is **11.99**
something that must be taken into account in relation to reasonableness under
s43G ERA. Further, if there is an exceptionally serious failure s43H ERA applies.
Clearly the seriousness of the relevant failure will also be a highly important consideration in relation to confidentiality and in some cases will be decisive.
However other factors might still need to be taken into account. Thus although
the public interest in disclosing past or proposed crimes will often be a determinative consideration, even in this context it has been recognized that other factors,
such as the person to whom disclosure is made and any countervailing public
interest in preserving confidentiality, needs to be considered as well as the nature
of the crime.[56] Thus, even where a disclosure relates to serious criminal conduct
there may, exceptionally, be a countervailing public interest which prevents confidentiality being overridden. In *Bunn v BBC* [1999] FSR 70, an application was
made to restrain the BBC from making reference in a television programme to an
interview with the police under caution by Mr Bunn, the former Deputy
Managing Director of Robert Maxwell Group plc. The interview was said to show
that Mr Bunn was engaged in conspiracy to defraud. The statement was also said
to contain material which would enable the public fairly to assess the workings
and efficiency of the Serious Fraud Office since it would be relevant to whether the
SFO had had sufficient material to proceed with the second criminal trial relating

---

[56] See also *Initial Services,* above para 11.22 (at 405) where Lord Denning MR emphasized the
overall qualification that disclosure must be justified in the public interest.

to the fraud by Robert Maxwell and his companies. Lightman J held that the statement made under caution was confidential in that it was only to be used for the purposes of criminal proceedings. Although Lightman J refused the injunction on the ground that the information was already in the public domain and on the ground of delay, he held that the public interest defence to the claim of breach of confidence would not have succeeded because there was a countervailing public interest in an accused person being able to make full disclosure in a statement to the police without fear of that statement being used for extraneous purposes.

11.100   In *Cream v Banerjee* Sedley LJ concluded that the principal matter which the *Echo* wanted to publish was 'incontestably a matter of serious public interest' and he said that the 'essential story' was one which, whatever its source, no court could properly suppress. However as we have already noted it appeared to be important to him that Ms Banerjee had exhausted other responses and Sedley LJ did not say that the matter was of 'exceptionally serious' public interest. Earlier cases such as *Initial Services* envisage that there may be a class of failure which requires disclosure to the public as a whole without reference to considerations of whether other routes have been followed already or are not applicable. If the protected disclosure provisions were to be a guide, this would indicate that the courts would have to be satisfied that the relevant failure is exceptionally serious, rather than merely serious, to allow general disclosure in a case where other routes have not been followed and would be applicable. However whilst the seriousness of the matter is an important consideration, such a limitation would unduly limit the weighing of the public interest in each case by reference to the test of proportionality, and run counter to Lord Nicholls' emphasis that the protected disclosure provisions are not intended to cut down the circumstances where the public interest may justify disclosure.

11.101   **Whether the relevant failure is continuing or is likely to occur in future**   In *Schering Chemicals* one factor that clearly weighed with the court was that the drug which was the subject of the intended broadcast was no longer in production; there was thus no continuing risk of damage to the health of the user whatever the risk might or might not have been when the drug was being used.

11.102   **Whether the disclosure is made in breach of a duty of confidentiality owed by the employer**   Whether the disclosure is made in breach of a duty of confidentiality owed by the employer to any other person who is not mixed up in the wrongdoing is clearly relevant. In *In re A Company* (albeit a second tier/regulatory case) Scott J said that details about the claimant's clients' personal affairs should be regarded as confidential information and should be so treated by all the claimant's employees: if there were any question or threat of general disclosure by the defendant of confidential information concerning any details of the affairs of any of its clients, there could be no answer to the claim for an injunction. However the fact that third party confidences might be disclosed can only be a factor, not a bar. Many disclosures of relevant failures will involve at least some information being disclosed concerning third parties because they will be the 'victims' of the iniquity or the hazard. Of course it will usually be possible for their identities to be protected even if the facts of their cases have to some extent to be revealed.

Action which the employer or regulator might reasonably be expected to have taken   As noted above, the fact that disclosure on an internal or regulatory basis had apparently not succeeded in the *Cream v Banerjee* case was a key factor in Sedley LJ's view that the first instance decision should be reversed.   **11.103**

Whether in making an internal disclosure the worker complied with an author-ized procedure   We are not aware of any case where a worker's compliance with a whistleblowing procedure has been a factor in a court's decision as to whether disclosure was in the public interest. However its express inclusion in s43G ERA may be taken as indicative of its materiality to the overall assessment of whether the public interest is in favour of disclosure.   **11.104**

The nature of the information

Whilst the protected disclosure provisions might be regarded as providing a checklist of relevant considerations in relation to wider disclosure, it is clear that the checklist cannot be regarded as comprehensive. This follows from that fact that ss43G and 43H themselves do not purport to identify all factors that might be relevant to the assessment of whether disclosure is reasonable. One factor which is omitted is the issue as to the degree of confidentiality or the nature of the privacy interest in relation to the information. This may however be an important consideration in assessing whether disclosure should be ordered in the public interest, and the need to consider this is in accordance with the requirement to apply proportionality.   **11.105**

Privileged information   Where the information is not only confidential but also subject to legal professional privilege the public policy against disclosure is partic-ularly strong. In this context the cases suggest that disclosure will only be justified in cases involving 'iniquity'. For these purposes iniquity includes all forms of fraud and dishonesty but does not extend beyond dishonesty to include disrep-utable behaviour or a failure to maintain good ethical standards.[57] It is sufficient that the solicitor's advice is sought in furtherance of or in relation to the fraud or crime[58] or that the disclosure relates to evidence gathered by fraudulent or   **11.106**

---

[57] *Gamlen Chemical Co (UK) v Rochem (No. 2)* (1980) 124 SJ 276 (CA), per Goff LJ; *Barclays Bank plc v Eustice* [1995] 1 WLR 1238 (CA), *per* Schiemann LJ at 1248D,1250D; *Nationwide Building Society v Various Solicitors* [1999] PNLR 52, Blackburne J. But see *ISTIL Group v Zahoor* [2003] 2 All ER 253 (Lawrence Collins J) suggesting a wider power on public interest grounds to refuse injunctive relief to restrain use of privileged documents. The decision is criticized in Hollander, *Documentary Evidence*, 9th edn (London: Sweet & Maxwell, 2006) p 420–421, paras 20–21.

[58] *Barclays v Eustice, per* Schiemann LJ at 12S1E–1252C, 1251E; *Nationwide v Various Solicitors*.

criminal conduct.[59] It is not necessary to show that the solicitor was aware of the iniquity. Even within the category of privileged communications, however, the court is required to weigh the public interest in confidentiality in the particular circumstances against the public interest in disclosing iniquity having regard to the seriousness of the alleged iniquity and the circumstances in which the privilege is claimed.[60]

11.107   **The contractual/non-contractual dichotomy**   An additional consideration might be the nature and source of the confidentiality obligation. Confidential information might have differing degrees of importance and secrecy, ranging from trade secrets which remain protected after the termination of employment, to lower levels of confidential information which is covered by implied confidentiality obligations during employment. A related distinction may also be drawn between obligations arising under contract and other confidentiality obligations which impliedly arise from particular relationships.

11.108   This distinction was significant in *Campbell v Frisbee* [2003] ICR 141. Ms Frisbee was employed by Naomi Campbell to provide management services under a weekly contract for services. Ms Frisbee supplied information to the *News of the World* which published an article about sexual encounters between Ms Campbell and Joseph Fiennes and the efforts made to keep secret the fact of these encounters—particularly from the man to whom Ms Campbell was engaged to be married. The newspaper paid Ms Frisbee £25,000 for the information. Ms Frisbee had orally agreed to keep confidential any information that she learnt about Ms Campbell in the course of her work and also had entered into a written confidentiality agreement in the form of a letter which included, in particular, that no information would be disseminated to the media without Ms Campbell's express written consent and that the confidentiality agreement would continue beyond the duration of the professional relationship between the parties. It was accepted by Ms Frisbee that it was an implied term of the confidentiality agreement that she would not divulge to the media or any third party any information, whether true or false, about Ms Campbell which Miss Frisbee claimed to have learnt in the course of working for Ms Campbell and also that, by reason of the relationship between them, Ms Frisbee owed to Ms Campbell a duty of confidence.

---

[59] *Dubai Aluminium Co v Al Alawi* [1999] 1 All ER 703; [1999] 1 Lloyds Rep 478 (Rix J).

[60] See *Derby v Weldon (No 7)* [1990] 1 WLR 1156, *per* Vinelott J at 1173A–F; *Barclays v Eustice*, *per* Schiemann LJ at 1249H–1250D where it is was suggested that the cloak of privilege was less likely to be lifted where advice is sought as to something that has already been done and then for the purposes of imminent litigation, than where advice is sought as to how to structure a fraudulent transaction. See also *Istil Group Inc and another v Zahoor and another* [2003] EWHC 165 (Ch); [2003] 2 All ER 252 and *Kuwait Airways Corporation v Iraqi Airways Corporation* [2005] EWCA Civ 286.

Ms Campbell claimed damages or an account of profits arising from breach of the **11.109**
confidentiality agreement and the duty of confidence. In her defence Ms Frisbee
contended that there had been a course of unacceptable behaviour by Ms Campbell
(including an alleged assault). This, she said, constituted a repudiation of her contract which she accepted, bringing their relationship to an end and thus discharging her from the confidentiality obligations. An alternative defence was that
Ms Frisbee was entitled to disclose the information to the newspaper because it was
in the public interest that this information should be published. Ms Campbell obtained
summary judgment. Ms Frisbee appealed to Lightman J who dismissed her appeal
([2002] 2 EMLR 656) but his judgment was reversed by the Court of Appeal who
held that it was arguable that a duty of confidentiality expressly assumed under
contract carried more weight, when balanced against the restriction to the right to
freedom of expression, than a duty of confidentiality that was not buttressed by
express agreement.[61] If that contractual obligation had been discharged by repudiation of the contract Ms Frisbee might have had a defence to the claim based
upon the non-contractual claim, albeit the court appears to have been unenthusi-
astic about the possibility. These were considerations that do not arise under the
express requirements in relation to protected disclosures, though they might be
considered material as part of the overall test of reasonableness for wider disclosures.

(3) Proportionality

Whilst it is possible to identify important considerations which apply both in the **11.110**
context of protected disclosures and balancing of public interest, in the context of
a defence to confidentiality ultimately these considerations must be filtered into
an assessment of proportionality. The *LRT* case, referred to at paras 11.39 and
11.54 above, provides an example of this. A further example is provided by the
decision in *Imutran Ltd v Uncaged Campaigns Ltd* [2001] 2 All ER 385 which
illustrates this in relation to wider disclosures. This concerned a claim for an
injunction in respect of the intended publication of leaked confidential documents regarding animal testing. Having referred to *Initial Services* and other
authorities in relation to the public interest defence, Morritt V-C noted that these
demonstrated:

(a) that the public interest in disclosure might outweigh the right of the claimant
to protect his confidences, and

---

[61] See also *London Regional Transport v The Mayor of London,* above para 11.39, referred to in
Campbell v Frisbee, where the view was expressed that there was no distinction to be drawn between
contractual and other duties of confidence, and *Attorney-General v Parry and MGN Limited* [2004]
EMLR 223 where it was said to be well arguable that a contractual duty should be given greater
weight.

(b) that the court will also consider how much disclosure the public interest required; the fact that some disclosure may be required does not mean that disclosure to the whole world should be permitted.

11.111 Morritt V-C proceeded to say at paragraph 21 that:

in addition the Human Rights Act 1998 requires the court, as a public authority, to take into account the right of freedom of expression conferred by Article 10 European Convention on Human Rights. . . . The effect of that article for present purposes is that any injunction, which by definition is a restriction on the exercise of the right to freedom of expression, must be justified as being no more than is necessary in a democratic society.

11.112 Various factors were then identified:

(a) the information contained in the documents received by the defendants from the anonymous sender were in their nature confidential;

(b) there could be no doubt that the defendants knew that the information contained in those documents was confidential;

(c) the defendants knew that Imutran had not known or consented to its documents being removed from its possession; and

(d) the circumstances as they existed did not justify the width of disclosure the defendants sought; the House of Lords had set up its ad hoc Select Committee to enquire into the very matters which concerned the defendants; the Home Secretary and the Council of RSPCA had called for reports and documents had been made available to GLPMA and UKXIRA; there was 'no impediment sought or in place such as to inhibit any regulatory authority from investigating all the matters on which the defendants expressed concern';

(e) when considering what was necessary in a democratic society and when paying particular regard to the importance of the right to freedom of expression it was relevant to consider which is the democratically selected responsible body or bodies and who would be the informed audience:

1. Parliament had considered the issue of animal experimentation in 1986 and had laid down a licensing and inspection system and a forum for and source of continuing consideration and advice in the Animal Procedures Committee, and

2. the RSPCA, GLPMA and UKXIRA all had an interest in investigating one or more of the matters which concerned the defendants, and

(f) the defendants' right to freedom of expression was an element in their democratic right to campaign for the abolition of all animal xenotransplantation or other experimentation but they could continue to do that whether the injunction was granted or not; the issue was whether they should be free to do so with Imutran's confidential and secret documents. However:

1. many of those documents were of a specialist and technical nature suitable for consideration by specialists in the field but not by the public generally, and

2. given the provisos to the injunction sought there would be no restriction on the ability of the defendants to communicate the information to those specialists connected with the regulatory bodies denoted by Parliament as having responsibility in the field.

In making this assessment Morritt V-C therefore took into account the nature of the information, the steps that it could be expected would be taken to deal with the concern aside from the disclosure, the width of the disclosure and that it went beyond what might be considered to be the informed audience having regard to the nature of the information. He concluded that the injunction sought did not go further than was necessary in a democratic society. Whilst paying particular regard to the importance of the right to freedom of expression, the Vice-Chancellor nevertheless concluded that the balance of convenience favoured the grant of the injunction sought because (a) if no injunction was granted the confidence would be destroyed and even if Imutran succeeded at trial the consequential damages would be entirely unquantifiable even if the defendants were able to pay them and (b) by contrast, if the defendants were successful at the trial they would then be able to publish anything they liked with the added benefit of knowing the views of the regulatory bodies and their experts and there was no suggestion that the delay in establishing their right would cause any damage. Whilst several of the considerations relied upon would have been material to whether there was a protected disclosure, the protected disclosure legislation cannot be said to have provided a key to balancing the competing interest. **11.113**

(4) Conclusions in relation to the application of PIDA provisions as a template

We have seen that considerations which are material to assessing whether there is a protected disclosure may also play an important role in relation to whether there is a public interest defence to confidentiality. It is clear, however, that the protected disclosure provisions are not being, and cannot be, simply applied as a 'pass or fail' test for protection. In particular: **11.114**

(a) Such a test would be inconsistent with the central importance of proportionality in considering the balancing of the interests in confidentiality and disclosure. Within s43G (wider disclosures) there is scope to give effect to proportionality in relation to the overarching reasonableness test. However it is first necessary to satisfy a series of 'pass or fail' tests such as that the disclosure is not for personal gain.

(b) As emphasized by Lord Nicholls in *Cream v Banerjee* the issues which arise in relation to confidentiality are not the same as those arising in relation to whether the added protected disclosure protection should apply. The focus in relation to a protected disclosure is on whether the worker acted properly in making the disclosure. Thus, for example, reasonable belief for the purposes of a qualifying disclosure is judged from the worker's perspective on the basis of information available to the worker: *Darnton v University of Surrey* [2003] IRLR 133. However when the court considers whether disclosure is in the public interest it need not (and should not) be confined to consideration of this from the worker's perspective.

(c) These differences are reflected in the differing approaches in relation to disclosure to a regulator, where the good faith test in protected disclosures is not necessarily an answer to a public interest defence to confidentiality. Similarly they are reflected in the wider public interest considerations which can justify disclosure or give rise to a defence and are not limited to the categories of relevant failures for the purposes of establishing a protected disclosure.

(d) In determining whether a disclosure is protected the position is considered as at the time when the disclosure was made, albeit the truth of the allegations may be material in relation to whether there was a reasonable belief. Again, the court is not so confined when it comes to considering whether to restrain disclosure or whether disclosure would amount to a breach of confidence.

(e) In some cases it will not be possible to apply the protected disclosure provisions with any certainty because the person who made the disclosure will not be available (and sometimes not identifiable) to give evidence. Thus, for example, where disclosure is made anonymously to a newspaper there might be no way of testing the good faith of the person who made the disclosure other than speculation.

11.115 Whilst it does not provide a 'pass or fail' test, however, the protected disclosure legislation can provide a helpful (though not necessarily exhaustive) checklist of important considerations to be taken into account, especially in relation to third tier/wider disclosures.

E. Agreements rendered void

11.116 In one significant respect PIDA protected disclosure provisions do modify contractual obligations and this might be material in relation to obligations of confidentiality. Section 43J of ERA provides an important mechanism for ensuring that those making protected disclosures cannot be silenced:

(1) Any provision in an agreement to which this section applies is void in so far as it purports to preclude the worker from making a protected disclosure.

1. This section applies to any agreement between a worker and his employer (whether a worker's contract or not), including any agreement to refrain from instituting or continuing proceedings under this Act or any proceedings for breach of contract.

As such, any clause or term in an agreement between a worker and his employer is **11.117** void insofar as it purports to preclude the worker from making a protected disclosure. The agreement may be in an employment contract, in a contract of a worker who is not an employee or in any other agreement between a worker and employee. This section therefore outlaws 'gagging clauses' although only insofar as they apply to a protected disclosure.

Accordingly insofar as it is established (or, in interim proceedings, likely to be **11.118** established) that the making of a disclosure would be a protected disclosure, a contractual confidentiality obligation could not be a basis to restrain disclosure. Nor could there be a claim for contractual damages where the disclosure was a protected disclosure. Irrespective of the issue considered above (see paras 11.107 and 11.108) as to the scope for non-contractual obligations to exist alongside contractual obligations, and whether they have less weight in the balancing exercise, it is difficult to conceive of circumstances where the court would restrain publication of information despite finding that a contractual restraint is void under s43J ERA.

It should also be noted that s43J covers settlement agreements of tribunal proceedings. **11.119** These very often contain confidentiality clauses as part-consideration for money paid in settlement. The employer might only be prepared to make a payment to an ex-employee if he can feel secure against the risk not only of further legal proceedings but also against the risk that his dirty linen will be washed—or further washed—in front of an interested public. This may be of particular importance where the employer is concerned to prevent the employee contacting a prescribed regulator under s43F. The provision would apply with equal strength and immediacy where a public body seeks to stop a worker contacting the sponsoring department under s43E. However confidentiality clauses in compromise agreements are in any event notoriously difficult to enforce and even without s43J it would have been difficult to obtain injunctive relief to prevent disclosure to a prescribed regulator or sponsoring department (see *In re A Company*).[62]

In the event that an employee accepts a specific sum in return for not making a **11.120** protected disclosure it is likely that (subject to a defence of change of position) the employer would be entitled to claim the return of that sum. Ordinarily money paid under a void contract can be reclaimed by means of an action for money had and received.[63] In *Credit Suisse First Boston (Europe) Limited v Padiachy*[64] in the context of a void term in relation to a transfer of undertaking, Longmore J said he could see no answer to a claim for the return of the money paid in consideration

[62] See above, paras 11.79ff.
[63] *Guinness Mahon & Co. Limited v Kensington & Chelsea LBC* [1999] QB 215.
[64] [1998] IRLR 504.

for entering into a void restrictive covenant. The position is less straightforward if a sum is paid in part in return for confidentiality and in part for other obligations in the settlement agreement, due to the difficulty of establishing a total failure of consideration. In the context of s203 ERA, in *Sutherland v Network Appliance Ltd* [2001] IRLR 12, the EAT held that the express words of s203, which stipulates that 'any provision in an agreement . . . is void *in so far as it purports* . . . to exclude or limit the operation of any provision of this Act' (emphasis added) rendered void only those provisions within the agreement in question which infringed s203. The rest of the agreement remained in existence and enforceable. However the EAT expressly noted that this was not a case where the payor (who has agreed and has paid ostensibly for the full and final settlement of all claims) asserted that it would be wrong that only some of those claims should turn out to be effectively compromised. It therefore did not address the issue which would arise if the employer, having paid for confidentiality and other settlement terms, did not wish the agreement to stand despite the confidentiality obligation being void by virtue of s43J ERA.

F. European Court of Human Rights decisions

11.121 In determining questions which arise in connection with Convention rights courts must take into account judgments of the European Court of Human Rights and opinions and decisions of the Commission where relevant to the proceedings.[65] This section therefore includes a brief survey of the European decisions in relation to the raising of issues of public concern.

11.122 The essential issue in the ECHR case law (dominated latterly by claims against Turkey by journalists subjected to legal proceedings for publishing information critical of the state) is whether the interference with the right to freedom of expression is justified. Article 10(2) requires that the interference be:

(a) prescribed by law, and
(b) necessary in a democratic society,
    1. in the interests of national security, territorial integrity or public safety;
    2. for the prevention of disorder or crime;
    3. for the protection of health or morals;
    4. for the protection of the reputation or rights of others;
    5. for preventing the disclosure of information received in confidence, or
    6. for maintaining the authority and impartiality of the judiciary.

---

[65] Section 2 of the Human Rights Act 1998.

(1) Prescribed by law

The ECHR has generally been willing to accept that the restriction is 'prescribed **11.123** by law' and to accept that it is for national authorities to interpret and apply domestic law.[66] In *Goodwin v United Kingdom* [1996] 22 EHRR 123 (at 139–141) the ECHR applied this principle in finding that the possibility of a journalist being required to disclose his sources was sufficiently 'prescribed by law' even though the court had to carry out a balancing exercise between competing public interests and had to be satisfied that disclosure was 'in the interests of justice'. More recently it has been said that, however clearly drafted a legal provision may be, there will inevitably be a need for interpretation by the courts. There will always be a need for elucidation of doubtful points and for adaptation to changing circumstances (*E.K. v Turkey* No. 28496/95, § 52, 7 February 2002).

(2) Legitimate aim

In practice the requirement of a legitimate aim has not been a substantial hurdle **11.124** of itself but instead has acted as an impetus to encourage states to identify the reasons for the restrictions and as a reference point against which to consider whether the restriction is indeed necessary. The most significant of the legitimate aims in the context of employees is the protection of the reputation and the rights of others and the prevention of the disclosure of information received in confidence. In most circumstances, other than the case where the employer acts in bad faith or imposes restrictions which have no rational relationship to the employment, a restriction of employee expression could be brought within one or both of these aims, albeit it might not be possible for the employer to show the *necessity* for the restriction.

In many cases where the restriction on freedom of expression relates to whistle- **11.125** blowing it would appear likely that the restriction on expression could be said to be aimed at protecting the rights of employers. In *B v United Kingdom* (1985) 45 D&R 41 a civil servant, who was also a local politician, participated in a television programme concerning safety at the atomic weapons research establishment at Aldermaston where he worked. The civil servant had been refused permission to speak on the programme and he received a severe reprimand which he challenged as being in breach of Art 10(1). The Commission found that there was an interference with free expression but that this was justified in order to protect the rights of the employers. Similar reasoning would apply in most whistleblowing cases since an employee would rarely have permission to criticize the employer, albeit in the particular circumstances protection of the employer's rights might not justify the interference. Indeed interference need not even be for the purpose of protecting

---

[66] See eg *Thorgeirson v Iceland* [1992] 14 EHRR 843.

legally recognized rights. In *X v U.K.* (1979) 16 D&R 101 the Commission was prepared to accept that protecting fellow members of teaching staff from being offended by a colleague's evangelical posters and stickers fell within the meaning of 'protecting the rights of others'. Thus the Commission was prepared to accept that there is a legitimate interest in protecting the rights of others not to be offended by speech.

11.126 Equally where the employee is involved in raising concerns about the employer, the imposition of a sanction might be regarded as being effected on the basis of protecting the employer's reputation. In *Morissens v Belgium* (1988) 56 D&R 127 a Belgian teacher was dismissed after she had sought to highlight discrimination against homosexuals by complaining on Belgian television that she was not appointed as a headteacher because she was gay. The Commission held that the dismissal was in pursuance of the legitimate aim of the protection of the reputation of those whom she had implicitly suggested had refused to promote her on grounds of her homosexuality.

11.127 Even in cases which would not appear to fit neatly into any of the recognized categories of legitimate aim, such difficulties have been overcome by a flexible application of the legitimate aim test. In *Vogt v Germany* [1996] 21 EHRR 205, for example, where a teacher was dismissed for her association with the German Communist Party, the insistence on political loyalty was imposed because, especially in the light of Germany's history, it was felt there was a need for democracy to be able to defend itself and that the civil service was the guarantor of the constitution and democracy. On its face it is not apparent that defence of the constitution falls within any of the legitimate aims which can be pursued but the ECHR appears to have accepted the German government's assertion that the restriction was aimed at protecting national security, preventing disorder and protecting the rights of others.

(3) Necessary in a democratic society and the margin of appreciation

11.128 Since there will usually be a legitimate aim which can be said to be pursued by the interference with the whistleblower's freedom of expression, in almost every whistleblowing case the key issue for determination will be whether the legitimate aim in question (such as protecting the employer's right to fidelity or confidentiality or to protection of its reputation) justifies the interference with free expression. In each case this is to be resolved by enquiring as to whether the aim is 'necessary' in a democratic society and the interpretation of this requirement and the evidential burden it imposes is therefore a matter of crucial importance to the whistleblower.

11.129 The ECHR has explained on several occasions (eg *Barthold v Germany* [1985] 7 EHRR 383 at para 55) that:

> whilst the adjective 'necessary', within the meaning of Article 10(2) of the Convention, is not synonymous with 'indispensable', neither does it have the flexibility of such

expressions as 'admissible', 'ordinary', 'useful', 'reasonable' or 'desirable'; rather it implies a 'pressing social need'. The Contracting States enjoy a power of appreciation in this respect, but that power of appreciation goes hand in hand with a European supervision which is more or less extensive depending on the circumstances; it is for the Court to make the final determination as to whether the interference in issue corresponds to such a need, whether it is 'proportionate to the legitimate aim pursued' and whether the reasons given by the national authorities to justify it are 'relevant and sufficient'.

Thus it must be shown that the interference: **11.130**

(a) corresponds to a 'pressing social need';
(b) is proportionate to the aim pursued or, as it is sometimes put,[67] there is a reasonable relationship of proportionality between the legitimate aim pursued and the means deployed to achieve that aim; and
(c) is justified by reasons which are relevant and sufficient.

Further the ECHR has often emphasized that the exceptions contained in **11.131** Art 10(2) are to be 'narrowly interpreted' and must be 'convincingly established'.[68] Nevertheless while these general pronouncements require a particularly close scrutiny of any purported justification for interfering with the whistleblower's right to free expression, the case law of the Commission and Court is considerably less reassuring. In applying the test of necessity, especially as regards the scope of the margin of appreciation to be permitted, the ECHR and/or the Commission has had regard in particular to the following factors:

(a) whether the whistleblowing touches on matters of public concern;
(b) the duties and responsibilities of employment;
(c) the manner of expression;
(d) the extent to which the accusations made by the whistleblower are well founded;
(e) the channel of communication used by the whistleblower;
(f) the nature of the employment; and
(g) whether the sanction is imposed by the state.

It is pertinent therefore to consider in turn how the application of these factors has **11.132** been applied and has influenced, or is likely to influence, the degree of protection afforded to the whistleblower.

(4) Does the whistleblower raise matters of public concern?

Unsurprisingly, in seeking to rely upon Art 10 it will be in the interest of **11.133** the whistleblower to emphasize that the matters raised are of public concern.

---

[67] Case 29183/95 *Fressoz and Roire v France* [2001] 31 EHRR 2, para 56 (ECJ).
[68] See *Vogt v Germany; Handyside v The United Kingdom* [1976] 1 EHRR 737, para 49; *Lingens v Austria* [1986] 1 EHRR 407, para 41; *Jersild v Denmark* [1994] 19 EHRR 1, para 31; *Goodwin v United Kingdom*, para 40.

In *Thorgeirson v Iceland*[69] (not an employment case) the applicant made claims of police brutality. The Icelandic government contended in response for a distinction between political discussion in which freedom of expression should have full rein and 'discussion of other matters of public concern' in which expression could be restricted. This would potentially have provided a severe constraint on the freedom of the whistleblower. However the ECHR expressly rejected the proposition that the wide limits of acceptable criticism in political discussion do not apply equally to other matters of public concern. In *Steel and Morris v UK (Application no. 68416/01)* [2005] 41 EHRR 403 (the *Mclibel* case) at para 88 the court acknowledged the breadth of matters that are of public concern:

> The Court must weigh a number of factors in the balance when reviewing the proportionality of the measure complained of. First, it notes that the leaflet in question contained very serious allegations on topics of general concern, such as abusive and immoral farming and employment practices, deforestation, the exploitation of children and their parents through aggressive advertising and the sale of unhealthy food. The Court has long held that 'political expression', including expression on matters of public interest and concern, requires a high level of protection under Article 10.

11.134 Equally the margin of appreciation for the state in interfering with free expression is correspondingly narrower in cases of political speech, and speech in relation to matters of public concern, than in other cases. A similar approach was taken in *Barthold v Germany* (above, para 11.129) where the applicant was quoted in a newspaper interview as being critical of the absence of emergency veterinary services at night. Proceedings were brought on the basis that this infringed professional guidelines restricting advertising. Injunctions were issued under Germany's competition laws restraining the applicant from reporting to the press the difficulties in relation to the night service (except in professional journals) and the problems experienced by his own practice. The ECHR held that although this interference with expression was in pursuit of the legitimate aim of the protection of rights of other vets, it was not necessary in a democratic society. The newspaper article had sought to inform the public about the situation in Hamburg in respect of veterinary services at a time when new legislation was being considered. While the illustrations given by the applicant might have had the effect of publicizing his own veterinary practice, the ECHR considered that this was secondary to the raising of a matter of public concern. The ECHR specifically expressed concern that, as the German court had decided, an injunction could be imposed merely on the basis of an intention to act for a commercial motive, observing that this could have a chilling effect in discouraging others from contributing to public debate.

---

[69] Above n 66.

Where a whistleblower seeks to raise issues of concern over the management of the **11.135** employer, there may well be a question as to whether in the circumstances this raises issues of public concern. Some assistance in relation to this might be derived from the decision of the ECJ in *Fressoz and Roire v France*.[70] The weekly satirical newspaper *Le Canard Enchaîné* published an article referring to salary increases awarded to Mr Jacques Calvet who was Peugeot's chairman and managing director. The article was accompanied by extracts from Mr Calvet's tax assessments. The tax assessments could only have been obtained by virtue of disclosure in breach of confidence by a tax official, albeit the identity of that tax official could not be identified. The journalist who reported the story and the editor of *Le Canard Enchaîné* were convicted of handling the stolen photocopies. They then claimed that this was a breach of Art 10 of the Convention. In upholding this complaint, the ECHR noted that the article related to a matter of public concern in that it was published during an industrial dispute at Peugeot over pay and showed that the company chairman had received large pay increases whilst opposing the employees' pay claims. The ECHR rejected the argument advanced by the French government that the disclosure of the remuneration of one person, even if he was the head of a major private company, did not contribute to debate on a matter of public interest and that the particular situation at Peugeot was too specific to be a matter of public interest.

The approach of the court in *Fressoz* suggests that, at least in relation to employers **11.136** that are substantial undertakings, a narrow argument to the effect that employment disputes raise matters of only private concern is unlikely to be successful. However the ECHR also emphasized that, although the publication of tax assessments was prohibited, the information which they contained was not confidential and that it was particularly important to protect the entitlement of the press to impart information and ideas on matters of public interest. The court was not called upon to consider the position of the unidentified tax official who had disclosed the tax assessments to the press.

(5) Duties and responsibilities

It may well be that a more restrictive approach would be taken where the disclo- **11.137** sure is by an employee, especially if made otherwise than to the employer. Both the Commission and the ECHR have emphasized the duties and responsibilities involved in freedom of expression and it has been recognized that such duties and responsibilities require restrictions on the employee's freedom of expression. Thus, in *Morissens v Belgium* (above para 11.126), where a teacher made accusations of discrimination by her employers, the Commission noted that the applicant had

---

[70] (2001) 31 EHRR 2.

accepted a responsible post in the provincial education service and that she had therefore accepted certain restrictions on the exercise of her freedom of expression as being inherent in her duties. Having regard to her professional responsibilities, the suspension of the applicant without pay was reasonably justified for the protection of the reputation of the teaching establishment where she worked and the reputation of her superiors.

11.138 Nevertheless reference to an employee's duties and responsibilities is unlikely to be decisive. Employees do assume duties of fidelity to the employer but the issue for the Court and Commission is how the tension between such duties and the norm of free speech is to be resolved. In *Morissens*, for example, the Commission also emphasized that the teacher had chosen to make her accusations on television without providing any proof for her claims. Nor was there any suggestion that she had previously raised these matters internally.

(6) Manner of the expression

11.139 One manifestation of the weight given to the duties and responsibilities of employment, perhaps unsurprisingly in the light of the need for a continuing workable relationship between employer and employee, is in relation to the significance attached to the way in which the whistleblower criticizes the employer.

11.140 In non-whistleblowing cases where matters of public concern have been raised, a measure of intemperate speech has been accepted. In *Thorgeirson*, where a non-employee made allegations of police brutality, the government argued that even if there had been a factual basis for the allegations of police brutality the applicant had overstepped the reasonable limits of criticism by using malicious, insulting and vituperative language in condemning the police and in calling them 'beasts in uniform'. In rejecting this argument the ECHR conceded that the articles written by the applicant were framed in particularly strong terms but denied that this could be regarded as excessive in the light of the matters of public concern which they raised and the impact which they were designed to have.

11.141 The approach in *Thorgeirson* may be contrasted with two whistleblowing cases, one concerning a public health service employee and the other concerning a police officer. In both these cases, although the applicant claimed to be raising matters of serious public concern, the Commission was not prepared to investigate further into this because of the intemperate way in which the applicants had criticized their employers. In *Tucht v FRG* 9336/81 (unreported) the applicant was dismissed from his position as a specialist in mental and lung diseases in a regional public health service in Germany. After being refused promotion he sent numerous letters to his superiors heavily criticizing their attitude and the organization and working of the regional public health service. These letters were copied to the regional parliament, trade unions, professional associations, colleagues and political parties. After many warnings he was dismissed from the civil service for various disciplinary offences. These included insulting his employees, publicizing abusive criticisms and communicating confidential information to third parties. He claimed that his dismissal was unjustified on the basis that he was merely exercising his right freely to criticize the 'System'. The Commission however accepted that the applicant was dismissed, not because of the fact that he was criticizing his superiors, but by reason of the abusive and offensive form that this criticism had taken. Having regard to the duties and responsibilities which his position carried, the interference with the applicant's freedom of expression was held to be necessary for the protection of the rights of others by preventing the disclosure of information received in confidence and by protecting the reputation of others. Indeed on this basis the Commission found the application to be inadmissible without having regard to the detail of the criticisms made by the applicant and, apparently, without considering whether the criticisms were such as could provide a valuable contribution to the effective working of the 'System' (in the form of the regional public health service).

A similar approach was adopted by the Commission in *De Jong v The Netherlands* **11.142** 10280/83. In that case a police officer complained that he had been transferred and then honourably discharged from the police on the grounds of the opinions which he had expressed. The applicant, who was a former chief sergeant of the Dutch national police, had strongly criticized persons, policies and situations within both the police and the judiciary. He had done so both privately and publicly. The Commission held that the applicant had been dismissed, not because of the fact that he was criticizing his superiors, but due to the abusive and offensive form the criticism had taken. As in *Tucht* it was held that having regard to the duties and responsibilities which his position carried the interference with his freedom of expression rights was necessary for the protection of the reputation and rights of others and for preventing disclosure of information received in confidence. Again the Commission appears to have found that the application was inadmissible without giving any weight to the value of such criticisms to public debate. Indeed the Commission was prepared to accept that the criticisms must have been confidential merely because the applicant was able to voice them only by virtue of the experience gained in his employment, irrespective of whether the information disclosed was already in the public domain. Certainly the Commission's decision on admissibility does not disclose whether any attempt was made to identify what, if any, information was confidential.

The decisions in *Tucht* and *De Jong* might be seen as supporting a submission that **11.143** it is permissible to impose a detriment for the way in which a worker behaves when blowing the whistle. This issue is addressed in Chapter 7. We suggest however that the decisions do not support this contention. The Convention creates a floor of rights and, therefore it is suggested that it would not be appropriate to rely on *Tucht* or *De Jong* as a basis for narrowing the scope of protection set out in the protected disclosure provisions of the ERA.

(7) Whether the accusations are supported by evidence

11.144   In *Thorgeirson* the ECHR emphasized that in most cases where matters of public concern are raised there is no general requirement to show that there is a sufficient evidential basis. However in *Morissens* the Commission took account of the absence of evidence in support of the allegations which the applicant made in relation to her employers. It appears to have been implicit that it was for the applicant at least to provide some proof that the allegations were well founded. This would go beyond an obligation to act in good faith since there was apparently no suggestion that the applicant in *Morissens* had acted in bad faith. However it may be that this decision should be treated with some circumspection since it preceded the important case of *Thorgeirson* and the Commission does not appear to have considered the case law in relation to the need for a greater degree of protection in relation to speech upon matters of public concern.

(8) The recipient of the information

11.145   We have seen, in both the protected disclosure provisions of the ERA and the general law on the domestic principle of public interest disclosure, the emphasis on the nature of the intended recipient of the disclosure. So too under the Convention a further factor which is often emphasized in considering the necessity of interference is the means used for the communication and the audience to be targeted. In non-employment cases one theme running through the case law has been an emphasis upon the role of the press as a watchdog and in imparting information and ideas.[71] By contrast, in cases where concern is expressed by employees about their employer, disclosure to the press or other media may be considered less deserving of protection (at least unless preceded by a genuine attempt to raise the matter with the employing organization) than in cases where disclosure is to an appropriate regulatory body. Thus in *Morissens* the Commission took account of the fact that the applicant's comments had been made on television, and that she had therefore used a 'means the impact of which is both wide and immediate'.

11.146   This might be contrasted with *Grigoriades v Greece* (1998) 4 BHRC 43. The applicant, a journalist, claimed to have discovered a series of abuses committed against conscripts in the course of his military service as a reserve officer on probation. Criminal proceedings brought against him before the national court failed but

---

[71] *Lingens v Austria* (1986) 8 EHRR 407, para 41; *Thorgeirson v Iceland*, para 63; *Goodwin v UK* (above, para 11.123).

a disciplinary penalty was imposed so that he had to spend additional time in the army. The language used by Mr Grigoriades in his articles about the army included a venomous attack on the army as 'a criminal and terrorist mechanism which, by creating an atmosphere of intimidation and reducing to tatters the spiritual welfare of radical youth, clearly aims at transforming people to mere parts of a mechanism of domination'. The Greek government stressed the abusive contents of the letter and the need to protect the authority of the army and relied upon the wide margin of appreciation enjoyed by the national authorities. In finding that there had been a breach of Art 10, the ECHR emphasized that the letter was not sent to the press but to the commanding officer and one other officer. As such, together with the fact that the letter did not contain any insults directed against the recipients of the letter it was held that any effect on military discipline must have been insignificant.

(9) Nature of the employing organization

In a number of cases which do not involve whistleblowing, the Commission has paid attention to the nature of the employing organization in assessing whether interference with free expression was justified. A breach of the obligation of fidelity has been considered to be particularly serious and to justify a sanction where the views expressed inhibit the employee's ability to perform his duties. In *van der Heijden v The Netherlands* (1985) D&R 42, for example, the applicant's employment by an immigration foundation in Holland was terminated on the basis of his membership of a political party hostile to the presence of foreign workers in the Netherlands. The Commission held that the interference with the applicant's freedom of expression was justified because it was reasonable for the employer to have some discretion concerning the composition of its staff and because, having regard to the applicant's professional duties, the employer could reasonably take account of the adverse effects which his political activities might have on the employer's reputation, particularly in the eyes of the immigrants whose interests it sought to promote. Similarly in *X v United Kingdom* (above, para 11.125), where a school teacher was dismissed for failing to obey an instruction that he was not to advertise his political, moral or religious beliefs by posters or stickers on school premises, the Commission found that the interference was justified and took into account the fact that the teacher was employed in a non-denominational school. This approach again provides little comfort to the prospective whistleblower seeking to widen the protection offered by the Public Interest Disclosure Act. It may well be that the concerns which an employee raises inhibit his continuing performance of his duties by causing a breakdown of trust with the employer. It might also be that an employee seriously damages the employer's reputation by blowing the whistle on matters of concern at the workplace. The risk of this being relied on as a basis to take action against the employee will be all the greater if an employee fails to meet the

11.147

requirements of the Public Interest Disclosure Act, for example by disclosing his or her concerns other than to the employer where this is not a protected disclosure.

(10) Is the sanction imposed by the state?—the scope of the positive obligation to protect the whistleblower

11.148   Although Art 10(1) proclaims that everyone has the right to freedom of expression, a complaint can only be made if the interference has been by a public authority. This requirement is satisfied where an employer relies upon the courts to provide a sanction against interference with free expression, such as by awarding an injunction or damages.[72] However where the interference is by way of a disciplinary measure imposed directly by the employer without the need for recourse to the court, there is then no scope for a claim unless it can be established that the state ought to have taken positive steps to protect freedom of expression. In *Rommelfanger v Federal Republic of Germany* (1989) 62 D&R 151 the Commission was required to consider the scope of the positive duty upon the state to protect free expression. The applicant was employed in a Catholic hospital and was dismissed because he had expressed in a newspaper an opinion which was not in conformity with the position of the Church. He signed, together with fifty others, a letter to the weekly magazine, *Stern*, criticizing the attitude of leading personalities in medical organizations to abortion legislation which had been introduced some three years earlier. He was given notice of termination. He then appeared on television to defend his views. Mr Rommelfanger was initially successful in challenging the dismissal but the Federal Constitutional Court decided that the Labour Courts had not given sufficient weight to the principle of church autonomy. The Commission held that the dismissal of the physician employee by a Roman Catholic foundation was an act of a private employer. The fact that in German law the Catholic Church could be regarded as a corporation of public law did not make the dismissal an act of the state. The Commission also held that the state would not be in breach of any positive obligation to protect the employee's free speech rights provided that it ensured that 'there is a reasonable relationship between the measures affecting freedom of expression and the nature of the employment as well as the importance of the issue for the employer.'

11.149   Consistently with the approach endorsed in *Vogt*, the Commission did not accept the German government's view that Rommelfanger had waived entirely his right to freedom of expression by entering into the employment contract, but accepted that his right to freedom of expression was limited to some extent by the duty of loyalty to his employer. Having noted that the views expressed by Rommelfanger on abortion were contrary to the convictions and value judgements which the

---

72   For example, *van der Heijden v The Netherlands*.

Church considered to be essential to the performance of its functions in society, the Commission concluded that the requisite reasonable relationship between the expression and the nature of employment and the importance of the issue to the employer was satisfied. The matters raised by the whistleblower will often be closely related to the employment and will touch on matters of great importance to the employer and *Rommelfanger* may be not all that encouraging to the extent that it suggests that the freedom of expression can be restricted on those matters. Nevertheless, in raising the prospect of positive obligations upon the state to protect free expression the Commission, it at least provided a basis for reliance upon Art10 even where a sanction is imposed upon the whistleblower by a private employer. It may yet be that, if the extent of such duties is considered in the context of an employee disclosing matters of public concern in relation to the employer, a more stringent requirement might be imposed upon the employer.

(11) Conclusion on the ECHR authorities

On many occasions the ECHR has emphasized the importance of the rights   **11.150**
provided by Art10. Neither the ECHR nor the Commission has yet focused directly on the situation of the whistleblower. However the cases in analogous areas permit some tentative conclusions as to the likely treatment of the whistleblower. Those wishing to argue in favour of extending the protection offered by the protected disclosure provisions of ERA, whether by a generous construction of that statute or of other legislation (such as in relation to unfair dismissal) or by a direct remedy against public authority, will emphasize the importance given to freedom of expression and the emphasis given to protection of speech in relation to matters of public concern (*Thorgeirson*; *Barthold*).

On the other hand, both the ECHR and Commission have recognized that   **11.151**
employment involves duties and responsibilities. The nature of these duties will depend in part on the express terms of the contract (*Morissens*) and in part on terms to be implied from the employment relationship, such as duties of loyalty (*Rommelfanger*) and confidentiality (*Tucht*). Even where the whistleblower raises matters of public concern protection may be less extensive than in a non-employment context. Thus an employee who raises matters of public concern in an intemperate way may, consistently with Art10, be disciplined on the grounds of the way the issue has been raised (*Tucht*; *De Jong*). Similarly, discipline of a whistleblower is more likely if the matter is first raised with the mass media rather than being raised internally or with an appropriate regulatory body (*Grigoriades*, *Morissens*). It may be that the decisions in *Thorgeirson* and *Vogt* will signal a more hospitable climate for the whistleblower. Nevertheless the Commission and Court have so far failed to give clear guidance as to when the whistleblower can be confident that the European Convention will offer protection. Even if the whistleblower uses temperate language and an appropriate channel of communication, it is as yet unclear

what degree of proof s/he must also attain in order to support the allegations (*Morissens*). Nor has consideration yet been given to the scope of a positive duty upon the state to ensure that private employers do not penalize the whistle-blower, albeit it seems that there is a positive duty to protect free expression (*Rommelfanger*). There remains little indication in the ECHR case law, therefore, to indicate that it can be relied upon to expand on the protection provided by the domestic courts, as well as under PIDA, for those who raise disclosures in the public interest.[73]

G. Criminal law

11.152 In this section we consider the principal criminal provision relating to 'confidentiality',[74] the Official Secrets Act 1989 ('OSA') which replaced the Official Secrets Act 1911. Under s1(1) a person who is or has been a member of the security and intelligence services, or a person notified that he is subject to the provisions of this subsection, is guilty of an offence if without lawful authority he discloses *any* information, document or other article relating to security or intelligence which is or has been in his possession by virtue of his position as a member of any of those services or in the course of his work while the notification is or was in force. 'Disclosing information relating to security or intelligence' includes making any statement which purports to be a disclosure of such information or is intended to be taken by those to whom it is addressed as being such a disclosure.

11.153 Under s1(3) a person who is or has been a Crown servant or government contractor is guilty of an offence if, without lawful authority, he makes a *damaging disclosure* of any information, document or other article relating to security or intelligence which is or has been in his possession by virtue of his position as such. A disclosure is damaging if it causes damage to the work of, or of any part of, the security and intelligence services; or it is of information or a document or other article which is such that its unauthorized disclosure would be likely to cause such damage or which falls within a class or description of information, documents or articles the unauthorized disclosure of which would be likely to have that effect.

---

[73] The same remark might be made with still more force as to the approach of the European Court of Justice in this area: see in particular *Connolly v Commission (Staff Regulations)* [2001] EUECJ C–274/99 (6 March 2001) in which the ECJ upheld the decision to discipline an official of the Commission for publishing without permission, and then having serialized in *The Times*, a book entitled '*The Rotten Heart of Europe—The Dirty War for Europe's Money*' in which he was critical of the Commission's policies.

[74] There are others, and for consideration of them and a fuller treatment of the 1989 Act and the background to it see Cripps, above n 1, chapter 3.

Specific defences are provided by s1(5): that the discloser proves that he did not **11.154**
know, and had no reasonable cause to believe, that the information, document or
article in question related to security or intelligence or, in the case of an offence
under s1(3), that the disclosure would be 'damaging'.

Further offences are provided for by s4 and apply to a person who is or has been a **11.155**
Crown servant or government contractor who is guilty of an offence if without
lawful authority he discloses any information, document or other article to which
s4 applies and which is or has been in his possession by virtue of his position as such.
Section 4 applies to various classes of information obtained by law enforcement
agencies. It is a defence for a person charged with an offence under s4 in respect of
any other disclosure to prove that at the time of the alleged offence he did not
know, and had no reasonable cause to believe, that the information, document or
article in question was information or a document or article to which s4 applies.

Various provisions (referred to below) provide for members and former members of **11.156**
the security services to express concerns within the service, within the government
and executive and to seek permission to make wider disclosure of those concerns.

In *R v Shayler* [2002] UKHL 11; [2003] 1 AC 247 the principal question for the **11.157**
House of Lords was whether, as a result of the coming into force of the Human
Rights Act 1998, there could be a defence to the offences under the OSA that
disclosure was necessary in the public interest to avert damage to life or limb or
serious damage to property, or to expose serious and pervasive illegality or iniquity
in the obtaining of warrants and surveillance of suspected persons, at common law.
Moses J, and then the Court of Appeal, had rejected this argument. The House of
Lords ruled to similar effect. It was plain that the only defences were those
expressed in the statute. Lord Bingham said (at para 20) that the sections left no
room for doubt, and if they did the 1988 White Paper, which was a legitimate aid
to construction and which had expressly dealt with and rejected the idea of a
public interest defence, made the intention of Parliament clear beyond argument.
The Human Rights Act did not alter this position. Article 10(1) which contained
the right to free expression, was subject to Article 10(2) which provides that freedom of expression could be restricted provided that restriction was prescribed by law
and directed to one or more of the objectives specified in the article and shown
by the state concerned to be necessary in a democratic society. 'Necessary' was not
synonymous with 'indispensable' nor did it have the flexibility of such expressions
as 'admissible', 'ordinary', 'useful', 'reasonable' or 'desirable'.[75] The questions were:

(a) Did the interference with freedom of expression correspond to a pressing
social need; was it proportionate to the legitimate aim pursued?

---

[75] Referring to *Handyside v United Kingdom* (above n 68), 754, para 48.

(b) Were the reasons given by the national authority to justify it relevant and sufficient under Art 10(2)?[76]

11.158 The OSA did restrict Shayler's right to free expression. But that restriction was directed to permissible objectives (ie national security, territorial integrity, public safety and the prevention of disorder or crime). The questions were whether the restrictions were necessary, met a pressing social need and were proportionate.

11.159 Lord Bingham said that the acid test was whether, in all the circumstances, the interference with the individual's Convention right prescribed by national law was greater than was required to meet the legitimate object which the state sought to achieve. His Lordship noted that the ban on disclosure in the OSA was not absolute. A member or former member of the security and intelligence services had various means of recourse:

(a) disclosure could be made to the staff counsellor, a high-ranking former civil servant, in respect of concerns relating to the work of the service which it had not been possible to allay through the ordinary processes of management–staff relations;

(b) concerns about the lawfulness of what the service had done or was doing could be disclosed to (among others) the Attorney-General, the Director of Public Prosecutions or the Commissioner of Metropolitan Police and these officers were subject to a clear duty, in the public interest, to uphold the law, investigate alleged infractions and prosecute where offences appear to have been committed, irrespective of any party affiliation or service loyalty; and

(c) concerns about misbehaviour, irregularity, maladministration, waste of resources or incompetence in the service could be disclosed to the Home Secretary, the Foreign Secretary, the Secretaries of State for Northern Ireland or Scotland, the Prime Minister, the Secretary to the Cabinet or the Joint Intelligence Committee. Disclosure could also be made to the staff of the Comptroller and Auditor General, the National Audit Office and the Parliamentary Commissioner for Administration.

11.160 A further safeguard was that a former member could seek authorization from his former superior or the head of the service to make a wider disclosure. Consideration of a request for authorization should never be a routine or mechanical process: it should be undertaken bearing in mind the importance attached to the right of free expression and the need for any restriction to be necessary, responsive to a pressing social need and proportionate. If a request for permission were refused it could be the subject of an application for judicial review and in any application for judicial review alleging an alleged violation of a Convention right

---

[76] *The Sunday Times v The United Kingdom* [1979] 2 EHRR 245, 277–278, para 62

the court will now conduct a much more rigorous and intrusive review than was once thought to be permissible (citing Lord Steyn in *R (Daly) v Secretary of State for the Home Department* [2001] 2 AC 532, 546–548) with the application of the proportionality approach as opposed to the less intensive traditional approach.

Finally s9(1) of OSA provides that the consent of the Attorney-General is required **11.161** before any prosecution is instituted for an offence under (among other sections) ss1(1) and 4(1) and (3). The Attorney-General would not give his consent to prosecution unless he judged prosecution to be in the public interest. He is unlikely to consent if the disclosure alleged is trivial or the information disclosed stale and notorious or the facts are such as would not be thought by reasonable jurors or judges to merit the imposition of criminal sanctions. The consent of the Attorney-General was required as a safeguard against ill-judged or ill-founded or improperly motivated or unnecessary prosecutions.

Whilst the tenor of Lord Hope's speech might be thought to have expressed **11.162** a degree of misgiving with the absence of a general public interest defence within the OSA, he nevertheless agreed with Lord Bingham's conclusions as did the rest of their Lordships. In effect a member or former member of the security services has no right, even as a last resort and even in the face of the most serious iniquity, to make a general disclosure. There is however an extensive system of internal disclosure with the safeguard of judicial review to oversee its proper functioning.

12

PROTECTION OF THE IDENTITY
OF INFORMANTS

A. Victimization	12.02	(1) Protection for informants through s10 of the Contempt of Court Act		12.15
B. Anonymity of informants and the fairness of disciplinary and dismissal procedures	12.03	(2) The public interest defence to a *Norwich Pharmacal* application		12.21
C. Forcing disclosure of the identity of informants	12.09			

A prospective whistleblower (in this context the expression 'informant' is more **12.01** apposite) may be deterred from making a disclosure if his or her identity will become apparent to the perpetrator of the wrongdoing or someone associated with the perpetrator. There is a recognized public interest that there should be disclosures of wrongdoing and also in extending protection to informants. However a balance has to be struck between the protection afforded to the informant and the rights of those who are the subject of the information disclosed.

A. Victimization

A whistleblower whose employer fails to take reasonable protective steps to **12.02** prevent detrimental treatment by fellow employees or others by maintaining the confidentiality of the disclosure or otherwise may have a claim under s47B ERA. There might also be a claim of unfair dismissal under s103A if an employee leaves in circumstances amounting to constructive dismissal. We consider the ingredients which would need to be satisfied for such claims in Chapters 7 and 8. We also consider the ways in which these issues are approached through the use of whistle-blowing procedures in Chapter 16.

B. Anonymity of informants and the fairness of disciplinary and dismissal procedures

12.03 The difficulties which arise in relation to protecting the identity of an informant may be particularly acute in the context of one employee making allegations against a colleague. An employer risks being subject of complaint by both the whistleblower and the person the subject of the allegations. Especially within the context of disciplinary proceedings, the person subject to the allegations will need to have sufficient details of the allegations and this might of itself reveal the identity of the whistleblower. Further, it may be argued that the employee who is being disciplined cannot properly defend himself without knowing the identity of the accuser, perhaps in order to show a malign motive.

12.04 Guidance has developed as to how a reasonable employer would be expected to proceed.[1] The starting point is *Linfood Cash and Carry Limited v Thomson* [1989] IRLR 235. In that case the EAT (Wood J) set out guidance for employers in dealing with informant evidence against employees who were accused of misconduct, (theft of credit notes) where the informants wish to remain anonymous:

1. The information given by the informant should be reduced into writing in one or more statements. Initially these statements should be taken without regard to the fact that in those cases where anonymity is to be preserved, it may subsequently prove to be necessary to omit or erase certain parts of the statements before submission to others—in order to prevent identification.
2. In taking statements the following seem important:
   (a) date, time and place of each or any observation or incident;
   (b) the opportunity and ability to observe clearly and with accuracy;
   (c) the circumstantial evidence such as knowledge of a system or arrangement, or the reason for the presence of the informer and why certain small details are memorable;
   (d) whether the informant has suffered at the hands of the accused or has any other reason to fabricate, whether from personal grudge or any other reason or principle.
3. Further investigation can then take place either to confirm or undermine the information given. Corroboration is clearly desirable.
4. Tactful inquiries may well be thought suitable and advisable into the character and background of the informant or any other information which may tend to add or detract from the value of the information.
5. If the informant is prepared to attend a disciplinary hearing, no problem will arise, but if, as in the present case, the employer is satisfied that the fear is genuine

---

[1] Each case must be considered on its own particular facts however, and in *Sainsburys Supermarkets Limited v Hitt* [2003] IRLR 23 the Court of Appeal confirmed that the range of reasonable responses test (the need to apply the objective standards of the reasonable employer) apply to the investigation and procedure adopted as much as to the reasonableness of a decision to dismiss.

then a decision will need to be made whether or not to continue with the disciplinary process.

6. If it is to continue, then it seems to us desirable that at each stage of those procedures the member of management responsible for that hearing should himself interview the informant and satisfy himself what weight is to be given to the information.
7. The written statement of the informant—if necessary with omissions to avoid identification—should be made available to the employee and his representatives.
8. If the employee or his representative raises any particular and relevant issue which should be put to the informant, then it may be desirable to adjourn for the chairman to make further inquiries of that informant.
9. Although it is always desirable for notes to be taken during disciplinary procedures, it seems to us to be particularly important that full and careful notes should be taken in these cases.
10. Although not peculiar to cases where informants have been the cause for the initiation of an investigation, it seems to us important that if evidence from an investigating officer is to be taken at a hearing it should, where possible, be prepared in a written form.

12.05 The *Linfood* guidance therefore envisaged that the information provided by the informant, suitably edited to prevent his/her identity, should be supplied to the employee who is the subject of the allegations, and that management conducting a disciplinary hearing against the person subject to the allegations should themselves interview the informant. In some cases, however, even this might be problematic. This was the situation considered by the EAT in *Ramsey v Walkers Snack Foods Limited/Hamblet v Same* [2004] IRLR 754. The context was 'the necessity of obtaining information about dishonesty[2] in a factory in a close-knit community where the slightest whiff of cooperation with the management could have the most serious consequences'. The particular issues were:

(a) the unwillingness of informants to sign a statement unless it had been sufficiently edited so as to remove any risk of identifying the maker of the statement from its content, and
(b) the informants' unwillingness to be exposed to further questioning on their statements by managers within the investigatory and/or disciplinary process (other than the human resources officer who took the original statements) for risk of their identities being revealed with the resulting reprisals that they feared.

12.06 The EAT said that the employment tribunal had made 'the clearest of findings' that the offer of anonymity given by the employer to the informants was not unreasonable in the circumstances of the case. The informants who had come forward had done so expressly on the basis that their identity would remain confidential.

---

[2] In the form of theft from the production line.

In those circumstances the tribunal found that the respondents genuinely and reasonably believed that no further information would be provided unless it was on an entirely confidential basis; and that was the offer made to the workforce. The tribunal found that the respondent genuinely and reasonably believed in the informant employees' expressions of fear. It was reasonable for that anonymity to be extended so that neither the decision maker nor even the investigating officers were able to directly test that which the informant had to say, but had to rely substantially on the belief of the human resources officers that the informants were reliable and trustworthy. However the employment tribunal heard evidence as to the approach of the human resources officer and the fact that she had explored the detail of their evidence with them. Also she knew the workforce well enough to cover the point made by Wood J in *Linfood* concerning the need to consider the character and background of the informants and whether there was likely to be any form of personal grudge in play.

12.07   The demands of anonymity meant that even in their original form the statements could not contain the sort of detail that the *Linfood* guidelines suggested they should contain, but the tribunal had made the clearest of findings that the informants were not willing to put their name to paper unless there was sufficient editing.[3] In the circumstances the EAT upheld the tribunal's finding that dismissals for theft were fair even though the statements given to the employees had been lacking in detail and the informants had not been questioned by management involved in the disciplinary process. The interest in encouraging the informants to come forward, and honouring the promise of anonymity, was found to be compelling.

12.08   In *Linfood* and *Ramsey* the essential elements of the alleged offence could be communicated to the accused without revealing the identity of the informant, albeit

---

    [3] See also *Asda Stores Limited v Thompson and others* [2002] IRLR 245 (EAT) where the claimants applied to the ET for a disclosure order in respect of the witness statements taken from informants who had been promised anonymity. The ET granted the order but the EAT said that it was within the power of an employment tribunal to direct disclosure of documents in anonymized or redacted form, and the ET in that case should have made such a direction in order to conceal the identity of the witnesses and maintain the employer's promise of confidentiality to those had made the statements. The case returned to the EAT on issues relating to the extent to which the employees' lawyers could participate in the redaction process: see [2004] IRLR 598. A promise of anonymity was again upheld in *Fairmile Kindergarten v MacDonald* (UKEAT/0069/05/RN) where the claimant was alleged to have struck a child. The child's parents were promised anonymity by the respondent's solicitor, who had compiled a report upon the basis of which the claimant had been dismissed. The ET chairman ordered disclosure of the identities of the parents and their child. On the respondent's appeal (unfair dismissal and sex discrimination) the EAT (Lady Smith) held that it was not necessary for the claimant's claim that she know those identities. The issue of whether or not the claimant had in fact struck the child was irrelevant; the issue was whether the respondent had acted on the basis of the information before it (the report of the solicitor) and whether it had done so reasonably. In these circumstances, the tribunal should have been slow to interfere with the promise of anonymity. The interests of justice did not require that it be breached.

in *Ramsey* in particular the statements provided were lacking in detail. This was not the case in *Surrey County Council v Henderson* (EAT/0326/05, 23 November 2005), where it was alleged against the employee that various sources had claimed that he had made threats of violence towards various parties, and he was not told the identity of persons who said they had been threatened. His complaint of unfair dismissal was upheld by the employment tribunal but the EAT allowed the employer's appeal on the basis that the ET had applied the wrong test as to whether the dismissal was substantively fair. The question then arose as to whether the decision could be upheld on the basis that it was plainly and unarguably correct since, having not been given the basic details of the allegations, the employee had been given no opportunity to defend himself properly. The EAT said it could see the force of those submissions. However it noted that this was a new point since the previous cases relating to informants had not concerned a situation where it had not been possible to give the employee the basic details of the allegations due to the need to protect the informants. In those circumstances the EAT was not persuaded that such an outcome was so plain and obvious that they could affirm the decision of the tribunal and the case was remitted.

C. Forcing disclosure of the identity of informants

In the cases discussed above the question for the tribunal was, in the end, whether **12.09** the employer acted reasonably in dismissing the employee. An accused employee might also have an interest in knowing the identity of his accuser in order to protect his reputation. An organization might have a legitimate interest in finding the source of a leak so that action can be taken against the employee who has been prepared to disclose confidential information before and may do so again.

The court's jurisdiction to force disclosure of the identity of an informant (and **12.10** ancillary information or documentation) takes its name from *Norwich Pharmacal Co. v Commissioners of Customs and Excise* [1974] AC 133. The *Norwich Pharmacal* jurisdiction allows a claimant to seek disclosure from an 'involved' third party who had information enabling the claimant to identify a wrongdoer, so as to be in a position to bring an action against the wrongdoer where otherwise he would not be able to do so. In *Norwich Pharmacal* Lord Reid said:[4]

> . . . if through no fault of his own a person gets mixed up in the tortious acts of others so as to facilitate their wrong-doing he may incur no personal liability but he comes under a duty to assist the person who has been wronged by giving him full

---

[4] At page 175.

information and disclosing the identity of the wrongdoers. I do not think that it matters whether he became so mixed up by voluntary action on his part or because it was his duty to do what he did. It may be that if this causes him expense the person seeking the information ought to reimburse him. But justice requires that he should co-operate in righting the wrong if he unwittingly facilitated its perpetration.

12.11   The required disclosure may take any appropriate form, not only by way of production of documents, but also providing affidavits, answering interrogatories or attending court to give oral evidence. Since *Norwich Pharmacal* the courts have extended the application of the basic principle:[5]

(a) it is not confined to circumstances where there has been tortious wrongdoing and is now also available where there has been contractual wrongdoing: *P v T Limited* [1997] 1 WLR 1309; *Carlton Film Distributors Ltd v VCI plc* [2003] FSR 47; and

(b) it is not limited to cases where the identity of the wrongdoer is unknown: relief can be ordered where the identity of the claimant is known, but where the claimant requires disclosure of crucial information in order to be able to bring its claim or where the claimant requires a missing piece of the jigsaw: see *Axa Equity & Law Life Assurance Society plc v National Westminster Bank* (CA) [1998] CLC, 1177; *Aoot Kalmneft v Denton Wilde Sapte* [2002] 1 Lloyds Rep 417; see also *Carlton Films*;

(c) further, the third party from whom information is sought need not be an innocent third party—he may be a wrongdoer himself: see *CHC Software Care v Hopkins and Wood* [1993] FSR 241 and Hollander, *Documentary Evidence*, 9th ed (London: Sweet & Maxwell, 2006) p 93 footnote 11; and

(d) the relief is a flexible remedy capable of adaptation to new circumstances: *Ashworth Hospital Authority v MGN Ltd* [2002] 1 WLR 2033 at 2049F (Lord Woolf).

12.12   The three conditions to be satisfied for the court to exercise the power to order are:

(a) a wrong must have been carried out, or arguably carried out, by an ultimate wrongdoer;

(b) there must be the need for an order to enable action to be brought against the ultimate wrongdoer, and

(c) the person against whom the order is sought must:
    i. be mixed up in and so have facilitated the wrongdoing, and
    ii. be able or likely to be able to provide the information necessary to enable the ultimate wrongdoer to be sued.[6]

---

[5] See Lightman J in *Mitsui & Co Ltd v Nexen Petroleum UK Ltd* [2005] EWHC 625 (Ch) (29 April 2005) at paragraph 18.

[6] *Mitsui*, paragraph 21.

Scott V-C dealt with a *Norwich Pharmacal* application in *P v T Limited*[7] where P, **12.13**
a senior employee, was notified that his employer had received serious allegations
about him from a third party. He was not told what the allegations were or by
whom they were made other than that they related to gross misconduct in the
way he had conducted himself with external contractors. The employer stated
that it would not disclose more as to the nature of the allegations since this would
disclose the identity of the informant and the employer considered that the informant's request for anonymity was reasonable. P was dismissed for gross misconduct. In subsequent proceedings the employers admitted unfair and wrongful
dismissal but P also sought an order against the employers compelling them to
disclose the precise nature of the allegations against him and the identity of the
informant. Scott V-C made the order notwithstanding that no wrongdoing by the
informant had yet been made out. There were potential claims of defamation
(which would depend upon the information being false) and malicious falsehood
(which would depend on the information being given maliciously). P could not
establish that these claims could be made out unless the order was granted. Justice
demanded that the order be made in order to give P a chance to clear his name.

Whilst the informant in *P v T Limited* was an outside source, the same considera- **12.14**
tions would have been relevant if it had been another employee. However there
would then be the additional complication that by revealing the identity of the
employee, the employer might be said to be subjecting the employee, who may
have made a protected disclosure, to a detriment. That is not necessarily an insuperable difficulty. In most situations the proper course would be for the employer
not to proceed with the disciplinary action unless at least able to put the substance
of the allegations to the employee against whom the allegations are made and, as
we have seen, guidelines have evolved as to the proper approach. Indeed Scott
V-C said that the conduct of the employer in *P v T Limited* was outrageous.
Further, if the employer is then ordered by the court to disclose the identity of the
informant, it can be said that any detriment which the informant worker then
suffers is not on the ground of having made the disclosure but on the ground of
the employer's obligation to comply with the order of the court.

(1) Protection for informants through s10 of the Contempt of Court Act

Special protection is offered to the media against *Norwich Pharmacal* applica- **12.15**
tions. Section 10 of the Contempt of Court Act 1981 provides under the heading
'Sources of Information':

> No court may require a person to disclose, nor is any person guilty of contempt of
> court for refusing to disclose, the sources of information contained in a publication

---

[7] Also reported as *A v Company B Limited* [1997] IRLR 405.

for which he is responsible, unless it be established to the satisfaction of the court that disclosure is necessary in the interests of justice or national security or for the prevention of disorder or crime.

12.16 Section 10 was enacted to reflect Art 10 of the European Convention, which is considered in more detail in Chapter 11. It provides:

(1) Everyone has the right to freedom of expression. This right shall include freedom to hold opinions and to receive and impart information and ideas without interference by public authority and regardless of frontiers . . .

(2) The exercise of these freedoms, since it carries with it duties and responsibilities, may be subject to such formalities, conditions, restrictions or penalties as are prescribed by law and are necessary in a democratic society, in the interests of national security, territorial integrity or public safety, for the prevention of disorder or crime, for the protection of health or morals, for the protection of the reputational rights of others, for preventing the disclosure of information received in confidence, or for maintaining the authority and impartiality of the judiciary.

12.17 The test set out in s10 of the Contempt of Court Act enables the court to distinguish between those cases where the employee is raising issues of public concern and other cases where there is no wider public interest to be protected beyond the general interest in freedom of expression. In *Camelot v Centaur Communications Limited*,[8] for example, the Court of Appeal upheld an order of Maurice Kay J against a magazine ordering it to return documents which would lead to the identification of an employee of Camelot who had leaked confidential draft year-end accounts. Schiemann LJ (at paras 12 to 20) set out the following principles:[9]

(a) There is an important public interest in the press being able to protect the anonymity of its sources.

(b) The law does not, however, enable the press to protect that anonymity in all circumstances.

(c) When assessing whether an order forcing disclosure of the source should be made, a relevant but not conclusive factor is that an employer maight wish to identify the employee so as to exclude him from future employment.

(d) Whether sufficiently strong reasons are shown in a particular case to outweigh the important public interest in the press being able to protect the anonymity of its sources, will depend on the facts of the particular case.

(e) In making its judgment as to whether sufficiently strong reasons are shown in any particular case to outweigh the important public interest in the press being able to protect the anonymity of its sources, the domestic court will give great weight to the judgments, in particular recent judgments, made by the

---

[8] [1998] IRLR 80.
[9] By reference to *X Ltd v Morgan Grampian (Publishers) Ltd* [1991] 1 AC 1 (HL); *Goodwin v United Kingdom* [1996] 22 EHRR 123 (ECHR).

European Court of Human Rights in cases where the facts are similar to the case before the domestic court.

Whilst there was no continuing threat to Camelot by further disclosure of the draft accounts, there was unease and suspicion amongst the employees of the company which inhibited good working relationships. There was a risk that an employee who has proved untrustworthy in one regard might be untrustworthy in a different respect and reveal the name of, say, a public figure who had won a huge lottery prize. Schiemann LJ emphasized that this was not a case of disclosing iniquity, nor was it a whistle-blowing case.[10] He continued:[11]

> there is a public interest in protecting sources. But it is relevant to ask, 'what is the public interest in protecting from disclosure persons in the position of the source in the present case?' Is it in the public interest for people in his position to disclose this type of information? Embargoes on the disclosure of information for a temporary period are a common and useful feature of contemporary life. It does not seem to me that if people in the position of the present source experience the chilling effect referred to by the ECHR the public will be deprived of anything which it is valuable for the public to have.

12.18

The effect of disclosing the identity of one source who has leaked unimportant material might be to have a chilling effect on the willingness of other sources to disclose material which is important. However, 'the well-informed source is always going to have to take a view as to what is going to be the court's reaction to his disclosure in the circumstances of his case'.[12]

12.19

The decision in *Camelot* was followed by Neuberger J in *O'Mara Books Limited v Express Newspapers plc* [1999] FSR 49 where stolen manuscripts of the book *Fergie—Her Secret Life* were found in the possession of two of the defendants and they were ordered to disclose their source. Neuberger J noted that whoever had stolen the manuscript had done so with a view to making a profit. Further, there was a likelihood that the source was an employee of either the publishers or their American printers. As in *Camelot* the existence of a dishonest employee was damaging to employer/employee relations and to relations between employees. There was also an obvious risk of the dishonest employee making further unlawful disclosures. As such the only public interest against disclosure was the general public interest (underlying s10 of the Contempt of Court Act) in encouraging freedom of expression and the interests of justice were clearly in favour of disclosure.[13]

12.20

---

[10] Paragraph 23.
[11] At paragraph 25.
[12] Schiemann LJ in *Camelot* at p 138.
[13] See also *John Reid Enterprises Limited v Pell* [1999] EMLR 675, Carnwarth J.

(2) The public interest defence to a *Norwich Pharmacal* application

12.21 Neither *Camelot* nor *O'Mara* were concerned with the case of a whistleblower and this aspect does not seem to have been suggested in *P v T Limited*. Where a whistleblower makes a disclosure covered by the provisions of ERA inserted by PIDA it is, we suggest, unlikely that this would be regarded as wrongdoing or that the interests of justice require disclosure. This is however subject to an important qualification. At the point at which the court comes to consider whether to require disclosure of the identity of the whistleblower it might not be possible to identify whether the disclosure was made in accordance with the protected disclosure provisions of the ERA. Even if an allegation was reasonably believed to be substantially true, and even if it is in fact true, only a disclosure in the course of obtaining legal advice would be protected if not made in good faith. Yet testing good faith will often be impossible without disclosure of the identity of the whistleblower. As such, any reference to the protected disclosure provisions as a guide to material considerations in relation to whether the informant's identify should be protected, will in many cases be only an imprecise guide because not all the criteria for a protected disclosure can be tested. We suggest, however, that it remains a useful guide in weighing competing considerations as to whether to order disclosure.

12.22 This is borne out by the more recent detailed consideration of s10 and its relationship with Art 10 at an appellate level in *Ashworth Hospital Authority v MGN Limited*, in the Court of Appeal ([2001] 1 WLR 515) and then the House of Lords ([2002] 1 WLR 2033) which was followed by the decisions of Gray J and the Court of Appeal in the proceedings subsequently brought by Mersey Care Trust against Robin Ackroyd[14] and, eventually, the decision at full trial of those proceedings by Tugendhat J.[15]

12.23 This litigation originated in the publication by the *Daily Mirror* of extracts from the 'PACIS' medical records of the Moors murderer, Ian Brady, who was being held at the hospital run by Ashworth (the hospital subsequently became the responsibility of Mersey Care NHS Trust). MGN declined to disclose its source. When it was ordered by Rougier J to do so (and the order confirmed by the Court of Appeal and subsequently the House of Lords) it transpired that Mr Ackroyd, an investigative journalist, was the *Mirror's* source. Ackroyd was in turn made the subject of an application for an order that he disclose *his* source(s), admitted to be 'at Ashworth', whose identity Ackroyd had promised not to disclose.

12.24 In the House of Lords in *Ashworth Hospital Authority* Lord Woolf CJ, at para 26, said that 'the exercise of the [*Norwich Pharmacal*] jurisdiction requires that there

---

14 [2002] EWHC 2115 (QB) and [2003] EWCA Civ 663/ [2003] EMLR 36 respectively.
15 *Mersey Care NHS Trust v Ackroyd* [2006] EWHC 107 (QB) (7 February 2006).

should be wrongdoing . . . of the person whose identity the claimant is seeking to establish . . .'. Subsequently in the Court of Appeal in *Mersey Care Trust* (at para 65) May LJ stated that he was prepared to assume without deciding that, if there were no wrongdoing by the source, because the source had a public interest defence to a claim against him by the hospital, then the *Norwich Pharmacal* jurisdiction would not be established for want of a wrongdoer. However the Court of Appeal did not consider this issue further because it considered that the appeal succeeded on grounds which were available to Mr Ackroyd even if the source were a wrongdoer.

At the trial Tugendhat J accepted the principle suggested by the *dicta* of Lord **12.25**
Woolf and May LJ as to the need to establish wrongdoing by the source. He further concluded that in a claim just for a disclosure order, the burden of proving that there was wrongdoing by the informant fell on the Trust even though in a claim against the informant the burden would probably have been upon the informer to establish a public interest defence. The judge further referred to the difficulties in establishing that the source had acted in the public interest, without direct evidence from the source:

> the court may gain little assistance from the interpretation or use that the journalist or a subsequent publisher places on the information disclosed. The manner in which the story is reported, if it is reported, may or not be what the source intended. Journalists and publishers are not the puppets of their sources. They may not know, or may fail to understand, the source's purpose, and they may have purposes of their own which are different.[16]

Plainly therefore if the court had been required simply to apply the template of the **12.26**
protected disclosure provisions it would be difficult to do so since key evidence as to whether the disclosure was in good faith would be absent. However it was emphasized that, in this context, the test of whether the source had a public interest defence for having disclosed medical records was an objective one. It was not enough that the source might have intended to act in what he or she thought was the public interest. Nevethertheless, the tests which play an important role in the protected disclosure template were taken into account. In all the circumstances the court concluded that there was no such public interest defence, having regard in particular to the nature of the information disclosed and the failure to explain why there were not other persons in the NHS or the police to whom the disclosures could be made, or that internal or limited disclosed had been made and had not had the appropriate effect.

However the degree of wrongdoing that the judge had found to have taken **12.27**
place at the hospital was a relevant consideration in relation to other questions.

---

[16] Paragraph 70.

In particular, the facts that the source did not commit a wrong against Ian Brady, and that his or her purpose was to act in the public interest, formed part of the factual matrix by which the judge reached his eventual conclusion, as an application of the discretionary and proportionality tests resulting from the synthesis of the equitable remedy and Art 10. In his judgment it had not been convincingly established that there was, by the time of the trial, a pressing social need that the sources should be identified. An order for disclosure of Mr Ackroyd's sources would not be proportionate to the pursuit of the hospital authority's legitimate aim to seek redress against the source, given the vital public interest in the protection of a journalist's source. In other words the balance that had gone in favour of disclosure in the *Camelot* and *O'Mara* cases went the other way in the circumstances of *Mersey Care Trust*.

13

WHISTLEBLOWING AND COPYRIGHT

A. Infringement	13.02	(5) 'Fair'	13.16
B. Defence of fair dealing	13.03	C. Public interest defence	13.21
(1) 'Purpose'	13.04	The effect of the passing of the Human	
(2) Criticism or review of that or		Rights Act 1998 (the HRA)	13.28
another work	13.05	D. Interrelation of copyright	
(3) 'Reporting current events'	13.09	protection and PIDA	13.42
(4) Sufficient acknowledgment—			
'identifying the author'	13.14		

A potential whistleblower who is considering speaking out will often be concerned **13.01** to be able to provide evidence in support of his allegations. The employee may, for example, wish to make copies of research gathered in the course of employment if that research demonstrates a health and safety concern. Alternatively the employee may wish to make and disclose copies of internal memoranda which evidence impropriety. In these circumstances, especially if there is a risk that he will be acting outside the protection of the Public Interest Disclosure Act 1998, the potential whistleblower, may have to consider not only whether there is a risk of a claim of breach of confidence, but also a risk of a breach of copyright.[1]

---

[1] In addition to general provisions relating to infringement of copyright, specific obligations apply in relation to data within the meaning of the Data Protection Act 1998 (DPA), as amended by the Freedom of Information Act 2000. The substantive provisions of the DPA came into force on 1 March 2000. Under s55 of the DPA, it is an offence for a person knowingly or recklessly to obtain or disclose personal data (or the information contained in such data), or to procure the disclosure to another person of that information, without the consent of the data controller. However, it is a defence to show that the action was necessary for the purpose of preventing or detecting a crime or that disclosure was justified in the public interest.

A. Infringement

13.02 Copyright will be infringed where there is unlicensed use of a work, for example by copying or reproducing all or a substantial part of the work. Most documents (being original literary works) and photographs (being artistic works) will be included as works within the meaning of the Copyright Designs and Patents Act 1988 (CDPA).[2] Ordinarily the author of a work will be the first owner of the copyright in that work.[3] However where the work is made by an employee in the course of his employment, the employer will be the first owner of the copyright subject to any agreement to the contrary.[4] Similarly the Crown will be the first owner of copyright in works produced by an officer or servant of the Crown in the course of his duties.[5] In ascertaining whether work was carried out in the course of employment or in the course of duties, the court will have regard to whether the skill, effort and judgement expended by the employee or officer in creating the work fell within the scope of the normal express or implied duties of the employee or officer or within any special duties assigned to him. The employer will not have copyright in the work merely because it was created in working hours and might be a useful accessory to the contracted work.[6] In addition, even where an employee creates a work other than in the course of his employment, the employer may be the owner of that work in equity if the work is created in breach of the employee's fiduciary duty to the employer.[7]

B. Defence of fair dealing

13.03 So far as the whistleblower is concerned, the most relevant defences are the public interest and, to a lesser degree, the fair dealing defences. As to the fair dealing defence, the most relevant provisions are contained in s30 CDPA, as amended by the Copyright and Related Rights Regulations 2003. This provides, with the amendments shown by the words in square brackets:

> (1) Fair dealing with a work for the purpose of criticism or review, of that or another work or performance of a work, does not infringe any copyright in the work provided that it is accompanied by a sufficient acknowledgment, [and provided that the work has been made available to the public.]

---

[2] ss1,4 CDPA.
[3] s11 CDPA.
[4] s11(2) CDPA.
[5] s163 CDPA.
[6] *Stephenson Jordan & Harrison Limited v MacDonald* [1952] RPC 10; *Noah v Shuba* [1991] FSR 14.
[7] *Service Corporation International plc v Channel Four Television Corporation* [1999] EMLR 83 at 91. See also *Nottingham Univerity v Fishel* (2001) RPC 367.

[(1A) For the purposes of subsection (1) a work has been made available to the public
if it has been made available by any means, including:
    (a) the issue of copies to the public;
    (b) making the work available by means of an electronic retrieval system;
    (c) the rental or lending of copies to the public;
    (d) the performance, exhibition, playing or showing of the work in public;
    (e) the communication to the public of the work,
but in determining generally for the purposes of that subsection whether a work has
been made available to the public no account shall be taken of any unauthorised act.]

(2) Fair dealing with a work (other than a photograph) for the purpose of reporting
current events does not infringe any copyright in the work provided that
(subject to subsection (3)) it is accompanied by a sufficient acknowledgment.

(3) No acknowledgment is required in connection with the reporting of current
events by means of a sound recording, film, [or broadcast where this would be
impossible for reasons of practicality or otherwise.]

(1) 'Purpose'

In *Pro Sieben Media AG v Carlton UK Television Limited* [1999] 1 WLR 605 the   **13.04**
Court of Appeal explained that it is not sufficient that the person seeking to rely
upon the defence of fair dealing subjectively intended the work to be for the purpose of criticism or review or for reporting current events, or sincerely believed
that this was the effect of the work. Whether that is the purpose of the work is to
be determined objectively, although the motive of the infringer of the copyright
might be relevant in ascertaining whether there has been fair dealing. The Court
of Appeal in *Pro Sieben Media AG* concluded that the judge at first instance had
wrongly decided that the use of copyright material was not for the purpose of criticism and review because he had focused too much on the purposes, intentions
and motives of those involved in the planning and production of the programme,
and focused too little on the likely impact on the audience.

(2) Criticism or review of that or another work

The fair dealing defence in s30(1) CDPA enables the potential whistleblower to   **13.05**
use a copyright work only for the purpose of criticizing that work or another work.
The criticism can be strongly expressed, and even unbalanced, without forfeiting
the fair dealing defence. Any remedy for malicious or unjustified criticism rests in
an action for defamation, although the work must be genuinely concerned with
criticism or review rather than an attempt to dress up an infringement in the guise
of criticism or review.[8] Criticism of a work need not be limited to criticism of style.
It can extend to criticism of the thoughts or ideas to be found in the work and its

---

[8] *Per* Robert Walker LJ in *Pro Sieben Media AG* (CA) at 613D; *Time Warner v Channel Four*
[1994] EMLR 1 *per* Henry LJ at 14.

social or moral implications.[9] Ideas or philosophy underlying a certain style of eg journalism, as manifested in the works themselves, could be the subject of criticism which fell within s30 of the CDPA; there is no requirement that the criticism and review contained specific reference to the work in question.[10]

13.06 In *Pro Sieben Media AG v Carlton UK Television Limited* [1998] FSR 43 Laddie J, at first instance, emphasized that it was not sufficient to use the copyright work for the purpose of criticizing something other than the work or another work. Laddie J explained that criticism of the work or another work need not be the only purpose and could be used as a springboard to attack something else. However criticism of the work or another work must be a significant purpose. In *Pro Sieben* the defendants, as part of a series of programmes on chequebook journalism, made a programme including the case of Mandy Allwood who had become pregnant with eight children after undergoing fertility treatment. As part of the programme, the defendants used footage from a programme made by the claimant about Ms Allwood's case. Laddie J concluded that the use of the copyright footage by the defendant was for the purpose of criticism of the decision to pay for an interview rather than for the purpose of criticism of the claimant's programme. As such, he concluded that it was not a criticism or review of that work or another work as required by s30(1). The Court of Appeal did not take issue with Laddie J's analysis that the criticism must be of the work or another work. However it concluded that, on the facts, the use of the copyright footage was for the purpose of criticism or review of the claimant's report, and of other newspaper material, as the fruit of chequebook journalism. This was in turn used as an illustration of the theme that chequebook journalism is inimical to the truth.

13.07 In many cases this approach will be wide enough to provide protection to the whistleblower. In a case where a whistleblower seeks to rely on documentary evidence which has been copied and is to be disclosed in breach of copyright, it will often be possible to show that the whistleblower is criticizing the ideas or themes contained in those documents. In other cases, however, the whistleblower will not be criticizing either the work or the ideas contained in it. In *Lion Laboratories Limited v Evans* [1985] 1 QB 526 (CA), for example, on leaving employment with the claimant, two of the defendants removed confidential internal memoranda which cast doubt on the accuracy of breathalyser equipment. This material was offered to a newspaper for publication. Although an allegation was made both of breach of confidence and breach of copyright, in refusing an interim injunction the Court of Appeal considered only the common law defence of public interest

---

[9] *Hubbard v Vosper* [1972] 2 QB 84 *per* Lord Denning at 94F; *per* Megaw LJ at 98D; *Time Warner v Channel Four TV per* Henry LJ at 15; *Pro Sieben Media AG* (CA) at 614H–615B.

[10] *Fraser-Woodward Ltd v (1) British Broadcasting Corporation (2) Brighter Pictures Ltd* (2005) FSR 36.

and not the statutory defence of fair dealing. The memoranda were to be used as evidence but there does not appear to have been criticism either of those documents or the ideas they contained. If, however, the documents had additionally suggested that the results should not be made public then the criticism of that sentiment, expressed in the document, would have qualified as criticism of the work.

It should be noted that the amendments to ss30(1) and 30(1A) of the CDPA **13.08** made by the 2003 Regulations, as set out above, restrict the statutory defence of fair dealing with a work for the purposes of criticism and review, to a work that has been made available to the public.

(3) 'Reporting current events'

A potential whistleblower may seek to show that disclosing documents in breach **13.09** of copyright constitutes reporting current events within s30(2) CDPA. The CDPA does not contain any definition of what constitutes a current event. Unless this is given a very liberal interpretation it might be difficult for a potential whistleblower to fall within the scope of this section. In many (but not all) cases the potential whistleblower will wish to bring to light matters which have not yet been placed in the public spotlight and as such, on a narrow view, might not be regarded as an 'event'. The whistleblower might also be concerned not merely about something which happened on a particular occasion but have an ongoing concern, such as failings in health and safety practice at the workplace.

Some commentators have argued that 'current events' should be given a liberal **13.10** meaning since it is prima facie in the public interest that the public should be informed regarding matters of public concern.[11] This view has received judicial support.[12] At first instance in *The NLA v Marks & Spencer plc* [1999] EMLR 369, Lightman J expressed the view that the report need not be made in the media or be open to the public or accessible to the public. He added that the publication of a report or article in the press might itself constitute a current event, but the reporting of current events does not extend to publishing matters which are merely currently of interest but are not current events, or to publishing matters not previously known and of historical interest alone. Publication of matters which are not current events can only be justified if reasonably necessary to understand, explain or give meaning to a report of current events.[13]

---

[11] Laddie, Prescott and Vitoria, *The Modern Law of Copyright and Designs* (2000) 3rd ed. (London; Butterworths, 2000) para 20.15 at p 753.

[12] *Pro Sieben Media AG* (CA); *The NLA v Marks & Spencer plc* [1999]) EMLR 369, Lightman J at 381–382.

[13] *The NLA v Marks & Spencer*, at p 382. It should be noted that the decision of Lightman J was reversed in the Court of Appeal [2000] 3 WLR 1256, but the court found it unnecessary to rule on the fair dealing defence. In the House of Lords [2001] 3 All ER 977, the decision of the Court of Appeal was upheld, but no argument was heard on the defence of fair dealing.

13.11 The liberal approach to what is 'current' was illustrated by the decision of Jacob J at first instance in *Hyde Park Residence v Yelland* (1999) EMLR 654. In August 1998 the *Daily Mirror* printed an article in which Mohammed Al-Fayed repeated an allegation that, shortly before their accident in August 1997, the Princess of Wales and Dodi Al-Fayed had visited Mohammed Al-Fayed's Villa Windsor in Paris. He claimed that they had been accompanied by an Italian designer and were planning to get married and live in the house. The former chief security officer at Villa Windsor, Mr Murrell, had made two video stills which demonstrated that the couple had only been at the villa for 28 minutes. He took these to *The Sun* to support his claim that there had been only a short tour of the house by Diana and Dodi, and that there had been no discussion of any plans to live there. *The Sun* printed the story and published the stills. The security company which had employed Mr Murrell brought proceedings against him and *The Sun* for breach of confidence and breach of copyright. Both claims failed. It was argued that there could be no defence of fair dealing under s30(2) of the CDPA since the event in question, being the tour of the villa, had taken place a year prior to publication. Jacob J emphasized that this was too narrow an approach. It was sufficient that the report was topical and, even aside from the fact that Mohammed Al-Fayed had recently repeated his allegations, the events at Villa Windsor were still very much under discussion. The decision of Jacob J was reversed by the Court of Appeal,[14] but the court accepted for the purposes of the appeal that the media coverage in question could be described as 'current events' when those words were construed liberally.[15] The Court of Appeal rejected the fair dealing defence on the basis that the dealing with the work was not fair.

13.12 In other cases, the general approach has been to assess whether there has been a report as to something which can legitimately be regarded as an 'event' having regard to the newsworthiness of the matter. In *Pro Sieben*, for example, the Court of Appeal, in concluding that media coverage of Ms Allwood's case was itself a current event, referred to the volume and intensity of media interest in the case. A similar approach appears to have been taken in *PCR Limited v Dow Jones Telerate Limited* [1998] FSR 170. The claimant issued cocoa reports concerning the status of cocoa crops around the world. The defendant, a specialist commodity news service, published articles containing substantial quotations from the reports. Lloyd J accepted that the fact that the reports had come out into the market, and their impact on the market, was 'news' and, as such, a current event. However in *Associated Newspapers Group plc v News Group Newspapers Limited* [1986] RPC 515 Walton J took the view that the publication of an exchange of letters between

---

[14] [2001] Ch 143.
[15] *Per* Aldous LJ at p 226.

the Duke and Duchess of Windsor was not the sort of current event with which the statute was concerned.

In any event an artificially wide interpretation of what constitutes a current event **13.13** may be unnecessary if it is instead possible to rely on a public interest defence. The scope of such a defence is considered below.

(4) Sufficient acknowledgment—'identifying the author'

Subject to the exception in s30(3) CDPA, there can be no fair dealing defence **13.14** under s30 CDPA unless the infringing copy is accompanied by a 'sufficient acknowledgment'. As to this, s178 CDPA provides that:

> 'sufficient acknowledgment' means an acknowledgment identifying the work in question by its title or other description, and identifying the author unless:
> (a) in the case of a published work, it is published anonymously;
> (b) in the case of an unpublished work, it is not possible for a person to ascertain the identity of the author by reasonable inquiry.

Accordingly it is not sufficient to identify the copyright owner. The author must **13.15** also be identified.[16]

(5) 'Fair'

Even where a publication has been for one of the purposes set out in s30 CDPA, **13.16** the dealing must be shown to be fair in all the circumstances. Fair dealing is a matter of degree to be assessed on the basis of fact and impression in each case.[17] The dealing must be fair for the approved purpose and the court will take into account such matters as the amount of the extract taken, its proportion to any criticism (where s30(1) applies), the purpose of the infringement and the motive of the person infringing the copyright.[18]

The purpose for which the copyright has been infringed is likely to be particularly **13.17** important in the context of whistleblowing. Where the copyright work is being used in conjunction with raising matters of public concern, copying of very substantial extracts may be fair dealing. In *Hubbard v Vosper* [1972] 2 QB 84 (CA), Mr Vosper wrote a book critical of Scientology which contained substantial extracts from books and bulletins about Scientology by L Ron Hubbard. In holding that there was an arguable defence of fair dealing, and refusing an interim

---

[16] *Express Newspapers plc v News (UK) Limited* [1990] FSR 359.
[17] *Pro Sieben Media AG* (CA) *per* Robert Walker LJ at 613B; *Hubbard v Vosper,* above n 9, *per* Lord Denning MR at 94C, *per* Megaw LJ at 98F.
[18] See *Hubbard v Vosper* ibid *per* Lord Denning MR at 94B–C; *Associated Newspaper Group,* above para 13.12, at 518; *BBC v BSB Limited* [1992] Ch 141 at 157–158; *PCR Limited v Dow Jones,* above para 13.12 at 185–186; *Pro Sieben Media AG* (CA); *Hyde Park Residence Ltd v Yelland* [2000] 3 WLR 215.

injunction, the Court of Appeal took account of the fact that Vosper claimed to be seeking to expose Scientology to the public and to criticize and condemn Scientology. This was contrasted with an infringement of copyright in order to attack or compete with a trade rival. In such circumstances there is far less likelihood of establishing fair dealing,[19] albeit this is not an absolute bar to there being fair dealing.[20]

13.18   The circumstances in which the potential whistleblower obtains or discloses the infringing copyright may also be relevant. In *Beloff v Pressdram Limited* [1973] 1 All ER 241 the claimant, who was the political and lobby correspondent for *The Observer*, wrote an internal memorandum to her editor stating that she had had a conversation with a named member of the government to the effect that, if the Prime Minister was to be run over by a bus, Mr Maudling would become Prime Minister. She then published an article criticizing *Private Eye's* attitude to Maudling. *Private Eye* then published a reply attacking the claimant in personal terms and incorporating in full her internal memorandum. The editor of *The Observer* purported to assign the copyright in the memorandum to the claimant and she then brought an action for infringement of copyright. Ungoed-Thomas J held that there was no valid assignment but if there had been, no fair dealing defence would have been established. Publication of information known to have been leaked and which could not have been pursued without the leak, was unjustifiable for the authorized purposes of criticism or review and was not fair dealing.

13.19   In *Time Warner Entertainments Company LP v Channel Four Television Corporation plc* [1994] EMLR 1 the Court of Appeal distinguished *Beloff* on the grounds that it related to an unpublished work. In *Time Warner* the Court of Appeal was concerned with whether there had been a breach of copyright in use of extracts from the film *A Clockwork Orange* which had already been released. The Court of Appeal emphasized that criticism and review of a work already in the public domain which might otherwise constitute fair dealing, would seldom if ever be rendered unfair because of the method by which the copyright was obtained. This would be of little comfort for the whistleblower or those seeking to publish the matters disclosed by the whistleblower where, as in the ordinary case, the whistleblower seeks to make public matters which are not already in the public domain. It is however unlikely that the surreptitious circumstances in which copyright may have been infringed would be a bar to a fair dealing defence where a whistleblower raises matters of public concern. This would be inconsistent with the public interest defence and with the judicial recognition that a distinction is to be drawn between whistleblowing cases and other disclosures: *Camelot v Centaur*

---

[19] See also *Associated Newspaper Group*, above para 13.12 at 518; *Pro Sieben Media AG* (CA); *Walter v Steinkopff* [1892] 3 Ch 489; *Weatherby v International Horse Agency & Exchange Limited* [1910] 2 Ch 297.
[20] *BBC v BSB Limited* [1992] Ch 141 at 158.

Communications Limited [1998] IRLR 80 (CA). As the Court of Appeal noted in *Time Warner*, if confidential material is improperly disclosed the remedy usually lies in an action for breach of confidence.

In any event, the circumstances in which the copyright is obtained and disclosed is **13.20** merely one factor to be taken into account. It is unlikely, especially where the disclosure relates to a matter of public concern, that this would be sufficient to render the dealing unfair. In *Hubbard v Vosper* the Court of Appeal specifically rejected the claim that there could be no fair dealing defence in relation to unpublished Scientology memoranda. The court recognized that there might be such general interest in the unpublished material that it is legitimate to criticize it, or the ideas contained in it, without there being any infringement of copyright.[21] However, decisions which relate to the fair dealing defence for the purposes of criticism or review in a work that has not been made available to the public will need to be revisited, or studied with care, having regard to the amendments to s30(1) and (1A) inserted by the 2003 Regulations, and set out above (at para 13.03).

C. Public interest defence

Whilst it might be prudent for a potential whistleblower to seek to meet the **13.21** requirements for a fair dealing defence, where matters of public concern are raised, the question may arise as to whether the whistleblower can rely on a defence of public interest to claims for copyright infringement. Section 171(3) of the CDPA specifically provides for the preservation of:

> any rule of law preventing or restricting the enforcement of copyright, on grounds of public interest or otherwise.

The scope of the public interest defence in relation to claims for breach of confi- **13.22** dence is considered in Chapter 11 above. However, the Court of Appeal has observed that the basis of the court's jurisdiction to allow a public interest defence in copyright claims was not the same as that which arose in the defence of public interest in a breach of confidence action.[22]

The availability of a general common law public interest defence in the context of **13.23** infringement of copyright has been recognized in a number of cases at least since 1972. It was recognized in *Beloff v Pressd'am* at 259H, where Ungoed-Thomas J explained that:

> fair dealing is a statutory defence limited to infringement of copyright only. But public interest is a defence outside and independent of statutes, not limited to copyright cases and is based on a general principle of common law.

---

[21] *Per* Lord Denning MR at 95A–B
[22] *Hyde Park Residence v Yelland*, above n 18.

13.24 Further recognition was given to the availability of a public interest defence to infringement of copyright in *A-G v Guardian Newspapers (No.2)* [1990] 1 AC 109 (HL). The House of Lords required the *Sunday Times* to account for the profits made in serialization of the book *Spycatcher* written by Peter Wright. Lord Keith explained that, in calculating profits, no account was to be taken of any sums paid to Peter Wright or his publishers for the copyright because no claim for these sums would have been enforceable. This was because there was no copyright in a work the publication of which was brought about contrary to the public interest.[23] Similarly Lord Jauncey noted that there could be no enforceable copyright in *Spycatcher* since it 'reeked of turpitude'.[24]

13.25 In two whistleblowing cases involving allegations of infringement of copyright, reliance has been placed on the public interest defence and the court has not considered it necessary to refer to the fair dealing defence. It was on the basis of a common law public interest defence that an interim injunction was refused by the Court of Appeal in *Lion Laboratories* (para 13.07 above). The judgment of Stephenson LJ (with whom O'Connor LJ agreed) might be explained on the basis that, although Stephenson LJ recognized that the courts would not restrain a breach of copyright where there was just cause or excuse for infringing the copyright, this was consistent with public interest being a factor relevant to discretionary injunctive relief rather than as a substantive defence. However Griffiths LJ stated expressly that he considered that the defence of public interest applied to breach of copyright in addition to breach of confidence.

13.26 A substantive defence of public interest was also recognized in a whistleblowing context in *Service Corporation International plc v Channel Four Television Corporation* [1999] EMLR 83. One of the defendants, Mr Anderson, was employed by an operator and owner of funeral homes as a trainee funeral director. In fact during the period of his employment he was working under cover and covertly made a film which purported to show corpses being subjected to disrespectful and abusive treatment and coffins with corpses in them being used as rubbish bins. The claimants sought to restrain the showing of the film on Channel Four, claiming that it had been made in breach of confidence and as a result of trespass and also that the claimants owned the copyright in the film. Injunctive relief was refused. Unsurprisingly, in relation to the claim of infringement of copyright Lightman J concluded that there were good prospects of establishing a public interest defence at trial, raising questions not only as to the funeral home where the filming took place but also as to whether the state of affairs revealed might be prevalent in the claimants' funeral homes or in the industry generally.

---

[23] *Per* Lord Keith at 262G–263A.
[24] At 294D.

There are other examples of cases in which the courts have recognized some form   **13.27**
of public interest defence in copyright cases.[25] In *Hyde Park Residence Ltd v Yelland*
[2001] Ch 143, referred to at paragraph 13.11 above, the Court of Appeal held
that the CDPA did not give a court a general power to enable an infringer to use
another's copyright in the public interest, although the court had an inherent
jurisdiction preserved by s171(3) CDPA, to refuse to enforce an action for infringement of copyright where enforcement would offend against the policy of the law.
The court held, by a majority of two to one (Mance LJ dissenting), that although
it was not possible to define the circumstances in which a court would be entitled
to invoke the jurisdiction, they had to derive from the work in question and not
from the ownership of the copyright, and included, for example, circumstances in
which the work in question either (a) was immoral, scandalous or contrary to
family life, or (b) was injurious to public life, public health and safety, or the administration of justice, or (c) incited or encouraged others to act in such a way. On the
facts of the case, the Court of Appeal found that there was nothing in the circumstances which required the court to refuse to enforce the copyrights provided by
the CDPA. As we discuss below, however, following the advent of the Human
Rights Act, the Court of Appeal has preferred the dissenting view of Mance LJ as
to the scope of the public interest defence.[26]

The effect of the passing of the Human Rights Act 1998 (the HRA)

Before the passing of the HRA, the public interest defence had been found to   **13.28**
apply not only in cases in which the defendant had infringed copyright in order to
reveal some form of impropriety, but also to cases in which disclosure was otherwise held to be in the public interest.[27]

The passing of the HRA has created a potential tension between copyright protec-   **13.29**
tion and freedom of expression. This means that the authorities decided before it
came into force need to be approached with caution.

The decision of the Court of Appeal in *Ashdown v Telegraph Group* [2002] Ch 149   **13.30**
must now be considered to be the leading case on the interaction between the
right to freedom of expression in Art 10 of the European Convention on Human
Rights, and a claim for infringement of copyright and the remedies for infringement, and on the public interest defence.

---

[25] *Lion Laboratories v Evans*, above para 13.07; *Church of Scientology v Miller*, *The Times*, 23 October
1987; *Beggars Banquet Records Ltd v Carlton Television* (1993) EMLR 349; *ZYX Music Gmbh v King*
(1995) EMLR 281; *PCR Ltd v Dow Jones*, above para 13.12; *Service Corp. International v Channel Four
Television Corp.*, *The Independent*, 14 May 1998.
[26] *Ashdown v Telegraph Group* [2002] Ch 149 (CA) (see para 13.33 below).
[27] Eg *Lion Laboratories*, and *PCR Ltd v Dow Jones*, above para 13.12.

13.31 The facts of the case were as follows. The claimant had kept diaries whilst he was the leader of a major political party. After he gave up the leadership, he prepared the material for publication and showed it in strict confidence to the press and publishing houses. Included in the material was a minute of an important political meeting in October 1997. A copy of the minute reached the political editor of the defendant newspaper, which published articles about it, quoting verbatim from a substantial part of the minute. The claimant brought an action against the defendant claiming breach of confidence and copyright infringement, and seeking injunctions and damages or an account of profits. An application for summary judgment in respect of the copyright claim was resisted on the grounds that, when considering whether actionable breach of copyright had occurred, or any appropriate remedies for breach, the court should have regard to the Art 10 right to freedom of expression, which required the court to give individual consideration to the facts of each case in order to assess the impact of Art 10. The judge at first instance granted the claimant's application for summary judgment.

13.32 The Court of Appeal held that rare circumstances could arise where the right to freedom of expression came into conflict with the protection afforded by the CDPA, and that in those circumstances the court was bound so far as possible to apply the CDPA in a manner that accommodated the right to freedom of expression, which made it necessary for the court to look closely at the facts of individual cases. In most cases it would be sufficient simply to decline the discretionary relief of an injunction, while recognizing that, if a newspaper considered it necessary to copy the exact words used by another, it should in principle indemnify the author for any loss caused to him or account to him for any profit made as a result of copying his work.

13.33 The Court of Appeal held that the circumstances in which the public interest defence to breach of copyright in s171(3) of the CDPA might override copyright were not capable of precise categorization or definition. Since the coming into force of the HRA, there was the clearest public interest in giving effect to the right of freedom of expression in those rare cases where it trumped the rights in copyright conferred by the CDPA. While s171(3) permitted the defence of public interest to be raised, it would be rare for the public interest to justify copying the form of a work to which copyright attaches. In reaching this conclusion, the Court of Appeal disagreed with the way in which the majority of the Court of Appeal in the *Hyde Park Residence* case sought to circumscribe the public interest defence as tightly as they did, and preferred the conclusions of Mance LJ in his dissenting judgment, in which he said that whilst the public interest defence for infringement of copyright and breach of confidence was not necessarily to be equated, 'the circumstances in which the public interest may override copyright are probably not capable of precise categorisation or definition'.

On the facts of the *Ashdown* case, the court rejected any fair dealing defence under **13.34**
s10(1) or 10(2). The appeal was dismissed.

In the light of the *Ashdown* case, there are two ways of giving effect to the right of **13.35**
freedom of expression in copyright cases. The first is by refusing injunctive relief,
and leaving the copyright owner to his remedies by way of damages or an account
of profits. This is not an application of the public interest defence. It is a question
of applying the CDPA so as to accommodate the Art 10 right to freedom of
expression.

The second way is to permit the use of the public interest defence under s171(3). **13.36**
This will be in rare cases only, where it is in the public interest for the copyright
work to be reproduced without the reproducer being exposed to infringement
proceedings. The Court of Appeal has made it clear that the defence is not limited
to cases where copyright has been infringed in order to reveal acts of impropriety,
and that the circumstances in which public interest may override copyright are
not capable of precise categorization or definition. The HRA requires the court to
look at each case carefully on its own facts.

The Court of Appeal expressed the view that the refusal of an injunction would **13.37**
usually be sufficient to give effect to freedom of expression. However, it is not clear
in what circumstances the courts will consider that this is not appropriate, and
will allow the application of the public interest defence, the effect of which is to
deny the copyright owner all his statutory remedies. Commentators have suggested that, where the defendant is not a newspaper, but, for example a person of
limited means, and where a notional royalty for use of the copyright work would
be unaffordable by the defendant, then the use of the public interest defence
might be permitted.[28]

In these circumstances, it is difficult to give specific examples of cases in which the **13.38**
public interest defence is likely to be successful. Such cases will be rare. Examples
of recent cases in which the public interest defence in copyright claims has been
squarely rejected by the courts include *Imutran Ltd v (1) Uncaged Campaigns Ltd
(2) Daniel Louis Lyons* [2001] 2 All ER385, and *HRH Prince of Wales v Associated
Newspapers Ltd* [2006] EWHC 522 (Ch).

In the present state of the law, it is suggested that the whistleblower should be **13.39**
slow to assume that the public interest defence embodied in s171(3) CDPA will
be successful, unless the facts of the case overwhelmingly indicate that the public
interest requires that copyright protection under the CDPA should be overridden.
In that regard, it must be remembered that the fact that disclosure of copyright

---

[28] See eg *Copinger and Skone James on Copyright*, 15th edition, (London: Sweet & Maxwell, 2005)
para 22.85.

material would be of interest to the public is not the same as disclosure being in the public interest.

13.40 Similarly, the whistleblower should be slow to assume that the right to freedom of expression under Art 10 will be sufficient to 'trump' the copyright owner's right to peaceful enjoyment of his property, unless the infringement in question is actually necessary in the public interest.

13.41 The whistleblower may be better advised to consider the public interest defence to a claim for breach of confidence, the principles of which are not the same as those which apply in the case of copyright infringement under s171(3). In any event, it will always be better for the whistleblower if he is able to rely on the statutory defences to a claim for copyright infringement, such as the rights of fair dealing contained in s30(1) and (2) CDPA.

D. Interrelation of copyright protection and PIDA

13.42 There is no express provision in PIDA addressing the extent to which a whistle-blower is entitled to infringe copyright in order to supply evidence to support a protected disclosure. The evidence collected and disclosed, whether or not in breach of copyright, will form part of a qualifying disclosure provided only that, in the reasonable belief of the worker, it tends to show one or more of the matters listed in s43B ERA. The infringing copy will itself be the means by which the requisite information is disclosed. As such, if the requirements for a protected disclosure are met, the worker will have the right not to be subjected to a detriment by his employer for disclosing the protected information notwithstanding that, in making the dislcosure, or in order to do be able to do so, he infringed copyright. Having regard to the policy underlying PIDA, the courts are unlikely to accept a submission that the detriment was due not to the disclosure but to the manner in which it took place, being an infringement of copyright.[29] Equally, having regard to the policy of PIDA, it is most unlikely that injunctive relief would be granted to enforce copyright where the infringement is part of or in support of a protected disclosure. There might be an infringement of copyright in preparing to make the disclosure, for example where the worker copies copyright material for this purpose. In principle it would be open to the employer to distinguish this from the protected disclosure itself: *Bolton School v Evans* [2006] IRLR 500 (EAT). However it would still be necessary to show that this, rather than the subsequent disclosure, was the reason (or in the case of dismissal the principal reason) for any act or deliberate failure to act causing detriment.

---

[29] See paras 7.68–7.70 above; *Shillito v van Leer (UK) Limited* [1997] IRLR 495 (EAT); *Goodwin v Cabletel UK Limited* [1997] IRLR 665 (EAT); *Hossack v Kettering BC* (EAT/ 1113/01, 29 November 2002).

14

DEFAMATION

A. The prima facie case	14.02
B. Justification	14.04
C. Qualified privilege	14.05
(1) The 'duty and interest' test	14.05
(2) The Public Interest Disclosure Act 1998	14.12
(3) Malice	14.14
(4) Third tier/wider disclosures	14.18

As well as facing disciplinary action, the whistleblower may find himself on the **14.01** receiving end of a claim in defamation; a fate that may also await any media entity or third party which republishes his allegations. The full law of defamation is beyond the scope of this book but here we deal with those features that are of most relevance to the whistleblower.

A. The prima facie case

Any publication to third parties of material that refers to and is defamatory of a **14.02** living and identifiable person gives rise to a prima facie cause of action in libel or slander.[1] Since the essence of whistleblowing is communication with another, publication to a third party will invariably occur and this appears to be the case even where publication has been by one employee or officer of a company to another solely concerning the company's affairs.[2] Furthermore, given that a statement is, according to the traditional test, defamatory if it tends 'to lower the claimant in

---

[1] The distinction between the two being, in essence, that publication in writing or some other permanent form will constitute libel while spoken or otherwise transient publication will generally constitute slander.

[2] *Riddick v Thames Board Mills* [1977] QB 893 (CA) (although note the dissenting judgment of Lord Denning MR).

the estimation of right thinking members of society generally',[3] a whistleblower seeking to expose malpractice is likely to find it almost impossible to avoid publication of defamatory material. In the circumstances, and bearing it in mind that a defamatory statement can be held to refer to a person even when that person is not named,[4] a whistleblower's actions will more often than not give rise to a prima facie cause of action. The fact that the whistleblower might not have intended to publish a defamatory statement and/or to refer to a given individual will, in relation to the prima facie case, be of no assistance as the law deems such matters irrelevant.

14.03 Once the claimant has discharged the task of establishing a prima facie case, the burden of proof shifts to the whistleblower (and to any other republisher of the latter's allegations that might be sued) to make out one of the recognized defences to libel proceedings.[5] These are now a dozen or so in number, but we will deal solely with those that are most likely to be of relevance in the whistleblowing context, namely justification and qualified privilege.

B. Justification

14.04 If a defendant is able to show that his allegations are true in substance and in fact he will, in all but the most exceptional circumstances, have an absolute defence to an action for defamation. For a plea of justification to be made out it is not necessary to establish the truth of every detail that formed part of the relevant allegations; only the sting or substance of the defamatory statement need be justified.[6] In every defamation action the court starts with the presumption that the words complained of are false and the onus thus lies upon the defendant to prove the contrary. Across the full range of defamation cases the difficulties faced by defendants in consequence of this burden of proof are generally of greater concern in theory than in practice. However, it is clear that, where whistleblowing is at issue, significant difficulties may be encountered. For example, there will inevitably be instances where a whistleblower is unable to provide the court with full particulars

---

[3] *Sim v Stretch* [1936] 2 All ER 1237. See also *Parmiter v Coupland* (1840) 6 M&W 105 (would the offending words 'injure the reputation of another by exposing him to hatred, contempt or ridicule'?) and *Youssoupoff v MGM Pictures Ltd* (1934) 50 TLR 581 (do the words cause the claimant to be 'shunned and avoided'?).

[4] For example, a fellow employee responsible for the operation or management of a department about which allegations of malpractice are made by a whistleblower might be referred to, and thus defamed, even if he is not named.

[5] None of these is specifically designed to take account of whistleblowing and all have material shortcomings in that context. This perceived deficiency has led to as yet unsatisfied calls for the introduction of an additional statutory defence (see, for example, 'Whistleblowers and the Law of Defamation: Time for Statutory Privilege?' by Lewis [2005] 3 Web JCLI).

[6] See *Belt v Lawes* (1882) 51 LJQB 359 and *Sutherland v Stopes* [1925] AC 47.

of the malpractice he has felt it necessary to disclose. In these circumstances, and in cases where the whistleblower subsequently finds his revelations to have been in error, he will be obliged to have recourse to the alternative defence of qualified privilege.

C. Qualified privilege

(1) The 'duty and interest' test

Where a statement is published in circumstances of qualified privilege this will **14.05** provide a defence to libel proceedings even though the statement is defamatory and untrue, unless the person making the statement was actuated by malice. A variety of circumstances might give rise to such privilege, but in cases of first tier disclosure a whistleblower will almost certainly be well advised to consider whether what is known as the 'duty and interest test' applies. This test was most succinctly expressed by Lord Atkinson in *Adam v Ward*:[7]

> A privileged occasion is an occasion where the person who makes a communication has an interest, or a duty, legal, social or moral, to make it to the person to whom it is made, and the person to whom it is made has a corresponding interest or duty to receive it. This reciprocity is essential.

In some cases of first tier disclosure there may be a legal duty to make the **14.06** disclosure—either to an appropriate regulatory body or to the employer. Even if there is no legal duty, an employee may be under a moral or social duty to blow the whistle. As to whether there is a social or moral duty, the test was enunciated by Lindley LJ in *Stuart v Bell*:[8]

> Would the great mass of right minded men in the position of the defendant have considered it their duty under the circumstances to make the communication?

In many cases the legal, moral or social duty will arise out of the whistleblower's **14.07** position as an employee. In particular the whistleblower may be able to rely on the dictum of Blackburn J in *Davies v Snead*[9] that the requisite duty arises:

> [w]here a person is so situated that it becomes right in the interest of society that he should tell to a third person certain facts.

As under PIDA, the identity of the recipient of the disclosure will be a very **14.08** important consideration when determining the presence or otherwise of privileged circumstances. It is not sufficient that the whistleblower believes that the person to whom the disclosure is made had the requisite interest. In general the recipient

---

[7] [1917] AC 309 at 334. See also *Loveless v Earl* [1999] EMLR 530 (CA) where, in addition to requiring a common and corresponding interest, the Court of Appeal applied a test of whether the communication was 'warranted by any reasonable occasion or exigency'.

[8] [1891] 2 QB 341 at 350.

[9] (1870) LR 5 QB 608 at 611.

must in fact have the requisite interest[10] and where publication is made to a person not having such an interest qualified privilege will not apply.[11] That said, a publication may in certain circumstances be privileged notwithstanding the absence of the necessary reciprocity between the duty to make the disclosure and the interest in receiving the information; for example if it is made in the ordinary course of business or if it is otherwise reasonably necessary or if it is the only effective way of discharging a duty or protecting an interest.[12]

14.09 In relation to disclosure to another employee in a supervisory position or to an employer, the whistleblower will almost always be able to rely on the principle that there is a common interest as between employees in a business and between employees and the employer in the success of the business and the way it is carried on.[13] In most cases the common interest or duty is likely to be equally apparent in relation to other first tier disclosures such as disclosure to an appropriate regulatory authority or disclosure to a trade union in order to obtain advice.

14.10 In the important and as yet unreported case of *Halpin v Oxford Brookes University*[14] an unsuccessful attempt was made to exclude qualified privilege on the basis that the publication was made in breach of a contract of employment. The claimant was employed in the University's Business School and complained that he had been defamed in an internal memorandum circulated by the Head of the Business School which was critical of his performance. The head of the school plainly had an interest or duty in relation to the claimant's performance and the memorandum was circulated to others who had a corresponding duty or interest to receive the information. It was argued, however, that circulation of the criticisms without allowing the claimant to comment on them was a breach of the disciplinary procedure and constituted a repudiatory breach of his contract of employment. It was then suggested that since the communication was in breach of contract there could be no defence of qualified privilege. The Court of Appeal rejected this logic and, in doing so, emphasized the importance of employees being able to raise internally matters of concern to employing organizations. As Neill LJ explained:

> it remains an important public interest that people should be able to communicate freely and frankly on matters of mutual concern. It seems to me to be beyond argument therefore that managers in large organisations must be free to have free and frank discussions on all matters relating to the organisation in which the parties to the

---

[10] *Hebditch v MacIlwaine* [1894] 2 QB 54 (CA).

[11] See, for example *Watt v Longsdon* [1930] 1 KB 130 where publication by a company director of allegations concerning the sexual misconduct of an employee were held to be privileged when made to the chairman of the company but not to be privileged when made to the employee's wife. See also *Tench v G. W.Ry.* (1873) 33 UP Can QB 8 and *Mutch v Robertson* (1981) SLT 217.

[12] *Edmondson v Birch* [1907] 1 KB 371; *Pullman v Hill* [1891] 1 QB 524; *R v Lancs CC Police Authority, ex p Hook* [1980] QB 603.

[13] *Bryanston Finance v de Vries* [1975] QB 703 (CA); *Hunt v G.N.Ry.* [1891] QB 189.

[14] 30 November 1995.

discussion have a proper mutual interest. The protection of the individual who may be defamed is that the privilege to communicate is qualified privilege only. It can be destroyed by malice. But I cannot accept that a manager can be prevented from expressing an honest and relevant opinion merely by reason of the fact that the matter or person discussed might have been dealt with in some other way.[15]

It should be noted that a particularly liberal approach to the defence of qualified privilege has, for well over a century, generally been adopted where a defamatory statement consists of an allegation against a person with responsibilities to the public, provided that the allegation is made bona fide to a person with a proper interest in the subject matter.[16] This approach has only been reinforced by the advent of Art 10 of the European Convention on Human Rights guaranteeing freedom of expression and by the series of cases that have followed in the wake of the decision of the House of Lords in *Reynolds v Times Newspapers Ltd*[17] (see below).   **14.11**

(2) The Public Interest Disclosure Act 1998

PIDA does not provide a whistleblower with specific protection against proceedings for defamation. If such proceedings were to be brought by the employer these might be regarded as subjecting the worker to a detriment within s47B ERA. However, nothing in PIDA would appear to afford protection from proceedings brought by another employee or by a third party who claims to have been defamed. Notwithstanding this, it might be felt to be contrary to the underlying policy of the Act if a worker could be the subject of defamation proceedings despite having made a protected disclosure. On this basis a worker who makes a protected disclosure could argue that he should by definition also succeed in a defence of qualified privilege in relation to that disclosure, particularly as the duty and interest test mirrors the structure of PIDA to a very significant degree.   **14.12**

However, this specific point has not, as far as we are aware, yet been determined by the court. Similar uncertainty exists in relation to the converse position where a worker publishes a defamatory statement in circumstances that do not amount to a protected disclosure under PIDA. It could be argued that qualified privilege should not apply in such circumstances on the basis that the Act encapsulates the balance struck by Parliament between the public interest in encouraging disclosure of matters of public concern and the interests of the employer and/or those others   **14.13**

---

[15] For another case in which the relationship between defamation and rights under an employment contract was explored see *Friend v CAA* [1998] IRLR 253 where the Court of Appeal held that allegations made against an employee during the course of a formal disciplinary process concerning that individual were protected by the defence of *volenti non fit injuria* where the disciplinary procedure formed part of the employee's contractual terms of employment.

[16] For example, *Couper v Lord Balfour of Burleigh* (1913) SC 492; *A v B* (1907) SC 1154; *Purcell v Sowler* [1891] 1 QB 474.

[17] [1999] 3 WLR 1010.

about whom the allegations are made. Against this it might be said that the Act does not, in any context, purport to define in comprehensive fashion the actions that might properly be taken by a whistleblower or, for that matter, the circumstances in which an employer can take action against a whistleblower.[18] For this and other reasons it does not necessarily follow that, provided the duty and interest test is satisfied, a defence of qualified privilege should fail merely because the worker would not have been entitled to the higher level of protection under PIDA.

(3) Malice

14.14 Any duty and interest-based plea of qualified privilege will be defeated where the claimant can show that, in publishing defamatory material, the defendant was actuated by malice. The defendant will have acted maliciously in this context if he used the privileged occasion for some purpose other than that for which the occasion was privileged.[19]

14.15 Thus, for example, if a whistleblower's dominant purpose was not to reveal malpractice but to injure the claimant, the defence will not be available. The fact that the defendant did not believe that what he said was true should usually be conclusive evidence of malice. The use of excessive language in the circumstances of the case might itself be indicative of malice but there must be something so extreme in the words used to afford evidence that the publication was actuated by malice. Although recklessness as to the truth of what was being alleged will suffice to establish malice, it is not sufficient for a claimant to show that the defendant was careless, impulsive or irrational in arriving at his belief or that he was improvident, credulous or stupid.[20] If a defendant honestly believed his statement to be true, he does not lose the protection of qualified privilege because he had no reasonable grounds for so believing.

14.16 It is also important to distinguish between the objective test which is applied for ascertaining the meaning of what has been published and the subjective test for malice. It may be that, applying the objective test, the words published have a defamatory meaning and that the defendant had no honest belief in the truth of that meaning. However, there will still be no malice if the defendant has an honest belief that the words have a different meaning which, at the time of publication, he honestly believed to be true.[21]

---

[18] For example, even where a disclosure is not protected an employee might still be protected against unfair dismissal.

[19] *Per* Lord Nicholls in *Tse Wai Chun Paul v Cheng* (Court of Final Appeal, Hong Kong) FACV No. 12 of 2000, [2001] EMLR 777, a decision followed by the High Court in *Sugar v Associated Newspapers Ltd* (unreported, 6 February 2001), QBD and in *Branson v Bower* [2001] EMLR 809 QBD.

[20] See the classic exposition on malice of Lord Diplock in *Horrocks v Lowe* [1975] AC 135 (HL) endorsed by Lord Nicholls in *Tse Wai Chun Paul v Cheng* above.

[21] *Loveless v Earl*, above n 7.

A large degree of latitude is thus given to those who publish in privileged circum- **14.17**
stances and, in consequence, the likelihood of a plea of malice being successfully
made out should not be exaggerated. In *Sugar v Associated Newspapers Ltd* [22] Eady
J, the senior libel judge and a man having more than 30 years of experience as a
libel practitioner, observed that he personally had only come across one case in
which a finding of malice was made against a defendant. [23]

(4) Third tier/wider disclosures

While it forms no part of the purpose of this chapter to review fully the means by **14.18**
which a media entity might seek to defend itself against a defamation claim arising
out of its coverage of material originating with a whistleblower, the development in
recent years of the defence of what is known among practitioners as *Reynolds*
qualified privilege (otherwise 'responsible journalism')[24] would clearly have a
significant impact upon cases resulting from third tier/wider disclosures.

Until very recently circumstances only rarely arose in which a general duty to pub- **14.19**
lish information to the world at large would in practice be recognized by the
court. [25] However, in *Reynolds v Times Newspapers Ltd*. [26] the House of Lords (while
ostensibly adhering to the conceptual foundation of duty and interest qualified
privilege) upheld what was effectively a public interest defence in cases of defamation. In cases where *'the public was entitled to know the particular information'*[27]
(an issue to be determined by reference to all the circumstances of the case and
particularly to ten specific criteria identified in the judgment of Lord Nicholls[28])
the media will now be protected where it publishes defamatory statements even if
these should prove to be untrue. [29]

---

[22] (Unreported, 6 February 2001), QBD.

[23] Although he himself subsequently doubled that figure with his finding of malice in *Lillie and Reed v Newcastle City Council* [2002] EWHC 1600 QB.

[24] Although the use of this phrase was frowned upon by the Court of Appeal in *Jameel v Wall Street Journal Europe* [2005] 4 All ER 356.

[25] See *Blackshaw v Lord* [1984] QB 1.

[26] [1999] 3 WLR 1010.

[27] *Per* Lord Nicholls at p 1020C.

[28] At p 1027C–F.

[29] The manner in which *Reynolds* has been applied at first instance and by the Court of Appeal has rarely found favour with the media, which has complained of the imposition of unreasonably stringent requirements upon the practice of journalism. These complaints finally fell on receptive ears in the House of Lords which, in the case of *Jameel v Wall Street Journal Europe UKHL* 44 [2006], was highly critical of the approach that had been adopted by the courts below and gave extensive guidance as to how *Reynolds* ought to be applied in future. It is also of some interest that, when considering the obligations of a journalist presented with allegations by a whistleblower, Lord Hutton (in his *Report of the Inquiry into the Circumstances Surrounding the Death of Dr David Kelly CMG*) appeared to envisage the imposition of far more stringent requirements upon the media than have ever been contemplated by the court when considering pleas of qualified privilege under *Reynolds*.

14.20 In the absence of case law on the point, the interaction between the *Reynolds* defence and the position of the whistleblower who has provided information to the media entity in question, is difficult to define. Where the court finds publication of the relevant information to the world at large to have been in the public interest then it might be thought obvious that the whistleblower's original disclosure to the media was also in the public interest. However, it is unclear whether the *Reynolds* umbrella extends to cover the media's sources against claims in defamation and, if it does not, it is easy to envisage arguments to the effect that the duty and interest test is not, in the circumstances of a particular case, satisfied by disclosure to the media rather than to, say, the appropriate regulatory body. It is also easy to contemplate circumstances in which the court would be only too keen to deny a supposed whistleblower the protection it is willing to afford a media defendant that has conducted itself responsibly; most obviously where a 'whistleblower' has acted maliciously in making statements he knows to be untrue to a newspaper which unfortunately has had no reason to doubt the truth of what it is being told and has published accordingly.[30]

14.21 One factor that is likely to minimize the number of occasions upon which this kind of interaction falls to be considered by the court is the media's continued entitlement to preserve the anonymity of its confidential sources. Although the Nicholls criteria require the court to assess the nature and extent of the defendant's inquiries prior to publication, the Court of Appeal has held that, given the statutory protection afforded to a journalist who does not wish to disclose his source,[31] the identification of a source should not be a necessary element of a defence of responsible journalism.[32] Thus if a whistleblower obtains an undertaking of confidentiality before he speaks with a journalist it is most unlikely (barring the application of the relevant exemptions under the Contempt of Court Act) that the court will compel the latter to disclose his identity.

---

[30] It is the apparent and not the actual reliability of the source that is relevant. See *GKR Karate (UK) Ltd v Yorkshire Post Newspapers Ltd & others* [2000] 2 All ER 931.

[31] Section 10 of the Contempt of Court Act 1981.

[32] *Gaddafi v Telegraph Group* [2000] EMLR 431.

PART III

THE OBLIGATION TO BLOW
THE WHISTLE

15

OBLIGATIONS TO BLOW THE WHISTLE

A. *Bell v Lever Brothers*	15.02	(2) Implied contractual reporting obligations other than misdeeds	15.42
B. **Implied reporting obligations under the contract of employment**	15.10	(3) Do employees have implied contractual obligations to disclose their own wrongdoing?	15.44
(1) Reporting wrongdoing of others	15.10	(4) Conclusion as to the scope of the contractual duty of disclosure	15.56
Blowing the whistle on subordinates	15.10	C. **Directors and employees who owe fiduciary obligations**	15.57
Blowing the whistle on superiors	15.17		
Blowing the whistle on employees of similar seniority	15.24	D. **Duty to investigate**	15.66
Express terms of the contract	15.26	E. **Interface with PIDA**	15.68
Seriousness of the wrongdoing	15.27	F. **Statutory and regulatory obligations to disclose information**	15.71
Continuing wrongdoing	15.29		
Deliberate concealment	15.34		
Has there been a specific request?	15.36	G. **Clarification by a whistleblowing policy**	15.76
Is there someone with whom to raise concerns?	15.40		

15.01 The Public Interest Disclosure Act 1998 does not impose any sanction upon an employee for failing to blow the whistle. However the public policy considerations which led to legislation protecting those who make protected disclosures, and in particular the disasters which might have been avoided had the whistle been blown, might also be thought to justify imposing *obligations* of disclosure. This chapter considers the extent to which there may be a positive obligation upon employees to blow the whistle in particular circumstances, whether under the contract of employment, arising out of fiduciary obligations or pursuant to specific statutory obligations.

A. *Bell v Lever Brothers*

15.02 In recent decisions,[1] emphasis has been placed on the distinction between (a) duties of disclosure which might arise out of the fiduciary obligations of directors and of employees who are subject to such obligations, and (b) the disclosure obligations which otherwise might arise in certain circumstances under the contract of employment. A further distinction, which has recently been the subject of reconsideration by the courts, has been drawn between disclosure of the wrongdoing of others (even if it implicates the employee making the disclosure) and disclosure of an employee's own wrongdoing. We address each of these matters below. In each case, however, the distinctions drawn have reflected in large part a need to distinguish the decision of the House of Lords in *Bell v Lever Brothers Limited* [1932] AC 161 (HL). The decision has held a baleful influence over this area of law for many decades, but the developing recognition that obligations of disclosure are sometimes appropriate has been facilitated by distinguishing the decision and, more recently, substantially confining it to its own facts.

15.03 In *Bell v Lever Bros*, Messrs Bell and Snelling entered into contracts of employment with Lever Bros, but were appointed as directors and respectively as chairman and vice-chairman of Lever's subsidiary company, Niger Company. Lever held over 99 per cent of the shares of Niger. Neither Bell nor Snelling was a director of Lever. During their appointments Bell and Snelling each made personal profits by speculating in Niger's business. However before Lever became aware of this, the service contracts of Bell and Snelling were terminated and severance agreements were entered into with Lever Bros pursuant to which substantial severance payments were made by Lever to the employees. Upon becoming aware of the secret profits, Lever sought to recover the severance payments arguing that Bell and Snelling were under an obligation to disclose their misdeeds in making the secret profits prior to the conclusion of the severance agreements and those agreements were voidable as a result of their failure to do so. This argument was accepted by the Court of Appeal but rejected by a majority of the House of Lords, which held that Lever was bound by the compromise in the absence on the part of the defendants (as found by the jury) of any fraudulent representation or of any fraudulent concealment. Lord Atkin said:[2]

> unless this contract can be brought within the limited category of contracts *uberrimae fidei* it appears to me that this ground of defence must fail. I see nothing to

---

[1] *Item Software (UK) Limited v Fassihi* [2004] IRLR 928 (CA); *Tesco Stores Limited v Pook* [2004] IRLR 618.

[2] At p 227.

differentiate this agreement from the ordinary contract of service; and I am aware of no authority which places contracts of service within the limited category I have mentioned . . . Nor can I find anything in the relationship of master and servant, when established, that places agreements between them within the protected category . . . The servant owed a duty not to steal, but, having stolen, is there super-added a duty to confess that he has stolen? I am satisfied that to imply such a duty would be a departure from the well established duties of mankind and would be to create obligations entirely outside the normal contemplation of the parties.

Lord Thankerton similarly rejected the proposition that an employee had to confess his own wrongdoings to the employer. He said (at 231):   **15.04**

in the absence of fraud, which the jury has negatived, I am of opinion that neither a servant nor a director of a company is legally bound forthwith to disclose any breach of the obligations arising out of the relationship so as to give the master or the company the opportunity of dismissal . . .

In *Item Software (UK) Limited v Fassihi* [2004] IRLR 928 (CA) Arden LJ (at para   **15.05**
53) identified two material differences between the approaches of Lord Atkin and Lord Thankerton. First, Lord Thankerton equated the position of an employee with that of a director, whilst Lord Atkin left the position open, and the issue did not arise on the facts. Second, there were indications in Lord Atkin's speech that whether a duty of disclosure arose would depend on the particular circumstances.

In a number of subsequent cases, in the context of considering the scope for a duty   **15.06**
to make disclosure, *Bell v Lever Bros* has been distinguished. In *Sybron Corp v Rochem* (see below), the Court of Appeal distinguished *Bell* principally on the basis that it was concerned with whether an employee had a duty to confess his own wrongdoing. It was not therefore to be taken as authority as to whether an employee has a duty to report on the wrongdoing of others. As Stephenson LJ noted (at 124), it was 'puzzling' that no one who dealt with *Bell* appeared to have considered whether Bell or Snelling had an obligation to report each other's wrongdoing. Indeed Lord Atkin said in the course of his speech (at 228) that:

it is said that there is a contractual duty of the servant to disclose his past faults. I agree that the duty in the servant to protect his master's property may involve the duty to report a fellow servant whom he knows to be wrongfully dealing with the property.

In *Sybron Corp v Rochem* Fox LJ further noted that *Bell v Lever Bros* was also   **15.07**
distinguishable on the basis that it related to past rather than ongoing wrongdoing, whilst Kerr LJ emphasized that *Bell v Lever Bros* did not deal with a case where concealment of wrongdoing was fraudulent.

Subsequently it has been emphasized that neither Bell nor Snelling were directors   **15.08**
of Lever Brothers (with whom the severance agreement was entered into), as opposed to its subsidiary company, and that it is therefore not authority as to whether there might be a fiduciary obligation to disclose wrongdoing: *Fassihi*; *Tesco Stores Limited v Pook* [2004] IRLR 618. More generally, in *Fassihi* Arden LJ

(with whose judgment Holman J and Mummery LJ agreed on this issue), emphasized that all that needed to be decided in *Bell v Lever Bros* was that in their particular circumstances neither Bell nor Snelling owed a duty to disclose their misdeeds to the employer. It did not therefore decide that there could never be such a duty on the part of the employee. Substantially this indicated that the decision could be confined to its own facts.[3]

15.09 The decision in *Bell v Lever Bros* may therefore no longer obstruct the path to development of positive obligations upon employees to disclose wrongdoing. However this in turn begs the question as to the circumstances in which such obligations would be acknowledged.

B. Implied reporting obligations under the contract of employment

(1) Reporting wrongdoing of others

Blowing the whistle on subordinates

15.10 As noted above, in *Sybron Corporation v Rochem Limited* [1984] 1 Ch 112 the Court of Appeal emphasized that *Bell v Lever Brothers* did not stand in the way of an obligation to report on the wrongdoing of other employees. In *Sybron* the employers sought to recover sums paid out to an ex-employee, Mr Roques, under a pension and life assurance scheme. Roques was employed by Gamlen Chemical Co. (UK) Limited, a subsidiary of the Sybron Corporation group. He was the most senior employee for Gamlen's European operations and had power of hiring and firing over the whole of the European zone. Various employees of Gamlen and Sybron Corp secretly set up rival organizations to act in competition with Sybron and Gamlen and traded through these rival companies whilst still employed by Sybron or Gamlen.

15.11 The judge found that the conspiracy would not have got off the ground if Roques had disclosed to Sybron that which, in the judge's view, he ought to have disclosed, namely the activities of his fellow conspirators and fellow employees. Instead Roques had seen to it that nothing was passed to Sybron. He was not prepared to report what was going on and so to risk losing his pension. Before Sybron discovered what was happening, Roques duly retired and started to receive pension payments. When the conspiracy became apparent Sybron claimed that the pension payments

---

[3] But see *Hydra plc and another v Anastasi and others* [2005] EWHC 1559 (20 July 2005) where *Bell v Lever Bros* was relied on as still establishing that, in the absence of fiduciary obligations, employees are not obliged to disclose their own past misconduct or breaches of contract.

were made under a mistake of fact. Sybron sought return of them, alleging that the pension policies had been agreed, and the payments under them made because it was believed that Roques was entitled to his pension rights when in fact he was not: he could have been summarily dismissed for serious misconduct.

In these circumstances, the Court of Appeal upheld the finding that Roques had **15.12** acted in breach of duty in not disclosing the wrongdoing, and had thereby induced a mistake of fact by Sybron, in implementing a pension agreement with Rocques rather than exercising their rights in relation to the agreement. This was so irrespective of the fact that by reporting on others he would also have implicated himself in the wrongdoing.

The Court of Appeal recognized that there is no general rule that in every case an **15.13** employee must disclose any information which he or she has about breaches of duty by fellow employees. Indeed Stephenson LJ (at 127) endorsed the view of the first instance judge (Walton J) that 'the law would do industrial relations generally no great service if it held that such a duty did in fact exist in all cases'.

As to where a duty to report arises, Stephenson LJ explained that: **15.14**

> whether there is such a duty depends on the contract and on the terms of employment of the particular servant. He may be so placed in the hierarchy as to have a duty to report either the misconduct of his superior, as in *Swain v West (Butchers) Ltd.* [1936] 3 All ER 261, or the misconduct of his inferiors, as in this case.

Stephenson LJ also endorsed the view expressed at first instance that: **15.15**

> the duty must, in my view, depend upon all the circumstances of the case, and the relationship of the parties to their employer and *inter se*.
>
> . . . where there is an hierarchical system, particularly where the person in the hierarchy whose conduct is called into question is a person near the top who is responsible to his employers for the whole of the operation of a complete sector of the employers' business—here the European zone—then in my view entirely different considerations apply.
>
> . . . A person in a managerial position cannot possibly stand by and allow fellow servants to pilfer the company's assets and do nothing about it, which is really what Mr. Munby's submissions would come to when applied to the present type of case. Certainly at all events where the misconduct is serious and the servant is not discharged immediately it must be quite obvious that, as part of his duties generally, the senior employee is under a duty to report what has happened as soon as he finds out, and further to indicate which steps (if any) he has taken to prevent a repetition thereof . . . . Of course, this all depends upon the duties of the relevant employee under his contract of service. In the present case there was a well-recognised reporting procedure, whereunder the zone controller, Mr. Roques, was expected to make reports as to the state of matters in his zone every month. It may possibly be argued that in such a case the duty to report was not an immediate duty but one to be fulfilled at the next reporting date; so be it, because even if this is correct no such report was ever made by Mr. Roques to his superiors.

15.16 *Sybron* may therefore be regarded as an extreme case. Roques occupied a very senior position in the employing organization, there was a recognized reporting structure under which he was required to make reports in relation to matters within his zone and there was serious wrongdoing by subordinates within his zone which was clearly a matter which ought to have been dealt with in the monthly reports. Further, the wrongdoing was serious and, as Fox LJ emphasized (at 129E–F), it was ongoing. Indeed Kerr LJ emphasized, in the light of Rocques' reporting duties, that the circumstances amounted to fraudulent breach of his duties in covering up and deliberately concealing the conduct of his subordinates. The case therefore begs the question as to the extent to which the duty to report wrongdoing would extend to less extreme circumstances.

Blowing the whistle on superiors

By senior employees

15.17 Although in *Sybron* the Court of Appeal emphasised that Roques was required to report the misdeeds of his subordinates, it was also his managerial status, with its attendant reporting duties, that was important. As acknowledged in *Sybron*, it is clear from the decision of the Court of Appeal in *Swain v West (Butchers) Limited* [1936] 3 All ER 261 that the duty to disclose misdeeds is not necessarily confined to reporting upon subordinates. Mr Swain was employed as the general manager of the employers' business and as such was responsible for the business as a whole except that he was subordinate to the managing director. However, he followed certain unlawful orders of the managing director involving the selling of incorrectly labelled meat. Swain was asked about this by the chairman of the employers and told that if he provided proof of the managing director's dishonesty he would not be dismissed. Swain provided the requisite information, thereby implicating himself in the fraud. He was then dismissed.

15.18 The Court of Appeal held that Swain could not enforce the agreement to the effect that he would not be dismissed because he was already under an obligation to report the managing director's wrongdoing and there was therefore no consideration for the agreement with the Chairman. The Court of Appeal emphasized that Swain's contract provided that he was to do all in his power to 'promote, extend and develop the interests of the company'. Of itself this might appear unremarkable. However this was in a context where Swain had control of the business and was responsible for seeing that it was conducted honestly and efficiently by all who came under his control.

15.19 More recently, in *RGB Resources plc (in liquidation) v Rastogi and others* [2002] EWHC 2782, a senior employee was held to be arguably under an implied obligation to report the wrongdoing of (slightly) more senior colleagues. The fourth defendant, Mr Patel, was the 'Senior Vice-President—Structured Finance'. RGB's business (against which large amounts of money had been borrowed) was in fact largely fictitious and, some time prior to RGB's collapse, its auditors had resigned because of their misgivings about the audit trail. In an action brought by the liquidators in the name of the company, it was claimed that Patel owed his employer a duty to investigate and report on the wrongdoing of his co-defendants, who were each directors of the company. The question for the Court was whether this case was arguable, since Patel's application was for summary judgment on the basis that it had no reasonable prospect of success. Laddie J dismissed the application and rejected the contention that there was a general rule that, before a duty to report wrongdoing on the part of fellow employees could be imposed, the defendant employee had to be in a supervisory position *vis-à-vis* those employees:

> Whether or not Mr Patel was under a duty to report wrongdoing by his co-defendants is a matter of fact which is dependent upon a multitude of factors, including the terms of his contract of employment, his duties and his seniority in the company. One of the relevant factors will be the nature of the wrongdoing and its potential adverse effect on the company. Where, as here, the alleged wrongdoing went to the very survival of the company, it is more likely that the court would imply a duty to report.

15.20 Laddie J noted that in *Sybron* Stephenson LJ had indicated that such a duty might include a duty to report the wrongdoing of superiors and concluded:

> at all material times, Mr Patel was a very senior executive of RBG concerned with arranging the bank borrowing . . . it is readily arguable that he was under a duty to report wrongdoing or suspected wrongdoing by others.[4]

15.21 The decision also addressed the issues of to whom the wrongdoing should have been reported, and as to whether there was a duty to investigate, which we consider further below.

Less senior employees

15.22 In the case of less senior employees the courts are likely to be much more reluctant to find that there is a duty to report the misdeeds of superiors or colleagues at the same level. Such reluctance is evident in the decision of the majority of the EAT in *Ladbroke Racing Limited v King*, Daily Telegraph, 21 April 1989. Following the dismissal of a manager for gross misconduct, including falsification of records and removing money from the shop, an investigation was carried out into the conduct of his subordinates. This revealed that the subordinate employees had, on their manager's instructions, been involved in serious breaches of the rules including allowing unauthorized betting and failing to reconcile the cash. The employer's rules provided that it would not be an answer to a breach of those rules that this

---

[4] Paragraph 40.

had been condoned by management. The subordinate employees were dismissed for their breaches of the rules and for failing to report the breaches of the rules by their manager. By a majority, the EAT held that the dismissal was unfair. There was no sufficiently clear express term upon which the employer could rely in order to impose an express duty to report the manager's misconduct. Nor was there a breach of the implied term of trust and confidence because this left a discretion in the employees and, in the EAT's view, the employees had not acted unreasonably in choosing not to report their manager's misconduct.

15.23　One difficulty in imposing an implied obligation of disclosure even on junior employees is the difficulty of reconciling this with the emphasis in *Sybron* that there is no general duty of disclosure on all employees. This was emphasized by Pumfrey J in *Cantor Fitzgerald International v Tradition (UK) Limited* (12 June 1998, Pumfrey J). A claim was brought by Tradition for infringement of copyright. It was alleged that Tradition's employed programmers had constructed a computer programme for Tradition which reproduced a code written for the claimant, their former employer. The employees had told Tradition that they were not copying the code. Tradition brought third party proceedings against one of the employees (Mr Gresham) and sought leave to serve out of the jurisdiction. This was refused on the basis that there was no good arguable case. Tradition argued that the employee was under an implied duty to disclose the misconduct of his fellow employees in copying the code. Pumfrey J concluded that this was unlikely to succeed. There was nothing to distinguish Mr Gresham from the ordinary run of comparatively junior employees, he had no managerial responsibility and had worked under the direction of a director of Tradition who was principally responsible for any infringement of copyright.

Blowing the whistle on employees of similar seniority

15.24　In *Sybron* Stephenson LJ took the view (approving a *dictum* of Walton J at first instance that referred to *Bell v Lever Bros*):

> it would be very difficult to have submitted, with any hope of success, that Messrs Bell and Snelling, having been appointed to rescue the affairs of their employers' African subsidiary in effect jointly, ought to have denounced each other.

15.25　This cannot however be taken as setting out any general principle that employees at a similar level or in joint management do not have a responsibility to report as to each other's conduct. First, as also noted by Stephenson LJ, the issue as to whether there was an obligation to report on the wrongdoing of others was not addressed by the House of Lords in *Bell v Lever Bros*, save for Lord Atkins's mention that there might be a duty to report on theft by a fellow employee. Second, the principles in *Sybron*, *Swain* and *Rastogi* emphasize the need to consider all the circumstances, including management responsibilities which might entail reporting duties. *Rastogi* was a case where the defendant was only slightly less senior than the directors he should have reported about. Indeed, rather than being of the same seniority, Bell was Chairman of Niger Company and Snelling was Vice-Chairman and Bell was entitled to a higher salary. In any event, it would be strange if a person in a managerial position had a responsibility to report on wrongdoing both by those more senior (as in *Swain*) and those less senior (as in *Sybron*) but not in respect of those at the same level.

Express terms of the contract

The express terms of the contract may impose a clear obligation to disclose wrong- **15.26** doing. In *Swain* there was some emphasis on the fact of the express duty to 'promote, extend and develop the interests' of the employer. The obligation might, however, arise from the circumstances of the employment irrespective of the express terms. By way of example, in *Sybron* no reliance was placed on any express terms of the service agreement. Further, a similar obligation to that in *Swain* is likely to apply to most senior employees and directors (and would certainly have applied to Bell and Snelling).

Seriousness of the wrongdoing

The nature of the wrongdoing is likely to be highly important and may be crucial. **15.27** If the wrongdoing is sufficiently serious this might of itself be sufficient to give rise to a duty of disclosure to the employer. An employee at any level would surely be expected to report if he/she was for example aware of a serious imminent health risk. In *Bell*, as we have seen, Lord Atkin (at 228) suggested that there might be a duty on employees to protect the employer's property to the extent of reporting a theft by a fellow employee. Although Lord Atkin explained this on the basis of the duty to protect the employer's property, it might also have been explained on the basis of the implied duty of fidelity or on the basis that an employee who kept quiet about such a theft would thereby seriously damage the requisite mutual trust and confidence between employer and employee. Indeed as we discuss below,[5] in *Lister v Hesley Hall Limited* [2001] ICR 665 (HL) some of the speeches in the House of Lords contemplated an obligation even to confess one's own wrongdoing or the consequences of it in the context of particularly serious harm (sexual abuse), and in *The Zinnia* [1984] 2 Lloyds Rep 211 seriousness of harm supported an implied disclosure obligation even in an arm's-length commercial context.

Where, on the other hand, the employee in a managerial position reasonably takes **15.28** the view that the matter can be dealt with without disclosure to a more senior level, then it is obviously going to be more difficult to argue (in the absence of an express term) that there was a duty to refer the issue nonetheless. In the *Swain* case, discussed

---

5 At paras 15.52–15.55.

above Swain was junior to the miscreant and there was no question of his being able to institute disciplinary action himself. However even if a wrongdoing employee has been dismissed or disciplined, there might still be an obligation on the employee taking the disciplinary action to report on the reasons for having done so. If this is not properly communicated the employer might be exposed to the risk of a claim for negligence if it subsequently provides a reference indicating that there is no reason to doubt the loyalty or probity of the ex-employee.

Continuing wrongdoing

15.29   As noted above, in *Sybron* Fox LJ placed emphasis on the fact that the misconduct was continuing, whereas in *Bell* there was only a question as to past misconduct. It is apparent that Fox LJ regarded this as one factor to be weighed in the balance in favour of requiring disclosure rather than as necessarily being determinative. Certainly this may be important. The seriousness of the matter and the urgency of disclosure to the employer will be all the more obvious in the case of ongoing misconduct.

15.30   The lesser importance of past wrongdoing may be seen as reflected in the decision in *Hands v Simpson Fawcett and Co Limited* (1928) 44 TLR 295. The claimant, whose contract with the defendants as a commercial traveller provided that he was to use a car for carrying samples, was convicted of driving the car 'to the common danger' and his licence was suspended for 3 months. The defendants dismissed him, arguing that the misconduct in driving the vehicle justified them doing so, but further that he ought to have informed them that he had previously been convicted of being drunk in charge of a car and dangerous driving. Both pleas failed. Finlay J said that the non-disclosure of the earlier motoring offences did not justify repudiation: this was not a contract like an insurance contract requiring the claimant to state all the material facts.

15.31   There are however dangers in placing too much importance on whether the misconduct is ongoing. Irrespective of whether the misdeed has been completed, an employer might have an interest in rooting out the culprit. The misdeed might be such as to cast doubt on whether the culprit is a sufficiently trustworthy employee and there may be concern not only to prevent the same misconduct in future but also other misconduct. In *Camelot v Centaur Communications Limited* [1998] IRLR 80, for example, the Court of Appeal was faced with an application to disclose documents which would reveal the identity of an employee of Camelot who leaked a copy of Camelot's draft accounts to a journalist. There was no danger of a further leak of the same nature due to injunctions or undertakings already given in relation to that information and the passage of time. However, the Court of Appeal accepted that an employee sufficiently disloyal or untrustworthy to make the initial disclosure could not be relied upon to refrain from revealing other confidential information such as, in the case of Camelot's employees, the names and addresses of lottery winners.[6]

Further it is doubtful whether *Bell* can itself properly be regarded as a case which **15.32** related solely to past misconduct. At the time when the severance agreements were entered into there were no longer any secret profits being made and the jury found that there was no deliberate concealment of the secret profits. However Bell and Snelling held their senior positions at the time when they were engaged in making secret profits. At that time the misconduct was ongoing but it was not held that at that stage there was any duty to disclose the misconduct. If there had been such a duty, then it would have been strongly arguable that Lever Brothers had suffered loss of the sums paid by way of severance payments by reason of the breach of contract by Bell and Snelling.

Conversely it seems very unlikely that the decision in *Sybron* would have been any **15.33** different even if there was only past misconduct, for example because the wrongful competition had been brought to an end. Roques had a managerial responsibility, and also had an express obligation to report matters within his zone every month. As such he was certainly under an obligation to report the misconduct by other employees.

Deliberate concealment

In *Bell* there was a specific finding that the non-disclosure of wrongdoing was not **15.34** fraudulent. As noted above, in *Sybron* Kerr LJ drew attention to this as a point of distinction from *Bell*. In *Fassihi*, Arden LJ also referred to this consideration whilst noting it was unnecessary to decide a point in relation to this.

Deliberate or fraudulent concealment is not however a prerequisite of liability. **15.35** Where, as in *Sybron* and *Swain*, there is an express or implicit positive obligation arising from employment to report wrongdoing, for example due to a senior managerial role of the employee, there would then be a duty to exercise reasonable care and skill in relation to that duty. A breach of the duty might therefore arise from careless oversight rather than deliberate concealment. Further, as Lightman J observed in *BCCI v Ali (No.1)* [1999] IRLR 226, there is a logical difficulty in taking account of deliberate concealment. In the context of considering whether there was an obligation upon BCCI to disclose its fraud to its own employees, Lightman J noted (at para 16) that he could not see how questions of fraudulent concealment could arise unless BCCI was under a duty to disclose. Nevertheless, *Sybron* provides some support for the argument that dishonesty in taking deliberate steps to conceal information, may be relied upon to indicate a positive obligation.

---

6 See, further, Chapter 12 on informants.

Has there been a specific request?

15.36 Similarly it might be important that an employee fails to supply information as to wrongdoing despite receiving a specific request. First, there may then be a positive representation that there is no further relevant information, rather than merely non-disclosure. Second, the obligation of disclosure may then be supported by the claim of a failure to obey lawful and reasonable instructions.

15.37 *Bell* was concerned with the duty on an employee to volunteer information concerning his own wrongdoing. As Lord Atkin put it, if the employer 'wishes to protect himself he can question his servant and will then be protected by the truth or otherwise of the answers'.[7] Employers who require their employees periodically to sign a statement confessing any breach or breaches of duty might conceivably find themselves to be in breach of the implied term of trust and confidence. On the other hand, where the express terms of the contract impose a clear obligation to report wrongdoing this may make a difference; certainly in *Swain*, emphasis was placed on the fact that there was an express duty to 'promote, extend and develop the interests' of the employer. That duty was rather vaguely expressed however: specific reporting duties may be of more relevance in a modern context.

15.38 Termination compromise agreements in respect of senior employees often contain warranties that the employee has disclosed any prior breaches of duty of which he or she is aware. A negative answer in this respect would ground an entitlement to set aside the resulting agreement. Similarly, in order to secure employment in the first place employees will usually be required to give, with varying degrees of formality and detail, information about themselves. Once again it would be open to an employer to avoid any contract formed on the basis of incorrect representations and, unsurprisingly, it has been held that a positive misrepresentation will be a good reason for the dismissal. In *Birmingham District Council v Beyer*,[8] Mr Beyer was a well-known trade union activist. By October 1975 he was convinced (and no doubt correctly so, as Wood J said), that no large employer who recognized him or his name would give him a job unless he could be shunted off into some narrow and restricted field where his zeal could find no outlet. He therefore deceived the Birmingham Corporation into giving him a job by giving a false name and a bogus reference. He was quickly identified and summarily dismissed on the grounds of gross misconduct. He tried unsuccessfully to get other work with the Corporation until, in September 1976, he managed to slip past the barrier and, as an inconspicuous member of a three-man gang, was taken on by the Corporation at a site where his face and his name were unknown to the local site agent. Within a couple of hours the intelligence system disclosed to the individual

---

[7] Above para 15.02, at p 228.
[8] [1977] 1 IRLR 211.

who had dismissed him a year earlier that Beyer was with the Corporation once more. Beyer was immediately dismissed on the ground that he was the man who had grossly deceived the Corporation a year earlier. Reversing the ET, the EAT said that dismissal for the previous year's deception was fair and Beyer could not qualify for a claim for unfair dismissal.[9]

However it is not an essential factor in all cases that there be a specific request or instructions. In *Sybron* there was indeed a duty to make monthly reports and in *Swain* the employee was expressly asked to blow the whistle on the managing director. However it was made clear in *Swain* that the duty to report acts of which Swain was aware and which he knew were not in the interests of his employer arose irrespective of any specific request. This was reaffirmed in *Sybron* (*per* Stephenson LJ at 126G). **15.39**

Is there someone with whom to raise concerns?

In *Rastogi* (see para 15.19) it was argued that there was no duty to report wrongdoing because the directors to whom the matter could be reported were implicated in the wrongdoing. This was rejected on the basis that there were members of the board against whom no accusations of wrongdoing had been made. Laddie J also held that there was an arguable duty to report to the company's auditors. He declined to consider (on the facts of the case before him) whether there was or might be a duty to report to the SFO, the police or the company's solicitors. **15.40**

The decision therefore illustrated that the fact that the concerns relate to the board does not necessarily exclude a duty of disclosure if there is an appropriate outside body with whom to raise concerns. However uncertainty as to with whom a concern should be raised might point against the implication of a positive obligation. A clear whistleblowing policy would help to avoid this difficulty. **15.41**

(2) Implied contractual reporting obligations other than misdeeds

It is also apparent that where an employee has managerial functions he/she may be required to report on matters other than the misdeeds of employees. In *Swain* Greer LJ noted that it was Swain's duty to report acts which he knew were not in his employer's interests. It appears to have been accepted that this flowed from Swain's overall responsibility for the business. Similarly the speeches of Lords Steyn and Hobhouse in *Lister*, to which we refer below,[10] seem to assume a duty to report a sufficiently serious concern to the employer. **15.42**

---

[9] Statutory duties and absolutions from obligations to disclose on job applicants are contained in the Rehabilitation of Offenders Act 1974 Exemptions Order 1975 SI 1975/1023; see Chapter 12.
[10] See paras 15.52–15.55.

15.43   In some cases the obligation may be obvious, such as reporting health and safety problems. However considerable difficulty arises in relation to identifying the precise scope of this obligation. There might also be difficult issues as to whether there is an obligation to disclose wrongdoing outside work which tarnishes the image of the employer. This problem could be partially resolved on the basis that in such marginal cases it would be for the manager in the first instance to assess, acting honestly in what he believes is in the employer's interests, whether the matters were such that he or she could deal with them without troubling superiors, or whether it would be necessary to take such matters further in order to protect the employer's interest. As we discuss further below, this would be consistent with the position in relation to duties of disclosure arising out of fiduciary obligations, where the fiduciary obligation is to act in the way the employee in good faith considers to be in the best interests of the company (*Fassihi*).[11]

(3) Do employees have implied contractual obligations to disclose their own wrongdoing?

15.44   Traditionally *Bell v Lever Brothers* has been taken as authority for the proposition that, whilst an employee may be obliged to blow the whistle on others, there is no obligation for an employee to disclose his or her own wrongdoing. However this was qualified in *Item Software (UK) Limited v Fassihi* [2003] IRLR 769 (HC); [2004] IRLR 928 (CA).

15.45   The directors of Item included Mr Dehghani, the managing director and the defendant, Mr Fassihi, who was the sales and marketing director. A major part of Item's business was the distribution of software products for Isograph. Item decided to negotiate more favourable terms with Isograph. At the same time, Fassihi secretly approached Isograph with his own proposals which involved establishing his own company, RAMS, to take over the contract. Meanwhile he encouraged Dehghani to press Isograph for terms more favourable to Item. Agreement was nearly reached by Dehghani with Isograph but the negotiations failed because Dehghani insisted on terms that Isograph was not prepared to accept. Isograph then terminated the contract by giving 12 months' notice. Item now discovered Fassihi's misconduct, and he was summarily dismissed. Item brought proceedings against Fassihi alleging, amongst other things, that he was in breach of duty in failing to disclose to Item his own wrongdoing in negotiating behind Item's back.

15.46   At first instance Strauss QC, sitting as a High Court Judge, suggested that *Bell v Lever Bros* was authority for the proposition that an employee is not obliged under

---

[11] At para (1); see above para 15.05.

his contract of employment to disclose his own misconduct at or after the time it is committed even where it is in the employer's interest to take action against the employee or to prevent further misconduct or to secure the business or profit which the employee might have misappropriated. Nor is there a duty to disclose the misconduct where the employee later enters into a contract to vary or terminate his employment contract, even if the misconduct would be a material matter to take into account. The judge identified three bases for disapplying the general rule. First, as in *Sybron*, particular aspects of the employee's functions might require disclosure of relevant facts even if this involved the employee owning up to his own misconduct. Second, disclosure might be required in cases of fraudulent misconduct, and third, by virtue of his director's duties, Fassihi was obliged to disclose the secret profit made by appropriating the company's contract. In relation to the first ground, Fassihi's misconduct gave rise to a 'superadded' duty to disclose his own misconduct. He was involved in the negotiations between Item and Isograph and his contractual obligations of fidelity and care required him to disclose important information known to him which was relevant to those negotiations. If he had learned that a third-party rival distributor had been trying to sabotage the negotiations with Isograph then it would have been his duty to tell Dehghani of this: the fact that the rival was himself did not relieve him of the duty. That it would also separately have been in Item's interest to know of the misconduct in order to deal with Fassihi would not have justified the imposition of a duty but Fassihi was bound to disclose facts which were relevant to the ongoing negotiations with Isograph.

15.47 The Court of Appeal upheld the decision but focused on the fiduciary obligations to make disclosure. However, in relation to ordinary contractual obligations, the Court of Appeal commented that *Bell v Lever Brothers* was not authority for the proposition that in no circumstances could an employee be under such an obligation. Arden LJ raised two possibilities:

(a) One route might be to conclude that no logical distinction can be drawn between an employee disclosing his or her own wrongdoing, and disclosing that of others, especially as the latter course might involve disclosing the employee's own wrongdoing.

(b) The second possibility was to rely upon the developing jurisprudence in relation to trust and confidence.

15.48 The superadded duty found at first instance was consistent with the first of these possibilities, essentially applying a similar analysis to that in *Sybron* but in the context of disclosing his own wrongdoing. Further, once the decision in *Bell v Lever Bros* is acknowledged no longer to be a barrier, there is no good reason to draw the philosophical distinction between confessing wrongdoing where no-one else is involved, and reporting on the conduct of others. Rather, when it comes to taking into account the various factors which might be relevant (as indicated above), the fact that the disclosure is only about an employee's *own* wrongdoing would be relevant but might not be decisive. It would be highly important if the reporting obligation arises out of responsibility for subordinates in a hierarchical structure, where it might be more difficult to spell out a duty to report an employee's own misconduct. But it may be that the employee has reporting responsibilities for a particular part of the business of which the employee is a part, in which case spelling out a duty to report the wrongdoing need not necessarily pose a difficulty.

15.49 The second possibility identified by Arden LJ was that a disclosure duty might be developed as part of the obligation not without reasonable cause or excuse to act in a manner likely to destroy or seriously damage the requisite relationship of trust and confidence. This was considered by Lightman J in *BCCI v Ali (No. 1)* [12] where it was held that BCCI was not under any duty to disclose to its employees the fraudulent manner in which it had been carrying on its business even though this conduct put at risk the employees' own reputation. Lightman J was sceptical of the possibility of reliance on the trust and confidence term as a basis for developing positive disclosure obligations. In that case it was argued that the (mutual) duty of trust and confidence involved an obligation on the employer to warn of breaches of contract which might give rise to risks to 'the physical, financial and psychological welfare of the employee'. Lightman J commented (at para 19) that:

> there is indeed much to be said for relaxing the rule which exempts employers and employees alike from any duty to disclose to the other their breaches of duty, for disclosure may be essential to enable the other party to take urgent steps to cure, control or mitigate the consequences of such breach; such disclosure may be necessary to protect the other's 'physical, financial and psychological welfare'. The price of any relaxation is however a high one. The T and C term is a mutual obligation of employer and employee. An employee's conduct may cast a stigma on an employer even as an employer's conduct may cast a stigma on an employee. Far from providing better protection for employees, the development represented by treating the T and C term as imposing duties of disclosure of wrongdoing may well be calculated to create more onerous burdens on employees than on employers. A duty on an employee to disclose eg that he took a day's sickness leave when not genuinely ill or used his employer's telephone or stationery for private use may be thought intolerable. A duty to confess wrongdoing whether on the part of employer or employee may be thought to require standards extravagant and unattainable in the workplace.

15.50 Lightman J referred to *University of Nottingham v Eyett* [1999] IRLR 87 in which Hart J rejected a submission that the implied trust and confidence term included a positive obligation on an employer to advise employees as to how best to exercise valuable pension rights under an employment contract. Hart J emphasized that such a term had potentially far-reaching consequences and that a cautious approach was therefore appropriate. It was necessary to consider how well such a

---

[12] See above, para 15.35.

positive obligation would cohere with the other default obligations implied by law. Lightman J considered that this pointed strongly against a duty to confess wrongdoing. Further the approach in *Eyett* was endorsed by the Court of Appeal in *Crossly v Faithful & Gould Holdings Limited* [2004] ICR 1615. In that case it was emphasized that with most implied obligations it was obvious what an employer was required to do or not do. A proposed implied term to take reasonable care for the economic well-being of an employee was rejected in part because of considerable difficulty in seeing what the employer would be required to do. Equally it might be contended that a duty to disclose wrongdoing would involve considerable uncertainty as to what must be disclosed and to whom, especially as there is no current obligation upon employers to introduce whistleblowing procedures.[13] Nor could this be answered on the basis that matters should be disclosed if they amount to protected disclosures. Aside from the uncertainty that might exist as to what is a protected disclosure, this does not necessarily provide an adequate touchstone since the legislation may cover only minor breaches of obligations as well as serious failures.

It may be countered that, applying the test in *Eyett*, a positive obligation to **15.51** disclose an employee's own wrongdoing where a failure to do so, if discovered, would destroy trust and confidence, coheres well with the scope of the existing positive obligations to disclose the wrongdoing of others. It is the distinction between disclosing one's own wrongdoing and that of others which is difficult to explain. Equally, lack of certainty as to when the duty arises may be said to be no greater than in relation to whether there is a duty to disclose the wrongdoing of others. A duty to confess wrongdoing, whether on the part of the employer or the employee, might indeed require 'standards extravagant and unattainable in the workplace', as Lightman J suggested, if every wrongdoing had to be confessed. Such a duty to confess would become impossibly onerous if it applied in every case, by for example imposing a duty on an employee to confess taking a day's sick leave when not genuinely ill. However there is already a need for the courts to ascertain in what circumstances and in relation to which wrongs an employee might owe a contractual duty to disclose the wrongdoing of others. Whether or not framed under the guise of the implied terms of trust and confidence,[14] the same process of reasoning could equally apply to ascertaining in what circumstances

---

[13] In 33 ILJ 278 Lewis argues against introducing a general duty to report wrongdoing in the light of the uncertainty this would produce, and that instead express terms should be imposed and accompanied by detailed procedures which make clear what is required of employees and provide protection against victimization for those who invoke them.

[14] But if framed in terms of the duty of trust and confidence this would have the limiting effect that the breach would necessarily be repudiatory (*Morrow v Safeway Stores plc* [2002] IRLR 9 (EAT)), whereas at present this may not necessarily be the case: see *Fulham Football Club (1987) Limited v Tigana* [2004] EWHC 2585 at para 103.

an employee should be required to disclose his own wrongs. There would be nothing extravagant in a requirement that an employee who, as in *Sybron*, is under an express or implied duty to report misconduct by reason of his position in the employer's organization, should be under a duty to report his own theft from the employer. Limits on the duty could be identified by reference to such matters as the position of the employee in the organization and the nature of the wrongdoing.

15.52 The irrationality of an immutable principle that employees need not disclose their own wrongdoing was perhaps tacitly recognized by some of the speeches in the decision of the House of Lords in *Lister v Hesley Hall Limited* [2001] IRLR 472. The claimants had been boarders at the defendants' school for maladjusted and vulnerable boys. They were subjected to repeated acts of sexual abuse by a warden, Mr Grain. Many years later a police investigation led to Grain being convicted of a large number of offences against the claimants. The claimants then brought actions for damages for personal injury against the defendants on the basis that they were vicariously liable for the torts committed by Grain. The county court judge felt constrained[15] to accept the defendants' argument that they were not vicariously liable for the acts of Grain because those acts were outside the course of employment. However the claimants still succeeded because the judge accepted that the employers were vicariously liable for Grain's failure to report his intentions to the defendants before the acts of sexual abuse were committed. The Court of Appeal held that if (as was the case in their view) the wrongful conduct was outside the course of employment, then the warden's failure to prevent or report that conduct was not within the scope of employment so as to make the defendants vicariously liable for that failure if they were not vicariously liable for the wrongful act itself. The House of Lords overruled earlier authority and allowed the claimants' appeal that the defendants were vicariously liable for the assaults.

15.53 The issue of liability in respect of the failure to disclose therefore became peripheral. Lord Steyn said[16] that it was not necessary to express a view on the argument based on Grain's alleged breach of a duty to report his sexual intentions or the consequences of his misdeeds, but he noted that this line of argument might require further consideration. If an employee was aware of a physical injury sustained by a boy as a result of his conduct, it might be said to be part of his duties to report this fact to his employers. He questioned why, if that was so, the same would not be true of psychological damage caused by his sexual abuse of a boy? Lord Hobhouse[17] noted that the judge had found that it was part of both the duty of the carers towards the claimants and of Grain towards his employers to report to them

---

[15] Because of the Court of Appeal's earlier decision in *Trotman v North Yorkshire County Council* [1999] IRLR 98.
[16] At paragraph 29.
[17] At paragraph 62.

any incident which was relevant to the health and well-being of the claimants and the Court of Appeal were mistaken in not attaching more validity to this way of putting the claimants' case. There were a whole succession of breaches of the duty to care for the claimant by Grain. The fact that the defendants might not have been liable for some of them did not alter the fact that the defendants would have been liable for the others. All it did was to put the former class of acts into the same category as acts done by some third party but of which, or of the consequences of which, Grain was aware. As the trial judge had pointed out, there might have been a groundsman at the school and he might have been the abusing party; Grain might have discovered what had happened and the distress it had caused to the boy but then had done nothing about it. The defendants might not be liable for what the groundsman did because he was employed to look after the grounds, not to have anything to do with the boys (or—he might have added—might have been employed by someone else). But the defendants would be liable for the breach of Grain who was employed to care for the boys and their welfare. The liability of the defendants might not be so grave or extensive as if Grain had been the abuser himself, but it would in principle be capable of existing. Lord Millett[18] declined to base liability on Grain's failure to report his own wrongdoing to his employer which was an 'artificial and unrealistic' approach. Even if such a duty did exist, on which he preferred to express no opinion, he thought it would be a duty owed exclusively to the employer and not a duty for breach of which the employer could be vicariously liable. The same reasoning would not, of course, necessarily apply to the duty to report the wrongdoing of fellow employees, but it was not necessary to decide this.

The speeches in *Lister*, other than that of Lord Millett, therefore provide some **15.54** indication that an implied obligation to confess own wrongdoing, or the consequences of it, may sometimes arise, and that consideration of factors such as the other duties of the employees and, in particular, the seriousness of the concern, are likely to be important. In the context of arm's-length commercial contracts it has also been acknowledged that duties of disclosure might arise where required to avoid serious harm, even though the disclosure must be by the party in the wrong. In *The Zinnia* [1984] 2 Lloyds Rep 211 there was a claim by shipowners against ship repairers following work done by the latter to reline the stern tube. In carrying out the repair, the repairers were supposed to use six-and-a-half sheets of Tufnol but instead they used only one-and-a-half sheets of Tufnol and five sheets of other material. The ship subsequently, and whilst in mid-voyage, suffered major damage in the engine room leading to dry-docking and, of course, loss and expense. Staughton J held that it had not been proved that the incorrect material

---

[18] Paragraph 84.

had caused the damage but he accepted that the ship repairer owed a duty to inform the owners that part of the material used was not Tufnol. At page 218 he said:

> it is . . . . a novel concept that a contractor who has broken his contract may be under a duty to inform the other party; I know of no authority to that effect and none was cited. At times, self interest will suggest that course, if the defect can be remedied cheaply and might otherwise cause great loss. Motor manufacturers, on occasion, recall cars of a particular model for some modification . . . . But at other times self-interest may point in the opposite direction. In the circumstances of this case, bearing in mind the unlikelihood of the stern tube being examined for four years unless a casualty occurred, the fact that the rules of the classification society had been infringed, and the possible danger to life at sea as well as very valuable property, I consider that [the repairer was] under a duty to inform the owners . . . . I would say that the duty arose from an implied term in the contract, rather than as a part of a general contractual duty of care.

15.55   In practical terms, an obligation on an employee to report his own wrongdoing might have little impact on the conduct of the employee. This was implicit in the concerns raised by Lord Millett in *Lister* as to a duty to confess one's own wrongdoing being 'artificial and unrealistic'. A person who is prepared to carry out a theft, for example, is unlikely to be willing to disclose his own wrongdoing merely because of a contractual obligation to do so. However, this concern was countered by Arden LJ (at para 66) in *Fassihi*, on the basis that 'two wrongs do not make a right: the fact that a director is unlikely to comply with a duty is not a logically sustainable reason for not imposing it if it is otherwise appropriate'. Further, the issue has often arisen in the context of seeking to set aside a contract such as a severance package. Where there has been a misrepresentation there is no difficulty since the employer would be entitled to rescind for misrepresentation. Indeed this remedy could have been open in *Sybron* where the employee wrote misleading letters to his employer. In the absence of misrepresentation it may be necessary (as in *Bell*) to establish a duty of disclosure in order to prevent an employee, who was guilty of gross misconduct but concealed this from the employer, receiving a windfall from a severance payment made by the employer in ignorance of the employee's conduct.

(4) Conclusion as to the scope of the contractual duty of disclosure

15.56   While there will be many cases where there is obviously a duty to disclose misdeeds or other significant concerns, in other cases, as emphasized in *Sybron*, an assessment of all relevant circumstances will be necessary. The following matters, whilst not an exhaustive list, are likely to be of particular significance:

(a)   the express terms of the contract;
(b)   any works rules or policies clarifying the scope of the duty;
(c)   any rules clarifying the procedure for raising concerns and to whom they are to be raised;
(d)   whether there has been a request to the employee for disclosure;
(e)   the seniority of the employee and his or her place in the employer's hierarchy;

(f) whether the employee has managerial responsibilities and the scope of those responsibilities;

(g) by whom any such wrongdoing was committed;

(h) the nature and seriousness of the wrongdoing or other matter to be disclosed;

(i) the degree of connection between the wrongdoing and the employment;

(j) whether the wrongdoing or other matter is of a continuing nature and/or is likely to continue unless reported;

(k) whether there has been deliberate concealment by the employee; and/or

(l) whether the wrongdoing has been by others.

C. Directors and employees who owe fiduciary obligations

In some cases, in addition to their contractual obligations, employees also owe **15.57** fiduciary obligations to their employer which require separate consideration in relation to duties of disclosure. This will obviously be the case in relation to employees who are directors. It may also apply to very senior employees.[19] Less senior employees might also acquire fiduciary obligations arising out of their specific obligations where they can be regarded as having placed themselves in a position where they must act solely in the interests of the employer: see *Nottingham University v Fishel* [2000] IRLR 471.

In relation to the core fiduciary duties, Elias J summarized the position in *Fishel* **15.58** at paras 83–84:[20]

> In *Bristol and West Building Society v Mothew* [1998] 1 Ch 1 at 18, Lord Millett elaborated on this analysis, and identified the duties which classically arise from such a fiduciary relationship:
>
> > 'A fiduciary is someone who has undertaken to act for or on behalf of another in a particular matter in circumstances which give rise to a relationship of trust and confidence. The distinguishing obligation of a fiduciary is the obligation of loyalty.

---

[19] See *Tesco Stores Limited v Pook*, above n 1, where an employee who was 'just below board level' was treated as having fiduciary obligations. In *Shepherds Investments Ltd & anor v Walters & ors* [2006] EWHC 836 (Ch) (12 April 2006) it was submitted that seniority was not sufficient to give rise to fiduciary obligations, and that the analysis in *Nottingham University v Fishel* [2000] IRLR 471 needed to be applied. The court did not need to resolve this as it held that the employee was a *de facto* director.

[20] Directors' duties have been the subject of a recent comprehensive review and analysis in the decision of Lewison J in *Ultraframe (UK) Ltd v Fielding* [2005] EWHC 1638. There is a long line of authorities to the effect that a director/fiduciary has a duty not to take opportunities which arise that might put him in conflict with his or her duties to the company. A director/fiduciary has a duty to exploit every opportunity of which he or she becomes aware for the benefit of the company, the only exception being if the company permits the taking of the opportunity personally after full and frank disclosure and full and informed consent. These principles will often merge or overlap with the duty to disclose wrongdoing. See *Keech v Sandford* [1726] Sel Cas 1 King 61, *Boardman v Phipps* [1967] 2 AC 46, *IDC v Cooley* [1972] 1 WLR 443, *Island Export Finance v Umunna* [1986] BCLC 460. Where a director/fiduciary obtains a benefit in breach of fiduciary duty thus defined, she or he is liable to account *even if* the beneficiary could not itself have obtained that benefit or opportunity; see *IDC v Cooley*.

> The principal is entitled to the single-minded loyalty of his fiduciary. This core liability has several facets. A fiduciary must act in good faith; he must not make a profit out of his trust; he must not place himself in a position where his duty and his interest may conflict; he may not act for his own benefit or the benefit of a third person without the informed consent of his principal. This is not intended to be an exhaustive list, but it is sufficient to indicate the nature of fiduciary obligations. They are the defining characteristics of the fiduciary.'

It is vital to recognise that although the key feature identified is the obligation of loyalty, that has a precise meaning, namely the duty to act in the interests of another. This is the fundamental feature which, in this category of relationship at least, marks out the relationship as a fiduciary one.

15.59 One basis for requiring disclosure of wrongdoing by a fiduciary arises out of the prohibition on making a secret profit. This was considered in *Horcal Limited v Gatland* [1983] IRLR 459 (Glidewell J); [1984] IRLR 288 (CA). The defendant, Mr Gatland, was the managing director of the claimant building contractors. At a time when he was negotiating to purchase the company, he was telephoned by a customer about carrying out some work. Since he was in any event going to be taking over the company, he decided to keep the proceeds of the work for himself, whilst paying the expenses. However the deal then changed and instead of buying the company he entered into an agreement pursuant to which he resigned and was paid for past services. At the time of the agreement he still intended to keep the profits from carrying out the work for the customer, but he did not receive the profits until after the agreement was entered into. At first instance the judge (Glidewell J) held that there was no breach of fiduciary duty at the time of entering the agreement because, although he had decided to keep the profits, he had not yet received them. This finding was upheld by the Court of Appeal. However Glidewell J held that if the profits had been received there would have been a duty to disclose this prior to entering the agreement. *Bell* was treated as distinguishable on the basis that only Lord Thankerton had dealt with duties of a director, and in any event neither Bell nor Snelling were directors of Lever Bros with whom the severance agreement was entered into. In the Court of Appeal Goff LJ recorded the competing arguments as to whether there was a duty of disclosure prior to entering into the agreement, but did not express a concluded view because there had at that time been no breach of fiduciary duty. However he commented that there was much force in the submission for the defendant that:

> putting fraud on one side, there is no general duty on directors or employees to disclose a breach of duty on their part. As I understood his argument he recognised that in the case of fiduciaries, such as directors, if they have failed to account for secret profits which they have made, then their failure to account must necessarily involve in consequence a failure to reveal a breach of duty which had given rise to that duty to account.

15.60 This therefore recognized an implicit obligation of disclosure in relation to secret profits. Beyond this, Goff LJ was sceptical as to whether there was a duty to disclose any breach of duty as this 'could lead to the extravagant consequence that a director might have to make what Mr Powles has called a "confession" as a prerequisite of such an agreement'. [21]

However in subsequent decisions, albeit again in the context of secret profits, an **15.61** obligation of disclosure of own wrongdoing has been identified as arising out of fiduciary obligations. In *Tesco Stores Limited v Pook* [2004] IRLR 618 Mr Pook, a very senior manager just below board level, was found to have taken a bribe. It was accepted by the judge (Peter Smith J) that there was no duty on an employee to disclose breaches of contract which did not involve a fiduciary element, but he held that there was a positive duty to disclosure breaches of fiduciary duty. Had Pook done so his contract of employment would have been immediately terminated by Tesco with the result that certain rights to share options would not have accrued to Pook. Peter Smith J emphasized the lack of logic in an obligation to disclose the wrongdoing of others, but not to confess an employee's own wrongdoing.[22]

Subsequently, in *Fassihi*,[23] the Court of Appeal has emphasized the need to focus **15.62** on the fiduciary obligation to act in what the fiduciary in good faith considers to be the best interests of his company. Arden LJ (at paragraph 41) said that it was not correct that a fiduciary owed a separate and independent duty to disclose his own misconduct to his principal or, more generally, to disclose information of relevance and concern to the employer, because this would lead to a proliferation of duties and arguments about the breadth of those duties. Instead the answer lay in the fundamental duty of loyalty. Fassihi could not reasonably have come to the conclusion that it was not in the interests of Item to know of his breach of duty and he could not fulfil his duty of loyalty except by telling Item about his setting up of RAMS, and his plan to acquire the Isograph contract for himself.

This approach cuts through much of the difficulty with regard to directors. **15.63** However it should not be assumed that there is a duty upon a director to disclose all that the company would wish to know. That is going too far. First, the requirement is one of good faith—it is not a test of whether it is in fact in the interests of the employer that the information be disclosed but whether the employee in good faith considers this to be the case. The scope of a director's duties will also depend upon how the business of the company is organized and what part the director could reasonably be expected to play,[24] and the scope of the director's responsibilities are

---

[21] Paragraph 16.

[22] See also *van Gestel v Cann* (31 July 1987, CA which concerned an agreement between the managing director and the employer's principal shareholder for the managing director to resign and transfer his shares in return for the principal shareholder taking over guarantees of the employer's overdraft. It was said that, in the context of an allegation that the agreement had been entered into without disclosing the managing director's fraud, that 'it is only where the contract being entered into is one "*uberrimae fidei*", or where a fiduciary or similar relationship exists between the contracting parties, that the positive duty to disclose a fraud or a secret profit arises'.

[23] See above paras 15.05 and 15.45.

[24] *Framlington Group plc v Anderson* [1995] BCC 611 at 628H.

therefore likely to be highly relevant. Equally, much may depend upon the nature and seriousness of the matter which it is alleged should have been disclosed. In particular there is no breach of fiduciary duty in a director taking steps preparatory to setting up in competition after ceasing to be a director and accordingly it is difficult to see how a director's failure to disclose such steps could be a breach of a duty of disclosure, notwithstanding that disclosure would be in the employer's interest and the information is withheld out of self-interest.[25] Nor is there any duty upon a director to disclose that he or she has it in mind to act unlawfully and in breach of contract in the future before doing anything wrong.[26]

15.64 Disclosure obligations upon directors in respect of their own and other directors' wrongdoing and anticipated wrongdoing are sometimes an important feature in claims in relation to loss caused by conduct preparatory to setting up in competition with the employer. In *Midland Tool Limited v Midland International Tooling Limited* [2003] 2 BCLC 523, directors of the claimant formed a plan to leave in concert and take many of the employees of the business with them to set up a rival undertaking. At paragraph 89, having referred to *Balston Ltd v Headline Filters Ltd* [1990] FSR 385, Hart J said:

> a director's duty to act so as to promote the best interests of his company prima facie includes a duty to inform the company of any activity, actual or threatened, which damages those interests. The fact that the activity is contemplated by himself is, on the authority of *Balston*'s case, a circumstance which may excuse him from the latter aspect of the duty. But where the activity involves both himself and others, there is nothing in the authorities which excuses him from it. This applies, in my judgment, whether or not the activity itself would constitute a breach by anyone of any relevant duty owed to the company . . . A director who wishes to engage in a competing business and not disclose his intentions to the company ought, in my judgment, to resign his office as soon as his intention has been irrevocably formed and he has launched himself in the actual taking of preparatory steps . . .

15.65 The suggestion of a clear distinction between a director's own wrongdoing and that of others is no longer appropriate following *Fassihi*. In addition in *Shepherds Investments Ltd & anor v Walters & ors*[27] Etherton J said[28] that Hart J may have been 'too prescriptive' in saying that the director's obligation was to resign or disclose at the stage identified by Hart J. Etherton J did however agree with Hart J (at paragraph 128) that it is the duty of a director to inform the company of any actual or threatened activity of another, whether or not he himself is involved, which damages the interests of the company, and whether or not that activity would in itself constitute a breach by anyone of any relevant duty owed to the company. The difficulty lies in deciding when the preparatory steps have reached such a stage as to trigger the duty to disclose.

---

[25] *Balston Limited v Headline Filters Limited* [1990] FSR 385 at 412.
[26] *Horcal v Gatland*, above para 15.59.
[27] See above n 19.
[28] At para 108.

D. Duty to investigate

In addition to the duty to disclose wrongdoing, in some cases it might be possible   **15.66**
to establish that, due to the employee's duties, there is an obligation to investigate
the wrongdoing. This was addressed in *Rastogi* (see para 15.19 above). The judge
ruled that it was arguable that the fourth defendant, Mr Patel, was under an obligation to investigate and make inquiries as to whether there had been wrongdoing within the company. He said that there was no universal obligation to investigate
and the obligation to do so was likely to arise in fewer cases than those in which there
was an obligation to report wrongdoing that the employee became aware of without
investigation. Once again a major factor in deciding whether such an obligation
existed would be the terms of the contract of employment and the duties which the
employee had within the company. Patel was the, or one of the, interfaces with the
auditors, and they had resigned, a very serious step which would not be taken lightly.
He was accordingly under an arguable duty to make enquiries as to whether there was
anything untoward in the way the company was carrying on its business.

The extent to which there may be a duty to investigate is necessarily fact-sensitive.   **15.67**
However to the extent that the case law moves towards development of a duty to
investigate in cases where there are serious concerns, this will throw into sharper
relief the gap in protection under PIDA, where investigations leading up to a
disclosure are not protected: *Bolton School v Evans* [2006] IRLR 500.

E. Interface with PIDA

There might also be an issue in some circumstances as to the extent to which it is   **15.68**
necessary to modify the scope of the duty to disclose wrongdoing, or the remedies
for breach, in the light of PIDA. A worker has a right not to be subjected to a detriment on the ground that he has made a protected disclosure and a dismissal will be
unfair if the reason or the principal reason is that he has made a protected disclosure.
These provisions would not have assisted the employee in *Swain*, notwithstanding
that he was dismissed after disclosure of the misdeeds of the managing director, since
the reason for the dismissal was Swain's misconduct rather than the disclosure.

The position would have been less straightforward if Swain had not himself been   **15.69**
guilty of serious misconduct, but had only been willing to make partial disclosure
of the managing director's misconduct, perhaps due to concern about reprisals or
implicating other colleagues. On the Court of Appeal's analysis, Swain was plainly
obliged to make full disclosure of the wrongdoing. However if he had been dismissed
for failing to make full disclosure, he could now argue that it only became apparent
to the employers that he had additional information to disclose by reason of the limited disclosure he made, and that it was limited disclosure which was the principal

reason for the dismissal. This argument might be made with still greater force if, rather than having been asked for the information, Swain had voluntarily come forward to provide the partial disclosure and therefore exposed himself to the wrath of the employer for not telling more. The tribunal would need to consider, in addressing the 'reason why' question, whether the employer could demonstrate and be able to succeed on the basis that the dismissal was not by reason of the disclosure, but the misconduct in refusing to provide full information.

15.70 Certainly the protection provided by the Act might be undermined if an employer could justify victimization of an employee who comes forward to blow the whistle, but is reluctant to make fuller disclosure, on the grounds that the victimization was not due to the partial disclosure but due to breach of a duty to make fuller disclosure. By way of example, an employee may be under an express contractual obligation to report any incidences of theft of which he becomes aware. Pursuant to that duty, the employee may report that items have been taken from a shop where the employee is based. The disclosure might be made in the hope of encouraging the employer to improve procedures so as to deter a recurrence, but the employee may be reluctant to disclose the identity of the culprits. As a result of the employee's whistleblowing it might therefore be apparent to the employer that the disclosure is only partial, since the culprits have not been identified, and that the employee is therefore in breach of the express duty of disclosure. It is unlikely that the employer would be able to justify disciplinary action against the whistleblowing employee on the grounds of his failure to make fuller disclosure in circumstances where the awareness of the inadequacies of that disclosure have arisen out of the partial disclosure, being a protected disclosure under PIDA. Otherwise this could deter potential whistleblowers from coming forward and substantially undermine the purposes of the legislation.

F. Statutory and regulatory obligations to disclose information

15.71 In addition to contractual obligations of disclosure, the need for employees and professionals to blow the whistle on impropriety has been recognized by the implementation of selected statutory duties of disclosure. For example s33A of the Pension Schemes Act 1993[29] and s70 of the Pensions Act 2004[30] each deal with express duties to report breaches of the law and impose specific duties upon trustees and professional advisers to pension schemes to report what they have 'reasonable cause to believe' are relevant breaches of the law or other matters likely to be of material significance to the Previous Regulators and other regulators.

---

[29] Amended by the Social Security Contributions (Transfer of Functions, etc) Act 1999, Sch 1, para 44.
[30] Formerly s48 of the Pensions Act 1995.

Similar obligations have also been imposed upon auditors of banks, insurance **15.72** companies, building societies, persons authorized to carry out investment business and friendly societies. In each case there is a statutory duty to report to the regulator various matters relating to authorization criteria or (in the case of building societies and friendly societies) criteria of prudent management, which are likely to be of material significance to the regulator.[31] Various statutory duties are also imposed upon employees, amongst others, to assist with or provide information in relation to investigations.[32]

Statutory duties to disclose also apply in contexts other than financial matters. **15.73** Sections 330, 331 and 332 Proceeds of Crime Act 2002[33] make it a criminal offence for those who in the course of their employment acquire information that another person is engaged in laundering the proceeds of drug trafficking, to fail to disclose this to a constable as soon as reasonably practicable. Sections 19 and 20 of the Terrorism Act 2000[34] make similar provision in relation to failure to disclose financial assistance for terrorism. Employees also have a duty under reg12 of the Management of Health and Safety at Work Regulations[35] to inform the employer, and any other employee with specific responsibility for health and safety, of any work situation which the employee ought to have considered to represent a serious and immediate threat to health and safety or a shortcoming in the employer's protection arrangements for health and safety where the problem arises out of that employee's activities at work and has not previously been reported.

Additionally, in some other situations a duty is placed on members of a particular **15.74** profession or group positively to report misconduct or incompetence when they become aware of the same. By way of example:

(a) the duties of medical professionals are set out in the General Medical Council's publication, *Good Medical Practice*. The edition coming into force on 13 November 2006 provides (at para 43) that: 'If you have concerns that a colleague may not be fit to practise, you must take appropriate steps without delay, so that the concerns are investigated and patients protected where necessary. This means you must give an honest explanation of your concerns to an appropriate person from your employing or contracting body, and follow their procedures.'

---

[31] Auditors (Financial Services Act) 1986 Rules 1994 (SI 1994 No.526); Auditors (Insurance Companies Act 1982) Regulations 1994 (SI 1994 No. 449); Accountants (Banking Act 1987) Regulations 1994 (SI 1994 No. 524); Building Societies (Auditors) Order 1994 (SI 1994 No.525); Friendly Societies (Auditors) Order 1994 (SI 1994 No.132).

[32] Section 41 Banking Act 1987; s55(3) Building Society Act 1986; s434 Companies Act 1985; ss177 and 284 of the Financial Services and Markets Act 2000 now provide for the same power to investigate collective investment schemes; ss218, 219 and 235 Insolvency Act 1986; *Re Arrows* [1995] 2 AC 75 (HL).

[33] Formerly s52(1) of the Drug Trafficking Act 1994.

[34] Formerly s18A(1) of the Prevention of Terrorism (Temporary Provisions) Act 1989.

[35] SI 1992/2051, implementing in part Art 13 of Council Directive 89/391 on the Introduction of Measures to Encourage Improvements in the Safety and Health of Workers at Work.

It is notable that this refers to 'concerns' as triggering the duty, whereas the previous edition (at para 27) set out a similar duty as arising where the medical professional had '*grounds to believe* that a doctor or other healthcare professional may be putting patients at risk' (our emphasis). The new edition further provides (at para 44) that: 'If there are no appropriate local systems, or local systems do not resolve the problem, and you are still concerned about the safety of patients, you should inform the relevant regulatory body.'

(b) the Royal Pharmaceutical Society of Great Britain published in July 2005 *Raising Concerns—Guidance for Pharmacists and Registered Pharmacy Technicians*. Para 2 provides that 'a Pharmacist's or Pharmacy Technician's failure to act on concerns could constitute a breach of the Code of Ethics and form the basis of a complaint of professional misconduct'. Further they must not deter someone else from raising concerns and 'must co-operate fully with any formal inquiry into their own, a colleague's or other health professional's fitness to practise'.

(c) since 2002 there has been statutory regulation of the conduct of local councillors by way primarily of a code of conduct. In the Code of Practice issued under the Local Government Act 2000 there is a duty on local councillors to inform on other councillors in respect of breaches of the code. A failure to do so may lead to a complaint being made to the Standards Board for England of misconduct for which a councillor might be admonished, suspended or disqualified from public office.

(d) Prison Service Order No 1215 provides (3.1) that 'all staff working in the Prison Service must report wrongdoing by others in the Service that they either witness or become aware of. Failure to report wrongdoing by others may itself be a disciplinary offence. Anonymous reporters do not discharge their responsibility to report wrongdoing under this PSO.'

15.75 Whilst the various statutory and regulatory duties apply only in certain limited circumstances, they illustrate that where disclosure is particularly important it may be necessary to go beyond a permissive approach.

G. Clarification by a whistleblowing policy

15.76 So as to ensure that employees are apprised of relevant statutory duties of disclosure and in the light of the difficulties that may arise in ascertaining whether there is a common law duty of disclosure in particular circumstances, it will often be in the employer's interest to seek to identify, as part of a whistleblowing policy, the following matters:

(a) which employees are required to disclose misdeeds of others;

(b) in relation to what types of misdeeds and what other matters there is a duty to blow the whistle;

(c) to whom disclosure should be made and what procedures exist for making the disclosure;

(d) the disciplinary sanction for a breach of the duty of disclosure; and

(e) the fact that an employee should not be victimized for making the disclosure. (See more generally Chapter 16.)

Some whistleblowing policies have embraced positive duties. By way of example: **15.77**

(a) The New Charter Housing Trust policy cited in the Shipman Report at para 11.88 states 'As a Home and Community Support Worker you have a duty to report any concerns you may have in the provision of the service to our service users' (para 11.88).

(b) Reed Elsevier has produced a Code of Ethics and Business Conduct which requires workers to report any suspected violations of the code. The Code is extensive, covering outside interests, nepotism, fraud and false statements, bribery and competition violations to name just a few.

Especially where there are likely to be matters which are of particular concern **15.78** to the employer the prudent course would be to provide as specifically as possible for those matters which must be disclosed and by whom. As the EAT explained in *The Distillers Company (Bottling Services) Limited v Gardner* [1982] IRLR 48 (where an employee was disciplined for failing to report a theft of a case of whisky):

> if . . . this is a matter of great importance to the [employer], it would be reasonable to expect in their rules not merely a specific prohibition against misappropriation but a clear obligation placed upon employees who witness such behaviour to report it immediately. It is asking a lot of an employee to require him to report the misdemeanours of his colleagues, but if this is to be the rules it should. . . be very clearly spelled out.

This *dictum* was followed by the Employment Appeal Tribunal in *Ladbroke* **15.79** *Racing Limited v King*, Daily Telegraph, 21 April 1989. Delivering the majority judgment of the EAT, Wood J noted that if it was to be asserted that there was an express duty to report any breach of company rules, such a stipulation would have to be written clearly, if necessary in capital letters in the staff handbook.

In addition to spelling out clearly the obligation to report certain matters, it is also **15.80** likely to be important to identify the disciplinary consequences of failing to do so. This is particularly important if the employer is seeking to impose an onerous or unusual obligation, such as imposing wide obligations on employees with no managerial responsibility, or where the misconduct is to be regarded as gross misconduct.[36]

---

[36] *Dalton v Burton's Gold Medal Biscuits Limited* [1974] IRLR 45 (NIRC).

15.81 There may be significant advantages to the employer in including duties to blow the whistle in addition to setting out whistleblowers' rights and relevant procedures in a policy. In particular:

(a) if carefully drafted it would clarify the scope of the duty of disclosure;

(b) it might encourage a sense of corporate responsibility;

(c) it might encourage employees to bring serious matters to light where otherwise the temptation would be simply to ignore the matter;

(d) it would assist in entitling an employer to set aside a severance package or other agreement entered into with an employee guilty of (non-disclosed) wrongdoing; and

(e) it might entitle the employer fairly to impose a disciplinary sanction that would otherwise be regarded as too severe.

15.82 However the imposition of duties of disclosure is not without problems. In particular:

(a) as noted in *Distillers* any express duty going beyond that which would be implied in the ordinary course would have to be very clearly spelled out. The wider the obligation sought to be imposed, the greater the difficulty there might be in identifying this and then in consistently applying it.

(b) too wide an obligation upon employees carries the risk of the duties being too unspecific, damaging industrial relations and causing friction and suspicion between employees.[37] If a defensive attitude is then encouraged this might undermine corporate responsibility rather than encouraging it.

(c) even if there is a whistleblowing policy incorporating duties of disclosure, there may be difficulty where there is only partial disclosure. If a sanction is then imposed for failing to make full disclosure this might be regarded as being imposed as a result of the worker having made a protected disclosure and therefore be unlawful victimization under PIDA.

(d) the imposition of an obligation to raise concerns in an organization might be seen as suggesting that the organization needs to force staff to raise concerns in fear of the consequences, rather than because they believe it is the right thing to do and that they will be protected in doing so.

15.83 Notwithstanding these concerns, since employees will in any event be under implied duties of disclosure, including statutory duties, a whistleblowing policy could usefully clarify the scope of the duties and the procedures to be followed. In addition it might be that a whistleblowing policy could helpfully identify certain obvious areas where a duty of disclosure is to be required. Careful identification of duties of disclosure might be regarded as complementing PIDA, providing a rounded approach to encouraging the whistleblower to come forward.

---

37 See *Distillers*, above para 15. 78, at p 50 para 17.

PART IV

RULES, POLICIES, PROCEDURES AND PROBLEMS

16

WHISTLEBLOWING PROCEDURES IN THE PUBLIC AND PRIVATE SECTORS: WHY THEY ARE NEEDED AND WHAT THEY SHOULD CONTAIN

A. **Why?**	16.01	
B. **How?**	16.24	
(1) Why should concerns be raised?	16.25	
(2) Who should raise concerns?	16.26	
(3) How should a report be made?	16.27	
(4) When should the concern be raised?	16.28	
(5) Confidentiality or anonymity?	16.29	
(6) Protection	16.30	
(7) To whom should reports be made?	16.31	
(8) Process	16.32	
(9) Detriments, reprisals, victimization and dismissal	16.33	

(10) Advice or assistance	16.34
(11) Monitoring	16.35
(12) Review	16.36
(13) Advertising	16.37
(14) Training	16.38
C. **Public sector**	16.39
D. **Regulators**	16.45
E. **Examples**	16.48
F. **Only employees?**	16.51
G. **Data protection**	16.53
H. **Future?**	16.57

The essence of a whistleblowing system is that staff should be able to bypass the direct management line because that may well be the area about which their concerns arise, and that they should be able to go outside the organization if they feel the overall management is engaged in an improper course.

PCaW advice

A. Why?

A key aspiration of those who supported the introduction of PIDA was that it would encourage employers to develop appropriate procedures to encourage potential whistleblowers to raise their concerns within the employer organization. We have already considered the role of such procedures in defending against

16.01

whistleblowing claims at para 5.35 above. In the course of explaining why there would be no ceiling on compensation for dismissal by making a protected disclosure, the Secretary of State for Trade and Industry, Stephen Byers, stated:

> I hope that businesses, including small business, will adopt best practice to ensure that the measures we are introducing today will never need to be used, because the climate has been created that precludes the occurrence of such wrongdoing.

There is good reason, both in terms of good practice and in terms of the employer's self-interest, for the employer organization, whether large or small, to put in place adequate procedures to address concerns of staff. Encouraging staff to raise concerns first within the organization produces benefits on several levels. Firstly, it fosters a more healthy and accountable workplace where problems are likely to be 'nipped in the bud'. Secondly, should a concern arise it is more likely that the member of staff would raise the matter internally using the procedure set out. This degree of control provides the employer organization with every opportunity to address the concern and minimizes the need for external involvement or the involvement of regulators. Finally, the internal system means that, should a worker make an external disclosure without first having made the disclosure internally or waiting for the matter to be addressed in accordance with the internal procedure, it is more likely that the disclosure will not be a protected disclosure. In some organizations there will be an added advantage in the impression made on those outside the employing organization that good practice is being followed and that any concerns over malpractice are likely to be identified and addressed. This may be important in terms of fostering greater confidence among investors and in the market place, or on the part of an organization with whom the employer organization is tendering for work.

16.02   In this chapter we set out the reasons why a whistleblowing procedure, or more appropriately a confidential reporting procedure, is necessary and what it should contain. The case of *Lingard*[1] sends an important message regarding the use of such procedures and policies. The value of having such a procedure is much reduced if those administering and managing it throughout are not aware of its requirements and the importance of following it, preferably having gained this understanding from appropriate training. The tribunal decision showed a stark contrast between the language of the policy involved in this case[2] and the respondent's treatment of the claimant. Amongst the ET's findings was that one governor 'profoundly disapproved of the Claimant blowing the whistle on her colleague' and that he acted to her detriment because she had been 'disloyal by whistle-blowing'. It is this culture that, for the wellbeing of any organization, must be changed. It is only through training, and the use of policies and procedures, that managers and workers can be educated in the importance to the organization of whistleblowing.

---

[1] ET, Case No. 1802862/04, 16 December 2004; and see Appendix 9, case 68.
[2] The Prison Service Order 1215, which was best practice at the time (albeit not in force).

Under the chairmanship of Sir Alistair Graham, the Committee on Standards in **16.03**
Public Life stated:

> effective whistleblowing is . . . a key component in any strategy to challenge inap-
> propriate behaviour at all levels of an organization. It is both an instrument in support
> of good governance and a manifestation of a more open organizational culture.[3] . . .
> Where an individual case reaches the point of invoking the Act then this represents a
> failure of the internal systems in some respect. Either the employee has failed to
> follow the procedure (for whatever reason) or the procedures themselves have failed.
> In our view, therefore, any case where the Act is invoked should initiate a review of
> the whistleblowing procedures in that organization.[4]

These statements apply to any organization in the public, private or voluntary
sector.

Confidential reporting procedures should ensure that the worker and the organi- **16.04**
zation know when and how to raise concerns. By providing encouragement and
security for those raising concerns, and a structure for them to be raised, it is made
more likely that a report will be raised and if so, raised internally. In terms of the
obvious advantages one only has to consider the *Herald of Free Enterprise* ferry
disaster and the findings of Lord Justice Barry Sheen; the *Piper Alpha* disaster
and Lord Cullen's findings; the Clapham rail crash and Lord Hidden's inquiry;
the Matrix Churchill affair; Beverly Allitt and the inquiry by Sir Cecil Clothier;
Dame Janet Smith's Shipman inquiry; the BCCI inquiry by Lord Bingham; the
Bank of England's report on the collapse of Barings—all of which occurred despite
people possessing concerns and either not raising them or raising them and those
concerns not being listened to.

Likewise the organization should ensure that it is receptive to reports, consistent **16.05**
in the manner of its response to them and that, with a clear structure and guidance
to managers, it has security that reports will be raised internally with the recipient
knowing how to react. Crucially the use of a properly drafted procedure will
also reduce the risk of a damaging external disclosure. Indeed s43G(3)(f) ERA
specifically provides that, in a case where the worker has previously made a disclosure of substantially the same information to the employer, in assessing whether it
was reasonable to make a wider disclosure, the tribunal shall take into account
whether the worker complied with any authorized procedure. Centrally and perhaps most importantly a procedure will ensure that the critical information
reaches those who can act upon it.

---

[3] The Committee on Standards in Public Life published their 10th report[3] on 19 January 2005
paragraph 4.31, Crown Copyright. The Tenth Report of the Committee on Standards in Public
Life, *Getting the Balance Right: Implementing Standards of Conduct in Public Life*, is available on the
Committee's website, <http://www.public-standards.gov.uk> (Cm 6407).

[4] ibid at para 4.35.

16.06 In evidence submitted to the Committee on Standards in Public Life regarding the substance of whistleblowing procedures Guy Dehn and Anna Myers of Public Concern at Work (PCaW), warned:

> of the dangers of a prescriptive 'one size fits all' approach to whistleblowing policies because of the wide differences in the size, function, and constitution of public bodies and because the uncritical adoption of model procedures can lead to an unwitting tick-box approach to governance.[5]

16.07 Notwithstanding the need to be alert to the particular circumstances of the particular organization, PCaW identified four key elements to any procedure:

(1) Ensuring that staff are aware of and trust the whistleblowing avenues. Successful promotion of awareness and trust depend upon the simplicity and practicality of the options available, and also on the ability to demonstrate that a senior officer inside the organisation is accessible for the expression of concerns about wrong-doing, and that where this fails, there is recourse to effective external and independent oversight.

(2) Provision of realistic advice about what the whistleblowing process means for openness, confidentiality and anonymity. While requests for confidentiality and anonymity should be respected, there may be cases where a public body might not be able to act on a concern without the whistleblower's open evidence. Even where the whistleblower's identity is not disclosed, 'this is no guarantee that it will not be deduced by those implicated or by colleagues'.

(3) Continual review of how the procedures work in practice. This is a key feature of the revised *Code on Corporate Governance*, which now places an obligation on the audit committees of listed companies to review how whistleblowing policies operate in practice. The advantage of this approach is that it ensures a review of action taken in response to the expression of concerns about wrongdoing; it allows a look at whether confidentiality issues have been handled effectively and whether staff have been treated fairly as a result of raising concerns.

(4) Regular communication to staff about the avenues open to them. Creative approaches to this include the use of payslips, newsletters, management briefings and intranets, and use too of Public Concern's helpline, launched in 2003 and available through subscription.[6]

16.08 The Committee on Standards therefore provided the following recommendation (R 38):

> Leaders of public bodies should reiterate their commitment to the effective implementation of the Public Interest Disclosure Act 1998 and ensure its principles and provisions are widely known and applicable in their own organisation. They should commit their organisations to following the four key elements of good practice i.e.
>
> (i) ensuring that staff are aware of and trust the whistleblowing avenues;
> (ii) provision of realistic advice about what the whistleblowing process means for openness, confidentiality and anonymity;
> (iii) continual review of how the procedures work in practice; and
> (iv) regular communication to staff about the avenues open to them.

---

[5] ibid at para 4.38.
[6] ibid at para 4.43.

These recommendations are sound for any organization in any sector.

The Committee concluded that: **16.09**

> the statutory framework (Public Interest Disclosure Act 1998) is a helpful driver but must be recognised as a 'backstop' which can provide redress when things go wrong not as a substitute for cultures that actively encourage challenge of inappropriate behaviour. We have recommended that leaders of public bodies should commit themselves to follow the elements of good practice.

Mere compliance with the statutory obligations in relation to protected disclosures   **16.10**
is therefore only the starting position. Although there is no statutory requirement to have a whistleblowing or confidential reporting procedure, public organizations in particular are expected to seek to change the culture in an organization where necessary. A policy and procedure is the start and not the end of an organization's commitment to whistleblowing. Private organizations should also consider these statements closely and consider what their commitment is to a cultural change in their organization.

The Government's response to recommendation R38 of the Tenth Report of the   **16.11**
Committee on Standards in Public Life[7] stated:

> the Government agrees on the importance of ensuring that staff are aware of and trust the whistleblowing process, and on the need for the boards of public bodies to demonstrate leadership on this issue. It also agrees on the need for regular communication to staff about the avenues open to them to raise issues of concern. There is some guidance on raising issues of concern for staff of public bodies but the Government accepts that it would benefit from some updating. It will therefore revise and reissue the Cabinet Office guidance for NDPB staff and board members making clear the requirement for effective and clear procedures for raising issues of concern, as well as the requirements of the Public Interest Disclosure Act 1998.

Policies must therefore be tailored specifically for the particular organization, taking   **16.12**
into account its structure and functions. A properly drafted procedure can ensure that focus is given to specific interests so that particular sources of corruption or inappropriate behaviour can be addressed. For example, a care home is more likely to place emphasis on preventing the abuse of residents whereas a bank is more likely to focus on financial regularity.

Some organizations have for over a decade encouraged the use of confidential   **16.13**
reporting or suggestion schemes to utilize the resource available within an alert and conscientious workforce. In the United States, for example, there exist financial incentives to encourage workers to suggest anything from improvements in production line systems to design faults on aircraft. From 1986 in these cases the defendant is liable for triple the amount of damages suffered by the claimant.

---

[7] Text available at <http://www.cabinetoffice.gov.uk/propriety_and_ethics/documents/cspl10.pdf>.

The case of *United States ex rel. Merena v. SmithKline Beecham Corp*[8] resulted in the largest award to date. The United States received $333,976,266 and the three 'relators' recovered 17 per cent namely $52,049,126 in total.

16.14 Such awards are not available only to US citizens. In the case of *United States ex rel. Copeland v Lucas Western, Inc. et al* filed in September 1993 by Frederick Copeland, the Department of Justice's press release records that 'LWI pleaded guilty to 37 felony counts of making false certifications to the Department of Defense that 35 AMAD and two ADU gearboxes had been fully inspected in accordance with the applicable contractual requirements, when, in fact, they had not'.[9] In a settlement with a payment of $88 million to the United States Mr Copeland, a British machinist at the company, received 21 per cent, namely $19,360,000.

16.15 This is not an approach which has been generally adopted in the UK,[10] and indeed the protected disclosure legislation is expertly framed as being to protect disclosures made in the public interest rather than for personal gain.[11] There is no statutory mechanism for a share of any savings to be made available to a whistleblower. There are however examples of rewards for information, such as the Community Action Trust awards available for police informants. One obvious criticism of a system of rewards for blowing the whistle is that in light of a potentially large-scale fraud, a whistleblower might wait until the fraud has occurred before disclosing the wrongdoing to increase the sum from which they will receive a percentage—especially where any damages are tripled.

16.16 There is nothing expressly to prevent a contractual agreement within an organization to enable internal whistleblowers the opportunity to receive a payment, perhaps even calculated as a share of any losses stopped.[12] It would require careful and specific drafting. In a press release of 16 March 2006[13] the Department of Justice stated that it estimated 'the United States has recovered more than $8 billion since 1986 through *qui tam* suits under the False Claims Act'. This allows private citizens with knowledge of fraud against the US to file a lawsuit on the government's behalf and if the claim is successful to receive between 15 and 25 per cent of the

---

[8] The decision of Donald W van Artsdalen, SJ on 8 April 1998 in the District Court for the Eastern District of Pennsylvania awarding this amount is available on line at <http://www.paed.uscourts.gov/documents/opinions/98D0360P.pdf>.

[9] <http://www.usdoj.gov/opa/pr/Pre_96/October95/523.txt.html>.

[10] But see *Virgo Fidelis Senior School v Boyle* [2004] IRLR 268 (EAT) in relation to the scope for awards of exemplary damages, discussed in Chapter 9.

[11] See the discussion of *Street v Derbyshire Unemployed Workers' Centre* [2005] ICR 97 (CA) in Chapter 4.

[12] But note that s43L ERA provides that only rewards payable by or under any enactment are to be disregarded for the purposes of determining whether a disclosure was for purposes of personal gain, and there may be a danger that the good faith of a whistleblower could be challenged on the basis that the motive for the disclosure was personal gain rather than the public interest.

[13] <http://www.usdoj.gov/usao/mie/press/2006/2006-03-16_rcooper.pdf>.

government's recovery in a case that the government joins. It therefore appears to work and is something larger organizations should at least consider.

There has been research conducted into the number of organizations which have **16.17** whistleblowing policies in place. There are also policies freely accessible through the internet showing that organizations ranging from government departments to small businesses recognize the importance of whistleblowing procedures and have implemented individual policies.

Since 1998 there has been a substantial increase in the number of organizations **16.18** adopting and drafting tailor-made whistleblowing or confidential reporting procedures. Following a limited survey in 1999[14] it was considered that the public sector had a 95 per cent chance of having a procedure set against 63 per cent in the private sector.[15] In 2000 Middlesex University undertook a survey of 600 colleges and universities showing over 91 per cent had such policies in place with 48 per cent coming into operation within the previous 12 months. As for the NHS, after the Shipman Inquiry, a 2003 survey[16] revealed 99 per cent of Trusts had a 'confidential reporting/whistleblowing' procedure.

The reasons for the implementation of such policies may be diverse.[17] However in **16.19** 2006 Professor Lewis concluded that the prominent reasons given in the public sector, where there has been the highest take-up, were for 'good practice or compliance with the law'.[18]

In 2005 PCAW published its biannual report stating that, of 1500 calls to its free **16.20** confidential legal advice line for whistleblowers, 53 per cent were from the private sector and 35 per cent were from the public sector with the remainder coming from the voluntary sector.[19] These figures show a substantial decrease in the number of concerns from the public sector, whilst those from the private sector increased. PCAW's previous biannual report of 2003 (which reviewed 2001 and 2002) and their 2001 report (that reviewed 1999 and 2000) highlight this change. The 2003 report showed that of concerns raised with them, 45 per cent were from the public sector, 42 per cent were from the private sector and 13 per cent were from the voluntary sector. In the 2001 report the public sector accounted for 49 per cent, private 40 per cent and voluntary 11 per cent. It would seem that the public sector, with its more widespread and systematic implementation of whistleblowing

---

[14] 114 organizations.
[15] 'The contents of confidential reporting/whistleblowing procedures in the UK: some lessons from empirical research', Professor Lewis, Middlesex University (2006) (Lewis (2006)).
[16] Lewis, Ellis & Kyprianou 2003: 'A survey of confidential reporting/whistleblowing procedures in National Health Service Trusts'. Middlesex University.
[17] ibid, Lewis (2006).
[18] ibid, page 18, paragraph 1 of conclusions, Lewis (2006).
[19] PCAW's Biannual Review published November 2005.

procedures, appears to be handling more concerns internally without the need for workers to seek advice externally from this specialist charity.

16.21 Underlying these statistics is the principle that a workforce where those in charge understand the advantages and have implemented a whistleblowing procedure will be more likely to realize concerns need to be addressed and handled appropriately and in a pro-active manner.

16.22 Further, if an organization has not even implemented any policy then it is more likely they will not recognize a qualifying disclosure without external advice—and the need for this might not be identified sufficiently quickly. One example is the case of *Boughton v National Tyres & Autocentre Ltd*[20] where the tribunal's finding of a failure to investigate and treat the concern seriously may be linked to the respondent's failure to have a policy or procedure. The tribunal highlighted the absence of a whistleblowing policy or procedure, and proceeded to criticize the investigation and the feedback.

16.23 Finally there remains one final persuasive reason to adopt and to encourage staff to use the whistleblowing procedure. If any worker is considering whether or not to become involved in malpractice, the existence of the policy and its correlation with the likelihood of colleagues raising their suspicions provides a good disincentive, as it increases the chances of the perpetrators being caught.

B. How?

16.24 A policy must be more than a tepid statement issued to tick a box under a compliance regime. The specimen policies in Appendix 5 are, we suggest, useful examples of how organizations in different sectors have approached the drafting of procedures. Whilst these may stimulate options for consideration it is essential that any procedure is written for the particular organization, taking into account its size, its business and its workforce to name but a few variables. Once drafted it may also need a degree of consultation and, if applicable, union agreement. The basics options for consideration are:

(1) Why should concerns be raised?
(2) Who should raise concerns?
(3) How should a report be made?
(4) When should the concern be raised?
(5) Should reports be anonymous or confidential?
(6) The degree of protection?
(7) To whom should reports be made?

---

[20] See Appendix 9, case 21.

(8) Process?

(9) Detriments, reprisals, victimization and dismissal.

(10) Advice or assistance.

(11) Monitoring.

(12) Review.

(13) Advertising.

(14) Training.

We shall now address each of these options in turn.

(1) Why should concerns be raised?

All organizations would be well advised to encourage workers to raise matters.   **16.25**
Encouragement must be clear with statements of support and to prevent retribution.

A whistleblowing policy must provide guidance as to why there exists the protection within PIDA and why workers are being encouraged to raise matters—setting out clearly that they are protected in doing so and that it would be better to raise a concern and to be wrong, than not to raise it at all.

The policy should be clear that all forms of alleged malpractice found to have occurred, be occurring or going to occur will be treated extremely seriously.

It may assist to make clear at the start of the document that matters may be raised in confidence and that such confidences will be maintained as far as possible.

(2) Who should raise concerns?

The legislation covers workers.[21] It would be helpful to spell out in the policy each   **16.26**
person covered within the work of the organization.

There is much to be said for increasing the applicability of the policy to include those external to the organization and those who have critical information. These would include contractors, suppliers, customers and users. It may be that those with whom the employing organization is contracting could be included and specifically sent a copy of the procedure. See further paras 16.51–16.52 below.

Depending on the organization it may be prudent to open up the confidential reporting system to members of the public. For example the City of London's procedure states it:

> . . . applies to all members of the public, employees, building contractors and those contractors working for the City of London on City of London premises, for example, agency staff, cleaners and caterers. It also covers suppliers and those providing

---

[21] See Chapter 6.

services under a contract with the City of London in their own premises, for example care homes. It does not apply to Police Officers as they have a separate, specific procedure to follow.[22]

(3) How should a report be made?

16.27 Is it necessary for all reports to be in writing? There is much to be said for a confidential hotline for matters to be discussed, initially confidentially, before reports are written, perhaps whilst matters are either imminent or fresh in the mind of the worker. The person who will receive such phone calls must, however, be trained and be prepared to listen to concerns. This hotline can be used to assist the individual. Obviously records will need to be maintained of those who call and what they state and if the matter appears appropriate the worker should be encouraged to provide written statements if time permits.

When reports are to be made in writing many organizations use the same route for confidential reports as they do for grievances. We believe that an alternative route should be seriously considered, with confidential reports considered as materially different to grievances.

A large organization might suffer delay or reports could be suppressed if they have to pass through a large cumbersome hierarchy. The best analysis is to consider how long the organization would want a very serious allegation to take for it to get to someone who can act upon it. Whilst matters can be referred back down, a simple three-stage process has many advantages. Restricting the number of people who are aware of the report and its contents in turn restricts those capable of meting out detriments—and the defence to allegations of detriments is made easier. It ensures that the recipient will be better able to recognize serious concerns requiring immediate action and those that can be investigated more rigorously. It will ensure a practical similarity in treatment of the reporter. Finally it reduces the need for all line managers to be trained on how to respond to reports as opposed to how they respond to grievances. Three stages also provide the opportunity for a decision, a review of that decision and an appeal, if necessary.

Mention should be made that if the employee chooses the wrong route or the wrong person with whom to raise their concern that they will not be disciplined. It must not be forgotten that a policy is there to encourage openness and accountability.

(4) When should the concern be raised?

16.28 PIDA covers past acts, present acts and future acts. Surprisingly some procedures neglect to address this important issue. It must be clear that the procedure covers them all.

---

[22] <http://www.cityoflondon.gov.uk/Corporation/about_us/departmental/AntiFraud_Corruption_Strategy/whistle_blowing_policy.htm>.

The users of the procedure need to know when it is they should use the procedure. Given that PIDA protects for internal disclosures those who possess a reasonable belief tending to show a relevant failure, even though the belief may prove to be wrong,[23] guidance should be provided to workers as to when they should raise concerns, perhaps giving examples and expressly stating that:

(a) they need not be certain, and

(b) they will not suffer any consequences of raising a mere suspicion[24] provided it was not done maliciously or otherwise in bad faith.

Some organizations and professional bodies make it a requirement that concerns be reported (as discussed in Chapter 15). If this is the case in the organization it may be that the policy should distinguish specifically between those (usually) professionals and other workers to whom the requirement does not apply.

Examples at this stage are crucial for the worker to understand how much belief they should have before they report concerns. It may be that merely overhearing allegations will be considered sufficient—provided they have some evidential credibility as opposed to mere 'tittle tattle'.

It is important that clear guidance explains that the confidential reporting procedure is distinct and separate from the grievance procedure. Whilst the protection extends to breaches of the worker's contract, such a matter would normally be raised as a grievance.

(5) Confidentiality or anonymity?

16.29 Anonymous reporting is not recommended and is often considered the 'cloak of the malicious'. Whilst anonymity can provide some assurance to the informant it cannot provide protection to the worker under the protected disclosure legislation— if the informant was anonymous how can they establish they suffered a detriment, or were dismissed on the grounds of the disclosure if they were unknown? Most importantly, an anonymous informant might not provide sufficient information for action to be taken. So whilst there are organizations that have anonymous telephone numbers where messages may be left, we do not encourage this method. Finally the culture that is to be fostered is one where the informant raises a concern because it is right to do so. The need for an anonymous reporting line may be symptomatic of something wrong within the organizational culture.

---

[23] See Chapter 3.

[24] This sets the threshold lower than the test for a qualifying disclosure, but we suggest that is appropriate in order to develop a culture where workers are encouraged to raise concerns internally.

In the US, the Sarbanes–Oxley Act of 2002 (SOX) requires the Audit Committee of publicly held US companies, and their EU-based affiliates, and non-US companies listed on one of the US stock markets, to establish procedures for 'confidential, anonymous' reporting by employees of concerns in relation to accounting and auditing matters (s301(4) SOX). There are equivalent provisions, providing for anonymous reporting, in the Nasdaq and New York Stock Exchange rules.

This was considered in a (non-binding) opinion adopted on 1 February 2006 by the 'Article 29 Data Protection Working Party', which is a working party consisting of data protection commissioners in the EU. The Working Party was firmly against encouragement of anonymous reporting, and also noted that it raised a problem in relation to the requirement that personal data should only be processed fairly. It recommended that if anonymous reports are investigated, there should be an emphasis on doing so with greater speed than other complaints because of the risk of misuse.

Whilst anonymous reporting is to be discouraged, confidentiality is an important principle. The procedure or policy must explain what 'confidential' means practically to the worker and to the recipient of the information.

It may be that the organization can commit not to disclose the name of the informant unless necessary. In reality, however, the likelihood is that if disciplinary action is to be taken then the informant's name may be disclosed.

What is important is that if the informant's name is to be disclosed the informant must be informed that it is going to be. The situation in *Boughton,* where information about the manager was disclosed on a tape to an area manager, only for the tape to be returned to the informant days later by the perpetrator, can only undermine the worker and his confidence in the employer.

(6) Protection

16.30 It is crucial that an organization makes a clear statement in support of concerns being raised and that it will protect the whistleblower against suffering detriments as a consequence. Such a statement would also be well advised to include a message that even if the concern raised in good faith is wrong, the reporter will not suffer as a consequence. There should be strong statements that best endeavours will be used to prevent victimization or retribution and that such action will be considered gross misconduct. Some discussion that all acts of detriment will be considered as gross misconduct will support a worker and may also serve as a deterrent to those considering such acts.

Some organizations have provided protection by way of an undertaking from the head of the organization, for example the Chief Executive's undertaking within the Higher Education Funding Council for Wales set out in their Whistleblowing Policy.[25] This states:

> Provided that a member of staff raises a Qualifying Disclosure in good faith, and follows the procedures set out in this policy, the Chief Executive . . . makes the following commitment:
>
> > That the member of staff will not be disciplined or subjected to any other detriment to his or her career as a result, even if the concern turns out to be mistaken.

(7) To whom should reports be made?

Professor Lewis notes that the majority of organizations in his survey made provision for reports to be initially to line managers.[26] **16.31**

As stated above, we believe that this is not necessarily the most effective means or route for a procedure to adopt, especially within large organizations. It is beneficial to have a specific route for raising such concerns, distinct from that for raising grievances. One of the recommendations of the Article 29 Working Party (see para 16.29) was to have a separate dedicated unit to receive the report. This reduces concerns as to fairly processing personal data as fewer people have access to the data and those to whom the report is made may develop expertise on dealing with such matters. One additional reason to those set out above is that workers are used to making statements and/or complaints to their line manager. Practically speaking, if they are to report to someone with whom they do not have a working relationship, they are more likely to consider them independent. They are more likely only to refer concerns about which they have reasonable grounds for suspecting malpractice. It distinguishes the confidential reporting system from all the other grievances and personal matters which line managers are required to address. Finally, it also prevents a line manager from suppressing or preventing a concern from being raised further.

Some larger private organizations may have non-executive directors with whom concerns might be raised. In public organizations such as schools, governors have been used. All procedures should finish with the most senior person in the organization being a capable, if not final, recipient of a report.

If there are prescribed bodies applicable to the organization (eg government departments), reference should be made to them in the policy and procedure and the circumstances when concerns may be raised with them. For example, some NHS Trusts have specifically enabled staff to raise matters direct with the Department of Health.

---

[25] Paragraph 22, Version 4, September 2005.
[26] 'The contents of confidential reporting/whistleblowing procedures in the UK: some lessons from empirical research'—Professor Lewis, Middlesex University (2006) paragraph 7 of its conclusions.

If there is a particular regulator applicable to the organization then the circumstances when reference should be made should be set out to the workers (if not at all times). For example, the FSA's whistleblowing policy provides 'or if you feel unable to talk to anyone internally for whatever reason, you can contact: the nominated official at the Treasury'[27] going on to provide his name, contact details including telephone and e-mail address.

(8) Process

16.32 We advocate that, in a manner similar to a disciplinary procedure, the confidential reporting procedure should be prescriptive as to the process to be followed. It should be clear as to when a step should occur and there should be time estimates for each step (though this may need to be considered in the specific circumstances of the particular report).

Set objectives should include:

1. Who reports to whom and how.
2. The investigation:
   a. Who investigates? It is sensible to have a named person or level of individual responsible for the investigation. The person who is responsible for the investigation need not be the person who received the information and there is good reason to separate the two.
   b. What do they investigate? The initial investigation would usually be into whether there is any evidence to support the concerns raised. The investigation should not be into who is responsible for the malpractice 'at this stage' but whether there is malpractice as reported. Focusing on this issue ensures the organization considers the malpractice and not the personalities involved.
   c. How should it be investigated?
      (i) It may be that there can be two stages of investigation. The first stage could be to find if there is any prima facie evidence of the malpractice reported. Once malpractice is thought to exist then a second stage can occur where the personalities are then investigated. Some malpractice can be investigated initially without the need to interview other staff—if for example one is dealing with financial malpractice there should be independent evidence that supports the report. Other circumstances, such as the abuse of one resident by a member of staff, are clearly more difficult. Any investigation however should be in a manner containing procedural safeguards similar to a disciplinary investigation.

---

[27] © Financial Services Authority.

(ii) Some investigations may need to take place without the alleged perpe-trator being aware, sometimes with external involvement from other organizations such as the police. The procedure should explain that this may occur to determine whether any grounds for further investi-gation have been found.

(iii) It should be stated that sometimes it will be necessary to suspend workers on full pay during the investigation and that such a suspension is not a disciplinary act.

d. To whom do they report?

(i) Depending on the size of the organization it is necessary to make it clear to whom any investigation will report.

(ii) What will be their remit? For example if the initial investigation is restricted to the malpractice it might be that the reporting process starts with a feedback to the nominated recipient of the information. If there appears to be malpractice then it may be the matter is then referred for disciplinary action, if necessary, or for further investiga-tion into who is the perpetrator.

(iii) It is essential that whoever makes the decision to continue or discon-tinue any investigation is capable of accounting for that decision and that some explanation is provided to the worker who made the disclo-sure. Such feedback is then capable of a review or appeal and provides another opportunity for the allegation to be scrutinised.

3. Decision:

a. Any investigation will involve a conclusion. There are three possible results: insufficient evidence and a further investigation; insufficient/no evidence and no further investigation; evidence of malpractice or other relevant failure.

b. This decision must be reported to someone or a body responsible for this procedure.

c. The decision needs to be communicated to the person who made the dis-closure to enable them to provide feedback or appeal or seek a review.

4. Feedback?

a. It is important that workers receive feedback on their concerns. If no feed-back is given but there is good reason for the organization not taking the report further, the worker is better able to make an external disclosure and be protected under PIDA.

b. The feedback must maintain confidentiality in any information regarding any sanctions imposed.

5. Satisfaction:

a. The person making the disclosure must be provided with an opportunity to challenge or review any decision not to take matters further. For any such challenge to be credible it would be recommended that the reporter receives a decision with reasons.

b. If a three- or two-stage process is adopted this enables a review and/or an appeal.

Any organization would be best advised to ensure that the minimum process adopted is that of the statutory grievance procedure. Given that tribunals so far have been quick to hold that mere letters of complaint should be treated as a grievance,[28] it is highly likely that a report made under a confidential reporting procedure might be considered a grievance. One alternative would however be to make it clear that the confidential reporting system is not to be used for grievances. However such a statement would not prevent a tribunal from holding that one is.

(9) Detriments, reprisals, victimization and dismissal

16.33 Above we have stated the importance of clear statements against detriments being caused in response to whistleblowing and the need perhaps to have detrimental treatment classed as gross misconduct or a dismissable offence.

There must however be within the procedure some advice to the worker as to what they should do if they consider they have suffered or are suffering a detriment. It may be they are referred directly to the grievance procedure. However there is some sense in keeping such matters within the remit of the confidential reporting system.

The worker must be asked to provide evidence and the necessary particulars: what, when, how and who is responsible. A simple form would focus the mind of the person who believes they are suffering a detriment.

Likewise, there must be compliance with the statutory grievance procedure: a process of investigation, a hearing and a decision with a right to appeal.

It is considered that by continuing to keep confidential reporting matters within this defined procedure those responsible for dealing with the matter are more likely to be concerned and aware of the need to ensure that, if detriments have been suffered, they are quickly stopped and remedial action taken, or if they are considered not to have occurred for the worker to feel that their concerns have been taken seriously and they have been listened to sympathetically. It is likely that those involved in the confidential reporting procedure will be better able to meet the requirements of PIDA and to better prevent an external disclosure.

(10) Advice or assistance

16.34 Those reporting should be enabled to attend meetings and hearings with a colleague or a union representative. A good procedure would also provide the worker

---

[28] See eg *Shergold v Fieldway Medical Centre* [2006] ICR 304 (EAT); *Draper v Mears Limited* [2006] IRLR 869 (EAT).

with some assistance as to whom they can contact internally and, if necessary, externally for assistance. Advice can be non-committal and such advice will be confidential. Reference should be made to the possibility of union assistance. If possible, especially where there is a recognized union, there should be a union contact name provided. The workers should be informed of their right to take independent legal advice.

Reference may be made to PCaW who advocate the raising of concerns internally and provide free confidential advice to prospective whistleblowers. Some NHS Trusts in the UK specifically refer to their existence in their policy.

(11) Monitoring

The following would appear relevant issues that require some form of monitoring   **16.35**
if the system and its effectiveness are to be considered for improvement. This monitoring can be undertaken each time a concern is raised by a form in an anonymized format that could contain the following:

1. How were they aware of the procedure?
2. Did they seek advice before raising a report?
3. Did they raise matters orally or in writing?
4. Had they raised the matter previously and if so to whom and what was the outcome?
5. What is the subject matter of the report? It may be that options are given here, ie by reference to the categories of relevant failure in s43B ERA.

The following information should also be maintained:

1. How long was the investigation?
2. What was the outcome?
3. Was the worker making the disclosure satisfied with that outcome?
4. Have they raised any matters relating to detriments?

(12) Review

It may be that a board will want a review of the policy annually or biannually to   **16.36**
consider the effectiveness of the policy. Warning signs will be that the procedure is not used or that it is used wrongly by staff.

(13) Advertising

A whistleblowing policy is useless unless it is known about. PCaW suggest   **16.37**
novel methods such as the use of the employer's payslips to continually remind workers of the procedure. It is assumed that any procedure would be included within any induction checklist.

Workers are often given much information in staff handbooks, but this documentation tends to be read only when the worker encounters a problem. Whilst we advocate the distribution of procedures for each and every employee, we recognize the ease of access to intranet procedures. This can have its drawbacks too: our experience is that when an employee considers what they should do in response to their concern, unless the events are imminent and dangerous, the options are most often considered and decisions made away from the workplace. If an employee is not also sent such a procedure he may not have it available at the crucial moment.

The successes of the policy should be publicized internally (without compromising the confidentiality of the report).

A good policy can also be highlighted to customers or clients. This highlights the organization not only as open, but as perhaps a safer organization with which to contract or deal.

(14) Training

16.38 Training of those to whom concerns will be reported should be considered essential. Training of managers and of the workforce as to the advantages of confidential reporting, whilst expensive, can be one of the most effective means of ensuring a change in a culture at an organization. Some organizations ensure that one person is trained to a sufficient level that they can then in turn train others.

C. Public sector

16.39 The Audit Commission has reported that:

> only 50 per cent of the employees in the local government and health bodies which have used the Commission's self-assessment tools were aware of the Public Interest Disclosure Act, and the protection this affords an employee making a disclosure concerning fraud and corruption.[29]

16.40 The standing terms of reference of the Nolan Committee, established in 1994, which later became the Committee on Standards in Public Life are:

> to examine current concerns about standards of conduct of all holders of public office, including arrangements relating to financial and commercial activities, and make recommendations as to any changes in present arrangements which might be required to ensure the highest standards of propriety in public life.

---

[29] The Tenth Report of the Committee on Standards in Public Life, *Getting the Balance Right: Implementing Standards of Conduct in Public Life*, is available on the Committee's website, <http://www.public-standards.gov.uk> (Cm 6407).

In their third report the Committee recognized[30] the importance of whistleblowing. **16.41**
The Committee published their tenth report[31] on 19 January 2005. As set out
above this report again underlines the importance of whistleblowing procedures
in the public sector.

It would now appear remiss for a public sector employer not to have a proper **16.42**
procedure. Where however attention is required is not in the writing of the procedure, but on the startling evidence of the Audit Commission as to the knowledge
of the workforce of the existence and purpose of any such procedure.

At present employment tribunals have a statutory requirement to consider **16.43**
compliance with ACAS codes of practice, albeit this is relevant but not decisive.
There is also scope, however, for tribunals to be shown the above significant
statements of the need for whistleblowing procedures and to take into account
a failure to implement an appropriate procedure as probative on matters such as
why an organization failed to investigate or failed to take a concern seriously.

Some sectors have policy packs prepared by the relevant government department. **16.44**
For example, the Department of Health in 2003 included the following:

- introductory booklet explaining what whistleblowing is and a practical summary
  of the Public Interest Disclosure Act 1998 (PIDA);
- an implementation guide to help organisations successfully introduce whistleblowing policies;
- tools to help with the implementation of policies (including an implementation
  checklist, draft policy and PowerPoint presentation for staff);
- a summary of cases brought under PIDA (including a small number of NHS
  ones); and
- HSC 1999/198. [Health Service Circular]

The policy pack also includes copies of two posters. The posters have been designed
so that they can be adapted by NHS employing organizations to include details of
named individuals that staff can approach to discuss concerns in confidence.[32]

D. Regulators

Guy Dehn of PCaW provided evidence on the adoption by regulators of whistle- **16.45**
blowing procedures to the Committee on Standards in Public Life record:

> He drew our attention to variable practice on whistleblowing, both among regulators
> and across the public sector. We were told that 'there are a lot of differences' in the way
> in which regulators regard whistleblowing. While some, like the Audit Commission

---

[30] *Standard of Conduct in Local Government*, Third Report of the Committee on Standards in Public
Life, July 1997, Cm3702–1, page 48 of the Report.
[31] See above n 29.
[32] Crown Copyright.

and the Financial Services Authority, have embraced the concept and communicated it very effectively, others have not. [As a consequence the Committee made the following recommendation]

Recommendation 37:
All regulators should review their procedures for handling whistleblowing by individuals in bodies under their jurisdiction, drawing upon best practice (for example the Audit Commission and Financial Services Authority).

16.46 The Government's response to the Tenth Report of the Committee on Standards in Public Life[33] responded to Recommendation 37 stating:

the Better Regulation Executive, set up following recommendations of the Hampton Report *Reducing Administrative Burdens* and the Better Regulation Task Force Report *Less is More*, is considering how this recommendation might be addressed as they consider the recommendations of both reports concerning regulators.[34]

16.47 As stated above it is recommended that the policy identifies the relevant regulators for the organization. If the regulator is not statutorily prescribed then the organization should consider whether it wants to provide access to a body which may not be required under the Act, and may not provide protection under s43F ERA, albeit there is an argument for some protection under contract law.[35] As discussed in Chapter 5, the effect of permitting disclosure to an outside body may be that the disclosure is regarded as made under an authorized procedure within the meaning of s43C(2) ERA.

E. Examples

16.48 In Appendix 5 there are examples of policies from various sectors.

16.49 There have been several Employment Tribunal cases where the failure to follow an established procedure has been mentioned by the tribunal. In *Holmes v Grimsby College*[36] comment is made on the failure to follow the procedure; however, 'that does not derogate that he complied with the statutory format in disclosing that information'. A procedure ought therefore to set out the elements of PIDA.

16.50 In *Jeffrey v The London Borough of Merton*[37] the Employment Tribunal specifically found that the disclosure of allegations (in relation to recruitment) firstly on the internet and not first through the respondent's whistleblowing procedure meant the disclosure was not protected. This is a helpful reminder that where a procedure exists and it is not used by the worker a tribunal will look for an explanation.

---

[33] Text available at <http://www.cabinetoffice.gov.uk/propriety_and_ethics/documents/cspl10.pdf>
[34] Crown Copyright.
[35] See eg *In re A Company's Application* [1989] 1 Ch. 47.
[36] See Appendix 9 case 59.
[37] See Appendix 9 case 62.

F. Only employees?

As discussed above there is much support for the extension of whistleblowing **16.51** procedures to those external to an organization, ensuring that regardless of the relationship of the contracting parties, a contractor can be certain matters will be brought to their attention. This is of particular use in the public sector, for example by local authorities. Given the number of agencies and organizations providing services for and to local authorities, it would make commercial sense to ensure that those individuals knew of the local authorities' procedures, if not making it a condition of the contract with the organization providing goods or services to the authority.

In the private sector the case of *Montgomery v Universal Services Handling Ltd* **16.52** *(in Liquidation)*[38] is a good example. Here, there were real problems encountered by staff trying to raise their concerns and, despite efforts to prevent wrongdoing, the critical information did not reach the organization most affected by the breach until long after the complaint was first made. In this particular case it was not until American Airlines became aware that up to 300 tons of freight was being presented as 'x-rayed', when in fact it had not been, that action was taken. Putting aside the grave security issues, this is an example of why the use of contractual confidential reporting lines between contracting organizations (Universal Services) and the contractor (American Airlines) should be seriously countenanced. These might have been avoided if there had been a contractual requirement that staff working upon contracts have received a copy of a whistleblowing policy, and it would make it more likely that those contracting to provide services were more reluctant to cut corners or to mislead the client for commercial gain. At the very least, however, a condition of a contract must be that the contractor has a whistleblowing policy.

G. Data protection

As noted above (para 16.29), in its opinion of 1 February 2006, the Article 29 **16.53** Data Protection Working Party addressed issues as to the compatibility of whistleblowing policies with EU data protection rules. The opinion was limited to the fields of accounting, internal accounting controls, auditing matters, fight against bribery, banking and financial crime, but the principles set out may be regarded as having wider application to cases where (as will usually be the case) processing of personal data is involved.

---

[38] See Appendix 9 case 76.

16.54 Article 7 of Directive 95/46/EC sets out the legitimate purposes for which personal data may be processed. The Working Party concluded that article 7(f) was likely to apply, which provides that personal data may be processed if necessary for the purposes of the legitimate interests pursued by the data controller or by the third party or parties to whom the data is disclosed, although this requires a balance with the fundamental rights and freedoms of the data subject.[39] A different rationale would be required where processing of sensitive data is involved—which includes personal data consisting of the commission or alleged commission of any offence by the data subject (s2(g) Data Protection Act 1998 (DPA)). The potential circumstances in which the data may be processed are set out in the Data Protection (Processing of Sensitive Personal Data) Order 2000 (SI 2000/417). The most likely basis is Article 2(1) of the Schedule to SI 2000/417. This applies where the processing (a) is in the substantial public interest, (b) is necessary for the purposes of the prevention or detection of any unlawful act and (c) must necessarily be carried out without the explicit consent of the data subject being sought so as not to prejudice those purposes.

16.55 Pursuant to Directive 95/46/EC, (a) personal data must be processed fairly and lawfully, (b) personal data must be collected for specified, explicit and legitimate purposes and not be used for incompatible purposes, and (c) the processed data must be adequate, relevant and not excessive in relation to the purposes for which they are collected and/or further processed. Having regard to these principles, the Article 29 Working Party emphasized the need not only to ensure protection for the person making the report, but also for the person subject to the allegations.

16.56 Particularly with this in mind, the Working Party set out a number of proposals:

1. Anonymous reports should not be encouraged but confidentiality should be maintained (see para 16.29 above).
2. A possible limit on the number of persons entitled to report alleged improprieties or misconduct through whistleblowing schemes or who may be incriminated through the scheme. (We doubt that this is a helpful restriction, especially if the scheme does not ordinarily proceed on the basis of anonymous reports.)
3. The permissible subject matter of the report should be tied to the corporate governance issues for which the report is established. (This proposal is to be seen in the context of the limited ambit of the Working Party's opinion. In practice the permissible subject matter of the complaint may be limited by being tied to the heads of relevant failure in s 43B ERA, and by personal grievances being dealt with separately as part of the grievance procedures.)

---

[39] This corresponds with paragraph 6 of schedule 2 of the Data Protection Act 1998.

4. Personal data processed by a whistleblowing scheme should be deleted promptly and usually within two months of the completion of the investigation unless legal proceedings or disciplinary measures are initiated against the incriminated person or the whistleblower.
5. Personal data relating to matters found to be unsubstantiated should be deleted without delay.
6. Data subjects should be informed about the existence, purpose and functioning of the scheme.
7. The person accused in the report should be informed by the person in charge of the scheme as soon as reasonably possible after the data concerning them is recorded. By way of exception, where there is substantial risk that such notification would jeopardize the employer's ability to investigate effectively, notification may be delayed for as long as this risk exists.
8. The scheme should take the necessary steps to ensure that the information disclosed will not be destroyed.
9. The scheme should ensure compliance with the right, including the right of the person subject to the complaint, to access to the data and the right to rectify incorrect, incomplete or outdated data. However this should not include access to the identity of the person making the report except in cases of maliciously making a false statement.
10. A specific unit should ideally be set up within the employing organization dedicated to handling whistleblowers' reports and leading the investigation. It should comprise a limited number of specifically trained and dedicated people, and should be separate from other parts of the company including the HR department. There should also be steps to ensure that concerns within the ambit of the scheme are specifically transmitted to this group.
11. Where the scheme is provided by external service providers, there should be appropriate measures to ensure that the providers adopt similar safeguards.

H. Future?

With the need now to have raised a grievance, and to have enabled the respondent **16.57** to address those grievances, as a condition precedent to issuing a claim within an employment tribunal, it is a short step to ensure that all organizations possess a 'confidential reporting procedure'. As we have noted, this would not of itself be sufficient unless further steps are taken such as sufficiently publicizing the procedure and ensuring staff operating it are sufficiently well-trained. But the requirement to possess such a procedure may be a further step in bringing about a change in organizational cultures so that those with public interest concerns feel able to raise them internally and without delay.

APPENDICES

1. Relevant extracts from the Employment Rights Act 1996   411
2. Relevant Statutory Instruments   427
3. Relevant Hansard Extracts   435
4. Extracts from Nolan Committee on Standards in Public Life   447
5. Extracts from the Shipman Report   459
6. Sample Whistleblowing Policies   465
7. Case Study   489
8. Appellate Whistleblowing Cases   497
9. Employment Tribunal Whistleblowing Cases   539
10. Precedents   599
11. Introduction to Public Concern at Work Guide to PIDA   613
12. Useful Addresses   621

Relevant extracts from the Employment Rights Act 1996

(as amended by the Public Interest Disclosure Act 1998
and the Employment Relations Act 1999)

PART IV A
PROTECTED DISCLOSURES

Meaning of "protected disclosure"

43A. In this Act a "protected disclosure" means a qualifying disclosure (as defined by section 43B) which is made by a worker in accordance with any of sections 43C to 43H.

Disclosures qualifying for protection

43B.—(1) In this Part a "qualifying disclosure" means any disclosure of information which, in the reasonable belief of the worker making the disclosure, tends to show one or more of the following—
- (a) that a criminal offence has been committed, is being committed or is likely to be committed,
- (b) that a person has failed, is failing or is likely to fail to comply with any legal obligation to which he is subject,
- (c) that a miscarriage of justice has occurred, is occurring or is likely to occur,
- (d) that the health or safety of any individual has been, is being or is likely to be endangered,
- (e) that the environment has been, is being or is likely to be damaged, or
- (f) that information tending to show any matter falling within any one of the preceding paragraphs has been, is being or is likely to be deliberately concealed.

(2) For the purposes of subsection (1) it is immaterial whether the relevant failure occurred, occurs or would occur in the United Kingdom or elsewhere, and whether the law applying to it is that of the United Kingdom or of any other country or territory.

(3) A disclosure of information is not a qualifying disclosure if the person making the disclosure commits an offence by making it.

(4) A disclosure of information in respect of which a claim to legal professional privilege (or, in Scotland, to confidentiality as between client and professional legal adviser) could be maintained in legal proceedings is not a qualifying disclosure if it is made by a person to whom the information had been disclosed in the course of obtaining legal advice.

(5) In this Part "the relevant failure", in relation to a qualifying disclosure, means the matter falling within paragraphs (a) to (f) of subsection (1).

Disclosure to employer or other responsible person

43C.—(1) A qualifying disclosure is made in accordance with this section if the worker makes the disclosure in good faith—
- (a) to his employer, or
- (b) where the worker reasonably believes that the relevant failure relates solely or mainly to—
    - (i) the conduct of a person other than his employer, or
    - (ii) any other matter for which a person other than his employer has legal responsibility,
    to that other person.

(2) A worker who, in accordance with a procedure whose use by him is authorised by his employer makes a qualifying disclosure to a person other than his employer, is to be treated for the purposes of this Part as making the qualifying disclosure to his employer.

Disclosure to legal adviser

43D. A qualifying disclosure is made in accordance with this section if it is made in the course of obtaining legal advice.

Disclosure to Minister of the Crown

43E. A qualifying disclosure is made in accordance with this section if—
    (a) the worker's employer is—
        (i) an individual appointed under any enactment by a Minister of the Crown, or
        (ii) a body any of whose members are so appointed, and
    (b) the disclosure is made in good faith to a Minister of the Crown.

Disclosure to prescribed person

43F.—(1) A qualifying disclosure is made in accordance with this section if the worker—
    (a) makes the disclosure in good faith to a person prescribed by an order made by the Secretary of State for the purposes of this section, and
    (b) reasonably believes—
        (i) that the relevant failure falls within any description of matters in respect of which that person is so prescribed, and
        (ii) that the information disclosed, and any allegation contained in it, are substantially true.
(2) An order prescribing persons for the purposes of this section may specify persons or descriptions of persons, and shall specify the descriptions of matters in respect of which each person, or persons of each description, is or are prescribed.

Disclosure in other cases

43G.—(1) A qualifying disclosure is made in accordance with this section if—
    (a) the worker makes the disclosure in good faith,
    (b) he reasonably believes that the information disclosed, and any allegation contained in it, are substantially true,
    (c) he does not make the disclosure for purposes of personal gain,
    (d) any of the conditions in subsection (2) is met, and
    (e) in all the circumstances of the case, it is reasonable for him to make the disclosure.
(2) The conditions referred to in subsection (1)(d) are—
    (a) that, at the time he makes the disclosure, the worker reasonably believes that he will be subjected to a detriment by his employer if he makes a disclosure to his employer or in accordance with section 43F,
    (b) that, in a case where no person is prescribed for the purposes of section 43F in relation to the relevant failure, the worker reasonably believes that it is likely that evidence relating to the relevant failure will be concealed or destroyed if he makes a disclosure to his employer, or
    (c) that the worker has previously made a disclosure of substantially the same information—
        (i) to his employer, or
        (ii) in accordance with section 43F.
(3) In determining for the purposes of subsection (1)(e) whether it is reasonable for the worker to make the disclosure, regard shall be had, in particular, to—
    (a) the identity of the person to whom the disclosure is made,
    (b) the seriousness of the relevant failure,
    (c) whether the relevant failure is continuing or is likely to occur in the future,
    (d) whether the disclosure is made in breach of a duty of confidentiality owed by the employer to any other person,

(e) in a case falling within subsection (2)(c) (i) or (ii), any action which the employer or the person to whom the previous disclosure in accordance with section 43F was made has taken or might reasonably be expected to have taken as a result of the previous disclosure, and

(f) in a case falling within subsection (2)(c) (i), whether in making the disclosure to the employer the worker complied with any procedure whose use by him was authorised by the employer.

(4) For the purposes of this section a subsequent disclosure may be regarded as a disclosure of substantially the same information as that disclosed by a previous disclosure as mentioned in subsection (2)(c) even though the subsequent disclosure extends to information about action taken or not taken by any person as a result of the previous disclosure.

Disclosure of exceptionally serious failure

43H.—(1) A qualifying disclosure is made in accordance with this section if—

(a) the worker makes the disclosure in good faith,

(b) he reasonably believes that the information disclosed, and any allegation contained in it, are substantially true,

(c) he does not make the disclosure for purposes of personal gain,

(d) the relevant failure is of an exceptionally serious nature, and

(e) in all the circumstances of the case, it is reasonable for him to make the disclosure.

(2) In determining for the purposes of subsection (l)(e) whether it is reasonable for the worker to make the disclosure, regard shall be had, in particular, to the identity of the person to whom the disclosure is made.

Contractual duties of confidentiality

43J.—(1) Any provision in an agreement to which this section applies is void in so far as it purports to preclude the worker from making a protected disclosure.

(2) This section applies to any agreement between a worker and his employer (whether a worker's contract or not), including an agreement to refrain from instituting or continuing any proceedings under this Act or any proceedings for breach of contract.

Extension of meaning of "worker" etc. for Part IV A

43K.—(1) For the purposes of this Part "worker" includes an individual who is not a worker as defined by section 230(3) but who—

(a) works or worked for a person in circumstances in which—

(i) he is or was introduced or supplied to do that work by a third person, and

(ii) the terms on which he is or was engaged to do the work are or were in practice substantially determined not by him but by the person for whom he works or worked, by the third person or by both of them,

(b) contracts or contracted with a person, for the purposes of that person's business, for the execution of work to be done in a place not under the control or management of that person and would fall within section 230(3)(b) if for "personally" in that provision there were substituted "(whether personally or otherwise)",

[(ba) Works or worked as a person performing services under a contract entered into by him with a Primary Care Trust or Local Health Board under section 28K or 28Q of the National Health Service Act 1977,]

[(bb) Works or worked as a person performing services under a contract entered into by him with a Health Board under section 17J of the National Health Service (Scotland) Act 1978,]

(c) works or worked as a person providing general medical services, general dental services, general ophthalmic services or pharmaceutical services in accordance with arrangements made—

(i) by a Primary Care Trust or Health Authority under section 38 or 41 of the National Health Service Act 1977, or

(ii) by a Health Board under section 25, 26 or 27 of the National Health Service (Scotland) Act 1978, or [(ca) Works or worked as a person performing services under a contract entered into by him with a Health Board under section 17Q of the National Health Service (Scotland) Act 1978,]

(d) is or was provided with work experience provided pursuant to a training course or programme or with training for employment (or with both) otherwise than—

(i) under a contract of employment, or

(ii) by an educational establishment on a course run by that establishment;

and any reference to a worker's contract, to employment or to a worker being "employed" shall be construed accordingly.

(2) For the purposes of this Part "employer" includes—

(a) in relation to a worker falling within paragraph (a) of subsection (1), the person who substantially determines or determined the terms on which he is or was engaged,

[(aa) in relation to a worker falling within pargraph (ba) of that subsection, the Primary Care Trust or Local Health Board referred to in that paragraph,]

[(ab) in relation to a worker falling within paragraph (bb) of that subsection, the Health Board referred to in that paragraph,]

(b) in relation to a worker falling within paragraph (c) of that subsection, the authority or board referred to in that paragraph, and]

[(ba) in relation to a worker falling with in paragraph (ca) of that subsection, the Health Board referred to in that paragraph, and]

(c) in relation to a worker falling within paragraph (d) of that subsection, the person providing the work experience or training.

(3) In this section "educational establishment" includes any university, college, school or other educational establishment.

Application of this Part and related provisions to police

43KA.—(1) For the purposes of—

(a) this Part,

(b) section 47B and sections 48 and 49 so far as relating to that section, and

(c) section 103A and the other provisions of Part 10 so far as relating to the right not to be unfairly dismissed in a case where the dismissal is unfair by virtue of section 103 A,

a person who holds, otherwise than under a contract of employment, the office of constable or an appointment as a police cadet shall be treated as an employee employed by the relevant officer under a contract of employment; and any reference to a worker being "employed" and to his "employer" shall be construed accordingly.

(2) In this section "the relevant officer" means—

(a) in relation to a member of a police force or a special constable appointed for police area, the chief officer of police;

[(b) in relation to a member of a police force seconded to the Serious Organised Crime Agency to serve as a member of its staff, that Agency; and]

(d) in relation to any other person holding the office of constable or an appointment as police cadet, the person who has the direction and control of the body of constables or cadets in question.

Other interpretative provisions

43L.—(1) In this Part—

"qualifying disclosure" has the meaning given by section 43B;

"the relevant failure", in relation to a qualifying disclosure, has the meaning given by section 43B(5).

(2) In determining for the purposes of this Part whether a person makes a disclosure for purposes of personal gain, there shall be disregarded any reward payable by or under any enactment.

(3) Any reference in this Part to the disclosure of information shall have effect, in relation to any case where the person receiving the information is already aware of it, as a reference to bringing the information to his attention.

PART V

PROTECTION FROM SUFFERING DETRIMENT IN EMPLOYMENT

Rights not to suffer detriment

Protected disclosures

47B.—(1) A worker has the right not to be subjected to any detriment by any act, or any deliberate failure to act, by his employer done on the ground that the worker has made a protected disclosure.

(2) ... [*Repealed*] This section does not apply where—

(a) the worker is an employee, and

(b) the detriment in question amounts to dismissal (within the meaning of that Part).

(3) For the purposes of this section, and of sections 48 and 49 so far as relating to this section, "worker", "worker's contract", "employment" and "employer" have the extended meaning given by section 43K."

Enforcement

Complaints to industrial tribunals

48.—(1) An employee may present a complaint to an employment tribunal that he has been subjected to a detriment in contravention of section 44, 45, [46, 47 or 47A].

[(1A) A worker may present a complaint to an employment tribunal that he has been subjected to a detriment in contravention of section 45A.]

(2) On such a complaint it is for the employer to show the ground on which any act, or deliberate failure to act, was done.

(3) An employment tribunal shall not consider a complaint under this section unless it is presented—

(a) before the end of the period of three months beginning with the date of the act or failure to act to which the complaint relates or, where that act or failure is part of a series of similar acts or failures, the last of them, or

(b) within such further period as the tribunal considers reasonable in a case where it is satisfied that it was not reasonably practicable for the complaint to be presented before the end of that period of three months.

(4) For the purposes of subsection (3)—

(a) where an act extends over a period, the 'date of the act' means the last day of that period, and

(b) a deliberate failure to act shall be treated as done when it was decided on;

and, in the absence of evidence establishing the contrary, an employer shall be taken to decide on a failure to act when he does an act inconsistent with doing the failed act or, if he has done no such inconsistent act, when the period expires within which he might reasonably have been expected to do the failed act if it was to be done.

(5) In this section and section 49 any reference to the employer includes, where a person complains that he has been subjected to a detriment in contravention of section 47A, the principal (within the meaning of section 63A(3)).

Remedies

49.—(1) Where an employment tribunal finds a complaint under section 48 well-founded, the tribunal—

(a) shall make a declaration to that effect, and

(b) may make an award of compensation to be paid by the employer to the complainant in respect of the act or failure to act to which the complaint relates.

(2) [Subject to subsections (5A) and (6)] the amount of the compensation awarded shall such as the tribunal considers just and equitable in all the circumstances having regard to—

(a) the infringement to which the complaint relates, and

(b) any loss which is attributable to the act, or failure to act, which infringed the complainant's right.

(3) The loss shall be taken to include—
  (a) any expenses reasonably incurred by the complainant in consequence of the act, or failure to act, to which the complaint relates, and
  (b) loss of any benefit which he might reasonably be expected to have had but for that act or failure to act.

(4) In ascertaining the loss the tribunal shall apply the same rule concerning the duty of a person to mitigate his loss as applies to damages recoverable under the common law of England and Wales or (as the case may be) Scotland.

(5) Where the tribunal finds that the act, or failure to act, to which the complaint relates was to any extent caused or contributed to by action of the complainant, it shall reduce the amount of the compensation by such proportion as it considers just and equitable having regard to that finding.

(5A) Where—
  (a) the complaint is made under section 48(1ZA),
  (b) the detriment to which the worker is subjected is the termination of his worker's contract, and
  (c) that contract is not a contract of employment,
  any compensation must not exceed the compensation that would be payable under Chapter II of Part X if the worker had been an employee and had been dismissed for the reason specified in section 101 A.

(6) Where—
  (a) the complaint is made under section 48(1A),
  (b) the detriment to which the worker is subjected is the termination of his worker's contract, and
  (c) that contract is not a contract of employment,
  any compensation must not exceed the compensation that would be payable under Chapter II of Part X if the worker had been an employee and had been dismissed for the reason specified in section 103A.

PART X
Unfair Dismissal

CHAPTER I
Right not to be Unfairly Dismissed

The right

The right

94.—(1) An employee has the right not to be unfairly dismissed by his employer.

(2) Subsection (1) has effect subject to the following provisions of this Part (in particular sections 108 to 110) and to the provisions of the Trade Union and Labour Relations (Consolidation) Act 1992 (in particular sections 237 to 239).

Circumstances in which an employee is dismissed

95.—(1) For the purposes of this Part an employee is dismissed by his employer if (and, subject to subsection (2) and section 96, only if)—
  (a) the contract under which he is employed is terminated by the employer (whether with or without notice),
  (b) he is employed under a contract for a fixed term and that term expires without being renewed under the same contract, or
  (c) the employee terminates the contract under which he is employed (with or without notice) in circumstances in which he is entitled to terminate it without notice by reason of the employer's conduct.

(2) An employee shall be taken to be dismissed by his employer for the purposes of this Part if—
  (a) the employer gives notice to the employee to terminate his contract of employment, and

(b) at a time within the period of that notice the employee gives notice to the employer to terminate the contract of employment on a date earlier than the date on which the employer's notice is due to expire;

and the reason for the dismissal is to be taken to be the reason for which the employer's notice is given.

Effective date of termination

97.—(1) Subject to the following provisions of this section, in this Part 'the effective date of termination'—

(a) in relation to an employee whose contract of employment is terminated by notice, whether given by his employer or by the employee, means the date on which the notice expires,

(b) in relation to an employee whose contract of employment is terminated without notice, means the date on which the termination takes effect, and

c) in relation to an employee who is employed under a contract for a fixed term which expires without being renewed under the same contract, means the date on which the term expires.

(2) Where—

(a) the contract of employment is terminated by the employer, and

(b) the notice required by section 86 to be given by an employer would, if duly given on the material date, expire on a date later than the effective date of termination (as defined by subsection (1)),

for the purposes of sections 108(1), 119(1) and 227(3) the later date is the effective date of termination.

(3) In subsection (2)(b) 'the material date' means—

(a) the date when notice of termination was given by the employer, or

(b) where no notice was given, the date when the contract of employment was terminated by the employer.

(4) Where—

(a) the contract of employment is terminated by the employee,

(b) the material date does not fall during a period of notice given by the employer to terminate that contract, and

(c) had the contract been terminated not by the employee but by notice given on the material date by the employer, that notice would have been required by section 86 to expire on a date later than the effective date of termination (as defined by subsection (1)),

for the purposes of sections 108(1), 119(1) and 227(3) the later date is the effective date of termination.

(5) In subsection (4) 'the material date' means—

(a) the date when notice of termination was given by the employee, or

(b) where no notice was given, the date when the contract of employment was terminated by the employee.

(6) ... [*Repealed*]

Fairness

General

98.—(1) In determining for the purposes of this Part whether the dismissal of an employee is fair or unfair, it is for the employer to show—

(a) the reason (or, if more than one, the principal reason) for the dismissal, and

(b) that it is either a reason falling within subsection (2) or some other substantial reason of a kind such as to justify the dismissal of an employee holding the position which the employee held.

(2) A reason falls within this subsection if it—

(a) relates to the capability or qualifications of the employee for performing work of the kind which he was employed by the employer to do,

(b) relates to the conduct of the employee,

(c) is that the employee was redundant, or

(d) is that the employee could not continue to work in the position which he held without contravention (either on his part or on that of his employer) of a duty or restriction imposed by or under an enactment.

(3) In subsection (2)(a)—

(a) 'capability', in relation to an employee, means his capability assessed by reference to skill, aptitude, health or any other physical or mental quality, and

(b) 'qualifications', in relation to an employee, means any degree, diploma or other academic, technical or professional qualification relevant to the position which he held.

(4) Where the employer has fulfilled the requirements of subsection (1), the determination of the question whether the dismissal is fair or unfair (having regard to the reason shown by the employer)—

(a) depends on whether in the circumstances (including the size and administrative resources of the employer's undertaking) the employer acted reasonably or unreasonably in treating it as a sufficient reason for dismissing the employee, and

(b) shall be determined in accordance with equity and the substantial merits of the case.

(5) . . .[*Repealed*]

Protected disclosure

103A. An employee who is dismissed shall be regarded for the purposes of this Part as unfairly dismissed if the reason (or, if more than one, the principal reason) for the dismissal is that the employee made a protected disclosure.

Assertion of statutory right

104.—(1) An employee who is dismissed shall be regarded for the purposes of this Part as unfairly dismissed if the reason (or, if more than one, the principal reason) for the dismissal is that the employee—

(a) brought proceedings against the employer to enforce a right of his which is a relevant statutory right, or

(b) alleged that the employer had infringed a right of his which is a relevant statutory right.

(2) It is immaterial for the purposes of subsection (1)—

(a) whether or not the employee has the right, or

(b) whether or not the right has been infringed;

but, for that subsection to apply, the claim to the right and that it has been infringed must be made in good faith.

(3) It is sufficient for subsection (1) to apply that the employee, without specifying the right, made it reasonably clear to the employer what the right claimed to have been infringed was.

(4) The following are relevant statutory rights for the purposes of this section—

(a) any right conferred by this Act for which the remedy for its infringement is by way of a complaint or reference to an employment tribunal,

(b) the right conferred by section 86 of this Act,

(c) the rights conferred by sections 68, 86, 146, 168, 169 and 170 of the Trade Union and Labour Relations (Consolidation) Act 1992 (deductions from pay, union activities and time off) [and

(d) the rights conferred by the Working Time Regulations 1998.]

(5) In this section any reference to an employer includes, where the right in question is conferred by section 63A, the principal (within the meaning of section 63A(3)).

CHAPTER II
REMEDIES FOR UNFAIR DISMISSAL
Introductory

Complaints to employment tribunal

111.—(1) A complaint may be presented to an employment tribunal against an employer by any person that he was unfairly dismissed by the employer.

(2) Subject to subsection (3), an employment tribunal shall not consider a complaint under this section unless it is presented to the tribunal—

(a) before the end of the period of three months beginning with the effective date of termination, or

(b) within such further period as the tribunal considers reasonable in a case where it is satisfied that it was not reasonably practicable for the complaint to be presented before the end of that period of three months.

(3) Where a dismissal is with notice, an employment tribunal shall consider a complaint under this section if it is presented after the notice is given but before the effective date of termination.

(4) In relation to a complaint which is presented as mentioned in subsection (3), the provisions of this Act, so far as they relate to unfair dismissal, have effect as if—

(a) references to a complaint by a person that he was unfairly dismissed by his employer included references to a complaint by a person that his employer has given him notice in such circumstances that he will be unfairly dismissed when the notice expires,

(b) references to reinstatement included references to the withdrawal of the notice by the employer,

(c) references to the effective date of termination included references to the date which would be the effective date of termination on the expiry of the notice, and

(d) references to an employee ceasing to be employed included references to an employee having been given notice of dismissal.

The remedies: orders and compensation

112.—(1) This section applies where, on a complaint under section 111, a tribunal finds that the grounds of the complaint are well-founded.

(2) The tribunal shall—

(a) explain to the complainant what orders may be made under section 113 and in what circumstances they may be made, and

(b) ask him whether he wishes the tribunal to make such an order.

(3) If the complainant expresses such a wish, the tribunal may make an order under section 113.

(4) If no order is made under section 113, the tribunal shall make an award of compensation for unfair dismissal (calculated in accordance with sections 118 to 127A . . . [*repealed*]

Orders for reinstatement or re-engagement

The orders

113.—An order under this section may be—

(a) an order for reinstatement (in accordance with section 114), or

(b) an order for re-engagement (in accordance with section 115),

as the tribunal may decide.

Order for reinstatement

114.—(1) An order for reinstatement is an order that the employer shall treat the complainant in all respects as if he had not been dismissed.

(2) On making an order for reinstatement the tribunal shall specify—

(a) any amount payable by the employer in respect of any benefit which the complainant might reasonably be expected to have had but for the dismissal (including arrears of pay) for the period between the date of termination of employment and the date of reinstatement,

    (b) any rights and privileges, (including seniority and pension rights) which must be restored to the employee, and

    (c) the date by which the order must be complied with.

(3) If the complainant would have benefited from an improvement in his terms and conditions of employment had he not been dismissed, an order for reinstatement shall require him to be treated as if he had benefited from that improvement from the date on which he would have done so but for being dismissed.

(4) In calculating for the purposes of subsection (2)(a) any amount payable by the employer, the tribunal shall take into account, so as to reduce the employer's liability, any sums received by the complainant in respect of the period between the date of termination of employment and the date of reinstatement by way of—

    (a) wages in lieu of notice or ex gratia payments paid by the employer, or

    (b) remuneration paid in respect of employment with another employer,

    and such other benefits as the tribunal thinks appropriate in the circumstances.

(5) . . . [*Repealed*]

Order for re-engagement

115.—(1) An order for re-engagement is an order, on such terms as the tribunal may decide, that the complainant be engaged by the employer, or by a successor of the employer or by an associated employer, in employment comparable to that from which he was dismissed or other suitable employment.

(2) On making an order for re-engagement the tribunal shall specify the terms on which re-engagement is to take place, including—

    (a) the identity of the employer,

    (b) the nature of the employment,

    (c) the remuneration for the employment,

    (d) any amount payable by the employer in respect of any benefit which the complainant might reasonably be expected to have had but for the dismissal (including arrears of pay) for the period between the date of termination of employment and the date of re-engagement,

    (e) any rights and privileges (including seniority and pension rights) which must be restored to the employee, and

    (f) the date by which the order must be complied with.

(3) In calculating for the purposes of subsection (2)(d) any amount payable by the employer, the tribunal shall take into account, so as to reduce the employer's liability, any sums received by the complainant in respect of the period between the date of termination of employment and the date of re-engagement by way of—

    (a) wages in lieu of notice or ex gratia payments paid by the employer, or

    (b) remuneration paid in respect of employment with another employer,

    and such other benefits as the tribunal thinks appropriate in the circumstances.

(4) . . . [*Repealed*]

Choice of order and its terms

116.—(1) In exercising its discretion under section 113 the tribunal shall first consider whether to make an order for reinstatement and in so doing shall take into account—

    (a) whether the complainant wishes to be reinstated,

    (b) whether it is practicable for the employer to comply with an order for reinstatement, and

    (c) where the complainant caused or contributed to some extent to the dismissal, whether it would be just to order his reinstatement.

(2) If the tribunal decides not to make an order for reinstatement it shall then consider whether to make an order for re-engagement and, if so, on what terms.

(3) In so doing the tribunal shall take into account—

    (a) any wish expressed by the complainant as to the nature of the order to be made,

(b) whether it is practicable for the employer (or a successor or an associated employer) to comply with an order for re-engagement, and

(c) where the complainant caused or contributed to some extent to the dismissal, whether it would be just to order his re-engagement and (if so) on what terms.

(4) Except in a case where the tribunal takes into account contributory fault under subsection (3)(c) it shall, if it orders re-engagement, do so on terms which are, so far as is reasonably practicable, as favourable as an order for reinstatement.

(5) Where in any case an employer has engaged a permanent replacement for a dismissed employee, the tribunal shall not take that fact into account in determining, for the purposes of subsection (l)(b) or (3)(b), whether it is practicable to comply with an order for reinstatement or re-engagement.

(6) Subsection (5) does not apply where the employer shows—

(a) that it was not practicable for him to arrange for the dismissed employee's work to be done without engaging a permanent replacement, or

(b) that—

(i) he engaged the replacement after the lapse of a reasonable period, without having heard from the dismissed employee that he wished to be reinstated or re-engaged, and

(ii) when the employer engaged the replacement it was no longer reasonable for him to arrange for the dismissed employee's work to be done except by a permanent replacement.

General

118.—(1) ... [*Repealed.*] Where a tribunal makes an award of compensation for unfair dismissal under section 112(4) or 117(3)(a) the award shall consist of—

(a) a basic award (calculated in accordance with sections 119 to 122 and 126), and

(b) a compensatory award (calculated in accordance with sections 123, 124, 126 [and 127A(l), (3), and (4)]).

Basic award

119.—(1) Subject to the provisions of this section, sections 120 to 122 and section 126, the amount of the basic award shall be calculated by—

(a) determining the period, ending with the effective date of termination, during which the employee has been continuously employed,

(b) reckoning backwards from the end of that period the number of years of employment falling within that period, and

(c) allowing the appropriate amount for each of those years of employment.

(2) In subsection (l)(c) 'the appropriate amount' means—

(a) one and a half weeks' pay for a year of employment in which the employee was not below the age of forty-one,

(b) one week's pay for a year of employment (not within paragraph (a)) in which he was not below the age of twenty-two, and

(c) half a week's pay for a year of employment not within paragraph (a) or (b).

(3) Where twenty years of employment have been reckoned under subsection (1), no account shall be taken under that subsection of any year of employment earlier than those twenty years.

(4) Where the effective date of termination is after the sixty-fourth anniversary of the day of the employee's birth, the amount arrived at under subsections (1) to (3) shall be reduced by the appropriate fraction.

(5) In subsection (4) 'the appropriate fraction' means the fraction of which—

(a) the numerator is the number of whole months reckoned from the sixty-fourth anniversary of the day of the employee's birth in the period beginning with that anniversary and ending with the effective date of termination, and

(b) the denominator is twelve.

(6) ... [*Repealed*]

Compensatory award

[amended by the Employment Relations Act 1999]

123.—(1) Subject to the provisions of this section and sections 124, [126, 127 and 127A(1), (3) and (4)] the amount of the compensatory award shall be such amount as the tribunal considers just and equitable in all the circumstances having regard to the loss sustained by the complainant in consequence of the dismissal in so far as that loss is attributable to action taken by the employer.

(2) The loss referred to in subsection (1) shall be taken to include—

(a) any expenses reasonably incurred by the complainant in consequence of the dismissal, and

(b) subject to subsection (3), loss of any benefit which he might reasonably be expected to have had but for the dismissal.

(3) The loss referred to in subsection (1) shall be taken to include in respect of any loss of—

(a) any entitlement or potential entitlement to a payment on account of dismissal by reason of redundancy (whether in pursuance of Part XI or otherwise), or

(b) any expectation of such a payment,

only the loss referable to the amount (if any) by which the amount of that payment would have exceeded the amount of a basic award (apart from any reduction under section 122) in respect of the same dismissal.

(4) In ascertaining the loss referred to in subsection (1) the tribunal shall apply the same rule concerning the duty of a person to mitigate his loss as applies to damages recoverable under the common law of England and Wales or (as the case may be) Scotland.

(5) In determining, for the purposes of subsection (1), how far any loss sustained by the complainant was attributable to action taken by the employer, no account shall be taken of any pressure which by—

(a) calling, organising, procuring or financing a strike or other industrial action, or

(b) threatening to do so,

was exercised on the employer to dismiss the employee; and that question shall be determined as if no such pressure had been exercised.

(6) Where the tribunal finds that the dismissal was to any extent caused or contributed to by any action of the complainant, it shall reduce the amount of the compensatory award by such proportion as it considers just and equitable having regard to that finding.

(7) If the amount of any payment made by the employer to the employee on the ground that the dismissal was by reason of redundancy (whether in pursuance of Part XI or otherwise) exceeds the amount of the basic award which would be payable but for section 122(4), that excess goes to reduce the amount of the compensatory award.

Limit of compensatory award etc

124.—(1) The amount of—

(a) any compensation awarded to a person under section 117(1) and (2), or

(b) a compensatory award to a person calculated in accordance with section 123, shall not exceed [£58,400]

(2) ... [*Repealed*]

(3) In the case of compensation awarded to a person under section 117(1) and (2), the limit imposed by this section may be exceeded to the extent necessary to enable the award fully to reflect the amount specified as payable under section 114(2)(a) or section 115(2)(d).

(4) Where—

(a) a compensatory award is an award under paragraph (a) of subsection (3) of section 117, and

(b) an additional award falls to be made under paragraph (b) of that subsection,

the limit imposed by this section on the compensatory award may be exceeded to the extent necessary to enable the aggregate of the compensatory and additional awards fully to reflect the amount specified as payable under section 114(2)(a) or section 115(2)(d).

(5) The limit imposed by this section applies to the amount which the employment tribunal would, apart from this section, award in respect of the subject matter of the complaint after taking into account—

    (a) any payment made by the respondent to the complainant in respect of that matter, and

    (b) any reduction in the amount of the award required by any enactment or rule of law.

Interim relief

Interim relief pending determination of complaint

128.—(1) An employee who presents a complaint to an employment tribunal—

    (a) that he has been unfairly dismissed by his employer, and

    (b) that the reason (or, if more than one, the principal reason) for the dismissal is one of those specified in section 100(l)(a) and (b), [101A(d),] 102(l)[103 or 103A.],

    may apply to the tribunal for interim relief.

(2) The tribunal shall not entertain an application for interim relief unless it is presented to the tribunal before the end of the period of seven days immediately following the effective date of termination (whether before, on or after that date).

(3) The tribunal shall determine the application for interim relief as soon as practicable after receiving the application.

(4) The tribunal shall give to the employer not later than seven days before the date of the hearing a copy of the application together with notice of the date, time and place of the hearing.

(5) The tribunal shall not exercise any power it has of postponing the hearing of an application for interim relief except where it is satisfied that special circumstances exist which justify it in doing so.

Procedure on hearing of application and making of order

129.—(1) This section applies where, on hearing an employee's application for interim relief, it appears to the tribunal that it is likely that on determining the complaint to which the application relates the tribunal will find that the reason (or, if more than one, the principal reason) for his dismissal is one of those specified in section 100(l)(a) and (b), [101A(d),] 102(1), [103 or 103A.]

(2) The tribunal shall announce its findings and explain to both parties (if present)—

    (a) what powers the tribunal may exercise on the application, and

    (b) in what circumstances it will exercise them.

(3) The tribunal shall ask the employer (if present) whether he is willing, pending the determination or settlement of the complaint—

    (a) to reinstate the employee (that is, to treat him in all respects as if he had not been dismissed), or

    (b) if not, to re-engage him in another job on terms and conditions not less favourable than those which would have been applicable to him if he had not been dismissed.

(4) For the purposes of subsection (3)(b) 'terms and conditions not less favourable than those which would have been applicable to him if he had not been dismissed' means, as regards seniority, pension rights and other similar rights, that the period prior to the dismissal should be regarded as continuous with his employment following the dismissal.

(5) If the employer states that he is willing to reinstate the employee, the tribunal shall make an order to that effect.

(6) If the employer—

    (a) states that he is willing to re-engage the employee in another job, and

    (b) specifies the terms and conditions on which he is willing to do so,

    the tribunal shall ask the employee whether he is willing to accept the job on those terms and conditions.

(7) If the employee is willing to accept the job on those terms and conditions, the tribunal shall make an order to that effect.

(8) If the employee is not willing to accept the job on those terms and conditions—
    (a) where the tribunal is of the opinion that the refusal is reasonable, the tribunal shall make an order for the continuation of his contract of employment, and
    (b) otherwise, the tribunal shall make no order.
(9) If on the hearing of an application for interim relief the employer—
    (a) fails to attend before the tribunal, or
    (b) states that he is unwilling either to reinstate or re-engage the employee as mentioned in sub-section (3),
    the tribunal shall make an order for the continuation of the employee's contract of employment.

Order for continuation of contract of employment

130.—(1) An order under section 129 for the continuation of a contract of employment is an order that the contract of employment continue in force—
    (a) for the purposes of pay or any other benefit derived from the employment, seniority, pension rights and other similar matters, and
    (b) for the purposes of determining for any purpose the period for which the employee has been continuously employed,
    from the date of its termination (whether before or after the making of the order) until the determination or settlement of the complaint.
(2) Where the tribunal makes such an order it shall specify in the order the amount which is to be paid by the employer to the employee by way of pay in respect of each normal pay period, or part of any such period, falling between the date of dismissal and the determination or settlement of the complaint.
(3) Subject to the following provisions, the amount so specified shall be that which the employee could reasonably have been expected to earn during that period, or part, and shall be paid—
    (a) in the case of a payment for any such period falling wholly or partly after the making of the order, on the normal pay day for that period, and
    (b) in the case of a payment for any past period, within such time as may be specified in the order.
(4) If an amount is payable in respect only of part of a normal pay period, the amount shall be calculated by reference to the whole period and reduced proportionately.
(5) Any payment made to an employee by an employer under his contract of employment, or by way of damages for breach of that contract, in respect of a normal pay period, or part of any such period, goes towards discharging the employer's liability in respect of that period under subsection (2); and, conversely, any payment under that subsection in respect of a period goes towards discharging any liability of the employer under, or in respect of breach of, the contract of employment in respect of that period.
(6) If an employee, on or after being dismissed by his employer, receives a lump sum which, or part of which, is in lieu of wages but is not referable to any normal pay period, the tribunal shall take the payment into account in determining the amount of pay to be payable in pursuance of any such order.
(7) For the purposes of this section, the amount which an employee could reasonably have been expected to earn, his normal pay period and the normal pay day for each period shall be determined as if he had not been dismissed.

Application for variation or revocation of order

131.—(1) At any time between—
    (a) the making of an order under section 129, and
    (b) the determination or settlement of the complaint,
    the employer or the employee may apply to an industrial tribunal for the revocation or variation of the order on the ground of a relevant change of circumstances since the making of the order.

(2) Sections 128 and 129 apply in relation to such an application as in relation to an original application for interim relief except that, in the case of an application by the employer, section 128(4) has effect with the substitution of a reference to the employee for the reference to the employer.

Consequence of failure to comply with order

132.—(1) If, on the application of an employee, an industrial tribunal is satisfied that the employer has not complied with the terms of an order for the reinstatement or re-engagement of the employee under section 129(5) or (7), the tribunal shall—

(a) make an order for the continuation of the employee's contract of employment, and

(b) order the employer to pay compensation to the employee.

(2) Compensation under subsection (l)(b) shall be of such amount as the tribunal considers just and equitable in all the circumstances having regard—

(a) to the infringement of the employee's right to be reinstated or re-engaged in pursuance of the order, and

(b) to any loss suffered by the employee in consequence of the non-compliance.

(3) Section 130 applies to an order under subsection (l)(a) as in relation to an order under section 129.

(4) If on the application of an employee an employment tribunal is satisfied that the employer has not complied with the terms of an order for the continuation of a contract of employment subsection (5) or (6) applies.

(5) Where the non-compliance consists of a failure to pay an amount by way of pay specified in the order—

(a) the tribunal shall determine the amount owed by the employer on the date of the determination, and

(b) if on that date the tribunal also determines the employee's complaint that he has been unfairly dismissed, it shall specify that amount separately from any other sum awarded to the employee.

(6) In any other case, the tribunal shall order the employer to pay the employee such compensation as the tribunal considers just and equitable in all the circumstances having regard to any loss suffered by the employee in consequence of the non-compliance.

CHAPTER III
OTHER INTERPRETATION PROVISIONS

Employees, workers etc

230.—(1) In this Act 'employee' means an individual who has entered into or works under (or, where the employment has ceased, worked under) a contract of employment.

(2) In this Act 'contract of employment' means a contract of service or apprenticeship, whether express or implied, and (if it is express) whether oral or in writing.

(3) In this Act 'worker' (except in the phrases 'shop worker' and 'betting worker') means an individual who has entered into or works under (or, where the employment has ceased, worked under)—

(a) a contract of employment, or

(b) any other contract, whether express or implied and (if it is express) whether oral or in writing, whereby the individual undertakes to do or perform personally any work or services for another party to the contract whose status is not by virtue of the contract that of a client or customer of any profession or business undertaking carried on by the individual;

and any reference to a worker's contract shall be construed accordingly.

(4) In this Act 'employer', in relation to an employee or a worker, means the person by whom the employee or worker is (or, where the employment has ceased, was) employed.

(5) In this Act 'employment'—

(a) in relation to an employee, means (except for the purposes of section 171) employment under a contract of employment, and

(b) in relation to a worker, means employment under his contract;
and 'employed' shall be construed accordingly.

[(6) This section has effect subject to sections 43K and 47B(3); and for the purposes of Part XIII so far as relating to Part IV A or section 47B, "worker", "worker's contract" and, in relation to a worker, "employer", "employment" and "employed" have the extended meaning given by section 43K.]

APPENDIX 2

Relevant Statutory Instruments

PUBLIC INTEREST DISCLOSURE (PRESCRIBED PERSONS) ORDER 1999

(SI 1999/1549)

NOTES

Made: 5 June 1999.
Authority: Employment Rights Act 1996. s 43F.
Coming into force : 2 July 1999.
The Schedule contained in this Order was wholly substituted by the Public Interest Disclosure (Prescribed Persons) (Amendment) Order 2003, SI 2003/1993, art 2; commencement 1 October 2003. All substitutions (and subsequent amendments) are printed here.

1 Citation and commencement

This Order may be cited as the Public Interest Disclosure (Prescribed Persons) Order 1999 and shall come into force on 2nd July 1999.

2 Prescribed Persons

(1) The persons and descriptions of persons prescribed for the purposes of section 43F of the Employment Rights Act 1996 are the persons and descriptions of persons specified in the first column of the Schedule.

(2) The descriptions of matters in respect of which each person, or persons of each description, specified in the first column of the Schedule is or are prescribed are the descriptions of matters respectively specified opposite them in the second column of the Schedule.

SCHEDULE[1]

Article 2

First Column *Persons and descriptions of people*	*Second Column* *Descriptions of matters*
Accounts Commission for Scotland and auditors appointed by the Commission to audit the accounts of local government bodies.	The proper conduct of public business, value for money, fraud and corruption in local government bodies.
Audit Commission for England and Wales and auditors appointed by the Commission to audit accounts of local government, and health service, bodies.	The proper conduct of public business, value for money, fraud and corruption in local government, and health service, bodies.
Certification Officer.	Fraud, and other irregularities, relating to the financial affairs of trade unions and employers' associations.
Charity Commissioners for England and Wales	The proper administration of charities and of funds given or held for charitable purposes.
The Scottish Ministers.	The proper administration of charities and of funds given or held for charitable purposes.
Chief Executive of the Criminal Cases Review Commission.	Actual or potential miscarriages of justice.
Chief Executive of the Scottish Criminal Cases Review Commission.	Actual or potential miscarriages of justice.
Civil Aviation Authority.	Compliance with the requirements of civil aviation legislation, including aviation safety.
[Office of Communications.	Matters relating to— (a) the provision of electronic communications networks and services and the use of the electro-magnetic spectrum; (b) broadcasting and the provision of television and radio services; (c) media ownership and control; and (d) competition in communications markets.][2]
The competent authority under Part IV of the Financial Services and Markets Act 2000.	The listing of securities on a stock exchange; prospectuses on offers of transferable securities to the public.

---

[1] Substituted by the Public Interest Disclosure (Prescribed Persons) (Amendment) Order 2005. SI 2003/1993 art 2 Schedule.

[2] Inserted by SI 2005/2646, arts 2, 3(1) Schedule.

First Column *Persons and descriptions of people*	Second Column *Descriptions of matters*
Commissioners of Customs and Excise.	Value added tax, insurance premium tax, excise duties and landfill tax. The import and export of prohibited or restricted goods.
Commissioners of the Inland Revenue.	Income tax, corporation tax, capital gains tax, petroleum revenue tax, inheritance tax, stamp duties, national insurance contributions, statutory maternity pay, statutory sick pay, tax credits, child benefits, collection of student loans and the enforcement of the national minimum wage.
Comptroller and Auditor General of the National Audit Office.	The proper conduct of public business, value for money, fraud and corruption in relation to the provision of centrally-funded public services.
Auditor General for Wales.	The proper conduct of public business, value for money, fraud and corruption in relation to the provision of public services.
Auditor General for Scotland and persons appointed by or on his behalf under the Public Finance and Accountability (Scotland) Act 2000 to act as auditors or examiners for the purposes of sections 21 to 24 of that Act.	The proper conduct of public business, value for money, fraud and corruption in relation to the provision of public services.
Audit Scotland.	The proper conduct of public business, value for money, fraud and corruption in public bodies.
[Gas and Electricity Markets Authority.	The generation, transmission, distribution and supply of electricity, participation in the operation of an electricity interconnector (as defined in section 4(3E) of the Electricity Act 1989) and activities ancillary to these matters. The transportation, shipping and supply of gas through pipes, participation in the operation of a gas interconnector (as defined in section 5(8) of the Gas Act 1986) and activities ancillary to these matters.][3]
. . .	. . .[4]
. . .	. . .
. . .	. . .
[Water Services Regulation Authority.][5]	The supply of water and the provision of sewerage services.

Continued

---

[3] Inserted by SI 2005/2464 arts 2, 3(3) Schedule.
[4] Revoked by SI 2005/2464, arts 2, 3(2), 4.
[5] Substituted by SI 2005/2035 reg 17.

First Column *Persons and descriptions of people*	*Second Column* *Descriptions of matters*
[Convener of the Water Customer Consultation Panels and any member of those panels.	The supply of water and the provision of sewerage services.
Water Industry Commission for Scotland.	The supply of water and the provision of sewerage services.][6]
Water Industry Commissioner for Scotland.	The supply of water and the provision of sewerage services.
Director of the Serious Fraud Office.	Serious or complex fraud.
Lord Advocate, Scotland.	Serious or complex fraud.
Environment Agency.	Acts or omissions which have an actual or potential effect on the environment or the management or regulation of the environment, including those relating to pollution, abstraction of water, flooding, the flow in rivers, inland fisheries and migratory salmon or trout.
Scottish Environment Protection Agency.	Acts or omissions which have an actual or potential effect on the environment or the management or regulation of the environment, including those relating to flood warning systems and pollution.
Food Standards Agency.	Matters which may affect the health of any member of the public in relation to the consumption of food and other matters concerning the protection of the interests of consumers in relation to food.
Financial Services Authority	The carrying on of investment business or of insurance business; the operation of banks and building societies, deposit-taking businesses and wholesale money market regimes; the operation of friendly societies, benevolent societies, working men's clubs, specially authorised societies, and industrial and provident societies; the functioning of financial markets, investment exchanges and clearing houses; money laundering, financial crime, and other serious financial misconduct, in connection with activities regulated by the Financial Services Authority.
General Social Care Council.	Matters relating to the registration of social care workers under the Care Standards Act 2000.
Care Council for Wales.	Matters relating to the registration of social care workers under the Care Standards Act 2000.

---

[6] Inserted by SI 2005/3172 art 11 Schedule pt 2, para 5.

First Column *Persons and descriptions of people*	Second Column *Descriptions of matters*
Scottish Social Services Council.	Matters relating to the registration of the social services workforce by the Scottish Social Services Council.
Children's Commissioner for Wales.	Matters relating to the rights and welfare of children.
Health and Safety Executive.	Matters which may affect the health or safety of any individual at work; matters, which may affect the health and safety of any member of the public, arising out of or in connection with the activities of persons at work.
Housing Corporation.	The registration and operation of registered social landlords, including their administration of public and private funds and management of their housing stock.
Local authorities which are responsible for the enforcement of health and safety legislation.	Matters which may affect the health or safety of any individual at work; matters, which may affect the health and safety of any member of the public, arising out of or in connection with the activities of persons at work.
[Independent Police Complaints Commission.	Matters relating to the conduct of a person serving with the police (as defined in section 12(7) of the Police Reform Act 2002) or of any other person in relation to whose conduct the Independent Police Complaints Commission exercises functions in or under any legislation.][7]
Information Commissioner.	Compliance with the requirements of legislation relating to data protection and freedom of information.
Scottish Information Commissioner.	Compliance with the requirements of legislation relating to freedom of information.
[Commission for Healthcare Audit and Inspection.	Matters connected with— (a) the provision of health care for the purposes of the National Health Service (where "health care" has the same meaning as in section 45(2) of the Health and Social Care (Community Health and Standards) Act 2003); (b) the provision of independent health services within the meaning of section 5A(8) of the Care Standards Act 2000; or (c) any activities not covered by (a) and (b) in relation to which the Commission for Healthcare Audit and Inspection exercises its functions.

Continued

[7] Inserted by SI 2004/3265 art 2, Schedule.

First Column *Persons and descriptions of people*	Second Column *Descriptions of matters*
Commission for Social Care Inspection.	Matters relating to the provision of regulated social care services as defined in the Care Standards Act 2000, and the inspection and performance assessment of English local authority social services as defined in section 148 of the Health and Social Care (Community Health and Standards) Act 2003.][8]
[National Assembly for Wales.	Matters relating to the provision of Part II services as defined in section 8 of the Care Standards Act 2000 and the Children Act 1989.
	Matters relating to the inspection and performance assessment of Welsh local authority social services as defined in section 148 of the Health and Social Care (Community Heath and Standards) Act 2003.
	Matters relating to the review of, and investigation into, the provision of health care by and for Welsh NHS bodies as defined under the Health and Social Care (Community Health and Standards) Act 2003.
	The registration and operation of registered social landlords, including their administration of public and private funds and management of their housing stock.][9]
Scottish Commission for the Regulation of Care.	Matters relating to the provision of care services, as defined in the Regulation of Care (Scotland) Act 2001.
[Pensions Regulator.][10]	Matters relating to occupational pension schemes and other private pension arrangements.
Office of Fair Trading.	Matters concerning the sale of goods or the supply of services, which adversely affect the interests of consumers.
	Competition affecting markets in the United Kingdom.
[Office of Rail Regulation.][11]	The provision and supply of railway services.
Standards Board for England.	Breaches by a member or co-opted member of a relevant authority (as defined in section 49(6) of the Local Government Act 2000) of that authority's code of conduct.
Local Commissioner in Wales.	Breaches by a member or co-opted member of a relevant authority (as defined in section 49(6) of the Local Government Act 2000) of that authority's code of conduct.

[8] Substituted by SI 2005/2464 arts 2, 3(5) Schedule.
[9] Substituted by SI 2005/2464 arts 2, 3(6) Schedule.
[10] Substituted by SI 2005/2464 arts 2, 3(7).
[11] Substituted by the Railways and Transport Safety Act 2003 s16(4), (5); sch 3, para 4.

First Column *Persons and descriptions of people*	Second Column *Descriptions of matters*
Standards Commission for Scotland and the Chief Investigating Officer.	Breaches by a councillor or a member of a devolved public body (as defined in section 28 of the Ethical Standards in Public Life etc (Scotland) Act 2000) of the code of conduct applicable to that councillor or member under that Act.
Treasury.	The carrying on of insurance business.
Secretary of State for Trade and Industry.	Fraud, and other misconduct, in relation to companies, investment business, insurance business, or multi-level marketing schemes (and similar trading schemes); insider dealing. Consumer safety.
Secretary of State for Transport.	Compliance with merchant shipping law, including maritime safety.
Local authorities which are responsible for the enforcement of consumer protection legislation.	Compliance with the requirements of consumer protection legislation.
Local authorities which are responsible for the enforcement of food standards.	Compliance with the requirements of food safety legislation.
A person ("person A") carrying out functions, by virtue of legislation, relating to relevant failures falling within one or more matters within a description of matters in respect of which another person ("person B") is prescribed by this Order, where person B was previously responsible for carrying out the same or substantially similar functions and has ceased to be so responsible.	Matters falling within the description of matters in respect of which person B is prescribed by this Order, to the extent that those matters relate to functions currently carried out by person A.]

THE PUBLIC INTEREST DISCLOSURE ACT 1998 (COMMENCEMENT) ORDER 1999

(SI 1999/1549)

The Secretary of State, in exercise of the powers conferred on him by section 18(3) of the Public Interest Disclosure Act 1998, hereby makes the following Order:—

Citation

1. This Order may be cited as the Public Interest Disclosure Act 1998 (Commencement) Order 1999

Commencement

2. The Public Interest Disclosure Act 1998, so far as not already in force, shall come into force on 2nd July 1999.

APPENDIX 3

Relevant *Hansard* Extracts

GENERAL

Lords Committee stage, 5 June 1998

Lord Nolan (col 614):

My three years in a previous incarnation as chairman of the Committee on Standards in Public Life persuaded me of the urgent need for such a measure. That view was shared by all my fellow committee members. I congratulate the noble Lord, Lord Borrie, and his colleagues at Public Concern at Work for so skilfully achieving the essential but delicate balance in this measure between the public interest and the interests of employers.

PUBLIC INTEREST MEASURE

Standing Committee D: Wednesday 11 March 1998

Mr Richard Shepherd (Aldridge-Brownhills) [co-promoter of the Bill (with Lord Borrie)]:

. . .

As with its predecessors, the Bill's purpose is to make it more likely that where there is malpractice that threatens the public interest, a worker will raise the concern in a responsible way rather than turn a blind eye. The Bill seeks to achieve that by offering workers protection against victimisation if they raise their concern in the ways specified.

. . .

The Bill is, as its name implies, a public interest measure. Were it merely an employee rights measure, I doubt that I would be able to inform the committee that its objectives are supported by the Institute of Directors, the Confederation of British Industry and the Committee on Standards in Public Life as well as the Trades Union Congress.

Lord Borrie (co-promoter of the Bill, introducing in Lords for 2nd reading—11 May 1998):

As I hope I have made clear, this measure will encourage people to recognise and identify with the wider public interest and not just their own private position. It will reassure them that if they act reasonably to protect the legitimate interests of others who are being threatened or abused, the law will not stand idly by should they be vilified or victimised.

SECTION 43B(1)(D): HEALTH AND SAFETY

Standing Committee D: Wednesday 11 March 1998

The Minister of State, Department of Trade and Industry (Mr Ian McCartney):

. . .

Several consultees expressed doubts about the effect of the subsection, which relates to danger or damage to the environment or to health and safety. They have argued, and I agree with them, that it is unnecessary and could be counter-productive.

Some processes are inherently damaging or dangerous. We would not want the full protection of the law to apply to, for example, a worker who discloses that his boss smokes, drives a car, or quite legitimately manufactures hazardous chemicals. If, however, his boss smokes in a munitions factory, that might be a different matter, as might the fact that the firm pollutes a river by discharging poisonous waste into it, or that the manufacturing process cuts corners on safety, or that the disposal of dangerous chemical by-products is unregulated. Disclosures about such matters will be covered by the Bill.

The subsection was intended to exclude the trivial and the mundane. However, it could have deterred people from raising issues of proper concern and led to legalism and complex case law.

The Government are satisfied that the Bill contains sufficient safeguards to ensure that workers will not be encouraged to disclose trivial matters or concerns. Individuals must act in good faith if they are to attract protection. External disclosures are protected only if a worker acts reasonably.

Industrial tribunals will take into account what has happened and the seriousness of the matter. They are unlikely to agree that a worker has acted reasonably where a matter is trivial or if the Health and Safety Executive is satisfied that everything has been done correctly. I do not think that new section 43B(3) adds to the necessary safeguards and it could cause confusion about what is meant by 'normal use' or the type of danger normally associated with it. I commend the amendment as a reasonable clarification of the proposal.

Section 43B(3): exclusion if disclosure involves an offence

An amendment in relation to this was tabled by Lord Wedderburn at the Lords Committee Stage on 5 June 1998. The amendment sought to limit the restriction of criminal offences in subs43B(3) to where the worker acted knowingly or recklessly in committing the offence The amendment was withdrawn.

He explained the amendment as follows (at col 613):

> The whole philosophy of the Bill would appear to be based on a worker taking reasonable action on the basis of reasonable belief. That does not in any way summarise fully the terms of what will be new Sections 43C, 43G and 43H on which we shall no doubt spend more time later. The thread that I found was that if a worker is behaving reasonably, he might on the whole be able to slip through these hoops.

> However, that is certainly not so with regard to one subsection. I refer to the case of a worker who in good faith and reasonably, so he believes, wants to disclose to a proper person some misfeasance of Maxwellian proportions. He may find that unintentionally he has transgressed some strict rule of the criminal law. We no longer teach our students that *mens rea* or a guilty mind is necessarily part of a criminal offence. If that employee is working with someone who is hacking information from another programme—a few years ago we made that a crime—he may not know that that information is coming from a young hacker, who will probably be aged about 12 because in order to get a really good hacker one has to go down the age range, that employee will be committing a crime. However, the worker sitting next to him, who then wants to disclose the matter, may be an accessory. In certain circumstances, I would be prepared to argue that he could be a principal.

> The example that is usually given is of someone finding that he is acting contrary to by-laws. That arises especially where a worker is giving the information, on paper, as it were, in a place where he is not supposed to do that. It is easy to find by-laws that may be transgressed. It has been suggested to me that there may be situations in which such an employee could innocently trespass with others into private property and find that he was part of an aggravated trespass under the Police and Criminal Evidence Act.

In such circumstances, the amendment suggests that that employee may be made to lose his protections under the Bill—that is what is at stake in subsection (3)—if he commits any criminal act with or without mental intent. The amendment retains the loss of protection where the worker has acted either knowingly or recklessly in that way. The word 'recklessly' covers a wide ground. As the noble and learned Lord, Lord Denning, once put it, it is the man who turns a blind eye. Other members of the judiciary have described it as including 'Nelsonian knowledge.' I accept that. Indeed, I am asking for a small area of ground in which the worker maintains the possibility of protection under the rest of these provisions when he knows none of the elements, and has failed to inquire into any of the elements, which constitute a criminal offence.

. . .

If the employee has reason to take advice, that still falls within the provisions of the Bill. Surely it is not a circumstance which should remove the protection of disclosure by a worker wholly taken by surprise at his criminality. I fear the day when the worker is deprived of his protection when others are not merely because of what may be the accident of criminality in the actions in which he has joined. I take it that the provisions would cover the position of a worker who is part of a group which could be said to be a conspiracy, aiming at the same venture; the acts of one being attributed as the acts of all.

This is a small amendment, based on what many people believe to be the philosophy of the Bill, which is that if workers act reasonably, are sensible, and take advice when they obviously should, they will be protected in a broad sense. We think that subsection (3) offends that. We do not believe that there is any problem with the Official Secrets Act. Anyone who is subject to that Act will know that they have to get things cleared. We thought that we should table this small amendment for your Lordships' consideration.

Lord Haskell, responding for the Government, explained the rejection of the amendment as follows (cols 615–616):

We believe that the amendment is both unnecessary and undesirable. In some cases lack of knowledge is already a defence against breaches of statutory prohibitions on disclosure, and one example of that is the Official Secrets Act. In such cases the amendment would assist workers. However, ignorance of the law in other cases is no excuse. The Bill must not undermine the statutory provisions that Parliament has put in place. If individuals ought to be able to disregard the law because they did not know of its existence, that should be provided in the statute itself, not just in the particular circumstances covered by this Bill. The effect of the amendment is that employers could be prohibited from disciplining an employee who had committed a criminal offence. That cannot be right.

I turn to the particular case of the hacker raised by my noble friend Lord Wedderburn. Section 43B(3) in Clause 1 excludes from protection disclosures which involve a criminal offence, but that does not mean that there must necessarily be a conviction or a criminal prosecution for the section to apply. My noble friend Lord McCarthy referred to the Bill being reasonable. I believe that if the matter went before a tribunal a high standard of proof would be required before the tribune could decide whether an offence had been committed. That would ensure a fair hearing for the employee. Nor would it be the same as finding the individual guilty of a criminal offence. But clearly it would be wrong to protect workers who had broken the law and the Bill cannot do so.

Lord Borrie commented (at col 616) referring to the public interest element in any disclosure:

This Bill is meant to encourage any worker in any workplace who discovers a malpractice of some kind, whether it is financial, a breach of safety regulations or the commission of a criminal offence by the employer—several examples were given by me and other noble Lords during Second Reading—to disclose those matters in the public interest. It is not concerned with a worker who wishes to disclose some malpractice for his own ends, possibly to try to gain a private advantage. As the title of the Bill clearly indicates, it is concerned with the public interest. In our society and the general scheme of things because the law states that a criminal offence can be committed only when it takes place knowingly or recklessly, or where it is a strict liability offence, as my noble friend Lord Wedderburn has indicated, it is very difficult to say that the commission of a criminal offence by a discloser can nonetheless be in the public interest. That is the difficulty I face in supporting the amendment.

Lord Borrie and Lord Nolan both argued that a criminal standard of proof would apply. (Lord Wedderburn disagreed and said the ordinary civil tests of balance of probability would apply). Lord Borrie said (at col 616):

> I am most grateful to the noble and learned Lord, Lord Nolan, not only for his support for the Bill but for his comment that, as and when a matter of this kind comes before an industrial tribunal, because a worker, having disclosed some malpractice, is victimised or dismissed, if it is faced with the argument on the part of the employer that the employee, by disclosing the malpractice, has committed a criminal offence that must be proved before that tribunal to the criminal standard; that is, beyond reasonable doubt. The case cited by the noble and learned Lord, Lord Nolan, was one decided by the former Lord Chief Justice, the noble and learned Lord, Lord Lane, who held that in disciplinary proceedings involving a solicitor, where it was alleged that a professional had committed a serious crime, the tribunal should apply the criminal standard of proof. Having in mind the situations that may arise under this Bill, the consequences for the reputation and employability of an employee who is dismissed because he is thought to have committed an offence of some kind will be no less grave than those for a professional such as a solicitor who is struck off as a result of allegations of a serious crime affecting his professional integrity. Therefore, I respectfully agree with the noble and learned Lord, Lord Nolan. I suggest that it is safe to assume that an industrial tribunal will follow that precedent and adopt the criminal standard of proof in applying Section 43B(3).

Lord Borrie said he could see greater force in the point in relation to strict liability offences, especially re Government secrecy, but took comfort in the fact that these were to be reviewed in relation to the Freedom of Information Bill. He concluded (at col 617) that:

> It seems to me that at the end of the day in a public interest disclosure Bill it is not appropriate to say that it is in the public interest to disclose things that are under the existing law criminal. Let us rest on the belief that many strict liability offences that currently exist perhaps should not exist and can be argued against in due course when we discuss the freedom of information Bill.

ABSENCE OF EXPRESS PROVISION FOR DISCLOSURE TO UNION: s43C(1)(B), 43D

Lords Committee Stage on 5 June 1998

Baroness Turner tabled an amendment to provide for disclosure 'to an independent adviser falling within the terms of sections 9 and 10 of the Employment Rights (Dispute Resolution) Act 1998.'

In rejecting this Lord Haskell (for the Government) emphasized the primacy of internal disclosures (at col 621):

> When my noble friend Lord Borrie spoke to the first amendment, he reminded us that we want to encourage the use of proper internal procedures. That is why the purpose of Section 43C in Clause 1 of the Bill is to encourage workers to raise their concerns with the employer first, whether directly or through proper internal company procedures. They need only act in good faith in doing so, which is deliberately not an onerous condition.

> The Bill is therefore very much in line with the Government's partnership approach, which seeks to encourage greater co-operation between employers and workers and trade unions.

Lord Haskell and Lord Borrie emphasized the difference between lawyers and unions in relation to obligations of confidentiality and also the problems with unions' dual individual and collective role. Lord Borrie said (at cols 625–626):

> Where a person is approached for confidential legal advice, protection under Section 43D will apply. As with all disclosures for legal advice, Section 43B(4) ensures that the lawyer cannot do as he pleases with the information. That is a most important point. As it stands, the amendment would not impose on advice agencies and unions the linked obligation under Section 43B(4). Unless the advice agency or union accepts that the information is subject to clear obligations of confidence, it will be free to do as it pleases with the information.

> It is possible that certain advice agencies—or, indeed, unions—will accept as a matter of practice strict obligations of confidence. However, the amendment does not deal with that aspect of the matter. . . . One solution would be to say that the disclosures to unions under the provision should be subject to obligations of confidence. Therefore, that would make it the same as disclosures to lawyers. But to do so would have a significant effect on the role of unions in labour relations. It would mean that the information could be used for no other purpose than the one to which the client had agreed. It could not be used in the course of general negotiations with the employer. More significantly, if the information related to some safety risk, but the whistle blower decided that he did not want to raise it or pursue it, it would not be open to the union to take up the matter itself even though the well-being of some of its members might well be affected.

> Without such an obligation of confidence as a *quid pro quo* to trade union officials being equated with lawyers, one possible effect of the amendment would be to give irresponsible whistle blowers a potential passport to media and more public disclosures if they were to find an individual union member or officer who would brief the media. The publication would be effected by that person on his own behalf. The employer would have no recourse against the employee whose disclosure would be protected. We are sure that this is an unintended effect of the amendment because, as my noble friend Lady Turner said on Second Reading, disclosures to the irresponsible and sensational parts of the media should not be encouraged.

In response Lord Wedderburn (at col 626) made the following point:

> Does my noble friend recognise the fact that this point is always made about trade union officials? Indeed, it is never made about anyone else. There is a clause in the Bill, though not very well drafted, about lawyers; but surely that does not alter the very simple fact—as the Court of Appeal has pointed out on many occasions—that there is a law of confidence. . . .

> If it is confidential information, it will be a breach of confidence to impart it other than in the public interest. That does not depend on any aspect of the Bill but it does apply to all the other people involved, such as those that the Minister suggested would be proper first targets; for example, the auditors and advisers of the company, trade union officials and all sorts of other people. They are all equally governed by the law of the land. If you want to put in something about lawyers you may do so, but you had better look first at their fees.

Lords Report stage—19 June 1998

Baroness Turner tabled an amendment, specifically to amend s43C to add: 'or (c) to an official of an independent trade union authorised by the union to accept such disclosure.' This was again opposed on the basis of the emphasis on encouraging internal disclosures and it was noted that unions could appoint a union legal adviser and a hotline and recognized unions could provide for disclosures through whistleblowing policies.

Lord Haskell said (at cols 1801–1802):

> I assure my noble friend that the Government object to her amendment not because they believe that trade unions are leaky vessels which should not be entrusted with disclosures but

because the best way of resolving these difficult issues is through procedures established for the purpose.

Of course, we know very well that trade unions handle a great deal of confidential material. They are used to dealing with it responsibly with the employer on the basis of trust. The Government are not in any way suggesting that unions are irresponsible or untrustworthy. Indeed, they have set out their support for trade unions in the *Fairness at Work* White Paper which will ensure unions have a voice to be heard with the employer where employees want this. Individuals will also have the right to be accompanied by their union or a work colleague in disciplinary or grievance hearings.

However, our starting point for this Bill is to encourage co-operation between employers and employees at all levels in identifying and resolving concerns within the company. The amendment would undermine this aim, and could jeopardise the widespread support behind the Bill. It would in effect open up so-called internal disclosures, and transform them into 'external' disclosures.

The best way to resolve a problem is through the use of proper internal procedures. The Bill as drafted encourages employers to set up easily accessible procedures which will encourage employees to raise and resolve their concerns through their employer, so that the employer can take any necessary action and the employee can be reassured that the matter is being handled properly. In some cases, of course, there may be such a conflict, and the Bill provides the necessary alternative routes for disclosure. There is wide protection where disclosure is made to a prescribed person under Section 43F. More generally, protected disclosures can be made to external bodies if the individual acts reasonably under Section 43G if he has been first to the employer or has good grounds for not doing so; or under Section 43H if it is an exceptionally serious failure.

Trade unions can have a valuable role to play in procedures, and in many cases it will be appropriate for them to have a formal role so that disclosure to them would be covered by Section 43C(2). Unions may well seek to ensure that their role is formalised in this way. However, whether or not they do so will be a matter for them to agree with the employer.

In addition, unions can organise themselves in other ways to ensure that individuals have protection if they discuss confidential matters. I understand that at least one union has set up a 'whistleblowers' legal hotline. Other unions have general inquiry points for legal advice. Disclosures made to union-based legal advisers in these ways will of course be protected under Section 43D. . . .

Lord Borrie emphasized that it did not fit with s43(C)(1)(b) (at cols 1801–1802):

Subsection (b) demonstrates that the 'other responsible person' refers to the person responsible for the malpractice because it is his misconduct which is in issue or because he has a legal responsibility for the malpractice.

This clause is absolutely at the heart of the Bill because this is the provision which will assert and help to ensure that those who are responsible for the concern or malpractice—be it crime, other kinds of illegality, danger to health or safety—are made aware of the concern and can investigate it.

The effect is that if the concern proves well-founded and there is concern on behalf of the public interest, the employer will, in law, be accountable for the response. Your Lordships will all recall the tragic loss of life in connection with the Zeebrugge ferry. Even though the official inquiry found that on five occasions staff had voiced concerns that the ferries were sailing with their bow doors open, the company was not liable in criminal law, as the board—known in law as the controlling heart and mind of the organisation—had not been informed on those concerns and was unaware of the resultant risk.

By contrast, when four schoolchildren were killed during a canoeing expedition at Lyme Bay, the managing director of the Outward Bound centre was gaoled for two years because a member of staff had written to him with a clear and graphic warning about the grave risk to life if safety standards were not dramatically and considerably improved. Unable to give good reason as to why he had ignored that warning, the managing director was the very first person in the United Kingdom to be gaoled for what is called corporate manslaughter. Therefore, what will be Section 43C of the 1996 Act signals that concerns should be raised with those who, in law, are responsible for the matter—normally the employer. However, where someone else is legally responsible, then it will be that person.

In practical terms the clause as it stands, unamended, is right to emphasise the vital role of those who are in law accountable for the conduct or practice in question. To accept my noble friend's amendment would confuse the very principle of accountability that the Bill and its supporters, including many trade unions, wish to see developed. It would suggest that it is enough simply to tell an authorised union official and that there is no need to tell the employer or the person responsible in law for the conduct or malpractice.

In relation to the role of unions, Lord Borrie said (at cols 1802–1803):

Finally, I should like to offer my noble friend some reassurance about the role of unions. Both I and the Minister in Committee—and the Minister again today—have indicated that unions will play a major role in developing the new law. Where a union is recognised, my noble friend will know that those behind the Bill consider it almost inevitable that the union will be given an important role to play in the organisation's—that is, the employer's—own whistle-blowing procedures. If I may say so, I believe that that is accepted by my noble friend and those who sponsored her amendment in Committee.

The issue which I believe has troubled my noble friend—and continues to trouble her—is what happens when the union is not part of those procedures, no doubt because it has not been recognised. Both I and government spokesmen have assured the House that disclosures in such cases to unions are capable of protection under what will be Sections 43G and 43H.

As my noble friend is aware, if there are problems in practice, a case can be made and the Government pressed to ensure that unions might be prescribed under Section 43F....

Where a union is not part of an organisation's whistle-blowing procedure, I ask: what help can a union easily and safely offer a member who is concerned about malpractice or misconduct? I believe that the answer is a practical one, clearly catered for in the Bill. For example, the Transport Salaried Staffs' Association offers telephoned legal advice through its national legal office. As my noble friend will recognise, disclosures in such circumstances—that is, the detailed asking for and giving of advice—are fully protected under what will be Section 43D. That simple service not only protects the worker and promotes the role of the unions; it also helps preserve the public interest within the framework of the Bill.

The union itself has a collective as well as an individual role to play. I note that my noble friend Lord McCarthy said in Committee on 5th June (col. 627 of *Hansard*) that if the union thought that giving the kind of advice that we are discussing could compromise it in collective bargaining, perhaps the union would not give that advice. Of course, that is true, but it does not really help the situation because the union has an individual role through union officials to its members and also has a collective role. It will not be very helpful in the former if it suddenly has to stop and say, 'Well, this might be relevant to something that we are engaged in as a union in collective bargaining.' I suggest that the sort of telephone hotline that I mentioned to a union lawyer, whether or not he is employed internally or externally, would be the best and most helpful way forward to ensure that the whistle blower is fully protected.

Section 43G(3)(d)

Standing Committee D: Wednesday 11 March 1998

Mr Ian McCartney

. . .

The amendment would ensure that tribunals take into account the damage that may occur to a third person by disclosure. The tribunal may already take that into account, but it is not obliged to do so. One example might be that of a doctor's receptionist who disclosed medical records in good faith and in accordance with information available to her. But she could be wrong and the patient might have suffered an irreversible invasion of privacy.

Another example might arise out of a business relationship. A bank employee might disclose that one of the bank's clients appeared to be insolvent. That could be very damaging to the client, who trusted the bank's duty of confidentiality to protect him. It would certainly damage his relationship with the bank and there might be damage to the bank's wider reputation and future business. Any potential damage might be justified by the circumstances, but the amendment has neither the intention nor the effect of suggesting that a duty of confidence to a third party will override all other factors. It would merely ensure that the tribunal will take that and any damage caused into account.

Mr Richard Shepherd:

As originally drafted, the Bill did not require tribunals to give weight to whether the information was confidential and, if so, what damage the disclosure may have caused to the third party whose confidence had been breached.

In consultations, the Minister and I agreed that any cross-reference to the law of confidence in the Bill was inappropriate for a number of reasons. First, we were keen to make the public interest in all disclosure of wrong-doing the pre-eminent factor. Secondly, we feared that it would not be sufficiently clear to employers and employees how this area of case law might apply if there were some umbilical link. Thirdly, we recognized that workers who reported a serious wrong-doing should not forfeit protection because it later transpired that that information was not in law confidential. When the courts have granted or refused an injunction to stop the disclosure of that same confidential information, the view of the Minister, with which I acquiesced, was that those decisions should be relevant, but not binding on the tribunal. As such, no reference was made to the law of confidence in the Bill.

During consultation, the point was made that there are some particularly important obligations of confidence for example, those owed by a doctor to his patient or a bank to its customer. A fear was expressed that the Bill as drafted might unwittingly permit or encourage a secretary in a doctor's surgery or a clerk in a bank to disclose a concern about malpractice or misconduct without regard to the fact that that information was subject to an important obligation of confidence owed by the employer to a third party. The amendment has been tabled simply to allay those fears. Its purpose is not to thwart protection simply because the information was subject to a routine claim of confidentiality. It covers those exceptional cases in which there is a particularly important duty of confidence, as between doctors and patients, when a worker's disclosure breaches that duty and harms the third party. In such cases, it is right that the tribunal should consider the breach and the degree of any harm that it causes in deciding whether the disclosure was reasonable.

Section 43H

Standing Committee D: Wednesday 11 March 1998

Amendment to introduce reasonableness test into s43H:

Mr Ian McCartney

> The Government firmly believe that where exceptionally serious matters are at stake, workers should not be deterred from raising them. It is important that they should do so, and that they should not be put off by concerns that a tribunal might hold that they should have delayed their disclosure or made it in some other way.

> That does not mean that people should be protected when they act wholly unreasonably: for example, by going straight to the press when there would clearly have been some other less damaging way to resolve matters. A matter might have been remedied earlier by the employer, or an allegation might have been proved entirely false. That might have become clear if the worker had raised it with a responsible body first. The Bill could cause significant damage to employers, and fears were raised that the balance of the Bill was tipped too far against the employer in such circumstances.

> The amendment will encourage people to act reasonably even in serious matters, but it should not make them afraid that they will lose protection when they do so. It restores the balance between the need to make a disclosure and the need to do so in an effective and reasonable manner. Such disclosures should not be made in an offhand, rushed way to the press, as if that were the first or only way to raise the complaint or allegation. The amendment re-tilts the balance to an even keel by recognising employers' needs as well as the dangers of discouraging urgent and serious disclosures.

Lord Borrie (introducing in Lords for 2nd reading—11 May 1998):

> This requirement within the Bill's structure that the concern should have been raised first does not apply where the worker can demonstrate a reasonable belief that he will be victimized or that evidence of the malpractice will be destroyed or covered up. Equally, no such conditions presently exist where the matter is exceptionally serious, such as the sexual abuse of a minor, an issue addressed in Section 43H.

Lords Committee Stage on 5 June 1998

Lord McCarthy tabled an amendment to s43H(1)(d) to tone down the exceptionally serious failure test and replace it with: 'he believes on reasonable grounds that the relevant failure is of a very serious nature.'

Lord McCarthy emphasized the difficulty in knowing whether a failure was exceptional and the importance of this due to the s43G(2) gateway requirements. He commented (at col 629) that:

> it might be asked what the difference is. 'Exceptional,' might relate to a matter that cannot be known. There might be some databank indicating the average, the mean, the norm; and it might then be said that the matter was an exception: that only 4 per cent or 8 per cent of illegalities were of this kind, and this one was therefore exceptional. It would be very difficult for anybody to be certain that a complaint was exceptional. I find it an exceptional word. It would be easier to operate if the matter was 'very serious'. A 'serious' matter would not be trifling, incidental or unimportant; and a matter that was 'very serious' would be the same, only more so. We should not then get into this 'roundabout', whereby we are trying to calculate whether a matter falls within the top 5 per cent. of illegality. We therefore believe it more reasonable and sensible to change the wording on the face of the Bill in the way that we suggest.

Lord Haskell (for the Government) emphasized the rare circumstances in which it was intended that s43H would apply (at cols 629–630):

> New Section 43H provides protection for workers who make disclosures about exceptionally serious failures. The intention is to provide as clear an indication as possible that the order of seriousness—if I may put it that way—is greater than that for other disclosures. The new section is meant to apply only in very rare cases. The purpose of inserting 'exceptional' is to indicate that the case is indeed a rare case. Nobody wants individuals disclosing confidential information to other bodies unless the circumstances are exceptional.
>
> However, we all recognise that there will be concerns that are rare, but so grave that they need to be disclosed and dealt with as soon as possible. We believe that the current wording conveys that very clearly. In our view, the proposed amendment is less unambiguous, and leaves room for doubt as to how this section should be interpreted in practice.
>
> We believe that the best way to convey the order of seriousness under new Section 43H is by referring to failures that are objectively judged to be exceptionally serious. There may be disclosures which are very serious, but hardly exceptional, and such disclosures would be protected under other provisions in the Bill.
>
> I realise that my noble friend Lord McCarthy has some concerns about whether an individual will be able to judge if a matter is exceptionally serious. He mentioned that issue at Second Reading. It is a very fair point. He raised it in the context of guidance on the Bill.
>
> Public Concern at Work will be liaising with the CBI and the TUC in developing guidelines. These will provide a user-friendly explanation of the Bill, and the best practical way for workers to proceed if they are worried about wrongdoing or failures in the workplace. That will be of considerable practical value to employers and workers alike.
>
> In addition, the Department of Trade and Industry will be issuing its own guide to workers' rights under the Bill. . . .

Section 47B: Detriment: Threats

Lords Committee Stage on 5 June 1998

Lord Wedderburn tabled an amendment in relation to threats of detriment. He referred to *Mennell v Newell and Wright (Transport Contractors) Ltd* [1997] IRLR 519 (CA) as indicating that threats would not otherwise be covered. The Government rejected this on the basis that threats would come within the definition of detriment and the amendment was unnecessary and would cast doubt on the meaning of other existing detriment provisions.

Lords Haskell explained (at col 634):

> Our understanding of how this would work can be illustrated by an example. An employee who has made a disclosure to the employer could be threatened with relocation to a remote branch of a company, for instance, where promotion prospects are poorer. That kind of threat is a detriment and even though the worker can be assured that the employer could not lawfully carry out the threat, the fear of the threat may well amount to detrimental action. Any threat which puts a worker at a disadvantage constitutes in itself detrimental action. Certainly, such a threat would be contrary to the openness which we hope to see between employers and employees working together in dealing with wrongdoings or failures under the Bill.
>
> The wording of the Bill follows the drafting of existing provisions of the Employment Rights Act 1996, which provides protection against detrimental treatment on specified grounds such as carrying out duties of a health and safety official. These provisions have not caused difficulties of interpretation, but to use different wording in this case, as suggested by the amendments, we feel would cast doubt on whether threats were covered in those other cases.

A separate point was made that threats to prevent disclosures being made would not be covered as there would not be protection until the disclosure was made. In response it was said that what was merely in somebody's head could not be covered, and if it was mentioned to someone that a disclosure was going to be made, that would itself be a disclosure. It was said that whilst there might be some circumstances that could be imagined, if the legislation was found not to be working in practice this could then be addressed.

As to this Lord Haskell said (at col 635):

> . . . it seems to me most unlikely that such a situation would arise. Normally, a disclosure made to the employer or via internal procedures is likely to get through, rather than be merely attempted.

> But even if the worker passes information on internally and it does not reach the right person who is responsible for dealing with such matters, it seems to me that a tribunal is likely to find that the employee has disclosed to the employer and is protected, provided that he acted in good faith.

> These amendments could allow workers to argue that although they had failed to follow the correct procedures, they had intended to do so and so had attempted to make a protected disclosure. This would of course undermine the clear procedures set out in the Bill. The Bill already contains provision in Section 43J to prevent employers placing 'gagging' restraints on employees. The amendments could be misinterpreted to enable workers to use the threat of disclosure as a bargaining counter with their employers, rather than working in partnership with them to resolve the concerns. This would be contrary to the spirit of the Bill.

Lord Borrie said (at col 635):

> . . . as soon as the employee talks to someone who is a senior person—a manager or someone in line management—he is part of the organisation of the employer and a disclosure to him, talking to him, is a disclosure within new Section 43C, and therefore there comes about the protection against victimisation and so on in the legislation. So I cannot see the value of the amendment dealing with intention. As for 'attempt,' the attempt involves, as I understand it, some sort of move towards disclosure which has not been completed. There may be some marginal value in that, but it requires the strong imagination of my noble friend to think that that adds something to the Bill.

APPENDIX 4

Extracts from Nolan Committee on Standards in Public Life

First Report of the Committee on Standards in Public Life

Chairman Lord Nolan

Volume 1: Report

[May 1995]

We recommend that departments and agencies should nominate one or more officials entrusted with the duty of investigating staff concerns raised confidentially.

54. We recognise that this represents something of a novelty, although the use of confidential appeal systems and hotlines is not uncommon in the private sector. Structured in the way we suggest, however, such a system could be introduced within the framework of the constitutional conventions governing the work of civil servants and their relations with Ministers. We accept the Government's view that most issues can safely be resolved by the normal mechanisms within departments and agencies. We think, however that the prevention of corruption and maladministration is hampered if an individual civil servant has to identify him or herself as a complainant before superiors who may have direct influence over his or her career. That has been found to be a powerful disincentive to 'whistleblowers' in other organisations. The independent charity, Public Concern at Work, has set out Good Practice Guidelines which recommend that employees are offered confidential routes to raise concerns.* Indeed, the result of failing to provide a confidential system for matters of conscience is, ironically, to encourage leaks, which are damaging to the cohesiveness of civil service bodies and weaken the relationship between Ministers and civil servants.

'Whistleblowing'

112. One of the conditions which can lead to an environment in which fraud and malpractice can occur, according to the Metropolitan Police, is the absence of a mechanism by which concerns can be brought to light without jeopardising the informant.† The Audit Commission figures (see Table 3) show that information from staff is a major contribution to the detection of fraud and corruption in the NHS. Concerned staff were instrumental in uncovering serious irregularities at two colleges of further education.‡ As Public Concern at Work, a leading charity in this field, told us in their submission, 'if there is a breach of the standards appropriate in a public body it is likely that the first people to suspect it will be the staff who work there'.

---

* Public Concern at Work, First Annual Report (1994), page 12.
† Metropolitan Police, Fraud Squad, Public Sector Corruption Unit, written evidence.
‡ As described to us by the Chairman and Chief Executive of the Further Education Funding Council.

Table 3: Method of detection of proven fraud and corruption in the NHS, over 3 years to 1994.

Information from staff	22%
Information from patients	9%
Accidental	8%
Internal controls	22%
Internal audit	18%
External audit	10%
Other	11%

Source: Audit Commission, in *Protecting the Public Purse 2: Ensuring in the NHS*, 1994

113. However, it seems that staff concerns come to light despite rather than because of the system. We are not aware of any central guidance for executive NDPBs, and whilst the NHS have issued comprehensive central guidance,* the Audit Commission's 1994 report found that none of the 17 NHS bodies they visited had well-publicised system which informed staff whom they should contact if they suspect fraud and corruption.

114. There is public concern about 'gagging clauses' in public employees' contracts of employment, which prevent them from speaking out to raise concerns about standards of propriety. Where a loyal employee has concerns about impropriety, making public allegations in the media is unlikely to be their first recourse. However, without some way of voicing their concern, and without some confidence that it will be taken seriously and dealt with if necessary, they may feel they have no other option. We agree with the sentiment expressed by Robert Sheldon MP, Chairman of the public Accounts Committee that 'public money must never be allowed to have silence clauses'. On the other hand, we would not wish to encourage vexatious or irresponsible complaints which undermine public confidence in institutions without due cause. We believe the best way to achieve this balance is to develop sound internal procedures backed by an external review.

115. Non-executives often see themselves as a safeguard against such problems but staff may be suspicious or reluctant to approach them. The Audit Commission found a third of the NHS staff they interviewed would take no action in the face of impropriety because of fears of losing their jobs if they 'rock the boat'. Alan Langlands, the Chief Executive of the NHS, recognised that, 'a sustained effort is required to ensure that these guidelines are properly carried through, both in spirit and in detail at local lever'. As Public Concern at Work point out, 'although the employee is well placed to sound the alarm, he or she has most to lose by raising the matter'.

116. In Chapter 3, we propose that each government department and agency nominate an officer to provide a clear route for staff concerns about improper conduct. This will be supported by a further route of appeal to the Civil Service Commissioners. The NHS guidance suggests that NHS bodies might wish to designate such an officer.

We recommend that each executive NDPB and NHS body that has not already done so should nominate an official or board member entrusted with the duty of investigating staff concerns about propriety raised confidentially. Staff should be able to make complaints without going through the normal management structure, and should be guaranteed anonymity. If they remain unsatisfied, staff should also have a clear route for raising concerns about issues of propriety with the sponsor department.

---

* Guidance for staff on relations with the public and the media, issued by the NHS Management Executive, June 1993.

Local Public Spending Bodies

Further and Higher Education Bodies (including universities)
Grant-maintained schools
Training and Enterprise Councils and local Enterprise Companies
Registered Housing Associations

Second Report of the Committee on Standards in Public Life

Chairman Lord Nolan

Volume 1: Report

Blowing the Whistle

41. All organisations face the risks of things going wrong or of unknowingly harbouring malpractice. Part of the duty of identifying such a situation and taking remedial action may lie with the regulatory or funding body. But the regulator is usually in the role of detective, determining responsibility after the crime has been discovered. Encouraging a culture of openness within an organisation will help: prevention is better than cure. Yet it is striking that in the few cases where things have gone badly wrong in local public spending bodies, it has frequently been the tip-off to the press or the local Member of Parliament—sometimes anonymous, sometimes not—which has prompted the regulators into action.

42. Placing staff in a position where they feel driven to approach the media to ventilate concerns is unsatisfactory for both the staff member and the organisation. We observed in our first report that it was far better for systems to be put in place which encouraged staff to raise worries within the organisation, yet allowed recourse to the parent department where necessary. In the course of the present study, we received evidence from the independent charity, Public Concern at Work, which specialises in this area. They proposed that an effective internal system for the raising of concerns should include:

- a clear statement that malpractice is taken seriously in the organisation and an indication of the sorts of matters regarded as malpractice
- respect for the confidentiality of staff raising concerns if they wish, and the opportunity to raise concerns outside the line management structure
- penalties for making false and malicious allegations
- an indication of the proper way in which concerns may be raised outside the organisation if necessary.

43. We agree. This approach builds on some aspects of existing practice, for example the duty of accounting officers in education bodies to notify the funding councils of the misuse of public funds. It goes further by inviting *all* staff to act responsibly to uphold the reputation of their organisation and maintain public confidence. It might help to avoid the cases when the first reaction of management faced with unwelcome information has been to shoot the messenger.

R2. Local public spending bodies should institute codes of practice on whistleblowing, appropriate to their circumstances, which would enable concerns to be raised confidentially inside and, if necessary, outside the organisation.

44. In the next three chapters we examine the main issues sector by sector, before drawing some general conclusions in chapter 6.

96. In practice, it seems that universities and funding councils have struck a practical bargain between the benefits of autonomy and the need for accountability. We agree with the maxim that 'the exact counter-balance to autonomy is accountability'. As HEFCE argued, that meant that

universities could be required to act reasonably, not to misuse public funds, not to withhold information from HEFCE, and not to ignore probity, value for money, or good governance—all requirements that can be imposed without infringing academic freedom.

97. That view does not lead us to underestimate the true importance of academic freedom if properly defined. The right of individuals to pursue lines of research and publication which may be unpopular or controversial seems to us to be fundamental to the success of universities, reflected in the debates of senates and the like, as an academic institution. By extension, it has created a tradition of freedom of speech within a university which is an important check on impropriety. Comparisons with the requirements of confidentiality normal in a commercial business are misleading and misguided, as Sir Michael Davies observed in his visitorial report on University College, Swansea: 'the point is that neither the University of Wales nor the University College Swansea is a "company" in the profit-making or any other sense. They are academic institutions.' He added that, when drawing the line between the exercise of proper academic freedom and unacceptable dissent, 'the fact that it is a line to be drawn in an adult academic world and not in a commercial jungle is of profound importance'.

R7. Institutions of higher and further education should make it clear that the institution permits staff to speak freely and without being subject to disciplinary sanctions or victimisation about academic standards and related matters, providing that they do so lawfully, without malice, and in the public interest.

Confidentiality clauses

98. In Chapter 1 we discussed the importance for organisations of setting up a proper system of whistleblowing within the organisation. Yet cases of misconduct and maladministration involving a risk to public funds will occur from time to time. In some cases, the embarrassment to the institution has been such that disincentives to whistleblowing, in the form of confidentiality clauses, have been used.

99. In their report *Severance Payments to Senior Staff in the Publicly Funded Education Sector*, the Public Accounts Committee observed that 'we are strongly opposed to the "gagging" clause such as that which was included in the original severance agreement [at the University of Huddersfield]. Such a restriction should not be employed to prevent disclosure of the use of public funds'. We have come across instances in higher and further education of clauses in service and severance contracts which place extremely wide restrictions on the ability of staff to discuss with outsiders events within the body in which they work. There may of course be a place for restrictions of some sort in these contracts: genuinely confidential material may need to be protected and severance agreements may contain personal details which the individual would want to keep private. Yet it is against the public interest for confidentiality clauses to inhibit the disclosure of maladministration or the misuse of public funds.

100. The charity Public Concern at Work provided us with an extract from the standard contract for staff in new universities and colleges of further education. In part it reads:

> *15.3 Confidential information must be determined in relation to individual employees according to their status, responsibilities or the nature of their duties. However, it shall include all information which has been specifically designated as confidential by [the institution] and any information which relates to the commercial and financial activities of [the institution], the unauthorised disclosure of which would embarrass harm or prejudice [the institution].*

101. We consider that this clause is unacceptably wide and will tend to inhibit staff from raising concerns in the public interest, even with the proper authorities. If clauses of this type are necessary, for example, to protect commercially sensitive details of a forthcoming purchase, they should contain a statement of a public interest exception, permitting staff to raise matters with the funding councils

or some other outside person or body, such as the Visitor. Protecting institutions from embarrassment cannot be weighed in the balance with ensuring the proper conduct of public business.

R8. Where it is absolutely necessary to include confidentiality clauses in service and severance contracts, they should expressly remind staff that legitimate concerns about malpractice may be raised with the appropriate authority (the funding council, National Audit Office, Visitor, or independent review body, as applicable) if this is done in the public interest.

Third Report of the Committee on Standards in Public Life

Chairman Lord Nolan

Volume 1: Report

Whistleblowing

193. The Local Government (Access to Information) Act 1985 imposed demanding standards of openness on local government, which compare favourably with other parts of the public sector. We received some evidence, notably from the local media, that these standards were not always observed, which, if true, would be reprehensible. The statutory arrangements, however, seem to us to be very much in line with the best practice we have recommended for other public bodies. High standards of openness should be coupled with a positive approach to whistleblowing. This is a matter on which we have, in our previous reports, adopted a consistent and firm approach which has been fully accepted by government. In our first report we recommended that:

> . . . each . . . [public] body should nominate an official or board member entrusted with the duty of investigating staff concerns about propriety raised confidentially. Staff should be able to make complaints without going through the normal management structure, and should be guaranteed anonymity.

194. We made similar recommendations in our second report. The essence of a whistleblowing system is that staff should be able to by-pass the direct management line, because that may well be the area about which their concerns arise, and that they should be able to go outside the organisation if they feel the overall management is engaged in an improper course.

195. We consider that local government should be expected to adopt this approach, and we note that the LGMB has produced recommendations on these lines. In some ways there is less need for local government employees to go to external sources, because there will usually be opposition councillors only too ready to pick up on matters of concern. That may not be a desirable way to ventilate an issue, however, and it would be sensible for councils to adopt the following approach:

- creating a route for confidential whistleblowing within the management structure, perhaps as part of the duties of the monitoring officer:
- permitting staff to raise matters in confidence with the local government ombudsman or district auditor:
- allowing access to some other external body, such as an independent charity.

196. In all cases the usual test would apply that the concerns are raised in good faith and without malice, in order for the whistleblower to be immune from disciplinary sanctions for breach of confidence.

R26 Every local authority should institute a procedure for whistleblowing, which would enable concerns to be raised confidentially inside and, if necessary, outside the organisation. The Standards Committee might well provide an internal destination for such complaints.

> *'We are not adversarial at all. We are inquisitorial and we set out to have a common aim with complainants and local authorities which is (a) to get at the truth and (b) to cooperate to try to put things right not just for the complainant but also for other people so that they do not suffer the same consequences. Our concern is that enforcement might change that, that it might become adversarial, that it might become much more like the courts and we think that might not be in the interests of complainants.* **Edward Osmotherley, Chairman, Commission for Local Government in England**

> *'Overall, and to our disappointment as a strong supporter of the Ombudsman in principle, our experience is of a service which is not living up to its potential. Inevitably the Ombudsman deals with contentious cases and frustrated individuals who use the service as a last resort. This can colour*

perceptions of its effectiveness. Nevertheless, we have encountered genuine problems with both the scope of the Ombudsman's powers and the complaint procedures for individuals. On too many occasions the public are left dissatisfied with the service provided by local authority and by the sanctions available to them when seeking redress. In many cases this dissatisfaction is not related to the question of whether a local authority has handled an issue fairly or not.' **Tony Burton, Head of Planning and Natural Resources, Council for the Protection of Rural England**

R31 Local authorities should ensure that people who receive services through a contractor to the local authority have access to a properly publicised complaints system.

258. We commented in chapter 4 about the importance of whistleblowing systems in local government. We have considered whether it would be realistic to recommend that organisations tendering for local authority services should be required, by a contract term, to have their own confidential mechanisms for reporting malpractice. The existence of such a mechanism is now considered best practice within the private sector and we would not wish to discourage organisations tendering for local authority contracts from putting their own systems in place. We recognise, however, that in the short term the existence of such procedures will be the exception rather than the rule. We therefore believe it is important that local authorities should seek to provide, through their contracts, access to their own internal whistleblowing procedures for the staff of contracting organisations. This could involve requiring the contracting organisation to declare, as part of the contract, that any confidentiality clauses relating to its staff should not apply in relation to a formal reference by that member of the staff to the council's internal whistleblowing procedures.

R32 Staff of contracting organisations should have access to the local authority's whistleblowing procedures.

'A combination of mid-career changes and early retirement has launched a skilled and potentially predatory class of knowledgeable senior local authority managers into the market place. Their skills and knowledge, gained in a local authority setting, are not only potentially of advantage to any new employer organisation offering them a job, but also potentially to the disadvantage of their former local authority.' **David Winchurch, Chief Executive, Walsall Metropolitan Borough Council**

'We believe that there are many examples of officers who have been responsible or very closely involved in the award of contracts to private sector organisations or in the award of grants to voluntary organisations who, shortly after the decision of the authority concerned, have then taken up employment with those organisations. Most members of the public would clearly regard that as an abuse. We believe it is one that should be prevented and we believe that it is capable of prevention and capable of being policed at the local level.' **Steven Bundred, Member, Society of London Treasurers, and Chief Executive, Camden Borough Council**

'I think it is an illustration of the potential conflict situation, inasmuch as it may tempt certain officers, or members also for that matter, to promote the contracting out of services with a view to their taking positions in it. That is the danger. How real a danger it is, I do not know, but it is around sufficiently for a mechanism to be required to test it.' **Sir Jeremy Beecham, Chairman, Association of Metropolitan Authorities (now Chair, Local Government Association)**

Review of Standards of Conduct in Executive NDPBs, NHS Trusts and Local Public Spending Bodies

Fourth Report of the Committee on Standards in Public Life

Chairman Lord Nolan

Common Themes

14. There is a number of issues which apply to all the bodies covered in this review which have force in more than one area of the report.

Whistleblowing

66. Responses on whistleblowing were patchy. Most executive NDPBs had formal procedures for staff to raise concerns over malpractice which were outlined in staff handbooks or codes of conduct. These allowed individuals to raise concerns confidentially with line management in the first instance. The individual then had the option to take the matter further with a nominated officer within the executive NDPB, and then to a nominated individual within the sponsor department. However some executive NDPBs had no such procedures or statement of confidentiality. Nor was there any indication that such procedures were being considered within those organisations.

67. The response we received from Public Concern at Work (the leading organisation in this field) noted that of the fourteen public bodies who commissioned them to help introduce a whistleblowing policy, one-qauarter had some difficulty distinguishing between a whistleblowing policy from a grievance procedure. In these organisations, Public Concern at Work were not convinced that staff would have sensed a genuine commitment that management wanted concerns to be raised.

68. The responses to our questionnaire noted that the whistleblowing arrangements had been put to the test in only four cases. The first two instances were (in general terms) allegations of dishonesty and/or conduct incompatible with high standards of regularity and propriety; and allegations of financial misconduct. A third case did not specify the occasions on which the arrangements had been used; and the fourth case related to personnel issues and not the use for which the mechanism was devised.

69. All organisations face the risks of things going wrong or of unknowingly harbouring malpractice. In these days of greater openness of government, those organisations who do not have arrangements to give staff the opportunity to act responsibly to uphold the reputation of the organisation and maintain public confidence, will be looked upon as failing in their duty adequately to protect the public purse.

70. It is clear that executive NDPBs and their sponsor departments are making efforts to provide avenues which enable staff to raise concerns about misconduct and malpractice, while offering safeguards about confidentiality. However, much still needs to be done to encourage a culture of openness within some organisations. **It is important that all Departments, executive NDPBs and NHS bodies should institute codes of practice on whistleblowing, appropriate to their circumstances, so as to enable concerns about malpractice to be raised confidentially inside and, if necessary, outside the organisation.** It is important that these arrangements are well publicised within organisations so that staff are left in no doubt about the avenues open to them. The proposal by Richard Shepherd MP to introduce a 'Public Interest Disclosure Bill' in the current Parliamentary session is likely to receive support from the Government, and will require a whole-hearted response from public sector bodies.

Getting the Balance Right
Implementing Standards of Conduct in Public Life

Tenth Report of the Committee on Standards in Public Life

CHAIRMAN: SIR ALISTAIR GRAHAM

4. Embedding the Seven Principles of Public Life into Organisational Culture

4.1 Embedding the Seven Principles of Public Life into organisational culture is a common thread that runs through this report. Our analysis and recommendations in Chapters 2 and 3 are specifically designed to introduce proportionate arrangements to do just this in the area of public appointments by government departments and in the conduct of councillors in local government.

4.2 In this final chapter we review some of the key generic components that can be applied more widely in all public sector bodies to enhance their governance arrangements in an effective and pro- portionate manner. Inevitably much of this concerns learning and drawing upon good practice in specific areas for more general application across the public sector. This is not always straightfor- ward. While it appears that many of us can readily recognise a healthy organisation with ethical behaviour at the heart of its culture (ie part and parcel of everyday operations) we all find it more dif- ficult to describe the constituent[s] parts which have made it so.

4.3 However intangible the issue of culture appears, the Committee believes that it is critical to deliv- ering high standards of propriety in public life in a proportionate and effective manner. Learning from good practice must play a central role and we have identified three key areas for improvement:

. . .

(iii) **'Whistleblowing'—or more accurately—a culture that encourages the challenge of inap- propriate behaviour at all levels.** We have sought to distinguish between the 'media' driven definition of whistleblowing and the role it can play internally in a healthy ethical organisa- tional culture. Here, more than in any other area we have considered, the principle of Leadership is paramount if organisations are to truly 'live out' the procedures that all have in place. The statutory framework is a helpful driver but must be recognised as a 'backstop' which can provide redress when things go wrong not as a substitute for cultures that actively encour- age challenge of inappropriate behaviour. We have recommended that leaders of public bodies should commit themselves to follow the elements of good practice developed by Public Concern at Work, the leading organisation in this field.

. . .

Whistleblowing

4.31 Whistleblowing is the 'pursuit of a concern about wrongdoing that does damage to a wider public interest' [Public Concern at Work, 22/96/05]. It is therefore part of the continuum of the communication process which begins with raising a wrongdoing with a line manager, but goes beyond that if the line manager does not deal with it or is not the appropriate person to be approached [Guy Dehn 15.06.04 508]. As the Committee noted in its Third Report [15, page 48], the essence of a whistleblowing system is that staff should be able to by-pass the direct management line, because that may well be the area about which their concerns arise, and that they should be able to go outside the organisation if they feel the overall management is engaged in an improper course. Effective whistleblowing is therefore a key component in any strategy to challenge inappropriate behaviour at all levels of an organisation. It is both an instrument in support of good governance and a manifestation of a more open organisational culture.

4.32 This is the first time the whistleblowing issue has been examined by this Committee since the Public Interest Disclosure Act became law, giving protection from victimisation to those who have raised issues of concern.

...

4.34 In the first three years of the Act, employees lodged over 1,200 claims alleging victimisation for whistleblowing. Two-thirds of these claims were settled or withdrawn without any public hearing. Tribunals reached full decisions in 152 cases. This has raised issues about whether it should be necessary for there to be legal protection for those raising concerns, or whether this should be tackled beforehand in the form of creating an organisational culture which promotes openness in the work place, so that these concerns are raised before it becomes necessary to invoke legislation.

4.35 Firstly, it is important to reiterate that the Act is a statutory 'backstop' to ensure that employees who follow prescribed procedures for raising concerns are not victimised or suffer detriment as a result. Where an individual case reaches the point of invoking the Act then this represents a failure of the internal systems in some respect. Either the employee has failed to follow the procedure (for whatever reason) or the procedures themselves have failed. In our view, therefore, any case where the Act is invoked should initiate a review of the whistleblowing procedures in that organisation.

4.36 Secondly, it is important to distinguish between the popular media-driven definition of a successful 'whistleblower' taking his or her 'story' directly to the press or other (non-regulator or non-prescribed) external bodies and 'real' internal whistleblowing. Successful whistleblowing, in terms of a healthy organisational culture is when concerns are raised internally with confidence about the internal procedures and where the concern is properly investigated and, where necessary, addressed. During the course of our inquiry there were a number of high profile 'so called' whistleblowing cases involving government departments. It is not for this Committee to comment on individual cases. However, just as where the invoking of the Act should trigger a review of whistleblowing procedures in an organisation, so should the unauthorised disclosure of information by those who cite public interest reasons. Such reviews should in no way be seen or taken as any admission of culpability by the organisation involved. A review is critical in such circumstances to demonstrate to other employees the commitment to 'living out' effective whistleblowing procedures and to learn whether there were issues of organisational culture which may have contributed to the unauthorised disclosure.

> What I tend to see, obviously from a journalist's point of view, is what reaches the media. It is when the whistleblowing arrangements do not work within an organisation then they sort of explode into the public domain.
>
> [Douglas Fraser, Political Editor of the Sunday Herald, 17.06.04 1262]

4.37 The evidence the Committee received indicates that public service leaders do recognise the importance of proper whistleblowing procedures and the integral part this plays in a healthy organisational culture:

> We have not gone so far as to teach Welsh schoolchildren the declension of, 'I brief, you leak, he, she or it blows the whistle'. I think the issue is that we believe that whistleblowers, without being artificially stimulated or encouraged to blow the whistle, have adequate protection if they do see something that they believe should have the whistle blown on it, to do what they should do at that point, which is to blow the whistle.
>
> [The Rt Hon Rhodri Morgan AM 7.07.04 2426]

> Perhaps I should just say that I think—and would like to say unambiguously—that the right of people to whistleblow, using the appropriate channels, is fundamental and absolutely important . . . Anyone working in the public sector who has a problem of this nature must feel that they can make their point known in an appropriately protected and safeguarded way.
>
> [Sir Jon Shortridge 7.07.04 2427]

I think the existence of whistleblowing will often highlight a lack of maturity in an organisation in terms of being able to deal with contentious issues in an effective, straightforward and sensible way. I do feel with other things that this [your] Committee has promoted that the focus on whistleblowing and the approach that has been developed over the last five/ten years has resulted in good progress.

[Sir Alan Langlands, 13.07.04 2877]

4.38 Public Concern at Work, the leading campaigning charity in the whistleblowing area, provided the Committee with comprehensive evidence, which repays careful reading [Public Concern at Work 22/96/01–15; Guy Dehn, Anna Myers, 15.06.04]. They warned of the dangers of a prescriptive 'one size fits all' approach to whistleblowing policies because of the wide differences in the size, function, and constitution of public bodies and because the uncritical adoption of model procedures can lead to an unwitting tick-box approach to governance.

4.39 Public Concern at Work drew our attention to variable practice on whistleblowing, both among regulators and across the public sector. We were told that 'there are a lot of differences' in the way in which regulators regard whistleblowing. While some, like the Audit Commission and the Financial Services Authority, have embraced the concept and communicated it very effectively, others have not [Guy Dehn 15.06.04 605].

4.40 This differential approach can be confusing and where the concept is not effectively communicated, disadvantageous to the challenge of inappropriate behaviour. It underlines the importance of our recommendation for public bodies to share good practice across organisational and sector boundaries. Regulators are not exempt from this. Indeed, as we pointed out in Chapter 1, cross-fertilisation is one of the principles of strategic regulation.

Recommendation

R37 All regulators should review their procedures for handling whistleblowing by individuals in bodies under their jurisdiction, drawing upon best practice (for example the Audit Commission and Financial Services Authority).

4.41 There is also a differential approach across the public sector. A key determinant of the effectiveness of the whistleblowing arrangements in a public body is the willingness of the board to demonstrate leadership on this issue. This means reviewing procedural arrangements, the extent to which they are trusted, awareness levels throughout the organisation, and reviewing how people who used the procedures were treated [Guy Dehn 5.06.04 630].

4.42 It is therefore of concern that the Audit Commission has found that only 50 per cent of the employees in the local government and health bodies which have used the Commission's self-assessment tools were aware of the Public Interest Disclosure Act, and the protection this affords an employee making a disclosure concerning fraud and corruption [Audit Commission, 22/85/04].

4.43 Public Concern at Work emphasised key elements of good practice for organisations to ensure their whistleblowing arrangements are fit for purpose and integral to their organisational culture. This Committee emphatically endorses this good practice which can be summarised in four key elements:

(i) Ensuring that staff are aware of and trust the whistleblowing avenues. Successful promotion of awareness and trust depend upon the simplicity and practicality of the options available, and also on the ability to demonstrate that a senior officer inside the organisation is accessible for the expression of concerns about wrongdoing, and that where this fails, there is recourse to effective external and independent oversight.

(ii) Provision of realistic advice about what the whistleblowing process means for openness, confidentiality and anonymity. While requests for confidentiality and anonymity should be respected, there may be cases where a public body might not be able to act on a concern without the whistleblower's open evidence. Even where the whistleblower's identity is not disclosed, 'this is no guarantee that it will not be deduced by those implicated or by colleagues'.

(iii) Continual review of how the procedures work in practice. This is a key feature of the revised Code on Corporate Governance, which now places an obligation on the audit committees of listed companies to review how whistleblowing policies operate in practice. The advantage of this approach is that it ensures a review of action taken in response to the expression of concerns about wrongdoing; it allows a look at whether confidentiality issues have been handled effectively and whether staff have been treated fairly as a result of raising concerns.

(iv) Regular communication to staff about the avenues open to them. Creative approaches to this include the use of payslips, newsletters, management briefings and Intranets, and use too of Public Concern's helpline, launched in 2003 and available through subscription.

Recommendation

R38 Leaders of public bodies should reiterate their commitment to the effective implementation of the Public Interest Disclosure Act 1998 and ensure its principles and provisions are widely known and applicable in their own organisation. They should commit their organisations to following the four key elements of good practice i.e.

(i) **Ensuring that staff are aware of and trust the whistleblowing avenues;**

(ii) **Provision of realistic advice about what the whistleblowing process means for openness, confidentiality and anonymity;**

(iii) **Continual review of how the procedures work in practice; and**

(iv) **Regular communication to staff about the avenues open to them.**

APPENDIX 5

Extracts from the Shipman Report

(5TH SHIPMAN INQUIRY REPORT OF DAME JANET SMITH, 9 DECEMBER 2004, CM 6394)

INTRODUCTION

In Chapters 8 and 9, I have considered how various people did or did not come to suspect that Shipman might be killing his patients and what, if anything, those with concerns felt able to do about raising them. I have also considered in Chapter 10 the position of two doctors who did not suspect that Shipman was deliberately doing wrong but who believed that he had given an inappropriate dose of morphine to a patient, with disastrous results. They did not report their concerns to anyone in authority.

. . .

The term 'whistleblower' is . . . a convenient shorthand way of describing the person who brings information about some form of misbehaviour to the attention of those outside his/her organisation. None of the people to whom I have referred at paragraph 11.2 could properly have been termed 'whistleblowers' had they taken their concerns to the police, the primary care organisation or (in the case of Mrs Foley and Mrs Simpson) to their employers. Mrs Bambroffe was not 'blowing the whistle' when she voiced her concerns to Dr Booth; nor was Dr Reynolds when she made her report to the Coroner. Mrs Simpson was not 'whistleblowing' when she spoke to her line manager of her concerns. None of those persons worked within the same organisation as Shipman; they were merely voicing their concerns to those who they felt were the appropriate authorities.

Another feature which set those people apart from the typical 'whistleblower' was the fact that most of them were far from confident that their concerns were justified. They were not seeing to make a complaint or to air a grievance about something that they knew to be wrong. Indeed, one of the factors that inhibited them from speaking out was their concern that they might be proved to be wrong and their fear of the consequences of such an error.

The public generally becomes aware of an incident of 'whistleblowing' when things have gone wrong—usually when the 'whistleblower' has been dismissed from his/her employment for breach of his/her duty of confidentiality or has suffered some other detriment. In some cases involving national security, 'whistleblowers' have even been prosecuted. When it appears that the 'whistleblower' has been motivated by genuine and well-founded concerns, public opinion tends to support the 'whistleblower' and the feeling is that s/he has done his/her public duty. Nevertheless, the message that emerges from media reports of 'whistleblowing' cases is in essence a negative one; namely that those who put their heads above the parapet and dare to speak out are liable to be penalised in some way. I do not think it is helpful to confuse that negative message with a discussion of how people with genuine and legitimate concerns affecting the public interest can be helped to bring forward those concerns in a responsible and effective manner.

I recognise that the meaning of the term 'whistleblower' has recently been extended somewhat. It is now sometimes used to describe a person who reports his/her concerns within the organisation to which those concerns refer, or even to describe a member of the public who raises concerns about a person or organisation with which s/he has no personal connection at all. It is used also to describe the raising of concerns which are less serious in nature than those that have formed the basis of the most celebrated 'whistleblowing' cases. Many of the witnesses to the Inquiry used the term 'whistleblowing' virtually synonymously with 'the raising of concerns.'

I propose to avoid using the expression 'whistleblowing' wherever possible. However, the term has come into such general use that many organisations now have what they call 'whistleblowing' policies, which are really policies to assist employees to 'raise concerns' in an appropriate way, giving them an assurance that they will be taken seriously and will not be victimised as a result of their action. Because the term 'whistleblowing' is used in this way by some, I will occasionally have to use it myself in this Chapter, as I did in Chapter 9. Otherwise, I shall not.

Serving the Public Interest

The raising of genuinely held concerns about issues of public importance is to be encouraged. The public interest may be served in many different ways, such as by the prevention or detection of crime, by the prevention of accidents or by the protection of the public purse. I have already mentioned some natural barriers to the raising of concerns encountered by those who harboured concerns about Shipman. Others include the fear of being seen as a troublemaker or 'maverick,' the fear of recriminations and a feeling of impotence grounded in the belief that, even if the report is made, nothing will be done about it. There may be a concern that making a report might lead to proceedings for defamation. There may be anxiety that the report of a concern will be interpreted as an attack on an individual or body whereas no such attack may be intended. There may be a fear that the group or team of which the person to be criticised is a member will rally round him/her and will ostracise the person who has raised the concern.

It is now generally recognised that the raising of a concern within the organisation in which it arises is usually preferable to more public disclosure. There are several reasons for this. There is a proper public interest in ensuring that genuinely confidential information is kept confidential. There is also a real public interest in promoting the internal accountability of organisations. Of course, some mistakes and misdeeds are so important that it is only right that the general public should be made fully aware of them; there are, however, many occasions when it would be preferable, in the public interest, that the organisation responsible for an error should be able to correct it and learn from it without any outside involvement. Disclosure to the press can attract a disproportionate degree of publicity with adverse consequences for all. The organisation is 'put on the back foot' by the unexpected disclosure and can become defensive and secretive. There is a tendency for attention to be focussed on the messenger rather than on the message and the 'whistleblower' may suffer reprisals. In brief, no one benefits.

The task of devising a system is relatively easy. The real challenge is in developing a culture where every member of a group, team, department or profession feels a sense of responsibility for the actions of the others. Where what is in issue is a question of poor clinical performance, that sense of responsibility may lead, first, to an attempt to assist the person who is performing badly to improve, but should extend, if necessary, to making an official report to an appropriate person. There is also a need to develop a culture in which, when a concern is raised about the conduct of practice of one member of a group, the rest of the group does not 'close ranks' and ostracise the person who has spoken out. In the last few years, real attempts have been made to improve the position of people who raise concerns.

Improving the Position for the Future

It appears to me that the position of any person seeking to raise a concern is now very much better than it was even six years ago, when the PIDA was passed. I think that the PIDA has been of great value, both in the relief it has provided for individuals and also in changing general attitudes. However, I am sure that more remains to be done. Mr Dehn told the Inquiry that the operation of the PIDA had been found to be less than perfect in some respects and it was intended that its operation should be reviewed with a view to introducing amendments. That being so, I propose to make some suggestions as to how the PIDA should be amended.

Possible Changes to the Public Interest Disclosure Act 1998

It is perhaps worth saying again that the object of any legislation of this kind must be to encourage persons to bring forward genuinely held concerns where the bringing of those concerns, whether subsequently found to be right or wrong, is in the public interest

Use of the Word 'Disclosure'

As I have said, the PIDA refers generally to the making of '*disclosures.*' To my mind, the use of that word conveys the presumption that the 'disclosed' facts are true. What is in fact happening is that concerns or information (that may be true or false) are being 'reported.' I would suggest that thought be given to the possible substitution of the word 'report' for the words '*disclose*' and '*disclosure.*'

Extension of the Categories of Persons Prescribed under Section 43F

In the context of raising a concern about a doctor or nurse or other healthcare worker, it is not satisfactory that '*disclosure*' or report made to the GMC or to the Healthcare Commission does not attract second tier protection. If and when the legislation is amended, I suggest that the Healthcare Commission, all the healthcare regulators and possibly even the Council for the Regulation of Healthcare Professionals (now known as the Council for Healthcare Regulatory Excellence) should be included in the list under section 43F of the Act. I note that the Ledward Inquiry Report recommended that second tier protection should be given to workers reporting a doctor to the GMC.

Good Faith

As I have explained above, no disclosure (except a disclosure made to a legal adviser in the course of obtaining legal advice) can be a qualifying disclosure unless it is made '*in good faith.*' When Mr Dehn gave evidence, in September 2003, he was asked about his understanding of that phrase. His response suggested that PCaW generally advised that '*good faith*' equated to honesty. He said:

> I think two things—and this was an issue that came up slightly with the discussion after the Bristol Inquiry reported—is that the good faith test or the reference to good faith was very much certainly in my understanding—subject to what you and the Chairman would say—is in the narrow legal meaning of 'good faith,' as in honesty or an absence of predominant or improper motive rather than in this sort of slightly more common meaning of 'good faith' meaning sort of 'virtuous'. So we generally say that the phrase 'good faith' if we are speaking to a public audience is we equate that with honesty. In other words, it is a disclosure that is made honestly.

I can see the force of PCaW's argument. If employers are able to explore and impugn the motives of the 'messenger,' when trying to justify having taken action against him/her, many 'messages' will not come to light because organisations like PCaW will have to advise those who come to them for advice that, if their motives can be impugned, they may not be protected by the PIDA. The Court of Appeal emphasised that someone in Mrs Street's situation was not totally without remedy; she lost the 'automatic protection' of the PIDA but retained the right to argue that, in all the circumstances, her dismissal had been unfair. That is undoubtedly so, but anyone advising her before she made her disclosure would have had to give very cautious advice. The effect of receiving that cautious advice might well have meant that she would have kept quiet. This would be unfortunate if the information affected, for example, patient safety in a healthcare setting. It is clear that, prior to the decision in *Street* at least, PCaW did not advise those who sought its advice that the presence of mixed motives would defeat a claim to automatic protection under the legislation.

It also appears that some organisations operate a policy which guarantees their employees greater protection than is, in fact, provided by the PIDA. Mr Alan Turner, consultant urologist and, since 1993, Medical Director of Peterborough Hospitals NHS Trust, provided the Inquiry with a copy of the whistleblowing policy operated by his Trust. Its language does not have the clarity that would be desirable in an Act of Parliament but its message is tolerably clear. It says:

> No disciplinary action will be taken against someone who makes a disclosure in good faith regardless of whether or not it is substantiated. (Of course, we do not extend this assurance to someone who maliciously raises a matter they know to be untrue).'

The phrase *'in good faith'* in that context, juxtaposed with the state of mind of a person who *'maliciously raises a matter'* s/he knows to be untrue, would not appear to require the absence of mixed motives that the PIDA has been held to require. The policy of the New Charter Housing Trust contains the following paragraph, which again goes further than the PIDA:

> If it is discovered you have abused this confidential reporting process and have maliciously or in bad faith or without reasonable belief raised unfounded allegations, we will treat this as a very serious disciplinary matter. No-one who comes forward in good faith and/or with a reasonable belief has anything to fear even if it turns out that their concerns were unfounded.

Although the words *'in good faith'* appear in that policy, it would seem that a person with 'mixed motives' would not have *'anything to fear'* so long as s/he had *'a reasonable belief'* even if his/her concerns were unfounded.

It seems to me that the assurances given in these two policies are pitched to give the level of protection that the PIDA ought to give—and that PCaW would like it to give—but does not. I think that there should be public discussion about whether the words *'in good faith'* ought to appear in the PIDA. In my view, they could properly be omitted. The three tiered regime of the PIDA, with its incrementally exacting requirements, should afford sufficient discouragement to those minded maliciously to raise baseless concerns. I think that it would be appropriate also if the preamble to the PIDA made it plain that the purpose of the PIDA is to protect persons disclosing information, the disclosure of which is in the public interest. That would serve to focus attention on the message rather than the messenger. The public interest would be served, even in cases where the motives of the messenger might not have been entirely altruistic.

The onus should not, in my view, be on an individual to establish *'reasonable belief'* in the case of internal disclosures and disclosures to external regulators. The public interest would, in my view, be best served by substituting 'suspicion' for 'belief'. The Tameside Families Support Group suggested this and I agree with its suggestion.

I am also of the view that to apply the *'reasonable belief'* test to reports of concern to *'prescribed persons'* sets the threshold for protection too high. In determining whether disclosures to *'prescribed persons'* attract protection, this test requires a *'reasonable belief'* that the information disclosed and any allegation contained in it is *'substantially true'*. This may be desirable and appropriate when the information is a matter is of firsthand observation but the position is different when the information is secondhand, perhaps a strong rumour or suspicion. The individual concern might well not be in a position to say that s/he reasonably believes *'that the information disclosed, and any allegation contained in it'* is *'substantially true'* although she might strongly suspect that to be the case and that suspicion might well warrant investigation. In an area where the natural tendency will be for people to 'sit tight' or 'keep quiet' I take the view that to apply as a threshold 'reasonable belief in substantial truth' will result in the regulators remaining unaware of cases of which they should be aware.

The third *'reasonable belief'* test, applicable, for example, to disclosures to the media, depends on the worker having the *'reasonable belief'* that his employer will 'respond badly' to the allegation, before an external disclosure (other than to a regulator) becomes protected. I do not regard this as being so onerous. It is far less exacting to expect a worker to be able to explain the basis for a belief about the likely response of his/her employer than it is to require justification of a belief about a state of affairs of which s/he may have only partial knowledge or understanding.

The problem could be resolved in the particular example I have given by imposing a requirement that each GP practice have a policy authorising disclosures to be made directly to the PCT. That is desirable and, indeed, it is contemplated by the draft policy to which I refer in paragraph 11.72. However, there may be other situations in which the problem cannot be resolved so easily. I have in mind, for example, the position of an employee in a small firm or business who begins to suspect that his/her employer may be defrauding clients. He or she is likely to feel unable to raise the matter within the firm, yet may not feel sufficiently certain to make a report to the police. A report made to a trade or professional organisation would attract protection under the PIDA only at the third tier, with all the additional hurdles that must be overcome before protection is secured. A possible but unwieldy option would be for the range of *'protected persons'* to be extended. The preferable solution—and I suggest this for consideration only—may be to consider requiring all employers to specify a third party recipient for expressions of concern. Provision could be made to allow third tier disclosures by employees of employers who did not take this step to be treated as second tier disclosures. I recognise that this suggestion is outside my Terms of Reference but, if the PIDA is to be reviewed, it occurs to me that it might help for such a provision to be included.

I mention in passing that the protection that the common law gives against proceedings in defamation is rather wider than that given under the PIDA to workers who have suffered a detriment on account of making a disclosure. The effect of the decision in *Horrocks* to which I have referred, is that, at common law, if it appears that the person making the allegation had mixed motives, judges and juries should not closely scrutinise those motives to ascertain which was predominant. Instead, they should concentrate on whether the person believed in the truth of what s/he said. If the words *'in good faith'* were removed from the PIDA, the test under the PIDA would be brought more closely into line with the test for 'malice' in defamation proceedings. It would seem to me to be desirable that the tests should be as close as possible so that a person thinking of making a report can be safely advised about his/her position in respect of both types of proceedings. It would also bring the test to be applied under the PIDA closer to the terms of many whistleblowing policies currently in force.

CONCLUSIONS

The value of the honest raising of concerns within the healthcare services should not, in my view, be underestimated. Together with patient complaints, of which I shall say more later in this Report, it provides an important source of information about clinical performance and has a vital role in clinical governance. The culture that for many years effectively prevented the raising of such concerns is changing but the old attitudes have not yet by any means died out. It is important, in my view, that those in positions of leadership, whether in managerial positions or at the head of the professions, should be committed to openness of reporting, not only by endorsing policies and the like but by practising what they preach.

I have already suggested a number of ways in which the momentum for change can be kept up. I have suggested amendments to the PIDIA which would, if implemented, strengthen the position of those who raise concerns. I shall not repeat those suggestions here. I have also suggested that policies for the raising of concerns across different sections of the healthcare services should be promulgated. I have called for the provision of an advice service available to any person, whether or not a healthcare professional, so as to provide the advice, encouragement and reassurance necessary for them to bring forward concerns which it is in the public interest to report.

Sample Whistleblowing Policies

A. CIVIL SERVICE

Department for Culture Media and Sport's Whistleblowing procedure.

Aim

1. The aim of this policy is to provide staff with a procedure for reporting any unlawful conduct at work and to reassure them that they can feel confident in exposing wrongdoing without any risk to themselves.

Context

2. All of us at one time or another may have concerns about what is happening at work. Usually these concerns can be easily resolved. However, when they are about unlawful conduct, fraud, dangers to the public or the environment, or other malpractice, it can be difficult to know what to do.

3. Many people in this situation worry about reporting their concerns and may feel inclined to keep such concerns to themselves, perhaps because the concern is only a suspicion or it could be described as none of their business. They may not want to feel that they are being disloyal to colleagues, management or to the Department. They may also have concerns about being branded as a trouble maker or even about their own job security or prospects.

Public Interest Disclosure Act 1998

4. The **Public Interest Disclosure Act** came into force on 2 July 1999. It enables workers who 'blow the whistle' about wrongdoing to complain to an employment tribunal if they are dismissed or suffer any other form of detriment for doing so.

5. The legislation covers workers in the public sector (with some exceptions, eg those who work in the security services) as well as the private sector. For Civil Servants, this legislation needs to be considered alongside the appeals mechanism contained in the **Civil Service Code**.

What type of disclosure will qualify for protection?

6. A disclosure will qualify for protection ('a qualifying disclosure') if, you reasonably believe, it tends to show one or more of the following has occurred, is occurring or is likely to occur:

- A criminal offence (eg: theft and fraud).
- A failure to comply with a legal obligation.
- A miscarriage of justice.
- Endangering of an individual's health and safety.
- Damage to the environment.
- Deliberate concealment of information tending to show any of the above.

When are disclosures protected?

7. A qualifying disclosure will be protected under the Act when it is made in good faith:

- To your employer.
- To a body or person other than your employer. *
- To a legal adviser in the course of obtaining legal advice.
- To a Minister of the Crown.
- To a prescribed body or person, provided that you reasonably believe that the relevant failing falls within matters prescribed to that body or person and that the information is substantially true. For a list of prescribed persons, please refer to the section on **other sources of information**.

   *Provided that you reasonably believe that the relevant failure relates solely or mainly to the conduct of that body or person, or relates to a matter over which the body or person has legal responsibility.

Circumstances in which disclosures are not protected

8. The legislation does not introduce a general protection for whistleblowers in all circumstances. Individuals who make disclosures will not be protected by the Act if they commit an offence by making the disclosure (**eg breach of the Official Secrets Act**)—[please refer to Annex A of this link for a basic guide to the Act].

How to use the DCMS Whistleblowing Procedure

9. The Department's Whistleblowing procedure should be followed if you wish to make a disclosure to your employer. It can be used to report bad practice which threatens the interests of others or the Department. The procedure to follow in order to raise a concern internally is described in the next section.

10. For some instances of possible malpractice, you will need to read this procedure in conjunction with other policies which are already in place. For example, if your concern is about fraud, you should also read the DCMS Fraud policy. The DCMS Fraud policy sets out your responsibilities regarding both the prevention of fraud and the procedures to be followed where a fraud is detected or suspected. It also explains what fraud is if staff are in doubt. Channels for reporting concerns relating to fraud will normally be as described in the next section of this policy, or depending on the circumstances, as laid down in 'Who to report to' in Annex A of the DCMS Fraud Policy.

11. If your concern is regarding the violation of the expected standard of conduct of staff, the following table sets out the other policies with which this policy will need to be read.

Possible examples of bad practice and Policy to be read in conjunction with the DCMS Whistleblowing procedure

- Misuse of information acquired in the course of work—**Confidentiality and the use of official information**.
- Violation of the Official Secrets Act—**Confidentiality and the use of official information**.
- Receiving gifts, hospitality or benefits which could compromise an individual's personal judgement or impartiality—**Gifts and Hospitality**.
- Violation of the Data Protection Act—**Data Protection Act 1998**.

12. If your concern is one of a personal nature you should follow the Department's **Complaints Procedure.** If you believe that you are being required to act in a way which is illegal or improper and you want to appeal under the Civil Service Code, you should follow the procedure set out in the **Civil Service Code** section.

13. **If something is troubling you which you think we should know about, please tell us straight away. We would rather that you raised the matter when it is just a concern rather than wait for proof.**

How to raise a concern internally

14. The procedure to follow if you want to raise a concern internally is as follows:

If you have a concern about malpractice, you should raise it first with your **line manager.** This may be done orally or in writing.

If you do not feel able to do so, for whatever reason, please raise the matter with your **Head of Division,** or your **Director** if you suspect that the Head of Division is party to the malpractice. If you do not wish to use your Divisional 'chain of command', or alternatively, if you are a line manager to whom an issue has been reported, you can raise the matter with the **Head of Personnel and Central Services Division; the Head of Finance; or Head of Internal Audit.**

Please say if you want to raise the matter in confidence so that appropriate arrangements can be made.

If these channels have been followed and you still have concerns, or if you feel that the issue is so serious that you cannot discuss it with any of the above, you can raise the matter directly with the Permanent Secretary.

Our Assurances to you

15. The Department will not tolerate the harassment or victimisation of anyone who raises a genuine concern under this policy. Provided you are acting in good faith, it does not matter if it later transpires that you were mistaken; you will not be subject to disciplinary action as a result.

16. Of course, this assurance does not extend to someone who maliciously raises a matter they know is untrue. Disciplinary action may be taken against staff who deliberately make false allegations.

Confidentiality

17. The Department recognises that you may want to raise a concern in confidence under this policy. If you ask us to protect your identity by keeping your confidence, we will not disclose it without your consent. However, in some circumstances, this may make it more difficult to fully investigate the matter. If the situation arises where we are not able to resolve the concern without revealing your identity, we will discuss with you how we can proceed.

Anonymity

18. Remember that if you do not tell us who you are, it will be much more difficult for us to look into the matter or to protect your position or to give you feedback. Accordingly, while we will consider anonymous reports, this policy is not designed to deal with concerns raised anonymously.

How we will handle the matter

19. Once you have told us of your concern, we will look into it to assess initially what action should be taken. You may be asked how you think the matter might best be resolved.

20. If you request, we will write to you summarising your concern and setting out how we propose to handle it. We will tell you who is dealing with the matter, how you can contact him/her and whether your further assistance may be needed.

21. It may be decided that a formal investigation is necessary; in most cases this will be the responsibility of the Head of Personnel and Central Services Division.

22. We will give you as much feedback as we properly can, and if requested, we will confirm our response to you in writing. However, we may not be able to tell you the precise action we take, where this would infringe a duty of confidence owed by us to someone else.

If you are dissatisfied

23. If you are unhappy with our response or with the outcome of the investigation, under the Civil Service Code you may report the matter to the Civil Service Commissioners. While we cannot

guarantee that we will respond to all matters in the way that you might wish, we will try to handle the matter fairly and properly.

24. For further guidance on how to appeal under the Civil Service Code please refer to the **Civil Service Code** section.

Independent advice

25. If after reading this policy, you are unsure whether to use this procedure or you want advice at any stage, you may contact your Departmental trade union representative. A qualifying disclosure will be protected if you make it to your Departmental trade union representative, but only if any formal action you subsequently take under the Public Interest Disclosure Act is in line with the procedure outlined at paragraph 14.

26. Alternatively, you may obtain legal advice, independently, through Public Concern at Work. This is an independent charity and is a leading authority on public interest whistleblowing. They can be contacted on 020 7404 6609 and their web address is **http://www.pcaw.demon.co.uk/**

27. A qualifying disclosure is protected if you make it in the course of obtaining legal advice. When preparing to seek legal advice you should be careful only to give details of the information you propose to disclose *to your legal adviser.* Otherwise there may be a risk that you will make **a** disclosure that will not be protected by the Public Interest Disclosure Act. Do not make a disclosure over a help-line, use one only to seek an appointment with a legal adviser.

Other sources of information

28. Other sources of information include:

The **Directory of Civil Service Guidance (section on Whistleblowing);** and

The **DTI Guide to the Public Interest Disclosure Act** (a short employment relations booklet which includes a list of prescribed persons and their areas of responsibility)

B. Banking

Standard Chartered Policy

Group Instruction

11th December 1997

Speaking up Policy

Introduction

Trust and integrity are vital to the Group. We must be able to trust each other to behave honestly. Our customers must be able to trust in the Bank absolutely.

Misconduct and malpractice breach trust and endanger the Bank's reputation and, in some cases, licences. The best way of protecting trust is for staff who have genuine suspicions about wrongdoings to speak up. Usually, staff will raise concerns with their line management but there will be times when this might not be possible.

This policy tells you what to do in such a case. Any report which you make will be listened to, investigated and treated in confidence. Victimisation of anyone who comes forward will not be tolerated. Remember 'speaking up' is an essential principle of our compliance policy.

What should I speak up about?

Any actual or planned wrongdoing or bad practice which:

- is against the law
- is against banking regulations
- does not comply with the Group rules or the Code of Conduct.

What if I have a grievance?

The system is not intended to deal with staff grievances, for which separate procedures exist.

What if I'm not sure of my facts?

You don't have to be 100% sure. If you have a genuine suspicion then come forward and explain your concerns. It may just be a mistake in the system or process, rather than deliberate wrongdoing. In any event, don't leave it until it is too late.

Won't I be thought malicious?

If you genuinely act in the best interests of the Bank and its employees, then your actions will be viewed as courageous, not malicious.

Wouldn't it be disloyal?

No—quite the opposite! Your action will help protect the interests of our Bank. Staff involved in wrongful behaviour are the ones who are being disloyal. They are putting at risk not only the achievements of their business, but possibly those of the Group as a whole.

Who should I speak to?

If you can, then you should speak to your line manager. However, the Bank accepts that there will be certain circumstances when staff could feel uncomfortable doing this. Compliance officers will therefore act as alternative first points of contact—his or her number is in your directory.

Can I come forward anonymously?

Yes. But it is much harder to investigate suspicions which are reported anonymously—and often it is impossible. It is best to declare your identity if you can.

Can I bring a colleague along?

Yes—if you wish.

What will happen next?

Your Compliance Officer will discuss with you whether anyone else needs to be put in the picture in order for your suspicions to be investigated and, if so, who. They will not mention your involvement to your line manager or anyone else implicated without your consent.

Will it be in confidence?

Every effort will be made to protect your confidence. The principle will always be to involve as few people as possible. Although you may be asked if you can provide further information, you will not be directly involved in the investigation.

What will be the consequences for me?

You will not be blamed for speaking up or for any failure to speak up earlier. Staff may have taken time to form their suspicions, or to build up the courage to act on them. However, those who have been actively involved in wrongdoing will not have automatic immunity from disciplinary or criminal proceedings.

How will I know whether action has been taken?

Your Compliance Officer will give you feedback on the outcome. Any investigation may take some time but you will be told in due course whether your suspicions were well founded and (where possible) what action is being taken about them.

C. Care Home

Leonard Cheshire

November 1998

Reasons for policy

Leonard Cheshire recognises that there are, from time to time, situations where employees/volunteers became aware of bad practices which can affect the well being of users of services, and the long-term reputation of the organisation. Suspecting or even knowing of such bad practice may cause contradictory feelings; for example employees or volunteers may be worried about raising such issues or want to keep their concerns to themselves. They may feel that raising the matter would be disloyal to colleagues, managers or to Leonard Cheshire. They may have decided to say something but find that they have spoken to the wrong person or raised the issue in an appropriate way and feel they still want to pursue it. This policy and procedure has been introduced to enable employees and volunteers to raise their concerns at an early stage. Leonard Cheshire wants matters raised when they are a concern rather than wait for proof.

Policy statement

1. Leonard Cheshire acknowledges its duty to encourage and empower employees and volunteers to speak out when they encounter bad practice.
2. All staff employed at Leonard Cheshire have a duty to care and assist people who use Leonard Cheshire Services. This duty extends to having an obligation not to overlook bad practices, but to speak out and seek to correct it.
3. No one who raises a genuine concern about bad practice will be at risk of losing their job or suffering any form of retribution as a result of doing so.
4. Trustees expect all people in management positions to recognise their responsibilities in this matter and to adopt and implement this policy and to adhere to its procedures with regard to whistleblowing by any employee or volunteer.

This Policy has accompanying Procedures which must be followed.

This Policy statement has been agreed by the Trustees of Leonard Cheshire and is mandatory on all its Departments and Services.

Whistleblowing

These Procedures should be used in conjunction with the relevant policy document.

Procedures

Introduction

- Bad practices may occur from time to time in the operation of Leonard Cheshire Services.
- Leonard Cheshire is committed to the principle that disclosing bad practice is good practice.
- These procedures are designed to enable and encourage employees and volunteers to raise concerns about bad practices without fear of reprisals, and to reassure employees and volunteers that such matters will be dealt with seriously and effectively by the organisation.
- The procedures apply to ALL employees and volunteers unless expressly stated otherwise.
- Managers of services, local committees and central and regional staff are required to implement these procedures and to ensure that all employees and volunteers are aware that they are available.
- The type of malpractice covered by the Whistleblowing Policy and Procedures includes:
  - Failure to uphold professional standards of practice and/or behaviour; (eg abuse in all its forms, breaches of confidentiality)
  - Danger to health and safety (eg ignoring manual handling regulations)
  - Criminal activity including fraudulent and corrupt behaviour; (eg theft, fraud)
  - Breach of legal duties; (eg staffing arrangements)
  - Cover-up of the above.

There are existing procedures in place to enable employees to lodge a grievance relating to their own employment. The Whistleblowing Policy is intended to cover concerns that fall outside the scope of those procedures and is not a substitute for Leonard Cheshire's Grievance Procedures. There is a separate Complaints Procedure for service users.

How to raise a concern

If employees or volunteers suspect malpractice they should act promptly and follow the procedure detailed below. The earlier they raise their concern the easier it is to take action. They will need to explain to the person they contact the reasons for their concerns and give as much information as they possibly can. It will help if they keep notes of the dates, times and details of their concerns but, even if they don't have all this information, it is important that they raise their concerns anyway.

– Employees/volunteers should raise their concerns about bad practices with one of the following people (list 1):

  • Their supervisor, line manager, volunteer co-ordinator; or
  • The local health and safety representative; or
  • The manager of the Service/Sections/Department; or
  • The local committee chairman.

– If they are not reassured by the response they receive from the person they have contact with in list 1, or they do not feel able to contact any of the above, they should raise their concerns with one for the following people (list 2):

  • The Regional Complaints Coordinator; or
  • The Regional Health & Safety Coordinator; or
  • The Regional Director (or any other Director); or
  • The Manager Internal Audit (Finance) c/o Wales & West Regional Offices; or
  • Any Trustee; or
  • The Head of Standards at Leonard Cheshire's Central Office, Millbank.

  It will help considerably at this stage if they are able to put their concerns in writing. This will assist the person carrying out any investigation into their concern.

– All people listed above will be trained to deal with concerns raised through these procedures.

– The intention in these procedures is that wherever possible any employee's or volunteer's concerns should be raised within Leonard Cheshire, in the ways outlined above. If, however, they feel unable to raise the matter in this way they may contract the Registration and Inspection Department of the relevant Local Authority, or in matters relating to fraud or corruption, the external Auditor PricewaterhouseCoopers.

Independent Advice

If at any stage in the procedures employees or volunteers are unsure about what to do and would like independent advice they may like to discuss their concerns with someone at Public Concern at Work (PCaW). PCaW is an independent charity staffed by lawyers which offers confidential free legal and practical advice on how people can raise concerns about malpractice at work. They can also give advice on who else employees or volunteers may contact and about what legal protection may be available. The most enquiries that PCaW receive are from people working in the health and care fields. PCaW's legal helpline can be contacted on 0171 4040 6609.

Professional associations and trade unions can also offer advice to members considering raising concerns.

Safeguards:

– Harassment or victimisation of whistleblowers will not be tolerated. Information about available support for whistleblowers will be offered to any employee or volunteer who whistleblows by the person they contact within Leonard Cheshire (lists 1 and 2).

– Every effort will be made to ensure that the employee's or volunteer's identity is kept confidential if they so wish. However, it must be appreciated that an investigation process may reveal the source of the information. Leonard Cheshire may need them to give evidence at disciplinary or criminal proceedings. If it becomes necessary to reveal the employee's or volunteer's identity in order to pursue the investigation, this will be discussed with them at the earliest stage. In such circumstances it may affect Leonard Cheshire's ability to continue the investigation, if they do not agree to be identified.

– If an allegation is made in good faith but it is not confirmed by any investigation, no action will be taken against them. If however, they maliciously make false allegations, disciplinary action will be taken against them.

– Leonard Cheshire hopes that all employees and volunteers will feel able to put their name to the allegation, as concerns expressed anonymously are more difficult to investigate. If employees or volunteers raise a concern anonymously their identity may be deduced. If, contrary to this policy, they then suffer reprisals, it may be difficult to show that this was the result of raising the concern.

How Leonard Cheshire will respond

– All concerns raised under these procedures must be followed up and documented.

– The action taken will depend on the nature of the concern. The matters raised may be:
  • Investigated internally;
  • Referred to the police;
  • Referred to the external Auditor;
  • Form the subject of an independent inquiry.

– Initial enquiries will be made to determine whether an investigation is appropriate, and if so, what form it should take. Concerns or allegations which fall within the scope of specific procedures (for example the Grievance Procedure) will normally be referred for consideration under those procedures.

– If requested, within 5 working days of a concern being received, the person raising the concern will be written to by the person in Leonard Cheshire who received it. The letter will acknowledge that the concern has been received and provide information on who is dealing with the matter and who to contact if they have any questions.

– So that the person who raised the concern can be sure that the matter has been properly addressed, they will be given feedback on how their concern has been handled and the outcome of any investigation. However, Leonard Cheshire may not be able to disclose full details due to confidentiality in relation to other people involved or due to legal constraints, in which case this will be explained.

D. NHS

Sandwell and West Birmingham NHS Trust Policy

Subject: Whistleblowing

1.0 Introduction

The Public Interest Disclosure Act (1998) provides legal protection for employees from dismissal, victimisation or other detrimental treatment when they raise genuine concerns at work in relation to:

- Criminal offences or failure to comply with legal obligations
- Miscarriages of justice
- Dangers to health and safety
- Damage to the environment
- Any attempt to cover up any of the above

In addition, the Trust recognises that all employees have both a right and a responsibility to express any concerns that they may have relating to the delivery of patient care and the overall provision of health services.

This policy provides the basis by which legitimate concerns can be fairly, effectively and speedily aired and responded to by the use of internal mechanisms. The policy sets out that concerns should initially be raised at a local level with the facility for employees to register concerns directly with a designated Non-Executive Director if necessary. This provides the Trust with the opportunity to address concerns and for remedial action to be taken where appropriate.

2.0 Aims

2.1 To ensure that the Trust meets its legal obligations under the Public Interest Disclosure Act 1998.

2.2 To encourage a culture where individual employees can speak out freely and report any genuine concerns at the earliest possible opportunity in the confidence that they will be taken seriously and will not be victimised as a result.

3.0 Objectives

3.1 To define the process by which employees can report genuine concerns.

3.2 To set out a clear procedure for investigating concerns.

3.3 To ensure that all genuine concerns reported are treated seriously and appropriately.

3.4 To ensure that action, where appropriate, is taken and improvements made.

4.0 Definitions

Whistleblowing is the disclosure by a member of staff of information that relates to some danger, criminal activity, failure to comply with a legal duty, standards of care, unethical conduct, miscarriage of justice, danger to health and safety or the environment, be it of the Trust or fellow employees.

5.0 Basic Principles

5.1 All employees have a responsibility to report any genuine concerns in a reasonable and responsible way. If an investigation confirms that an employee has made a disclosure for malicious or vexatious reasons this could lead to disciplinary action.

5.2 An employee who raises a genuine concern in accordance with this policy will not be at risk of any form of retribution as a result provided that they acted in good faith. The Trust will not tolerate harassment of any individual who does decide to whistleblow. Any such action will be dealt with in line with the Trust's Disciplinary and Appeals Procedure.

5.3 This procedure is intended to provide a mechanism for individual employees to raise matters of concern. It is not intended to replace the Trust's Grievance and Disputes Procedure.

5.4 All employees are encouraged to consult and seek guidance from their professional organisation, statutory bodies such as the Nursing and Midwifery Council or the General Medical Council or their local trade union. This will complement existing professional or ethical rules/guidelines and codes of conduct on freedom of speech including the NMC Code of Professional Conduct for Registered Nurses and the General Medical Council Guidance on Contractual Arrangements in Healthcare.

5.5 The Trust recognises that there may be circumstances when an employee feels that it is necessary to report their concerns to an external body. The appropriate regulatory bodies prescribed by legislation are listed in Appendix A. Wider disclosures to the police, media, MPs and non-prescribed regulatory bodies are protected if they are reasonable and not made for personal gain, (see point 7.2).

6.0 Procedure for Raising Concerns

6.1 In the first instance the employee should raise their concerns with their line manager.

The line manager should always:

- take all concerns seriously and investigate them
- recognise the difficulty the employee may have in raising them
- give the employee an unequivocal guarantee that where they raise concerns responsibly and reasonably they will be protected against victimisation
- seek advice from other healthcare professionals where appropriate

If the employee's concerns relate to suspected fraud their first point of contact should be the Counter-Fraud Specialist within the Trust's Internal Audit team.

6.2 The line manager should meet with the employee within 2 working days of the matter being raised.

6.3 The line manager should notify the individual of the outcome within 5 working days of their meeting. Where action is not considered appropriate, the employee should be given an explanation of the reasons behind this decision.

6.4 If a member of medical staff wishes to raise an issue of concern about a colleague's performance they have a duty under their General Medical Council registration to raise it in the first instance with the Trust's Medical Director. (See Procedure for Doctors to Report Concerns about the Conduct, Performance or Health of Medical Colleagues SHC/HR/032).

6.5 If an employee does not feel it is appropriate to raise their concerns with their line manager or continues to feel concerned after feedback from their line manager he/she may write to the designated Non-Executive Director via the Director of Governance Development. The Non-Executive Director will acknowledge their letter within 7 days of receipt and make arrangements to meet with the employee to discuss their concerns.

6.6 If the Non-Executive Director decides that it would be appropriate for an investigation to take place, he/she will decide who is to investigate. This will normally be an appropriate Executive Director. The Non-Executive Director will be responsible for deciding on the time scales for the investigation and will keep the employee regularly informed of progress in writing. On completion of the investigation, the Non-Executive Director should advise the employee in writing of the outcome. A copy of this letter must be sent to the Chief Executive for information and for appropriate follow-up action.

6.7 Where the matter in question is of a particularly serious nature (for example in relation to criminal or unlawful behaviour) it may be necessary to inform the appropriate external body (for examples of such prescribed regulatory bodies see Appendix A). Where this is necessary the Trust will support the employee throughout the process and maintain their anonymity within the Trust as far as is possible.

7.0 Wider Disclosures

7.1 The Trust hopes that this policy and procedure will give employees the confidence to raise concerns internally. However, it is recognised that there may be circumstances where they can properly report matters to outside bodies other than the prescribed regulatory bodies, This includes circumstances where employees are dissatisfied with the outcome of the internal investigation.

7.2 Staff may, after taking advice from their professional body, trade union or the independent charity, Public Concern at Work, wish to raise their concerns with their MP, the police, the media or non-prescribed regulators. Such wider disclosures are protected if they are reasonable in all the circumstances and are not made for personal gain. The whistleblower must also meet one additional precondition to win protection for a wider disclosure. This is either that:

- He or she reasonably believed that he or she would be victimised if he or she had raised the matter internally or with a prescribed regulator OR
- he or she reasonably believed the evidence was likely to be concealed or destroyed if disclosure is made to the employer OR
- The concern had already been raised with the employer or a prescribed regulator

Employees need to be aware that such action, if entered unjustifiably could result in disciplinary action.

Public Concern at Work—an organisation which provides free legal advice about how to raise a serious work related issue—can be contacted by telephone on 020 7404 6609 or via e-mail helpline@ pcaw.co. Further information can be obtained via the organisation's website—www.pcaw.co.uk.

8.0 Monitoring and Review

The Non-executive Director will be responsible for monitoring the number of complaints under the policy, how they have been handled and their outcome. An annual report will be made to the Trust Board.

9.0 Training

9.1 Reference to this policy will be made during the Trust Corporate Induction course.

9.2 Awareness sessions for both employees and managers will be held on introduction of the policy.

10.0 Financial Implications

Any financial implications including meeting the costs of any legal actions instituted against an employee who has followed the Trust's procedure will be met within existing budgets.

Appendix A—Prescribed Regulatory Bodies

NHS Executive

Department of Health

Health and safety dangers—Health and Safety Executive or local authority

Environmental dangers—Environmental Agency

Utilities—OFTEL, OFFER, OFWAT, OFGAS, Rail Regulator

Financial services and the City—Financial Services Authority, Stock Exchange

Fraud and fiscal irregularities—Serious Fraud Office, Her Majesty's Revenue and Customs (HMRC)

Public Sector finance—National Audit Office, Audit Commission, Accounts Commission for Scotland

Company law and competition breaches—Office of Fair Trading, Department of Trade and Industry

Others—Charity Commission, Civil Aviation Authority, Occupational Pensions Regulatory Authority

Mental Health Commission

Nursing and Midwifery Council

General Medical Council

Health Professions Council

Royal Pharmaceutical Society of Great Britain

The above list is not exhaustive.

E. Police

Merseyside Police Force: Doing the Right Thing—Whistleblowing Policy

1 Statement of the Policy

Merseyside Police fully recognises the need to provide a mechanism and appropriate support for staff who report inappropriate behaviour in the workplace.

This policy is seen as a major contributor to creating a climate in which staff at all levels feel a genuine obligation to maintain the integrity of the Police service by reporting wrongdoing. It is our intention to continue to develop a Force culture in which such actions are viewed as the right thing to do.

All staff should feel that they can report corruption, dishonesty and malpractice openly with the support of colleagues and managers.

Department of Origin:	Professional Standards Unit
Author / Post Holder:	D/Chief Inspector AW
Related Reference Documents:	Public Interest Disclosure Act 1998
Date agreed / endorsed by BMG:	16 March 2005
Date published in *Billboard*:	
Date of last Review:	16 March 2005

2. General Principles

All staff have the responsibility to report suspected corrupt, dishonest and unethical behaviour by others within Merseyside Police. In cases where it is felt necessary to report a complaint of inappropriate behaviour, which does not meet the standards required in the Force Diversity or Dignity at Work Policies, consideration should be given to the use of Fairness at Work (Grievance) Procedure in the first instance.

In some instances staff may wish to remain anonymous in making such reports. Whilst this policy encourages openness in the reporting of information, there will be provisions made for those occasions when members of staff wish to remain anonymous.

All information reported under the terms of the policy will be treated in absolute confidence by managers at all levels.

Staff who identify themselves when making reports should do so in the knowledge that they may be required to give evidence. This may be in a criminal prosecution or Misconduct / Police Staff Disciplinary Hearing.

The Force recognises the importance of ensuring staff confidence in the use of this policy and is committed to making every effort to obtain corroboration prior to any appropriate action being taken.

All staff will be supported by the Force in any situation in which they are required to give evidence.

3. Scope

This Policy applies to all members of the wider police family (all police officers, employees and volunteers) within Merseyside Police.

4. Legislative Procedure

Public Interest Disclosure Act 1998

The purpose of this legislation is to ensure that information in the public interest is brought to the attention of an appropriate person in order that wrongdoing may be dealt with promptly.

The legislation provides statutory protection against victimisation and unfair dismissal to individuals who make 'protected' disclosures in good faith about certain acts of wrongdoing or work place dangers.

These are summarised below:

- A criminal offence
- The breach of a legal obligation
- A miscarriage of justice
- A danger to the Health & Safety of an individual
- Damage to the environment
- Deliberate covering up of information relating to the above

The Police Reform Act 2002, extended the provisions to Police Officers.

All staff are now protected by this legislation and can lodge a complaint with an Employment Tribunal if they have been harmed as a result of making a protected disclosure.

F. EDUCATION

Procedures for all Employees in Schools with Delegated Budgets

Model Grievance Procedure

Setting up the Procedure

1. The aim of this procedure is to enable employees of Oxfordshire County Council in schools to raise concerns about their own employment. It has been drawn up following consultation with all the recognized Trade Unions and Associations.

2. If an employee wants to raise a concern about the alleged behaviour of someone who is not employed by the governing body of their own school, they may use this Procedure. If, as a result, the governing body concludes that action is necessary which is outside their power but within the power of the County Council, the governing body can require the County Council to take this action. For example, they can require that the Director for Learning & Culture initiates a disciplinary investigation.

3. If a school employee wants to raise a concern about other aspects of the school's or the Council's operations the appropriate route is likely to be the 'Raising Concerns at Work ('Whistleblowing') Procedure'.

4. The Procedure cannot be used to deal with concerns raised by former employees or others who are not employed at the school. They may have recourse to the Complaints Procedure or the Whistleblowing Procedure instead.

Responsibilities of the Governors

5. The governing body must establish a procedure by which employees may seek redress for any grievance relating to their work at the school. They must draw up a Grievance Procedure in consultation with the County Council (through Education Personnel) or formally adopt this Model one, and publicise it to their employees.

6. When drawing up their Procedure, they should decide whether or not to allow a further appeal to the County Council. If this right of appeal is to be granted, the following paragraph should be inserted in the Procedure at paragraph 3.7, replacing the one shown: "There is a further right of appeal to a panel of County Councillors, whose decision is binding on all parties."

7. Governors must ensure that appropriate support is given both to the employee raising the grievance and to any employee against whom allegations have been made under this Procedure and that both parties are kept fully informed of progress.

This Procedure should be printed out and given to any employee who expresses a wish to invoke the Grievance Procedure

Oxfordshire County Council Model Grievance Procedure for School Employees

1. Introduction

1.1 The aim of this procedure is to enable employees of the County Council in schools to raise concerns about their own employment. It has been drawn up following consultation with all the recognized trade Unions and Associations.

1.2 If an employee wants to raise a concern about the alleged behaviour of someone who is not employed by the governing body of their own school, they may use this Procedure. If, as a result, the governing body concludes that action is necessary which is outside their power but within the power of the County Council, the governing body may require the County Council to take this action. For example, they can require that the Director for Learning & Culture initiates a disciplinary investigation.

1.3 If a school employee wants to raise a concern about other aspects of the school's or the Council's operations, the appropriate route is likely to be the 'Raising Concerns at Work ('Whistleblowing') Procedure'.

2. Raising Concerns about your Employment

2.1 Oxfordshire County Council aims to promote good employee relations by encouraging employees to raise concerns about matters affecting their employment at an early stage.

As a general principle you should raise concerns about matters affecting your employment first with the person you believe is causing you concern and if this does not resolve the matter, next with your usual manager. S/he will treat these concerns seriously and deal with them promptly.

2.2 The Council recognises that in special circumstances it may be inappropriate for you to approach your usual manager with your concern. A number of alternative routes may be appropriate depending on the nature of the concern (eg: your School's Adviser, Education Personnel, Health & Safety Adviser, a more senior manager).

2.3 If you are the Headteacher the usual route will be to the Chair of Governors unless s/he is already involved.

2.4 You may choose to be supported and accompanied by your Trade Union Representative or a colleague at any step.

2.5 You should notify your manager within three months of any event which gives rise to a grievance. A Grievance which is not notified within this timescale will be disregarded unless you can demonstrate a good reason why it should still be considered. One example of 'good reason' could be a lengthy period of sickness absence. Another could be where you feel that a number of events over a period of time have had a cumulative impact on you and it is only the most recent one which is within the three-month time limit; your manager or governors may then agree that earlier incidents may also be taken into account.

G. LOCAL AUTHORITY

Whistleblowing Policy

1. Introduction

1.1 The Nolan Committee's 1997 report into standards of conduct in local government recommended that every local authority should introduce a procedure for 'whistleblowing' that would enable any individual to raise concerns about conduct.

1.2 The Government accepted the need for an established whistleblowing procedure and the *Public Interest Disclosure Act 1998* was introduced to protect whistleblowers who were dismissed or suffered detriment as a result of their action.

2. Definitions used in this Policy

2.1 The term *'whistleblowing'* in this policy refers to the disclosure of information by employees or others in respect of illegal acts, malpractice or wrongdoing.

2.2 The term *'in good faith'* means honesty in the conduct of any concerns raised.

2.3 The term *'responsible officer'* refers to the officer investigating any concern raised.

2.4 This policy covers any illegal acts, malpractice or wrongdoing by any person. This could include:

- any employee of Oxford City Council;
- any councillor or co-opted member of Oxford City Council;
- any person acting in a representative role for Oxford City Council
- any contractor, partner, consultant or supplier of service to Oxford City Council.

2.5 The 'Authority' means the Oxford City Council.

3. Policy Statement

3.1 Oxford City Council is committed to the highest possible standards of openness, integrity and accountability. In line with that commitment it expects employees and others with serious concerns about any aspect of the Council's work to come forward and voice those concerns. It is recognised that as a result of voicing concerns certain cases will need to proceed on a confidential basis.

3.2 This policy is intended to encourage and enable individuals to raise serious concerns with the Council rather than overlooking a problem or 'blowing the whistle' outside the Council.

4. Aims and Scope of the Policy

4.1 This policy aims to:

- **encourage** any individual to raise concerns about possible malpractice
- **provide** avenues for concerns to be raised, giving feedback on any action taken
- **ensure** that a response is given to any concern and provide advice on how to proceed if this response is not satisfactory
- **assure** any individual that they will be protected from reprisals or victimisation for acts of whistle-blowing made in good faith.

4.2 The Authority has a number of different policies and procedures in place which relate to standards of behaviour at work. These include Discipline, Grievance, Diversity and Recruitment and Selection. Employees are encouraged to use the provisions of these procedures where appropriate. There may be times, however, when the matter is not about personal employment matters and needs to be handled in a different way. Examples may be:

- a criminal offence
- suspected fraud and/or corruption
- damage to the environment
- the unauthorised use of public funds
- breach of Council Financial Procedure Rules
- breach of legislation

4.3 This list is not exhaustive and any serious concerns that individuals have about conduct of officers, members or others acting on behalf of the Council can be reported under the Whistleblowing Policy.

5. Safeguards

5.1 An individual should have nothing to fear from reporting a concern since he or she will be merely doing their duty to the Authority and to the community. However, it is acknowledged that the decision to raise a concern can be difficult and safeguards must be put in place.

Harassment or Victimisation

5.2 The Authority will not tolerate harassment or victimisation and will take action to protect a whistleblower when they raise a concern in good faith. Harassment or victimisation of a whistleblower will be treated as a serious disciplinary offence which will be dealt with through the Council's Disciplinary Procedure.

Confidentiality

5.3 All concerns raised will be treated in confidence and every effort will be made to protect an individual's identity where this is requested. However, the investigation process may reveal the source of the information and the individual may be required to come forward as a witness.

Anonymous Allegations

5.4 This policy encourages individuals to put their names to allegations.

5.5 Concerns expressed anonymously are much less powerful, but they will be considered at the discretion of the Authority. In exercising this discretion, the factors to be taken into account would include:

- the seriousness of the issue raised;
- the credibility of the concern; and
- the likelihood of confirming the allegation from attributable sources.

Untrue Allegations

5.6 If an individual makes an allegation in good faith, but it is not confirmed by the investigation an employee will suffer no detrimental treatment as a result of raising a concern. If, however, allegations are deliberately false or malicious this will be treated as a disciplinary offence which will be dealt with through the Authority's Disciplinary Procedure.

6. Whistleblowing Procedure

Reporting a Concern

6.1 If any employee has a legitimate concern this should be raised with the responsible officer. Normally this would be their supervisor or their supervisor's line manager. This course of action depends on the seriousness and sensitivity of the issues involved and who is suspected of the malpractice.

6.2 A line manager may consider that he or she is unable to address an employee's concern. If this is the case the employee must be advised on how the matter will be progressed. The options for the line manager are to refer the complaint to the Chief Executive, to a senior Officer in the Department, not the Director, nominated to deal with whistleblowing concerns, or any appointed Scrutiny Officer. One of these options must be chosen in consultation with the employee.

6.3 Where the line manager passes on responsibility for the complaint, the Chief Executive, the senior officer in the Department concerned, or the Scrutiny Officer will become the responsible officer.

6.4 Concerns can be raised directly with a Director, the Chief Executive, or the Council's Monitoring Officer by:

a) an employee who does not wish to raise a concern with line management and
b) any other person

6.5 Concerns about officers can be raised with the Leader of any political group by any councillor. The Leader concerned must ensure that the procedure detailed in this document is followed.

6.6 If there is concern about fraud or corruption of any sort this can be addressed to any of the officers listed under 6.4 or, alternatively, to the Internal Audit Business Manager.

6.7 Individuals are encouraged to raise concerns in writing and should include:

- the background and history of the concern (giving relevant dates)
- the reason why the individual is particularly concerned about the situation.

6.8 Those who do not feel able to put their concern in writing, can be interviewed by the responsible officer. The responsible officer will write a brief summary of the interview which will be agreed by both parties.

6.9 Although individuals are not expected to prove the truth of an allegation, they will need to demonstrate that there are sufficient grounds for concern.

6.10 Employees may invite their Trade Union or professional association to raise a matter on their behalf.

6.11 However the concern is reported it should be made clear that it is being raised in accordance with the provisions of the Whistleblowing Policy. This will have the effect of ensuring that the agreed procedures are followed and help to avoid misunderstanding.

How the Authority will Respond to Concerns

6.12 The action taken by the Authority will depend on the nature of the concern. The matters raised may for example:

- be investigated by management, internal audit or through the disciplinary process
- be referred to the Police
- be referred to the District Auditor
- form the subject of an independent inquiry.

6.13 In order to protect individuals and the Authority, initial enquiries will be made by the responsible officer to decide whether an investigation is appropriate and, if so, what form it should take. The overriding principle which the Authority will have in mind is the public interest. Concerns or allegations which fall within the scope of existing procedures, for example, racial discrimination will normally be referred for consideration under those procedures.

6.14 Some concerns may be resolved by agreed action without the need for an investigation.

6.15 Within ten working days, the responsible officer will write to the individual who has raised the concern:

- acknowledging that the concern has been received;
- indicating how the matter will be progressed;
- giving an estimate of how long it will take to provide a final response;
- telling them whether any initial enquiries have been made; and
- telling them whether further investigations will take place, and if not, why not.

6.16 The amount of contact between the responsible officer and the individual will depend on the nature of the matters raised, the potential difficulties involved and the clarity of the information provided. If necessary, further information will be sought from the individual.

6.17 When any meeting is arranged an individual can, if they so wish, be accompanied by a Trade Union or professional association representative or a friend.

6.18 The Authority will take steps to minimise any difficulties which an individual may experience as a result of raising a concern. For instance, if employees are required to give evidence in criminal or disciplinary proceedings, the Council will advise them about the procedure.

6.19 If the concern raised is very serious or complex, an inquiry may be held.

6.20 The Authority accepts that anyone raising a concern needs to be assured that the matter has been properly addressed. Subject to legal constraints, the Authority will report to the whistleblower within 10 working days of the conclusion an investigation.

7. Taking a Complaint Further

7.1 This policy is intended to provide an avenue to raise concerns within the Authority. If after seeking advice an individual feels it is right to take the matter outside of this process the following are possible contact points:

• the local Council member (if you live in the area of the Council)
• the District Auditor
• the Health and Safety Executive
• a government department
• a solicitor
• the Police
• a Member of Parliament

This list is not intended to be exhaustive.

7.2 If an individual does take the matter outside the Council, they need to ensure that they do not disclose confidential information. This can be checked with the Monitoring Officer who will also advise on ways to proceed.

8. The Monitoring Officer

8.1 The Council's Monitoring Officer reporting to the Standards Committee has overall responsibility for the maintenance and operation of this policy. The Monitoring Officer maintains a record of concerns raised and the outcomes (but in a form which does not endanger confidentiality) and will report all concerns raised to the Standards Committee.

[Announcement circulated to staff follows]

Oxfordshire County Council

Raising Concerns at Work, Grievances and Whistle-blowing

1. The aim of this policy is to enable employees of Oxfordshire County Council to raise concerns directly with the County Council, either about their own employment **(grievance)** or about other aspects of the Council's operations **(whistle-blowing).** This does not remove an employee's right to raise concerns in other ways where appropriate such as through the agencies listed in paragraph 46 below. Separate procedures exist for school staff and uniformed fire-fighters which are available from Directorate HR Officers.

Introduction

2. The Council is committed to the highest possible standards of:

a) Openness and inclusiveness
b) Accountability
c) Integrity

In line with that commitment, we encourage employees with serious concerns about any aspect of the Council's work to come forward and express those concerns.

3. In the large majority of cases, employees with concerns should share these with their line manager. However, the Council recognises that, from time to time, this may not be appropriate.

4. The Council will provide all reasonable protection for employees who raise genuine concerns in good faith.

5. The Chief Executive, as Head of the Paid Service, and the Assistant Chief Executive, as the Council's Monitoring Officer, have overall responsibility for this policy. Directors are responsible for the management of services and staff within their directorates.

6. Directors will be responsible for ensuring that appropriate personal support is given both to the employee raising the concern and to any employee against whom allegations have been made under this procedure, and for ensuring that both parties are kept informed of progress.

7. If an employee raises a concern in good faith but it is not subsequently confirmed by investigation, no action will be taken against him/her. If however, an employee raises a concern frivolously, maliciously, or for personal gain, disciplinary action may be taken against him/her.

Raising Concerns about Your Own Employment (Grievances)

8. The Advisory, Conciliation and Arbitration Service (ACAS) defines a grievance as an issue raised by an employee with management, about his/her work, or about his/her employer's clients' or fellow workers' actions which affect him/her. These concerns may be those directly arising from the contract of employment such as promotion issues, changes in work assigned and performance evaluation. They may be issues such as bullying, harassment or racism. See paragraph 30 for a list of related policies and procedures which may apply.

9. The Council aims to promote good employee relations by encouraging employees to raise such concerns about matters affecting their employment at an early stage. As a general principle, you should raise concerns about matters affecting your employment with your line manager in the first instance. Your line manager will treat these concerns seriously and should deal with them promptly.

10. The Council recognises that in some circumstances it may be inappropriate for you to approach your line manager with your concern. A number of alternative routes may be appropriate depending on the nature of the concern (eg Human Resources Officer, Health & Safety Adviser, a more senior manager).

11. In some cases, mediation may be agreed upon as a possible helpful way to address the issues. This may include where concerns relate to relationships between two or more parties and both sides are willing to abide by the agreements which arise from the process, and where no other formal action is required, such as disciplinary action.

Right to be Accompanied

12. You may choose to be accompanied by your Trade Union Representative or a work colleague at any step under this procedure.

How to Raise a Concern about Your Own Employment—Grievance Procedure General Points:

13. Most issues related to your employment which might cause you concern can be resolved by informal discussion, eg change to your working pattern which makes it difficult for you to get to work on time because of your caring responsibilities, perceived unfair allocation of work, lack of training etc.

14. If you have a concern about the behaviour of a colleague you should, wherever possible, first try to resolve this informally directly with that individual.

15. It is in everyone's interests to address a concern swiftly without the need to use the formal procedures if possible. You may wish to involve a HR Officer, work colleague or Trade Union representative in order to assist in doing this.

16. Even when a concern is being dealt with informally, it is helpful for all parties to keep a record of any discussions and agreed actions. Where issues are discussed between an employee and his/her line manager, this record should be retained as part of the supervision records. Both parties are then able to refer to such notes in any subsequent formal action should the matter fail to be resolved.

17. You should note that this procedure aims to ensure that concerns are addressed promptly so that there is an opportunity for appropriate action to be taken. A concern that has not been notified, without good reason, within 3 months of the events which gave rise to it, will normally be disregarded unless there are exceptional circumstances.

18. As a result of following this procedure, the manager or Panel hearing the grievance may decide that it is necessary to investigate the actions of another employee and they may recommend that a disciplinary investigation be carried out.

19. Please note that a separate procedure applies if you wish to raise concerns about your salary or grade or your pension. The Raising Concerns at Work procedure is also not appropriate for the following issues which are subject to a collective disputes procedure between the County Council and a trade union: matters relating to income tax, National Insurance and rules of the Local Government Pension Scheme or to matters which are outside the authority of the County Council. See paragraph 30 for a list of related policies and procedures.

Step 1 (Informal)

20. If you wish to raise a concern you should discuss this initially with your line manager as soon as possible. In presenting your concern you should identify a) what your concern is, b) how you are disadvantaged and c) what redress you are seeking. It is important to give as much evidence as possible, as your line manager will have to decide whether there is sufficient evidence to proceed formally. If s/he decides that there is insufficient evidence to proceed formally, s/he will respond to you indicating that no action can be taken.

21. Your line manager will attempt to resolve your concern. S/he may need to consult or involve other employees and/or managers in order to do this. S/he will respond to you as soon as possible and in any case within 10 working days.

22. Where it is not possible to give a full response within this timescale, your line manager will explain the reasons and indicate when you will be given a fuller response.

Step 2 (Formal)

23. The Steps outlined below should be followed in situations where, after raising an issue with your line manager about your employment, you feel that it has not been resolved fairly within a reasonable timescale.

24. If you still feel that your concern has not been addressed or you do not receive a response within 10 working days, you should inform your line manager in writing, again within 10 working days.

25. Your line manager will then arrange a meeting at an early date with an appropriate senior manager and your directorate HR Officer. The aim of this meeting will be to resolve outstanding issues. Where appropriate, and with mutual agreement, an external mediator may be consulted.

26. You will be notified in writing of the decision within 10 days and of your right of appeal.

Step 3 (Appeal to Director)

27. If you still feel your concern has not been resolved, or if your line manager fails to carry out the actions set out in Step 2, you should appeal **in writing to your Director,** again within 10 working days. You will need to give reasons in writing as to why you wish to appeal. Examples could be, faults in procedure, new evidence that could not have been available at the first meeting, a perverse decision.

28. Your Director will respond in writing within 10 working days.

Step 4 (Appeal to the Democracy and Organisation Committee Tribunal Panel)

29. If you still feel that your concern has not been addressed, you may refer the matter to the County HR Manager within 10 working days of receipt of your Director's response. He/she will arrange for you to have your appeal heard by the Tribunal Panel of the Democracy and Organisation Committee.

30. Special policies exist for the following circumstances, some of which have separate procedures to follow, and you should refer to the appropriate policy document, which is available from your Directorate HR Officer.

- Comprehensive Equality Policy
- Equal Pay
- Dignity at Work
- Health & Safety Guidance
- Redundancy
- Stress at Work

Further Right of Appeal

31. Using this procedure does not affect your right to refer issues to an Employment Tribunal. However, you should be aware that your right to take a case to an Employment Tribunal may be affected if you do not first raise the grievance in writing with the Council and wait a further 28 days before presenting the tribunal claim.

32. Wherever possible, a concern should be dealt with before an employee leaves employment. However, in cases where the process has not already been started at the point at which the employee leaves, the former employee should then write to their manager setting out the grievance as soon as possible, and not later than three months after leaving employment and the Council will respond in writing.

Raising Other Concerns ('Whistleblowing')

33. 'Whistleblowing' is defined as 'raising concerns about misconduct within an organisation or within an independent structure associated with it' (Nolan Committee on Standards in Public Life). Since the Nolan Committee legislation has been enacted which deals with whistleblowing. In the legislation it is called a protected disclosure. The Public Interest Disclosure Act 1998 (the 'PIDA 1998') amends the Employment Rights Act 1996 and protects employees from suffering a detriment in their employment or being dismissed by their employer if they make certain disclosures in accordance with the legislation.

34. You have certain common law confidentiality obligations to your employer. However, in a limited set of circumstances the PIDA 1998 may override these obligations if you reveal information about your employment or the work of the Council.

35. Any serious concerns you have about any aspect of the Council's service provision or about the conduct of Council employees, elected members or others acting on behalf of the Council, should be reported using the following procedure. Your concern must relate to something which:

a) Is against Council's Standing Orders and policies or
b) Falls below established standards or practice or
c) Amounts to improper conduct, including something you believe may be;
   • Against the law
   • Is a failure to comply with a legal obligation
   • Is a possible miscarriage of justice
   • A Health & Safety risk
   • Damaging the environment
   • Misuse of public money
   • Corruption or unethical conduct
   • Abuse of clients or service users
   • Deliberate concealment of any of these matters
   • Any other substantial and relevant concern

These issues could have arisen in the past, be currently happening or likely to happen in the future.

The PIDA does not protect an employee who would be breaking the law in making the disclosure.

36. All concerns will be treated sensitively and with due regard to confidentiality and where possible every effort will be made to protect your identity if you so wish. Nevertheless, this information will need to be passed on to those with a legitimate need to have this information and it may be necessary for you to provide a written statement or act as a witness in any subsequent disciplinary proceedings or enquiry. This will always be discussed with you first.

37. Where concerns are expressed anonymously the relevant Director, County HR Manager and the Solicitor to the Council will decide how to proceed. An investigation may be carried out, depending on the nature of the allegations and the evidence/information presented.

How to Raise a Concern ('Whistleblowing')

Step 1

38. If you wish to raise a concern normally you should raise this initially with your Line Manager. This can be in person or in writing. In clarifying your concerns, it may be helpful for you to refer to the Council's Code of Conduct for Officers which sets out the standards expected of its employees.

39. The Council recognises that sometimes it may be inappropriate for you to approach your line manager with your concern. A number of alternative routes may be appropriate depending on the nature of your concern. For example, you could approach a more senior manager in your directorate, your HR Officer, your Director or one of the following

- The Chief Executive
- The Monitoring Officer
- The Solicitor to the Council
- The Head of Finance
- Internal Audit Services
- Your local County Councillor

40. Although you are not expected to prove beyond doubt the truth of your concerns, you will need to demonstrate that you have sufficient evidence or other reasonable grounds to raise them.

41. You may wish to obtain assistance in putting forward your concern from your HR Officer, a Trade Union representative or a colleague. You may choose to be represented by a Trade Union representative or colleague at any meetings that are required.

Step 2

42. The manager with whom you have raised your concern will acknowledge its receipt as soon as possible and will write to you within 10 days with the following:

- An indication of how the concern will be dealt with
- An estimate of how long it will take to provide a final response
- Whether any initial enquiries have been made
- Whether further investigations will take place, and if not why not
- Information on employee support services

43. Advice for managers and County Councillors on dealing with concerns is available from Directorate HR Officers, the County HR Unit, the County Legal Services or Financial Services.

Step 3

44. Initial enquiries will be made to decide whether an investigation is appropriate in each case. Where an investigation is necessary, it may take the form of one or more of the following;

- An internal investigation by management, which may, for example, take the form of a disciplinary investigation or an investigation by the Internal Audit Services
- A referral to the Police
- A referral to the Council's external auditor,
- The setting up of an external independent inquiry

Step 4

45. The Council will inform you in writing of the outcome of any investigation or any action taken, subject to the constraints of confidentiality and the law.

46. **If you do not feel your concern has been addressed adequately you may raise it with an independent body such as one of the following as appropriate;**

- The Council's external auditor
- Your Trade Union
- The Citizens Advice Bureau

- A relevant professional body or regulatory organisation
- A relevant voluntary organisation
- The Police
- The Local Government Ombudsman
- The Equal Opportunities Commission
- The Commission for Racial Equality
- The local Race Equality Council
- The Disability Rights Commission

You must make the disclosure in good faith; you must not make the disclosure for personal gain and you must reasonably believe the information disclosed and any allegation in it to be substantially true; and in all the circumstances it must be reasonable for you to make the disclosure.

47. If there is an issue of an exceptionally serious nature which you believe to be substantially true, you do not make the disclosure for personal gain and if, in all the circumstances, it is reasonable for you to make the disclosure, then you may disclose the issue to someone other than those listed in paragraph 46.

In determining whether it is reasonable for you to have made a disclosure regard shall be had to the identity of the person to whom the disclosure is made.

48. You have a duty to the Council not to disclose confidential information. This does not prevent you from seeking independent advice at any stage nor from discussing the issue with the charity Public Concern at Work on 020 7404 6609 and www.pcaw.demon.co.uk, in accordance with the provisions of the Public Interest Disclosure Act 1998.

Review of the Procedure

49. This policy has been reviewed with reference to the ACAS Code of Practice on Discipline and Grievance Procedures (June 2004) and an impact assessment has been undertaken to take account of the Race Relations (Amendment) Act 2000 and discrimination legislation more generally. Confidential monitoring is undertaken of the procedures in order to gather data to help establish whether the policy is operated in a fair and consistent manner. In undertaking monitoring the Council will not identify individuals.

50. This policy will be reviewed by the Head of Human Resources in October 2005.

Head of Human Resources

Revised October 2004

Albanian
Bengali
Chinese
Hindi
Punjabi
Urdu

Alternative formats of this publication are available on request. These include other languages, large print, Braille, audiocassette, computer disk or email.

Case Study

THE SCENARIO

1. X is employed by Megaphones Ltd in a call centre as a team leader.
2. He applies for promotion but is unsuccessful. He seeks feedback from his manager Y, but this leads to a vicious argument between them in which Y says that X is useless and X contends that Y cannot manage. X reports the incident to the company's HR Director.
3. A month after the argument, the company indicate that they are proposing to make a number of staff redundant. X tells his manager that the proposed redundancies could breach employment legislation. His manager tells him that this is not his (X's) concern.
4. Around the same time X becomes suspicious that his manager is breaching the company's data protection policy. He stays late one evening to investigate further. He finds evidence that suggests there has been a breach, prints out some company material and takes it home. He tells his manager's manager of the alleged breach and gives him a copy of the relevant material.
5. Within the next month:
    (i) so far as X can tell there is no investigation into his allegations about the breach of the data protection policy;
    (ii) X's manager calls him names ('slacker' 'sneak', 'the terrorist') in front of his team and peers; and
    (iii) X is the only team leader not to be offered overtime.
6. As a result of this X has problems sleeping and develops nervous rashes.
7. X is called to see his manager's manager and is told that he is to face a disciplinary hearing. The charge is that he breached the company's security policy by taking home copies of the material about his manager's activities.
8. As he comes out of the meeting, X, who is feeling very anxious, sees his manager who smiles and asks if he 'enjoyed' his meeting. X swears loudly at his manager. The incident is overheard by various members of staff. X is suspended that day because of the swearing.
9. X has always thought that the financial accounting of Megaphones Ltd was 'a bit dodgy' and posts his concerns on an internet site and also writes to his MP about the subject. He adds at the end the concern about his manager breaching the company's data protection policy.
10. X resigns and claims constructive dismissal.

ISSUES

Introduction

Whistleblowing claims tend to be both very fact sensitive and potentially quite technical. In considering the questions below, which are mainly focused on disclosures to the employer, it is important to follow the structure of the relevant provisions of the Employment Rights Act 1996 (ERA).

The questions need to be asked in a structured way; usually

(a) is there a disclosure; if so
(b) is the disclosure qualifying; if so
(c) is the qualifying disclosure protected; if so

(d) (i) detriment:
- what is the act/deliberate failure to act?
- does the act/deliberate failure to act cause detriment?
- is the detriment on the ground of the qualifying protected disclosure?

    (ii) dismissal:
- is there a dismissal?
- if so is the reason or principal reason that the employee made the protected disclosure?

(e) what is the remedy?

(1) Are there any protected disclosures?

For a protected disclosure to arise there will first need to be a *qualifying* disclosure within s43B ERA, ie

(a) any disclosure of information (which may include something already known to the employer),

(b) which, in the reasonable belief of the worker making the disclosure,

(c) tends to show a relevant failure, including that a criminal offence has been committed, is being committed or is likely to be committed; or that a person has failed, is failing or is likely to fail to comply with any legal obligation to which he is subject.

In order to be protected, a qualifying disclosure will need to be made in accordance with any of ss43C to 43H ERA.

Section 43C(1)(a) is most likely to be relevant in this case. It requires:

(a) the disclosure to be made in good faith,

(b) to the employer (or to an other person where in accordance with a procedure whose use by the discloses is authorized by the employer).

See also ss43F (disclosure to prescribed person), 43G (disclosure in other cases) and 43H (disclosure of exceptionally serious failure).

The following disclosures need to be considered.

(i) X reports the argument with Y to the company's HR Director

If Y's conduct is reasonably believed by X to amount to a breach of a term of the employment contract (most probably the implied duty of mutual trust and confidence) then, depending on what information X discloses to the HR director, this could conceivably be a qualifying disclosure. (See *Parkins v Sodexho* [2002] IRLR 109 EAT—a legal obligation which arises from a contract of employment falls within s43B(1)(b).)

The disclosure is clearly to the employer. However, for the disclosure to be protected, X will also need to make the disclosure in good faith (see below).

(ii) X tells his manager that the proposed redundancies could breach employment legislation

If X simply indicates that the redundancies *could* breach the legislation, this is most unlikely to amount to a qualifying disclosure. Section 43B(1)(b) requires the disclosure to be one which in the reasonable belief of the worker tends to show that a person '*is likely* to fail to comply' with a legal obligation. The worker must reasonably believe that the information disclosed tends to show that it is probable or more probable than not that there is a failure to comply, mere possibility is insufficient (see *Kraus v Penna plc* [2004] IRLR 260 EAT). Note also that the reasonableness of the belief relates to the information, not to the legal obligation, so if no legal obligation exists as an objective fact, the worker cannot rely on a belief that it did exist having been reasonable. (However, see *Bolton School v Evans* [2006]IRLR 500 where the EAT held that the protection is not lost merely because the employer might be able to show that, for reasons not immediately apparent to the employee, the legal obligation will not apply or that he has some defence to it.)

If, however, a legal obligation does exist, then even if the allegations are objectively incorrect, the worker might still have a reasonable belief that the information tends to show a relevant failure. The focus is on the information known to the worker at the time of making the disclosure (see *Darnton v University of Surrey* [2003] IRLR 133 (EAT)).

(iii) X tells his manager's manager of the alleged breach of the data protection policy

This may be a qualifying disclosure but the position will depend on the nature of the alleged breach. If it is a breach of the Data Protection Act 1998 (or the contract of employment) then it is likely to fall within the *legal obligation* provision in s43B(1)(b). It may also fall within the *criminal offence* provision in s43B(1)(a). X will need to reasonably believe that the information disclosed tends to show the relevant failure.

The disclosure is clearly to the employer, but the disclosure will have to have been made in good faith in order to be protected.

For the disclosure to have been made in good faith, it will be insufficient for X to have a reasonable belief. A disclosure may be not in good faith if an ulterior motive was the dominant or predominant purpose. (See *Street v Derbyshire Unemployed Workers' Centre* [2004] IRLR 687 CA). Hostility to the person against whom the allegation is made may be found to be an ulterior motive, although a whistleblower is 'hardly likely to have warm feelings for the person about whom . . . disclosure is made' (Wall LJ in *Street* at para 72). This will be a question of fact for the Tribunal. In this case there may be an issue as to whether X has an ulterior motive of hostility to Y arising out of their earlier argument.

However, the onus of proving lack of good faith is on the employer and is not lightly to be found, absence of good faith being both a serious allegation and exceptional in an employment relationship. (See *Lucas v Chichester Diocesan Housing Association Ltd* (EAT10713/04/DA) & *Bachnak v Emerging Markets* (EAT/0288/05/RN).

(iv) X posts his concerns about financial accounting on an internet site

Whether this is a qualifying disclosure will depend on what X says and the matters discussed above. An expression of concern alone may well be insufficient to fall within s43B (see *Kraus v Penna* above).

If this is a qualifying disclosure, it is plainly not a protected disclosure within the scope of s43C, as it is neither to his employer nor in accordance with his employer's procedure.

In order to fall within s43G (which permits wider disclosure), the following are necessary:

(a) The worker makes the disclosure in good faith.
(b) He reasonably believes the information disclosed and any allegation contained in it are substantially true. *
(c) He does not make the disclosure for personal gain. *
(d) One of the following are met: *
   - when making the disclosure he reasonably believes that he will be subject to detriment if he discloses to the employer; or
   - he reasonably believes relevant evidence will be concealed or destroyed if he discloses to the employer; or
   - he has previously made a disclosure of substantially the same information to he employer.
(e) It is reasonable for him to make the disclosure in all the circumstances. *

Those marked * are requirements extra to those for first tier disclosures.

In order to succeed X will first need to be found to have acted in good faith (see above) and to meet the higher test of a reasonable belief that the information and allegations are substantially true. There is no suggestion of personal gain. He has not previously made a disclosure of substantially the same information (ie in relation to the financial accounting) so he will also need to establish a reasonable belief either that he will be subject to a detriment if he discloses to his employer or that relevant evidence will be concealed or destroyed. The precise nature of the allegations and the nature of the website might be relevant but it is likely to be difficult to establish that a posting on the internet is reasonable in respect of such information (see also question (vi) below) and this may cast doubt on the good faith of X.

We consider that posting on the internet would be most unlikely to be reasonable in this case, and that it is always likely to be difficult for a claimant to establish that it is reasonable. However the information posted and the nature of the internet site are part of the circumstances that have to be considered. A general rant about an employer in a chatroom seems bound to fail, but a short serious point in response to (say) a BBC website feature on abuse in care homes might (depending on the other facts) give rise to more of an arguable issue.

In order to fall within s43H it would be necessary for X to show, amongst other things, that the relevant failure was 'of an exceptionally serious nature'. This seems unlikely to be made out and very few cases have upheld claims under s43H.

(v) X writes to his MP about Megaphones Ltd's financial accounting

The position here is similar to that in relation to the website, except that (if all other requirements are satisfied) there might be more chance of establishing that disclosure to an MP is reasonable in all the circumstances than would be the case in relation to a posting on an internet site, perhaps especially if the MP has some particular interest in financial matters.

(vi) X refers on the internet site to his concern about his manager breaching the data protection policy

The position here is similar to the posting of concerns about financial accounting, except that the data protection allegations have already been raised with the employer (thereby satisfying that condition).

(vii) X refers to this concern in his letter to his MP

The position here is similar to the raising with the MP of concerns about financial accounting, except that the data protection allegations have already been raised with the employer (thereby satisfying that condition).

(2) What acts/deliberate failures to act and detriments should X claim?

The right under s47B is not to be subjected to any detriment by any act, or any deliberate failure to act, by his employer that took place *on the ground* that the worker has made a protected disclosure. (See *London Borough of Harrow v Knight* [2003] IRLR 140 EAT emphasizing the importance of following the wording of s47B).

In some cases the doing of the act or the deliberate failure and the suffering of the detriment might be in effect the same thing (eg where disciplinary action is taken). In other cases the act/failure to act and the detriment may clearly be separate.

Acts/deliberate failures to act:

(a) being called names by his manager in front of his team and peers;
(b) not being offered overtime;
(c) (possibly), the (apparent) failure to investigate;
(d) the decision to discipline him; and
(e) (possibly), a failure to support him as a whistleblower. (See *London Borough of Harrow v Knight* para 12—where it appears to be implied that failure to support could, where deliberate, form the basis of a claim.)

Detriments:

(a) loss of overtime;
(b) injury to feelings (including stress and anxiety); and
(c) (possibly) injury to health.

Clearly in relation to the (constructive) dismissal, X will be claiming that the reason or principal reason for dismissal was that he had made protected disclosures. Section 103A provides that a dismissal in such circumstances is automatically unfair. It is important to recognize that, before getting to PIDA questions, X must prove that he has been constructively dismissed on the normal tests.

(3) Were the acts/deliberate failures done on the basis of the disclosures?

Note that the test under s47B is whether the act/deliberate failure to act was done *on the ground of* the protected disclosure. The ground on which the employer acts requires an analysis of the conscious or unconscious mental processes which caused the employer to act, as in victimization in sex/race discrimination cases. It is not sufficient to show that 'but for' the disclosure the act or omission would not have occurred, nor merely that the act or omission was 'related to' the disclosure. (See *London Borough of Harrow v Knight*.)

Section 48(2) ERA provides that it is for the employer to show the ground on which any act, or deliberate failure to act, took place.

It will be a question of fact for the tribunal to decide. The following issues seem likely to arise in X's case.

(a) Can the employer prove any innocent explanation of the manager's name-calling? 'Sneak' in particular appears to be on the ground of whistleblowing.
(b) Can the employer prove why X was not offered overtime, other than because of the whistleblowing?
(c) Has there in fact been an investigation into X's allegations? If not, is there a credible explanation why?
(d) How have other staff who have breached the security policy been treated? Is there a credible explanation for any difference?
(e) Was any failure to support X deliberate (as opposed to merely insensitive or careless)? Was it based on hostility, conscious or unconscious, to X as a whistleblower?

In relation to the discipline applied, the protection under the ERA is against detriment/dismissal on the ground of the disclosure itself, not for any activity by the worker that is connected to the disclosure. Thus in *Bolton School v Evans*, where Mr Evans was found to have been disciplined by the employer which had genuinely believed that he had hacked into the computer system without authority and that he had only been disciplined for that reason, the EAT overturned the tribunal's decision that this was on the ground of his making a protected disclosure. The EAT commented:

> An employee cannot be entitled to break into his employer's filing cabinet in the hope of finding papers which will demonstrate some relevant wrongdoing which he can then disclose to the appropriate person. He is liable to be disciplined for such conduct, and that is so whether he turns up such papers or not. Provided that his misconduct is genuinely the reason for the disciplinary action, the employee will not be protected even if he does in fact discover incriminating papers.

If X establishes constructive dismissal, the company will need to establish the reason for dismissal.

(4) What compensation can X claim?

Section 49 ERA provides that if a detriment claim is upheld the tribunal shall make a declaration to that effect and may make an award of compensation to be paid by the employer to the complainant in respect of the act or failure to act to which the complaint relates. In making an award of compensation the tribunal must have regard to the infringement to which the complaint relates and any loss caused by the breach.

Section 124(1A) provides that the limit on compensatory awards does not apply to a dismissal that is automatically unfair under s103A.

Interim relief is available where the complaint is of unfair dismissal contrary to s103A. (See ss128–132 ERA.)

Detriment s49(2) ERA

X can claim in respect of:

(a) financial loss (loss of overtime);
(b) injury to feelings, and/or
(c) injury to health.

In relation to injury to feelings, the *Vento* guidelines are to be applied (see *Virgo Fidelis v Boyle* [2004] IRLR 268 (EAT)). Detriment suffered by whistleblowers should normally be regarded as very serious although the award is compensatory not punitive, so it is necessary to look at the injury to feelings suffered by the individual.

While not likely to be available to X, aggravated damages are potentially available depending on the particular circumstances including the way in which the complaint was handled. In *Boyle*, the EAT referred to a press release issued by the employer *after* the merits hearing in the tribunal as one of the factors in support of an award of £10,000 for aggravated damages, in addition to an award for injury to feelings of £25,000. The conduct of the employer was described as a 'travesty' and there was no apology or mitigation. There was no separate head of psychiatric damage claimed in that case.

Exemplary damages are potentially available on normal principles, ie oppressive, arbitrary or uncon-stitutional action by the servants of the government or where the respondent's conduct is calculated to make a profit for himself (see *Rookes v Barnard* [1964] AC 1129) but these do not apply here.

Dismissal

X can claim in respect of:

(a) basic award;
(b) unlimited compensatory award, but not
(c) injury to feelings.

While no injury to feelings can be claimed in relation to dismissal (*Dunnachie v Hull City Council* [2004] IRLR 727 (HL)), in a constructive dismissal case injury to feelings can be claimed right up to the employee's resignation (rather than up to the point at which the employer's conduct becomes so serious that it amounts to a repudiatory breach). (See *Melia v Magna Kansei Ltd* [2006] IRLR 117.)

(5) What is the relevance of X swearing at his manager?

The whistleblowing provisions of the ERA protect against detriment/dismissal on the ground of a protected disclosure rather than all conduct that is connected with the disclosure (see in a slightly different context *Bolton School v Evans*).

The company may try to argue that, even if X succeeds with his claim for constructive dismissal, X would have been dismissed in any event and that any compensation should be reduced accord-ingly. Alternatively the swearing might go to contributory fault (see *Perkin v St Georges* [2005] IRLR 934 and *Friend v CAA* (cited in [1998] IRLR 253)).

X is likely to argue that a fair disciplinary hearing of the swearing charge would have taken into account all the circumstances, including the stress he had been under as a whistleblower and the provocation from his manager, and that a fair dismissal was unlikely to have resulted.

(6) Is X justified in posting the concerns on the internet and to his MP?

See discussion of the relevant disclosures at (1) above.

(7) Might Megaphones Ltd take any action against X?

Megaphones Ltd might be tempted to claim that the allegation regarding their financial accounting is defamatory, but unless X says that he will not seek to justify the same it is unlikely that Megaphones Ltd can gain an injunction. Alternatively Megaphones Ltd might seek an injunction to restrain the misuse of confidential information but there is a public interest defence for X (see eg *Initial Services Ltd v Putterrill* [1968] 1 QB 396; *A-G v Guardian Newspapers (No 2)* [1990] 1 AC 109).

APPENDIX 8

Appellate Whistleblowing Cases

1. ALM MEDICAL SERVICES LTD v BLADON

[2002] IRLR 807; [2002] EWCA Civ 1085 (CA)

First appeal of PIDA case to Court of Appeal.

Key issues: (1) Test for substantially the same disclosure for s43G(2); (2) Case management.

Case Summary: Mr Bladon, a registered nurse, was employed by ALM from 14 June 1999 until 6 September 1999. He made disclosures concerning patient care and wellbeing, first by telephone to the PA of the MD. He was asked to put these concerns in writing and he did by fax to the MD on 22 August 1999. On 31 August 1999 Bladon spoke to the Nursing Home Inspectorate of the local authority who carried out an investigation on 1 September 1999. The Inspectorate wrote to the respondent on 8 September 1999. Following a disciplinary hearing the day before, Bladon received a written warning on 10 September 1999. On 16 September 1999 he was summarily dismissed. On 20 September 1999 Bladon presented an ET1 claiming 'unfair dismissal (Protected Disclosure)' based on the alleged detriment of the written warning and on his dismissal. He was represented by Unison.

The respondent's ET3 stated that Bladon's dismissal 'had nothing whatsoever to do with his allegations to the Nursing Inspectorate'. They claimed he was dismissed for serious breaches of contract regarding the proper discipline of a care assistant and a failure to investigate properly an incident of possible non-accidental injury to a resident. They also relied on shortcomings in his professional attitude to staff and that, while on leave from the respondent, he was supplied to another home of theirs without the management's knowledge. It was then claimed that he had acted in bad faith in making statements to staff on 15 September 1999 to the effect that he intended 'to close the [Respondent] down for good' and that he wanted the staff there to provide him with 'information and written statements citing any failings at Arundel Lodge for him to use as extra ammunition for his case against ALM'.

ET: held that he had been dismissed as a consequence of making a protected disclosure. The tribunal did not accept the respondent's explanation of the dismissal and concluded that the protected disclosures were the principal reason for the dismissal of Bladon.

The tribunal awarded £10,000 for the detriment (ie the written warning for having made a protected disclosure to the Inspectorate), and for his automatically unfair dismissal £13,075.06 compensation.

It was held that the disclosures related to the danger to the health or safety of a patient (s43B(1)(d)), to a failure or likely failure to comply with a legal obligation (s43B(1)(b)) and possibly to the potential commission of a criminal offence (s43B(1)(a)); that they were made in good faith (s43C(1)) and in the reasonable belief that the information communicated (which was substantially the same in the disclosures to both the employer and the Inspectorate) was true (ss43C(1)(a) and 43C(1)(b) respectively), with the motive of achieving an investigation, which took place and substantiated most of the allegations. They found that Bladon had acted reasonably in contacting Social Services nine days after his fax to the MD without waiting for him to return from holiday.

There was no notice of the disciplinary hearing, and no notice of the allegations against him.

EAT: during a preliminary hearing on 19 January 2001 the EAT determined not to allow ALM's appeal to proceed to a full hearing on the ground that it had no reasonable prospect of success. At this stage the focus of the appeal was on the conclusions of the ET as to whether Bladon had a reasonable belief in the matters raised with the Inspectorate; it was alleged that the tribunal erred in holding that the information disclosed to the Inspectorate was substantially the same as the information disclosed to the employer; and that it was perverse in holding that it was reasonable for Mr Bladon to make the disclosure to the Inspectorate. Whilst an application was made to amend the grounds of appeal to allege bias on the part of the chairman and for permission to adduce fresh evidence, this was refused. In relation to the phrase 'substantially the same' in s43G(2), EAT said (at para 31) that:

> it would, in our judgment, be wholly inappropriate for tribunals to embark upon an exercise of nice and detailed analysis of the disclosure to the employer, compared with the disclosure to the outside body, for the purpose of deciding whether the test in section 43G(2)(c) has been made out. The correct approach, in our judgment, is for tribunals to adopt a commonsense broad approach when decided whether or not the disclosure is 'substantially the same'.

Court of Appeal: Sir Andrew Morritt (Vice Chancellor), Mummery LJ, Rix LJ: on the application for permission to appeal, ALM sought to rely on additional grounds: an allegation that the chairman of the Employment Tribunal, accused of conducting the hearing in an unfair manner, did not disclose his prior association with Unison (on the ground that he was a partner and later a consultant with Unison's solicitors).

Lord Justice Mummery on 22 November 2001, requested the chairman to write a letter to the court commenting on the allegation of bias. The chairman's reply, dated 3 January 2002, made it clear that the proceedings in the Employment Tribunal were legally flawed by the decision not to permit ALM to call relevant evidence which it wished to put to Bladon in cross-examination. Mummery LJ said (at para 22):

> In order to reduce the risk of this happening in another case, I would suggest that there should be directions hearings in protected disclosure cases in order to identify the issues and ascertain what evidence the parties intend to call on those issues.

Result: rehearing by a fresh tribunal.

Detriment: final written warning. Value: £10,000 (pre *Virgo Fidelis* decision).

Sections considered: 43B(1)(a), (b), (c); 43C(1), (a), (b); 103A ERA.

Damages: Compensatory award—£13,075.06.

Cited: *Street v Derbyshire Unemployed Workers' Centre* [2005] ICR 97; *Boulding v Land Securities Trillium (Media Services) Limited* (EAT/0023/063, 3 May 2006); *The Trustees of Mama East African Women's Group v Dobson* (EAT/0219/05 and EAT/0220/05, 23 June 2005); *Lucas v Chichester Diocesan Housing Association* (EAT/0713/04, 7 February 2005); *Ganatra v London North Business Into Education Limited* (EAT/0498/04 and EAT/0499/04); *Arthur v London Eastern Railway Limited* [2006] EWCA Civ 1358.

2. Aspinall v MSI Mech Forge Limited

(EAT/891/01, 25 July 2002)

Key issue: 'Reason why' test.

Case Summary: The respondent makes fork lift truck arms. In 1999 Mr Aspinall was injured at work. He asked a colleague to make a video of a production process for evidence in support of his PI claim and his colleague agreed. The video was given to the claimant's solicitors. It was subsequently disclosed to the respondent's insurer's solicitors. The respondent did not view the video. The respondent was concerned that the video showed a secret and confidential process used by the company. During an investigation Aspinall was pressed to identify the name of his colleague who had made the video. He considered that he had been threatened that if he did not reveal the name of the person who took the video he would be sacked. He returned to work to find his clocking-in card missing and as a consequence Aspinall resigned, giving no reasons.

Note: the claimant resigned and immediately started work in a new job for which he had applied and been interviewed before the disciplinary process was contemplated.

Aspinall issued proceedings claiming unfair dismissal. On the day of the hearing the tribunal permitted the claim to be amended to include a claim under s103A.

ET: found no automatically unfair constructive dismissal. It found that making the video 'could' be a protected disclosure. However Aspinall left employment for his own reasons (so no dismissal). The company's actions were taken because of a breach of confidentiality rather than a disclosure about health and safety. The tribunal found the disappearance of the clocking-in card occurred without any involvement of the respondent. Regarding the warning that Aspinall would be sacked—it was accepted that no words were said and the tribunal found there was nothing upon which such a belief could reasonably have been entertained. This finding was at the heart of the appeal.

There were contemporaneous notes which the ET accepted as an accurate record. In those notes it was recorded that if Aspinall had provided the name of the person who took the video he would have been given a nine-month final written warning. Those notes also stated that if he did not do so, further action would be considered. The respondent cross-appealed the tribunal's decision to permit the amendment to include s103A.

EAT (HHJ Reid QC): regarding the notes: the tribunal were entitled to reach the conclusions of fact which they did.

The EAT allowed the amendment to plead s103A as it raised no new issues of fact and was simply another way of putting a claim for unfair dismissal. They confirmed that the claim did not raise a new claim under s47B (detriment). *Selkent* was considered.

> The claim failed as there was no dismissal and in any event if [constructive dismissal] had been established the reason or principal reason was not any protected disclosure but the perceived breach of confidentiality. Nor was there any detriment. For there to be detriment under section 47B 'on the ground that the worker has made a protected disclosure' the protected disclosure has to be causative in the sense of being 'the real reason, the core reason, the *causa causans*, the motive for the treatment complained of', to borrow the words of Lord Scott in the Race Relations case of *Chief Constable of West Yorkshire Police v Khan*.

Sections considered: 103A, 43B(1)(d), 47B ERA.

Issues considered: Late amendment to include PIDA claim. 'Reason why' question.

ET determined that making of a video could be a disclosure under s43B(1)(d), but this was doubted by EAT.

Result: No automatically unfair dismissal.

Detriment: not pleaded.

Damages awarded: none.

Cited: *Bolton School v Evans* [2006] IRLR 500 (EAT).

3. BABULA V WALTHAM FOREST COLLEGE

(EAT/0635/05, 31 March 2006)

Key Issue: Reasonable belief in relevant failure.

Case Summary: Mr Babula was a lecturer with the respondent. Another lecturer had divided students into Islamic and non-Islamic groups and stated to the Islamic group that he wished that a September 11 incident would occur in London, indicating his happiness with the events in

New York on 11 September 2001. The students and then Babula raised concerns that these observations amounted to a 'threat to national security and a possible criminal offence of incitement to racial hatred'. He then reported the matter to the CIA and FBI, where he was advised to report his concerns to the local police. The claimant asserted that the disclosure tended to show a criminal offence of incitement to commit racial hatred under s18 Public Order Act 1986.

ET: The Chairman at a preliminary hearing struck out the claim on the grounds that Babula did not possess a reasonable belief in a criminal offence under s18 Public Order Act 1986, or breach of a legal obligation (under the other lecturer's contract of employment).

EAT (HHJ Peter Clark): upheld the Employment Tribunal's finding.

Babula's pleaded case was that he reasonably believed that a criminal offence of incitement to racial hatred had been committed. That claim failed because the allegations only amounted to racial hatred, and it was conceded that no case was being advanced in relation to the Employment Equality (Religion or Belief) Regulations 2003 (paras 26–30):

> . . . the approach of Elias P in [*Bolton School v Evans*] is not whether Mr Jalil may have some defence to a criminal charge under Section 18 which may not have occurred to this Claimant, but whether the set of facts which he reasonably believed existed could possibly constitute the offence. Only if there is no reasonable prospect of his establishing that the facts could constitute the offence can this part of his claim properly be struck out as misconceived under Rule 18(7)(b).

> . . . I accept that the comment that he wished to see a 9/11 incident in the UK is capable of amounting to threatening words. The real question, identified by the Chairman, is whether such words are capable of evincing an intention to stir up racial hatred, that is hatred against a racial group.

> It is here, in my judgment, that the Claimant's pleaded case falls down. The racial group against whom the 9/11 remark was directed is simply not identified. It is not British citizens, but the group of students consisting of Jews and white Europeans. However, that group emerges from the division of the class into Islamic and non-Islamic students, a division based on religion, not race.

> In short, I have concluded that the Chairman was entitled to find that the words relied on were, on the Claimant's pleaded case, not directed to any racial group so as to found a reasonable belief that a Section 18 offence had been, was or was likely to be committed. The claim based on a Section 43B(1)(a) qualifying disclosure had no reasonable prospect of success.

> . . . his bid to establish a qualifying disclosure under Section 43B(1)(b) foundered on the distinction between racial and religious discrimination, as the Chairman found.

Result: No reasonable belief in the protected disclosure.

Detriment: not addressed.

Sections Considered: 43B(1)(a), (b) and (f) ERA.

Damages awarded: none.

4. Bachnak v Emerging Markets Partnership (Europe) Ltd

(EAT/0288/05, 27 January 2006)

Key issue: Burden of proof for good faith.

Summary: Mr Bachnak, an investment officer, was dismissed by EMP(E) Ltd, and subsequently brought an unfair dismissal claim. Among other things, he alleged that he had been dismissed as a result of making a number of 'protected disclosures' to his employer regarding the way in which the company was conducting its investment business. Bachnak claimed dismissal under s103A ERA.

ET: the tribunal rejected Bachnak's 'whistleblowing' claim, holding that some of his disclosures had not been made in 'good faith' and thus were not 'protected disclosures' within the meaning of either s43C or s43G ERA. Since the disclosures were not 'protected', s103A did not apply. In any event, the tribunal found, there was no causal link between Bachnak's disclosures and his dismissal, which was carried out for reason of misconduct. The tribunal went on to uphold Bachnak's alternative claim of 'ordinary' unfair dismissal under s98 ERA, since the employer had failed to follow a fair procedure. It decided, however, that it would not be just and equitable to award compensation because Bachnak had contributed to his own dismissal by 100 per cent.

Bachnak appealed to the EAT, contending that the burden should have been on EMP(E) Ltd to prove that he had acted in bad faith in making his disclosures. The tribunal, he submitted, had erred in proceeding on the basis that the burden of proof in this regard was neutral.

EAT (HHJ Peter Clark): the EAT, having referred to the decisions in *Lucas v Chichester Diocesan Housing Association Ltd* (EAT 0713/04) and *GMB v Fenton* (EAT 0484/04; 0798/02; 0046/03) agreed with Bachnak that the burden is on the employer to show that an employee made the relevant disclosures in bad faith. It thus rejected the tribunal's tentative suggestion that the burden was neutral. It also held that the onus of showing the reason for dismissal is on the employer once a protected disclosure is established.

Despite the tribunal's error over the burden as to good faith, the EAT declined to overturn the tribunal's decision on this issue. The tribunal had made firm findings of fact on the basis of the evidence presented to it, and its decision was in no way dependent on the burden of proof. Having heard the witnesses and considered the documentary evidence, the tribunal had found that two of Bachnak's disclosures had been made to strengthen his hand in negotiations for a new contract with EMP(E) Ltd. One had been made after Bachnak had been summoned to a meeting for copying documents without permission. The other had followed his suspension, and had been intended to put pressure on his employer not to dismiss him. These were findings of fact as to Bachnak's motive which were open to the tribunal to make and with which the EAT would not interfere. Bachnak's had been acting out of personal interest in making the disclosures and not out of public interest. The EAT therefore dismissed his appeal.

Result: no protected disclosure.

Detriment: none.

Sections considered: 103A ERA.

Damages awarded: none.

5. Bolton School v Evans

[2006] IRLR 500 (EAT)

Key issue: Reason for dismissal/detriment: distinction between making a protected disclosure and the previous investigation.

Case Summary: Mr Evans deliberately broke into the new computer system at the school to test and demonstrate the validity of his concerns over data security. He was disciplined and then resigned in protest at this and claimed he had been constructively unfairly dismissed. He also asserted that he had permission to try and break into the system.

ET: automatically unfairly dismissed (constructive dismissal) and the claimant suffered a detriment. If not automatic—he was still unfairly dismissed.

> We then turn to the issue of causation. The claimant must demonstrate that he has suffered a detriment on the grounds of a protected disclosure and, in order to succeed with his unfair dismissal case, that the protected disclosure was the reason or the main reason for his dismissal. The respondent argues that he had been dismissed not because he had disclosed matters of public interest but, rather, because he had without authority hacked into the computer system. The Tribunal reminds itself that the statutory scheme introduced by the Public Interest Disclosure Act 1998 is to encourage disclosures to be made internally, that is to say, to the whistleblower's own employer and that this is achieved by making protection readily available

so long as the worker raises his or her concern with the employer. Prior to the enactment of the Public Interest Disclosure Act, a worker who blew the whistle could expect to feel the full force of an organisation's disapproval by way of ostracism, criticism, poor appraisals, victimisation and even dismissal. The Tribunal is therefore acutely conscious of the policy behind the Public Interest Disclosure Act. Parliament, when framing the legislation, required an employer to have a reasonable belief in the matters being disclosed. This requirement was inserted in order to achieve a fair balance between the interests of the worker who suspects malpractice and those of an employer who could be damaged by unfounded allegations. It seems to us that it would emasculate the public policy behind the legislation for us to accept the respondent's submission that the claimant was the subject of disciplinary action not because he had blown the whistle on a suspected failure to comply with the legal obligation but rather because he had hacked into the respondent's computer system without authority. To allow an employer to defeat a Public Interest Disclosure Act case in this way would be to drive a coach and horses through the intention of the legislature that whistleblowers should have employment protection. Doubtless, had the claimant approached Mr Edmundson, Mr Brooker or anyone else for that matter, and simply said that he had a belief that the security system was inadequate, and had he been subject to disciplinary action and brought a similar complaint as he now does, the respondent would have sought to argue that he did not have the basis for a reasonable belief. The respondent cannot have it both ways. In order to obtain sufficient evidence to found a reasonable belief, the Claimant had to do more than simply express misgivings about what had happened over the summer of 2003. It is our view that the legislation must be construed purposively and the investigation undertaken by the employee to found his reasonable belief should not be divorced from the disclosure itself.

It is our judgment, therefore, that the claimant has established that the reason that disciplinary action was taken against him was because he made a protected disclosure.

Section 43B(3) ERA provides that a disclosure is not protected if the person making it commits a criminal offence in so doing. However the EAT held that Evans did not lose protection on this basis because the Computer Misuse Act 1990 only established criminal liability for unauthorized access to computers, and the Tribunal found that he was in fact authorized.

EAT (Mr Justice Elias): breaking into the computer system was not a disclosure. Informing relevant people that it could be broken into was a disclosure. Mr Evans was dismissed for breaking into the system which was not a protected act. The EAT explained (paras 64–68) that a distinction was to be drawn between the making of the disclosure (which was protected) and the previous investigation which was not protected:

> The Tribunal sought to justify its conclusion on policy grounds. It observed that if the Claimant had simply noted that the security system was inadequate and had been disciplined then the employers would have said that he had no reasonable grounds for his belief. The point is, however, it seems to us, that if he had done simply that there is no reason to suppose that he would have been subject to any disciplinary sanction at all. And even if he had, the law only protects him if he has reasonable grounds for his belief. It does not allow him to commit what would otherwise be acts of misconduct in the hope that he may be able to establish the justification for his belief.

> An employee cannot be entitled to break into his employer's filing cabinet in the hope of finding papers which will demonstrate some relevant wrongdoing which he can then disclose to the appropriate person. He is liable to be disciplined for such conduct, and that is so whether he turns up such papers or not. Provided that his misconduct is genuinely the reason for the disciplinary action, the employee will not be protected even if he does in fact discover incriminating papers. Success does not retrospectively provide a cloak of immunity for his actions, although he will then of course be protected with respect to the subsequent disclosure of the information itself.

> We have considered the point, which we recognise can be put forcefully in this case, that the Tribunal found that the Claimant did indeed have authority for testing the system. But we have

come to the view that this still does not bring his testing within the protected category for two reasons in particular.

First, this was not the understanding of the employers when they dismissed him. The Tribunal found that the School was wrong to consider that he had not been authorised, and that is of course highly relevant indeed to the question of whether he had been unfairly dismissed in the ordinary way, but it does not affect the reason why he was dismissed. Second, and in any event, it seems to us that the fact of authority would not of itself convert into a protected disclosure something that otherwise was not a disclosure.

We think there are two quite separate issues here. First, the conduct designed to demonstrate that the belief was reasonable and, second, the disclosure of the information itself which tended to show a breach of the relevant legal obligation. Putting it simply, it seems to us that the law protects the disclosure of information which the employee reasonably believes tends to demonstrate the kind of wrongdoing, or anticipated wrongdoing, which is covered by section 43B. It does not protect the actions of the employee which are directed to establishing or confirming the reasonableness of that belief. The protection is for the whistleblower who reasonably believes, to put it colloquially if inaccurately, that something is wrong, not the investigator who seeks either to establish that it is wrong or to show that his concerns are reasonable.

The EAT also considered the case of *Kraus v Penna plc* [2004] IRLR 260 (EAT) and the requirement that where reliance is placed on s43B(1)(b) there must be an actual legal obligation rather than merely a belief that one exists. As to this (paras 51–52):

We do not think that the protection is lost merely because the employer may be able to show that, for reasons not immediately apparent to the employee, the duty will not apply or that he has some defence to it. The information will still, it seems to us, tend to show the likelihood of breach. It is potentially powerful and material evidence pointing in that direction even although there may be other factors which ultimately would demonstrate that no breach is likely to occur.

There may indeed be cases where a relatively detailed appreciation of the relevant legal obligation is required before an employee can establish that he reasonably believed that the information tended to show that a breach of a legal obligation was likely. But it would undermine the protection of this valuable legislation if employees were expected to anticipate and evaluate all potential defences, whether within the scope of their own knowledge or not, when deciding whether or not to make that disclosure.

Result: remitted back to consider constructive dismissal. But leave to appeal has been granted ([2006] EWCA Civ 710).

Detriment: a warning.

Sections considered: 43A, 43B, 43C, 47B, 103A ERA.

Damages awarded: £26,118.13 which included an award of £3,000 for injured feelings resulting from the detriment.

6. The Brothers of Charity Services Merseyside v Eleady-Cole

(EAT/0661/00, 24 January 2002)

Key issue: Drawing inferences concerning reason for dismissal.

Case Summary: Mr Eleady-Cole was a full-time support worker in a hostel operated by the respondent. He raised concerns regarding his fellow workers' use of pornographic material and illegal substances at the residence. This disclosure was made through a telephone system (EAP) that was not confidential. Eleady-Cole was not confirmed in post at the expiry of his probationary three-months period. The respondent relied upon his conduct in other areas to support their decision not to confirm him in post.

ET: found the claim for unfair dismissal proven.

> What. . . was the reason for his dismissal? Was it a consequence of the protected disclosure, or not. The stated reason in the letter of dismissal was 'that your probationary period has been unsatisfactory in as much as that we have a number of concerns regarding your work performance and standards that we can not reconcile.' Presumably, although somewhat imprecisely worded, that was a reference to matters of either conduct or capability. Be that as it may, since the Applicant's service was of such short duration it would not be possible for him to bring a normal unfair dismissal claim. Had he been able to do so, then there must have been very serious doubts as to the adequacy of the reasons advanced for his dismissal and the degree of investigation. That, however, is not, of course, our direct concern in this instance, although not without significance in the general process of determining what was the true reason for dismissal. The Applicant's earlier appraisals were good. . . . That very favourable view then suddenly changed. Why, we ask? On the face of it, it appears mainly to be the unfavourable comments put forward by Mr Bonnar. These, on due consideration are in the main insubstantial, other than the question of proper treatment of the resident who had the 'attack'. That was a matter, however, where there was a possibility of a difference of opinion as to the proper course of action or treatment to be taken. Why would those who had, so far, been impressed by Mr Eleady-Cole suddenly, over what was a very short period of time, completely change their views and readily come to the conclusion that he was unfit to remain. Significant, the only new factor during that time was the protected disclosure made by the Applicant, and its consequences. In making the disclosure the Applicant, on the face of it, was performing a very real service for the Respondent. Something for which, one might properly think, gratitude would seem to be the appropriate response and certainly not dismissal. There is, however, an alternative scenario which is to the effect, here is someone who, on this occasion, has done good. However, taking a longer view, and disregarding the immediate situation, a view might then emerge to the effect, here is someone who has been a 'whistle blower' on this occasion: is it, therefore, possible that he might act in this way again in the future and thereby prove a source of, if nothing more, irritation. Is he going to 'rock the boat'? If he took such action in circumstances where, and perhaps more than once, he was shown to be right in what he did, might that be seen as something of a de-stabilising influence within the establishment? Taking all the known circumstances into account, with particular emphasis on the sudden change of view as to his abilities and qualities, the Tribunal concludes and finds, that the true reason for his dismissal was the making of the protected statement. Accordingly we find in his favour. He was unfairly dismissed.

EAT (Mr Commissioner Howell QC): The disclosure by a non-confidential telephone support service that passed on information to the respondent fell within s43C(2) ERA. However the appeal was allowed, in part on the basis that the tribunal's approach to drawing inferences had strayed too far into considering reasonableness rather than the reason for dismissal (paras 25, 30–31):

> We note . . . [in] the Tribunal's Extended Reasons, in referring to the recorded complaints as being of a somewhat 'trivial nature', they said that they 'certainly were not certain enough to determine [what] his probationary period was without some further enquiry being made at a higher level' adding that the Tribunal considered, and found that this was a matter which needed more detailed consideration before any final conclusion leading to dismissal could be reached. That appears to us to demonstrate that the Tribunal were not directing their attention at [this] point in their decision, as they should have been, to whether those complaints were *in fact* the reason which led to Mr Eleady-Cole's dismissal, rather than whether they would have *justified* a dismissal, as would have been the issue in a more normal unfair dismissal case.

> The Tribunal's explanation for how they came to draw the inferences they did relied too much on surmise as to what the reasons might have been in the absence of what they considered reasonable explanations, and too little on a reasoned explanation of their own having regard to specific findings of fact that ought to have been made. . . .

In this context, there was force in the submissions of Mr Spencer that under Section 103A where a finding of unfair dismissal in circumstances such as those in this case necessarily involves a finding that the reasons put forward by the employer were not genuine and that evidence given before the Tribunal was untruthful, it is incumbent on the Tribunal to base its conclusions on clear findings as to the primary facts about which of the persons before it were responsible for what happened, and to explain clearly how those findings lead causally to the conclusion that the protected disclosure had been the true reason for the employee's dismissal.

Result: remitted to a freshly constituted Employment Tribunal to consider the reason for dismissal.

Sections considered: 43C, 103A ERA.

Damages awarded: none at this stage

Cited: *De Haney v Brent Mind and Lang* (EAT/0054/03, 10 April 2003)

7. DARNTON V UNIVERSITY OF SURREY

([2003] IRLR 133 EAT)

Key Issue: Test of reasonable belief for qualifying disclosure.

Case Summary: Mr Darnton, a full-time lecturer, fell out with the head of his school over working hours shortly after starting work at the university. Following a meeting to agree hours of work, he criticized the head over his 'ridiculous' management style. There then followed a deterioration in the relationship, with Darnton accusing the head of 'serious academic malpractice' regarding unrealistic time periods for marking. The relationship further deteriorated. Darnton then made enquiries about the grievance procedure and, during this, proposed the termination of his employment on terms. He complained about bullying and harassment. A compromise was entered into that included terms of a single payment together with an agreement that he continue as an 'associate lecturer' for one year doing work valued at £20,000. Darnton obtained a new post at another university. He believed the university was still bound to pay for the agreed work; the respondent did not. Darnton wrote to the respondent complaining and demanding more compensation. He contended that this letter contained protected disclosures.

ET: considered the letter so as to 'carefully, isolate from it the disclosures as opposed to the general complaints, demands for money and vituperation and decide whether in the reasonable belief of the [claimant] that the information tended to show either that a criminal offence had been committed or that the respondents had failed to comply with any legal obligation to which they were subject'. They found there was no qualifying disclosure.

EAT (HHJ Judge Serota QC): remitted the claim back to the Employment Tribunal. The employment tribunal did not appear to have asked themselves the question required by s43B, namely whether, in Darnton's reasonable belief, the disclosure tended to show a relevant failure. It was submitted and accepted that in determining whether the information 'tends to show' a relevant failure, the employment tribunal should look at matters from the perspective of the worker, not on the basis of the facts they had found (para 32):

> We agree with the authors [of the 1st edition of this book] that, for there to be a qualifying disclosure, it must have been reasonable for the worker to believe that the factual basis of what was disclosed was true and that it tends to show a relevant failure, even if the worker was wrong, but reasonably mistaken.

The truth of the allegations would often be relevant to ascertaining reasonable belief, but all depends on the circumstances:

> We consider that as a matter of both law and common sense all circumstances must be considered together in determining whether the worker holds the reasonable belief. The circumstances

will include his belief in the factual basis of the information disclosed as well as what those facts tend to show. The more the worker claims to have direct knowledge of the matters which are the subject of the disclosure, the more relevant will be his belief in the truth of what he says in determining whether he holds that reasonable belief.

However, it is clear from the wording of the statute that the standard of belief in the truth of what is disclosed cannot be such as to require the employee making a qualifying disclosure, under s43B, to hold the belief that both the factual basis of the disclosure and what it tends to show are 'substantially true'.

The EAT also endorsed the commentary in the previous edition of this book as follows:

We have derived considerable assistance from *Whistleblowing: the new law* by John Bowers QC, Jeremy Lewis and Jack Mitchell. The learned authors write, at p 19, under the heading 'Reasonable belief in truth':

'To achieve protection under any of the several parts of the Act, the worker must have a "reasonable belief" in the truth of the information as tending to show one or more of the six matters listed which he has disclosed, although that belief need not be correct (s43B(1)). This had led some to criticise the statute as giving too much licence to employees to cause trouble, since it pays no regard to issues of confidentiality in this respect. Nor need the employee actually prove, even on the balance of probabilities, the truth of what he is disclosing. This is probably inevitable, because the whistleblower may have a good "hunch" that something is wrong without having the means to prove it beyond doubt or even on the balance of probabilities. [An example is the *Herald of Free Enterprise* disaster where no one had the resources to check on the hunch which several employees had about the safety of the bow doors.[1]] The notion behind the legislation is that the employee should be encouraged to make known to a suitable person the basis of that hunch so that those with the ability and resources to investigate it can do so.

The control on abuse is that it must have been reasonable for the worker to believe that the information disclosed was true. This means, we think, that the following principles would apply under the Act:

(a) It would be a qualifying disclosure if the worker reasonably but mistakenly believed that a specified malpractice is or was occurring or may occur.
(b) Equally if some malpractice was occurring which did not fall within one of the listed categories, the disclosure would still qualify if the worker reasonably believed that it did amount to malpractice falling within one of those categories.[2]
(c) There must be more than unsubstantiated rumours in order for there to be a qualifying disclosure. The whistleblower must exercise some judgment on his own part consistent with the evidence and the resources available to him. There must additionally be a reasonable belief and therefore some information which tends to show that the specified malpractice occurred . . .
(d) The reasonableness of the belief will depend in each case on the volume and quality of information available to the worker at the time the decision to disclose is made. Employment tribunals will have to guard against use of hindsight to assess the reasonableness of the belief in this respect in the same way as they are bound, in considering liability in unfair dismissal cases, to consider only what was known to the employer at the time of dismissal or appeal . . .'

---

[1] This sentence was omitted from the passage quoted by the EAT.
[2] But see the comments in *Kraus v Penna* [2004] IRLR 260 (EAT) at p 518 below, emphasizing that 'likely' means 'probable' or 'more probable than not'.

Result:

The employment tribunal . . . has departed from the statutory test: it did not ask whether [the Claimant] held the reasonable belief that what he was disclosing tended to show a relevant failure, but instead asked itself whether the factual allegations were correct. While, as we have said, determination of the accuracy of factual allegations may be a useful tool to determine whether the worker's belief is reasonable, reasonable belief must be based on facts as understood by the worker, not as actually found to be the case.

Result: remitted.

Sections considered: 43B; 43C, 43(5), 43F, 43G, 43H, and 43K ERA.

Damages awarded: remitted.

Cited: *Bolton School v Evans* [2006] IRLR 500 (EAT); *Street v Derbyshire Unemployed Workers' Centre* [2005] ICR 97; *Kraus v Penna plc* [2004] IRLR 260 (EAT).

8. De Haney v Brent Mind and Lang

(EAT/0054/03/DA, 10 April 2003)

Key issue: Qualifying disclosure.

Case Summary: Ms De Haney alleged she had been suspended and dismissed because she had made protected qualifying disclosures. One such disclosure was that she had complained that the appointment of a colleague had been in breach of the Equal Opportunities Policy.

ET: dismissed claim on facts. Held that her allegation as to what was said did not amount to a qualifying disclosure because (a) she did not in terms allege race discrimination, (b) the appointment did not happen in the way she alleged and c) the allegation was added late as a 'makeweight'.

EAT (HHJ McMullen QC): this was upheld (paras 23–25):

In our judgment the principles applicable to a case such as this can be derived from the following authorities. It must be asked in each case:

(a) Does the allegation made by an applicant include a failure to comply with an obligation under Section 43?
(b) Did the Applicant have reasonable belief in the factual basis of the allegation?
(c) Did the Respondent act on the ground of that disclosure?

The correct approach is set out in Darnton v University of Surrey [2003] IRLR 133 EAT. Judge Serota QC said at paragraph 29:

'In our opinion, the determination of the factual accuracy of the disclosure by the tribunal will, in many cases, he an important tool in determining whether the worker held the reasonable belief that the disclosure tended to show a relevant failure. Thus if an employment tribunal finds that an employee's factual allegation of something he claims to have seen himself is false, that will be highly relevant to the question of the worker's reasonable belief. It is extremely difficult to see how a worker can reasonably believe that an allegation tends to show that there has been a relevant failure if he knew or believed that the factual basis was false, unless there may somehow have been an honest mistake on his part.'

In *London Borough of Harrow v Knight* [2003] IRLR 140 (EAT), Mr Recorder Underhill QC, it was decided that in a claim under this section it is essential to show that the fact that the protected disclosure had been made caused or influenced the employer to act in the way complained of. See paragraph 16:

'It is thus necessary in a claim under s47B to show that the fact that the protected disclosure had been made caused or influenced the employer to act (or not act) in the way complained of: merely to show that "but for" the disclosure the act or omission would not have occurred is not enough (see *Khan*). In our view, the phrase "related to" imports a different and much looser test than that required by the statute: it merely connotes some connection (not even necessarily causative) between the act done and the disclosure.'

Court of Appeal: [2004] ICR 348: set aside the EAT's decision on the ground that the panel was not properly constituted. Remitted to the EAT.

EAT (HHJ Serota): again dismissed the appeal. The claimant had raised a concern about the appointment of a colleague in writing prior to her dismissal, but the allegation that her concerns in relation to this amounted to a protected disclosure was not contained in the Claim Form or De Haney's further particulars of her claim, but was first made in her witness statement. In those circumstances the EAT held that the tribunal had been entitled to find that the allegation was put in as a 'makeweight' and as such was not a qualifying disclosure (in that she did not hold the requisite reasonable belief).

Detriment: not invited to meetings; not considered for deputizing duties; failing to appraise.

Sections considered: 43A, 43B, 47B(1), 48(2) and 103A ERA.

Damages awarded: none.

9. Douglas v Birmingham CC and Governing Body of Canterbury Cross School and Boyle

(EAT/018/02, 17 March 2003)

Key issues: (1) Who is the employer for purposes of s43C ERA? (2) Scope of 'legal obligation' for qualifying disclosure.

Case Summary: Ms Douglas was an Afro-Caribbean school governor who claimed to have made a qualifying disclosure to the Chair of the Governing Body and also to another governor. Her concern was that the head teacher had refused to replace a member of staff who was retiring. She claimed this was a failure to comply with equal opportunities procedure.

ET: claim dismissed at a preliminary hearing on the basis that no disclosure was made.

EAT (HHJ McMullen QC): one disclosure made during a private conversation with another governor could not amount to a qualifying disclosure (paras 30–31):

> . . . Mrs Canning was being consulted for the purposes only of advice and the Applicant indicated that she would herself pursue the matter and did not want the matter to be handled on her behalf by Mrs Canning. The relationship was one of confidentiality and thus, at first sight and on close analysis thereafter, a statute which is designed in the public interest to protect disclosures ought not to apply to a private conversation between these two governors of the school.
>
> Thus, the Applicant falls at the first hurdle, in our judgment, since what she is disclosing to Mrs Canning is done in a confidential manner and not to her *qua* employer. . . .

It was found that an allegation that there had been a failure to follow the equal opportunities policy would be a failure of a legal obligation either because the school was enjoined to follow the policy or because a failure to follow it would result in a breach of the trust and confidence obligation (para 36):

> An allegation that a head teacher is engaged in a practice which conflicts with that obligation is, it seems to us, indicating that she is failing to comply or likely failing to comply with a legal obligation—both within the equal opportunities policies, which we have no doubt in so far as they are apt, are incorporated into the contracts of employment; and the anti-discrimination legislation.

Douglas was a 'worker' within s43K (para 43):

> The work she performs is for the Governing Body of the School. The definition of 'worker', therefore, in section 43K(1) applies to her. She was supplied by a contract of employment, effected by the City Council, to do work for the Governing Body of the School.

A disclosure to the Chair of Governors was to her employer or another responsible person within s43C(1)(b)(ii).

Result: appeal allowed.

Sections considered: 47B; 43 K; 230; 43A; 43B and 43C ERA.

Damages awarded: none.

10. METEOROLOGICAL OFFICE V EDGAR

[2002] ICR 149

Key Issue: Coverage for pre-PIDA protected disclosures. Could a claimant rely on a protected disclosure that pre-dated the coming into force of the Public Interest Disclosure Act 1998?

Case Summary: On 11 March 1999 Mr Edgar made a formal complaint of bullying and harassment to the respondent. This complaint was investigated and a report produced that was favourable to Edgar. The person against whom the complaint had been made was disciplined. Following a period of sick leave said to have been caused by this treatment Edgar returned to work to be informed he was being relocated away from the BBC Weather Centre. This decision, he claimed, had a detrimental effect on his career and earning capacity.

ET: claim could be brought. Edgar argued and it was accepted by the tribunal:

> that the purpose of the legislation is to protect employees. To accept the interpretation advanced on behalf of the Respondent, that the protected disclosure must post-date the coming into force of the Act, would be contrary to public policy and the 'public good construction' referred to in *Bennion on Statutory Interpretation*.

The tribunal held that the time for bringing a complaint ran from the date of the detrimental act or omission complained of. It could not have been Parliament's intention to require that the protected disclosure should have taken place after the Act came into effect.

EAT (HHJ Peter Clark): protected disclosures prior to PIDA coming into force were covered if detriment was post-Act.

Detriment: relocation.

Sections considered: 48(1)(a) ERA.

Damages awarded: none, as preliminary hearing over jurisdiction.

Cited: *Miklaszewicz v Stolt Offshore Limited* [2002] IRLR 344 (Court of Session).

11. EL-HOSHI V PIZZA EXPRESS RESTAURANTS LIMITED

(EAT/0857/03, 23 March 2004)

Key issue: Affirmation of contract. Policy approach in whistleblowing context.

Case summary: Mr El-Hoshi was claiming constructive dismissal. The respondent admitted that he had made a protected disclosure but took issue with whether he had suffered a detriment and whether that was as a result of the disclosure. As a fall-back position they asserted in any event that the contract had been affirmed after any alleged breach.

ET: while El-Hoshi was off work he constantly submitted sick notes covering the whole of the period. These were expressly in relation to depression. The tribunal held that his depression was due to the detriment. It decided that, while El-Hoshi had a legitimate claim for being subjected to a detriment, he was not constructively dismissed, for he had affirmed the fundamental breach of his contract.

EAT (HHJ McMullen QC): El-Hoshi did not affirm the contract by virtue of delaying his resignation by 3 months, during which he submitted sick notes and received statutory sick pay.

His illness was due to the detriment that had been inflicted upon him and the delay was therefore caused by that detriment.

> We also take the view that we have taken against the background of the protection given to 'whistle-blowers'. The reaction of this manager, to humiliate the Applicant, was bound to cause an effect upon the Applicant's health. This legislation is there to protect those people who raise issues of concern and which are acknowledged to be in the public interest. It would be an odd result if an employee who raised an issue were to find himself or herself dismissed, even constructively dismissed. Public policy is to protect and take a liberal view of employees who raise these issues and who pass the thresholds in Part IVA of the Employment Rights Act 1996 entitling them to claim that they are legitimate whistle-blowers.

Result: remitted to the Employment Tribunal to consider damages for unfair dismissal.

Detriment: being rostered to work four nights in the kitchen.

Sections considered: 47B(1) ERA.

Damages awarded: £9,640.75 (injury to feelings £3,500) before award for unfair dismissal.

12. EVERETT FINANCIAL MANAGEMENT LTD v MURRELL

(EAT 552–3/02 and 952/02, 18 December 2002)

Key issues: (1) Qualifying disclosure requires disclosure of information; (2) 'Reason why' question; (3) Affirmation.

Case summary: Mr Murrell claimed constructive dismissal caused by a protected disclosure. He was an equities dealer in the respondent's 'Elite Group'. He and 19 colleagues became concerned about a particular practice which they were required to carry out. They raised their concerns in a meeting and the next day they wrote a petition to directors seeking assurances that they were not 'engaged in any activity that is unlawful, could be construed as unlawful, in contravention of any SIB Principle/Regulation or could jeopardise our individual personal registration'. The respondent invited Murrell to set out any issues that would 'be dealt with under EFML's public disclosure policy'. Murrell was then informed that he was to be removed from the Elite Group, losing various perks, including an assistant. A few days later he was issued with a final written warning. After a further few days Murrell was suspended. During his suspension his solicitors wrote to the respondent stating the treatment he had received was because he had made a protected disclosure. Murrell was then invited to rejoin the Elite Group, which he accepted. Upon his return Murrell took issue over who was appointed as his assistant and then resigned.

ET: the majority concluded that he had been the object of victimization under s47B. In giving Murrell 'an assistant who was known to be underperforming, EFML had set up Mr Murrell to fail and that it was therefore only a matter of time before EFML took further measures against him'.

The minority took the view that there was no protected disclosure because it did not specifically name or identify a practice which could be identified as making a disclosure for the purposes of the Act.

EAT (HHJ Burke QC): found that the agreement entered into after Murrell's solicitor's intervention was an 'unequivocal affirmation of the contract of employment'. However neither party invited the EAT 'to remit this case to the Tribunal for determination of the critical issue as to when the affirmation. . . took place'. The EAT found that Murrell had affirmed the contract in full knowledge of all the alleged acts including the appointment of his assistant and accordingly 'as a matter of law the Tribunal cannot have held that there was a constructive dismissal on that date'. They found that the unfair dismissal claim must be dismissed.

Regarding causation the EAT took issue with the ET for failing to set out why they concluded that the purported disclosure was a reason or the principal reason for the dismissal. They highlighted (para 40) that 'prima facie the five month gap in which no steps were taken against Mr Murrell contra-indicated a connection between the two episodes'.

The EAT also found that he did not disclose any information falling within s43B at all. They referred to the fact that a number of concerns had been raised on the previous day (which of itself could not be and was not suggested to have been a qualifying disclosure) and thereafter simply sought assurances. Merely expressing a concern and seeking reassurance that there was no breach of a legal obligation did not involve a disclosure of information within s43B.

Result: Mr Murrell did not make a qualifying disclosure.

Detriment: providing an assistant who was not capable and thus setting the employee up to fail.

Sections considered: 47(b), 47B, 98(1), 98(2), 98(4), 103A ERA.

Damages awarded: £301,115.83 by ET, nothing by EAT.

13. FELTER V CLIVEDEN PETROLEUM COMPANY

(EAT/0533/05, 9 March 2006)

Key issues: Was there a legal obligation (s43B(1)(b))? Where there was a commercial contract between two commercial companies did that contract contain an implied obligation requiring the executive chairman of one of them to inform the other when 50 per cent of the shareholding was sold by its owner to Chinese companies?

Case Summary: Dr Felter was appointed director and Executive Chairman of an oil company, Cliveden SA. Cliveden owned eight geological basins, known as the 'Chad Convention', that were to be explored for oil. 50 per cent of Cliveden's interest in the Chad Convention was sold to a Canadian corporation, Encana. The deal was negotiated by Dr Felter. An agreement was entered into between Encana and Cliveden. It was common ground between the parties, and recorded by the EAT (at paragraph 25), that the agreement was 'impenetrable'. Subsequently 50 per cent of Cliveden's shares were sold to two Chinese companies. It was alleged by Dr Felter that he had made a protected disclosure by advising the respondent that it was obliged to tell Encana of the share sale before it took place or immediately afterwards.

ET: there was no implied legal obligation or express obligation to tell Encanca.

EAT (HHJ McMullen QC): dismissed the appeal. Following *Kraus v Penna* [2004] IRLR 260, the finding that there was no legal obligation was decisive of the issue. Notwithstanding the impenetrable nature of the agreements, and the difficult legal issues which arose as to what obligations should be implied under the agreement, there was no issue as to whether it was reasonable for Dr Felter to believe that there was a legal obligation.

They stated (para 15) '. . . the words "on the ground that" in s47B and "if the reason . . . for the dismissal" in s103A require the same approach'.

Result: appeal dismissed.

Detriment: released from position as chairman and member of board.

Sections considered: 43B(1)(b), 47B, 103A ERA.

Damages awarded: none.

14. FINCHAM V H M PRISON SERVICE

(EAT/0925/01/RN and EAT/0991/01/RN, 19 Dec 2001).

Key issue: Qualifying disclosure. To what extent must a breach of a legal obligation or other relevant failure be spelled out?

Case Summary: Ms Fincham was employed as Operations Support Grade Personnel and made allegations of harassment against two members of staff. Subsequently her fixed term contract was not renewed.

EAT (Mr Justice Elias): stated in paras 24, 30 and 32–33:

> The specific breaches of legal obligation relied upon were infringements of obligations under Health and Safety legislation, and the breach by the employer of the duty to respect the trust and confidence of the employee. We were referred to the decision of this Tribunal in *Parkins v Sodexho* [2002] IRLR 109, Judge Altman presiding, in which the Tribunal took a broad view of what would constitute a legal obligation within the terms of this section. That Tribunal held that it would include breaches of the contract of employment and we agree with that.
>
> . . .
>
> . . . What the Tribunal is saying is that the statement does not tend to show that health and safety was likely to be endangered. We found it impossible to see how a statement that says in terms 'I am under pressure and stress' is anything other than a statement that her health and safety is being or at least is likely to be endangered. It seems to us, therefore, that it is not a matter which can take its gloss from the particular context in which the statement is made. It may well be that it was relatively minor matter drawn to the attention of the employers in the course of a much more significant letter. We know not. But nonetheless it does seem to us that this was a disclosure tending to show that her own health and safety was likely to endangered within the meaning of subsection D.
>
> Mr Cramsie also contends that the Tribunal erred in law in paragraph 5 of its decision when it concluded that there had been no breach of the duty of trust and confidence. He said the Tribunal were wrong to require that disclosures must be looked at individually. He submitted that they could and should be looked at collectively in an appropriate case.[3] In our view there is no valid criticism that can be made at paragraph 5. If an employee complains on various occasions about the conduct of other employees that is not of itself demonstrating any breach of any duty by the employer at all. Of course there can be a breach of trust and confidence resulting from a whole series of acts of inattention or carelessness or any inconsiderate behaviour by an employer over a period of time.
>
> But there must in our view be some disclosure which actually identifies, albeit not in strict legal language, the breach of legal obligation on which the employer is relying. In this case the Tribunal found none. We have no reason to conclude that they erred in law in reaching that conclusion.

Result: remitted to a different ET.

Detriments: anxiety, demoralization; segregated at work; refused renewal of contract; refused promotion.

Sections considered: 47B, 43B(1)(b) and (d) ERA.

15. FLINTSHIRE COUNTY COUNCIL v SUTTON

(EAT/1082/02/MAA, 1 July 2003)

Key issue: Failure to support by reason of protected disclosures.

Case Summary: Mr Sutton was an audit manager with the respondent. He raised concerns regarding a payment purported to have been made on the grounds of 'redundancy' to someone who remained a member of the respondent's staff. The respondent investigated the matter. This gave rise to a suggestion that serving officers were involved in falsifying documents. The County Secretary (Mr Loveridge) instructed counsel to advise, but then instead of simply presenting his opinion to the full council, he paraphrased it and, in Sutton's belief, Loveridge passed off his own views as those of counsel.

---

³ But see *Flintshire v Sutton*, case 15 below.

Sutton put his criticisms of Loveridge to the respondent's *ultra vires* panel. He claimed he was then ostracized by Loveridge. Other concerns arose and Sutton sent Council members a memorandum accusing the respondent's Chief Offices of failing to comply with the Council's financial regulations as to cooperation and providing records for internal audit. The memo was leaked to the press. Sutton then sent three further memos to Council members raising concerns. In response to one of them, the Deputy Chief Executive wrote to Council members stating it would be necessary to consider what action to take 'in response to the inappropriate and misleading memorandum' sent by Sutton. He also wrote to the Nolan Committee and Public Concern at Work referring to alleged failures by senior officers of the respondent to comply with financial regulations. He then went off work for an extended time suffering from stress. The District Auditor's involvement and report had only unreserved praise and no criticism of Sutton's pursuit of the various investigations and emphasized the very serious procrastination and delay which had taken place in dealing with his concerns.

ET: found the following were protected disclosures: (1) the four memoranda to the Council were protected under s43G (and there was no good reason to distinguish between the four memoranda making up the sequence)[4], (2) a verbal challenge during a meeting was protected under s43C, (3) disclosures made to the District Auditor were protected under s43F and (4) the letters sent to outside bodies were protected under s43G ERA.

The tribunal further found that the respondent had acted or deliberately failed to act, subjecting Sutton to a detriment, in that it had failed to provide him with the support to which he was entitled. It further found that the failure to act had been on the ground of at least some of those disclosures (the four memoranda, the verbal challenge and, to a lesser extent the disclosure to outside bodies except the District Auditor).

The tribunal also rejected a limitation defence in relation to the s47B claim, on the ground that the respondent's course of conduct in failing to give support to Sutton after the *ultra vires* panel meeting continued up to the termination of employment. Also there were a series of similar failures.

It also found that Sutton had been constructively unfairly dismissed under s103A.

EAT (HHJ Peter Clark): Upheld findings of detriment and s103A dismissal by reason of protected disclosures to or about the Council—ss43C, 43F, 43G (para 26):

> the judgment of Mr Recorder Underhill QC in *London Borough of Harrow v Knight* . . . . It is for the Applicant to show that:
>
> (i)   he has made a protected disclosure;
> (ii) he has suffered some identifiable detriment;
> (iii) the employer has done an act or omission by which he has been subjected to that detriment and
> (iv) that act or omission had been done by the employer 'on the ground that' he had made the identified protected disclosure.

As to s43G, there was no need to show that precisely the same memoranda had been disclosed when making the earlier internal disclosure.

As to s48(4)(b): 'near impenetrable language . . . not . . . the Parliamentary draftsman's finest hour'.

In relation to constructive dismissal, there was an issue between the parties (para 28) as to whether a failure of the respondent to discharge the burden of showing the reason for dismissal meant it had no reason or that it had not disproved an inadmissible reason. The EAT did not address this because the tribunal had concluded that the reason why the respondent was in repudiatory breach of the implied trust and confidence term was their 'perception of the Applicant as a problem because he

---

⁴ Compare with the approach in *Fincham* in relation to whether disclosures could be looked at cumulatively in spelling out an allegation of breakdown of trust and confidence.

had made the relevant protected disclosures' and those protected disclosures were therefore the reason or principal reason for the dismissal.

Result: appeal dismissed.

Detriment: serious procrastination and delay; failing to keep Sutton informed of decisions. Employment Tribunal found that 'he did not receive the support from the Respondent to which he was entitled either in health or in sickness'.

Sections considered: 43A, 43B, 43C, 43F, 43G, 47B, 48(1A), 48(4)(b), 95(1)(c), 103A ERA.

Damages awarded: remedies hearing had not occurred before appeal.

16. Harrow LBC v Knight

[2003] IRLR 140 (EAT)

Key issue: Meaning of 'on the ground that' and the burden of proof in relation to that issue.

Case Summary: Mr Knight was a technical officer and in February 1999 raised concerns under the respondent's whistleblowing procedure that another officer might be complicit in breaches of health regulations by a business. The respondent appointed persons to investigate the allegations. By November 1999 Knight had become stressed and suffered a 'nervous breakdown'. The respondents failed to respond to any correspondence from him.

ET: the exacerbation of Knight's medical condition was 'related to the disclosure'. They accepted that he had suffered over the months, especially when his letters were ignored both by the chief executive and the investigators. He had not gained from this disclosure; rather he had suffered a detriment which was 'directly related to the protected disclosure that he had made'. The tribunal concluded that the complaint under s47B ERA succeeded.

EAT (Mr Recorder Underhill QC): in order for liability in this case to be established the tribunal has to find:

(1) a claimant has made a protected disclosure (or disclosures);

(2) that he had suffered some identifiable detriment (or detriments);

(3) that the Council had 'done' an act or deliberate failure to act (for short, an 'act or omission') by which he had been 'subjected to' that detriment; and

(4) that this act or omission had been done by the Council 'on the ground that' the claimant had made the protected disclosure identified at (1).

The act or omission identifiable from the tribunal's reasons was the respondent's failure to answer Knight's letters. It was necessary for Knight to show that:

> by 'doing' that omission (or those omissions) the Council 'subjected' him to the relevant detriment, ie to the resulting breakdown. Although the statutory language is arguably not very well-chosen, the position on the current authorities is that an employer subjects an employee to a detriment if he causes or allows the detriment to occur in circumstances where he can control whether it happens or not: *Burton v de Vere Hotels Ltd*, [1997] ICR 1, *per* Smith J at p 10 A–B.[5] It seems clear that the Tribunal thought that Mr Redmond's failure to answer Mr Knight's letters contributed to his breakdown; and it can also reasonably be inferred that the same is true of the Council's more general failure to look after him, if that be relevant. Those were conclusions which the Tribunal was entitled to reach.

---

[5] This is no longer good law: see *Macdonald v Advocate General for Scotland* and *Pearce v Governing Body of Mayfield Secondary School* [2003] IRLR 512 (HL).

'*On the ground that*':

> It is thus necessary in a claim under s47B to show that the fact that the protected disclosure had been made caused or influenced the employer to act (or not act) in the way complained of merely to show that 'but for' the disclosure the act or omission would not have occurred is not enough (see *Khan*). In our view, the phrase 'related to' imports a different and much looser test than that required by the statute: it merely connotes some connection (not even necessarily causative) between the act done and the disclosure.

Recorder Underhill also expressed the view that the effect of s48(2) ERA regarding the burden of proof for detriment was that if the employer failed to establish the reason, it did not necessarily follow that the reason was deemed to be a protected disclosure, but rather that the tribunal might have regard to this in drawing an inference (but need not do so).

As the Employment Tribunal had failed to consider on what ground the respondent had acted or failed to act the case had to be remitted.

Result: remitted to a fresh tribunal for re-hearing.

Detriment: Knight asserted three: (1) the loss of the opportunity to remain in the Department because he had failed to obtain the necessary professional qualification; (2) when the Council had wrongly disclosed confidential information to a third party with whom he was in litigation; (3) his nervous breakdown. The Employment Tribunal only found (3).

Sections considered: 47B(1) ERA.

Damages awarded: remitted.

Cited: *Bolton School v Evans* [2006] IRLR 500 (EAT); *Miller v 5m(UK)Limited* (EAT/0359/05, 5 September 2005); *The Trustees of Mama East African Women's Group v Dobson* (EAT/0219/05 and EAT/0220/05, 23 June 2005); *Flintshire v Sutton* (EAT/1082/02, 1 July 2003); *Odong v Chubb Security Personnel* (EAT/0819/02, 13 May 2003); *De Haney v Brent Mind and Lang* (EAT/0054/03, 10 April 2003); *Everett Financial Management Limited v Murrell* (EAT/552,553/02 and EAT/952/02, 24 February 2003).

17. Hinton v University of East London

[2005] EWCA Civ 532; [2005] IRLR 552

Key issue: compromise agreements.

Case Summary: Dr Hinton entered into a compromise agreement with the University. The agreement sought to compromise all claims against the University. In correspondence prior to the agreement Dr Hinton had alleged he had suffered detriments having made qualifying disclosures regarding financial irregularities. The case turned on whether the terms of the compromise agreement satisfied s203(3)(b) of the Employment Rights Act 1996 with regard to s47B of the Act.

ET: the following clause in a s203 agreement was held by the Tribunal not to prevent a claim being pursued under s47B:

> 9. Settlement
> 9.1 This Agreement is made without any admission of liability on the part of the University on the basis that its terms are in full and final satisfaction of all claims in all jurisdictions (whether arising under statute, common law or otherwise) which the employee has or may have against the University officers [sic] or employees arising out of or in connection with his employment with the University, the termination of his employment or otherwise including in particular the following claims which have been raised by or on behalf of the Employee as being claims which he may have for: . . .

Following this general provision there followed a list of numbered paragraphs 9.1.1 to 9.1.11, item-izing 11 particular kinds of claim at common law, under ERA and the Discrimination Acts. However the itemized list did not include reference to a claim falling under s47B of ERA.

The Employment Tribunal concluded that there was a 'grave omission' of the section in the list and that it was not included in the general provisions of 9.1 above.

EAT (EAT/0495/04, 22 October 2004, HHJ Ansell) held Hinton was precluded from pursuing a s47B claim as it was included in the provisions of 9.1. and that under s203 it is not necessary to par-ticularize precisely each claim being compromised. They find [para 25] 'on the section 203 issue we have no hesitation in agreeing with the [University's] submissions, and in particular we are satisfied that the *Lunt* case can be regarded as authority for the proposition that the words "relate to" simply refer to proceedings or claims which have been raised as opposed to the necessity of setting them out within the body of the compromise agreement.'

CA (Lord Justice Mummery, Lady Justice Smith and Sir Martin Nourse) reversed the EAT and restored the decision of the ET. The s47B claim was not particularized within the Compromise Agreement as required by s203.

Lord Justice Mummery said (in para 19) that he was in no doubt that contractually the terms were wide enough to cover the s47B claim. However (in paras 22 and 23) he said that the statute was not satisfied:

> For me the decisive point is in the formulation of the key question. I would formulate it in this way: how does the agreement relate to the particular proceedings under s47B? The opening part of clause 9.1, on which the university relies, is very general indeed: it relates to all claims 'arising under statute'. It relates to proceedings, but not to 'particular proceedings'. Particularity on this point is required, but it is missing from clause 9: no particular statute is stated expressly; no particular description is supplied of the legal nature or the factual basis of any proceedings 'arising under statute'; no mention is made of public interest disclosures or of any detriment suffered by Dr Hinton as a result of making them.
>
> This approach to the construction of s203 is consistent with the policy of the section and its language. Its practical consequences should not give rise to difficulties and it should provide clear guidance to the parties and their legal advisers.

He added in para 24:

> If actual proceedings are compromised it is good practice for the particulars of the proceedings and of the particular allegations made in them to be inserted in the compromise agreement in the form of a brief factual and legal description. If the compromise is of a particular claim raised which is not yet the subject of proceedings, it is good practice for the particulars of the nature of the allegations and of the statute under which they are made or the common law basis of the alleged claim to be inserted in the compromise agreement in the form of a brief factual and legal description.

Lady Justice Smith and Sir Martin Nourse agreed.

Result: the s47B (Detriment) claim had not been compromised.

Detriment: not set out by the CA or EAT.

Sections considered: 47B, 203 ERA.

Damages awarded: case remitted to Tribunal to determine if Hinton had suffered a detriment.

18. Hossack v Kettering BC

(EAT/1113/01, 29 November 2002)

Key issue: 'Reason why' issue. Is it permissible to discipline/dismiss for manner of disclosure?

Case Summary: Ms Hossack was appointed Policy Research Officer to the Conservative Group of the respondent Council. This particular position was supposed to be impartial so she was subject to disciplinary action for making a political speech which was both a breach of her contract and of the respondent Council's code of conduct. The Employment Tribunal expressly found that 'she saw herself very much as a campaigner and a politician and had difficulty in taking a back seat' and in so acting was 'very much the tail trying to wag the dog'. Hossack was commissioned to draw up a report on the sale by the Council of property for a councillor to submit to the District Auditor. The report drafted by her and handed to the councillor alleged the commission of criminal offences and made suggestions of wrongdoing. The councillor insisted these references be removed before it was submitted to the District Auditor. Hossack wrote to the District Auditor. The councillor became aware of this letter and other conduct that resulted in him requesting she be dismissed as she 'would not act as an adviser but appeared to want to act as a member of the Conservative Group and as a politician'. Hossack was dismissed. She complained of automatically unfair dismissal and having suffered a detriment.

ET: reason for dismissal was not the protected disclosure but Hossack's inability to distinguish her role from a political role.

EAT (Mr Justice Wall): it had been found that Hossack had made a protected disclosure but that this was not the reason for the dismissal. The cases on distinguishing between a protected act and the way it is done were considered. The EAT stated that there was force in the point that the legislation should not be undermined by too narrow a distinction and acknowledged (para 41) the:

> anxiety that a differentiation between the content of a disclosure and the manner in which it is made could, if not carefully analysed, emasculate the legislation. Plainly, any Tribunal approaching a protected disclosure will need to be alert to that danger.

However in this case the ET had this in mind and made no error of law. Hossack was not dismissed due to the protected disclosure but due to her inability to understand that her role was not a political one, and some of her comments made in her disclosures were evidence of this.

Result: appeal dismissed, no automatic unfair dismissal.

Sections considered: 43A, 47B and 103A ERA.

Damages awarded: none.

Cited: *Shillito v van Leer (UK) Ltd; Goodwin v Cabletel UK Ltd; Lyon v St James Press Ltd; Bass Taverns Ltd v Burgess; Smith v City of Glasgow City Council.* Considered in *Vaseghi v Brunel University* (EAT/0757/04 and EAT/0222/05, 3 November 2005) where, in the context of a claim of victimization (under the Race Relations Act) and trade union victimization, the EAT said:

> The precise factual background of *Hossack v Kettering Borough Council* EAT/1113/01, judgment delivered on 29 November 2002, is rather different on the factual basis. For the employee, it was argued that a differentiation between the content of a disclosure and the manner in which it [was] made could, if not carefully analysed, emasculate the legislation. The Employment Tribunal agreed that [in] approaching a protected disclosure [one] will need to be alert to that danger. It went on to say:
>
> > 'However, in our judgment, this Tribunal was so alert and its conclusions are not only, in our view, correct in law, they also accord with common sense and in no way offend against the spirit or letter of the legislation.'

Due to the efficiency and hard work of the Tribunal staff, the presiding judge was able to put before the parties a decision of Wood J called *Re York Trucks* EAT 10988. The facts of that case, were that the Respondent company owned a number of flats. An allegation was made by an employee, who was a cleaner, that she had been the subject of a serious sexual assault by one of those occupying the flats. It was claimed that the company had not taken the matter sufficiently seriously. In that case, Wood J accepted the position that the ET had properly found that the reason for dismissing the claim was because of the employee's disruptive behaviour in the way in which she raised the matter and that on the issue of causation, the Tribunal were entitled to find that.

19. Kraus v Penna plc

[2004] IRLR 260 (EAT)

Key issues: (1) Meaning of 'likely' in s43(1) re qualifying disclosure; (2) requirement for actual legal obligation (not merely reasonable belief of one) for s43(1)(b) ERA.

Case Summary: Mr Kraus alleged the HR services that he provided under contract for R1 to R2 had been terminated because he had advised that proposed redundancies 'could' breach employment legislation and leave a vulnerability to unfair dismissal claims.

ET: no qualifying disclosure. ET justified in striking out the claim as misconceived.

EAT (Mr Justice Cox): the word 'likely' in s43B(1)(b) requires more than a possibility or a risk that an employer might fail to comply with a relevant legal obligation. The information disclosed should, in the reasonable belief of the worker at the time it is disclosed, tend to show that it is probable or more probable than not that the employer will fail to comply with the relevant legal obligation. Therefore it was not sufficient merely to say that the company 'could' breach employment legislation (para 21):

> On his own account the information disclosed . . . was only that the company 'could' breach employment legislation and would be vulnerable to claims for unfair dismissal. At its highest, therefore, Mr Kraus's belief was limited at this early stage to the possibility or the risk of a breach of employment legislation, depending on what eventually took place. In our judgment this did not meet the statutory test of 'likely to fail to comply'. On his own account, Mr Kraus's case was that, after Mr Bolton moved the discussion on, he 'made a mental note to discuss this matter with him in private at a later date'. We bear in mind too that, as Mr Kraus would know, consultation on the reorganisation/redundancy programme would have to take place, which could affect the numbers of employees to be made redundant. As the tribunal recognised, in paragraph 8, there may have been sufficient volunteers for redundancy so as to avoid the need for, or reduce considerably, any compulsory redundancies. In our view, therefore, the tribunal did not err in finding, on the accepted facts, that the information disclosed could not be said to tend to show that Syltone were likely to fail to comply with its legal obligations. Whilst we accept that they made no express reference to Mr Kraus's reasonable belief, in considering this matter it was obvious on the accepted facts that the question of reasonableness did not arise. Mr Kraus did not himself believe that the information he disclosed to Mr Bolton tended to show that a failure to comply with a legal obligation was 'likely', in the sense of 'probable' or 'more probable than not'.

Also there must be a legal obligation for the purposes of s43B(1)(b) (para 29):

> The worker's 'reasonable belief' in terms of s43B(1) relates to the information which he is disclosing and not to the existence of a legal obligation which does not actually exist. If the employers are under no legal obligation, as a matter of law, a worker cannot claim the protection of this legislation by claiming that he reasonably believed that they were. His belief and the reasonableness of it relates to the factual information in his possession, namely what he perceives to be the facts and the basis on which he considers it reasonable to rely upon them. This can only properly be tested against the background of the legal obligation to which the employers are subject. If there is no obligation to which they actually are subject, the worker's suggestion that he reasonably believed they were cannot render a disclosure a protected one within ss43A and B.

This case therefore drew a distinction between (1) circumstances where the employer is clearly under some legal obligation and those circumstances where the employee reasonably but mistakenly believes there was a breach, and (2) a case where the employee reasonably but mistakenly believes that the employer was under a legal obligation which it has breached. Such a distinction undermines the protection and severely limits the scope of the protection. On the facts it simply could not be said that Kraus disclosed information which he believed reasonably tended to show that the respondent was likely to fail to comply with any obligation not to unfairly dismiss employees.[6]

Result: no disclosure as no legal obligation—appeal dismissed.

Detriment: the termination of the consultancy agreement.

Damages: none awarded.

Sections considered: 43A, 43B, 43C, 43L(3), 47B, 48(1A), 103A, 43K(1)(a), 43K(2)(a) ERA.

Cited: *Babula v Waltham Forest College* (EAT/0635/05, 9 March 2006); *Boulding v Land Securities Trillium (Media Services) Limited* (EAT/0023/06, 3 May 2006); *Felter v Cliveden Petroleum Company* (EAT/0533/05, 17 May 2006).

20. LUCAS V CHICHESTER DIOCESAN HOUSING ASSOCIATION LIMITED

(UKEAT/0713/04/DA, 7 February 2005)

Key issue: Burden of proof for good faith.

Case Summary: Ms Lucas's position whilst employed by the respondent was funded by the Brighton and Hove Corporation. She raised concern over financial irregularities involving 'X'. Lucas was confronted by X who stated they were 'extremely angry' about the allegation. Later X informed Lucas her hours and pay were to be reduced. She then raised her concerns with an employee of Brighton and Hove Corporation. X wrote to Lucas informing her of her dismissal because her 'strained relationship' was having an 'adverse effect' on the project.

ET: Lucas claimed automatic unfair dismissal contrary to s103A. The ET held that she had acted in bad faith.

EAT (HHJ McMullen QC): Issue—what is required to prove bad faith? Conclusion—it remains a 'heavy burden' to show disclosure in bad faith. Such an allegation must be clearly put to a claimant. The Employment Tribunal had no ground to determine that a 'deeply worsening relationship' and an assertion that the Claimant had raised her concern in 'spite' as opposed to the promotion of public interest was sufficient to found a case of 'bad faith'. This assertion had not been put in the ET3 or in cross examination and appeared first within the respondent's written legal argument. To find 'bad faith' there must be cogent evidence. Where there is an allegation of 'bad faith' it must be made explicitly and in advance and must be put before a claimant (para 39):

> Where an allegation is made that the disclosure was not made in good faith, the evidence as a whole must be cogent, for bad faith is a surprising and unusual feature of working relationships, and as Lord Nicholls said in *In Re H (Minors) (Sexual Abuse: Standards of Proof)* [1996] AC 563 at 586: 'The more serious the allegation the more cogent is the evidence required . . . to prove it.'

Result: case remitted to the same Employment Tribunal to determine whether Lucas was dismissed because she had made the disclosure.

Detriment: reduction in hours.

Sections considered: 103A, 43B, 43C ERA.

Damages awarded: remitted.

---

[6] For criticism of this approach see Chapter 3.

Cited: *Bachnak v Emerging Markets Partnership (Europe) Limited* (EAT/0288/05, 27 January 2006); *The Trustees of Mama East African Women's Group v Dobson* (EAT/0219/05 and EAT/0220/05, 23 June 2005); Doherty v British Midland Airways Limited (UKEAT/0684/04, 7,8 February 2005) applied *Lucas* in the context of dismissal for trade union activities.

21. Mama East African Women's Group v Dobson

(EAT/0219/05/ and EAT/0220/05, 23 June 2005)

Key issues:

(1) When a claimant has made a protected disclosure what is the correct test to determine whether the dismissal was for that reason?

(2) What is the assessment of compensation when the employer seeks to limit the compensation for unfair dismissal on the basis of its own failure to protect the employee from the consequences of her disclosure?

Case Summary: Ms Dobson was an English teacher to Somali women in Sheffield. Her disclosure alleging child mistreatment (criminal offence) took place on 10 May and she was dismissed on 24 May following the steps taken by the respondent, which concluded there was no evidence of mistreatment.

ET: looked at the reasons set out in the dismissal letter which advanced three bases for the dismissal. (1) false allegation (2) not following the procedure (3) breach of confidentiality. The respondent did however accept that, but for the disclosure, Dobson would not have been dismissed. The respondent's assertion that she had committed 'unprofessional conduct' by reporting 'unfounded' allegations cannot be sufficient for an employer in the social context of this legislation to avoid its connection to the protected activity. The reason or the principal reason the Tribunal found was that Dobson had raised a disclosure.

The respondent appealed in relation to Dobson's award on the fact that she would have been dismissed in any event as her students had lost confidence in her, because they were aware of her having raised her concern.

EAT (HHJ McMullen QC): the reason or principal reason for the dismissal was the disclosure. An Employment Tribunal must make clear findings as to what is in the mind of the person who dismisses. The reasons advanced by the respondent were inextricably linked to the disclosure (in this case the manner in which it was raised and the lack of substance). To permit such reasons to be a fair reason would undermine the purpose of the legislation. In relation to the award a respondent cannot use its own failure (here to maintain confidentiality and thus the loss in confidence) to reduce any award to which the claimant was entitled.

Result: automatically unfair dismissal. *Note:* The decision is now to be read in the light of the decision in *Bolton School v Evans* where the EAT rejected a similar policy argument by the ET and drew a distinction between the disclosure and the associated previous conduct: see further the discussion in Chapter 7.

Detriment: none.

Sections considered: 103A, 123 ERA.

Damages awarded: £12,035.76 for unfair dismissal and damages of £489.62 for wrongful dismissal.

22. Melia v Magna Kansei Limited

(UKEAT/0339/04/DA 16, 17 November 2004); [2005] ICR 874; [2006] IRLR 117 (CA)

Key issues: (1) (In CA): What is the boundary between detriment and dismissal claims? (2) (In EAT) reduction of compensatory award for pre-dismissal conduct.

Case Summary: Mr Melia worked as a senior designer for the Respondent who make parts for cars. He made a protected disclosure when he alleged that a colleague had assaulted him at work. Following the disclosure he was subjected to bullying. He was then suspended pending an investigation of an allegation of gross misconduct. In response, in November 2001, he resigned and claimed constructive dismissal and claimed this was by reason of his disclosure.

ET: concluded that he was subjected to a detriment on the ground that he made a protected disclosure and his dismissal was automatically unfair under s103A. However:

> prior to and unconnected with his dismissal, the applicant had committed an act, namely the serious misuse of the respondent's computer system, which was a blameworthy act for which he might, but not necessarily, have been fairly dismissed in any event.

The ET awarded £6,000 for the detriment having concluded that it should only award injury to feelings up to June 2001, rather than up until acceptance of the repudiatory breach. The repudiatory conduct which was directly tied to the dismissal was excluded.

EAT (Mr Justice Burton, President): increased the award in favour of the appellant by £600 to take into account two points on appeal (although the exact figure was agreed by the parties). First, whilst there was a deduction to Melia's award to take into account early payment of future benefits, there was no interest charged on payments in relation to past losses already sustained. Second, with regard to the exclusion of an award for legal fees that were incurred in drafting a compromise agreement, the EAT also upheld a reduction of 50 per cent in both the basic and compensatory award which had been made on the grounds that it was just and equitable to do so in the light of Melia's misconduct prior to dismissal. This reduction was made notwithstanding the tribunal's finding that the evidence of wrongdoing was:

> discovered after a concerted effort to find material which—as a result of the protected disclosure—could be used to ensure the termination of the claimant's employment, if possible without the need for any form of negotiated settlement.

The EAT (at para 55) note the force of the submission that employers should not be permitted 'to scrabble around after a protected disclosure to try to find some misconduct which it could then use as a justification or excuse for dismissal, or at any rate by way of self-defence to claim against it . . .' Indeed this in itself would appear to have been an unlawful detriment under s47B ERA. Notwithstanding this, the EAT considered that there was no basis to interfere with the tribunal's decision on this issue. There was no appeal on this point.

CA (Lord Justice Chadwick, Lady Justice Smith, Lord Justice Wilson): The appeal concerned the calculation of compensation for a detriment. Where a detriment occurs before the dismissal but forms part of the reason for the dismissal—how is compensation to be calculated when applying s123, which permits compensation for losses sustained in consequence of the dismissal, given that his detriment was sustained before his dismissal and is not taken out of s47B (and Part V) by the limitation in s47B(2)? Chadwick LJ stated that 'the proper meaning to be given to the phrase "the detriment in question amounts to dismissal" is that it excludes detriment which can be compensated under the unfair dismissal provisions. If the detriment cannot be compensated under the unfair dismissal provisions—for the reason that it is not a loss sustained in consequence of the dismissal—then there is nothing to take it out of s47B; and the provisions in s49, which require compensation for that detriment, should apply.' Within s47B(2) the word 'dismissal' means the date dismissal occurs and in relation to constructive dismissal this is the date of acceptance of the repudiatory breach.

Lady Justice Smith stated:

> if an employee suffers a detriment due to making a protected disclosure and is then dismissed by the employer, the employee will be entitled to compensation for the detriment under s47B of the Employment Rights Act up to the date of dismissal. That compensation may include compensation for personal injury and injury to feelings. He may also claim compensation for

the consequences of unfair dismissal, including a compensatory award under s123. But, say the respondents, the position is different with a case of constructive dismissal. There, the employee may only recover for the detriment he suffers until the time comes when the employer's conduct amounts to a repudiatory breach of the employment contract. If that were right, it would follow that an employee might suffer from gradually deteriorating and increasingly unlawful treatment by the employer, but if he does not resign immediately when the conduct has become bad enough to amount to a repudiatory breach, but waits some time before he accepts the breach, he will not be able to recover for the detriment he has suffered during that intervening period. I, for my part, cannot accept that Parliament should have intended so unjust a consequence.

Result: appeal dismissed—automatically unfair constructive dismissal.

Detriment: bullying.

Sections considered: 47B, 48, 49, 94, 95(1)(c), 97(1), 103A, 123 ERA.

Damages awarded: £6,000 for the detriment; basic award of £840 and a compensatory award of £11,601.87 was made by the ET, and increased by the EAT by £600, of which £300 was for delay in Mr Melia receiving payment, which was permitted by the CA.

23. Miklaszewicz v Stolt Offshore Ltd

[2002] IRLR 344 (Court of session)

Key issue: Coverage of pre-Act disclosures if dismissal post-PIDA.

Case Summary: Scottish case. Upon admitted facts of a public interest disclosure occurring in 1993 and the dismissal taking place in 1999—did the ET have jurisdiction to entertain the s103A complaint?

ET: no jurisdiction.

EAT (Lord Johnston): reversed decision:

> In our opinion, this statute is not properly to be regarded as having any retrospective effect at all in relation to the present case because we consider the crucial aspect to be the fact that the dismissal was effected after the legislation came into force. It is that act of the employer which requires the employee to claim a protected disclosure. It is a voluntary act on the part of the employer and it is not therefore, in our opinion, appropriate to regard the legislation as having taken away any rights available to him. . . . the issue is essentially one of status as can be divined from the *Whitechapel* case in relation to the state of widowhood. The disclosure having been made in 1993 acquires the status of a protected disclosure when it becomes relevant to an issue of dismissal subsequent to 1998 . . . Equally in cases of race or sex discrimination, the gender or the ethnic status of the claimant is established by birth. A claim is triggered by a discriminatory act and it is only that latter matter which must post-date the relevant legislation.

Result: remitted for full hearing.

Sections considered: 43A, 47B, 103A.

Damages awarded: none.

Cited: *Pinnington v (1) City and County of Swansea and (2) Governing Body of Ysgol Crug Glas School* [2005] ICR 685.

24. Milne v The Link Asset and Security Company Limited

(EAT/0867/04, 26 September 2005)

Key issues: No 'good faith', no 'reasonable belief' and no causal link between the disclosure and the resignation.

Case Summary: Mr Milne was a broker and manager for the respondent. The respondent operated an optional trust benefit tax scheme. Milne joined the scheme then raised concerns about it. Milne was suspended and disciplined regarding his conduct elsewhere. The Employment Tribunal was highly critical of the respondent's process. It found there was no reasonable ground for the disclosure. The Employment Tribunal however erred in their decision by referring to the claim being brought under s43B(1)(a) and not s43B(1)(b).

ET: no constructive dismissal and Milne should pay £5,000 to the Respondent towards its costs. There was no 'reasonable belief' of any illegality and the claimant's concerns related principally to his own financial position. The tribunal found:

> We accept that the applicant was genuinely concerned about the effectiveness of the . . . tax avoidance EBT offered to higher employees but we do not believe that this amounted to a genuine belief that the scheme was illegal.

> . . .

> So looking at this closely whilst recognising [the claimant] clearly did have some concerns about the [EBT] scheme we certainly did not believe this was a genuine belief as to illegality of the scheme, we do think the whistle blowing claim was opportunistic. We do not feel the [claimant] has acted in good faith in bringing the claim and that the [claimant] has done so to put pressure on the employer through litigation which is obviously not the purpose of the legislation. We believe the claim was an afterthought and we are surprised that it was raised by [the claimant].

> . . .

> the undeniable conflict and tension arising between the employer and employee was unrelated to the applicant's late opposition to the EBT. In this respect one further factor that has assisted us in reaching this conclusion is that the employee never mentioned his belief that his opposition to the tax scheme was a factor in the way in which he was treated either through the disciplinary process or when he resigned or even through his first solicitor's letter. Whilst we have already said that we would understand his lack of knowledge as to the legal significance of possible detriment through making a whistle blowing claim there is no reason why the fact of his concern should not have been highlighted in a more obvious way to the employers at an early stage. In any event we do not believe that there is a qualifying disclosure and therefore there is no protected disclosure and in any event we do not think that any future detriment suffered by the applicant (including this dismissal) was because of his ultimate reluctance to join the EBT.

EAT (Mr Justice Silber): there was no error of law in the tribunal's finding that there was no constructive dismissal.

In relation to whistleblowing, the tribunal made an error in treating the claim as under s43(1)(a) (criminal offence) rather than s43(1)(b) (legal obligation). It was argued that this was significant because of the differing mental elements. For s43(1)(b) it was only necessary to believe that the tax scheme was unlawful, not that there was a criminal *mens rea*. Also it was argued that the claimant was permitted to have a concern as to his own financial position because that was the nature of the scheme's illegality.

But EAT held that the matter was concluded by the tribunal's findings of fact that Milne did not act in 'good faith' and lacked the requisite 'reasonable belief'. Also the disclosure was not the reason for resignation—the ET was entitled to place emphasis on the fact that this was not raised during the disciplinary process or when he resigned.

Result: no whistleblowing claim. Costs order against Milne for £5000.

Detriment: none.

Sections Considered: 43A, 43B, 103A ERA.

Damages awarded: none.

25. MORRISON V HESLEY LIFECARE SERVICES LIMITED

(UKEAT/0262/03/DM and UKEAT/0534/03/DM, 19 March 2004)

Key issue: Good faith.

Case Summary: Mr Morrison was employed as a special support assistant. He resigned claiming constructive dismissal. During the hearing and on the fourth day of evidence with the sixth respondent witness, Morrison sought to move his claim to a dismissal for a reason connected with a protected disclosure but it was not until closing written submissions that there was the first express reference to a protected disclosure.

ET: considered the protected disclosure claim raised and stated that his evidence was such as 'to confirm the view of this tribunal that the applicant has regarded the protection which the law affords to "whistle blowers" as a weapon in the campaign he has waged against the respondent'. The tribunal dismissed his claim and ordered him to pay the respondent's costs. The costs order was made on the ground that his claim had not been brought in good faith.

In awarding costs the Employment Tribunal stated (para 20) that:

> costs should be awarded for three reasons. First, the Applicant's Counsel had advised that he could not discern the elements of a repudiatory breach of contract. The Applicant regarded the protection which the law affords to whistle blowers as a weapon in a campaign he has waged against the Respondent. He sought to carry out at an Employment Tribunal the function of a public enquiry into the running of the Respondent's establishments. That is an approach which the Tribunal found to be inappropriate.

EAT (HHJ McMullen QC): dismissed the appeal (paras 26 and 32):

> The legal principles appear to be as follow. A tribunal is to be given credit for decisions of fact which it makes, particularly when they go to issues of credibility. A finding on an issue such as reasonable belief or good faith is peculiarly fact sensitive and the decision of the Employment Tribunal would not likely be overturned based upon that matter . . .

> . . .

> We then turn to the costs issue. What might have at first sight appeared to be less than a firm finding of bad faith at the merits decision is put beyond doubt by the costs decision. The Tribunal regarded the conduct of the Applicant as unreasonable and misconceived. He was acting in bad faith in pursuing a campaign against the Respondent. We have mentioned to the parties a judgment of the Employment Appeal Tribunal in *Street v Derbyshire Unemployed Worker Centre* EAT/0508/02 which indicates that a claim for Public Interest Disclosure protection will not succeed even if there is reasonable belief in the truth of the matter put forward if it is put forward out of personal antagonism. We bear in mind that this legislation is designed to protect people who no doubt would be regarded as officious, at best and bloody minded at worst. It is in the public interest that people be protected if they make disclosures meeting the specific conditions, and do so in good faith reasonably believing the material before them. It is not Parliament's intention to protect those who simply wage a campaign against their employer. The finding by the Tribunal based upon both the conduct of the proceedings and upon the lack of good faith is an ample basis upon which the Tribunal could exercise its discretion when asked by the Respondent to award costs.

Result: no public interest disclosure.

Detriment: not set out.

Sections considered: 43C (good faith), 103A ERA.

Damages awarded: none.

Cited: *Street v Derbyshire Unemployed Workers' Centre* [2005] ICR 97.

26. ODONG V CHUBB SECURITY PERSONNEL

(EAT/0819/02/TM, 13 May 2003)

Key issues: Qualifying disclosure: legal obligation and reasonable belief.

Case Summary: Mr Odong was a security officer employed by the respondent. He was instructed to work in the relevant period for American Express. When Odong attended work the guard finishing the previous shift instructed him to make regular checks in three rooms because of a 'danger of overheating which might lead to a fire'. Odong refused to perform the task as (a) he suspected the previous guard did not have authority to instruct him as to what he must do and (b) the rooms were marked 'No Entry'. Odong did not therefore carry out the checks. On the next day at the start of his shift there was a written instruction provided by a manager to perform the tasks and Odong duly obliged. American Express became aware of his refusal and instructed Chubb to remove him. Odong asserted that the direction of his colleague was unlawful and unauthorized. He asserted he had made a public interest disclosure to his colleague when he refused to perform the tasks. He claimed that he had suffered a detriment in (a) his removal from his posting to American Express and (b) the failure to post him elsewhere thereafter.

ET: found that Odong was removed because he failed to obey a reasonable instruction to conduct temperature checks. The tribunal dismissed the claim that his removal was due to his protected disclosure.

EAT (Mr Recorder Luba QC): allowed the Appeal. They accepted that on the tribunal's findings of fact there was a qualifying disclosure under s43(1)(b) for 'failing or likely to fail to comply with a legal obligation' in that Odong had doubted that the person who gave the instruction to enter the room to carry out the checks had the authority to do so (paras 13, 20 and 21):

> . . . an Employment Tribunal in a protected disclosure case is to follow a particular sequence of analysis. The sequence of analysis proposed . . . is that the Tribunal should ask itself three questions. First, did the Applicant make a protected disclosure as defined? Second, was the Applicant subjected to a detriment by reason of an act or deliberate failure to act of his employer? Third, if so, was that act or deliberate failure to act done on the ground that the worker had made a protected disclosure?
>
> We accept that formulation . . . as broadly representing the correct approach.
>
> . . .
>
> In support of his submission, [Counsel] draws attention to the fact that there are several potential legal obligations which may have been infringed by Mr Bailey [who gave the instruction carry out the checks]. First, Mr Bailey may have been in breach of his own contract of employment with Chubb, if he was giving a fellow employee an unauthorised or illegitimate instruction. Second, insofar as Mr Bailey was acting as Chubb's representative in giving the instruction, the giving of an unauthorised instruction or an instruction beyond the terms of Mr Odong's contract of employment was a breach of that contract of employment. Thirdly, the instruction may have been in breach of legal obligations imposed by American Express Bank, as represented by the fact that they had described the rooms as 'No Entry' rooms. It is not necessary for Mr Odong to establish that, in fact, there was a failure to comply with any legal obligation in giving Mr Odong the instruction he was given. For the purposes of section 43B, it is sufficient if it was the reasonable belief of Mr Odong that the instruction was given in breach of legal obligations.
>
> . . . on the basis of the recent authority of this Tribunal in *Parkins v Sodexho Ltd* . . . that a breach of a term of a contract of employment is a sufficient breach, or a potentially sufficient breach, to come within section 43B(1)(b). In those circumstances, . . . the Tribunal, having found the facts that it did find, must have been satisfied that the conditions of section 43B(1)(b) were made out and insofar as they thereafter rejected the proposition that that section was satisfied,

they erred in law in doing so. As to the 'reasonable belief' component of the section 43B test, . . . the finding by the Tribunal that Mr Odong believed that the employer's representative (Mr Bailey) had no authority to give the instruction. Although the Tribunal do not expressly find that this was a reasonable belief, nor do they find that it was an unreasonable belief. In those circumstances it seems to us that there was material found by the Tribunal capable of amounting to a protected disclosure for the purposes of 43A and 43B of the 1996 Act.

Result: remitted to Employment Tribunal.

Detriment: removal of his posting to American Express and the failure to post Odong elsewhere thereafter.

Sections considered: 43A, 43B and 47B ERA.

Cited: *Parkins v Sodexho* [2002] IRLR 109.

27. OWENS V MITSUI BABCOCK ENERGY LIMITED

(EAT/0732/03, 12 March 2004)

Key issue: The tribunal should have decided whether the dismissal was unfair as contrary to s98 ERA even if they rejected the claim of automatic unfair dismissal contrary to s103A.

Case Summary: Mr Owens was a grinder for the Respondent. He raised a grievance regarding his expenses. He was sent to work at Sizewell. At the end of that posting Owens was asked to move to work at Tilbury power station and as he wanted to move back to Dungeness he believed this new move was as a consequence of his grievance. Owens refused to move and was dismissed for refusing to work at Tilbury.

ET: 'In relation to the qualifying disclosure issue, the finding of the Tribunal is that the Applicant did make a qualifying disclosure to his employers in good faith. However, it is the conclusion of the Tribunal that he did not suffer a detriment, nor was he dismissed as a result of the disclosure.' They concluded that Owens' dismissal was not on the grounds of his disclosure but was for refusing to work. The tribunal however did not consider the fairness of the respondent's procedure or its decision.

EAT (HHJ Wakefield): The respondent asserted that the fairness of the dismissal was not in issue as the claim was presented as an unfair dismissal as a consequence of the disclosure. The EAT found it was not. The ET1 had complained of unfair dismissal. The ET3 raised misconduct as the reason for the dismissal. The facts to be relied upon as regards s98 unfair dismissal were not new primary facts. In the present case the tribunal identified s98 unfair dismissal as an issue to be decided. They then wholly failed to go through the necessary stages to determine that issue. This was an error of law. Matter remitted to the Employment Tribunal.

Result: fairness of dismissal still relevant if not a protected disclosure.

Detriment: none found.

Sections considered: 103A ERA.

28. PARKINS V SODEXHO

[2002] IRLR 109 (EAT)

Key issues: (1) Meaning of legal obligations for purposes of qualifying disclosure; (2) Approach to assessing evidence on interim relief application.

Case Summary: This claim concerned an application for interim relief that was refused with a costs order being made against Mr Parkins. The disclosure was with regard to (para 6):

> two areas of work and he complained, or says that he complained, on one of them where he had to use a buffing machine, that he did not have supervision on site and in the event of

problems, he was instructed to telephone a supervisor off site in the evenings. He says now that that was a matter of health & safety and also gave rise to a breach of contract, which he properly complained of and as a result of his complaint he was dismissed.

ET: gave a narrow interpretation of s43B when they found against Parkins, stating:

that by instructing him to telephone his day supervisor Mr Daniels [the Respondent] was in breach of the contract of employment. We were not shown the contract of employment or the job description of Mr Parkins and we cannot say whether or not Mr Daniels was in breach of contract in instructing Mr Parkins to telephone to another manager rather than report directly to persons on site. However, it does not seem to us that an allegation of breach of contract of this nature could possibly fall within the language of Section 43B(i)(b)—ie failure to comply with any legal obligation. While everybody is obliged to comply with contracts of employment, we do not consider that an allegation of breach of an employment contract in relation to the performance of duties comes within the letter or spirit of the statutory provision.

EAT (HHJ Altman): allowing the appeal, the EAT said (para 18):

we do not agree with the assertion of the Employment Tribunal, where they say that 'an allegation of breach of an employment contract, in relation to the performance of duties, does not come within the letter or spirit of the statutory provision'. We find it difficult to define the spirit of this sort of legislation or to be confident that we know about it, but it certainly comes within the letter of the provision, on a literal interpretation. It seems to us that we do not need to go beyond that.

The EAT also commented on the process to be undertaken in relation to interim relief (paras 25–7):

We are driven to conclude, therefore, that in analysing such evidence as there was before them the Tribunal asked themselves what was the reason for dismissal and came to a decision upon it that it was not any of those which were put forward by the Appellant. Of course that would disentitle him to interim relief, but it was a wholly different process which the Tribunal were asked to engage upon. They went further than they needed; they evaluated the evidence, they decided which evidence they accepted and rejected and they came to a conclusion that they accepted the assertion of the Respondents, unsupported by evidence on the matter. In effect they left nothing for the final hearing to decide.

We do not know what conclusion the Employment Tribunal would have come to had they looked at the evidence that was being put forward and asked themselves whether it was likely that the Employment Tribunal would come to a conclusion in favour of the Appellant. It may well be that on the evidence before them they would have come to the same conclusion by a different route. But they would at the same time have left open the very important task for the main Tribunal of hearing witnesses, hearing them being cross-examined and deciding where the truth lay and how the issues of credibility were resolved.

That process was prevented, effectively, by steps which were based upon, inevitably, a cursory review of the evidence. Furthermore, in the light of what we have already found, it was based upon a conclusion which was deliberately restricted by the exclusion of any consideration of the contract, as a result of what we found to be the error of law that the contract of employment could not found an allegation of failure to comply with a legal obligation under Section 43B.

Result: remitted the application for interim relief to a different tribunal—to be heard at the same time as the application for unfair dismissal.

Detriment: not an issue.

Sections considered: 43B, 103A, 129 ERA.

Damages awarded: remitted.

Cited: *Milne v The Link Asset and Security Company Limited* (EAT/0867/04, 26 September 2005), *Street v Derbyshire Unemployed Workers' Centre* [2005] ICR 97; *Kraus v Penna plc* [2004] IRLR 260

(EAT); *Odong v Chubb Security Personnel* (EAT/0819/02, 13 May 2003); *Douglas v Birmingham City Council and others* (EAT/018/02, 17 March 2003); *Darnton v University of Surrey* [2003] ICR 615 (EAT).

29. Phipps v Bradford Hospitals NHS Trust

(EAT/531/02, 30 April 2003)

Key issue: Good faith.

Case Summary: Mr Phipps was employed by the respondent as a Consultant Surgeon. He wrote to the Medical Director raising concerns as to treatment of patients with breast cancer. A few months later he was dismissed, purportedly for misconduct but, Phipps contended, actually because of the disclosure he had made.

ET: the disclosure was not made in good faith. Phipps was not making a disclosure in good faith, in writing his letter to the Medical Director: rather he was seeking to demonstrate that his position was not to be challenged lightly by the Medical Director. He was dismissed by reason of conduct unrelated to the disclosure. The procedure was unfair but a 100 per cent reduction was made on the basis that he would certainly have been fairly dismissed if a fair procedure was followed. Also there was 90 per cent contributory fault.

EAT (HHJ Peter Clark): appeal dismissed. The tribunal made an error of fact in stating that the letter containing the protected disclosure had not been reviewed by Phipps's union when it had. But that was not sufficient to overturn the findings. There were ample other bases for the tribunal's finding that the disclosure was not in 'good faith' including that: (a) the issue raised had already been the subject of a report and discussion within the respondent, (b) immediately prior to writing the letter he had had a meeting with the Medical Director following an investigation of inter-personal relationships and Phipps was suspicious of him, (c) the failure to set out information in the letter or subsequently to enable the respondent to investigate.

Further, there was no error in the tribunal's finding as to reason for dismissal or reductions from the award.

Result: procedurally unfairly dismissed but 100 per cent *Polkey* reduction and 90 per cent contributory fault.

Detriment: none.

Sections considered: s47B, 103A ERA.

30. Pinnington v (1) City and County of Swansea and (2) Governing Body of Ysgol Crug Glas School

[2005] ICR 685 (CA)

Key issue: Deliberate failure to act in s47B ERA.

Case Summary: Mrs Pinnington was a nurse at a special needs school. She alleged that a policy of non-resuscitation of terminally ill children was being implemented at the school. An inquiry by the local council found no basis for the allegations. She was away from work on certificated sick leave from 17 September 1997 to 31 March 1998 suffering from stress and anxiety. She returned to work for a short period between 31 March and 29 April 1998 but then went of sick again and did not return prior to her dismissal. On 2 July 1998, after she had begun the second period away sick, she was suspended by the employer on the grounds of a breach of confidence about records relating to children at the school. Following a capability hearing (and thereafter an appeal) the claimant was dismissed with effect from 3 July 1999. PIDA only came into effect on the previous day, 2 July 1999. Later Pinnington was vindicated when the Secretary of State expressed concern over the resuscitation procedures operated at the school, by which time she was medically permanently unfit to return to work.

ET: the dismissal was fair and the principal reason for the dismissal of the claimant was capability due to illness, rather than the protected disclosures. No period earlier than 2 and 3 July 1999 was relevant because the protected disclosure provisions did not come into effect until 2 July 1999. Even in that short period she was prevented by ill-health from going to work. It was not simply a question of her having been suspended and that suspension still being in force. She was unable to go to work because of her ill-health.

EAT (HHJ McMullen QC): found that Pinnington had been fairly dismissed, despite the connection between the injury sustained by her and that injury being the reason for her dismissal. As to this (paras 69, 83, 88 and 90):

> We see no reason why similar objective standards, falling within a band of reasonable responses, should not also apply to the way in which employers 'inform themselves upon the true medical position' (*per* Phillips J in *East Lindsey District Council v Daubney* [1977] ICR 566) prior to dismissing on the grounds of ill health . . . Particular care needs to be taken in respect of claims of dismissal or detriment suffered by whistle-blowers, for, as Mummery LJ said in *A1M Medical Services Ltd v Bladon* [2002] IRLR 807:
>
> > 'The self evident aim of the provisions is to protect employees from unfair treatment (that is victimisation and dismissal) for reasonably raising in a responsible way genuine concerns about wrongdoing in the workplace. Provisions strike an intricate balance between (a) promoting the public interest and the detection, exposure and elimination of misconduct, malpractice and potential dangers by those likely to have early knowledge of them, and (b) protecting the respective interests of employers and employees. There are obvious tensions, private and public, between the legitimate interests and the confidentiality of the employer's affairs and in the exposure of wrong.'
>
> Causation is relevant to finding the reason for dismissal. This is because in *Edwards* . . . the EAT held that in certain circumstances it was relevant to look beyond the immediate reason (ill health) and consider whether the ill health of the Applicant was caused by the malicious act of the employer. If it was, that might make the dismissal unfair, notwithstanding all proper procedures relating to dismissal on the grounds of ill health had been complied with.
>
> It is of course possible that the decision-makers, . . . and their panels, considered there might be a connection between the protected disclosure, the illness and the dismissal. But the Tribunal found as a fact that their reason was simply the lack of capability due to ill health of the Applicant. . . . In the present case, even assuming the Applicant made a protected disclosure meeting all of the criteria of the Act, she is protected from dismissal only if the reason for the dismissal is the protected disclosure. Where another reason emerges, which is upheld as a matter of fact by the Employment Tribunal, it is easy to see, but hard for the employee to accept no doubt, that although the dismissal came after the protected disclosure the disclosure was not the reason for the dismissal . . . An employer who responds to a complaint with a detailed and thorough investigation is, in our judgment less likely unfairly to dismiss the complainant for that reason.

The EAT however did remit an issue as to detriment regarding the failure to terminate Pinnington's suspension that continued for one day after PIDA was brought into force. This was the focus of the appeal to the Court of Appeal.

CA (Mummery, Clarke and Wall LJJ): held that there was no issue to remit in relation to the two days that PIDA was in force. For Pinnington it was argued that there was a 'deliberate failure to act' by *not* terminating the suspension, which had been in force since 2 July 1998. This was rejected by the Court of Appeal on the basis that whilst there was a failure to act, in the sense of the failure to terminate the suspension, this was not a *deliberate* failure. There was neither any evidence of a deliberate failure nor any basis upon which one could be inferred. Prior to PIDA coming into force it had already been decided that she would be dismissed on grounds of capability and it was unrealistic in those circumstances to expect that they should have considered, on 2 July, terminating the suspension.

Result: claim failed.

Detriment: 2 days suspension; ostracism ; ill health.

Sections considered: 47B, 43C, 43E, 43F, 43G, 98(1), (2) and (3), 103A ERA.

Damages awarded: none.

31. Sim v Manchester Action on Street Health

(EAT/0085/01, 6 December 2001)

Key issue: Qualifying disclosure.

Case Summary: Dr Sim was a night service doctor for the respondent charity. In his claim he stated that:

> my dismissal appeared to relate to sickness absence and to my having previously raised concerns about the management of the organisation . . . I believe I was dismissed for reasons which may be contrary to the Public Interests Disclosure Act 1998, and were concerned with financial probity and safeguarding the health and safety of employees and clients of MASH.

EAT (Mr Justice Lindsay (President)): was critical of the way in which the claim was framed: 'expressions such as "I believe" and "may be" hardly suffice as a true allegation' for s103A. The EAT was also critical of the tribunal regarding Sim's status in that:

> so far as concerns Section 103A—one can only claim under that if an employee. There cannot be said to have been any adequately made claim at that stage under Section 47B of the Act.

As to the elements of a qualifying disclosure:

> the subject matter of protected disclosures and to whom they must be made and by whom and in what state of mind are all matters carefully regulated by the Employment Rights Act Sections 43B and 43C and need to have their constituent parts set out and specified in a claim even if only in brief or summary form. Concern as to financial probity falls short, as it seems to us, without further allegation, of 43B(1)(b). Concerns as to safeguarding the health and safety of employees also fall short, in our view, unless further amplified, of 43B(1)(d). It is not said, either, to whom the disclosure was made—compare Section 43C.

Result: appeal dismissed.

Detriment: not claimed.

Sections considered: 47B, 98, 103A, 230(3) ERA.

Damages awarded: none.

Cited: *Duffin v Deloitte and Touche Wealth Management Limited* (EAT/0453/03, 24 September 2003).

32. Street v Derbyshire Unemployed Workers' Centre

(2004) ICR 213 (EAT); [2005] ICR 97 (CA)

Key issue: Meaning of 'good faith'.

Case Summary: Mrs Street was an administrator for the respondent, which was partly funded by a borough council (BC). She raised concerns with the management committee of the respondent and wrote to the treasurer of the council making allegations against the respondent's co-ordinator including: allegations of fraud, working for other organizations on the council's time and requesting Street to do work for other organizations. The allegations were investigated and the co-ordinator exonerated. The respondent initiated disciplinary proceedings against Street for breach of trust and gross misconduct.

ET: found the disclosures fell within s43(1)(b). It held Street possessed a reasonable belief in the truth of the allegations (s43C) and that the disclosure to a member of the management committee of the respondent fell within s43C (disclosure to employer). The disclosure to the Treasurer was considered under s43G. The tribunal found however that none of the disclosures were protected disclosures because they were not made in 'good faith' and had been made due to 'personal antagonism' towards the co-ordinator.

Regarding 'reasonable belief' the tribunal found:

> there has been no suggestion that the applicant made the disclosure for personal gain. We then consider the matters set out in s43G(2) of which really the only relevant part is subsection '(a) that, at the time he makes the disclosure the worker reasonably believes that he will be subjected to a detriment by his employer if he makes a disclosure to his employer ...'. We find that such was the applicant's view of Mr Hampton that she did believe that a disclosure made to her employer would at best be ineffective and at worst would lead to what she believed had happened to others namely that if one was not for Mr Hampton one was perceived as being against him. Turning to s43G(3) we find that a disclosure to someone in Mr Earlam's position namely treasurer of the local authority which was a major funder of the respondent can properly be regarded as reasonable. Accordingly, in general terms we find that the applicant satisfies the vast majority of the conditions imposed by s43G.

In relation to good faith they found:

> accordingly in those circumstances we conclude that none of the disclosures made can be regarded as made in good faith but were instead motivated by the applicant's personal antagonism towards Mr Hampton fuelled in particular by his perceived treatment of Mr Skinner's and Councillor Williams' cases. It therefore follows that the applicant has not made a protected disclosure and accordingly that cannot be the reason for her dismissal ...

EAT (HHJ McMullen QC): held there was nothing inconsistent with a finding of 'reasonable belief' in the truth and raising a matter with 'ulterior' intentions.

> We reject the contention that the simple finding that the appellant believed the material, as far as she was aware, as being a complete answer. There is nothing inconsistent in an applicant holding such a belief that the material is true and yet promoting it for reasons which are based upon personal antagonism. It seems to us that what Lord Denning had in mind, albeit in a different context [*Secretary of State for Employment v ASLEF (No.2)*] ... was that the motive for which a person does a particular act can change its character from good to bad, and so here ... It is not, in our view, the purpose of the Public Interest Disclosure Act to allow grudges to be promoted and disclosures to be made in order to advance personal antagonism. It is, as the title of the statute implies, to be used in order to promote the public interest. The advancement of a grudge is inimical to that purpose ....

CA (Auld LJ, Wall LJ and Jacob LJ): the claimant sought to assert that an ulterior motive would have to be both malicious and predominant to amount to bad faith. Public Concern at Work, as an interested party, submitted that if an ulterior motive can vitiate the requirement of good faith, even where the disclosure is made honestly, it should only have that effect where: (1) it is so 'wicked or malicious' that it approaches 'dishonesty'; and (2) it is the predominant motive for the disclosure. The respondent submitted that the requirement of good faith must mean that the disclosure should be made for the purpose of disclosing one or more of those wrongdoings, not for some other ulterior motive such as personal antagonism to the person the subject of the disclosure, as the employment tribunal had found in this case. The Court of Appeal held that 'good faith' is more than just a reasonable belief in the truth. If the dominant or predominant reason for raising the concern was not in the public interest the tribunal can find that it was not made in good faith.

Auld LJ said (paras 53 and 56):

> In considering good faith as distinct from reasonable belief in the truth of the disclosure, it is clearly open to an employment tribunal, where satisfied as to the latter, to consider nevertheless whether the disclosure was not made in good faith because of some ulterior motive, which may or may not have involved a motivation of personal gain, and/or which, in all the circumstances of the case, may or may not have made the disclosure unreasonable. Whether the nature or degree of any ulterior motive found amounts to bad faith, or whether the motive of personal gain was of such a nature or strength as to 'make the disclosure for purposes of personal gain' or 'in all the circumstances of the case' not reasonable, is equally a matter for its assessment on a broad basis . . .

> . . . it seems more in keeping with the declared public interest purpose of this legislation, fair and a more useful guide to employment tribunals in conducting this sometimes difficult, sometimes straightforward, exercise—depending on the facts—to hold that they should only find that a disclosure was not made in good faith when they are of the view that the dominant or predominant purpose of making it was for some ulterior motive, not that purpose.

Lord Justice Wall said (para 68):

> . . . good faith is a question of motivation, and as a matter of general human experience, a person may well honestly believe something to be true, but, as in the instant case, be motivated by personal antagonism when disclosing it to somebody else. . . . Motivation, however, is a complex concept, and self-evidently a person making a protected disclosure may have mixed motives. He or she is hardly likely to have warm feelings for the person about whom (or the activity about which) disclosure is made. It will, of course, be for the tribunal to identify those different motives, and nothing in this judgment should derogate from the proposition that the question for the tribunal at the end of the day as to whether a person was acting in good faith will not be: did the applicant have mixed motives? It will always be: was the complainant acting in good faith? In answering this question, however, it seems to me that tribunals must be free, when examining an applicant's motivation, to conclude on a given set of facts that he or she had mixed motives, and was not acting in good faith. If that is correct, how is it to be done? I can see no more satisfactory way of reaching such a conclusion than by finding that the applicant was not acting in good faith because his or her predominant motivation for disclosing information was not directed to remedying the wrongs identified in s43B, but was an ulterior motive unrelated to the statutory objectives.

Result: appeal dismissed.

Detriment: not relevant.

Sections considered: 43A, 43B, 43C, 43E, 43F, 43G, 98(1), (2), 103A ERA.

Damages awarded: none.

Cited: *Bachnak v Emerging Markets Partnership (Europe) Limited* (EAT/0288/05, 27 January 2006); *The Trustees of Mama East African Women's Group v Dobson* (EAT/0219/05 and EAT/0220/05, 23 June 2005); *Lucas v Chichester Diocesan Housing Association* (EAT/0713/04, 7 February 2005); *Morrison v Hesley Lifecare Services Limited* (EAT/0262/03 and EAT/0534/03, 19 March 2004).

33. Virgo Fidelis Senior School v Boyle

[2004] IRLR 268 (EAT)

Key issues: (1) Quantum for injury to feelings in protected disclosure case; (2) Scope for aggravated and exemplary damages.

Case summary: Mr Boyle made a protected disclosure by writing a letter making explicit allegations against various members of the school staff to the Diocese, London Borough of Croydon and the

Convent de Notre Dame de Fidelité in France. He was bullied leading to inadequate cover and the onset of stress-related injuries.

ET: claim for detriment and automatic unfair dismissal made out—awarded £47,755 in damages.

EAT (HHJ Ansell): the guidelines in *Vento v Chief Constable of West Yorkshire Police (No 2)* [2003] IRLR 102 (CA) apply. Awards should be compensatory, albeit that the seriousness of the wrong normally affects the amount of harm (para 45):

> . . . we are firmly of the view that the Tribunal were in error in not having regard to the *Vento* guidelines, albeit that detriment suffered by 'whistle-blowers' should normally be regarded by Tribunals as a very serious breach of discrimination legislation.

The injury to feelings award was therefore reduced to £25,000 (reflecting that it was a very serious case) with no separate award for psychiatric damage.

As to aggravated damages (paras 64–5):

> it is clear from this Tribunal's decision that had they the power they would have made such an award and indeed their use of the word 'travesty' is an echo of the way in which the employer's conduct was described by Smith J in *Johnson*, together with the absence of any apology or mitigation. Indeed there were before the Tribunal two documents: a copy of a letter from the Chair of Governors and a copy of a press release from the London Borough of Croydon, following the merits hearing which showed not a jot of regret or remorse. Indeed the Governors described the original disclosure letter as 'totally reprehensible, unprofessional and unethical'.

> Adopting the Tribunal's findings of fact with regard to the School's conduct, we are of the view that a figure of £10,000 by way of aggravated damages should be awarded.

The EAT reviewed the cases on exemplary damages, starting with *Rookes v Barnard* [1964] AC 1129 (HL) which:

> identified the two circumstances in which exemplary damages might be available, namely (1) in the case of oppressive arbitrary or unconstitutional action by the servants of the Government and (2) where the defendant's conduct had been calculated by him to make a profit for himself. They defined those damages where the object was to punish or deter and which were distinct from aggravated damages, whereby the motives and conduct of the defendant aggravating the injury to the plaintiff would be taken into account in assessing compensatory damages. Lord Devlin made it clear in the course of his speech at page 412D–I that the fact that the injury to a claimant had been aggravated by the malice or by the doing of the injury would not normally be justification for an award of exemplary damages, aggravated damages would be sufficient in that type of case.

Whilst noting that awards of exemplary damages could be made if the above conditions were satisfied in a protected disclosure case, the EAT declined to make an award (paras 78–81):

> For our part we would venture to suggest that once the cause of action test no longer exists and the *Rookes v Barnard* test becomes fact sensitive rather than cause of action sensitive we see no reason why in principle exemplary damages could not be awarded, provided that the other conditions are made out. Clearly in the majority of cases aggravated damages would be sufficient to mark the employer's conduct.

> On the facts of this case there are also further difficulties. In the findings on liability the Tribunal had found that the School was a voluntary-aided school under the control of the London Borough of Croydon. We agree that the presence or otherwise of the London Borough of Croydon in the action was irrelevant. The question to be decided was whether the School (i.e. the Governors) were acting as servants or agents exercising executive power derived from the government, central or local.

> Miss McLynn sought to highlight the various pieces of evidence before the Tribunal which demonstrated the proximate relationship between the London Borough of Croydon and the

School, which included the requirement under the School's disciplinary procedure for them to seek consultation and advice from the London Borough of Croydon where disciplinary procedures could lead to dismissal, and the subsequent advice received that Sister Bernadette was a proper person to carry out the investigation.

Whilst we have not found this an easy issue, we conclude that the School in exercising their disciplinary powers were not acting as servants or agents of the executive, even at a local level. Further, whilst the actions of the School in dealing with Mr Boyle were criticised quite properly by the Tribunal, there was in our view not sufficient before them to enable them to say that this was oppressive, arbitrary or unconstitutional action.

Result: *Vento v Chief Constable of West Yorkshire Police (No. 2)* applies—award of £25,000 for injury to feelings and £10,000 aggravated damages.

Detriment: disciplining him.

Sections considered: 47B, 48, 103A, 123 ERA.

Damages awarded: £47,755; £45,000 for injury to feelings. Reduced as above on appeal.

Cited: *Pinnington v Swansea City and County Council and another* [2005] ICR 685; *Rookes v Barnard* [1964] AC 1129 (HL).

34. WELSH REFUGEE COUNCIL v BROWN

(EAT/0032/02, 22 March 2002)

Key issue: Reasonable belief for qualifying disclosure.

Case Summary: The Welsh Refugee Council was funded by the Home Office. Mrs Brown was informed in her first week by the Finance Officer of the Council that:

> Mr Yusuf would ask her for travelling expenses made out by cheque for cash without providing an invoice. He would cash the cheque at the local NatWest Bank and, Mrs Donovan suspected, he would then claim the same expenses from the Cardiff City Council who administered the payroll on behalf of the Home Office. Mrs Brown was told of other concerns. These included Mr Yusuf's alleged taking expenses for a particular event which he subsequently did not attend and his refusing to return the money to Mrs Donovan; his alleged paying of cash sums to people who were believed to be his friends for 'translation services' of which there were no records; his failure for several months to hand over a £200 grant to a refugee woman, and doubts as to the amount she ultimately received, and as to the signature on the receipt; his suspected deliberate spilling of ink over a queried signature on a landlord's bond.

Brown raised these concerns with a member of the management committee. The respondent then contended that Brown's appointment was 'invalid' because references had not been received and her employment was terminated. She claimed to have made a protected disclosure and therefore her dismissal was automatically unfair.

ET: found that:

> the reason for dismissal was that Mrs Brown made a disclosure to members of the respondents' management committee, in that there has been no other rational, credible, or satisfactory explanation for her dismissal and the respondents' conduct points to a determination to contrive her dismissal.

EAT (Mr Justice Holland): upheld the finding of automatically unfair dismissal (para 9):

> . . . a finding that Mrs Brown had a reasonable belief for these purposes necessarily connotes two component matters; thus it necessarily connotes that she did in point of fact believe what she was saying, that is, it necessarily connotes a subjective finding to that extent. Second and further, it connotes a finding that that belief was reasonable, that is, it was a tenable belief neither eccentric nor fanciful, it is a belief that withstands objective assessment.

As to the basis for the reasonable belief? (para 13):

> . . . How could the grounds be other than reasonable as a basis for further disclosure, given the source of the information? What else should Mrs Brown as regional coordinator have done, other than pass the material forward? Should she have kept silent pending her own investigation before passing the matter forward?

The EAT then went on to comment of the appeal that:

> At its best it was tactical. It could not possibly have been regarded as having any merit at all. The Council knew the grounds underpinning Mrs Brown's complaint. If it did not, it should have done. Given now two critical judgments, the first being that of the Employment Tribunal, the second being that of this Tribunal, cannot the Council now learn valuable lessons in the public interest that will help it devote its time and funds to its essential laudable purpose and will prevent it engaging in bad man management and hopeless litigation?

Brown sought her costs and they were ordered but reduced to a third due to error ensuring that the appeal was listed without having gone through a sift.

Result: automatically unfair dismissal.

Detriment: none pleaded.

Sections considered: 43A, 43B, 43C, 103A ERA.

Damages awarded: appeal prior to remedy hearing.

35. WILLIAMS v NORTH TYNESIDE COUNCIL

(UKEAT/0415/05/CK, 31 January 2006)

Key issue: Quantification of loss.

Case Summary: Miss Williams claimed that she was unfairly constructively dismissed on three grounds (ss100C, 103A and 104). She claimed as a consequence of making a protected disclosure she suffered a detriment. The protected disclosure related to the bullying and harassment by her manager, Mr Pringle. Williams raised her concerns as a grievance. She suffered the following detriments: the respondent refused to accept the grievance; Pringle refused to speak to her ; she was cold-shouldered by colleagues and not invited to meetings. During an adjournment the respondent admitted liability in respect of all Williams's claims.

ET: found Williams had unreasonably 'taken herself outside the world of work' when she enrolled on a four-year university course.

EAT (HHJ Burke QC): the tribunal erred in failing to calculate when Williams would reasonably have obtained a new job. Regarding pension losses the tribunal stated:

> Employment Tribunals are entitled to adopt a pragmatic and proportionate approach to the calculation of pension loss; and it would be wholly impracticable and disproportionate when only a short period was in issue for detailed and difficult or even actuarial calculations to be embarked upon.

Regarding aggravated damages Williams relied on these four allegations: (1) the respondent did not carry out a full and fair investigation into her allegations; (2) they offered no form of apology; (3) they made allegations against Williams's credibility, professional standing and capability; (4) they discussed her case with her previous employers. The tribunal erred in only considering damages for the actions during the hearing and not their actions during employment.

Result: remitted to the same tribunal to consider, if Williams had acted reasonably—when would she have obtained employment and at what rate? To consider three aspects of aggravated damages.

Detriments: the Employment Tribunal found life had been made very unpleasant for her over the last six to seven weeks in that the respondent refused to accept the grievance; Pringle refused to speak to her; she was cold-shouldered by colleagues and not invited to meetings.

Aggravated damages: the respondent did not carry out a full and fair investigation into her allegations. The respondent offered no form of apology. The respondent made allegations against Williams's credibility, professional standing and capability, discussing her case with her previous employers.

Sections considered: 47B, 100C, 103A, 104 ERA.

Damages awarded: detriment—£5,000 for injury to feelings; £2,257.17 as a compensatory award. (But the award has been remitted for reconsideration).

36. Woodward v Abbey National plc

[2006] IRLR 677 (CA)

Key issue: Employer liable for detriment imposed after employment.

Case Summary: The claimant claimed that some years after the termination of her employment, she was caused detriment by her ex-employers including by their not providing a reference for her due to her having been a whistleblower.

EAT: (Mr Justice Burton (President)) found that the Employment Tribunal and the EAT did not have jurisdiction to consider the claim as they could not distinguish and were thus bound by the Court of Appeal and therefore Woodward could not present a claim regarding her post-termination detriment.

Court of Appeal (Ward LJ, Maurice Kay LJ, Wilson LJ): claims could be brought for post-termination detriment.

In relation to other discrimination statues, post-termination victimization claims could be brought: *Rhys-Harper v Relaxion Group plc* [2003] ICR 867 (HL). The same applied here. Ward LJ (with whom Maurice Kay LJ and Wilson LJ agreed), observed that:

> Victimisation is established by showing *inter alia* the discrimination of the employee by 'subjecting him to any other detriment'—see s6(2) of the 1975 Act and s4(2) of the 1976 and 1995 Acts. Under s47B of the ERA a worker likewise has the right 'not to be subjected to any detriment'. Although the language and the framework might be slightly different, it seems to me that the four Acts are dealing with the same concept, namely, protecting the employee from detriment being done to him in retaliation for his or her sex, race, disability or whistle-blowing. This is made explicit by the long title to the Public Interest Disclosure Act 1998, which is, as I have already set out:
>
> > 'An Act to protect individuals who make certain disclosures of information in the public interest; to allow such individuals to bring action in respect of victimisation.' (Emphasis added)
>
> All four Acts are, therefore, dealing with victimisation in one form or another. If the common theme is victimisation, it would be odd indeed if the same sort of act could be victimisation for one purpose, but not for the other.

The various tests suggested in *Rhys Harper* in relation to whether relief should be afforded after termination of employment were summarized by Ward LJ in *Woodward* (at para 53 and referring in brackets to paragraph numbers in *Rhys Harper*):

(1) for Lord Nicholls, the employment relationship triggered the employer's obligation not to discriminate in all the incidents of the employment relationship whenever they arise, provided the benefit in question arises between the employer or former employer as such and the employee or former employee as such (44, 45);

(2) for Lord Hope the test was whether there is still a continuation of the employment relationship (114, 115).

(3) for Lord Hobhouse the test was one of proximity: does the conduct complained about have a sufficient connection with the employment (139) or a substantive and proximate

connection between the conduct complained of and the employment by the alleged discriminator (140);

(4) for Lord Rodger, one must look for a substantive connection between the discriminatory conduct and the employment relationship, with the former employer discriminating qua former employer (205);

(5) for Lord Scott, it depends on whether the relationship between employer and employee brought into existence when the employee entered into the employer's service is still in existence (200) or is still continuing notwithstanding the termination of the employment (204).

In other words Lord Hope and Lord Scott seem to tie the application of the Act to the continuance of the employment relationship whereas the majority look for a connection (variously described) between the former employee as such and the former employer as such.

On each of these tests references would be covered. More remote claims would still be problematic. Further, the Court of Appeal expressly left over the question as to whether the protected disclosure must precede the termination of employment.

Result: Court of Appeal reversed the EAT and ruled that *Fadipe v Reed Nursing Personnel* [2005] ICR 1760 could not stand with the decision of the House of Lords in *Rhys-Harper v Relaxion Group plc* [2003] ICR 867.

Detriment: poor reference after termination.

Sections Considered: 48 (and 47B) ERA.

Damages awarded: remitted back to the Employment Tribunal.

APPENDIX 9

Employment Tribunal Whistleblowing Cases

1. A v B & C* (2002)

Headline: Detriment: failure to investigate a complaint of sexual assault was a detriment justifying resignation.

Case Summary: Ms A was the personal assistant to the Managing Director (MD) of B company. The MD took Ms A on a business trip to New York and sexually assaulted her when she was 'drunk and insensible'. Ms A was too ill to work for 13 months, during which time police in the UK and US investigated the matter. When Ms A was ready to return, she wrote to the Financial Director saying what had occurred and pointed to the ongoing risk to B company's female staff. She said she would not work for the MD, who she thought should be investigated by the company's board and sacked. After 3 months there had been no news of any investigation or a considered response so Ms A resigned. ET held that Ms A's letter was a protected disclosure, and that B's failure to investigate was a detriment, so entitling Ms A to resign. Ms A was awarded £79,308.

Result: unfair constructive dismissal and detriment suffered.

Detriment: failure to investigate.

Damages: £79,308

2. A v X Limited

ET, Case no. 2102023/00, 9 March 2001 (Liverpool)

Headline: Reporting an allegation of sexual discrimination of another is a protected disclosure.

Case Summary: The claimant was aged 55. He reported an alleged case of sexual harassment. He claimed he suffered a detriment by being 'disciplined' because he reported an alleged case of unlawful sex discrimination.

The Employment Tribunal found that the respondent was:

> at pains to restrict any information which might be relevant coming to the attention of the Tribunal . . . and at times . . . the respondent was attempting to mislead the tribunal by leading it away from issues which the tribunal considered to be pertinent.

The claimant was a branch manager. He became responsible for another branch nearby. The claimant received a phone call from a subordinate, Mrs A, who was very upset. When he met with Mrs A she informed him that a senior manager had sexually assaulted her and committed acts of gross indecency towards her. These included touching her and exposing himself together with lewd comments. She claimed the acts had been going on for some time and she could no longer put up with the situation. The claimant stated they were very serious and believed they were criminal acts and should be reported to the police and the respondent. Mrs A begged him not to do so as her husband was unaware. He advised her to tell her husband and to make a formal complaint.

---

* Summary courtesy of Public Concern at Work.

Mrs A contacted the claimant again on a later evening regarding another act of the senior manager. He advised her to write everything down.

On the way to meet Mrs A the next day he spoke with Mrs B as to whether she knew anything about Mrs A. Mrs B said yes and stated that the senior manager had done the same to her, alleging harassment and lewd comments. On one occasion Mrs B said he had trapped her in the kitchen saying she could not get out until she complied with his request for sexual favours. He again advised Mrs B to speak to her husband who was unaware and to write the matters down. Upon meeting Mrs A she described the senior manager exposing himself and masturbating in front of her.

Mrs A and Mrs B told their husbands and asked the claimant to report the matter. He reported it to the chief executive and asked the police to be involved. The chief executive said he would get the head of personnel to sort the matter out. The head of personnel visited the claimant, instructed the claimant not to inform anyone and informed him that no investigation would take place as no complaints had been made. The claimant asked that an investigation should be undertaken in case staff needed help or counselling. The head of personnel then reprimanded the claimant for not following the correct procedure. The head of personnel stated that the regional director would be upset at his 'going over her head' and she would explain that he had done so as he didn't want to give these details 'to a woman'. The claimant protested as this was not true. The claimant was warned that if he divulged any information he would be dismissed for gross misconduct.

The claimant met with his regional manager who in the face of the allegations said without complaints they did not want to 'stir things up' by investigating.

Mrs A was interviewed in the presence of the claimant. The respondent insisted the claimant remained quiet and he conducted the interview in an intimidating matter. Mrs A was threatened with dismissal and an action for slander by Mr Y and asked if she realized Mr Y would lose his job and his marriage would break up. Mrs A stated she was prepared to report the matter to the police. Mrs B was interviewed in a similar fashion and the respondent asked both if they had been put under pressure by the claimant to report the matter.

The claimant was then accused of talking about the case which the claimant denied. The claimant spoke to the respondent to find out what was happening to which he was told it was 'none of his business'. The victims were interviewed again and they were told by the respondent that 'they could trust [him] least of all'. Each was threatened with slander and dismissal if they repeated the allegations. The respondent accused both Mrs B and Mrs A of lying and Mrs A of having an affair with the senior manager and of sexually harassing him.

The senior manager was dismissed. The claimant was then asked to meet with the respondent regarding a 'disciplinary matter' but the substance was not conveyed to him. He attended and was accused of a breach of confidentiality.

The respondent then held a disciplinary hearing with Mrs A and accused her of bringing an inappropriate item to work in her handbag, a vibrator. The Employment Tribunal found that in relation to this the respondent 'grossly invaded Mrs A's privacy' by disciplining her for the personal item in her handbag. The respondent issued the claimant with a written warning for his breach of confidentiality when there was no evidence of such a breach save for a comment in relation to the senior manager that he 'might not be back' which disclosed nothing and they accepted this was not a breach of confidentiality. The claimant responded to the written warning raising breaches of the disciplinary rules and the grievance procedure but the respondent did not respond.

The claimant went off on sick leave and the respondent was aggressive in their treatment of his absence. He resigned.

They found the respondent had intended to 'intimidate . . . Mrs A and Mrs B . . . so as to try to enforce a blanket of confidentiality' and treating their complaints in a 'partial and unsympathetic manner'. The Employment Tribunal noted that the respondent never offered 'an apology or counselling' to the victims.

The Employment Tribunal accepted that the consequences of the claimant's detriment went beyond the dismissal.

Result: the claimant was subjected to humiliating treatment and disciplined for having made a protected disclosure.

Detriment: humiliating treatment and being disciplined when there was no evidence.

Sections considered: 43B; 43C; 47B; 103A ERA.

Damages: £139,677.56 of which £5,000 for injury to feelings and £3,000 for psychiatric damages.

3. Dr. Alexander v Gloucestershire Partnership Mental Health Trust*

ET, Case No. 1400470/03 Bristol

Headline: No causal like between detriment and disclosure.

During her three-year employment at the Trust, Dr A raised multiple concerns and also pursued grievances against colleagues. Her attitude at work resulted in grievances being brought against her. Generally, Dr A's discontent stemmed from the way things were run; she was also not happy with the way the grievances were dealt with, and the proposed merger of the Trust with another trust did not help the situation.

Dr A resigned and claimed for constructive dismissal and race and sex discrimination. Helped by the BMA Advocacy Unit she included a claim for 'detriment in employment due to protected disclosures'. The Tribunal referred to her particulars of claim as a 'poorly prepared document' and observed that her claim under PIDA did not extend to her claim for dismissal.

Although the Tribunal recognized that amongst the 'mass of complaints and criticisms' made by Dr A there could have been protected disclosures, the only detriment that was within the ET time limit was 1) the decision of two of her colleagues to pursue their grievances against her, and 2) the Trust allowing such grievances to proceed. As the Tribunal had not been presented with any evidence to show that there was a link between these decisions and any protected disclosure Dr A might have made, her claim for detriment failed.

Result: no link between disclosure and detriment or resignation.

Detriment: grievances pursued against Dr A; the Trust allowing the grievances to proceed.

4. Allison v Sefton M.B. Council* (2001)

Headline: Detriment: neither the continuation of bad relations with his manager nor the transfer of the whistleblower to another office was a detriment.

Case Summary: Allison was an environmental health officer. He made a protected disclosure about the conduct of his manager—with whom there had been bad relations for some time—in the issuing of a noise abatement notice. The issue was investigated, though not rapidly. Allison's relations with his manager did not improve and then for operational reasons Sefton Council subsequently moved Allison to another office. ET held that the continuation of Allison's bad relations with his manager was not a detriment and that Allison's transfer to another office was not caused by the disclosure.

Result: detriment not caused by disclosure.

Detriment: transfer to another office.

Damages: none

---

* Summary courtesy of Public Concern at Work.

5. Almond v Alphabet Children's Services* (2001)

Headline: Detriment: offer of less work to a casual worker was a detriment.

Case Summary: Almond was a casual worker at a care home. ET held that after she made a protected disclosure (though to whom or about what is not stated in the summary decision), the care home offered her less work than they had previously.

Result: detriment occurred.

Detriment: offered less work

Damages: £1,000 for detriment.

6. Aziz v (1) Muskett (2) Tottenham Legal Advice Centre

ET, Case No. 2200560/01, 3 April 2002 (London Central)

Headline: The use of disclosures as leverage to bolster another claim is bad faith.

Case Summary: The claimant worked at the second respondent (the respondent). The disclosure was an allegation of breaches of their equal opportunities policy. The claimant was a temporary receptionist. She wanted a pay rise. She did not get it but believed she had been promised it. She presented a claim in the County Court. The respondent concerned as to the cost of defending that claim arranged for a member of the management committee, a solicitor, to meet the claimant. During this informal meeting an offer was made that should the claimant drop her claim the respondent would give the claimant a 'fresh start' and try and raise funds for positions the claimant could apply to work in. The solicitor stated she would be willing to sit on any interview panel.

When no money was offered and further negotiations broke down the claimant alleged that she possessed a tape recording of the meeting and that the solicitor had offered to 'fix a job for her by rigging an interview' and that the respondent had to settle the claim. If it was not settled the claimant would inform the Office of Solicitors Complaints, the local authority (funders of the respondent) and someone presenting a claim against the respondent. The claimant asserted she had a transcript of the tape recording.

The claimant sent the transcript (later claimed to be a disclosure) to the Law Society, MPs and the local authority.

The Employment Tribunal found her disclosures were not made in good faith. She had at the time a County Court claim against the respondent and had not withdrawn it at the time she raised her concerns. They found she embarked on this 'course of action as a way of putting pressure on the Centre to give her the pay rise'. Importantly they found the transcript to be inaccurate. Accordingly they found that the disclosures were neither qualifying nor protected.

Result: no disclosure and no good faith.

Detriment: none.

Sections considered: 43B; 47B ERA.

Damages: none.

Relevant cases cited: *Parkins v Sodexho Ltd* [2002] IRLR 109.

7. Azmi v Orbis Charitable Trust* (2000)

Headline: Causation less than 1 year: ET reject explanation that a whistleblower's failure of probation period was for alleged poor performance.

---

* Summary courtesy of Public Concern at Work.

Case Summary: Orbis was the UK fundraising part of a US-based international charity. Shortly after joining as the resource director, Azmi raised concerns internally about breaches of charity law and circular funding. Azmi also knew that her predecessor had recently sent similar concerns to the Charity Commission. On the day the Charity Commission made a formal request for information, Azmi was told she had failed her probation. Orbis claimed that the reason was Azmi's poor performance but the ET rejected this as Azmi had only just been appointed company secretary and had recently been taken to the US to meet the parent body.

Result: Azmi's probation ended because of disclosure.

Detriment: not claimed.

Damages: not known.

8. Azzaoui v Apcoa Parking UK Ltd

ET, Case No. 2302156/01, 30 April 2002 (London South)

Headline: Parking attendant raised concerns about targets forcing staff to issue false PCNs to meet targets.

Case Summary: The claimant, a parking attendant, stated that staff were 'forced into a position of issuing false PCNs in order to meet production targets . . . known to be inaccurate by management but were nevertheless allowed to be used by the Council'. He thought that senior management and Westminster Council should be made aware of his concerns. He set out these concerns in an incident report on 17 August 2000. On 23 January 2001 the claimant wrote to the Head of Parking at Westminster Council and various managers and the Employment Tribunal found this letter 'tended to show that criminal offences were being committed'. The Employment Tribunal found that the claimant possessed a genuine and reasonable belief that improper practices were taking place and he raised them in good faith.

The claimant was suspended on 30 January 2001. During two investigations the respondent focused on the claimant naming those who had been involved in the incidents described and did not focus on his own treatment. The claimant was charged with having caused a 'breakdown in trust and confidence' and summoned to a disciplinary meeting. The claimant refused to name individuals and he claimed his action did not prevent a proper investigation. The claimant was dismissed. The claimant appealed including making a plea that the 'respondent provide a better public service and a good working environment'. His appeal was unsuccessful because the claimant continued to refuse to name those involved.

The Employment Tribunal found the disclosure to Westminster fell within s43C(1)(b)(ii), finding that the principal reason for his dismissal was that he had made a protected disclosure in good faith. The comment 'it would often be the case that such informants would not wish to go so far as to divulge names of individual perpetrators, but to give a sufficient indication of the problem so that the employer can investigate. This employer had sufficient indications so as to focus their investigations if they seriously wished to do so'.

Result: automatically unfairly dismissed.

Detriment: none claimed.

Sections considered: 43B; 43C ERA.

Damages: settlement was reached but not recorded.

9. Bailey v Arrow Consultants Ltd

ET, Case No. 5000328/00, 10 October 2000 (Ashford)

Headline: Inland Revenue protected disclosure.

Case Summary: The respondent not attending, the finding was that the claimant had made a protected disclosure to the Inland Revenue, which was a prescribed regulator under s43F, and this was the reason for Bailey's summary dismissal.

Result: protected disclosure.

Detriment: none claimed.

Sections considered: 103A ERA.

Damages: £10,917.56.

10. BALMER V CHURCH VIEW LTD

ET, Case No. 2502583 Newcastle upon Tyne

Headline: Victimized to cover up wrongdoing of others.

Case Summary: Balmer was a diligent, if junior, member of staff in a care home. She was understandably shocked and frightened when she witnessed three co-workers repeatedly slapping an elderly resident about the head until he became upset and angry, and then withholding his meal. Balmer did not know what to do. Later after speaking about the incident to her partner, also a worker at the home, she raised the matter with a senior carer who said that she would report the matter to the manager. Shortly thereafter the manager asked Balmer to attend a meeting which she assumed was to discuss the incident she had reported.

At the meeting pressure was put on Balmer to say that she had been mistaken in what she had seen and in doing so the manager raised her voice and spoke in an intimidating manner. Balmer refused to retract her statement and two days later she was required to attend a disciplinary hearing. During the hearing Balmer was again asked to retract her statement, which, again, she refused to do and her employment was terminated for 'gross misconduct'.

A letter seeking to justify Balmer's dismissal stated that an investigation into the alleged abuse of the resident had concluded that the allegations were false. As Balmer had refused to acknowledge that she might have been mistaken in what she had seen, and that she had failed to report the incident promptly, it concluded that she had raised the matters with malicious intent. Balmer appealed her dismissal and the employer found that, given the allegations were false, the original dismissal was justified.

Balmer presented a claim for unfair dismissal and the ET said that she knew what she had seen, and there was no possibility of her having been mistaken. The ET noted the lack of evidence that the employer had investigated the incident and that it had not taken any notice of any of her grounds of appeal.

The ET found that the reason for Balmer's dismissal was 'inextricably linked' with her having told her employer about the treatment of the resident, which was a protected disclosure. The ET went on to find that A was victimized in order to cover up the wrongdoing of others and awarded damages for injury to feelings.

Result: unfair dismissal and detriment suffered.

Damages: unknown.

11. BARKNESS AND JOHNSTON V BOOKER TATE LIMITED

ET, Case No. 2500437; 2500438/02, 6 January 2004 (Newcastle)

Headline: Automatic unfair dismissal contrary to s103A. The claimants were not unfairly dismissed (including constructive dismissal) for making a protected disclosure as they did not make them in good faith.

Case Summary: The respondent provided management and technical personnel to the Government of Kenya. The substantive claim concerned a commercial agreement between Mumias Sugar Company Limited (MSC) and Busia Sugar Company (BSC) in Kenya. Mr Johnston was Chief Executive

Officer of MSC and Mr Barkness attended board meetings to give advice on financial matters and had responsibility for all financial matters of MSC. MSC was owned 71per cent by the Government of Kenya. BSC was also owned by the Government, the respondent and the Cane Development Corporation in Kenya. The claimants' concerns surrounded the need for due diligence to be performed prior to completion of a commercial agreement between MSC and BSC in Kenya. The Employment Tribunal found that a number of the disclosures were qualifying disclosures. They then went on however to decide they were not protected disclosures.

The Employment Tribunal found that the claimants had been advised by a lawyer that due diligence was not required prior to entering into a 'memorandum of understanding'—namely a statement of an intention to enter into a contract—as such a memorandum was not binding. That advice was not provided to the board or set out in correspondence. They went on to conclude that 'the protected disclosures were not made with good faith. They were made for an ulterior motive . . . indications were given that the Government of Kenya may very well wish them both to work for MSC if BTL were no longer in control of the management' later commenting 'the press had information which could only have come from the applicant'.

In relation to 'good faith' the Employment Tribunal commented that:

> The requirements of good faith must import more than a reasonable belief in wrongdoing. In the Tribunal's view it relates to the whistleblowers' motives. A whistleblower may act as such from a number of motives; some good; some not so good and some bad. The motive which is clearly protected is the motive to bring the wrongdoing to the employer's attention so that an investigation may take place and, or the wrongdoing righted in the public interest. However, a whistleblower may also make a disclosure with the motive, for example, of damaging a competitor for promotion; or in an attempt to ingratiate himself with his employer, knowing that he is party to wrongdoing and thereby to protect himself from punishment. It seemed to the Tribunal that in order to establish good faith, a whistleblower must prove that the predominant motive for his actions was to further the intentions of the Act that individuals should be protected who make disclosures in the public interest. The motive of the whistleblower can also change over time. The Tribunal must look at the facts to ascertain the whistleblower's motive. These facts can relate to the motives of the whistleblower both before and after the protected act.

Result: the Employment Tribunal found that the claimants did not have good faith.

Detriment: none claimed.

Sections considered: 103A; 43B; 43C; 43D; 43E ERA.

Damages: none.

Relevant cases cited: *Abernethy v Mott, Hay and Anderson* [1974] IRLR 213; *Parkins v Sodexho Ltd* [2002] IRLR 109; *Darnton v The University of Surrey* [2003] IRLR 133; *Shillito v Van Leer (UK)* [1997] IRLR 495; *Goodwin v Cabletel UK Ltd* [1997] IRLR 665; *Neary v Dean of Westminster* [1999] IRLR 288.

12. Mr R. Bekhaled v Pizza Express (Restaurants) Limited

ET, Case No. 2204249/2000, 25 January 2001 (London Central)

Headline: Persistence in allegations after investigations. Reasonable belief at outset but doubtful whether still true after investigation. Claim dismissed as no detriment and time limits. Being summoned to a disciplinary hearing for making a protected disclosure and there being 'informally warned' was not a detriment.

Case Summary: Mr Bekhaled complained regarding his working conditions. He suffered from asthma and he was concerned regarding the lack of ventilation, flour dust and long hours. He then complained that these conditions caused a deterioration in his health and about the refusal to permit him to transfer to a waiter position. He also alleged against his previous manager theft by his not ringing through orders made by customers.

Bekhaled did transfer and as a consequence his hours were reduced. The ET found that at the time he accepted the fewer hours because of his asthma. His complaint of theft was made after his transfer.

The complaint of theft was taken seriously and the respondent found that evidence produced by Bekhaled was 'consistent with [him] giving free food to customers' but that other records did not indicate there was a serious problem with shortages or losses. The claimant was called to a disciplinary hearing regarding 'unwarranted allegations' against his previous manager and that he had 'taken company property' [the evidence of his previous manager's wrongdoing] without authority. When he attended the meeting he was 'informally warned about his future behaviour'.

The ET were not impressed with Bekhaled's 'exaggerated' allegations as to the amount of money being taken. It found that the claimant did make a protected disclosure but that then doubted his 'good faith' and his 'reasonable belief' although the ET did not reach a concluded view on these issues as it held that Bekhaled was 'unable to establish any detriment as a result of his protected disclosure'. The Tribunal commented that 'we do not find it satisfactory that [he] was summoned to a disciplinary hearing and only then told the outcome of the investigation, even if . . . [he] suffered no detriment because he was not disciplined'.

The ET also stated that even if their finding that there was no detriment was wrong, the claim in relation to detriment was out of time.

Result: no detriment.

Detriment: none found, but this is difficult to justify. Being summoned to a disciplinary hearing following a protected disclosure is a detriment (see Chapter 7), especially where there was a finding that the disclosure was a protected disclosure. Then to receive an 'informal warning' is a further detriment.

Sections considered: 43B; 43C.

Damages: none.

13. BENNET v NEWSQUEST MEDIA (SOUTHERN) PLC*

ET, Case No. 1600464/03 Cardiff

Headline: Anonymity protected claimant from victimization.

Case Summary: Mr Bennet worked as Controller in the classified advertisements section of a regional newspaper. Due to overstaffing in this section, his employer decided to make one of three Controllers in the section redundant. Before the selection procedure was completed, an anonymous letter was sent to the Commission for Racial Equality containing allegations that the newspaper was institutionally racist and citing specific instances and names. CRE contacted the employer and there was an enquiry into these allegations. There was, however, nothing to support the allegations; indeed the newspaper had already disciplined one employee for making racist remarks before this investigation commenced. On the day that Bennet was informed that he had been selected for redundancy, he revealed that he was the author of the anonymous letter. After he was made redundant Bennet brought a claim for unfair dismissal under PIDA.

The Tribunal rejected Bennet's claim. It noted that, as a matter of common sense, victimization cannot occur if the whistleblower's identity is not known to the person in a position to victimize.

Result: no detriment.

Damages: none.

---

* Summary courtesy of Public Concern at Work.

14. Bhadresa v SRA (British Transport Police)* (2002)

Headline: Damages: aggravated damages and injury to feelings. Detriment: unfairly rejected for permanent post after whistleblowing.

Case Summary: Bhadresa was a senior barrister. British Transport Police (BTP) wanted her to run its legal department but, due to a recruitment freeze, this had to be done through an agency initially. Bhadresa was assured of a permanent post, her contract was renewed and she was given a 25 per cent pay rise. BTP then advised Bhadresa that it had to advertise the post under its rules but assured Bhadresa the position was hers. Before the interviews, Bhadresa discovered her line manager destroying prosecution files. Bhadresa reported this to the appropriate internal authority and was assured of confidentiality. Bhadresa's manager was suspended as the destroyed files were recovered from the rubbish bins. Bhadresa was cold-shouldered by colleagues and then allies of her manager conducted her interview. BTP appointed a less qualified lawyer and Bhadresa claimed under PIDA. The Employment Tribunal, having barred BTP from defending the case, held that Bhadresa was a worker, who had been subjected to a detriment.

Result: detriments suffered.

Damages: awarded £218,000, including £10,000 aggravated damages and £50,000 for injury to feelings.

15. Bhatia v Sterlite Industries (India) Ltd and ors

ET, Case No. 2204571/00, 2 May 2001

Headline: concerns over statements in IPO are protected disclosure. Likely failure to comply with NY Stock Exchange obligations. Illustration of application to foreign obligation.

Case Summary: the respondent is listed on the Indian National Stock Exchange and has business interests in mining, metals, manufacturing and telecommunications. The Chairman's office is in London. The claimant was the 'Vice-President—Mergers and Acquisitions'. On his arrival investment banks made presentations and one suggested the flotation of the optical fibre cable division of the respondent on the New York Stock Exchange via an Initial Public Offering ('IPO').

The claimant was asked by the Chairman to prepare a presentation for the initial IPO with the investment bank. The Chairman asked the claimant to include 'photonics' as an existing business line in the benchmarking exercise where the prospective company is valued against peer group companies. Photonics is a highly complex optical component at the cutting edge of communications technology. The claimant knew that the respondent did not have even a prototype of such a product and he said to the Chairman that photonics could not be included as the proposed listing on NASDAW had strict regulations and to include something in the registration document for the IPO would be in violation of the American Securities and Exchange Commission regulations and legislation leading to criminal and civil proceedings against the company and its directors. The Chairman became agitated and thereafter regularly berated the claimant.

The claimant raised his concerns with the CEO of the respondent and with other members of the senior management.

In a meeting on 10 July with the investment bank the claimant noticed that the draft IPO included several misrepresentations regarding the current revenues of the respondent and gave undue prominence to photonics revenue. The claimant told those present that the document was 'misleading in that photonics was a non-existent business line'.

The claimant then informed a further representative, the merchant bank's telecom and technology analyst, of his reservations and the inability of the respondent to produce the components required for photonics.

---

* Summary courtesy of Public Concern at Work.

The claimant then became involved in the negotiations to buy an Australian company, Western Metals. In a meeting with Western Metals' Managing Director it was agreed that, should the respondent purchase the company, the interests of ordinary shareholders would be protected—in particular convertible preference shares would be converted to ordinary shares according to a ratio.

Upon the claimant's return, when he discussed the negotiations with Western Metals the Chairman of the respondent became extremely angry stating he would ignore the agreement in relation to convertible preference shares. The claimant responded that such action would be illegal, believing the regulations in the Australian stock exchange would be the same as anywhere else in the world. The Chairman threw items at the claimant and stated 'get out of here immediately . . . you have not seen my negative side and I will make sure that you do not have a place on this planet. I will destroy you'.

The Employment Tribunal stated that the burden of proving that he was dismissed and that the reason (or principal reason) for his dismissal was that he had made a protected disclosure lies on the claimant. They found that it is 'immaterial whether the relevant failure occurred, occurs or would occur in the UK or elsewhere'.

They found that the respondent 'searched for every means it could find to resist his complaint . . . and to make counter-allegations against him, all with a view to avoiding liability to him' and that they sought to 'cloud matters and fabricate a reason for his leaving his employment to cover up the true one'.

The Employment Tribunal found that the claimant believed that the draft IPO tended to show a criminal offence was or was likely to be committed, or was likely to fail to comply with a legal obligation. They found that belief was reasonable. They found that the disclosures were made in good faith and he was dismissed because he made protected disclosures.

Result: the claimant was unfairly dismissed.

Detriment: none.

Sections considered: 43B; 43C; 43G ERA.

Damages: £805,384.34 (£700,000 was for commission to the date of the hearing following expert evidence). However the amount was amended to $148,500 following a second hearing promulgated on 5 April 2005.

Relevant cases cited: none.

16. BILL v D. MORGAN PLC

ET, Case No. 21012981/00, 2 May 2001 (Liverpool)

Headline: No qualifying disclosure where accountant raised concern as to irregularity as reasonable belief not established.

Case Summary: The claimant was an accountant who started with the respondent on 4 January 2000 and was dismissed on 30 June 2000. The claimant had sought discovery of documents which was refused by the respondent as a 'fishing expedition'.

The claimant had concerns relating to non-capitalization of capital costs; selling assets to officers below market value; incorrectly keeping invalid invoices on the books of the company; depreciating cars in excess of relevant limits; avoiding PAYE and NI by making deductions of salary gross; the VAT on a car used primarily for private purposes and inter-company charges made to a VAT-exempted subsidiary amongst other matters.

The Employment Tribunal found that the claimant raised these concerns and others with the Company Secretary and told her he was going to raise the matters with the auditors. The claimant was then dismissed.

The respondent contended that when the claimant raised the above concerns (and others) they were mistakes which were properly and subsequently amended. They relied on the lack of causation established by the claimant between the disclosures and his dismissal. The respondent however called no evidence and made a submission of no case to answer.

The Employment Tribunal found that PIDA 'required the applicant to satisfy the Tribunal that he had made a disclosure . . . the Tribunal recognised the applicant had a belief . . . but he had not established to the Tribunal's satisfaction that that belief was reasonable . . . no sufficient documentary or other evidence had been provided'.

They went on to find that whilst the claimant had raised matters 'the tenor of his evidence was that he simply challenged or queried certain matters with them, which was not sufficient under the Act which required a worker to disclose information through appropriate channels . . . In this case the applicant was simply drawing attention to matters he . . . considered to be errors/irregularities in accounting, which was pursuant to the specific duties for which he was employed, and was not therefore conduct covered by the Act.'

As to the reason for his dismissal the Employment Tribunal relied on the fact that the respondent did not refer 'to "whistleblowing" as a reason for his dismissal'.

The Employment Tribunal refused to review this decision.

Result: no disclosure or dismissal as a consequence.

Detriment: none.

Sections considered: 43A; 43C; 47B ERA.

Damages: none.

17. BLAIKIE v TRUSTEES OF MERTON HARD OF HEARING RESOURCE CENTRE

ET, Case No. 2305174/00, 13 February 2001 (London South)

Headline: Raising the need to tighten or improve financial arrangements is not sufficient to be a protected disclosure. There is a distinction between the effect of s43B(1)(b) on constitutional rules of a charity and legal obligations.

Case Summary: The claimant was the first full-time Director of the respondent, which receives most of its funding from the lottery board. The claim was determined against s43B(1)(b). They found the claimant with her experience was 'pointing out a number of areas mainly concerned with the financial procedures and arrangements . . . which needed "tightening up" or "improving"'. She accepted in evidence she was not accusing anyone of dishonesty.

The Employment Tribunal found 'the financial procedures [she] was advocating in her various proposals written and oral . . . we not accept that the sort of matters which she was proposing really amounted to qualifying disclosures at all'.

Result: no disclosure.

Detriment: none.

Sections considered: 43B; 103A ERA.

Damages: none.

18. BOLKAVAC v DYNCORP AEROSPACE OPERATIONS (UK) LTD*

ET, Case No. 3102729/01 Southampton

Headline: Allegations of trafficking girls for prostitution made in graphic and insulting terms. Qualifying disclosure—graphic and insulting terms irrelevant. Example of s43H, exceptionally serious failure.

Case Summary: Ms Bolkavac was employed between June 1999 and April 2001 as a police monitor attached to the International Police Task Force (IPTF) located in Bosnia Herzegovina. She became increasingly concerned about the issue of abuses to local women, including prostitution and trafficking

---

* Summary courtesy of Public Concern at Work.

and the involvement of UN personnel in such abuses. Although both the UN and DynCorp recognized that the problem existed and some UN personnel were involved, Bolkavac was concerned that the police monitors and those responsible for them were not recognizing the seriousness of the problem.

In October 2000, she sent a memorandum to about 50 recipients at both the UN and DynCorp. The contents described the nature of trafficking and abuse of women in graphic detail and also implied that some of the recipients would have a guilty conscience. This was not the first memorandum she sent. In July 2000 she had sent another memorandum on the same issues to a narrower audience.

After she had sent the second memo, Bolkavac was redeployed. The reason given to her at the time was that this was for her own good. The evidence heard by the Tribunal confirmed that her redeployment was, in fact, a demotion. In April 2001 Bolkavac was dismissed for 'gross misconduct', purported to arise from timesheet infringements that had occurred in 2000. Although Bolkavac's employment was, at all material times, outside the UK, she was able to bring a claim in the UK for unfair dismissal for having made a protected disclosure. See now *Lawson v Serco* HL [2006] IRLR 289.

The Tribunal recognized that where exceptionally serious matters are at stake, a worker should not be deterred from raising them. Bolkavac had not raised her concerns with the three most senior officers because she had felt that they were dismissive of her concerns or took the issue lightly. The Tribunal found that the failure of some elements of the UN, including IPTF, to take an adequate grip on the situation and do something about it was of an exceptionally serious nature, satisfying s43H requirements, and Bolkavac's October e-mail was a protected disclosure. The Tribunal found DynCorp's explanation of why she had been dismissed as 'completely unbelievable', and found that her dismissal was caused by the disclosure.

Result: Automatically unfair dismissal; detriment.

Damages: awarded £110,000 compensation, which included £15,000 for injury to feelings.

19. D Borah v Stonehill Park Auctions Ltd*

ET, Case No. 2202060/02 London Central

Headline: Financial irregularities regarding director raised with another director protected.

Case Summary: Mr Borah was employed as an accountant for a car auction company. After there was a change in management, he became concerned about the way that staff and directors would take petty cash from the till, and about the way that one of the directors in particular, (B), failed to replace or account for money taken. Although Borah had initially put in place a system whereby petty cash would be accounted for, over time this was gradually eroded and, eventually, ignored. Over a period of about nine months Borah raised his concerns with R, the chief auctioneer and one of the directors. B owed about £6,800 to the company, and Borah asked R to speak to B about repaying the money, as if it was not repaid it would need to be written off in the accounts. Borah also told R that there was a further £8,000 that B had not accounted for. Borah told R that he did not mean this as a criticism of B, but needed direction so that he could complete the accounts.

After this B phoned Borah and told him, in no uncertain terms, to keep his nose out of B's affairs otherwise he would see that Borah no longer worked for the company. R assured Borah that his job was secure, and that he should continue with the accounts. When, however, the irregularities continued, Borah not only raised his concerns again, but also took to keeping track of what appeared to be strange and unexplained transactions. Borah was then told by respondent that he was being made redundant, and that, for economic reasons, he would be replaced by a less qualified person on a part-time basis.

---

* Summary courtesy of Public Concern at Work.

Borah brought an ET claim for unfair dismissal because he had made a protected disclosure. The ET accepted that the concerns raised by Borah were raised in good faith, and amounted to protected disclosures. After raising these concerns he was threatened with dismissal; when he continued to raise concerns he was dismissed. Despite his repeated requests for the reasons for his dismissal, Borah's employer refused to provide any.

Result: automatically unfair dismissal.

Damages: awarded a total of £51,463, with the ET taking into account loss of future earnings, which amounted to £42,027 of the award.

20. BORLEY v SUFFOLK CC* (2002)

Headline: Causation: transfer of whistleblower not linked consciously or subconsciously with the disclosure.

Case Summary: Borley reported a scuffle between her manager and a youth in care. She was subsequently investigated for interfering with another witness to the incident and the charge was proved. Rather than give Borley a warning, her employing council decided to transfer her to another unit because of a breakdown in working relationships in the unit. The Employment Tribunal held that, while Borley made a protected disclosure and her transfer was a detriment, there had been no causal link in fact. The ET applied the legal test as to causation that 'motive is not a factor and intention is not necessary' and on the facts was satisfied that the council's decision was not linked 'consciously or subconsciously' with Borley's report of the assault.

Result: Detriment not caused by disclosure.

Detriment: transfer.

Damages: none.

21. BOUGHTON v NATIONAL TYRES & AUTOCENTRE LTD

ET, Case No. 1500080/00, 15 September 2000 (Bury St Edmunds)

Headline: Tape-recording of a conspiracy to reallocate losses so as to attribute them to a break-in was a protected disclosure. Failure to investigate adequately, and to provide objective support, amounted to a constructive dismissal by reason of a protected disclosure.

Case Summary: The claimant was a tyre fitter. He believed his manager was selling worn out lorry tyres and pocketing the proceeds.

In October 1999 the Peterborough depot reported a break-in. The claimant asserted there was no stock missing. The manager of Huntingdon decided to write off losses and put them down against the break-in at Peterborough. The claimant recorded these conversations. The claimant reported them to the regional manager who asked to hear the tapes and Boughton provided the tapes to him.

Some days later the claimant's manager returned the tape the claimant had given to the regional manager. The claimant was angered and concerned by this.

Thereafter the claimant was ostracized by the management. They did not assist him in loading his van with tyres; staff would get up and walk out of the tea room and gave him the cold shoulder. He resigned in November.

The ET found that the respondent had conducted an inadequate investigation into the claimant's disclosures, and then failed to provide support to him. This amounted to a repudiatory breach of contract, which was by reason of the claimant having made a protected disclosure.

Result: the claimant made a protected disclosure and was unlawfully dismissed as a result.

---

* Summary courtesy of Public Concern at Work.

Detriments: ostracized; did not assist him in loading his van with tyres; staff would get up and walk out of the tea room and give him the cold shoulder.

Sections considered: 47B; 103A ERA.

Damages: none recorded, presumably settled.

Relevant cases cited: none.

22. Dr Bright v Harrow and Hillingdon NHS Trust

ET, Case No. 2201389/00, 29 November 2000 (London Central)

Headline: consultant psychiatrist had insufficient basis for concern that nun's habit would alarm psychiatric patients. Disclosure not made in good faith in that she had ulterior motive—The nun's competence.

Case Summary: Dr Helen Bright was a locum consultant psychiatrist at the respondent. The first disclosure concerned was internal; the second was to the press. Dr Bright's practice and that of her department was not to wear uniforms. The claimant's concerns centred on a newly appointed Sister who, as a nun, wore a habit to work. She raised those concerns and they did not meet with approval.

The claimant then contacted a reporter at the *Evening Standard* who on 17 November 1999 wrote an article 'Doctor tries to ban nun's habit'. The ET noted the claimant did not 'consult her defence union before going to the press'. The claimant was then dismissed and a further article 'Doctor in row over nun loses her job' appeared on the front page of the Evening Standard.

The claimant relied on 'health and safety issues' as justification for her complaint about the nun. The ET found that no mention was made of health and safety in her disclosure letter or in subsequent letters to the respondent. If the claimant did have a 'reasonable belief' in the health and safety issue the ET found that this belief was not reasonable. They went on to find the claimant did not possess good faith in her concerns as her real motive was the competence of the nun.

The ET found the disclosures to the press were not 'reasonable in all the circumstances of the case'. They noted 'the Applicant made her disclosure to a well-known newspaper and not to any of her professional bodies for example the General Medical Council or her defence union'.

Result: no protected disclosure.

Detriment: a reference from the respondent.

Sections considered: 43B; 43 C; 43G (to the press) ERA.

Damages: none.

Relevant cases cited: *Central Estates (Belgravia) Ltd v Woolgar* [1971] 3 All ER 647. Lord Denning MR said 'good faith' meant 'honestly and with no ulterior motive'.

23. Brooks v Maharajah & Khan trading as Bridges Homes

ET, Case No. 3203857/03, 29 June 2004 (Stratford)

Headline: An internal report of an incident in a care home was a protected disclosure.

Case Summary: The respondents were unrepresented. The claimant was employed as a residential social worker in the respondent's care home. There was a serious incident where the police were called. The claimant also produced a report to the respondents. This was a protected disclosure as 'it tended to show that a person had failed to comply with a legal obligation . . . the health or safety of an individual had been endangered'. Pressure was applied to the claimant to alter her report as it contained matters prejudicial to the respondents. The claimant's contract was then terminated. The claimant had less than one year's service.

Result: unfair dismissal and detriment.

Detriment: a refusal to provide a reference following dismissal.

Sections considered: 47B; 103A ERA.

Damages: total award £35,661.08 (including continuing losses of £10,4005.40). For the detriment £10,000. Costs £1,260. Recoupment Regulations apply to £9,704.52.

Relevant cases cited: *Rhys Harper v Relaxion Group plc* [2003] IRLR 484; *Virgo Fidelis Senior School v Boyle* [2004] IRLR 268; *Dunnachie v Kingston upon Hull City Council* [2004] IRLR 287.

24. BUCKNOR V MAR CONTRACT CLEANING AND SUPPORT SERVICES LIMITED

ET, Case No.1101644/02 31 July 2003 (Ashford)

Headline: Causation: five-month gap between disclosure and dismissal indicated no link.

Case summary: Mr Bucknor was a cleaner for MAR. The initial claim was that he was unfairly dismissed and suffered race discrimination. Bucknor did not have one year's qualifying service and he amended his claim (at the start of the hearing) to one of dismissal because of a protected disclosure. His claim was that on a cleaning contract that required three cleaners only one had been attending between August and September 2001. On 31 December 2001 he informed his managers of this together with the client. MAR in their notice of appearance admitted that one of the reasons for his dismissal was for 'speaking to the client in spite of being prohibited from doing so' amongst other reasons.

The ET found that Bucknor made a protected disclosure: s43B(1)(b). However given that he was dismissed on 7 June 2002, over five months after the disclosure, the ET found that the reference to the 'speaking to the client' was in relation to another matter occurring on 28 August 2001. They found that the disclosure to the client was not a qualifying disclosure as it was not reasonable for him to make disclosure 'without waiting to see whether or not his employers would act on the disclosure'.

Result: no automatically unfair dismissal.

Note: this decision pre-dates *London Borough of Harrow v Knight*.

25. BUTCHER V THE SALVAGE ASSOCIATION

ET, Case No. 2204597/00, 4 July 2001 (London Central)

Headline: Whilst accounts were alleged to be 'misleading' experts agreed they breached no legal obligation.

Case Summary: The respondent is a company incorporated by Royal Charter and its business is to supply marine surveying services, principally to underwriters in London.

The claimant, Mr Butcher, was employed by the respondent as Chief Financial Officer. The Chief Executive disagreed with the way Mr Butcher presented financial reports to the respondent's governing committee. The choice of styles was presented to the committee, and it preferred the Chief Executive's position. Mr Butcher raised a concern internally that in being asked to adopt the approach of the Chief Executive to the financial reporting he was being asked to change figures and monthly management reports to the board in a way which he believed would be misleading. He addressed the governing committee about his complaints, but they were rejected.

Accounting experts for the claimant and the respondent both 'agreed that there was no relevant legal obligation arising out of the facts of the case . . .[the claimant's witness] confirmed that the professional obligation to which he referred in his report was not the same as a legal obligation'. The ET concluded that Butcher's concerns were about acting professionally and that it was 'contrived to seek to promote an issue as to professional ethics into a legal obligation'. It also rejected the contention that requirements of professional ethics were incorporated into his contract since the accounts were only internal (so there was no question of misleading a third party or the board—who were aware of the issues), and in preparing the accounts in the way required he was acting on the instructions of the board and the governing committee. The appeal on this issue was dismissed by the EAT at a preliminary hearing (EAT/988/01, 21 January 2002), and permission to appeal was refused by the Court of Appeal ([2002] EWCA Civ 867).

Result: no breach of a legal obligation.

Sections considered: 103A ERA.

26. Carroll v Greater Manchester Fire Service

ET, Case No. 2407819/00, 16 July 2002 (Manchester)

Headline: Fireman who blew the whistle on hoax calls to increase pay 'sent to Coventry'.

Case Summary: The claimant blew the whistle on a swindle involving hoax 999 calls made by firemen to boost their wages. Three part-time fire fighters were called before a hearing following a two-year investigation into allegations that retained firemen made hoax 999 calls to boost their wages. Following the hearing a leading fireman was told he had to leave the service. The claimant's involvement was found to have been revealed to his colleagues although the information was not disclosed maliciously. As a consequence he suffered detriments:

 (i) being sent to Coventry: the ET found that, given his job, this was a matter of substance;
 (ii) hiding his pay sheets: ET found this to be of minor significance;
 (iii) rifling his belongings: ET found this to be potentially dangerous;
 (iv) inciting evidence against him, and
 (v) being told to 'keep his mouth shut': the ET found these to be minor.

The respondent argued that the claimant 'gave as good as he got' and sought to apply the equitable maxim that the claimant needed to come with 'clean hands'.

The ET recognized the difficulty and 'lack of authority in respect of compensation for non-pecuniary loss'. They considered it sensible to have regard to discrimination cases and sought assistance from them. With the background of horseplay between the claimant and his colleagues they came to the conclusion that £1,000 was adequate.

Result: the claimant was awarded damages for detriment.

Detriments: set out above.

Sections considered: 43C and 47B ERA.

Damages: £1,000.

Relevant cases cited: none.

27. Cattrall v Plymouth TUC Unemployed Workers Centre*

ET, Case No.1700158/03 Plymouth

Headline: Letter from employee's solicitor was protected disclosure. Not providing access to grievance procedure a detriment.

Case Summary: In March 2002, after Cattrall had been employed for about six months, he had fallen down a flight of stairs whilst at work and sustained a back injury. He was off work for the next six months, during which time he instigated a personal injury claim. Before his accident Cattrall had raised general health and safety concerns with his employer. There had already been friction between Cattrall and his employer about the scope of his job, and whilst he was off sick there was further friction about his sick leave and sick pay entitlement.

In June 2002, in connection with the personal injury claim and whilst he was on sick leave, Cattrall's lawyers wrote on his behalf to the employer setting out the nature of his personal injury claim and also referring to various breaches of health and safety regulations.

---

* Summary courtesy of Public Concern at Work.

Cattrall returned to work in October 2002 and immediately asked for a copy of the grievance procedure and the Unison Health and Safety Report that the employer had commissioned. He then raised further concerns about health and safety risks with the newly appointed health and safety representative. The employer 'blanked' his request for a grievance hearing and, in December 2002, Cattrall resigned, claiming constructive unfair dismissal in the ET. His claim also included a claim for detriment and dismissal for having raised health and safety issues and making a protected disclosure.

The ET found that the June 2002 letter from Cattrall's solicitors on his behalf to his employers amounted to a protected disclosure. They said it was significant that, after Cattrall had submitted his resignation letter, his employer had failed to respond formally. On the back of the employer's remark that it was relieved that Cattrall had resigned, which the ET noted was 'illuminating', it said that the employer thought of Cattrall as a nuisance and found that the reason why the employer had not provided him with a grievance hearing was because he had raised health and safety issues and made a protected disclosure. This, along with the employer's other acts that breached the implied duty of mutual trust and confidence, amounted to a fundamental breach of contract and Cattrall's constructive dismissal was automatically unfair because of it.

Result: automatic unfair dismissal.

Detriment: refused access to grievance procedure.

28. Chard v Glendorgal Health Club*

ET, Case No. 1702071/03 Truro

Headline: Health and safety concerns.

Case Summary: Mr Chard was employed as a fitness instructor and initially had responsibility for cleaning the swimming pool, steam room, sauna and Jacuzzi. After his manager took over these cleaning responsibilities, Chard wrote to his employer expressing concern about the running of the health club and the inadequacy of his manager's performance. He specifically mentioned that the pool and its surrounding areas had not been cleaned for at least ten days, and there was a one-inch layer of green fungus on the floor in the steam room, which presented a health hazard. Chard was then called into the office and dismissed. He was told that the letter would cause a clash of personality between Chard and his manager. Chard successfully brought an ET claim for unfair dismissal for making a protected disclosure, with the ET accepting that the conditions described in his letter would pose a threat to the health and safety of any club member.

Result: automatic unfair dismissal.

Section considered: 43B ERA.

Damages: awarded £2,765 as compensation for loss of wages.

29. Chattenton v City of Sunderland City Council

ET, Case No. 6402938/99, 18 July 2000 (Newcastle upon Tyne)

Headline: Pornographic pictures downloaded by a colleague from the internet were a protected disclosure. Meaning of detriment—no detriment if all staff treated the same.

Case Summary: Mr Chattenton was a quality adviser in the IT department of the respondent. He discovered pornographic images on the computer he shared with another and alerted his employer to this. Chattenton was interviewed then went on holiday. Upon his return his office was locked and his possessions moved to an open-plan office. He was made to feel isolated by his managers and staff.

The ET found that there had been a protected disclosure. It was argued on the part of the respondent that the Act was not 'designed to discourage [sic] whistleblowing in regard to contractual matters

---

* Summary courtesy of Public Concern at Work.

between employee and employer but they were more to do with public matter such as corruption'. This was rejected by the ET but they found that Chattenton had not been subjected to a detriment. The move to an open-plan office was not directed at him. There was a move of all employees below senior management level to an open-plan area in order to deal with the problem that Chattenton had highlighted, and he was treated no differently from his colleagues in losing his own office.

Result: no detriment.

Query: being isolated by colleagues or managers could still be a detriment and no finding is made in regard to this.

Detriments: moving place of work; changing work; isolated by colleagues and managers.

Sections considered: 43B; 43C ERA.

Damages: none.

30. CHUBB AND ORS V CARE FIRST PARTNERSHIP LTD

ET, Case No. 1101438/99B, 13 July 2001 (remedies, 10 December 2001) (Ashford)

Headline: Concerns raised as to health and safety. Payment of sick pay not a detriment. Re-employing team leader who was the subject of the allegations not a detriment.

Case Summary: The six claimants, who were care assistants, raised concerns regarding health and safety with their employer and the local authority. The claimants relied on s44(1)(c) and (e) ERA (detriment for raising health and safety concerns) and claimed detriments in relation to protected disclosures under s47B. They then complained of unfair constructive dismissal. The respondent asserted that the claimants did not hold a 'reasonable belief' and put in issue whether they acted in 'good faith'. Their concerns centred on allegations of neglect or ill-treatment of residents which be claimed to have witnessed at a care house. The respondent further alleged the claimants knew the allegations were false.

The claimants complained to the local authority, the London Borough of Bromley. The ET thought it useful, and the local authority agreed, to provide copies of their notes from the initial disclosure and the reports following their investigation.

The ET found that the claimants possessed a reasonable belief in the truth of many acts (not that the events alleged occurred as a matter of fact). They upheld 35 different allegations including the following:

(1) Shopping done for residents would include sweets eaten by staff (held to be a qualifying disclosure made in good faith under s43B(1)(a)).

(2) Taking newspapers from residents. This caused residents to look for them which led the member of staff to say they had mislaid the paper. This was a health and safety concern as it would harm their well-being and undermine their belief in the reliability of their memory.

(3) Bruises on the wrists of one resident. This was a qualifying disclosure relating to health and safety made in good faith.

(4) If a resident was unwell the member of staff was reluctant to call a GP. This was a qualifying disclosure relating to health and safety made in good faith.

(5) Residents left unwashed and still in bed when they were not supposed to be. This was a qualifying disclosure relating to health and safety made in good faith.

(6) Not recording medication given. The ET took note of the Local Authority's commissioned reports that supported the allegation. This was a qualifying disclosure relating to health and safety made in good faith.

(7) Pushing a resident into her bedroom and shouting when she became incontinent. This was a qualifying disclosure relating to health and safety made in good faith.

(8) Serious mistakes in the administration of medication. This was a qualifying disclosure relating to health and safety made in good faith.

(9) Care plan altered to show resident was given drug when she had not. This was a qualifying disclosure relating to health and safety and forgery and was made in good faith.

(10) Failing to change catheter bag. This was a qualifying disclosure relating to health and safety made in good faith.

(11) Not giving painkillers when required. This was a qualifying disclosure relating to health and safety made in good faith.

(12) Being left in urine-soaked bed and not given adequate fluids. This was a qualifying disclosure relating to health and safety made in good faith.

(13) A resident falling and no GP being called, together with fact her bed was too close to a radiator. This was a qualifying disclosure relating to health and safety made in good faith.

(14) Washing a resident's face with a flannel dirty with faeces. This was a qualifying disclosure relating to health and safety made in good faith.

(15) A member of staff kicked a resident. This was a qualifying disclosure relating to health and safety made in good faith.

Upon receipt of these allegations the local authority organized an inter-agency meeting where police interviews were arranged and the purported culprit was suspended immediately.

The identity of the claimants became widespread knowledge and the ET found they were shunned by staff and the group soon became known as 'they'. One member of staff began to keep file notes of their shortcomings. Detriments continued and included pushing, hostile looks, being ignored, banging a vacuum cleaner into the legs of one of them.

The ET grouped the detriments into timeframes from which it could consider the claimants' decisions to resign and complaints of constructive dismissal. It considered that s44 (detriments for raising health and safety concerns) was likely to become 'increasingly academic' following PIDA.

The ET found that the respondent did not subject the claimants to any detriments after 2 July 1999 when they started sick leave. The payment of sick pay was not a detriment, but a contractual requirement. Further the culprit's return to work following her suspension was found not to be a detriment to the claimants. Finally, given that the claimants resigned between 18 October and 14 January the ET found their complaints of constructive dismissal were 'stale' and therefore out of time.

Result: they suffered detriments.

Detriment: see above for the list.

Sections considered: s43B; 44; 47B ERA.

Damages: between £1,000 and £1,500.

Relevant cases cited: *Miklaszewicz v Stolt Offshire Ltd* [2002] IRLR 344; *Cleveland Ambulance NHS Trust v Blance* [1997] *ICR 851*; *ICTS (UK) LTD v Tchoula* [2000] IRLR 643.

31. COKE V MOSS SIDE & HULME COMMUNITY DEVELOPMENT TRUST

ET, Case No. 2302271/01, 26 September 2001 (Manchester)

Headline: Allegations did not found reasonable belief that there had been a criminal offence.

Case Summary: This is a summary decision. It records that the respondent's Chief Executive Officer told the claimant to take steps to dismiss certain employees and to support allegations of misconduct when he knew these to be untrue. The ET was not satisfied that this amounted to a 'criminal offence' or that the non-renewal of the claimant's contract was as a direct result of his disclosure.

Result: no disclosure.

Detriment: none.

Sections considered: 43B(1)(a) ERA.

Damages: none.

Relevant cases cited: none.

32. Collins v National Trust

ET, Case No. 2507255/05 17 January 2006 (Newcastle upon Tyne)

Headline: s43H: disclosure to press.

Case summary: Mr Collins genuinely and reasonably believed that a draft report he disclosed to the press relating to contaminated land showed that the environment was likely to be damaged [s43B(1)(d) ERA], that health and safety was likely to be endangered with the potential to cause damage to workers and public, including children [s43B(1)(d) ERA] and that information about this was being concealed [s43B(1)(f) ERA]. The ET held that the reason for dismissal was the disclosure of the content of the report to the press in relation to the requirement that the disclosure be of an 'exceptionally serious nature' they accepted that to gain protection the relevant failure must be 'very serious indeed'. In concluding that this test was satisfied they took into account in particular that there were three relevant failures: damage to the environment, endangerment of health and safety to the public and concealment of information. The public were invited on to the land for recreational purposes. Children played there and were identified in the report as especially at risk. The National Trust was a well-known and well-respected conservation charity in which the public places special trust and confidence, and the disclosure related to land which the Trust owned and managed.

The ET accepted that the Trust may have acted reasonably in adopting a strategy of further consultation before disclosing the report. However it stressed that the fact that the Trust may have been acting reasonably did not necessarily imply that Collins had been acting unreasonably. In this case the ET concluded that he had been acting reasonably in the light of his genuine and reasonable concerns about public safety, that there was reason to believe that disclosure of the report would be delayed and that the public should be able to obtain their own advice on the risks indicated in the report.

They found he made the disclosure in good faith [s43H(1)(a)]; he reasonably believed the information disclosed was substantially true [s43H(1)(b)]; he did not make it for personal gain [s43H(1)(c)]; it was exceptionally serious [s43H(1)(d)]; the circumstances were such that it was reasonable for him to make the disclosure [s43H(1)(e)] given he was genuinely worried about public access to the site.

Result: automatically unfair dismissal.

Sections considered: 43A; 43B; 43H; 103A ERA.

33. Daniel v Toolmex Polmach* (2002)

Headline: Causation: restructuring of company and redundancy was not in consequence of the disclosure.

Case Summary: Mr Daniel had for 5 years been a sales director for Toolmex, which manufactured machine tools. In autumn 2000, a new shareholder wanted Toolmex to double turnover without further investment. The following spring, Daniel and two colleagues became concerned about four instances of possible false accounting. Daniel raised these with the head office in Poland, which sought to assure Daniel that the issues were in fact in order. In the early summer, senior personnel were replaced including the person Daniel's concern most related to. Additionally one of Daniel's concerned colleagues was promoted. In July, Daniel was told his post was being made redundant and was offered a lesser post. The Employment Tribunal held that the evidence of the restructuring 'clearly shows that the process was well in hand before any disclosure and could not have been a consequence of it'.

Result: no automatically unfair dismissal.

34. D'Offay v Initial Security Limited*

ET, Case No. 1402289/03 Bristol

Headline: Inaction and action due to the lack of competence of manager not protected disclosure.

---

* Summary courtesy of Public Concern at Work.

Case Summary: Mr D'Offay had worked in a shopping mall as a Security Manager for twelve years. He enjoyed his job. After a TUPE transfer of his contract, he became concerned that new reporting requirements meant that his employer was not crediting the mall with undermanned hours, as had been the practice in the past. He was worried that this might be fraudulent and raised his concern with a colleague (R) who was employed by the mall management company (MMC). R dismissed his concerns, but D'Offay then took them to a higher level. There was an investigation, and, as a result, D'Offay's employer lost the mall contract and his employment was taken over by Initial Security.

After the investigation, R's attitude towards D'Offay changed. The friendly relationship that had previously existed ceased, and D'Offay was effectively ostracized. D'Offay complained to his employer about the treatment he was getting, and his employer directed the grievance to MMC. His manager also led D'Offay to believe that his grievance was being looked into by Initial's legal department. In fact, nothing was done for the next six months.

D'Offay, working in a hostile environment, with no progression on his grievance and without management support, suffered from stress and he took sick leave. Seven months after he had first complained to his employer about the victimization, he was told that the matter had not progressed at all, indeed nothing had been done. Although D'Offay was offered a meeting to discuss these issues, he was unable to attend because of ill health. In his view his employer had no interest in protecting him and he resigned.

Although the ET accepted that D'Offay had made a protected disclosure, and had been harassed and victimized by R as a consequence, it found that the subsequent actions and inaction of his employer to protect him were not because he had made the protected disclosure but because of the lack of competence and training of management. His claim for detriment under s47 failed, as did his claim under s103A (although he was successful in his claim for constructive unfair dismissal).

Result: no automatic unfair dismissal, but constructive unfair dismissal.

35. DONOVAN v ST JOHNS AMBULANCE* (2001)

Headline: Qualifying disclosure: suspicion with no reasonable basis. Detriment: no difference in treatment before and after disclosure

Case Summary: Donovan was a facilities manager for a charity from 1995. In 1999 Donovan learned that the charity's facilities management work might be outsourced. While Donovan was repeatedly assured that his position would not be adversely affected and he would retain his job title, he remained anxious and went sick. Donovan then discovered that a trustee at the charity had a 3 per cent shareholding in the company that would take over the work and he raised this concern. The ET heard that while only shareholdings of 5 per cent were required to be disclosed, the relevant trustee did declare his interest shortly before Donovan resigned. The ET found that Donovan 'had worked himself into such a state as to be highly suspicious of the respondent's managers. This suspicion extended to the conduct of Trustees but had no reasonable or rational basis'. They therefore held that Donovan's disclosure was not protected. The Tribunal additionally observed that the charity sought to reassure Donovan throughout and that, as Donovan was treated no differently before and after the disclosure, there had been no detriment.

Result: no qualifying disclosure.

36. DRING v GMB* (2002)

Headline: Worker: union branch secretary a worker, while branch president not.

Dring, a branch president and branch secretary for GMB, claimed she was victimized for giving evidence in a sex discrimination claim being brought against GMB. On a preliminary point, the ET

---

held that Dring was a worker within PIDA in respect of her activities as branch secretary (for which she was paid £3–4,000 a year) but not in her position as branch president (to which she had been elected).

Result: a union branch secretary could present a complaint.

37. DUDIN V SALISBURY DISTRICT COUNCIL

ET, Case No. 3102263/03

Headline: s43F: disclosure to wrong prescribed body.

Case summary: Dudin disclosed bullying and harassment in the workplace to the Council's scrutiny panel. The ET found that the appropriate person was the Health & Safety Executive and that it was not a protected disclosure because it was not made in the prescribed manner, despite the fact that the scrutiny panel was responsible for reviewing decisions and actions of the Council.

Result: no protected disclosure to scrutiny panel.

38. DURRANT V NORFOLK SHEET LEAD LIMITED

ET, Case No. 1500257/01, 30 April 2002 (Norwich)

Headline: Allegation in heat of moment, not a disclosure.

Case Summary: The claimant was a lead worker and plumber. The claimant was dismissed on the purported ground of redundancy by being given a letter following no consultation. There followed an 'almighty row' where the claimant accused his employer of 'fraud and theft of golf clubs'. The ET found that after the dismissal there followed a 'war of attrition' while the respondents sought to 'gather evidence from other employees, some very junior, in order to establish that the [he] was . . . dishonest'. The ET found that whilst the dismissal was unfair (given the failure to warn or consult regarding the redundancy which they found should have been admitted) they stated Durrant had 'not established or begun to establish any link between the dismissal and his complaint . . .concerning the provision of scaffolding'. They concluded 'there was no protected disclosure. Further, if there was, it was not made in good faith.'

They commented 'we doubt very much if the draft of the statute envisaged it being used in such circumstances where an employee who is being dismissed in the heat of the moment accused his employer of some nefarious activity'.

Result: unfair dismissal—no protected disclosure as allegation made in the heat of the moment.

Detriment: none.

Sections considered: 43B; 103A ERA.

Damages: settlement was reached but not recorded.

39. DR EARDLEY; DR WALDRON V LIFELINE CARE LTD*

ET, Case No. 3300707/03; 3300708/03 Watford

Headline: Disclosure to employer and Director of Public Health. Detriment includes suspension.

Case Summary: Eardley and Waldron were employed as medical practitioners in one of Lifeline's single vaccine clinics. Lifeline was run by a Medical Director located in Australia. Eardley and Waldron had several concerns about the vaccines they administered, including possible deterioration, contamination, dosage and a reduced potency because of the age of the vaccines. They raised their concerns in several e-mails to Lifeline's MD, who responded by directing that protocols and arrangements be

---

* Summary courtesy of Public Concern at Work.

put in place by the doctors, as well as indicating that the situation had to be accepted. The doctors were not happy with this response and wrote to the Director of Public Health, setting out all their concerns.

The MD then notified the doctors that, for economic reasons, their contracts were terminated on 90 days' notice and they were suspended pending termination.

The doctors claimed in the ET for unfair dismissal and victimization by way of action short of dismissal under PIDA. The ET accepted that their suspension was because they had written to the Director of Public Health and awarded them damages to cover their salary for the period of their suspension. When considering the quantum of future losses the ET took into account the stigma of being associated with the respondent company and the MD, and the possibility of media reporting of ongoing proceedings between the two of them.

Result: suspension was detriment. Automatically unfair dismissal.

Damages: Eardley received total damages of £66,170 and Waldron received £54,930. In addition, both doctors were awarded £4,000 each for injury to feelings.

40. EASTELOW v TAYLOR* (2001)

Headline: Causation: no inference that employer knew of anonymous disclosures.

Case Summary: Shortly after starting work at a care home, Eastelow made complaints about her pay and conditions. She then began to make anonymous calls to the local Social Services inspectors about quality of care and fire risks. When a resident died and Eastelow's own conduct came under scrutiny, she was asked to an interview. At the interview Eastelow got angry and then took time off sick. The respondent then dismissed Eastelow for unreliability, disruptive conduct, sleeping on duty and taking time off without notice. Eastelow claimed the reason was her disclosure to the Social Services inspectors. The Employment Tribunal found no evidence that the respondent knew Eastelow had made the disclosures and, as they were anonymous, it was unable to infer that the respondent knew. PIDA claim dismissed.

Result: no automatic unfair dismissal.

41. ENGLAND v BALDWIN LTD (IN ADMINISTRATIVE RECEIVERSHIP)*

ET, Case No. 6001820/01 London Central

Headline: s43K—consultant not a worker.

Case Summary: England created a company (C) which employed only him, and which hired him out to perform consultancy work. He drafted a consultancy agreement on behalf of C, under which C was to provide consultancy services to The respondent. England was to carry out the consultancy service. The Tribunal found, as a matter of fact, that this contract was determined by England rather than by The respondent or a third party (ie C) and said that as it was clear that England was on an equal footing with the respondent he could not be a worker for the purposes of s43K.

Result: no jurisdiction, as not a worker.

42. EVERETT v MIYANO CARE SERVICES LTD

ET, Case No. 3101180/00, 6 April 2000 (Brighton)

Headline: Interim relief application. s43H disclosure that resident of a care home being badly treated not sufficiently serious.

Case Summary: The claimant was a care assistant and she telephoned Social Services regarding the treatment of a resident. The Employment Tribunal were satisfied that the complaint was a

---

* Summary courtesy of Public Concern at Work.

qualifying disclosure. The Employment Tribunal were satisfied that the disclosure was the principal reason for the dismissal. They however found that the disclosure was not a protected disclosure as the case fell within s43G and the claimant was unlikely to show that the conditions in s43G(1)(d) ERA were satisfied. The claimant stated that she had no reason not to tell her employer as he had always been approachable. In this case the ET concluded that the claimant did not have a 'pretty good chance' of success which is required for interim relief. The ET found that the treatment of the resident was not sufficiently serious, to be exceptional under s43H, for her to disclose the matter to Social Services first.

Result: no protected disclosure.

Detriment: none claimed.

Sections considered: 43G; 43H; 103A ERA.

Damages: none, case then settled.

Relevant cases cited: *Taplin v C Shippam Ltd* [1978] IRLR 450 (re: interim relief).

43. Fairhall v Safeway Stores plc

ET, Case No. 2104468/01, 12 June 2002 (Liverpool)

Headline: Despite the claimant being ostracized the respondent could do no more—so no detriment.

Case Summary: Mr Fairhall was a company vehicle washer/cleaner. He was aware that colleagues were stealing from the company. On one occasion Fairhall learned that one colleague was going to steal some diesel. He therefore told his manager to keep an eye on a particular van, with the result that the colleague was indeed caught attempting to steal and was dismissed. Rumours began that Fairhall had tipped off the boss.

Unknown to Fairhall, at a meeting he did not attend the boss had told others that Fairhall had not tipped him off. The attitude of the colleagues was to ignore him. Fairhall had to take time off work suffering with anxiety. The respondent met with him and they pointed out they could not force staff to socialize with him. On his return to work a colleague was offensive to Fairhall. The ET found there was hostility from colleagues saying things like 'you have to be careful what you say in here'. Later the existing lottery syndicate was abandoned and a new one started excluding Fairhall. Whilst Safeway reprimanded his colleagues they took no further action.

The ET found Fairhall had made a protected disclosure. They rejected Safeway's argument that merely passing on information was insufficient, since it was implicit that Fairhall had been inform-ing his employer that a theft was likely to be committed. But the ET found that Safeway had done all it reasonably could to ensure that social behaviour was appropriate. In relation to specific instances of abuse or comments made, the Tribunal concluded that Safeway could have done more. However the ET went on to find that the decision not to do more was not based on the disclosure but on the desire to ensure the department worked efficiently. The ET also noted that it was not argued that the treatment of Fairhall by his colleagues, as opposed to the failure of the employer to act, was a detriment for which Safeway might have been vicariously liable.

Result: despite the claimant suffering a detriment from a protected disclosure the respondent's fail-ure to act was not on the ground of the disclosure.

Detriment: ostracized.

Sections considered: 47B ERA.

Damages: none.

44. Fernandes v Netcom Consultants (UK) Ltd

ET, Case No. 2200060/00, 22 February 2000 (interim relief), 18 May 2000 substantively and 6 July 2000 (remedy).

Headline: Inappropriate expenses claims raised by junior member of staff was a protected disclosure.

Case Summary: A claim for interim relief resulted in the claimant's contract subsisting until the determination of his claim. The claimant (aged 58) was an accountant and he raised concerns regarding payments being made for expenses without receipts by the Managing Director and Chief Executive. There was at that time a cash flow crisis in the company and they had difficulties paying corporation tax and contributions to the pension fund. Fernandes also mentioned that bonuses were out of control. The credit card expenses were £14,000. In total there were transactions amounting to £316,456. The claimant did not support transactions which be believed were fraudulent.

The claimant was sent home whilst the matter was 'investigated'. The claimant was met by the Chief of Security worldwide for the respondent's group of companies. The resultant disciplinary action was taken against the claimant for non-payment of corporation tax 1998 and 1999, late payment of employee pension contributions and authorizing company reimbursement for Mr Woodhouse. The claimant's appeal was dismissed.

The Employment Tribunal did not accept that the non-payment of tax and the pension played any part in the decision to dismiss. They found that pressure was placed on Mr Fernandes to resign. They found the dismissal was due to the disclosure and they were 'fortified in this view by our conclusion that had the UK management team not seen the letter of 28 November and insisted on action against Mr Woodhouse, he would still be in post'.

Result: dismissed for raising concerns.

Detriment: none claimed.

Sections considered: 43B; 43C; 103A ERA.

Damages: £293,441.

Relevant cases cited: *Maund v Penwith District Council* [1984] IRLR 24.

45. Fielden v Total Fitness UK Limited*

ET, Case No. 2104937/03 Liverpool

Headline: Deterioration in a relationship on grounds of a disclosure, causing a dismissal, is automatically unfair.

Case Summary: Ms Fielden had worked for TF for less than a year. She raised allegations of dishonesty against a colleague (H). H knew about these allegations and that Fielden had raised them and, when he made unwarranted complaints about Fielden to TF, Fielden was dismissed.

Fielden successfully claimed PIDA protection for unfair dismissal. It was accepted that the allegation of dishonesty was a protected disclosure. The Tribunal accepted that TF genuinely did not consider this disclosure when taking the decision to dismiss Fielden. However, it still found that the reason for Fielden's dismissal (whether because of her attitude or because of the unsatisfactory relationship between Fielden and H) was the fact that she had made the protected disclosure.

Result: automatically unfair dismissal.

Damages: The Tribunal gave a compensatory award of £1,467.

46. Frost v Boyes & Co* (2000)

Headline: Qualifying disclosures: reporting rumours covered.

Case Summary: Frost was a supervisor in Boyes' store, with 10 years' service. She reported to a manager that a colleague, T, might be shoplifting. The manager did not reprimand T. Frost subsequently overheard a conversation in the canteen from which she understood the manager was about to commit an insurance fraud. When Frost reported this internally she also cited rumours she had heard

---

* Summary courtesy of Public Concern at Work.

that T was having an affair with the manager and had had an abortion. Frost was summarily dismissed for making malicious allegations after the manager and colleagues claimed it was all a joke. The ET decided that Frost had raised concerns in good faith, that the additional matters had not been invented but were rumours she had heard. Finding Frost a very serious-minded and intense woman, the ET upheld her PIDA claim.

Result: automatically unfair dismissal.

Damages: unknown.

47. Dr Gammon v Stoke Mandeville Hospital NHS Trust*

ET, Case No. 2700909/02 Reading

Headline. Detriments and a constructive dismissal claim were not based on a previously admitted protected disclosure. No later breach of contract occurred.

Case Summary: Dr Gammon was a Lead Clinician in the A&E department at the Trust. She raised concerns about the professional conduct and competence of a fellow consultant (B). For a number of reasons, including the Trust's perception that the problem stemmed from a personal conflict between Gammon and the other consultant, she believed that she suffered a detriment for having raised these concerns. In January 2002 she brought a claim in the ET under PIDA. The Trust and Gammon came to a negotiated settlement, with the Trust admitting liability in respect of Gammon's suffering as a detriment for having made a protected disclosure. The Trust and Gammon agreed that she should return to work. As part of this agreement, the Trust agreed to circulate a letter to the A&E department and other departments in the Trust, clearly stating that Gammon had acted properly and in good faith in raising her concerns. The Trust also agreed that there would be an investigation into the way the matter had been handled so that similar problems would be avoided in future; it was clear that this would not be an investigation into the specific concerns raised by Gammon. The intention was for Gammon to return to work in March 2002.

From the time that the agreed letter was circulated to staff in early January, Gammon took issue with the way that the Trust handled her return to work. She felt that the terms of her settlement agreement were being ignored and that she had difficulty in communicating with the Trust. At the end of January a newspaper article appeared in *The Observer* referring to clinical problems in the A&E department. Although Gammon had not contributed to the article, she still felt that she was being blamed by members of the Trust who suspected that she had disclosed documents to the press.

As a result of this article, the local MP became involved, worried about patient safety and questions were raised in the House of Commons. The Chief Executive's correspondence with the MP, reassuring him that there was no risk to patient safety was copied to consultants in the A&E department and within the Trust. Gammon saw this as a breach of the settlement agreement. She was also suspicious that meetings held to discuss her return to work in the A&E department were actually about her fitness to return to work. At this stage, Gammon was assisted by the BMA legal advisor and her own solicitor. Although the Chief Executive thought that it might help matters if Gammon and B met before she returned to work, Gammon was unwilling to countenance such a meeting as it had not been included in the settlement agreement. Despite these setbacks, the Trust agreed that Gammon should return to work on 18 February 2002. Gammon declined to attend a further meeting scheduled for 15 February, on which date she resigned. Gammon claimed constructive dismissal and brought a further claim under PIDA for detriment.

The ET felt that the suggestion that Gammon meet with the other A&E consultants before she returned to work was sensible management practice. It was clear that the Chief Executive and her

* Summary courtesy of Public Concern at Work.

senior management team were aspiring to put the previous problems behind them and move towards a harmonious return to work by Gammon. On the other hand Gammon and her advisers spent 'considerable time arguing and nit-picking on the minutiae' of the settlement agreement. Although the ET did not doubt the genuineness of Gammon's application it did remark that it felt that her advisers were seeking to impose decisions on management against the 'background of a nit-picking interpretation of the Settlement Agreement', describing their conduct as 'obdurate and uncooperative in the extreme'. It was unable to find that any of the matters alleged by Gammon had been a breach of her contract or the last straw, and her claim for constructive unfair dismissal failed, as did her claim for detriment under PIDA.

Result: no breach of contract therefore no detriment or constructive dismissal.

48. Goldman v Thomas Cook Retail Ltd*

ET, Case No. 3201925/02 Stratford

Headline: Disclosure to police. Delay prevents claim.

Case Summary: Mrs Goldman worked as Senior Sales Consultant in a travel agency. In the immediate wake of 9/11 a potential customer's behaviour and appearance made her suspect he might be a terrorist. Rather than raising her concerns about the customer through line management, she went directly to the police. When her employer found out she had done so it not only told her that she could not give the police any information because of the Data Protection Act, it also disciplined her on the basis that, in going to the police, she had breached client confidentiality. Goldman received a written warning for unauthorized disclosure of personal data and Thomas Cook information. The effect on Goldman was that she was signed off work for two weeks for 'acute stress'. She successfully appealed the written warning, which her employer then rescinded and an apology was given to her. She was still unhappy with the way the company had handled her disciplinary treatment and asked for a grievance hearing.

When Goldman saw a named terror suspect in a national newspaper, his resemblance to the customer she had raised concerns about caused Goldman to ask her line manager for a copy of the cctv tape of the day he called at the agency. She also contacted the police letting them know of her suspicions that it was the same man. Following a misunderstanding by her line manager as to when Goldman could be interviewed by the police, she took sickness absence. By this time, her grievance had not been heard. Whilst off sick, Goldman tried to negotiate a financial settlement. Four months after the suspected terrorist had walked into the travel agency, she resigned.

Goldman brought an ET claim for constructive unfair dismissal and included a claim for detriment under PIDA. Her employer conceded that Goldman's initial report to the police was a protected disclosure. The ET found unanimously that the disciplinary action which resulted in the written warning was a detriment and it was an action based directly on Goldman's going to the police (the protected act). The ET also agreed that the acute stress she had suffered was an identifiable detriment. Unhappily for Goldman, her claim for such detriment was made outside the time limit.

The ET also found that the events which followed Goldman's successful appeal of the disciplinary action were not caused or influenced by her having made the protected disclosure, and her claims in respect of them were dismissed.

Result: protected disclosure admitted but it did not cause her a detriment that was presented in time.

Damages: none.

---

* Summary courtesy of Public Concern at Work.

49. GREEN V FIRST RESPONSE TRAINING & DEVELOPMENT LTD*

ET, Case No. 2505042/03, 13 April 2002 (Thornaby on Tees)

Headline: Protected disclosure to funding college and Chartered Institute of Environmental Health.

Case Summary: Mr Green was employed by a company that provided training and education services to various organizations. Some of the courses were funded by the local council and by a local college. He had worked part-time but in December 2002 he was employed full-time as quality and curriculum development co-ordinator. He reported to the sole Director and shareholder (S) and, initially, S appreciated his efforts in re-organizing the business structure.

Shortly after his permanent appointment, Green became concerned about a discrepancy in the funding arrangements for the courses that the company provided. It seemed that the company was invoicing for more hours of training than were actually being provided to the students. He asked S about this and was assured that the discrepancy in hours was justified. When S failed to provide documentary evidence to support these assurances, Green's concerns grew. He approached S again and she said she would deal with it and get back to him.

In the early part of 2003 Green's relationship with his manager deteriorated. There were still issues about his contract terms, holiday entitlement and mileage claims and his contract had still not been signed. At the end of March, Green wrote to S that it was 'time to just get on' with the contract. Rather than address these issues, S told him she was terminating his employment on one month's notice of termination but wanted him to continue to work on a self-employed basis. Green refused this and agreed with S that, although his contract was to be terminated, he could continue working there until he found alternative work.

Green continued to work at the college and had continuing concerns about the way the courses were run. In early July 2003 he wrote to the Chartered Institute of Environmental Health (CIEH) as the examination body, expressing concerns about the manager's conduct of examinations. CIEH told him that they would investigate. Green also looked into the company's paperwork and records, and this led him to believe that S was submitting exaggerated and fraudulent claims for funding. At the beginning of August, he raised these concerns with the Principal of the funding college.

Green then formally raised a grievance about several issues, which included the falsification of examination papers and the fraudulent claims for funding. S called a meeting with Green on 11 August, which Green taped (without S's knowledge). In the meeting, S asked Green if he had contacted CIEH, and when he said yes, S said that this was gross misconduct. S wrote to Green the following day terminating his contract 'due to irretrievable breakdown of communication and trust'.

Green brought a claim for unfair dismissal under s103A. The ET was satisfied that the reason for Green's dismissal was that he had made protected disclosures to CIEH and the funding college. It found that it was absolutely clear that the material factor in S's mind was that Green had disclosed information to CIEH. This was reiterated in her letter of dismissal. The question then arose as to whether Green had made these disclosures in good faith, as was required under s43G(1)(i). The ET considered the EAT decision in *Street*, and was satisfied that Green had made the disclosure in good faith; he had been rightly concerned about the impact upon his own reputation, and that of his colleagues, had the wrongdoing come to light in other circumstances.

Result: Green's claim for unfair dismissal succeeded.

Relevant cases cited: *Street v Derbyshire Unemployed Workers Centre* [2005] ICR97 (CA).

---

* Summary courtesy of Public Concern at Work.

50. Green v Warren Grieg & Partners

ET, Case No. 1700579/03, 14 July 2003 (Truro)

Headline: No reasonable belief that a criminal offence had been committed.

Case Summary: A smattering of incidents over Mrs Green's three-year employment period caused her to go to the police twice. Green, who thought her former employer owed her money, believed that Warren Grieg and her former employer knew each other and were working together to prevent her from getting what was owed. When she saw correspondence from Warren Grieg's independent financial adviser, advising the firm to complete the 'money-laundering forms' she went to the police for the first time. The second time was after a colleague said it was important that Green remain with Warren Grieg until the end of the tax year.

At a meeting to discuss a pay review, Green told her employer's principal that, believing that there might be money laundering, she had gone to the police. The principal asked Green to give him time to think about what she had done over the weekend. On her way home, Green told a colleague that she thought she had been sacked because she had told the principal of her money-laundering fears.

When Green was dismissed for gross misconduct she brought a claim in the ET for unfair dismissal for having made a s43G protected disclosure.

The ET dismissed Green's claim finding that she had no reasonable grounds for her belief that a criminal act had been, was being or was going to be committed, and so she had not made a qualifying disclosure. Her belief was based on the references to money laundering she had seen in correspondence that was openly available in the public area of the office, and on (what the ET described as) her 'entirely irrational' belief that her past employer and Warren Grieg were working together to stop her being paid monies she believed were owing to her.

The ET also said that Green should have gone directly to her employer to seek clarification. Green had not thought to do this, and her first and only thought was to go to the police. The ET noted that, even if she had made a qualifying disclosure (which she hadn't) it would not have been a protected disclosure within s43G as Green had not shown that she reasonably believed she would be subjected to a detriment if she raised her concerns with her employer first.

Result: it was a fair dismissal.

Detriment: none claimed.

Sections considered: 103A; 43A; 98(4) and it appears they considered 43G ERA.

Damages: none.

Relevant cases cited: none.

51. Gulwell v Consignia plc

ET, Case No. 1602588/00, 10 June 2002 (Cardiff)

Headline: Disclosure not in good faith as made to obtain promotion, as a form of bullying of others and to get own way with other employees whom claimant wanted to be disciplined.

Case Summary: Mr Gulwell was a sales administrator at the Cardiff Sales Centre. The ET saw messages sent by the claimant that were 'impertinent'. Gulwell kept a diary on his colleagues, noting absences and hours worked. Consignia decided to take no action against Gulwell but also took no action against the person (unknown) who had ripped out the pages of his diary. Gulwell wanted to take further his grievance as to his diary. The matter was considered by the divisional sales manager who found the issue 'bizarre'. Gulwell was not satisfied and appealed, seeking an 'apology'. He applied for a promotion and Consignia 'bent over backwards' to ensure he was interviewed despite concerns regarding his personal attributes.

The respondent asserted that 'what was disclosed at the meeting . . . does not fall within the definition of "information" because Parliament must have intended to use that word specifically and not to use other words, for example "allegation" which might import something which lacks a degree of proof or substance'. The ET however found that 'rights . . . have to be widely construed . . . to encourage workers who are concerned about matters specified in the section to come forward'. They went on however to find that Gulwell did not act in 'good faith' and that he did not possess a 'reasonable belief'. They found Gulwell made the allegations 'to be appointed as sales adviser [a promotion] and were being used as a crude form of bullying tactics by the applicant as a fact-finding, fishing expedition . . . holding over a number of individuals what they perceived to be the threat that they would be drawn into a public forum'.

Result: the claimant to pay £10,000 costs to the respondent (11 October 2002).

Detriment: none.

Sections considered: 43B; 43C ERA.

Damages: none.

Relevant cases cited: *Parkins v Sodexho* [2002] IRLR 109.

52. HASSAN v YAFA* (2001)

Headline: Good faith: where concern is known to be untrue and disclosure is for ulterior motive, it was not made in good faith.

Case Summary: Hassan was a development officer at YAFA, a small charity. After three months, he was warned about dissatisfaction with his performance. At this time a dispute arose whether a £47 cheque drawn on the charity had in fact been signed by Hassan's father. Hassan and his father went to the police to no effect. Three months later—when his performance was again under close scrutiny—Hassan alleged in an open meeting that the management committee were a bunch of thieves. As a result, Hassan was dismissed. The ET held that the disclosure at the meeting was not in good faith as Hassan (a) had not mentioned his concern internally for 3 months, (b) knew no money was missing, and (c) his motive was to try to divert attention away from his own shortcomings.

Result: no protected qualifying disclosure.

53. HAVERS v OCS CLEANING SOUTH LTD

ET, Case No. 3100829/00, 3 October 2000.

Headline: Causation: protected disclosures may have set in train events leading to dismissal, but this was insufficient to establish causation—the claimant was dismissed for gross misconduct.

Case Summary: The claimant was a regional manager for the respondent's office cleaning business. She was dismissed without notice aged 59 following 12 years' service. The claimant raised with her regional director that two managers were sanctioning payments to persons who were not carrying out the work they were ostensibly paid for. An auditor was dispatched who found no hard evidence. The claimant was not shown a copy of the report. The claimant repeated her complaints to the divisional Managing Director when he was leaving a party. The two managers then made allegations of wage irregularities against the claimant. The claimant was asked to attend a meeting which she assumed was regarding the two managers but she was questioned regarding her own conduct. As a consequence she was summoned to a disciplinary hearing. The claimant was too unwell to attend and asked for documentary evidence to assist her defence. The respondent conducted a disciplinary hearing in the absence of the claimant and dismissed her.

The ET found the dismissal had nothing to do with the claimant's complaints.

Result: unfair dismissal but no causation.

Detriment: none.

Damages: £17,103.48.

---

* Summary courtesy of Public Concern at Work.

54. Hayden v Dorchester Trinity Club Ltd

ET Case No. 3102769/01, 17 January 2003 (Southampton)

Headline: No detriment pursuant to s47B.

Case Summary:* Mrs Hayden had worked for Dorchester Trinity Club for nearly two years, initially as a bar assistant and then as club steward. Dorchester Trinity was a substantial business with a high turnover; but it did not have professional management and at important times there was no treasurer.

For the first few months following Hayden's appointment as club steward, her performance was considered satisfactory by the committee. However, less than a year after her promotion, various incidents occurred where Hayden openly disregarded committee instructions. The committee discussed Hayden's conduct and she was also asked to attend a future committee meeting.

Before Hayden was asked to attend the next committee meeting, two incidents took place. The first was that the lottery machine was left unlocked after it had been emptied, the second involved a shortfall in the bar takings of just over £1,000. Hayden wrote to the chairman saying she had found the lottery machine unlocked, and that she presumed that he would instigate an immediate investigation. When Hayden discovered the bar takings shortfall she contacted the chairman, who told her to keep calm as he was sure it would be sorted out. With respect to the shortfall, the secretary had put the cash in the office safe but had failed to put a note to this effect in the till. After this incident Hayden wrote to the chairman, asking that he instruct the secretary and committee members to follow proper procedures in future. She told him that should a similar situation occur, she would contact the police at first instance.

After Hayden had attended the full committee meeting, she was notified of various disciplinary charges relating to her behaviour, including undermining the authority of the committee (by writing to bar staff telling them to serve committee members last), failing to follow the committee's instructions, inciting club users to complain about the lack of heating in the club and making a false claim for payment. She was given a final written warning and told that she had to establish an effective working relationship with the club secretary and her behaviour would be monitored over the following month. Hayden was given the right to appeal.

She resigned and brought a claim for unfair constructive dismissal and detriment under PIDA. Hayden's claim for detriments were 1) the final written warning and 2) the failure of the club to give her an assurance that the financial irregularities she had raised would be investigated.

With respect to the first detriment claim, the ET accepted that an obligation to comply with club rules and 'to manage its affairs with reasonable care, competence and diligence' was a common law obligation, and that negligent management of club affairs would constitute a breach of a legal obligation under s43(1)(b). However, although the ET found that Hayden's two letters to the chairman pointed out administrative errors that showed breaches of the club's legal obligations, and were therefore protected disclosures, it also noted that these were only minor breaches. The ET also accepted that a final written warning could amount to a detriment under PIDA.

In considering the second claim for detriment, the ET said it did not rule out the possibility that an employer's failure to promise that unlawful action would not take place in the future might constitute a detriment. However, a failure to promise to take positive action in the future, such as giving assurances, could not be a detriment for s47B purposes. In this case there was no significant irregularity, merely minor failures to follow procedure. These were rectified and explained practically immediately. The ET said that it followed that there was no need for any investigation or assurances that 'financial irregularities' would not be repeated. The ET said that even if Hayden's claims had been lodged within the time limit, they would have failed on the merits.

Result: no unfair constructive dismissal, no detriment and no automatically unfair dismissal.

---

* Summary courtesy of Public Concern at Work.

Detriment: the claimant asserted that the failure to promise to take positive action in the future, such as the giving of assurances, was a detriment. The ET rightly found that the giving of such assurances could not in these particular circumstances be said to be a detriment.

Sections considered: 43B; 47B; 103A ERA.

Damages: none.

Relevant cases cited: none.

55. HAYES V 1. REED SOCIAL CARE
2. BRADFORD METROPOLITAN COUNCIL

ET, Case No. 1805531/00, 16 October 2001 (Leeds)

Headline: It is possible to be a worker for two respondents on one contract.

Case Summary: Mr Hayes worked as a social worker for Reed and was assigned to the Bradford MBC's social services department. He raised various concerns relating to vulnerable young people, including allegations in relation to handling by Bradford of care proceedings concerning a boy aged 12 and in particular the decision to reduce contact with the boy's mother.

Bradford undertook an investigation into Hayes's practices. This identified concerns which the council passed to Reed. Reed suspended the claimant and Bradford stated it did not want Hayes to return to work with them. As a consequence of the concerns raised against the claimant, he was placed on a national 'stop list' denying him income and the ability to work.

The ET held that Hayes was a worker with both Reed and Bradford MBC. Whilst he was employed by Reed under s43K, Hayes was directed as to his work by Bradford. The ET found that the claimant made protected disclosures but that the respondent's decision to remove him from the case was because they saw his actions undermining the security of the boy's placement in foster care. The investigation into Hayes arose from concerns raised 'spontaneously' by others and therefore not as a reaction to his complaint. The decision to report Hayes was made by others on an 'opinion based on evidence gathered' and they were not 'influenced in reaching those opinions' by his protected disclosure. Accordingly the claim failed on causation.

Result: no causation and no detriment.

Detriment: being investigated and conclusions drawn. Being placed on a 'stop list'.

Sections considered: 43K; 43A, 43B ERA.

Damages: none.

Relevant cases cited: *Regis Europe Ltd v Kelly* EAT 28 May 1999.

56. HERRON V WINTERCOMFORT FOR THE HOMELESS

ET, Case No. 1502519/03, 11 August 2004 (Bury St Edmunds)

Headline: s43H: disclosure sufficiently serious.

Case summary: Herron was working out her notice having secured alternative employment when a former client who had previously attended stating 'her partner had threatened to set her on fire' died following serious burn injuries. Herron had wanted to inform the police but was instructed to wait until the police contacted Wintercomfort. Herron did report matters to the police when they contacted her and immediately they asked to take possession of Wintercomfort's file in relation to this client. The officer placed pressure on Herron to hand over the file immediately to which she initially refused on the grounds that she needed to speak to a superior. Having attempted to do so and failed, she handed over the file. Herron notified the manager the next day. As a consequence she was taken into a pre-disciplinary meeting which, when held, was heated, and her invitation to the staff barbecue was cancelled. Herron was then invited to a disciplinary hearing. She was found to have been guilty of 'gross misconduct' which resulted in her transfer to another office, her supervision and the formal withdrawal of the invitation to the barbecue.

The ET held that the disclosure 'warranted protection' under s43H relying on the fact the disclosure was made to the police.

Result: protected disclosure.

Detriments: transfer to another office, her supervision and the withdrawal of the invitation to the barbecue.

Sections considered: 43A; 43B(1) (a) and (d); 43G; 43H ERA.

Cited: *Virgo Fidelis Senior School v Boyle* [2004] IRLR 268; *Zaiwalla & Co v Wailia* [2002] IRLR 697.

Damages: £2,634.

57. Hittinger v St Mary's NHS Trust & Imperial College* (2001)

Headline: Worker with two employers.

Case Summary: Hittinger was the clinical governance manager for the Trust and had been introduced and supplied to do the work by Imperial College. On a preliminary point, both respondents had said Imperial College had determined her terms of engagement and hence it alone was the employer for PIDA. The ET held both respondents were Hittinger's employer within PIDA, as s43K(2) expressly states employer 'includes' not 'is'.

Result: two employers potentially liable.

58. Holden v Connex South Eastern Limited

ET, Case No. 2301550/00, 15 April 2002 (London South)

Headline: Health and Safety representative 'ruffled too many feathers' and in making protected disclosures suffered detriments then was unfairly constructively dismissed. Sufficient for qualifying disclosure that relied on information received after making appropriate enquiries. Rejection of time limit defence. Continuing detriment found.

Case Summary: The claimant started working for the respondent (albeit a predecessor) in 1974 and from 1977 to 2000 was a train driver. Amongst other responsibilities the claimant was responsible for health and safety issues from the end of 1992 and appointed H&S Rep at the start of 1993 pursuant to the H&S Act 1974. The claimant took his health and safety responsibilities seriously and raised many issues.

Some of the concerns raised were:

(i) 1996–7 to 1998—unsafe walkway. Despite assurances the walkway was not remedied. The claimant wrote three reports. During one meeting the respondent 'threatened' to take away the claimant's licence to drive trains.

(ii) March 1997—reported slippery platform. Requests for meetings ignored and no response to the report. December 1997 three drivers injured on the platform from slipping.

(iii) March 1997—dangerous chairs. The first report was submitted before an injury, the second report before a second injury. The claimant was ignored and he removed the chairs personally.

(iv) The claimant raised an issue regarding a dangerous tunnel on behalf of another driver. The respondent said the matter was for Railtrack and did nothing. The claimant posted a health and safety notice and then a train was damaged by debris falling from the ceiling of the tunnel.

---

* Summary courtesy of Public Concern at Work.

(v) The claimant raised concerns over the lack of suitable rest accommodation for non-smokers. He produced a nine-page report. Nothing was done. However the respondent produced a note that the claimant had been seen in the rest room talking to two safety representatives who were smoking. The claimant was not aware this note was placed on his personnel file.

(vi) The claimant took up the temperature in the cabs which was recorded at 43°. He raised concerns about concentration being affected by such conditions. The claimant later reported the problem direct to Her Majesty's Railway Inspectorate (HMRI). This convinced the claimant that if he wanted results he must complain direct.

(vii) The claimant raised issues regarding drivers' hours and rest periods. He correlated the incidents of 'signals passed at danger' (SPADs) to the lack of rest and heat.

(viii) The claimant was concerned that a new working package infringed the Railway (Safety Critical Work) Regulations 1994 which state 'every employer shall ensure . . . . that no employee undertakes any safety critical work for such number of hours as would be liable to cause him to fatigue and could endanger safety'. He raised this concern with the Managing Director of the respondent asking for a copy of the risk assessment linked to the increase in hours. His requests were ignored or refused. Whilst there was a report his concerns were 'brushed aside' and he was never provided with a copy.

(ix) The claimant performed his own assessment and it concluded that 11 out of 20 SPAD incidents were attributed to tiredness. He reported his findings to HMRI. This report, sent in January 1999, was also sent to the Director of the Office of Rail Franchising; the Secretary of State for the Environment; the Principal Inspecting Officer of Railways; and the General Secretary of ASLEF.

Each disclosure was either admitted to be protected or the ET found it to be so, as the claimant believed the information to be substantially true.

The Ladbroke Grove tragedy was as a result of a SPAD. The claimant sent a copy of his assessment (see (ix) above) to Lord Cullum who presided over the public inquiry into this disaster.

As a consequence of the claimant's behaviour the respondent became critical of him. For example, when dealing with health and safety concerns the claimant was eight minutes late leaving the station with an empty train at 4.08 am. He arrived at the first station on time. He was served with a disciplinary form and given a severe reprimand. After the SPAD report was seen by the press the claimant was disciplined further. Eventually the claimant resigned.

The ET found that the whole of the respondent's 'conduct can be treated as acts of continuing detrimental treatment . . . the conduct forms part of a series of similar acts and failures the last of which is in time'.

They found that Holden made protected disclosures and the requirements of ss 43G and 43F were satisfied in that he made them in good faith believing them to be substantially true. The two reports he sent to HMRI were protected disclosures.

They found that the first report 'ruffled feathers at head office, they were not pleased about it [and] had to sort the [claimant] out'. There followed 'particular attention to the [claimant] and paid minute detail to the [claimant's] conduct and issued disciplinary charges against him where in the normal course the conduct complained of would not have merited going down the disciplinary process'.

Result: the claimant was 'victimized' for making a public interest disclosure and unfairly constructively dismissed contrary to s103A ERA.

Detriment: many instances and importantly the cumulative effect was recognized by the Employment Tribunal.

Sections considered: 43B(1); 43 F(1); 43(G)(1), (3); 43H; 47B; 103A ERA.

Damages: total £54,320 including some costs and £18,000 for aggravated damages and injury to feelings.

Relevant cases cited: *Miklaszewicz v Stolt Offshore* [2001] IRLR 656; *Goodwin v CableTel UK Ltd* [1997] IRLR 665; *Shilito v van Leer (UK) Ltd* [1997] IRLR 495; *Mennell v Newell & Wright (Transport Contractors) Ltd* [1997] IRLR 519; *Edgar v The Met Office* EAT 2001 unreported.

59. HOLMES V GRIMSBY COLLEGE

ET, Case Nos.1087380/01; 1808249/01; 1801049/01, 26 February 2003

Headline: The claimant was subjected to a detriment.

Case Summary:* Mr Holmes was employed as a research assistant on a fixed-term contract, and also acted as a UNISON shop steward. As union representative he supported a colleague (R) who had brought various grievances against the college. At a meeting to resolve R's position, Holmes disclosed to the employer that two lecturers had been asked to amend and falsify registers to increase hours recorded on courses. The principal initiated an investigation, which found that although the registers had been altered, this was a practice that was not restricted only to Grimsby College but possible across the whole Further Education sector. 'Considerable sums of money' would need to be invested in order to deal with it. There had been some confusion as to whether R or Holmes had raised the issue, and the investigating report said that Holmes was wrongly claiming credit for the disclosure. It noted that this was not the appropriate way in which such a disclosure should have been made, that a responsible trade union official would have raised it directly with management and that the action could be seen as malicious with the deliberate intention of harming a line manager in the college.

Subsequently the college charged Holmes with gross misconduct for having used privileged information while acting in the capacity of union representative. At the disciplinary hearing the employer decided that Holmes had claimed to be a whistleblower but he had not used the correct Whistleblowing Procedure. Holmes was given a written warning for 'a serious offence of misconduct' that was to remain on his file for 12 months.

At about the same time the college had decided to cut back on staffing numbers for financial reasons. It was decided that Holmes's fixed-term contract would not be renewed. Although he applied for various posts within the college, Holmes was made redundant and claimed in the ET that he had been victimized for having made a protected disclosure.

The ET said that the core reason that the disciplinary sanction was imposed on Holmes was because he had made a protected disclosure and found in his favour. The information he revealed was accepted as correct by the college, and showed there had been a breach of a legal obligation to keep correct registers. The ET accepted that Holmes had raised the matter in good faith and said that it was unsatisfactory that he should have been charged with gross misconduct. It said it was surprising that Holmes was given a warning for such conduct, whilst the two lecturers who had been found to have falsified the records, although disciplined, were not treated as liable for dismissal. In this context, the ET said that the college's disciplinary sanctions were 'impenetrable'.

Result: having made a protected disclosure the claimant suffered a detriment in receiving a warning for gross misconduct for claiming he had made a protected disclosure.

Detriment: receipt of a warning for gross misconduct.

Sections considered: 43A; 43B; 47B; 103A.

Damages: the claimant had requested no financial award, having obtained similar employment, and he did not seek reinstatement. No assessment of the injury to the claimant's feelings as a consequence of his detriment was undertaken and therefore no award made.

Relevant cases cited: *Aspinall v MSI Mech Forge Ltd* EAT/891/01.

---

* Summary courtesy of Public Concern at Work.

60. Hough v Virtual Presence* (2001)

Headline: Reason: breach of confidence contrary to PIDA.

Case Summary: Hough was the Managing Director of Virtual Presence, which was being merged with another company. ET had no doubt that Hough's dismissal for breach of confidence was because he had raised concerns that false invoices were being used by M to support the merger proposal.

Result: automatically unfair dismissal.

Damages: awarded £123,677.

61. Hutcheson v The Key Group (KGI) South*

ET, Case No. 3100213/03 Brighton

Headline: Disclosure unknown to dismissing officer. No causation for claim.

Case Summary: Hutcheson was employed for less than a year when he was dismissed. He claimed for unfair dismissal under PIDA. He claimed that he had found out that the manager (D) at the branch where he worked was forging employee signatures on their P46 tax forms and that he had confronted D about this. There was no documentary evidence to support his claim, nor had Hutcheson raised his concerns to anyone else in the company.

On the other hand, the employer's evidence showed that the Finance Director (H) had made monthly recommendations that Hutcheson should be dismissed or made redundant as he had not contributed to the branch's performance. The only reason these recommendations had not been acted on was because the Operations Director (O) thought that Hutcheson should be given more time to make an impact.

The Tribunal dismissed Hutcheson's claim. It found that, even if D had forged signatures, and Hutcheson had raised concerns about this practice, it was not the principal reason for his dismissal. Although the dismissal was carried out by D, she was merely carrying out the instructions of O and H, neither of whom was aware of the allegations that Hutcheson had made against D. Neither was there anything to suggest that there was a conspiracy between these two directors and D.

Result: dismissal not linked to disclosure.

62. Jeffrey v The London Borough of Merton

ET, Case No. 2304242/02, 4 April 2003 (London South)

Headline: Setting up a website to ventilate grievances was not a public interest disclosure. Failure to raise first with employer indicated absence of good faith.

Case Summary: From the summary reasons the claimant produced a website critical of the respondent. The website indirectly referred to allegations of 'jobs for boys' and recruitment. However the claimant had never previously raised these concerns under the grievance procedure or whistleblowing procedure.

The ET found that it was not reasonable or in good faith for the claimant to make such allegations publicly, or threaten to make them public, when he had not previously raised them.

Result: no protected disclosure.

Sections considered: 43B and 43G ERA.

63. Johnson v Powerworld Limited*

ET, Case No. 2502218/02 Newcastle upon Tyne

Headline: Disclosure to Environmental Health protected.

---

* Summary courtesy of Public Concern at Work.

Case Summary: Johnson had worked as manager in a club where food and drink were served. Less than three months after he was employed, he found out that chilled and frozen food was being kept in fridges that were being switched off at night. He raised concerns about the effect this would have on the food with one of the directors who dismissed his concerns and told him to do nothing about the food. A few days later another member of staff told Johnson that the food in the freezer smelled bad. Johnson checked and found this to be the case, and the temperature in the freezers was 10° below what it should have been; further, some of the food showed evidence of being re-frozen. As the director had dismissed his concerns Johnson contacted the Environmental Health Department who told him that the food needed to be disposed of under supervision. Johnson's employer told him not to contact EDH and not to get rid of the food. The following day there was an EHD inspection of the club. Johnson told the inspector that the fridges and freezers had been switched off at nights and the food in the freezers was disposed of.

Johnson's employer dismissed him a few days later. Johnson successfully brought an ET claim with the Tribunal recognizing that he had been dismissed for making a protected disclosure to both his employer and an Environmental Health Officer.

Result: automatic unfair dismissal.

Damages: £12,789.

64. KAJENCKI V TORRINGTON HOMES*

ET, Case No. 3302912/01, 30 September 2002 (Watford)

Headline: Good faith. Disclosure made for ulterior motive.

Case Summary: Kajencki brought a claim for detriment under s47B. She had worked as the manager of a residential care home and, although initially her employer indicated that it was happy with her overall performance, there were difficulties in the employment relationship. She resigned and brought a claim for unfair dismissal and for detriment under s47B. During her employment, which was for less than a year, Kajencki had raised concerns with the Joint Inspection Unit about standards of food hygiene and staff training.

The ET considered whether this amounted to a disclosure under s43G, and found that although there was some basis to the information that she had disclosed, her disclosures were not made in good faith. It found that Kajencki had made the disclosures to secure effective control over the running of the home from her employer. The ET took into account that Kajencki had acted against her employer's interests by encouraging staff to present the JUI inspectors with their written complaints and found that she had been reckless in the statements she made relating to training. It accepted that Kajencki had raised concerns with her employer about staffing levels, and, although not identical, these concerns were, in general terms, substantially the same as the concerns she raised with the inspectors. However the ET was unable to find that Kajencki had reason to believe that her employer would conceal or destroy information relating to the failures she had referred to, and as manager of the home it was unreasonable for her to have made the disclosures as she did.

Result: no qualifying disclosure.

65. KAY V NORTHUMBRIA HEALTHCARE NHS TRUST

ET, Case No. 6405617/00, 29 November 2001 (Newcastle upon Tyne)

Headline: Satirical letter written to the press was a protected disclosure. Failure to remove final written warning pending appeal was a continuing act and the last in a series of acts, and continuous in that the policy of the Trust was to discourage such disclosures, which led to the sanction and the refusal to remove it.

---

* Summary courtesy of Public Concern at Work.

Case Summary: Mr Kay was a ward manager at Wansbeck Hospital. He was highly qualified. During Christmas and New Year, pending a government national beds enquiry, the claimant raised the issue of acute bed provision on two occasions with management in ward management meetings. He was told there simply were not the resources to make provision. On 3 January 2000 a course of action was decided following severe bed shortages. One proposal was to transfer medical and elderly care patients to a gynaecological ward in Ashington. Kay was not happy and wrote to the manager of the Medical Directorate.

Kay also wrote a letter picked up by the newspaper *The Journal* and he was contacted by a journalist and persuaded to change the beginning to 'Dear Mr Blair'. He refers to the closure between 1970 and 1997 of 200,000 beds in the NHS whilst at the same time the number of patients rose by the same figure. He concludes the letter:

> so Prime Minister, Mr Health Secretary and the NHS Management Executive, as you return bleary-eyed from your Christmas break (no doubt rested and well fed) spare a thought for this poor, sickly old patient lying hurting and exhausted on an NHS trolley . . . hang on a minute, we can't let patients lie around on trolleys; that would muck up the waiting time statistics. Quick Shove her into any bed you can find. What? We haven't got any beds! Well MAKE SOME. How about shoving those patients from the Elderly Ward into that old shed at the back—the one with the crib and baby in it? Yes, I know it's the Obs and Gynae Ward. They'll be fine there, even if they don't get any physiotherapy and the staff there haven't a clue about caring for elderly people. The old gerries won't complain; half of them are deaf or demented anyway. Tomorrow we can move them somewhere else—the laundry perhaps—with a bit of luck some of them might catch pneumonia there and create a few more beds. Happy New Year by the way. That new patient doesn't look too well, does she? No; poor old sod. Good job she's got the NHS to fall back on.

On 6 January the respondent was contacted by *The Journal* wanting to take Kay's photograph to accompany a story. The respondent's Mr Morgan gave permission. Mr Morgan asked for a copy of the letter but it was not sent for a couple of days.

The story was published under the heading 'Beds Chaos' with a picture of the claimant and colleagues outside the hospital in uniform where the name of the hospital could be seen.

There followed letters from the respondent to *The Journal*, a response from the claimant and he also wrote to the Prime Minister enclosing a copy of the newspaper letter.

On 24 January Kay attended a disciplinary meeting. He claimed the letter referred to national issues and denied it affected confidence, claiming it inspired confidence that real issues could be talked about. No grievance was ever raised by staff against the claimant.

The respondents then disciplined Kay and issued a final written warning finding he had acted in a 'totally unprofessional and totally unacceptable manner'.

He appealed citing Article 10 of the Human Rights Act and PIDA. His appeal was unsuccessful.

The ET quoted from Ian McCartney's report to the Commons that

> the Government firmly believe that where exceptionally serious matters are at stake, workers should not be deterred from raising them. It is important that they should do so, and that they should not be put off by concerns that a tribunal might hold that they should have delayed their disclosures or made it in some other way. That does not mean that people should be protected when they act wholly unreasonably; for example by going straight to the press when there would clearly have been some other less damaging way to resolve matters. The matter might have been remedied earlier by the employer, or an allegation might have been proved entirely false. That might have become clear if the worker had raised it with a responsible body first.

The ET found it was a protected disclosure that the claimant reasonably believed to be substantially true. They took into account the 'satirical skit' used to illustrate the alternative consequences of shortages. They accepted it was not for personal gain and that he had previously made a disclosure of substantially the same information to the respondent (s43G). They accepted that Kay was not aware of any other route to raise such matters than as he had and that it was in all the circumstances of the case reasonable.

They commented:

> much of the problem surrounding this case appears to have been the unwillingness of the respondent's officers to see the satirical nature of the way in which the [claimant] wrote. That is a manner of expressing himself which would be readily understood by most people. The [claimant] wrote a letter identifying no individuals and breaching no patient confidentiality. Against that he has received a final written warning which hangs over him for a potential three-year period. The effect is that other employees may be discouraged from making responsible use of their right to free expression . . . we think it right to construe the Employment Rights Act 1996 so as to protect the applicant's right under Article 10 and that it is fully proportionate for us to do so.

They found that it was the policy of the Trust to 'discourage employees from making this sort of disclosure and it was that policy which led to both the imposition of the sanction and the refusal to remove it'.

Result: claimant subjected to detriment on grounds of protected disclosure.

Detriment: final written warning for writing a letter published in a local newspaper and a failure to remove the warning on appeal was a detriment.

Sections considered: 43B; 43L(3); 43(G) ERA.

Damages: not decided.

Relevant cases cited: *Camelot v Centaur Communications Ltd* [1998] IRLR 80.

66. Leonard v Serviceteam Limited

ET, Case No. 2306083/01, 30 April 2002 (London South)

Headline: Automatically unfair dismissal s103A. Qualifying disclosure sufficient basis even though claimant did not know whether the allegations were true or not. Reasonable suspicion short of certainty sufficient.

Case Summary: The claimant raised a concern by letter. He was a plumber employed by the respondent who had contracts with local authorities. The material facts surround the claimant's attendance at a tenant's property: whilst there he was concerned the tenant would 'not let him do his job' as she was raising her voice and taking an aggressive posture. Whilst he did not feel in imminent threat of danger he left and telephoned his line manager, who was unavailable, so the claimant returned to the office and was seen by his newly appointed supervisor. That meeting did not sort the matter out. The claimant then attempted to speak to members of the respondent's management and as a consequence he wrote a letter setting out his concerns.

There was a dispute as to whether the claimant resigned before or was dismissed after the letter. The letter accused the supervisor of being involved in 'corruption matters'.

The ET found that the claimant had been dismissed. It postulated

> What is the legal position so far as the burden of proof is concerned? . . . We form the view that it is for [him] to demonstrate on the balance of probabilities that the reason, or principal reason, for his dismissal was because [he] made a protected disclosure. We consider that in a similar fashion to discrimination cases there may often be no direct evidence of the causation element within whistleblowing cases. . . . the case will depend on the inferences it is proper to find . . . in this case where there seems to have been a change of heart . . . following a letter sent that could include a qualifying disclosure . . . why [did] that change of heart [take] place . . . the Tribunal looks to the employer for an explanation and if none is put forward or there is an explanation but it is inadequate, then it would be legitimate for the Tribunal to infer that the dismissal was on whistleblowing grounds.

Interestingly the claimant gained the information on corruption from others and when he disclosed it 'he did not know if it were true or not'. However the ET rightly focused on whether the claimant held a belief and whether that belief was reasonable. They found that he had 'seen documents that in his view tended to implicate [the supervisor] which caused him to suspect' the corruption. They state 'to hold otherwise would seriously undermine the purpose of these statutory provisions'.

Result: dismissed for raising an allegation of corruption.

Detriment: none claimed.

Sections considered: 43B(1)(a), (d) ERA.

Damages: £1,000.

Relevant cases cited: none.

67. Lewer v Railtrack plc

ET, Case No. 2302352/00, 7 December 2000 (London South)

Headline: The worker was subjected to a detriment on the ground of his protected disclosure. Inferences drawn as to causation.

Case Summary: The claimant worked through an agency for the respondent at Waterloo as a computer systems engineer and in those circumstances the claimant was a worker pursuant to s43K.

There had been a spate of equipment disappearing from the room in which Mr Lewer worked. On one occasion a laptop disappeared from the room. The claimant found the missing laptop and informed the respondent of its location before a weekend. Over the weekend the laptop disappeared from that location. The location could only be accessed by a swipe card and the system showed that two individuals had entered the room. The respondent's security guard then informed the claimant that Mr A had entered and left carrying a bag. He also raised the fact that it would appear Mr A had also used a different card to enter the office.

The claimant raised his concerns regarding Mr A to the respondent.

The respondent terminated the claimant's contract on the basis of an allegation of fraudulently submitting improper timesheets following an in-depth study of the timesheets with the swipe-card system following an allegation of absenteeism. The allegation had not been raised with the claimant during the week following the alleged absence or with his employing agency.

The ET found that the disclosure was protected, falling within s43B(1)(a) and being made in good faith. They drew inferences that the dismissal was by reason of the protected disclosure.

The ET 'suggested' recognizing it did not have the power to order the retraction of the memo and a letter of apology with a reference regarding the claimant's work, to assist him prior to a remedies hearing.

Result: dismissal for protected disclosure.

Detriment: the decision to investigate the claimant; the decision to remove him; a memo critical of the claimant was widely circulated.

Sections considered:43 A; 43 B; 43C; 43K ERA.

Damages: £25,000 (agreed).

Relevant cases cited: none.

68. Lingard v HM Prison Service

ET, Case No. 1802862/04, 24 January 2005 (Leeds)

Claim: Constructive dismissal following protected disclosures then a breach of confidentiality and a failure to protect the claimant from detriments.

Headline: Failure to protect from detriments and a failure to treat her concerns properly caused automatically unfair constructive dismissal.

Case Summary: The claimant relied on five disclosures given the following headings:

(a) Falsification of history sheets:
   i. Alleged criminal offence and miscarriage of justice.
   ii. Protected Disclosure: the claimant had 'ample evidence' from the documents and from recognising handwriting to show that what had been an oral warning was misrepresented as a written one which could affect the prisoner's treatment within the prison. Breach of the Civil Service Code and Prison Service Handbook.

(b) '*Heil Hitler*' incident:
   i. Failure to comply with legal obligation.
   ii. Respondent conceded reasonable belief and the ET found the claimant's belief was that the gesture was intended to convey that the officer was behaving like a 'little Hitler'.

(c) '*Get slashed*' incident:
   i. A threat made by an officer to an inmate convicted of offences relating to children.
   ii. Failure to comply with a legal obligation and/or health and safety.
   iii. A prison officer had made the comment which was an incident of bullying a vulnerable prisoner. The ET found that this was not a protected disclosure in relation to a breach of a legal obligation of health and safety but that there was a failure to comply with the Civil Service Code and Prison Service Handbook making it a protected disclosure.

(d) Planting of pornography incident:
   i. The planting of photographs of children (including innocuous photographs such as ones from clothes catalogues) with a prisoner who had been convicted of offences relating to children.
   ii. Alleged criminal offence.
   iii. Respondent conceded if it was true this allegation would be a criminal offence and a breach of a legal obligation. The ET found the claimant did have a reasonable belief that another prison officer had incited the planting of the evidence—this belief was based on officers spreading a rumour he had planted such photographs and, whilst this alone may not have been sufficient, because the claimant heard the allegation from two sources, and in view of the officer's recent conduct, these two elements meant she did possess a reasonable belief.

(e) Assault on officer:
   i. Criminal offence and/or failure to comply with legal obligation; miscarriage of justice.
   ii. ET found that the assault genuinely took place even though the claimant's initial report was in the alternative. The ET concluded that, the recording of it breached the officers' legal obligation to keep accurate information which could have a serious impact on on the treatment of prisoners and in relation to release, parole and supervision.

Detriments found to have occurred:

(a) Identifying the claimant as the whistleblower to one of the perpetrators. This was found to have been done because the claimant had made the disclosure in the misguided belief he had an absolute right to know.

(b) Failing to follow the Prison Service Order 1215 to support and assist whistleblowers. The ET found there was a series of failures occurring 'mainly because different levels of management . . . deliberately took a decision to tell [the perpetrator] who the whistle-blower was'. They also comment 'although it is not necessary . . . [the detriments] also continued after the claimant resigned and after the Originating Application was presented'.

(c) Governor Forster's failure to afford the claimant 'protection, anonymity and support'. The ET found he 'failed to act appropriately with regard to the disclosure . . . and that he failed to afford the claimant proper protection, anonymity and support . . . because she had made a protected disclosure . . . [these acts or omissions led] directly to the claimant's resignation'. They found therefore these were acts forming part of the dismissal and not separate detriments.

(d) Governor Hodges' action. The ET found he 'gave no thought whatsoever to the claimant's protection'. They were concerned with his decision to inform the perpetrator immediately and 'conclude that that was done deliberately as a detriment to the claimant' and his subsequent failure to 'authorise and oversee an appropriate inquiry was on the same ground'.

(e) Governor Blakeman's actions. The claimant wrote to this Governor proposing various action. The ET found that he 'saw the claimant as "the problem"' and his evidence that the claimant had raised her concerns 'in the wrong way' was a 'belated attempt to justify the indefensible'. They found he completely failed to take any of the sensible actions which the claimant had suggested. These were found to have been 'done deliberately or subconsciously on the ground of the disclosures'.

(f) Governor Lowles' actions. The ET found he 'did not conduct a reasonable investigation . . . did not keep notes . . . failed to interview the claimant until . . . [she was] so alienated . . . she could no longer trust him [and] failed to acknowledge her complaint'. These were indicative of a failure to recognize the seriousness of her complaint.

(g) Collective failure of the respondent. The ET found pre-and post-resignation acts and that the 'Respondents totally failed to accept that the claimant was honest and genuine in her disclosure and was seriously at risk—principally . . . because they did not wish to face up to the unpleasant truths which were emerging'.

(h) Governor Slater's actions. The ET concluded that 'his failures to institute a proper Inquiry or even to acknowledge her complaint . . . were directly related to the disclosure'. It was, they found, his job to 'oversee the matter and to ensure that those persons who were responsible for supporting her did so and in that regard he failed significantly'. These were done directly on the ground of the disclosure.

(i) Governor Bullock. The ET found his actions were 'because he profoundly disapproved of the claimant blowing the whistle on her colleague'. The respondent tried to argue his conduct was on the ground of his friendship with the officer concerned; however they found it was on the ground of the claimant's complaints.

(j) Governor Phelan's actions. The ET found 'beyond belief that he could fail to recognise the serious difference between deliberately altering the type of warning recorded in the history sheets and simply correcting a mistake in them'. Having found he was not a 'gullible man' they had 'serious concerns about the reasons why he failed to recognise those concerns' and concluded that he 'failed to conduct a proper and reasonable Inquiry' failing to interview potentially relevant witnesses; failed to pass on the claimant's concerns regarding hostility and showed a total lack of urgency. They concluded that the possible effect of 'rocking the boat could have on his career had a major part to play in the low priority he gave to the Investigation' finding subconsciously that the detriments were nevertheless 'on the ground of the disclosure'.

(k) Mr Atherton's actions. Whilst he delegated action to Governor Slater, the ET found this did not 'absolve him from all responsibility' and his failure to act promptly 'indicates to us that he gave inadequate weight to the fact that there had been a public interest disclosure and the need to protect the claimant'.

Whilst the issue of delay in resigning and claiming constructive dismissal was live, the ET concluded that the claimant did not affirm the contract by 'accepting sick pay'.

The Employment Tribunal found that there had been 'failure by all involved to adhere to the requirements to support and assist whistleblowers, as set out in Prison Service Order 1215 (PSO 1215)'.

The ET found that 'the Act does not specifically state that an employer has a legal duty to investigate the disclosures which an employee makes'. They however go on to find that 'it is a detriment to a whistleblower to fail, deliberately or by maladministration or negligence to investigate legitimate concerns which directly affect the duties the whistleblower has to carry out, and which she was contractually obliged to disclose.' They continue that 'there would be a term implied into the contract of an employee that such matters would be investigated, although we do no not consider that it is necessary for us to determine this issue'.

Whilst the issue of delay in dismissal was live, the ET affirm the contract by resigning and claiming constructive concluded that the claimant did not 'accepting sick pay'.

Result: claimant resigned after having made a protected disclosure, the respondent failed adequately to protect her and therefore she was constructively dismissed. She was subject to a detriment under s47B.

Detriment: considerable, set out above, and the decision refers to her being called a grass and being told she should have 'kept her mouth shut', and hostility.

Sections considered: 43B; 47B; 48(1A); 103A ERA.

Damages: £477,600.

Relevant cases cited: *Parkins v Sodexho Limited* [2002] IRLR 109; *London Borough of Harrow v Knight* [2003] IRLR 140.

69. Llewelyn v Carmarthenshire NHS Trust* (2002)

Headline: Interim relief: no reasonable prospect.

Case Summary: Llewelyn, a consultant at the Trust, became concerned at the increasing use of nurses in his care to deliver expert services to GPs. A panel was set up to review the relevant services. This concluded in May 1999 finding that Llewelyn was primarily responsible for the irretrievable breakdown in his unit and should be replaced. Meanwhile a second panel had been set up under the auspices of the Royal College of Physicians. In November 1999 this concluded that Llewelyn was unsuitable to function as a consultant. After a period off sick, Llewelyn was suspended in June 2000 and dismissed in March 2001. In November 2000 Llewelyn had contacted the Audit Commission about his own position being a waste of public money and about other concerns. Llewelyn brought a claim for interim relief which failed. The Employment Tribunal held that on the level of evidence available to it, Llewelyn had no prospect of being able to dislodge the causal connection that his dismissal was due to the findings of the two reports rather than to his disclosures.

Result: no interim relief.

70. Maini v Department for Work and Pensions

ET, Case Nos. 2202378/01; 2203653/01 and 2203978/01, 15 October 2002 (London Central)

Headline: Allegations without supporting information did not amount to qualifying disclosures.

Case Summary: The claimant started work with the respondent in May 1991 and his employment ended in October 2001. The claimant's job was to visit claimants for benefits to discuss their cases and he was required to maintain a diary of these events. On 25 July 2000 the claimant was accused of making 'false entries in his diary'. Later it was clarified that he had been 'fictitiously entering names and National Insurance numbers in his diary'. On 8 September 2000 the claimant wrote two letters complaining. In the first he said he had been 'harassed by people . . . every day harassment, make fun of me and had a bitter hatred against me'. In the second he refers to 'huge amounts of corruptions on visits' later stating 'I can reveal a lot more organised corruption'. On a meeting of the same date the claimant said he wanted 'all aspects investigated and would like immediate action to be taken as there is corruption which needs to be investigated urgently'. On 19 September 2000 he wrote to the Chief Executive Officer suggesting he 'carry out very urgent investigation into the section part of Benefit Agency based in London. There is huge amount of corruptions and some of the things are very shocking and disturbing.'

The claimant relied on disclosures to the National Audit Office although the letter was not produced to the ET. He relied on a disclosure to the Chief Executive Officer dated 19 September 2000. The ET took into account the two letters of 8 October 2000.

---

* Summary courtesy of Public Concern at Work.

They found that the NAO and Chief Executive Officer letters were not protected disclosures as they merely made allegations and did not contain information tending to show one or more of the matters referred to.

As far as the 8 October 2000 letters are concerned the ET 'assume . . . (but without so finding) that they are capable of being qualifying disclosures. However we are unable to trace any possibility of the Applicant having suffered a detriment or being dismissed by reason of having written those letters'.

The Chairman refused to review this decision.

Result: no disclosure, but if a disclosure—no detriment or dismissal as a consequence.

Note: Maini was not represented. The ET adopted a very narrow (and we suggest erroneous) approach (compare *McCormack v Learning and Skills Council* below). The better approach would be to accept that the allegation of corruption engaged s43B(1)(a) and (b) (criminal offence or breach of a legal obligation) and to consider whether having regard to all the circumstances the claimant could reasonably believe this tended to show a breach of a legal obligation. A worker may often reasonably disclose little more than the bare allegation in the first instance, in the expectation of being invited to provide further details, and it would be inconsistent with the purpose of the legislation if this was necessarily unprotected on the basis that there was no supporting information disclosed.

Detriment: none alleged.

Sections considered: 43B; 103A ERA.

Damages: none.

Relevant cases cited: none.

71. Marchant v The Holiday Place* (2000)

Headline: Causation: no detriment against more vociferous whistleblowing colleagues.

Case Summary: Marchant, a travel consultant, put her name to staff concerns about the effects of telephone headsets in the office. Four months later, when colleagues had neck trouble, Marchant mentioned that she had read an article about the health risks of misusing headsets. Some months later, and within Marchant's first year, Holiday Place decided to make Marchant redundant due to a downturn in business. The following day, Marchant's mother complained to the health and safety inspectors who visited the office. Marchant was then dismissed and brought a PIDA claim. Marchant's claim failed as the ET held (a) Holiday Place applied 'first in, first out' redundancy selection, (b) the decision to dismiss had preceded the visit of the inspectors and (c) other colleagues had taken a more high profile role on the safety of the headsets and received no detriment.

Result: dismissal not related to a qualifying disclosure.

72. McCormack v Learning & Skills Council

ET, Case No. 3104148/01, 5 December 2002 (Southampton)

Headline: The claimant was not automatically unfairly dismissed pursuant to s103A.

Case Summary: The respondent is divided into 47 local offices of which the Bournemouth, Dorset and Poole office is one. The claimant was Deputy Director. The NAO was appointed as an external auditor to assist the respondent taking over the previous functions of the former TEC and Further Education Funding Council and it was agreed that the respondent was required to ensure better quality audit trails in the new organization. The claimant asserted she raised 'financial irregularities' with the external auditor from the NAO. The external auditor denied the claimant had used these words. There was some dispute over the actual concerns raised; however the respondent had admitted 'the Applicant believed that there were financial irregularities and that the Applicant complained to' the NAO external auditor.

---

* Summary courtesy of Public Concern at Work.

The ET found that the claimant had complained to the auditor regarding eight projects but did not specifically mention financial irregularities and was concerned with controls.

The claimant then on 18 July 2001 had an outburst during a management meeting and 'began what was described as a vitriolic attack' against a colleague, shocking those in attendance. As a consequence the colleague left the meeting and resigned.

The claimant later made a disclosure by letter to Mr Harwood, the Chief Executive of the respondent in Coventry. In her letter she complained of the disciplinary action taken against her, sex discrimination and bullying, without specifying details and ending with 'I have supported colleagues involved in trying to resolve financial irregularities, some of them very serious matters, including one where records were recreated retrospectively'.

Mr Harwood gave evidence that he did not see the letter and had left when the letter was faxed by the claimant. The claimant was suspended later that day.

McCormack, once suspended, was then dismissed during her probationary period.

The ET, dealing with a submission that there was a disclosure of information, stated 'we do not see how a person can disclose their belief without thereby disclosing information, and if we found that the Applicant had indicated either to Mr Harwood or to the auditor that she believed that there were "financial irregularities" we would be prepared to conclude that that in itself was a disclosure . . . within 43B(1)'.

McCormack claimed she had been dismissed for making disclosures about financial irregularities to (a) her employer and (b) the auditors.

The ET held that there was no qualifying disclosure. It stressed that the test of whether the claimant's belief was reasonable was an objective one. In relation to this it was noted that McCormack was comparatively new to the type of work she was doing and to the public sector and the ET considered that she had not carried out what were clearly reasonable enquiries before making any allegations. As such, although she had a subjective belief in the wrongdoing, the ET concluded that it was not a reasonable belief.

Regarding the disclosure to the auditor the ET applied s43F, noting that the NAO were a prescribed person under the Public Interest (Prescribed Persons) Order 1999 SI 1549. However the ET concluded that although McCormack believed the allegations were 'substantially true' (the higher test), her belief was 'not reasonable' when judged objectively.

Result: letters to the NAO and Chief Executive did not contain any information tending to show one or more of the matters set out in s43B(1). The ET 'assumed' the other letters were protected disclosures (without so finding) and could not 'trace any possibility' of the claimant having suffered a detriment by reason of those letters.

Note: this decision must be contrasted with *Maini* above.

Detriment: none claimed.

Sections considered: 43A; 43B; 43C(1); 43F; 103A ERA.

Damages: none.

Relevant cases cited: none.

73. McGreal v Kingsleigh Holdings Ltd

ET, Case No. 2400030/03, 29 January 2004 (Southampton)

Headline: The claimant raised concerns of financial irregularity using the grievance procedure for which he was suspended and then he resigned.

Case Summary: The claimant was a financial controller of the respondent. He resigned on 6 December 2002. He claimed constructive dismissal following treatment he received, claiming this was because he made a protected disclosure. The respondent was unrepresented and did not appear, having entered administration.

The claimant became aware of 'alarming irregularities in relation to payments . . . in cash and also a questionable . . . transfer of funds to Australia'. The claimant raised them under the grievance procedure. The claimant then raised them with Inland Revenue and Customs & Excise. He was suspended by being told to 'get out' by the Director of the company following the removal of his briefcase from his car and his mobile phone being confiscated.

When the claimant returned for the grievance hearing he was refused the right to be accompanied. When he returned rumours had circulated about his redundancy and he was not invited to a meeting to introduce the new Managing Director.

The claimant resigned.

McGreal was found to have made qualifying disclosures in that he reasonably believed that a criminal offence had been, or was likely to be, committed and that the directors were going to fail to comply with a legal obligation. His disclosures to his employers and to the Inland Revenue and Customs and Excise were also protected disclosures, having been made in good faith. The ET was satisfied that there was a breakdown of trust and confidence between McGreal and his employer and that his resignation amounted to constructive dismissal by reason of the protected disclosures.

Result: protected disclosure and detriment suffered.

Detriment: it is not clear from the decision what was claimed or found to be the detriment.

Section considered: 48 ERA.

Damages: Confidential settlement recorded 24 February 2005.

Relevant cases cited: none.

74. Mehdaoua v Demipower

ET, Case No. 2201602/04, 11 January 2005 (London Central)

Headline: Good faith: unexplained delay since alleged wrongdoing—fraud by manager—indicated lack of good faith.

Case summary: The disclosure concerned fraud in Demipower's Kentucky Fried Chicken stores. The fraud took place between 1997 and concluded in 2000 and related to the use of till voids and refunds. The disclosure took place in 2001. The ET found the delay in the absence of an explanation was a factor pointing to a lack of good faith. In relation to the detriments they found them to be 'minor and typical workplace difficulties'. Further when Mehdaoua first complained of the detriments he claimed they were victimization on the basis of his being summoned to appear as a witness in ET proceedings.

The ET concluded Mehdaoua 'did not act in good faith. First there is the delay in time, one year at least, between the fraud coming to an end and the disclosure being made, and no explanation for that delay in reporting it. Second, the disclosure was in fact only made when [Mr S] is dismissed, and appears to have been the reason for making the disclosure. Third in the Claimant's case the predominant reason for making it was to support [Mr S's] claim for unfair dismissal'.

Result: not a protected disclosure therefore no detriment nor automatically unfair dismissal.

Sections considered: 43B(1)(a); 43C; 47B; 103A ERA.

Cases cited: *Street v Derbyshire Unemployed Workers Centre* [2004] IRLR 687, CA.

75. Miller v 5m (UK) Ltd*

ET, Case No. 1101006/03 Ashford (EAT/0359/05, 5 September 2005)

Headline: s47B entitles award for injury to feelings.

---

* Summary courtesy of Public Concern at Work.

Case Summary: In considering whether it had the power to award compensation for injury to feelings, the ET relied on *Cleveland Ambulance National Health Service Trust v Blane* (The Times, 4 March 1997). In *Cleveland*, the EAT considered the effect of s149 of the Trade Union and Labour Relations Act 1992 (TULRA) and concluded that Tribunal's had the power to award compensation for injury to feelings.

Result: as s49(1) ERA contained words identical to s149 TULRA in material respects, the ET unanimously concluded that it had the power to make an award for injury to feelings in claims for detriment under s47B. The ET said that the arguments in favour of awards for injury to feelings in cases of trade union victimization were equally applicable in claims for detriment under s47B.

76. MONTGOMERY V UNIVERSAL SERVICES HANDLING LTD (IN LIQUIDATION)

ET, Case No. 2701150/03, 29 January 2004 (Reading)

Headline: Failure to x-ray air freight as required by airline was raised with Police, Department of Transport, Customs & Excise and then the Airline.

Case Summary:* The respondent's defence was struck out for complete non-compliance with the directions. The respondent was also debarred from taking any further part in the proceedings.

Montgomery worked as a night driver, delivering perishable foodstuffs to American Airlines for export by air from Heathrow. The perishable items should have been x-rayed before delivery, but Montgomery noticed that some consignments were not passed through the x-ray machine, although it was falsely certified that they had been x-rayed before being put on the plane.

Montgomery raised his concerns with colleagues and with his employer. About the same time the employer had taken the decision to reduce staffing levels and there was a lot of pressure to get work out and cut corners by avoiding the x-ray machine; indeed, a letter was sent to all staff telling them that the x-ray machines had to be by-passed, and staff had to 'like it or lump it'. Montgomery reported the practice to the Metropolitan Police at Heathrow who dismissed his concerns. He also raised his concern by sending a fax anonymously to the Department of Transport before going on holiday. When the practice continued, Montgomery notified Customs & Excise of what was happening, using their confidential reporting line.

Nine days after contacting Customs & Excise, Montgomery refused to deliver a consignment of fresh flowers he knew had not been x-rayed. Before the start of his next shift he was telephoned by the operations manager and told not to return to work as he was being 'let go'. No reason for the dismissal was given at this time, although, at a later date, Montgomery received a letter stating that it was 'due to redundancy'.

Montgomery, who had been employed for less than 12 months, claimed unfair dismissal under PIDA. The ET had no hesitation in finding that the real reason for his dismissal was that he had made protected disclosures, not only to his employer but, on different occasions to the police, the Department of Transport and Customs & Excise. It said that Montgomery had acted in an exemplary fashion to try to ensure the safety of air travellers and had brought blatant lapses of security practice to the attention of the appropriate authority.

(NB: Montgomery was awarded £39,000 although, as his ex-employer was in liquidation, he did not receive any money.)

Result: dismissal for having made a qualifying disclosure.

Note: Montgomery alleged his disclosures to the Metropolitan Police and the Department of Transport were made in accordance with s43F and they were found to have been made under s43F, but as these are not prescribed persons s43F did not apply to them.

---

* Summary includes material supplied by Public Concern at Work.

Detriment: none claimed.

Sections considered: 43B(1)(b); 43C; 103A ERA.

Damages: £39,000.

Relevant cases cited: none.

77. MOUNSEY V BRADFORD NHS TRUST* (2002)

Headline: Public disclosure: reasonable to go to media to defend colleague against unfair media coverage.

Case Summary: Mounsey was medical secretary to a consultant, P, who was concerned about quality of breast cancer services. Mounsey shared and adopted these concerns through and from 1999. In 2001 Mounsey was interviewed on Yorkshire TV and said that in her view P had been made a scapegoat. For giving this interview, the Trust instigated disciplinary proceedings and Mounsey then resigned. At the ET once the Trust learned that Mounsey had agreed to do the interview to counter media coverage about P which she thought had been unfair, the Trust conceded that Mounsey had made a protected disclosure.

Result: conceded protected disclosure.

Damages: to be decided.

78. MUSTAPHA V ProTX LTD AND ORS

ET, Case No. 2303086/99, 12 February 2001 (London South)

Headline: Routine differences of view lacking specificity did not amount to a qualifying disclosure.

Case Summary: The claimant was employed by the respondent as an accountant. She claimed that the respondent had been making various payments out of the usual financial set-up to various employees and/or contractors in breach of Inland Revenue rules and regulations. The claimant was dismissed within a month of her employment.

The ET stated it had considered 'whether . . . there was evidence that the main persons named . . . were intending to carry out or to attempt to carry out frauds on the Inland Revenue' and observed 'we came to the conclusion that certainly on the evidence before us there was no evidence that that had been the intention'. The ET went on to conclude that the claimant 'did not in fact make any qualifying disclosures in relation to the accounting issues in the case at any stage . . . our firm conclusion is that at no stage did she either orally or in writing flag up, say or assert anything which might be called an assertion amounting to a disclosure'.

Result: no protected disclosure.

Detriment: none.

Sections considered: 43; 43G ERA.

Damages: none.

79. O'CONNOR V MIND HALTON* (2001)

Headline: Causation: disclosure follows detriment.

Case Summary: O'Connor was told his post was being made redundant due to cuts in funding. On the day this was confirmed in writing, O'Connor wrote to his solicitors raising several concerns about the way affairs were conducted at his office. The ET held whether or not this was a protected disclosure, there could be no causation as the decision to make him redundant preceded his disclosure.

Result: no decision as to whether protected disclosure, since no causation of his redundancy.

---

* Summary courtesy of Public Concern at Work.

80. Olesinski v Tameside MBC

ET, Case No. 2400410/10, 23 February 2005 (Manchester)

Headline: Causation: submission rejected that performance-related dismissal was by reason of protected disclosure because disclosures affected performance.

Case summary: Olesinski was a contracts officer for Tameside MBC. She was aware of the European Community Regulations and Standing Orders aimed at eliminating potential corruption or favouritism in the awarding of contracts. Shortly after starting at Tameside during a meeting Olesinski formed the view that they operated practices that did not strictly comply with the Regulations and Standing Orders. In response to her concerns her line manager stated that they 'go over and above the Standing Orders' and that they were 'exempt from EC Regulations'.

Olesinski also took issue with the provision of work to her regarding licenses and leases with which she felt unqualified to deal.

Olesinski then in her work would raise issues with her line managers relating to the above issues. Her managers were found to have become 'frustrated' at her 'reluctance to deal with matters in the way in which they had traditionally done' which was 'placing unnecessary obstacles in the smooth operation of the Unit's functions'. Her probationary period was extended.

Having failed to obtain a satisfactory response Olesinski contacted Personnel. She was informed of and then raised her concerns through Tameside's whistleblowing procedure.

During the hearing the respondent 'acknowledged that there was some substance in the assertion that Standing Orders were not being complied with and that there could be a risk of EC Regulations being innocently broken'. Olesinski then had her probationary period extended again.

Tameside informed Olesinski of the conclusion of the whistleblowing investigation. The ET found however that Olesinski was at the same time 'having considerable difficulties in her work' upon which ground she was later dismissed on the grounds of capability.

Result: Olesinski made a protected disclosure. The extension of her probationary period was a detriment although it was not on the grounds of the disclosure and the dismissal was not for a reason connected to the disclosure, so not an automatically unfair dismissal. Her capability was the reason for the detriment and the dismissal but this was not connected to her disclosure.

Sections considered: 43A; 43B(1)(b); 47B(1); 103A ERA.

81. Owalo v Galliford Try Partnership Ltd

ET, Case No. 3203344/03

Headline: Reasonable belief: legal obligation; belief that employer would rectify a design problem was not a belief of a breach of a legal obligation.

Case summary: Owalo disclosed a design fault breaching building regulations, believing that it would be rectified. The ET found that this was not a protected disclosure as the belief was not that the employer was likely to breach a legal obligation (building regulation).

Result: no protected disclosure.

82. (1) Painter (2) Collins v Southampton Motor Auction Millbank Ltd*

ET, Case No. 3103894/03; 3103901/03 Southampton

Headline: Raising question regarding insurance of vehicles a protected disclosure.

---

* Summary courtesy of Public Concern at Work.

Case Summary: Painter and Collins collected and delivered cars to their employer's auction house. Some of these vehicles were not taxed, insured or MOT-tested, but, as was usual in the trade, they could lawfully be driven on the roads using trade plates. Painter was concerned that the trade plates he was given were not in the name of his employer, but in the name of another company, which was owned and operated by one of his directors (V). He raised this with V who made it clear that if Painter was unwilling to use the plate then there was no job for him. Painter left.

Collins was aware of this incident, and remonstrated with another director (B), letting him know he was unhappy that Painter had been dismissed, particularly as it involved insurance problems. B told Collins that any other person who raised the same matter would be treated in the same way. Collins also walked out.

Both Painter and Collins brought a claim for unfair dismissal. The ET accepted that both their concerns, raised with V and B respectively, about the insurance position and trade plates were protected disclosures. Taking all matters into account it found that the principal reason for the termination of both Painter and Collins's employment was that they had made such disclosures.

Result: automatically unfair dismissal.

83. P. C. v CCC LIMITED

ET, Case No. 2304244/01, 26 April 2002 (London South)

Headline: A grossly and irresponsibly overstated concern can still be sufficient to found reasonable belief, but it may not be made in good faith.

Case Summary: The dispute surrounds an act of sexual abuse. The claimant worked as a senior residential childcare worker in a care establishment, and he is a qualified social worker. He worked for 3 months and complained of unfair dismissal contrary to s103A.

The respondent operated several homes but the case concerned two which at the time had only male residents. One home 'A' housed boys aged 6 to 12, the second 'B' housed boys aged 12 to 16.

There was an allegation that two boys in house A had previously been abused. There was no evidence other than the claimant's testimony and the ET rejected it.

An issue arose over a new boy and personal hygiene. The member of staff working that night 'LW' had been unable to persuade the boy to wash his genitals. He telephoned RL who advised him as to how to approach the matter (despite this phone call taking place after bathtime). On handover the following morning LW relayed the issue to the claimant. The claimant denounced RL's advice. The claimant then spoke with RL about the incident. The claimant then on the next day telephoned MR to state that 'RL had been in the bathroom with [the boy] and had washed the child's genitals'. The claimant was asked the source, and he said RL. An urgent meeting took place between the claimant and the respondent. He repeated the allegation and raised another about a boy's use of a bunk bed.

There was then another urgent meeting between RL and the respondent. During this meeting they repeated the allegation to which RL apologized for the rushed change-over with the claimant and the ET found that RL then explained the misunderstanding.

The following night the claimant repeated the allegation against RL to another colleague. This allegation was reported to the respondent. The respondent then met with the claimant and he repeated his allegations. The claimant had been having working difficulties with staff and was given three options: resign, take annual leave and then return, or continue. The claimant sent a fax asking for minutes of the meeting concluding 'I do not feel I can continue my shifts until I am sure what action I need to take over this matter'. Two days later the claimant then contacted the local authority. The next day the respondent accepted the claimant's resignation. The ET found that the respondent was unaware of the disclosure to the local authority until after they had accepted PC's resignation.

The ET found five disclosures and it was conceded they were capable of being disclosures under s43B (1)(d), including in relation to washing/attempting to wash the boy's genitals, failing to follow a proper procedure when supervising the boy at bath time and the bunk bed issue. The ET found that the disclosures relating to following a proper supervision procedure at bath time and as to the bunk bed issue were qualifying disclosures. In relation to attending to wash the boy's genitals, the ET found that the claimant was only informed 'RL had attempted to persuade the child to wash himself'. The description of the act by the claimant had 'involved a material degree of invention'. However the ET found that whilst the allegation was 'grossly and irresponsibly overstated' the claimant had a reasonable belief.

Most of the allegations were found to have been made in good faith but the ET found that the allegation of washing the boy's genitals, when it was repeated with further detail added, was made in bad faith as it was a repetition with 'additional detail which was pure invention'.

Further, the ET found the reason for the dismissal was the claimant's refusal to work the shift he had been instructed to work. The claimant had failed to establish the causal link between the disclosure and the dismissal.

Result: whilst there were protected disclosures (as well as another disclosure made not in good faith) there was no causal link to the claimant's dismissal.

Note: given the claimant didn't work because of his concerns, this is an illustration of a distinction between a disclosure and conduct associated with the disclosure, and the principle that a causal connection with the disclosure is not sufficient to establish liability: see *London Borough of Harrow and Knight* [2003] IRLR 140 (EAT).

Detriment: being asked to sleep in—rejected.

Sections considered: 103A ERA.

Damages: none.

Relevant cases cited: none.

84. Perkin v St George's Healthcare NHS Trust*

ET, Case No. 2306256/02 (London South)

Headline: s103A principal reason for dismissal.

Case Summary: Perkin brought a claim under s103A which was dismissed by the ET as they were not satisfied that he had succeeded in casting any doubt on the Trust's principal reason for his dismissal as stated in their dismissal letter, ie his style of working and his manner of dealing with requests for information.

Result: no automatically unfair dismissal.

85. Pimlott v Meregrove Limited

ET, Case No. 1500625/01, 29 April 2002 (Bury St Edmunds)

Headline: Not an employee therefore cannot claim under s103A.

Case Summary: The claimant founded the respondent and was with his wife the controlling shareholder. The respondent manufactured wooden furniture. The Pimlotts looked to sell the respondent. There was an agreement which included the employment of the claimant to continue as an advisor following the purchase. The purchaser had purchased a similar company in the same business that was failing. The claimant was shown cheques that were to be paid and realized (looking only at outgoings) that these would exceed the overdraft. The respondent states that the claimant informed him to appoint a receiver. The claimant said he simply stated the respondent did not have

---

* Summary courtesy of Public Concern at Work.

enough money to meet the cheques. The ET preferred the respondent's recollection, taking into account the evidence of another witness who had worked with the claimant for many years.

Part of the agreement between the claimant and the purchaser caused a further payment to be made or a refund determined by the net asset value of the respondent. The claimant then signed the accounts (believing he was entitled to do so as the Director for the accounting period, despite not being a Director on signature). On the basis of those accounts the claimant sought payment of £84,976. The claimant made a telephone call to the respondent and asserted his claim and threatened legal action.

The respondent suspended the claimant. The reason was the improper signing of the accounts. The respondent then wrote that the figures in the accounts were not correct and dismissed the claimant. The dismissal letter referred to the allegations regarding the appointment of receivers.

The claimant relied on the disclosure relating to the breach of the legal obligation to pay wages and not to breach the overdraft agreement with the bank.

The ET concluded the claimant was not an employee and therefore could not claim a breach of s103A. They did not consider whether he was a worker.

Result: none.

Detriment: none.

Sections considered: 43B(1)(b); 43C; 103A ERA.

Damages: none.

Relevant cases cited: *Parkins v Sodexho Ltd* [2002] IRLR 109; *Secretary of State for Trade and Industry v Bottrill* [1999] IRLR 326.

86. Pipes v Bridgeford Lodge* (2002)

Headline: Causation: burden of proof on employer.

Case Summary: Bridgeford Lodge ran a care home for the elderly and employed Pipes as a care assistant and, after a year, as cook. Pipes reported to her manager a concern about oxygen for a resident, though the concern was not recorded as it should have been. Shortly thereafter Pipes was given a verbal warning for swearing within earshot of residents. Two months later a further incident of Pipes' bad language arose and she was summarily dismissed. Pipes won on PIDA even though she did not attend the ET as the evidence of Bridgeford Lodge was 'wholly unreliable' and it had failed to discharge the burden on it under PIDA.

Result: automatically unfair dismissal.

87. Power v Hampshire County Council
and The Governing Body of Hayling School

ET, Case No. 3101406/03 extended reasons sent 9 June 2004 (Southampton)

Headline: The claimant was subjected to a detriment having made a protected disclosure; s43C(1)(b)(ii) disclosure.

Case Summary: The claimant disclosed to the Chairman of the Board of Governors comments regarding the school's finances and that this tended to show that the school's Bursar was failing or likely to fail to comply with their legal obligations.

The outgoing First Deputy Head warned the claimant, who was to take that role, that she would be asked by the Bursar 'to sign cheques in circumstances where she would not know what the payment was for'. . . and that the Bursar 'took home more than his net salary'.

---

* Summary courtesy of Public Concern at Work.

The next term the claimant raised these matters with the Chairman of the Board of governors. The Governors determined to investigate the matters without recourse to the Head.

The respondent subsequently found that the claimant had made an 'error of judgement' in referring the matter to the Chairman of the Board of Governors. The ET found specifically that this was not an error and that she was 'a person who the Applicant reasonably believed to be a person who had legal responsibility in respect of the matter' pursuant to s43C(1)(b)(ii).

The ET found that the Head treated the claimant differently because he was aggrieved disclosures had been made by her to the Chairman, and that as a consequence it 'affected their professional relationship; he dealt with the Applicant formally and without warmth'. He delegated the claimant's authority to other staff in staff meetings and they found she felt 'disempowered and humiliated'. Later he produced a document for a meeting which questioned the claimant's 'professional competence and judgement with specific reference to the disclosure and accuses her of a lack of honesty' concluding he 'can trust in neither [her] judgement nor her honesty, I feel I cannot trust her as a colleague, especially in the traditional role of Deputy Head. I have serious reservations with regard to her competence and integrity particularly as an Acting Head . . . I do not believe, having on ability to trust the judgment of [her] that I can continue to support her work as an OFSTED Inspector'.

Result: the claimant suffered detriments following her disclosure.

Detriment: dealing with the claimant formally and without warmth; the Head writing that the claimant had no competence, a lack of integrity and judgement; that she had no honesty and that he could not trust her.

Sections considered: 43B; 43C; 47B ERA.

Damages: not known.

Relevant cases cited: none.

88. RICHARDS V THE TRUSTEES OF THE OXFORDSHIRE ADVOCACY DEVELOPMENT GROUP

ET, Case No. 2700261/00 Reading

Headline: Suspension on full pay to investigate a protected disclosure amounted to detriment.

Case Summary: From the summary reasons the claimant was a part-time coordinator with the respondent. The claimant made a protected disclosure and was suspended as a consequence. He was however fairly dismissed in relation to conduct.

Result: detriment suffered by suspension.

Detriment: suspension.

Sections considered: 47B and 103A ERA.

Damages: £1,000.

89. RIVAUD V EXETER CITY AFC LTD*

ET, Case No. 1701536/03 Exeter

Headline: Detriments were shouting and swearing. Constructive automatically unfair dismissal.

Case Summary: Rivaud was employed as Assistant Commercial Manager. His employer ran a football club. Within one month of starting work, Rivaud became aware that some of the players and the staff had not been paid. He also had received no wages. He investigated the company's paperwork

---

* Summary courtesy of Public Concern at Work.

and, in doing so, found out not only that gate receipts were not being paid into the company's bank, but that two of the three directors were taking out large sums of money on a regular basis.

Rivaud contacted the third director and told him of his concerns. When Rivaud went in to work the following day the other two directors shouted and swore at him. They accused him of industrial espionage and then suspended him with no pay. Rivaud went home. The following day he submitted a letter of resignation. He was, on the same day, contacted by the police in connection with a criminal investigation against the two directors.

Rivaud successfully claimed for constructive unfair dismissal. The ET found his resignation was because of the conduct of the two directors towards him, which amounted to constructive dismissal. The ET also found that Rivaud's disclosure to the third director was a protected disclosure, made in the belief that a criminal offence had been or was being committed, and was satisfied that Rivaud would not have been treated the way he had been (by the two directors), had he not made the protected disclosure.

Result: s103A: automatically unfair dismissal.

Detriments: shouting and swearing.

90. Robinson v Hartland Forest Golf Club* (2001)

Headline: Disclosure to prescribed regulator; detriment, suspension without pay.

Case Summary: 8 months after starting, Robinson became concerned that although HFGC was not VAT-registered, it charged its customers VAT. Robinson raised this concern with the Finance Director who told him to do as his conscience said. As a result, Robinson notified Customs & Excise. When the MD heard of this, he suspended Robinson without pay. The ET held that this was a detriment. Robinson, who then resigned, was awarded £2,000.

Result: suspension without pay is a detriment.

Damages: £2,000.

91. Saunders v Westminster Dredging Co Ltd*

ET, Case No. 1500083/00 Bury St Edmunds

Headline: Danger need not exist: perception sufficient. Health and Safety.

Case Summary: Saunders had been employed under a series of temporary contracts as a crew member on WD's barges. He was worried about safety issues on one particular barge. These included the stability of the barge in high seas and the system of changing crew at sea when they were required to jump from one barge to the next. There was also a problem with the bilge pump, a worn anchor chain and no guard rails around the cooking stove. Saunders felt that there was a 'climate of fear' on board, with temporary crew feeling unable to raise genuine concerns about safety matters for fear of not being selected for future employment, and he took it upon himself to complain about these matters to both the barge captain and the Superintendent. Saunders also complained to the Harbour Pilot about the seaworthiness of the barge.

Following a crew change, Saunders returned to shore on leave pending his next barge appointment. He was then informed, by telephone, that he was made redundant. He brought a claim for unfair dismissal under PIDA.

Having accepted that Saunders was a 'worker', the ET considered whether he had made a protected disclosure. It was satisfied that Saunders had complained to his employer about these safety issues.

---

* Summary courtesy of Public Concern at Work.

It said that circumstance of danger did not have to exist, but Saunders perceived that there were circumstances of risk to health and safety. The ET took into account his years of experience at sea, accepting that he had every reason to have anxiety for the health and safety of himself and his colleagues.

WD said that the decision to dismiss Saunders was because he did not have the necessary qualifications whilst another candidate for redundancy did. It said that it had decided to make Saunders redundant for this reason. The ET, however, found that WD was quite unable to support this, particularly as Saunders appeared to have equivalent qualifications. It also considered that although there was a contract term of 'last in, first out' at least four others were recruited after Saunders, and none of them had been made redundant.

The ET said that they were satisfied so that they were sure (and not just on a balance of probabilities) that the decisive consideration that led to Saunders's dismissal was that he had been grumbling about health and safety matters, and his dismissal was automatically unfair.

92. Scott v Building Management Services* (2002)

Headline: Employer's response to the disclosures.

Case Summary: Scott was responsible for certain alarms and electrical work for Building Management Services (BMS), a small firm. After 8 months when Scott attended a site where BMS had just fitted the electricity supply, the Fire Brigade was present and had put out a fire in a cupboard. Scott said the cause of the fire was that BMS had bridged a fuse with galvanised wire. He also said that his managers had removed the galvanized fuse and told Scott to say the Fire Brigade had removed it. Scott wrote to BMS about the incident but this received little or no attention. Two months later Scott was working at a primary school and saw dangerous live wires. When he reported this, BMS became angry. Scott wrote again and was then told there was no work for him. Two weeks later he was dismissed. The ET held that this was in breach of PIDA.

Result: s103A automatically unfair dismissal.

Damages: amount not known.

93. Sims v MASH* (2000)

Headline: Worker: unpaid secondee at charity not covered.

Case Summary: Sims, a doctor employed by an NHS Trust, was seconded most Tuesday nights to work for M, a charity dealing with prostitutes. Sims' time with M was paid for by the NHS Trust. When Sims failed to attend, as he often would, M would not complain, nor would it ask for sick notes when Sims was away ill, nor would it check on his time-keeping. Sims did not see himself as part of M but as someone who gave it services which his employer paid for. When M decided it no longer needed Sims' help, he claimed unfair dismissal under PIDA as he had previously raised concerns about financial issues. At a preliminary hearing The ET held Sims' claim would fail as he was neither an employee nor a worker within PIDA. On appeal, the EAT held there was no error in law in the Tribunal's analysis.

Result: not covered by PIDA as neither an employee nor a worker.

94. Smith v Age Concern (Manchester)

ET, Case No. 2407595/00, 11 July 2001 (Manchester)

Headline: Dismissal on ground of breakdown in trust and confidence where person subject to allegations unable to work with claimant was a dismissal by reason of making a protected disclosure.

---

* Summary courtesy of Public Concern at Work.

Case Summary: The claimant was a deputy manager of an Age Concern shop. She wrote a letter stating she was being 'hounded and harassed by' the new manager 'into considering resigning'. She states she was 'uneasy about [his] practices regarding the furniture shop' and raised issues regarding the use of a 'duplicate' receipt book instead of a 'triplicate' book. Further she mentioned 'petty cash missing'. Events she described culminated in an abusive phone call where the new manager was 'yelling . . . he would not be dictated to by any woman'.

The respondent wrote to the claimant summarizing her concerns and set up a meeting. The minute recorded that the manager's practices were such that she believed he was 'committing a criminal offence' amongst other matters. The respondent then interviewed the manager. That interview concluded with him stating he could not work with the claimant again.

The respondent responded to the claimant's concerns by stating that there was 'an irreparable break-down in trust and confidence' giving the claimant one month's notice.

The ET found that the letter and her comments during the meeting were a protected disclosure as the information tended to show the commission of a criminal offence. The ET found that the investigator during the meeting stated 'she could only give more information in the presence of' the manager which they find is 'outrageous'. They found the principal reason for the dismissal was the protected disclosure. The ET noted that 'it is not insignificant that [the investigator] was ignorant of the Public Interest Disclosure Act 1998'.

Result: s103A automatically unfair dismissal.

Detriment: none claimed.

Sections considered: 43B(1)(b); 103A ERA.

Damages: settlement was reached but not recorded.

Relevant cases cited: none.

95. Smith and ors v Ministry of Defence

ET, Case No. 1401537/04 and 1401899-904/04.

Headline: s43G ERA: disclosing conviction of child sex offender to press unreasonable.

Case summary: Smith and others became aware of a colleague's conviction for indecent assault on a child. A group of seven refused to work and the MOD refused to permit them to so refuse. The workers disclosed to the press that the colleague was a child sex offender, citing the proximity to a local nursery. The seven were dismissed for gross misconduct. The ET were not satisfied there was a danger to a local nursery.

Result: no protected qualifying disclosure under s43G.

96. Speyer v Thorn Security Group Limited and ors

ET, Case No. 2302898/03, 20 August 2004 (London South)

Headline: Good faith: disclosures made in good faith despite acting on instructions rather than in public interest.

Case Summary: The claimant started work for the third respondent on 14 May 1990 as an internal audit manager. At the time of his dismissal the claimant worked for fourth respondent. In 1998 the claimant then started to report to managers in the US but received no formal notification of a change of employer. Between 1995 and his dismissal the claimant worked outside the UK in Malaysia and Singapore. The claimant continued to progress and by his dismissal he had been appointed Vice-President.

Tyco International was the parent company of all four respondents. In 2002/03 the claimant was interviewed as part of an investigation by the Manhattan District Attorney into potential fraud and financial irregularity and in particular accounting and financial reporting. That investigation spread to the Far East and the claimant was interviewed. He was instructed to assist the investigators. He was interviewed in Singapore and once summoned to New York.

The claimant informed them of gross margin accounting arrangements but that he believed they were lawful, given their approval by Price Waterhouse Cooper. He informed the investigators of a fraud he had investigated in November 2002 in Korea, in which Korean government officials had been bribed by Tyco group employees contrary to both local laws and the United States Foreign Corrupt Practices Act. Having previously reported the matter to internal audit he did not believe he was informing them of anything they did not already know.

He also informed them of an accounting transaction under which construction contract losses of $50 million incurred on contracts performed in Singapore were divided between one respondent and a US Tyco company to minimize taxation liability, which the claimant believed was unlawful.

The claimant had during this process provided documentation and on 7 March 2002 he was requested to return to Singapore to collect further documents.

The claimant's Singapore office was locked, preventing access to the further material the claimant required. The claimant returned to England where he received notification of his dismissal by letter on 20 March 2003.

The ET found the claimant had made a qualifying disclosure. They state that 'we accept that as [he] did not, at the time believe that the PWC advice concerning gross margin accounting arrangements was unlawful, it is arguable that this falls outside the scope of section 43B(1), but this is a moot point . . . we consider that the information given by [him] about the Korean fraud also comes within section 43(b)(1)(a) . . . since section 43L(3) seems to suggest that the repetition of something previously known. . . may nonetheless be considered a disclosure'. As senior representatives of Tyco were present at the meetings between the claimant and the Manhattan District Attorney they were covered by s43C(1)(a).

The ET found that he was 'dismissed on the grounds that he had made the identified protective disclosures' and whilst the dismissal letter alleges 'gross misconduct' there was no evidence to show gross misconduct. They continue that 'the timing of the Applicant's dismissal so soon after the information had been given by him . . . leads us to conclude that the principal reason . . . was the protected disclosures'.

Result: the claimant made a protected disclosure.

Detriment: none relied upon.

Sections considered: 43B; 43C; 43L; 103A ERA.

Damages: total £307,646.41. Injury to feelings—£7,500 (assessed at bottom end of middle category).

Relevant cases cited: none.

97. Staples v Royal Sun Alliance* (2001)

Headline: Public disclosure: disclosure of breach of consumer law to a customer held reasonable.

Case Summary: Staples joined Royal Sun Alliance's estate agency division as a part-time negotiator. He raised internally concerns about health and safety of customers and the way financial services were being sold. Staples subsequently mentioned one concern to a customer. The ET held this disclosure was protected as (a) it concerned a breach of consumer law, (b) Staples had already raised it internally and (c) it was reasonable to tell the customer as 'we can quite understand why the applicant might feel obliged to inform potential customers so they would not be deceived'. However on evidence, The ET hold that the principal reason for his dismissal after two months was Staples' poor performance.

Result: protected disclosure did not cause dismissal.

---

* Summary courtesy of Public Concern at Work.

98. Vaux & McAuley v Bickerton* (2002)

Headline: Disclosure to prescribed regulator.

Case Summary: Vaux and McAuley were senior managers and were concerned that Bickerton was being asset-stripped, with assistance from people who were disqualified directors. They raised their concern internally and with the DTI. Bickerton's advertising of their posts amounted to constructive dismissal. The ET commended Vaux and McAuley for considerable courage.

Result: s103 automatically unfair constructive dismissal.

Damages: as both were quickly in good jobs, awards were £3,000 and £30,000 respectively.

99. Whitely v Manchester Seating Company Ltd*

ET, Case No. 2409217/03; 2400153/04 Manchester

Headline: s43D(1)(b) [legal obligation] and (c) [health and safety]: protected disclosure concerning state of wiring.

Case Summary: In May 2003 Whitely, a factory manager, raised concerns with senior management about the state of the electrical wiring in the machinist room. He advised that the plugs were overloaded and the extensions were overheating, and he pointed out that this contravened the fire regulations and could lead to prosecution. He was asked to obtain quotations for the required work, which he did, passing these on to his MD. Nothing was done. At the beginning of September he raised his concerns again. He was dismissed two weeks later, the reason given for his dismissal being that there had been repeated breakdowns in communications between whitely and other staff and that warehouse procedures had not been followed.

The ET accepted that Whitely reasonably believed that the overloading of the electric system was a failure to comply with a legal obligation and/or a health and safety risk, and his raising his concerns with the MD was a protected disclosure. The employer was unable to show any evidence that, prior to Whitely's dismissal, there had been any relationship issues with the other members of staff, or that warehouse procedures had not been followed, the ET found that Whitely's dismissal was because he had made the protected disclosure.

Result: s103A automatically unfair dismissal.

Damages: £9,363.

100. Wilgar v Ali t/a Wardour House*

ET, Case No. 1700692/04 Plymouth

Headline: Treatment of residents in care home reported to owner and National Care Standards Commission: protected disclosure.

Case Summary: Miss Wilgar had worked as the manager of a care home for the elderly for less than a year. Some of the residents were frail and vulnerable. When she suspected that one of the night carers was sleeping on duty, she told Mrs Ali, the owner of the home. The owner's view was that the culprit should be found, even suggesting a surprise visit which might catch them sleeping on the job. A short time after this incident Wilgar received an anonymous call. The caller warned that one of the residents was being mistreated on those nights when a particular care team were on duty. Following the tip-off, Wilgar paid a surprise visit to the resident's room and found the resident in a very distressed state. She had been tightly restrained by her nightclothes and bed sheets, and was lying directly on a plastic sheet. Wilgar immediately spoke to the care team on duty. She also contacted Ali and told her what had happened. Ali instructed Wilgar to telephone Ali's employment lawyers to

---

* Summary courtesy of Public Concern at Work.

find out what action could be taken against the carers. The lawyers told Wilgar that, as she had already spoken sharply to the team on duty, she should take no further action against them. Wilgar was unhappy with this advice.

Wilgar then issued a staff memo which she copied to Ali. The memo said that certain practices, such as restraining residents, putting plastic sheeting directly under them and sleeping during the night shift were unacceptable, and any member of staff found guilty of these practices would be disciplined and could even face dismissal. The next day, still unhappy that no action could be taken against the two carers, she phoned the National Care Standards Commission and complained. An inspector was sent to inspect the premises and Wilgar spoke to him at length about her concerns. Although Ali knew there had been a complaint to NCSC, she did not know that Wilgar was the complainant.

The week after the inspection, Wilgar asked a friend to phone in to say she was not well and would not be going in to work. When two days later, Wilgar had still not come back to work, Ali wrote to her saying that her conclusion was that Wilgar's absence meant that she had resigned. Although Wilgar tried to explain that her absence had been genuine, Ali issued her with a P45.

Wilgar's claim for unfair dismissal for having made a protected disclosure succeeded. The ET took into account that although she had only worked there for a short period of time, she held a senior position and Ali had been pleased with her work. They said that a reasonable employer would have asked after the health of an absent employee and, if they felt that she was about to resign, would have tried to find out what her intentions were. The speed with which Ali took Wilgar's absence as indicating her voluntary termination of employment was 'telling', and was because Wilgar had made the protected disclosure.

Result: s103A automatically unfair dismissal.

101. Williamson v Karl Suss (GB) Ltd

ET, Case No. 2702198/00, 2 March 2001 (Reading)

Headline: Wild allegations that chairman of employer was seeking to ruin British economy did not amount to reasonable belief in criminal offence.

Case Summary: The claimant was office manager from October 1987 to July 2000. The respondent manufactures and supplies machinery to produce microchips. She was concerned regarding 'the supply of spares and servicing to the respondent's' customers and 'increasingly long lead times for the supply of new machines'. Being on the receiving end of complaints the claimant relayed them to her German counterparts in the sales and service department in Munich.

The respondent was concerned by the claimant's action in faxing 300 pages to Munich in February 2000 cataloguing all the problems perceived by the claimant. The ET noted the respondent's concern regarding its tone regarding her counterparts in Munich and some customers.

The Chairman of the respondent flew to the UK to meet with the claimant. He expressed concern at her tone. During this meeting the claimant claimed that the Chairman and others were 'corrupt' and that they were involved in 'criminal activities . . . sabotaging the microelectronics industry to wreck the British economy'. She continued stating the Chairman 'and other culprits were corrupt and were members of the Nazi party'.

The respondent did not recall the allegation of 'corruption' and the ET preferred their evidence. The Chairman advised the claimant to reduce her hours and changed the person with whom she dealt in Munich.

There followed a separate dispute between the claimant and a local department store run by the John Lewis Partnership and she sent a fax to its Chairman. The fax was derogatory and offended him. The claimant had used the respondent's office facilities to further her own private grievances. Proximate to this incident the claimant also sent a fax to a customer of the respondent regarding non-payment, stating 'if you want to play, may I suggest you play Queen's Greatest Hits tracks 2, 16 & 17'.

The claimant was suspended and later dismissed for the above reasons and regarding concern surrounding a payment of £500. The claimant had declined to attend any meetings.

During the course of the hearing the claimant made further allegations which the ET found to be unreasonable. They found that her dismissal was fair and that it was unconnected to any disclosure, which was not a protected disclosure as any 'belief' in the allegations was not 'reasonable'.

Result: case dismissed and the claimant ordered to pay two-thirds of the respondent's costs.

Note: the Queen tracks quoted by the claimant are *Another one bites the dust*, *We will rock you* and *We are the Champions*, provided it was Volume 1 of the album. If it was the second volume then *Under pressure*, *The Show must go on* and *One vision* apply. Either volume seems poignant.

Detriment: none.

Sections considered: 43B; 103A ERA.

Damages: none.

Relevant cases cited: none.

APPENDIX 10

Precedents

FORM 1

CONFIDENTIALITY / INFORMANT / DELIVERY-UP INJUNCTION

CIVIL PROCEDURE RULES 1998 PART 25 PROVIDES THE RULES IN RELATION TO INTERIM REMEDIES AND THE PRACTICE DIRECTIONS.

DELIVERY UP ORDER

IN THE HIGH COURT OF JUSTICE QUEEN'S BENCH DIVISION

THE HONOURABLE MR/MRS JUSTICE 'X'

CLAIM NO:

BETWEEN:

DATED:

NAME, ADDRESS AND REFERENCE OF RESPONDENT:
THE DAILY RAG
1 SLEAZY STREET
LONDON **P4P ER5**

SEAL

BIG BUCKS PLC Applicant

- AND -

THE DAILY RAG LTD Respondent

PENAL NOTICE
IF YOU THE DAILY RAG LTD DISOBEY THIS ORDER YOU MAY BE HELD IN CONTEMPT OF COURT AND MAY BE IMPRISONED, FINED OR HAVE YOUR ASSETS SEIZED.

ANY OTHER PERSON WHO KNOWS OF THIS ORDER AND DOES ANYTHING WHICH HELPS OR PERMITS THE RESPONDENT TO BREACH THE TERMS OF THIS ORDER MAY ALSO BE HELD TO BE IN CONTEMPT OF COURT AND MAY BE IMPRISONED, FINED OR HAVE THEIR ASSETS SEIZED.

THE DAILY RAG LTD

THIS ORDER
An Application was made on _____ by Counsel for the Applicant, [and attended by Counsel for the Respondent] to Mr/Mrs Justice _____ who heard the application. The Judge read the witness statements listed in Schedule A and accepted the undertakings set out in Schedule B at the end of this Order.

As a result of the application **IT IS ORDERED** that:

1. Until [   ] or further Order of the Court, the Respondent shall be restrained whether by its directors, officers, employees or agents or any of them, or otherwise howsoever:
   (1) from making any use (to include the passing to any third party) of the report to the Board ('the Report'), referred to in the issue dated 29 July 2006 of The Daily Rag or any of its content and
   (2) from defacing, deleting any part of, or otherwise altering or tampering with the format or appearance of any and all documents and records which are the property of the Applicant.

2. The Respondent must immediately hand over to the Applicant's solicitors any of the listed items, which are in his possession or under his control, save for any computer or hard disk integral to any computer. Any items the subject of a dispute as to whether they are listed items must immediately be handed over to the Applicant's solicitors for safe keeping pending the resolution of the dispute or further order of the court. The Respondent must hand over:
   (1) the report to the Board or any extracts from it and all documents containing information derived from the Report.
   (2) all documents and records (in hard copy, digital or electronic form) which are the property of the Applicant.

PROVISION OF INFORMATION

3. The Respondent shall swear an affidavit within [two] days of the date of this Order:
   (1) confirming compliance with paragraph 2 of this Order.
   (2) to the extent that any copy of the Report or any other document belonging to the Applicant was, but is no longer, in the possession of the Respondent, and has not been returned to the Applicant, stating what has become of it.
   (3) stating when, how and to whom the Report or any of its contents has been disclosed by the Respondent.
   (4) identifying the person or people who disclosed the Report to the Respondent and what other information relating to the Applicant, or property belonging to the Applicant, was disclosed by that person or people to the Respondent and stating when and how the disclosure was made.

PROHIBTED ACTS

4. Except for the purpose of obtaining legal advice, the Respondent must not directly or indirectly inform anyone of these proceedings or of the contents of this order, or warn anyone that proceedings have been or may be brought against him by the Applicant until 4.30 pm on [date] or further order of the Court.

5. Until 4.30 on the return date the Respondent must not destroy, tamper with, cancel or part with possession, power, custody or control of the listed items otherwise than in accordance with the terms of this order.

COSTS

6. The costs of the Applicant's application shall be the Applicant's costs in the case.

RESTRICTIONS ON SERVICE

7. This order may only be served between [_____] am/pm and [_____]am/pm [and on a weekday].

EFFECT OF THIS ORDER

8. A Respondent who is an individual who is ordered not to do something must not do it himself or in any other way. He must not do it through others acting on his behalf or on his instructions or with his encouragement.

9. A Respondent which is a corporation and which is ordered not to do something must not do it itself or by its directors, officers, employees or agents or in any other way.

VARIATION AND DISCHARGE OF THIS ORDER

10. Anyone served with or notified of this Order may apply to the Court at any time to vary or discharge this Order (or so much of it as affects that person) but they must first inform the Applicant's solicitors [at least 48 hours beforehand]. If any evidence is to be relied upon in support of the application, the substance of it must be communicated in writing to the Applicant's solicitor in advance.

INTERPRETATION OF THIS ORDER

11. A Respondent who is an individual who is ordered not to do something must not do it himself or in any other way. He must not do it through others acting on his behalf or on his instructions or with his encouragement.
12. A Respondent which is not an individual which is ordered not to do something must not do it itself or by its directors, officers, partners, employees or agents or in any other way.
13. In this Order the words 'he' 'him' or 'his' include 'she' or 'her' and 'it' or 'its'.
14. Where there are two or more Respondents then (unless the contrary appears):
    (1) a reference to 'the Respondent' means both or all of them;
    (2) a requirement to serve on 'the Respondent' means on each of them; however, the order is effective against each Respondent on whom it is served; and
    (3) an Order requiring 'the Respondent' to do or not to do anything applies to all Respondents.

COMMUNICATIONS WITH THE COURT

All communications to the Court about this Order should be sent, where the Order was made in the Queen's Bench Division, to Room WG034, Royal Courts of Justice, Strand, London EC2A 2LL quoting the case number.

The telephone number is 0207 947 6009.

The offices are open between 10 am and 4.30 pm Monday to Friday.

SCHEDULE A

WITNESS STATEMENTS
The Applicant relied on the following witness statements—

Name	number of witness statement	date of statement	filed on behalf of
(1)			
(2)			

SCHEDULE B

The listed items:

15. The report to the Board or any extracts from it and all documents containing information derived from the Report.
16. All documents and records (in hard copy, digital or electronic form) which are the property of the Applicant.

SCHEDULE C

UNDERTAKINGS GIVEN TO THE COURT BY THE APPLICANT

17. If the court later finds that this order has caused loss to the Respondent, and decides that the Respondent should be compensated for that loss, the Applicant will comply with any order the court may make. Further if the carrying out of this order has been in breach of the terms of this order or otherwise in a manner inconsistent with the Applicant's solicitors' duties as officers of the court, the Applicant will comply with any order for damages the Court may make.

18. [The Applicant will-
    (1) on or before [date] cause a written guarantee in the sum of £[ ] to be issued from a bank with
        a place of business within England or Wales, in respect of any order the court may make
        pursuant to (1) above, and
    (2) immediately upon issue of the guarantee, cause a copy of it to be served on the Respondent.]

19. As soon as practicable the Applicant will issue and serve a claim form [in the form of the draft
    produced to the court][claiming the appropriate relief].

20. The Applicant will [swear and file a witness statement][cause a witness statement to be sworn
    and filed][substantially in the terms of the draft witness statement produced to the court][con-
    firming the substance of what was said to the court by the Applicant's Counsel/Solicitor].

21. [Anyone notified of this Order will be given a copy of it by the Applicant's legal representatives.]

22. The Applicant will not, without permission of the court, use any information or documents obtained
    as a result of carrying out this order nor inform anyone else of these proceedings except for the
    purposes of these proceedings (including adding further Respondents) or commencing civil proceed-
    ings in relation to the same or related subject matter to these proceedings until after the return date.

23. If this order ceases to have effect (for example, if the Respondent provides security or the Applicant
    does not provide a bank guarantee as provided for above) the Applicant will immediately take all
    reasonable steps to inform in writing anyone to whom he has given notice of this order, or whom
    he has reasonable grounds for supposing may act upon this order, that it has ceased to have effect.

24. [The Applicant will not without the permission of the court use any information obtained as a
    result of this order for the purpose of any civil or criminal proceedings, either in England and
    Wales or in any other jurisdiction, other than this claim.]

25. [The Applicant will not without the permission of the Court seek to enforce this order in any
    country outside England and Wales [or seek an order of a similar nature including orders con-
    ferring a charge or other security against the Respondent or the Respondent's assets].

SCHEDULE D

UNDERTAKINGS GIVEN BY THE APPLICANT'S SOLICITORS

26. The Applicant's Solicitors will serve upon the Respondent [together with this order][as soon as
    possible]—
    (1) a service copy of this order;
    (2) the claim form (with the Defendant's response pack) or, if not issued, the draft produced to
        the court;
    (3) an application notice for hearing on the return date;
    (4) copies of the witness statements and exhibits containing the evidence relied upon by the
        Applicant;
    (5) a note of any allegations of fact made orally to the court where such allegation is not
        contained in the affidavits or draft affidavits read by the judge;
    (6) a copy of any other documents provided to the court on the making of the application; and
    (7) a copy of the skeleton argument produced to the court by the Applicant's [Counsel/solicitors].

27. The Applicant's solicitors will answer at once to the best of their ability any question whether a
    particular item is a listed item.

28. Subject as provided below the Applicant's solicitors will retain in their own safe keeping all
    items obtained as a result of this order until the court directs otherwise.

29. The Applicant's solicitors will retain the originals of all documents obtained as a result of this
    order (except original documents which belong to the Applicant) as soon as possible and in any
    event within [two] working days of their removal.

NAME AND ADDRESS OF APPLICANT'S LEGAL REPRESENTATIVES

The Applicant's legal representatives are—
[*name, address, reference, fax and telephone numbers both in and out of office hours and e-mail*]

FORM 2

PARTICULARS OF CLAIM

Confidentiality / informant / delivery up

IN THE HIGH COURT OF JUSTICE   Claim Number: _____
QUEEN'S BENCH DIVISION

Between:

BIG BUCKS PLC

Claimant

- and -

THE DAILY RAG LTD

Defendant

PARTICULARS OF CLAIM

The Parties
1. At all times material to this action:
   (1) the Claimant has been a public limited company which has been authorized to run a game of chance, and
   (2) the Defendant was the proprietor and publisher of a weekly magazine bearing the title '*News that is fit to print*' ('the Magazine').

The Draft Statement
2. The Claimant's financial and accounting year ends on 31 March. In preparation for publication on 1 June 2006 of a preliminary financial statement, the Claimant prepared a report to the board ('the Report').
3. The Report and its contents:
   (1) constituted confidential information the property of the Claimant which was only to have been disseminated to third parties with the authority of the Claimant; and
   (2) had been passed in confidence to the Board of the Claimant for the sole purpose of enabling them:
      i. to audit the Claimant's draft accounts;
      ii. otherwise and generally to advise, as appropriate, on the contents of such document.

Copyright
4. Further the Report is an original literary work which was prepared by employees of the Claimant in the course of their employment with the Claimant and accordingly the Claimant is the first owner of the copyright in the Report.

Unauthorized disclosure of the Report
5. On a date of which the Claimant is unaware, but which fell prior to 28 June 2006, an individual or individuals ('the Informant(s)') whose identity is unknown to the Claimant, acting without the authority or knowledge of the Claimant, wrongfully caused and/or permitted a copy of the Draft Statement to be passed to a journalist employed by the Defendant ('the Journalist').

603

Equitable duty of confidence owed by the Defendant

6. The Journalist received the copy of the Report in circumstances where it was obvious that the Report had been disclosed in breach of an equitable duty of confidence owed to the Claimant.

7. Accordingly upon receipt of the Report the Defendant was under a duty not to use any part of the Report or divulge any part of its contents without the Claimant's consent.

Receipt and publication of the Report by the Defendant

8. Following the receipt by the Defendant of the Report, in the issue of the Magazine dated 29 June 2006 (published and/or distributed on the 1 July 2006) the Defendant published an article written by the Journalist under the heading '*Big Buck's chief's pay soars as lottery gives less and less to charity*' ('the Article'). The Article made express reference to (parts of) the Report as having been the source for the conclusions drawn by the Journalist and included extracts from the Draft Statement.

Breach of Confidence

9. Accordingly the Defendant has acted in breach of its equitable duty of confidence.

Infringement of copyright

10. Further:
    (1) by making unauthorized use of the Draft Statement, including printing extracts from the Report, the Defendant has infringed the Claimant's copyright in the Report.
    (2) the Defendant has in its possession custody or control in the course of its business, infringing copies of the Claimant's copyright work, the Report.

Wrongful interference with Property

11. Further the Defendant has failed or refused to return the copy or copies of the Report supplied to it without authority, notwithstanding a demand made for the return of such copies in a facsimile message dated 28 June 2006. Accordingly the Defendant has wrongfully interfered with the Claimant's property.

Duty of Disclosure

12. Further and in any event, the Defendant has become mixed up in, and has facilitated, the wrongdoing of the Informant(s). Accordingly the Defendant is under a duty to assist the Claimant by providing full information of matters within its knowledge relating to such wrongdoing, including information as to the identity of the Informant(s). The Claimant contends that such disclosure is in the interests of justice within the meaning of that phrase in section 10 of the Contempt of Court Act 1981. In particular:
    (1) it is likely that the Informant(s) is or are employed by either the Claimant or the Auditors and, as such, the Claimant and the Auditors have a legitimate interest in identifying a disloyal employee who will have access to confidential information of the Claimant and the Auditors.
    (2) it is in any event necessary to identify the Informant(s) so as to prevent further wrongful disclosures of confidential information.

Threat of further use of the Report.

13. Unless restrained by this Honourable Court, the Defendant threatens and intends to make further use of the Report and/or parts of it in breach of its equitable duty of confidence to the Claimant and by way of infringement of the Claimant's copyright interest in the Report.

Loss and damage / Account of Profits.

14. By reason of the matters set out above the Claimant has suffered loss and damage. Alternatively, and at the election of the Claimant, the Defendant is liable to account to the Claimant for the

profits earned by reason of its breach of the equitable duty of confidence and infringement of copyright.

15. Further the Claimant claims interest pursuant to the equitable jurisdiction of the Court, alternatively pursuant to section 35A of the Supreme Court Act 1981, on such sums as are found to be due to the Claimant at such rate and for such period as the Court shall think fit.

AND the Claimant claims:

(1) An injunction restraining the Defendant, whether by its directors, officers, employees or affects or any of them, or otherwise howsoever:

    i. from making any use (to include the passing to a third party) of the Report or any of its content; and

    ii. from infringing the Claimant's copyright interest in the literary work constituted by the Draft Statement; and

    iii. from defacing, deleting any part of, or otherwise altering or tampering with the format or appearance of any and all documents and records which are the property of the Claimant.

(2) An Order for the delivery up to the Claimant of all property belonging to the Claimant in its possession including:

    i. the Report and any extracts from it and all documents containing information derived from the Report, alternatively destruction upon oath of all such documents.

    ii. all documents and records (in hard copy, digital or electronic form) which are the property of the Claimant.

(3) An Order for disclosure by the Defendant of the identity of the Informant(s) and of the precise circumstances in which each and every piece of confidential information, or other property of the Claimant, received by the Defendant from the Informant(s) came to its attention and into its possession.

(4) Damages consequential upon the Defendant's wrongful interference with the Claimant's property.

(5) An Inquiry into the damages which have been, and may be, suffered by the Claimant by reason of the Defendant's wrongful use of confidential information the property of the Claimant and infringement of copyright.

(6) Alternatively, and at the election of the Claimant, an Account of profits made by the Defendant with the assistance of confidential information the property of the Claimant and/or by reason of the Defendant's infringement of copyright.

(7) Payment of the amount certified in answer to such Inquiry or Account as set out above.

(8) Interest pursuant to section 35A of the Supreme Court Act 1981 as above.

(9) Such further or other relief as the Court shall consider appropriate.

The Claimant believes the facts stated in this Particulars of Claim are true.

Signed: . . . .

Position or office held:

Date: . . . .

STATEMENT OF VALUE

FORM 3

THE GRIEVANCE LETTER

Mr T. Leaf
The Manor House
The Manor
London D0D GY1

Chairman
Big Bucks plc
Swell Place
Righteous Lane
London GR8 P4D

12 July 2006

GRIEVANCE

Dear Mr V. Rich,

I am writing following your decision to dismiss me summarily on 10 July 2006.

You dismissed me on the ground that I had made a disclosure of a confidential report to the Magazine the *Daily Rag*.

I informed you during the disciplinary hearing that I had disclosed the Report dated 1 June 2006 to the Magazine. All gambling cards are sold with the following information upon them—'You may lose, but 10 pence of every pound you spend goes to charity'.

I was asked on 1 June 2006 to photocopy a Report that was to be handed to the Board of Directors that afternoon. This report clearly set out that Big Bucks intend only to provide 8 pence to Charity, the remaining 2 pence being used to fund the Chief Executive's pay rise.

Given that the Board saw this report and as far as I am aware did nothing, I took a copy of that report and gave it to the *Daily Rag*.

I believe that my giving that Report to the *Daily Rag* was a public interest disclosure and that I suffered a detriment in being dismissed without you following the company's disciplinary procedure and that as you have dismissed me because of that disclosure my dismissal is automatically unfair.

I look forward to hearing from you.

T. Leaf.

FORM 4

RESPONSE TO GRIEVANCE LETTER

Chairman
Big Bucks plc
Swell Place
Righteous Lane
London GR8 P4D

Mr T. Leaf
The Manor House
The Manor
London D0D GY1

20 August 2006

Dear Mr Leaf,

Thank you for your letter dated 12 July 2006.

We have investigated your grievance. This response is pursuant to the modified grievance procedure as you were dismissed from Big Bucks on 10 July 2006 and you have agreed that the modified grievance procedure is to be followed.

The Report dated 1 June 2006 was a confidential report and is an original literary work which was prepared by employees of the Claimant in the course of their employment with the Claimant and accordingly the Claimant is the first owner of the copyright in the Report.

The Report was disclosed by someone unknown to the *Daily Rag*. We issued court proceedings against the *Daily Rag* and they were ordered by a High Court Judge to inform us who had provided them with a copy of the Report on 5 July 2006. In a statement written for the Court dated 4 July 2006, the journalist Mr V. Hugo stated that it was you who provided the Report to the *Daily Rag*.

We initiated a disciplinary investigation and we followed our disciplinary procedure. We do not accept that we failed to follow the disciplinary procedure. In such circumstances we do not believe you suffered a detriment by reason of your disclosure.

During the Disciplinary Hearing on 10 July 2006 that you attended with your Union Representative, you admitted removing the Report and providing it to the *Daily Rag*. Given that the Report contained confidential information of highly commercially sensitive information it was determined that you had acted in breach of the implied term within your contract of trust and confidence.

We note that you did not use our Whistleblowing procedure and seek to raise your concern with Father Ted as provided for in that procedure.

Finally it was stated within Mr V. Hugo's statement that he paid you £15,000 for the Report by a cheque made out to you from the *Daily Rag* dated 28 June 2006 which was cashed on 1 July 2006.

We note that you do not state specifically which legal obligation was being breached in the Report. We deny that you made a public interest disclosure. We also believe that, in providing the Report to the *Daily Rag* in circumstances where you were paid, you did not act in good faith in making your disclosure.

Yours truly,

V Rich.
Chairman, Big Bucks plc

FORM 5

Employment Claim

The Employment Tribunal now use a digital form available from <http://www.employmenttribunals.gov.uk>

It is now a statutory requirement that the Employment Tribunal's form is used.[1]

If the claim is only in relation to a detriment suffered then the claim must be described under the 'reasons for the claim' and 'other complaints' in section 9.1 of the form. If the claim is also for unfair dismissal then the necessary information for that claim will need to be placed in box 5.1.

The present Claim Form contains the following fields for information:

1. Your details. (questions 1.1 to 1.7)
2. Respondent's details. (questions 2.1 to 2.4)
3. Action before making a claim (questions 3.1 to 3.7)
   (1) It is important here to set out that the Claimant has raised their claim that they have suffered a detriment and or that their dismissal was automatically unfair pursuant to section 103A in a grievance letter as set out above and that you have waited 28 days for a response before issuing the claim.
4. Employment details. (questions 4.1 to 4.5)
5. Unfair dismissal / Constructive dismissal. (questions 5.1 to 5.7)
   (1) It is here at 5.1 that you explain why your dismissal was an unfair dismissal or constructive dismissal.
   (2) The following example sets out the essential elements required in section 5.1 for an unfair dismissal claim for having made a protected disclosure.

   5.1

   1. I started working for Big Bucks on 6 January 2006 as an assistant in the photocopying room.

   2. Big Bucks operate a gambling card sold nationally. The purchasers buy the card in the hope of winning money. It is sold with the following statement that is also used in advertising 'You may lose, but 10 pence of every pound you spend goes to charity'.

   3. On 1 June 2006 I was asked to photocopy a Report. The Report was drafted by Big Bucks' internal auditor and it stated that Big Bucks over the past year had only given 8 pence to Charity, the remaining 2 pence being used to fund the Chief Executive's pay rise.

   4. All gambling cards are sold with the following information upon them—'You may lose, but 10 pence of every pound you spend goes to charity'.

   5. I read the report as I was copying it and I was very upset by its content. It was clear to me from the contents of the report that Big Bucks were misleading the public over the amount of money it provided to charity. I believe that the report showed that Big Bucks breached a legal obligation to customers who purchased the card. I believe the report contained evidence of false accounting, theft or misappropriation of charitable assets and/or evidence of a material application of charitable funds for a non-charitable purpose. I believed the contents of the report were true as it was written by the Financial Director.

   6. I believed that if I had raised the matter with Big Bucks they would dismiss me.[2]

   7. I believed that if I had raised my concerns to Big Bucks they would destroy the report.[3]

---

[1] Schedule 1, The Employment Tribunal Rules of Procedure, Regulation 16, 1(3) requires that on or after 1 October 2005 a claim must be presented on a claim form which has been prescribed by the Secretary of State in accordance with regulation 14.

[2] Section 43G(2)(a)

[3] Section 43G(2)(b)

  8. *As the entire Board knew of the contents of the Report I didn't know who else to go to and so I called the* Daily Rag *and they told me they would expose Big Bucks to stop them.*

  9. *During my disciplinary hearing (which I set out in paragraph 9.1 below) Big Bucks stated they were dismissing me because of my disclosure to the* Daily Rag.

  10. *I believe that my giving that Report to the* Daily Rag *was a public interest disclosure in accordance with section 43G of the Employment Rights Act 1996 and that my dismissal was automatically unfair in that I was dismissed by reason of this disclosure.*

6. Discrimination. (questions 6.1 to 6.2)
7. Redundancy payments. (question 7.1)
8. Other payments you are owed. (questions 8.1 to 8.3).
9. Other complaints. (question 9.1)
 (1) It is at this point a detriment needs to be claimed.
  For example:
  1. *I made a protected disclosure as set out above.*
  2. *When Big Bucks called me into the disciplinary meeting the Chairman decided to dismiss me summarily.*
  3. *Big Bucks' disciplinary procedure states at paragraph 9.3 that no person can be summarily dismissed unless the decision is made by the Chief Executive and the Chairman of Big Bucks.*
  4. *The decision to dismiss me was taken by the Chairman alone who attended the disciplinary hearing and the Chief Executive was not in attendance.*
  5. *I believe I suffered a detriment as a consequence of my disclosure set out above by Big Bucks dismissing me without following the disciplinary procedure.*
10. Other information. (question 10.1)
11. Disability. (question 11.1).
12. Your representative. (questions 12.1 to 12.6).
13. Multiple cases.

FORM 6

RESPONSE TO A CLAIM

The Employment Tribunal now use a digital form available from <http://www.employmenttribunals.gov.uk>

It is now a statutory requirement that the Employment Tribunal's form are used.

Firstly you need to know the name and number of the case you are responding to.

1. Name of the Respondent Company or organization. (questions 1.1 to 1.8)
2. Action before the Claim. (questions 2.1 to 2.6)
3. Employment details. (questions 3.1 to 3.10)
4. Unfair Dismissal/Constructive dismissal. (questions 4.1 to 4.2)
5. Response. (questions 5.1 and 5.2)

   Question 5.2 enables a response to the claim:

   It is important to respond to the claim set out in paragraphs 5.1 and 9.1 of the Claim.

   a. Such as:

   5.2

   1. The Respondent shall reply to the numbered paragraphs of the Claimant's claim in paragraphs 5.1 and 9.1.

   5.1 of the Claim

   Paragraph 1

   2. Is admitted.

   Paragraph 2

   3. Is admitted.

   Paragraph 3

   4. It is admitted that on 1 June 2006 the Claimant was requested to photocopy a Report. The Report constituted confidential information the property of the Claimant which was only to have been disseminated to third parties with the authority of the Claimant. It is admitted that the Report stated that Big Bucks over the past year had only given 8 pence to Charity but it is denied that it stated any remaining 2 pence had been used to fund the Chief Executive's pay rise.

   5. The Respondent first became aware of a disclosure of the Report when the Report was published on 29 June 2006 by the Daily Rag *by the Journalist Mr V. Hugo under the heading 'Big Buck's chief's pay soars as lottery gives less and less to charity'.*

   6. As a consequence of this article the Respondent issued proceedings against the Daily Rag *who consequently, pursuant to an Order of the High Court, disclosed the circumstances of the Claimant's disclosure of the Report. Included within the information was the fact that the Claimant had been paid £15,000 for the Report.*

   Paragraph 4

   7. During the disciplinary meeting the Claimant accepted that he had disclosed the Report to the Daily Rag. *It is admitted that all gambling cards are sold with the following information upon them—You may lose, but 10 pence of every pound you spend goes to charity.*

   Paragraph 5

   8. It is denied that the Report shows that the Respondent was misleading the public about the amount of money it provided to charity. It is denied that the report showed that Big Bucks breached a legal obligation to customers who purchased the card or at all.

   9. It is denied that the Claimant believed that the report contained evidence of false accounting, theft or misappropriation of charitable assets and/or evidence of a material application of charitable funds for a non-charitable purpose and the Claimant is put to strict proof of the same.

10. It is denied that the Claimant made a protected disclosure.
11. It is further denied that the Claimant raised his concerns with the Daily Rag in good faith.
12. The Claimant failed to use the Respondent's internal whistleblowing procedure.
13. It is admitted that the Report was drafted by the Financial Director. It is denied that the Claimant made a protected qualifying disclosure.

Paragraph 6

14. Is denied save that it is admitted that the Claimant was dismissed because of his breach of confidence and theft of the Respondent's property that was sold to the Daily Rag.

Paragraph 7

15. Is denied and the Claimant is put to strict proof.

Paragraph 8

16. Is denied except that no admissions are made as to what the Daily Rag told the Claimant. The Claimant knew that he could raise any concerns under the Respondent's internal whistleblowing procedure.

Paragraph 9

17. Is admitted save that it was not a protected qualifying disclosure.

Paragraph 10

18. Is denied.

Part 9.1

Paragraph 1.

19. Is denied for the reasons set out above.

Paragraph 2

20. Is admitted save that the decision was made by the Chairman and the Chief Executive.

Paragraph 3

21. Is admitted.

Paragraph 4

22. Is denied. The Chairman discussed the proposed decision with the Chief Executive before it was made. The Chief Executive agreed the decision to dismiss the Claimant.

Paragraph 5

23. The Claimant did not make a protected or qualifying disclosure. Further and in the alternative the Claimant did not have good faith in raising his concern in that he was paid for the Report.
24. Further the Claimant did not raise the matter with an appropriate person, and the Daily Rag was not such a person.

6. Other information.
7. Your representative. (questions 7.1 to 7.6).

APPENDIX 11

Introduction to Public Concern at Work Guide to PIDA

Public Concern at Work have produced a Guide to the Public Interest Disclosure Act. It is currently being updated and is expected to be available in 2007. It will be published on the Public Concern at Work website: <http://www.pcaw.co.uk>. We are grateful to PCaW for providing the following advance copy of the updated introduction section of the Guide.

> There are obvious tensions, public and private, between the legitimate interest in the confidentiality of the employer's affairs and in the exposure of wrong. The enactment, implementation and application of the 'whistleblowing' measures and the need for properly thought out policies in the workplace, have over the last three years, received considerable publicity from various quarters, including the valuable activities of an independent charity, Public Concern at Work, established in 1993 and experienced in providing assistance to both employers and employees.
>
> Court of Appeal in *ALM Medical Service v Bladon* (2002) IRLR 807

> All organisations face the risks of things going wrong or of unknowingly harbouring malpractice. Part of the duty of identifying such a situation and taking remedial action may lie with the regulatory or funding body. But the regulator is usually in the role of detective, determining responsibility after the crime has been discovered. Encouraging a culture of openness within an organisation will help: prevention is better than cure. Yet it is striking that in the few cases where things have gone badly wrong in local public spending bodies, it has frequently been the tip-off to the press or the local Member of Parliament—sometimes anonymous, sometimes not—which has prompted the regulators into action. Placing staff in a position where they feel driven to approach the media to ventilate concerns is unsatisfactory both for the staff member and the organisation.
>
> *Committee on Standards in Public Life*
> Second Report (May 1996) p 21

These words from the Nolan Committee were said[1] to best summarize the purposes of the Public Interest Disclosure Act which, it should be stressed, applies across the private and voluntary sectors as well as to public bodies.[2] During the Bill's passage, Lord Nolan stated that his Committee had been persuaded of the urgent need for protection for public interest whistleblowers and he commended those behind the Bill 'for so skillfully achieving the essential but delicate balance in this measure between the public interest and the interests of employers'.[3]

---

[1] *Hansard* HL, 11 May 1998, Lod Borrie QC, col. 889.
[2] Parliamentary consideration of the Act can be found at *Parliamentarv Debates* HC, Standing Committee D, 11 March 1998; *Hansard* HC, 24 April 1998, cols. 1124–1144; *Hansard* HL, 11 May 1998, cols. 888–904; *Hansard* HL, 5 June 1998, cols. 611–639; and *Hansard* HL, 19 June 1998, cols. 1798–1804. While there was no debate at Second Reading in the Commons in 1997, the principles behind the legislation were debated the previous year—*Hansard* HC, 1 March 1996 cols. 1108 et seq. It should be noted that where the construction of this Act may be open to more than one interpretation, these annotations draw on the statements in Parliament not only of the Minister but of the promoters of the Bill (Richard Shepherd MP and Lord Borrie QC). This is because along with Ministerial statements, those of the promoter are recognized as relevant authority for purposes of construction when permitted under the rule in *Pepper v Hart* (1993) 1 All ER 42.
[3] *Hansard* HL, 5 June 1998, col. 614.

To achieve such a balance, the Act sets out a framework for public interest whistleblowing, which protects workers from reprisal because they have raised a concern about malpractice. Though the Act is part of employment legislation, its scope is wide and no qualifying periods or age limits restrict the application of its protection (s 7).

Only a disclosure that relates to one of the broad categories of malpractice can qualify for protection under the Act. These include (s.1, s.43B) concerns about actual or apprehended breaches of civil, criminal, regulatory or administrative law; miscarriages of justice; dangers to health, safety and the environment; and the cover-up of any such malpractice. Cast so widely, and with its emphasis on the prevention of the malpractice, and with the guarantee of full compensation, the Act requires the attention of every employer in the UK. While the main issues for practitioners and their clients are set out at the end of this General Note, the key issue for employers will be to reduce any risk of creating grounds for protected public disclosures. Such steps will include (a) introducing, reviewing and refreshing a whistleblowing policy; (b) promoting the policy effectively; (c) ensuring that the work-force understands that victimisation for whistleblowing is not tolerated; and (d) making it clear that reporting malpractice to a prescribed regulator is acceptable.

The most readily available protection under the Act (s.1, s.43C) is where a worker, who is concerned about malpractice, raises the matter within the organisation or with the person responsible for the malpractice. The purpose of this provision is to reassure workers that it is safe and acceptable for them to raise such concerns internally. It is thereby more likely that those in charge of the organisation (a) will be forewarned of potential malpractice, (b) will investigate it, and (c) will take such steps as are reasonable to remove any unwarranted danger. In this way, the Act aims to deter and facilitate the early detection of malpractice. Additionally, this approach furthers the principle of accountability because—should the concern subsequently prove to be well founded—the law can more readily hold people to account for their actions where it can be shown they had actual (as opposed to constructive or implied) notice of the malpractice.

As the short title makes clear, the Act (s.1 ss. 43E to 43H) also sets out the circumstances where the disclosure of the malpractice outside of the organisation is in the public interest and should be protected. In these provisions, the Act adopts and develops many of the signposts from the common law on whether particular information may, notwithstanding the fact it is confidential, lawfully be disclosed in the public interest. Before touching on the relationship between these new statutory provisions and the common law principles, there are two important points. First, the Act applies to all information, whether confidential or not. Secondly while it draws on the common law, it should be noted that these cases focused on whether the confidential information might itself be published (usually by a newspaper) or disclosed to a regulator, rather than whether the whistleblower who made that public interest disclosure should be protected from reprisal or sanction.

In some circumstances, the Act may impose requirements additional to those in the law of confidence. For a disclosure to be protected, (a) the whistleblower must make the disclosure in good faith; (b) as to all external disclosures, he needs to show some substantive basis for his belief; and (c) as to wider public disclosures—unless there is some legitimate reason why not—the concern should have been raised internally or with a prescribed regulator first. In other respects—such as factors to be weighed in deciding whether a wider public disclosure was reasonable under ss.43G and 43H— the Act requires tribunals to have regard to matters which are also considered at common law. While relevant cases from the law of confidence may provide helpful guidance to tribunals, they are not binding. Indeed the Act only requires tribunals to consider duties of confidence where the disclosure was in breach of a duty of confidence which was owed to a third party by the employer: s.43G(3)(d). For a comprehensive analysis of the case law in this area, the reader is referred to Dr Y Cripps' monograph *The Legal Implications of Disclosure in the Public Interest,* 2nd ed. (Sweet and Maxwell, London, 1994) and, more generally, to Toulson & Phipps *Confidentiality* (Sweet & Maxwell, London, 1996).

Background

The Act was introduced as a Private Member's Bill and promoted in the Commons by the Conservative MP Mr Richard Shepherd and in the Lords by the Labour peer Lord Borrie QC. It received strong support from the Government. The protection forms part of employment legislation and was put forward in the *Fairness at Work* White Paper (May 1998) Cm 3968 as one of the key new rights for individuals. However, it was primarily recognised as a valuable tool to promote good governance and openness in organisations, as can be seen not only from the Parliamentary debates on the Bill but from the references to it in the White Papers on Freedom of Information *Your Right to Know* (Dec. 1997) Cm 3818 and on *Modern Local Government* (July 1998) Cm 4014 and also in ministerial guidance to the NHS (*Freedom of Speech in the NHS,* letter from Health Minister to NHS Trust Chairs, 25 Sept. 1997). It was mostly on account of these wider implications for governance and their relevance across all sectors that the legislation received broad support from the Confederation of British Industry, the Institute of Directors and all key professional groups.

The legislation was closely linked to the work of the whistleblowing charity, Public Concern at Work, publishers of this text. Public Concern at Work was launched in 1993 by the author of these notes, Guy Dehn, under the guidance of, *inter alia,* Lord Borrie QC, the Rt. Hon. Lord Oliver of Aylmerton, Ross Cranston QC (lately the Solicitor General), Maurice Frankel (director of the Campaign for Freedom of Information) and Marlene Winfield (a health policy analyst). The present Chairman of Trustees is Michael Smyth, (litigation partner and head of public policy at Clifford Chance). Michael Brindle QC heads the Advisory Council, having succeeded the late Sir Ralph Gibson (a former head of the Law Commission and Appeal Court judge).

The background to the Act lies in the analysis by Public Concern at Work of a spate of scandals and disasters in the 1980s and early 1990s. Almost every public inquiry found that workers had been aware of the danger but had either been too scared to sound the alarm or had raised the matter in the wrong way or with the wrong person.

Examples of the former included:

- the Clapham Rail crash (where the Hidden Inquiry heard that an inspector had seen the loose wiring but had said nothing because he did not want 'to rock the boat'),
- the *Piper Alpha* disaster (where the Cullen Inquiry concluded that 'workers did not want to put their continued employment in jeopardy through raising a safety issue which might embarrass management'), and
- the collapse of BCCI (where the Bingham Inquiry found an autocratic environment where nobody dared to speak up).

Examples of where the concern was raised but not heeded included:

- the Zeebrugge Ferry tragedy (where the Sheen Inquiry found that staff had on five occasions raised concerns that ferries were sailing with their bow doors open),
- the collapse of Barings Bank (where the regulator found that a senior manager had failed to blow the whistle loudly or clearly), and
- the Arms to Iraq Inquiry (where the Scott Report found that an employee had written to the Foreign Secretary to tell him that munitions equipment was being unlawfully produced for Iraq).

Similar messages have come out of the inquiries into the abuse of children in care (over 30 reports of concern were ignored about the serial sex abuser Frank Beck) and investigations into malpractice in the health service. Two recent examples from the NHS are the Kennedy Inquiry into the high mortality rate amongst babies undergoing heart surgery at the Bristol Royal Infirmary and Dame Janet Smith's Inquiry into the serial killer Dr Harold Shipman (see <www.pcaw.co.uk> or more information).

Those behind Public Concern at Work took the view that such communication breakdowns were also likely to be a relevant issue in many of the thousands of accidents and frauds which caused death, serious injury and loss but which did not, because of their more modest scale, justify a public or judicial inquiry.

Dr Tony Wright, an independent minded Labour MP, first initiated the idea of a legislative framework for public interest whistleblowing in a promotional Ten Minute Rule Bill in 1995. He approached Public Concern at Work and the Campaign for Freedom of Information and asked if they would prepare a draft Bill. After its publication, it received broad support from all key interest groups. As a result, the Labour MP, Don Touhig introduced a revised bill in 1996, after he won a place in the private members' ballot. Although that Bill was unsuccessful, it had been strongly supported in and out of Parliament. Tony Blair MP—then leader of the Opposition—pledged that a future Government of his would introduce whistleblowing legislation on the same lines.

Within a few weeks of the election of Mr Blair's government in 1997, Public Concern at Work and the Campaign for Freedom of Information were asked by ministers to promote the Bill again through the private members' ballot. Conservative MP Richard Shepherd MP, a leading campaigner for openness and supporter of the earlier bills, was successful in the ballot. He used his place to introduce the Bill which became the Public Interest Disclosure Act. The Bill was championed for the Government by Department of Trade and Industry Minister Ian McCartney MP. Following consultation on the measures—undertaken by Public Concern at Work on behalf of the Government and Mr Shepherd—the Bill passed through Parliament supported by all sides. While the legislation would never have been enacted without the support of the new Labour Government, the Act is unusual in the extent to which its scope and detail were settled outside of the machinery of government.

OVERVIEW OF THE PROVISIONS

Commencement

The Act came into force on July 2nd 1999 in England, Wales and Scotland. Similar protection came into force on the 31st October 1999 in Northern Ireland.

Malpractice

The Act applies to people at work raising genuine concerns about crimes, civil offences (including negligence, breach of contract, breach of administrative law), miscarriages of justice, dangers to health and safety or the environment and the cover up of any of these. It applies whether or not the information is confidential and whether the malpractice is occurring in the UK or overseas.

Individuals covered

In addition to employees, it covers workers, contractors, trainees, agency staff, homeworkers, police officers and every professional in the NHS. The usual employment law restrictions on minimum qualifying period and age do not apply to this Act. It does not cover the genuinely self-employed (other than in the NHS), volunteers, the intelligence services or the armed forces.

Good faith

To be protected, most disclosures must be made in good faith. Essentially this means the disclosure is made honestly so that the concern can be addressed. Good faith can be vitiated where the disclosure is made for some other dominant improper motive.

Internal disclosures

A disclosure made in good faith to the employer (be it a manager or director) will be protected if the whistleblower has a reasonable belief the information tends to show that the malpractice has occurred, is occurring or is likely to occur. Where a third party or person is responsible for the malpractice, this same test applies to disclosures made to him. The same test also applies where someone in a public body whose leaders are appointed by ministers (e.g. the NHS and many 'quangos') blows the whistle direct to the sponsoring Department.

Regulatory disclosures

The Act makes special provision for disclosures to prescribed persons. These are regulators such as the Health and Safety Executive, the Inland Revenue and the Financial Services Authority. Such disclosures are protected where the whistleblower meets the tests for internal disclosures and, additionally, reasonably believes that the information and any allegation in it are substantially true and is relevant to that regulator.

Wider disclosures

Wider disclosures (e.g. to the police, the media, MPs, consumers and non-prescribed regulators) are protected if, in addition to the tests for regulatory disclosures, they are reasonable in all the circumstances and they are not made for personal gain.

A wider disclosure must also fall within one of four broad circumstances to trigger protection. These are that (a) the whistleblower reasonably believed he would be victimised if he had raised the matter internally or with a prescribed regulator; or (b) there was no prescribed regulator and he reasonably believed the evidence was likely to be concealed or destroyed; or (c) the concern had already been raised with the employer or a prescribed regulator; or (d) the concern was of an exceptionally serious nature.

Additionally for these public disclosures to be protected, the tribunal must be satisfied that the particular disclosure was reasonable. In deciding the reasonableness of the disclosure, the tribunal will consider all the circumstances, including the identity of the person to whom it was made, the seriousness of the concern, whether the risk or danger remains, and whether the disclosure breached a duty of confidence which the employer owed a third party. Where the concern had been raised with the employer or a prescribed regulator, the tribunal will also consider the reasonableness of their response. Finally, if the concern had been raised with the employer, the tribunal will consider whether any whistleblowing procedure in the organisation was or should have been used.

Protection

Where a whistleblower is victimised or dismissed in breach of the Act he can bring a claim to an employment tribunal for compensation. Awards are uncapped and based on the losses suffered. An element of aggravated damages can also be awarded. Presently where the whistleblower's claim is for victimisation (but not dismissal) he may also be compensated for injury to feelings. Where the whistleblower is an employee and he is sacked, he may within seven days seek interim relief so that his employment continues or is deemed to continue until the full hearing.

Confidentiality clauses

Gagging clauses in employment contracts and severance agreements are void insofar as they conflict with the Act's protection.

Secrecy offences

Where the disclosure of the information is found to be in breach of the Official Secrets Act or another secrecy offence, the whistleblower will lose the protection of the Public Interest Disclosure Act if (a) he has been convicted of the offence or (b) an employment tribunal is satisfied, to a high standard of proof approaching the criminal one, that he committed the offence.

Whistleblowing policies

Though the Act does not require organisations to set up or promote any particular whistleblowing policies, they are strongly recommended. The key elements of such arrangements, as endorsed by the *Committee on Standards in Public Life (supra),* are set out below.

Guidance on Whistleblowing Arrangements

Since its launch under the chairmanship of Lord Nolan, the Committee on Standards in Public Life has continued to highlight the role whistleblowing plays 'both as an instrument of good governance and a manifestation of a more open culture'. Emphasising the important role whistleblowing can play in deterring and detecting malpractice and in building public trust, the Committee has explained:

> The essence of a whistleblowing system is that staff should be able to bypass the direct management line, because that may well be the area about which their concerns arise, and that they should be able to go outside the organisation if they feel the overall management is engaged in an improper course.

In making this work, the Committee has said that 'leadership, in this area more than in any other, is paramount' and that the promotion of the whistleblowing arrangements is critically important. The Committee has long distinguished a 'real' internal whistleblower from an anonymous leaker to the press and has recently stressed that the Public Interest Disclosure Act should be seen as a 'backstop' for when things go wrong and not as a substitute for an open culture.

Good Policy

The Committee has recommended that a whistleblowing policy should make the following points clear:

a) The organisation takes malpractice seriously, giving examples of the type of concerns to be raised, so distinguishing a whistleblowing concern from a grievance,

b) Staff have the option to raise concerns outside of line management,

c) Staff are enabled to access confidential advice from an independent body,

d) The organisation will, when requested, respect the confidentiality of a member of staff raising a concern,

e) When and how concerns may properly be raised outside the organisation (e.g. with a regulator), and

f) It is a disciplinary matter both to victimise a bona fide whistleblower and for someone to maliciously make a false allegation.

Good practice

In its most recent report the Committee 'emphatically endorsed' additional elements of good practice drawn from Public Concern at Work's evidence that organisations should:

- ensure that staff are aware of and trust the whistleblowing avenues;
- make provision for realistic advice about what the whistleblowing process means for openness, confidentiality and anonymity;
- continually review how the procedures work in practice;
- regularly communicate to staff about the avenues open to them.

Responding to these recommendations on good practice in its White Paper of December 2005, the Government stated that it agreed 'on the importance of ensuring that staff are aware of and trust the whistleblowing process, and on the need for the boards of public bodies to demonstrate leadership on this issue. It also agrees on the need for regular communication to staff about the avenues open to them to raise issues of concern'.

Good audit

The Institute of Chartered Accountants in England and Wales has produced practical guidance for auditors and companies on the obligations in the revised Combined Code on Corporate Governance. Encouraging companies to follow our approach, the ICAEW recommends that boards reviewing their whistleblowing arrangements should ask the following questions:

- Is there evidence that the board regularly considers whistleblowing procedures as part of its review of the system of internal control?
- Are there issues or incidents which have otherwise come to the board's attention which they would have expected to have been raised earlier under the company's whistleblowing procedures?
- Where appropriate, has the internal audit function performed any work that provides additional assurance on the effectiveness of the whistleblowing procedures?
- Are there adequate procedures to track the actions taken in relation to concerns made and to ensure appropriate follow-up action has been taken to investigate and, if necessary, resolve problems indicated by whistleblowing?
- Are there adequate procedures for retaining evidence in relation to each concern?
- Have confidentiality issues been handled effectively?
- Is there evidence of timely and constructive feedback?
- Have any events come to the committee's or the board's attention that might indicate that a staff member has not been fairly treated as a result of their raising concerns?
- Is a review of staff awareness of the procedures needed?

Further guidance on best practice is available at <www.pcaw.co.uk>.

Practical Points

For employers and those who advise them, issues to bear in mind are:

a) employers should positively consider the benefits of introducing a whistleblowing policy. If they have one, they should review and refresh it and promote it effectively to staff;

b) employers should—whether or not as part of the policy—make it clear through the management line and across the organisation that it is safe and acceptable for workers to raise a concern they may have about malpractice;

c) where a worker raises a concern about malpractice, every effort should be made to ensure that the employer responds [and can show it has responded: s.43G(3)(e)] to the message, rather than shoots the messenger;

d) employers should recognise it is in their own interests to introduce and promote effective whistleblowing policies. This will not only help managers and staff separate the message from the messenger but will also reduce the likelihood that a public disclosure will be protected under the Act: s.43G(3)(f);

e) where a protected disclosure has been made, employers should take all reasonable steps to try and ensure that no colleague, manager or other person under its control victimises the whistleblower: s.2;

f) where an employer is satisfied with its response to a concern but the worker is not, the employer should consider notifying the regulator as an alternative to finding itself in a protracted dispute with its worker;

g) the implications of the Act on confidentiality clauses [s.43J] in severance agreements and employment contracts should be borne in mind by advisers and their use by employers should be carefully reviewed;

h) employers should consider whether to revise their arrangements with key contractors to provide that those who work for key contractors have access to the employer's whistleblowing policy insofar as the concern affects it;

i) disclosure to a prescribed regulator is protected [s.43F] *whether or not* the concern had first been raised internally. It is important to note that where the worker reasonably believes he will be victimised if he goes to a prescribed regulator, he will be entitled to protection if he makes a wider, public disclosure: s.43G (2)(a). Accordingly employers should make it clear that reporting concerns to a prescribed regulator is acceptable;

j) any attempt to suppress evidence of malpractice is now particularly inadvisable since (a) a reasonable suspicion of a 'cover-up' is itself a basis for a protected disclosure: s.43B(1)(f); (b) a disclosure to the media is more likely to be protected: s.43G(2)(b); and (c) there is less scope for keeping such matters private by a gagging clause: S.43J;

k) if the employer is a public body where at least one of its Board members is a ministerial appointee, it should have a policy which authorises and facilitates whistleblowing direct to the sponsoring department: S.43E;

l) depending on the employer's particular business, it is advisable that—at a senior level—it reviews its relationship with any regulator prescribed in its key areas of activity; and

m) Board members and/or senior managers designated to handle whistleblowing issues should receive appropriate training.

For individuals and those who advise them, issues to bear in mind are:

a) while the Act covers most of the workforce there are a few notable exceptions; (see overview above);

b) if the worker is seeking to engineer a claim to protect himself or is seeking to use the Act to obtain or improve a settlement, it is most unlikely his disclosure will in law be protected;

c) if the worker seeks advice about how to raise a concern, it is suggested that making an initial disclosure under S.43C should be considered as the preferred step as the Act's protection most readily applies here;

d) if the worker wishes to pursue a concern, it is suggested that making an external disclosure under S.43F or 43G should be considered as protection under 43C can be jeopardised if the concern descends into a dispute with the employer about its response to it;

e) the worker is likely to face real problems with causation [ss. 2, 5 and 6] if he blows the whistle anonymously. This is because for a worker to win protection the tribunal must be satisfied that the worker was victimised by the employer because (and hence the employer knew that) he had blown the whistle;

f) if the worker is to disclose information externally because of fear of victimisation or fear of a cover-up or because of the seriousness of the matter, it is suggested that disclosures to ministers [s.43E] and to prescribed regulators [s.43F] are considered first, even though a wider disclosure may also be protected [ss.43G(2) and 43H];

g) if the worker is to make a public disclosure of information [s.43G or S.43H], there are two rules of thumb: (a) a disclosure to a body whose duty it is to investigate the malpractice is likely to be more readily protected; and (b) where the public interest will be equally protected by disclosures to two bodies, the disclosure which causes less damage to the employer is likely to be more readily protected;

h) as to media disclosures [ss.43G and 43H], these are more likely to be protected (a) where the information was not confidential; (b) where, if it was confidential, there is or was a cover-up and there is no prescribed regulator; (c) where less public disclosures had failed to secure a reasonable response; or (d) where the matter was exceptionally serious and the client can show the media was a reasonable recipient of the disclosure;

i) if the worker suffers victimisation short of dismissal, he is also protected [s.2];

j) if the worker is an employee and is dismissed, he can within the first seven days apply for an interim order [s.9] - though these are not readily granted; and

k) where a worker has a shopping list of concerns, an employment tribunal may take this as an indication that there is more to the case than public interest whistleblowing.

Note: this is part of the annotations to the Act prepared by Guy Dehn of PCaW. The complete annotations appear on <www.pcaw.co.uk>.

Useful Addresses

Action on Elder Abuse	Astral House 1268 London Road, London SW16 4ER	\<http://www.elderabuse.org.uk/\> Tel: (++44) (0)20 8765 7000 Fax: (++44) (0)20 8679 4074
Audit Commission	1st Floor, Millbank Tower, Millbank, London SW1P 4HQ	\<http://www.audit-commission.gov.uk/\> Tel: (0)20 7828 1212 TextTel: (0)20 7630 0421 Fax: (0)20 7976 6187
Department for Environment, Food and Rural Affairs (DEFRA)	Nobel House, 17 Smith Square, London SW1P 3JR	\<http://www.defra.gov.uk/\> Defra Helpline by Tel on 08459 33 55 77 (+44) (0)20 7238 6951. minicom/textTel: 0845 300 1998 The fax number is (0)20 7238 2188; from outside the UK: +44 (0)20 7238 2188
	(For enquiries relating to the Environmental Information Regulations) Judith Cullen, Environmental Information Unit, Information Management Division, Defra, 1E Whitehall Place West, 3-8 Whitehall Place, London SW1A 2HR	(For enquiries relating to the Environmental Information Regulations) Tel: (0)20 7270 8887
Environment Agency	25th Floor, Millbank Tower, 21/24 Millbank, London SW1P 4XL Note: The EA has offices across England and Wales. These are divided into eight regions and each region has a number of areas within it. Each area office is reponsible for the day-to-day management of their local area. Contact the general enquiries number to locate the relevant office.	General Enquiries: 08708 506 506 Hazardous Waste Registration number: 08708 502 858 Agricultural Waste Registration: 0845 603 3113 Floodline: 0845 988 1188 Incident hotline: 0800 807060 minicom service is available: 08702 422 549

Financial Services Authority	25 The North Colonnade, Canary Wharf, London E14 5HS	Main switchboard From UK: (0)20 7066 1000 From overseas: (+44) 20 7066 1000 Consumer Helpline From UK: 0845 606 1234 (call rates may vary) From overseas: (+44) 20 7066 1000 Complaints against the FSA From UK: (0)20 7066 9870 From overseas: (+44) 20 7066 9870 Fax: From UK: (0)20 7066 1099 From Overseas: (+44) 20 7066 1099
Health & Safety Executive	Rose Court, Southwark Bridge, London SE1 9HS	<http://www.hse.gov.uk/> Tel: 0845 345 0055
Information Commissioner	Freedom of Information Information Commissioner, Wycliffe House, Water Lane, Wilmslow SK9 5AF	Tel: 01625 545 700 Fax: 01625 524 510
Insurance Ombudsman Bureau	Financial Ombudsman Service, South Quay Plaza, 183 Marsh Wall, London E14 9SR	<http://www.financial-ombudsman.org.uk/> Tel: (0)20 7964 1000 Fax: (0)20 7964 1001
Law Centres Federation	Duchess House, 18–19 Warren Street, London W1P 5DB	<http://www.lawcentres.org.uk/> Tel: (0)20 7387 8570 Fax: (0)20 7387 8368
Local Government Ombudsman London boroughs north of the River Thames (including Richmond but not including Harrow or Tower Hamlets), Essex, Kent, Surrey, Suffolk, East and West Sussex, Berkshire, Buckinghamshire, Hertfordshire and the City of Coventry	Tony Redmond, Local Government Ombudsman, 10th Floor, Millbank Tower, Millbank, London SW1P 4QP	<http://www.lgo.org.uk> Tel: (0)20 7217 4620 Fax: (0)20 7217 4621

Local Government Ombudsman London Borough of Tower Hamlets, City of Birmingham, Solihull MBC, Cheshire, Derbyshire, Nottinghamshire, Lincolnshire, Warwickshire and the North of England (except the cities of Lancaster, Manchester and York)	Anne Seex, Local Government Ombudsman, Beverley House, 17 Shipton Road, York YO30 5FZ	\<http://www.lgo.org.uk\> Tel: 01904 380200 Fax: 01904 380269
Local Government Ombudsman London boroughs south of the River Thames (except Richmond) and Harrow; the cities of Lancaster, Manchester and York; and the rest of England, not included above	Jerry White, Local Government Ombudsman, The Oaks No 2 Westwood Way, Westwood Business Park, Coventry CV4 8JB	\<http://www.lgo.org.uk\> Tel: 024 7682 0000 Fax: 024 7682 0001
Department of Constitutional Affairs— Freedom of Information and Data Protection	Has responsibility for Freedom of Information and Data Protection matters in order to improve people's understanding of their rights and responsibilities and promote openness in the public sector. Information Rights Division, Department for Constitutional Affairs, 6th Floor, Selborne House, 54 Victoria Street, London SW1H 6QW	Tel: (0)20 7210 8034 Fax: (0)20 7210 8388 Website: \<http://www.dca.gov.uk/foi/index.htm\>
National Association of Citizens' Advice Bureax	Myddelton House, 115–123 Pentonville Road, London N1 9LZ	\<http://www.citizensadvice.org.uk\> Tel: (0)20 7833 2181 Fax: (0)20 7833 4371
National Society for the Prevention of Cruelty to Children (NSPCC)	42 Curtain Road, London, EC2A 3NH	Tel: 0800 800 500 (24-hour Child Protection Helpline) Website: \<http://www.nspcc.org.uk\>

Office for the Supervision of Solicitors	Victoria Court, 8 Dormer Place, Leamington Spa, Warwickshire CV32 5AE.	<http://www.lawsociety.org.uk> Tel: 01926 820082/3
Office of Rail Regulation	Office of Rail Regulation, 1 Kemble Street, London WC2B 4AN	Tel: (0)20 7282 2000 Fax: (0)20 7282 2040 <http://www.rail-reg.gov.uk>
Office of Fair Trading	Office of Fair Trading, Fleetbank House, 2–6 Salisbury Square, London, EC4Y 8JX. The Consumer Regulations Enforcement Division; Competition Enforcement Division; Markets and Policy Initiatives Division can all be contacted on the general number and e-mail.	<http://www.oft.gov.uk> Tel: 08457 22 44 99, or email enquiries@oft.gsi.gov.uk You can also contact OFT Enquiries through switchboard on (0)20 7211 8000. For merger enquiries, contact (0)20 7211 8915 /8917 / 8918. Cartels hotline (0)20 7211 8888.
Parliamentary and Health Ombudsman	If you need to make a complaint about a UK government department, or one of its agencies or the NHS in England: The Parliamentary and Health Service Ombudsman, Millbank Tower, Millbank, London SW1P 4QP	Tel: Helpline 0845 015 4033 Or email phso.enquiries@ombudsman.org.uk Fax: (0)20 7217 4000
Public Concern at Work	Public Concern at Work, Suite 301, 16 Baldwins Gardens, London EC1N 7RJ	Tel: (0)207 404 6609 Fax: (0)207 404 6576 9am to 6pm <http://www.pcaw.co.uk>
Scottish Information Commissioner	Office of the Scottish Information Commissioner, Kinburn Castle, Water Lane, St Andrews KY16 9DS	Tel: 01334 464610 Fax: 01334 464611
Standards Board for England	1st Floor, Cottons Centre, Cottons Lane, London SE1 2QG	Tel: 0845 078 8181 Fax: (0)20 7378 5001 <http://www.standardsboard.co.uk>
The Pensions Regulator	The Pensions Regulator, Napier House, Trafalgar Place, Brighton BN1 4DW	<http://www.thepensionsregulator. gov.uk/> Tel: 0870 6063636 Fax: 0870 2411144

The Welsh Administration Ombudsman	Fifth Floor, Capital Tower, Greyfriars Road, Cardiff CF10 3AG	Fax: 0845 601 0987 Website: <http://www.ombudsman.org.uk>
UK Central Council for Nursing, Midwifery and Health Visiting	23 Portland Place, London W1N 4JT	Tel: (0)20 7333 6541 Website: <http://www.ukcc.org.uk/cms/content/home/>

INDEX

Abbey National
  triumph of the whistleblower 1.21
**ACAS (Advisory, Conciliation and Arbitration
  Services)** 10.74, 10.76
accountability
  first tier disclosure 5.04
addresses, useful App 13
adr *see* alternative dispute resolution (ADR)
advertising
  policy on whistleblowing 16.24, 16.37
advice or assistance
  policy on whistleblowing 16.34
**Advisory, Conciliation and Arbitration Services
  (ACAS)** 10.74, 10.76
agency workers
  workers 6.10–6.13
aggravated damages 9.61–9.65
agreements
  protected disclosures, not to make 2.09, 2.10,
    11.116–11.120
Allitt, Beverly 16.04
alternative dispute resolution (ADR)
  Advisory, Conciliation and Arbitration
    Services (ACAS) 10.74, 10.76
  arbitration 10.76–10.78
  conciliation 10.74, 10.75
  generally 10.71–10.73
  mediation 10.79–10.86
  options 10.74–10.93
  settlement agreement 10.87
  specific issues to whistleblowing 10.88–10.93
anonymity
  informants 12.03–12.08
appeal cases on whistleblowing App 8
arbitration 10.76–10.78
armed forces
  persons protected under PIDA 6.33–6.35
  workers 6.33–6.35
Arms to Iraq scandal
  public interest immunity certificate 1.20
  Scott Report 1.20
Ashworth Special Hospital
  patient abuse 1.17
automatically unfair dismissal
  protected disclosure 2.09

bailment 11.11
Bank of Credit and Commerce International SA
  Bingham Inquiry 1.06, 16.04
  blind eye, turning a 1.06
  momentum for reform 1.23
banks 15.72
Barings Bank
  Bank of England report on 16.04
  blind eye, turning a 1.07
***Belgrano*, sinking of the** 1.14
Bell v Lever Brothers 15.02–15.09
Bingham Inquiry 1.06, 16.04
Birmingham Royal Orthopaedic Hospital
  cancer misdiagnosis 1.12
blaming the messenger
  Bolsin, Dr Stephen 1.15
  Bristol Royal Infirmary case 1.15
  British Biotech case 1.16
  European Commission fraud 1.18
  generally 1.13
  Millar, Andrew 1.16
  patient abuse 1.17
  R v Ponting 1.14
blind eye, turning a
  Barings Bank 1.07
  BCCI 1.06
  Clapham rail disaster 1.05
  Piper Alpha disaster 1.04
Bolsin, Dr Stephen 1.15
breach of confidentiality
  detriment, right not to suffer 7.66, 7.67
breach of contract
  protected disclosure 2.09
Bristol Royal Infirmary case
  blaming the messenger 1.15
British Biotech case
  blaming the messenger 1.16
Brown, Gary 1.21
building societies 15.72
burden of proof
  constructive dismissal 8.14
  detriment, right not to suffer 7.76–7.81
  dismissal for making protected disclosure
    not protected disclosure, showing 8.20–8.27
    ordinary unfair dismissal 8.19

burden of proof (*cont.*)
   good faith 4.34–4.37
   unfair dismissal 8.19

cancer misdiagnosis
   Birmingham Royal Orthopaedic
      Hospital 1.12
   deaf ear, turning a 1.12
   Malcolm Inquiry 1.12
case management
   application for order 10.15–10.18
   discussions 10.13, 10.14
   Employment Tribunal
      applying for order 10.15–10.18
      case management discussions (CMD)
         10.13, 10.14
   refusal of order 10.18
   review of order 10.17
case study App 7
child abuse
   deaf ear, turning a 1.10
   Kirkwood Inquiry 1.10
   Leicestershire County Council children
      homes, in 1.10
Civil Service
   codes 1.26
claim forms
   cause of action 10.03–10.05
   Employment Tribunal 10.02–10.06
   mandatory use 10.02
   responses 10.07–10.09
   tactical issues 10.09
   time limit 10.02
Clapham rail disaster
   blind eye, turning a 1.05
   Hidden Inquiry 1.05, 16.04
   momentum for reform 1.23
Clothier Inquiry 16.04
CMD (Case Management Discussions)
   10.13, 10.14
codes
   Civil Service 1.26
   FSA 1.26
   introduction 1.26
   NHS 1.26
common law 2.10
compensation for dismissal
   dismissal for making protected
      disclosure 8.01
   unfair dismissal 8.01
compensatory award
   limit 2.10
   unfair dismissal 9.19–9.22

complaints to Employment Tribunal
   extension of time 8.39
   statutory grievance procedures 7.90–7.96
   time limits 7.97–7.99, 8.39
conciliation 10.74, 10.75
confidentiality
   bailment 11.11
   breach of duty 3.03
   contractual duties 11.02, 11.04–11.11
   criminal law 11.152–11.162
   Data Protection Act 1998 11.13
   duties outside contract 11.11, 11.12
   Employment Tribunal 10.38
   friends 11.13
   implied term 11.04
   intellectual property rights 11.13
   Official Secrets Acts 11.152–11.162
   policy on whistleblowing 16.24, 16.29
   professionals 11.13
   property 11.11
   sources of obligations to maintain 11.13
   third tier disclosure 2.10
   trade secrets 11.04
   trust, breach of 11.11
constructive dismissal 8.14–8.16
Contempt of Court Act 1981 12.15–12.20
contract of employment
   definition 6.03
   implied reporting obligations *see* **reporting**
      obligations under contract of employment
   principles 6.04
contributory fault
   unfair dismissal 9.09, 9.23–9.30
copyright
   fair dealing defence
      criticism or review 13.05–13.08
      fair 13.16–13.20
      generally 13.03
      purpose 13.04
      reporting current events 13.09–13.13
      sufficient acknowledgment 13.14, 13.15
   generally 13.01
   infringement 13.02
   interrelationship with PIDA 13.42
   research documents 13.01
corporate manslaughter
   Lyme Bay canoe disaster 1.11
costs
   amount 10.62
   circumstances of order 10.52
   generally 10.47–10.54
   good faith 10.48
   limited power to award 10.47

costs (*cont.*)
  misconceived proceedings 10.54, 10.56–10.60
  overstated cases 10.50
  power to award 10.47
  specified sums 10.62
  timing of order 10.53
  vexatious 10.54, 10.55
  wasted 10.63–10.69
COT3 form 10.87
cover-ups
  relevant failures 3.80, 3.81
criminal disclosures
  data 3.84
  protectable information
    consequential procedural issues 3.89
    exclusion 3.82–3.88
    standard of proof 3.90, 3.91
criminal offence
  public interest defence 11.30
  relevant failures 3.56
    minor offences 3.56
Crown employees
  persons protected under PIDA 6.22
  workers 6.22
Cullen Inquiry 1.04, 16.04
culture
  disloyalty 16.02
  education 16.02
  need to change 1.01
  reluctance of whistleblowers to come
    forward 1.22
  secrecy 1.22
  whistleblower, affecting 1.01

damages *see also* **remedies**
  aggravated 9.61–9.65
  exemplary 9.66, 9.67
Darnton **guidance** 3.04–3.10
deaf ear, turning a
  cancer misdiagnosis 1.12
  child abuse 1.10
  generally 1.08
  Lyme Bay canoe disaster 1.11
  Zeebrugge ferry disaster 1.09
defamation
  generally 14.01
  justification 14.04
  prima facie case 14.02, 14.03
  qualified privilege
    duty and interest test 14.05–14.11
    malice 14.14–14.17
    PIDA and 14.12, 14.13
    wider disclosures 14.18–14.21

detriment, right not to suffer
  act or deliberate failure to act 7.27–7.33
  age limits 7.06
  anti-discrimination guidance 7.10, 7.11, 7.12
  approach 7.03
  breach of confidentiality 7.66, 7.67
  burden of proof 7.76–7.81
  complaints to Employment Tribunal
    act extending over a period 7.100, 7.101
    series of similar acts or failures 7.102
    statutory grievance procedures 7.90–7.96
    time limits 7.97–7.102
  deployment of existing models of protection
    7.07–7.10
  generally 2.09
  inferences, drawing 7.82–7.89
  Khan guidance 7.11, 7.12, 7.44–7.55
  limitation to employment field 7.26
  meaning of detriment
    Khan guidance 7.11, 7.12
    post-termination detriment 7.17–7.25
    scope for post-termination claims 7.22–7.25
    Shamoon guidance 7.11, 7.12
    Woodward v Abbey National plc 7.17–7.21
  Nagarajan guidance 7.44–7.55
  'on the ground that'
    act or deliberate failure by employer 7.75
    breach of confidentiality 7.66, 7.67
    burden of proof 7.76–7.81
    conduct associated with the disclosure
      7.57–7.65
    detriment 7.75
    disclosure and manner of disclosure
      distinguished 7.68–7.74
    distinction between disclosure and acts
      connected with it 7.56–7.74
    failure in the investigation of the subject
      matter of disclosure 7.75
    inferences, drawing 7.82–7.89
    Khan, guidance in 7.44–7.55
    meaning 7.75
    Nagarajan guidance 7.44–7.55
  original model for mechanism 7.08
  overview of provisions 7.01–7.06
  post-termination detriment 7.17–7.25
    Woodward v Abbey National plc 7.17–7.21
  pre-existing models of protection 7.07–7.10
  protected disclosures 7.01
  psychiatric damage 9.54
  qualifying period, no 7.06
  remedies
    adjustment of awards 9.72, 9.73
    aggravated damages 9.61–9.65

detriment, right not to suffer (*cont.*)
  remedies (*cont.*)
    causation 9.51
    feelings, injury to 9.40–9.53
    injury to feelings 9.40–9.53
    knowledge 9.52, 9.53
    non-compliance with statutory disciplinary
      procedures 9.72, 9.73
    overview 9.36–9.39
    personal injury 9.54–9.60
    psychiatric damage 9.54
    victimization by dismissal of worker who is not
      an employee 9.68–9.71
  Shamoon guidance 7.11, 7.12
  subjection by the employer
    London Borough of Harrow v Knight 7.34, 7.35
    third parties, action by 7.40–7.43
    vicarious liability 7.36–7.39
  third parties, action by 7.40–7.43
  threat of a detriment 7.13–7.16
  trade unions 7.08
  vicarious liability 7.36–7.39
  Woodward v Abbey National plc 7.17–7.21
directors
  Bell v Lever Brothers 15.02–15.09
disciplinary procedures
  anonymity of informants 12.03–12.08
  fairness 12.03–12.08
disclosure
  criminal *see* **criminal disclosures**
  Employment Tribunal
    applicable principles 10.28–10.34
    confidentiality 10.38
    form of application 10.36
    injustice, no party should suffer 10.33
    non-parties 10.35
    oppression 10.34
    proportionality 10.34
    relevance of document 10.30
    restrictions 10.37–10.40
    self-incrimination 10.39, 10.40
    use of tribunal powers 10.33
  protected *see* **protected disclosure**
  qualifying *see* **qualifying disclosure**
  second tier disclosures *see* **regulatory disclosures**
  third tier disclosures *see* **wider disclosures**
  wider *see* **wider disclosures**
dismissal for making protected disclosure *see also*
  remedies
  automatically unfair 8.01
  burden of proof
    not protected disclosure, showing 8.20–8.27
    ordinary unfair dismissal 8.19
  compensation for dismissal 8.01

  constructive dismissal 8.14–8.16
  extension of time 8.39
  identifying principal reason for
    dismissal 8.11–8.13
  industrial action, unofficial 8.18
  interim relief 8.01
  minimum service qualification, no 8.01
  more than one reason for dismissal 8.03
  non-protected disclosures 8.28–8.38
  not protected disclosure, showing 8.20–8.27
  ordinary unfair dismissal and 8.03–8.10
  pre-PIDA position 8.01, 8.02
  reason for dismissal 8.11–8.13
  redundancy, selection for 8.17
  scope of protection 8.01
  time, extension of 8.39
  unofficial industrial action 8.18
  workers 8.01
dismissal procedures
  anonymity of informants 12.03–12.08
  fairness 12.03–12.08
doctors
  Shipman Inquiry report 1.29–1.31
drug trafficking 15.73

employee
  definition 6.02
  identity of employer 6.05, 6.06
  more than one employer, where 6.37
Employment Rights Act 1996
  extracts App 1
  section 43B *see also* **qualifying disclosure;**
    reasonable belief; relevant failures
    overview 3.01–3.03
Employment Tribunal
  additional information 10.19–10.27
  case management
    applying for order 10.15–10.18
    case management discussions (CMD)
      10.13, 10.14
  cases App 9
  claim forms 10.02–10.06
  complaints to
    acts extending over a period 7.100, 7.101
    series of similar acts or failures 7.102
    statutory grievance procedures 7.90–7.96
    time limits 7.97–7.102
  confidentiality 10.38
  costs *see* **costs**
  COT3 form 10.87
  disclosure
    applicable principles 10.28–10.34
    confidentiality 10.38
    form of application 10.36

Employment Tribunal (*cont.*)
disclosure (*cont.*)
injustice, no party should suffer 10.33
non-parties 10.35
oppression 10.34
proportionality 10.34
relevance of document 10.30
restrictions 10.37–10.40
self-incrimination 10.39, 10.40
use of tribunal powers 10.33
hearings
no case to answer, submission of 10.43–10.46
private, sitting in 10.41, 10.42
legal professional privilege 10.93
no case to answer, submission of 10.43–10.46
procedure
additional information 10.19–10.27
case management 10.13–10.18
claim forms 10.02–10.06
costs *see* **costs**
disclosure *see* disclosure *above*
hearings 10.41–10.46
no case to answer, submission of 10.43–10.46
private, sitting in 10.41, 10.42
response to claim form 10.07–10.09
response to claim form 10.07–10.09
self-incrimination 10.39, 10.40
settlement agreement 10.87
employment tribunals
levels of claims to 1.27
Enron scandal 1.26
environment, damage to
meaning 3.79
public interest defence 11.34
relevant failures 3.79
European Commission fraud
blaming the messenger 1.18
European Convention on Human Rights *see also*
European Court/Commission of Human
Rights decisions
development of law 11.14
privacy, right to 11.01, 11.14–11.18
European Court/Commission of Human Rights
decisions
conclusions on authorities 11.150, 11.151
democratic society, necessary in 11.128–11.132
duties and responsibilities 11.137, 11.138
evidence supporting accusation 11.144
generally 11.121, 11.122
legitimate aim 11.124–11.127
manner of the expression of matter of public
concern 11.139–11.143
margin of appreciation 11.128–11.132
nature of employing organization 11.14

prescribed by law 11.123
public concern, raising matters of 11.133–11.136
recipient of information 11.145, 11.146
scope of positive obligation to protect the whistleblower 11.148, 11.149
evidence
first tier disclosure 5.02
regulatory disclosure 5.22
wider disclosures 11.94, 11.95
exceptionally serious matters
wider disclosures 5.38

fair dealing defence
criticism or review 13.05–13.08
fair 13.16–13.20
generally 13.03
purpose 13.04
reporting current events 13.09–13.13
sufficient acknowledgment 13.14, 13.15
feelings, injury to 9.40–9.53
fiduciary obligations
obligation, whistleblowing 15.57–15.65
financial interests of investors/public, damage to
11.38, 11.39
first tier disclosure
accountability 5.04
employer or other responsible person
accountability 5.04, 5.11
conduct of person other than employer 5.05, 5.09
disclosure to the employer 5.03, 5.11
legal responsibility 5.07
other authorized procedures and 5.12
other responsible person 5.07–5.09
overview 5.02
reasonable belief 5.10
section 43C(1)(a) 5.03
section 43C(1)(b) 5.04
solely or mainly conduct of the other person
5.06, 5.08
evidence 5.02
generally 5.01
government-appointed bodies 5.16
importance of provisions 5.02
legal advice, disclosures in the course of
capacity in which legal advice sought 5.15
from whom legal advice sought 5.14
overview 5.13
meaning 2.08, 5.01
Ministers of the Crown 5.16
Public Concern at Work view 5.07
reasonable belief 5.10
section 43C 5.02–5.12
section 43D 5.13–5.15
section 43E 5.16

fixed-term contracts
unfair dismissal 7.04
forcing disclosure of identity of informant
12.09–12.27
fraud
European Commission 1.18
friendly societies 15.72
friends
confidentiality 11.13
FSA
codes 1.26

geographical scope
protectable information 3.94
good faith
burden of proof 4.34–4.37
honesty, not synonymous with 4.04–4.06
illegitimate purposes 4.08–4.15
legitimate purposes 4.08–4.15
meaning
honesty, not synonymous with 4.04–4.06
illegitimate purposes 4.08–4.15
legitimate purposes 4.08–4.15
predominant non-public interest motive
4.16–4.33
ulterior motive must be predominant or
dominant motive 4.07
overview 4.02, 4.03
personal gain 4.20
predominant non-public interest motive 4.16–4.33
reform 4.51, 4.52
regulatory disclosure 5.17, 11.79–11.86
Shipman Inquiry report 4.01, 4.19, 4.23
Street v Derbyshire Unemployed Workers' Centre
concerns about decision 4.38–4.44
support of decision, arguments in 4.45–4.50
ulterior motive must be predominant or dominant
motive 4.02, 4.03
wider disclosures 11.89–11.93
Graham Committee 16.03

Hansard extracts App 3
health and safety risks
employment legislation 15.73
likelihood of danger 3.74
potential harm 3.75
public interest defence 11.33
reasonable belief 3.73
relevant failures 3.73–3.78
trivial concerns 3.76–3.78
Herald of Free Enterprise 1.09, 16.04
Hidden Inquiry 1.05
honesty
good faith not synonymous with 4.04–4.06

House of Commons staff 6.36
House of Lords staff 6.36

immorality, alleged 11.46–11.48
industrial action, unofficial 8.18
Industrial Relations Law Bulletin
Whistleblowers at Work (1997) 1.01
informants
anonymity 12.03–12.07
Contempt of Court Act 1981
12.15–12.20
forcing disclosure of identity 12.09–12.27
meaning 12.01
victimization 12.02
injury to feelings 9.40–9.53
insurance companies 15.72
intellectual property rights 11.13
interim relief
dismissal for making protected
disclosure 8.01
protected disclosure 11.02
public interest defence 11.59–11.61
investigate, duty to 15.66, 15.67
investment business 15.7

just cause and excuse as defence to breach of duty
see **public interest defence**
justification
defamation 14.04

Kirkwood Inquiry 1.10
knowledge
remedies 9.52, 9.53

legal obligation
actual 3.64, 3.65
different jurisdiction, in 3.58
level of protection 2.08
meaning 3.61
moral obligations 3.62
professional obligations 3.63
public interest defence 11.31
qualifying disclosure 2.08
relevant failures 3.57–3.70
seriousness 3.60
threshold 2.08
legal professional privilege 10.93
protectable information 3.92, 3.93
Leicestershire County Council
abuse in children's homes 1.10
local councillors 15.74
Lyme Bay canoe disaster
corporate manslaughter 1.11
deaf ear, turning a 1.11

Malcolm Inquiry 1.12
Matrix Churchill affair 16.04
media
    Contempt of Court Act 1981 12.15–12.20
mediation 10.79–10.86
medical professionals 15.74
Millar, Andrew 1.16
Ministers of the Crown
    first tier disclosure 5.16
miscarriage of justice
    meaning 3.72
    public interest defence 11.32
    relevant failures 3.71, 3.72
monitoring
    policy on whistleblowing 16.24, 16.35
moral obligations 3.62

national security
    persons protected under PIDA 6.33–6.35
    workers 6.33–6.35
NHS
    codes 1.26
    persons protected under PIDA 6.14, 6.15
    Shipman Inquiry report 1.29–1.31
    workers 6.14, 6.15
no case to answer, submission of
    Employment Tribunal 10.43–10.46
Nolan Committee 1.22, 1.23, 2.01,
    16.40, 16.41, App 4
non-executives
    persons protected under PIDA 6.32
    workers 6.32
Norwich Pharmacal action 12.21–12.27

obligation, whistleblowing
    Bell v Lever Brothers 15.02–15.09
    fiduciary obligations 15.57–15.65
    generally 15.01
    implied reporting obligations *see* **reporting**
        obligations under contract of employment
    interface with PIDA 15.68–15.70
    investigate, duty to 15.66, 15.67
    policy on whistleblowing 15.76–15.83
    regulatory obligations to disclose information
        15.71–15.75
    statutory obligations to disclose information
        15.71–15.75
Official Secrets Acts 11.152–11.162

Parliamentary staff
    persons protected under PIDA 6.36
patient abuse
    Ashworth Special Hospital 1.17
    blaming the messenger 1.17

payments for whistleblowing 16.13–16.16
PCaW (Public Concern at Work) 1.23, 1.24
pensions 15.71
personal gain
    wider disclosures 5.24
persons protected under PIDA
    agency workers 6.10–6.13
    armed forces 6.33–6.35
    Crown employees 6.22
    employees
        contract of employment 6.03
        definition 6.02
        workers *see* **workers**
    national security 6.33–6.35
    NHS 6.14, 6.15
    non-executives 6.32
    Parliamentary staff 6.36
    police officers 6.18–6.21
    trainees 6.16, 6.17
    volunteers 6.24–6.31
pharmacists 15.74
Piper Alpha disaster 16.04
    Cullen Inquiry 1.04, 16.04
    momentum for reform 1.23
police officers 2.10
    internal grievance procedures 6.19
    persons protected under PIDA 6.18–6.21
    relevant officer 6.21
    workers 6.18–6.21
policy on whistleblowing
    advertising 16.24, 16.37
    advice or assistance 16.34
    confidentiality 16.24, 16.29
    consultation 16.24
    detriment 16.24, 16.33
    dismissal 16.24, 16.33
    drafting 16.24
    examples 16.24, 16.48, App 5
    failure to follow 16.49, 16.50
    how should report be made 16.24, 16.27
    matters for consideration 16.24
    monitoring 16.24, 16.35
    process 16.24, 16.32
    protection 16.24, 16.30
    reprisals 16.24, 16.33
    review 16.24, 16.36
    specimen 16.24, 16.48, App 5
    tailor-made policies 16.18, 16.19
    timing of raising concern 16.24, 16.28
    to whom should reports be made 16.24, 16.31
    training 16.24, 16.38
    undertakings from head of organization 16.30
    union agreement 16.24
    victimization 16.24, 16.33

policy on whistleblowing (*cont.*)
  when to use procedure 16.24, 16.28
  whistleblowing 1.28, 15.76–15.83
  who should raise concerns 16.24, 16.26
  why should concerns be raised 16.24, 16.25
  writing, report in 16.27
Ponting, Clive 1.14
precedents App 10
prison staff 15.74
private information
  confidentiality *see* confidentiality
  contractual duties 11.04–11.10
  Data Protection Act 1998 11.13
  duties in respect of 11.04–11.18
  European Convention on Human Rights
    11.14–11.18
  generally 11.01–11.03
  just cause and excuse as defence to breach of duty
    see public interest defence
  outside contract, duties 11.11, 11.12
  privacy obligation
    identification 11.04–11.18
  public interest defence *see* public interest
    defence
private sector 16.52
procedures, whistleblowing *see also* policy on
    whistleblowing
  cultural factors 16.02
  examples 16.48–16.50
  failure to follow 16.49, 16.50
  future of 16.53
  organizational changes necessary for 16.05
  payments for whistleblowing 16.13–16.17
  public sector 16.39–16.44
  purpose of procedures 16.04
  rationale of procedures 16.01–16.23
  reasons for raising concerns 16.25
  regulators 16.45–16.47
  scope 16.51, 16.52
  tailor-made policies 16.18, 16.19
professional obligations 3.63
professionals
  confidentiality 11.13
  medical 15.74
proportionality
  protected disclosure 11.110–11.113
protectable information *see also* qualified
    disclosure; reasonable belief;
    relevant failures
  criminal disclosures
    consequential procedural issues 3.89
    exclusion 3.82–3.88
    standard of proof 3.90, 3.91

geographical scope 3.94
legal professional privilege 3.92, 3.93
overview of s 43B ERA 3.01–3.03
reasonable belief
  all circumstances relevant to 3.24
  basis for the information disclosed 3.11–3.20
  Darnton guidance 3.04–3.10
  reasonable suspicion or concern 3.21–3.23
protected disclosure
  agreements not to make 2.09, 2.10,
    11.116–11.120
  automatically unfair dismissal 2.09
  breach of contract 2.09
  concept 2.09
  detriment, right not to suffer *see* detriment, right
    not to suffer
  dismissal for making *see* dismissal for making
    protected disclosure
  flow chart 2.05, 2.13
  interim relief 11.02
  meaning 2.05
  pre-commencement of PIDA 2.12, 2.13
  proportionality 11.110–11.113
  purpose of regime 11.02
  qualifying disclosure, existence of 2.05
  redundancy 2.09, 8.17
  scheme of PIDA 1998 2.04
  template, as
    assessment 11.114, 11.115
    balancing interests 11.72
    Banerjee approach 11.64–11.71
    first tier disclosures 11.73, 11.74
    generally 11.02
    proportionality 11.110–11.113
    regulatory disclosures 11.75–11.87
    wider disclosures 11.88–11.109
  tiers of protection *see also* first tier disclosure;
      regulatory disclosure; tiers of disclosure;
      wider disclosures
psychiatric damage 9.54
public awareness 1.27, 1.28
Public Concern at Work (PCaW) 1.23, 1.24,
    16.06–16.09, 16.20, 16.45, App 12
public interest defence *see also* private
    information
  balancing interests
    context in which balancing act
        carried out 11.58
    domestic law 11.50–11.57
  categories
    corresponding to protected disclosure regime
        under ERA 11.29–11.34
    crime 11.30

public interest defence (*cont.*)
  categories (*cont.*)
    environment, damage to the 11.34
    health and safety concerns 11.33
    legal obligation 11.31
    miscarriage of justice 11.32
    not covered by protected disclosure regime of
      ERA 11.35–11.49
  context in which balancing act carried out 11.58
  development of defence 11.21–11.28
  environment, damage to the 11.34
  financial interests of investors/public, damage to
    11.38, 11.39
  health and safety concerns 11.33
  Human Rights Act 1998, effect of 13.28–13.41
  immorality, alleged 11.46–11.48
  interim relief 11.59–11.61
  legal obligation 11.31
  miscarriage of justice 11.32
  misleading public 11.40–11.45
  move from 'iniquity' 11.23–11.27
  nature of information that can form
    basis of 11.49
  Norwich Pharmacal action 12.21–12.27
  not covered by protected disclosure regime of
    ERA, information
    financial interests of investors/public, damage
      to 11.38, 11.39
    generally 11.35
    immorality, alleged 11.46–11.48
    misleading public 11.40–11.45
    self-regulatory schemes, breaches of rules of
      11.36, 11.37
  old 'iniquity' principle 11.21, 11.22
  overview 11.19, 11.20
  self-regulatory schemes, breaches of rules of
    11.36, 11.37
  threatened publication 11.62, 11.63
  types of information forming basis of defence
    11.29–11.49
Public Interest Disclosure Act 1998
  aim 2.02
  amendment 2.10
  background 1.24
  beyond the Act 1.25
  commencement 2.11–2.13
  copyright law, interrelationship with 13.42
  levels of protection 2.06, 2.07
  Northern Ireland 1.24
  operation 2.10
  outside of protection, whistleblowers 2.10
  persons protected under
    employees 6.02–6.06

    territorial jurisdiction 6.39
    workers *see* **workers**
  pre-commencement protected disclosures
    2.12, 2.13
  Private Member's Bill introducing 1.01, 1.23,
    2.01, 2.02
  protected disclosure *see* **protected
    disclosure**
  qualifying disclosure *see* **qualifying
    disclosure**
  repeals 2.10
  Royal Assent 2.11
  scheme 2.04–2.09
  standard of proof 3.90, 3.91
  structure
    generally 2.01–2.03
    initial observations on 2.10
    scheme 2.04–2.09
  territorial scope 2.11, 6.39
  theme of Act 1.25
  tiers of protection 2.08
Public Interest Disclosure Bill 1.23,
  2.01, 2.02
public interest immunity certificate
  Arms to Iraq scandal 1.20

qualified privilege
  duty and interest test 14.05–14.11
  malice 14.14–14.17
  PIDA and 14.12, 14.13
  wider disclosures 14.18–14.21
qualifying disclosure
  definition 3.02
  good faith 2.08
  legal advice, disclosures in the course of
    obtaining 2.08
  meaning 2.06
  reasonable belief *see also* **reasonable belief**
    all circumstances relevant to 3.24
    basis for information disclosed 3.11–3.20
    Darnton guidance 3.04–3.10
    generally 2.06
    reasonable suspicion or concern 3.21–3.23
  relevant failures *see also* **relevant failures**
    categories 2.06, 2.10, 3.52–3.81
    cover-ups 3.80, 3.81
    criminal offence 3.56
    environment, damage to 3.79
    legal obligation 3.57–3.70
    miscarriage of justice 3.71, 3.72
    scope 3.03
    statutory provisions 3.02
  scheme of PIDA 1998 2.04

qualifying disclosure (*cont.*)
  statutory definition 3.02
  'tends to show'
    extent to which disclosure spells out relevant
      failure 3.30–3.36
    future failures, disclosures in relation to likely
      3.42–3.51
    information requirement 3.37, 3.38
    truth of allegation 3.25–3.29
    unknown to recipient, information need
      not be 3.39–3.41

R v Ponting 1.14
reasonable belief
  all circumstances relevant to 3.24
  assessment 3.04–3.10
  basis for information disclosed 3.11–3.20
  credible sources 3.20
  Darnton guidance 3.04–3.10
  first tier disclosure 5.10
  generally 2.06
  health and safety risks 3.73
  reasonable suspicion or concern 3.21–3.23
  regulatory disclosure
    information and allegation disclosed are
      substantially true 5.21
    relevant failure falling within prescribed
      description 5.19
  subjective test 3.04
  tenable belief 3.19
redundancy
  protected disclosure 2.09, 8.17
**Reed Elsevier Code of Ethics and Business
  Conduct** 15.77
regulatory disclosure
  evidence 5.22
  generally 5.01
  good faith 5.17, 11.79–11.86
  level of protection 2.08
  meaning 2.08, 5.01
  overview 5.17
  prescribed persons 5.18, App 2
  rationale for protection 11.76
  reasonable belief
    information and allegation disclosed
      are substantially true 5.21
    relevant failure falling within prescribed
      description 5.19
  recipient of disclosure, importance of 11.77, 11.78
  section 43F 5.17–5.22
  seriousness of wrongdoing 11.87
  statutory provisions 5.17
  threshold 2.08

time at which recipient prescribed 5.20
relevant failures
  categories 2.06, 2.10
  cover-ups 3.80, 3.81
  criminal offence 3.56
  environment, damage to 3.79
  health and safety risks 3.73–3.78
  legal obligation 3.57–3.70
  meaning 3.03
  miscarriage of justice 3.71, 3.72
  scope 3.02
  statutory provisions 3.02
remedies
  aggravated damages 9.61–9.65
  causation 9.51
  compensation 9.14–9.18
  compensatory award 9.19–9.22
  contributory fault 9.09, 9.23–9.30
  detriment, right not to suffer
    adjustment of awards 9.72, 9.73
    aggravated damages 9.61–9.65
    causation 9.51
    feelings, injury to 9.40–9.53
    injury to feelings 9.40–9.53
    knowledge 9.52, 9.53
    non-compliance with statutory disciplinary
      procedures 9.72, 9.73
    overview 9.36–9.39
    psychiatric damage 9.54
    victimization by dismissal of worker
      who is not an employee 9.68–9.71
  feelings, injury to 9.40–9.53
  knowledge 9.52, 9.53
  non-compliance with statutory disciplinary
    procedures 9.72, 9.73
  overview 9.01, 9.36–9.39
  psychiatric damage 9.54
  re-engagement 9.03–9.18
  reinstatement 9.03–9.18
  terms of re-engagement 9.13
  unfair dismissal
    back pay 9.14–9.18
    compensation 9.14–9.18
    compensatory award 9.19–9.22
    contributory fault 9.09, 9.23–9.30
    interim relief 9.31–9.35
    overview 9.01, 9.02
    permanent replacements 9.11
    practicality of compliance 9.06–9.08
    re-engagement 9.03–9.18
    reasons 9.12
    reinstatement 9.03–9.18
    terms of re-engagement 9.13

remedies (*cont.*)
  victimization by dismissal of worker who is not an
    employee 9.68–9.71
reporting obligations under contract of
  employment
  continuing wrongdoing 15.29–15.33
  deliberate concealment 15.34, 15.35
  express terms of contract 15.26
  need for 16.02
  other than misdeeds, reporting obligations
    15.42, 15.43
  others, reporting wrongdoing of
    continuing wrongdoing 15.29–15.33
    deliberate concealment 15.34, 15.35
    express terms of contract 15.26
    seriousness of wrongdoing 15.27, 15.28
    similar seniority, employees of 15.24, 15.25
    someone with whom to raise concerns
      15.40, 15.41
    specific request 15.36–15.39
    subordinates 15.10–15.16
    superiors 15.17–15.23
  own wrongdoing, disclosure of 15.44, 15.45
  scope of duty 15.56
  seriousness of wrongdoing 15.27, 15.28
  similar seniority, employees of 15.24, 15.25
  someone with whom to raise concerns
    15.40, 15.41
  specific request 15.36–15.39
  subordinates 15.10–15.16
  superiors 15.17–15.23
rewards 16.13–16.16

Scott Report 1.20
second tier disclosures *see* **regulatory**
  disclosures
self-incrimination
  Employment Tribunal 10.39, 10.40
self-regulatory schemes, breaches of rules
  of 11.36, 11.37
settlement agreement 10.87
Sheen Inquiry 16.04
Shipman Inquiry report 1.29–1.31,
  4.01, 16.04
  extracts App 5
  good faith 4.01, 4.19, 4.23
  whistleblowing policies 15.77
statutory instruments, relevant App 2
subordinates
  reporting obligations under contract of
    employment 15.10–15.16
suffer detriment, right not to *see* **detriment,**
  right not to suffer

superiors
  reporting obligations under contract of
    employment 15.17–15.23

territorial scope
  Public Interest Disclosure Act 1998 2.11, 6.39
third tier disclosures *see* **wider disclosures**
threatened publication
  public interest defence 11.62, 11.63
tiers of protection *see also* **first tier**
  disclosure; regulatory disclosure; wider
  disclosures
  generally 2.08
  second tier *see* **regulatory disclosures**
  third tier disclosures *see* **wider disclosures**
  three tiers 5.01
trade secrets 11.04
trade unions
  detriment, right not to suffer 7.08
  policy on whistleblowing, agreement to 16.24
  wider disclosures 5.37
trainees
  persons protected under PIDA 6.16, 6.17
  workers 6.16, 6.17
training
  policy on whistleblowing 16.24, 16.38
trust, breach of 11.11

unfair dismissal
  automatically unfair dismissal
    generally 2.09
    protected disclosures 8.01
  burden of proof 8.19
  compensation for dismissal 8.01
  compensatory award 9.19–9.22
  contributory fault 9.09, 9.23–9.30
  disclosures not given protection, relevance
    of 2.10
  fairness 8.03
  fixed-term contracts 7.04
  more than one reason for dismissal 8.03
  non-protected disclosures 8.28–8.38
  potentially fair reasons for dismissal 8.03
  protected disclosure, dismissal for making *see*
    dismissal for making protected
    disclosure
  reason for dismissal 8.11–8.13
  remedies
    back pay 9.14–9.18
    compensation 9.14–9.18
    compensatory award 9.19–9.22
    contributory fault 9.09, 9.23–9.30
    interim relief 9.31–9.35

unfair dismissal (*cont.*)
  remedies (*cont.*)
    overview 9.01, 9.02
    permanent replacements 9.11
    practicality of compliance 9.06–9.08
    re-engagement 9.03–9.18
    reasons 9.12
    reinstatement 9.03–9.18
    terms of re-engagement 9.13
    right not to be unfairly dismissed 8.03
United States
  awards in 16.13, 16.14

van Buitenen, Paul 1.18
vexatious costs 10.55
vicarious liability
  detriment, right not to suffer 7.36–7.39
victimization
  informants 12.02
  policy on whistleblowing 16.24, 16.33
  wider disclosures and reasonable belief
    in 5.26
volunteers
  persons protected under PIDA 6.24–6.31
  workers 6.24–6.31

wasted costs 10.63–10.69
  amount of order 10.70
  when can orders be made 10.69
whistleblower
  anonymity 12.03–12.08
  Contempt of Court Act 1981 12.15–12.20
  forcing disclosure of identity
    12.09–12.27
  meaning 1.01
  reluctance 1.22
  resource, as 1.01
  role 1.26
  triumph of
    Abbey National 1.21
    generally 1.19
    Scott Report 1.20
  typical matters raised by 1.01
  victimization 12.02
whistleblowing
  change, need for 1.22
  codes *see* **codes**
  meaning 1.01
  policy *see* **policy on whistleblowing**
  reform, need for 1.23
  use of term 1.23
wider disclosures
  approach of legislation to 5.23

assessment of all the circumstances 5.36
confidentiality 2.10
contractual/non-contractual dichotomy
  11.107–11.109
cover-up, reasonable belief in 5.27
duty of confidentiality owed to third party
  5.33, 11.102
evidence 11.94, 11.95
exceptionally serious matters 5.38
generally 5.01
good faith 11.89–11.93
identity of person to whom disclosure
  made 5.30
meaning 2.08
nature of information 11.105, 11.106
overview 5.23
personal gain 5.24
preconditions
  cover-up, reasonable belief in 5.27
  generally 5.25
  previous internal disclosure 5.28
  victimization, reasonable belief in 5.26
previous internal disclosure 5.28
privileged information 11.106
qualified privilege 14.18–14.21
reasonableness
  action reasonably expected to have
    taken 11.103
  assessment of all the circumstances 5.36
  authorized procedure, compliance
    with 11.104
  continuation of relevant failure
    5.32, 11.101
  duty of confidentiality owed to third party
    5.33, 11.102
  generally 5.29
  identity of person to whom disclosure
    made 5.30, 11.98
  previous disclosures 5.34
  seriousness of failure 5.31, 11.99, 11.100
  third party owed confidentiality duty
    5.33, 11.102
  whistleblowing procedures 5.35
section 43G 5.23–5.37
seriousness of failure 5.31, 11.99, 11.100
statutory provisions 5.23
third party owed confidentiality duty
  5.33, 11.102
third tier disclosures, as 5.01
threshold 2.08
trade union 5.37
victimization, reasonable belief in 5.26
whistleblowing procedures 5.35

workers
  agency workers 6.10–6.13
  armed forces 6.33–6.35
  Crown employees 6.22
  definition
    extended 6.09
    key elements 6.08
    limits on 6.23–6.36
    section 43K 6.09
    section 230(3) 6.07, 6.08
    summary 6.38
  dismissal for making protected disclosure 8.01
  expatriate workers 6.39

  more than one employer, where 6.37
  national security 6.33–6.35
  NHS 6.14, 6.15
  non-executives 6.32
  overseas 6.39
  Parliamentary staff 6.36
  police officers 6.18–6.21
  summary of position on 6.38
  trainees 6.16, 6.17
  volunteers 6.24–6.31

Zeebrugge ferry disaster
  deaf ear, turning a 1.09